The New Humanities Reader

FIFTH EDITION

RICHARD E. MILLER
Rutgers University

KURT SPELLMEYER
Rutgers University

CENGAGE
Learning·

Australia · Brazil · Mexico · Singapore · United Kingdom · United States

CENGAGE
Learning®

**The New Humanities Reader,
Fifth Edition**

Richard E. Miller and
Kurt Spellmeyer

Product Director: Monica Eckman

Product Manager: Kate Derrick

Senior Content Developer:
Leslie Taggart

Content Developer: Karen Mauk

Content Coordinator: Danielle
Warchol

Product Assistant: Marjorie Cross

Managing Media Developer:
Cara Douglass-Graff

Marketing Manager: Lydia Lestar

Art and Cover Direction,
Production Management, and
Composition: PreMediaGlobal

Manufacturing Planner:
Betsy Donaghey

Rights Acquisitions Specialist:
Ann Hoffman

Cover Image: © Daniel Bendjy/
iStockphoto, © Samer Chand/
iStockphoto, © Jezper/
Shutterstock, © Johan Swanepoel/
Shutterstock, © La Vieja Sirena/
Shutterstock, © photofriday/
Shutterstock, © Galyna Andrushko/
Shutterstock

For product information and
technology assistance, contact us at **Cengage Learning
Customer & Sales Support, 1-800-354-9706.**

For permission to use material from this text or product,
submit all requests online at **www.cengage.com/permissions**.
Further permissions questions can be e-mailed to
permissionrequest@cengage.com.

Library of Congress Control Number: 2013952128

Student Edition:

ISBN-13: 978-1-285-42899-4

ISBN-10: 1-285-42899-4

Cengage Learning
200 First Stamford Place, 4th Floor
Stamford, CT 06902
USA

Cengage Learning is a leading provider of customized learning solutions with office locations around the globe, including Singapore, the United Kingdom, Australia, Mexico, Brazil, and Japan. Locate your local office at **www.cengage.com/global**.

Cengage Learning products are represented in Canada by Nelson Education, Ltd.

To learn more about Cengage Learning Solutions, visit **www.cengage.com**.

Purchase any of our products at your local college store or at our preferred online store **www.cengagebrain.com**.

Printed in the United States of America
2 3 4 5 6 7 17 16 15 14

Contents

Karen Armstrong, *Homo religiosus*   1

Is God a father? Is heaven a place? Do we have immortal souls? None of these questions, Armstrong maintains, were important to religion in the past. Instead, for tens of thousands of years, religion was seen as an art of consciousness designed to restore our natural sense of connection to the world.

Leslie Bell, *Selections from* Hard to Get: Twenty-Something Women and the Paradox of Sexual Freedom   24

More women than men now get bachelor's degrees, master's degrees, and Ph.D.s. Women make up nearly half the graduates from schools of medicine and law. They can become corporate CEOs, and they can even run for President. But are women free to be sexual?

Cathy Davidson, Project Classroom Makeover   47

The Internet has transformed publishing, the music industry and other forms of entertainment, but what about education? Combining responsiveness to personal needs with a capacity for collaboration, Web-based education might be poised to produce a renaissance of learning. Or is it?

Susan Faludi, The Naked Citadel   72

A reporter describes the legal battle—and the cultural meltdown—that ensues when The Citadel, an all-male military academy, admits its first female recruit.

In Laramie, Wyoming, the murder of a gay college student puts the town under the media microscope. From one perspective, we see citizens struggling to spin their public image. From another perspective, we might be able to detect the first signs of genuine cultural change.

When we decide on what to eat, do we really make free choices? Consumers face a staggering variety at the store, and no one is holding a gun to our heads when we stuff our faces with cheese puffs. But food companies spend millions on research designed to create nearly unbreakable addictions.

Can art be more powerful than a dictatorship? This is the question posed by an account of a women's reading group in the days following the establishment of the Islamic Republic of Iran.

The violence we find today in popular culture—television, movies, advertising, and the new media—has its roots in the artistic avant-garde, which continues to define the cutting edge. How can our society back away from violence when sadism has become so thoroughly interwoven with the ways we feel, think, and imagine?

When applied to the reality of war, words like *honor, valor, courage,* and *sacrifice* may be profoundly dishonest. O'Brien's short story asks its readers to take another look at a subject that no one can claim to understand fully, not even those who have found themselves in the thick of battle.

For more than a century, people have believed that the structure of the brain was fixed at birth and more or less unchangeable thereafter. But the writings of people who have lost their sight suggest that the brain can rewire itself to a degree that scientists have only started to recognize.

The phenomenon known as Human-Elephant Conflict—as measured by events where elephants destroy villages and crops, attacking and killing humans—is on the rise. Elephants, who travel in herds and mourn their dead, are profoundly social creatures. The collapse of elephant culture, brought on by predation, stress, and trauma, may point to what lies ahead for human culture.

Jean Twenge, An Army of One: *Me* 486

What it means to have a self has changed over the course of the past thirty years. While Baby Boomers set out to transform the world, Generation Me seeks out fun as the highest value and promotes self-esteem as the greatest good. Drawing on data taken from 1.3 million young people, Twenge argues that this obsessive focus on the self is not just bad for society, it's also bad for the individual.

Ethan Watters, The Mega-Marketing of Depression in Japan 512

As the American way of life spreads across the world, so do our ideas about mental health. Even though we think of mental illness as a scientific fact, the big pharmaceutical companies know that selling antidepressants in Japan starts with the effort to export our model of the mind. Has pharmacology become a form a cultural imperialism?

Tim Wu, Father and Son 533

The creators of the Internet imagined a virtual democracy where everybody would be equal, but now, thanks to companies like Bell, the Internet might emulate past monopolies by offering preferential treatment to elite customers. Can Google save that day for net neutrality—and does it want to try?

Thematic Contents

Nature and Culture

Religion and Secularity

The Mind

Politics and Culture

Preface

This book is based on a single idea that might seem far from revolutionary: students starting college should write about nonfiction that thoughtfully explores the major issues of their time. Although the university is changing—some would say past all recognition—most people even now would accept the value of such reading for young adults in transit from their home communities to a larger and often confusing world. One claim universities have always made is that higher education has the power to impart a broader view: if not a magic key to the universe, then at least a few useful paradigms that can make events in the world more coherent. And now those paradigms circulate through the medium of nonfiction prose.

The prose argument—the essay—could be described as the genre of our time, enjoying the same pride of place held by poetry in the Renaissance or by novels in the nineteenth century. The essay enjoys this preeminence because in its form it communicates the ungrounded, exploratory character of thinking in the twenty-first century. The most complex, cutting-edge knowledge now—in physics, for example, or cognitive science—shares with blog posts and Twitter feeds an implicit sense of moving forward to something that has yet to be revealed. In an era when the past feels remote and we imagine knowledge to be infinite, the metaphor of connection has replaced the old search for origins and the hope of getting to the ultimate truth. It's possible to say that the Internet has taught us the value of connecting, but the Internet itself might represent only one expression of an essayistic logic at work in our culture well before 1990, the year Tim Berners-Lee completed his programming for the World Wide Web. A logic of connection had already become essential to survival in a world dominated by science and technology, and caught up in the first wave of globalization, when languages, philosophies, and forms of life collided in new ways. Connecting is what we have learned to do when we bump up against incompatibles, and where the alternative to reaching out is closing down on our options. Reaching out is better than closing down: this is the essay's deep logic.

Small wonder, then, that nonfiction prose keeps turning up wherever thinking has gone beyond the boundaries of the already-known. Simone de Beauvoir's *The Second Sex* went beyond a critique of inequality by insisting women have the power to create their own identities, independent of male projections and desires. *Silent Spring*, the book that first brought to public view the environmental crisis, qualifies as an extended essay too, and so does *An Inconvenient Truth*, which has directly or indirectly reached millions of people around the world. Whether we are readers of *Foreign Affairs*, *Harper's*, *Science*, or *JAMA*, we look to nonfiction prose when we need to navigate the complexities of politics, health, human relations, history, computer science, or engineering. Civic life in general and culture broadly speaking become legible for us only when they find their place in the sentences and paragraphs of arguments that might range from one computer screen to many hundreds of pages.

In a period we could call the "Age of Nonfiction," teaching prose that deals with contemporary issues should hardly seem like a revolutionary act—though, remarkably, it is for many reasons. First, we might find it shocking when we stop to think that throughout the whole span of their high school years, generations of young Americans never cast their eyes on nonfiction prose except in the form of textbooks—aimed for commercial reasons well below the reading level of the target audience. Convention and bureaucracy conspire to ensure that Holden Caulfield and Huck Finn dominate a space for inquiry which might be shared with world events, new technologies, and changes in a market system rigged to ensure that most young Americans start their adult lives hopelessly in debt. Needless to say, literary art has enormous value, but educators in the English speaking world have too often presupposed that discourse in a "philosophical" vein lies beyond the reach of ordinary minds, who can't get any thinking done without vivid imagery and lively narrative. The Common Core movement now promises to make a place for nonfiction in K-12, but the rise of the education industry, which threatens to take the "public" out of public schools, hardly inspires much confidence that students will read what they really need to know or be encouraged to think differently.

A second impediment to the teaching of contemporary nonfiction is a prejudice deeply ingrained in the culture of the humanities themselves. No one in the humanities needs to be argued into seeing the past as "another country"—distant, difficult to understand, essential to recover, and quite unlike the "now." But this belief takes for granted the obviousness and transparency of our present moment, although the present is actually at least as opaque and baffling as the past. Nothing is more mysterious to us—enigmatic, multifaceted, and potentially dangerous—than the period we are living through. Only in retrospect can events take on the apparent clarity we find in our history books, with well-defined periods, a cast of characters, and linear trajectories. Of all the "other countries" we will ever know, the present is the most "other" of them all, even if we have been trained to see it as unworthy of close attention. Naturally an understanding of the past is essential for an intelligent response to the here and now, but why have the humanities so willingly postponed an encounter with contemporary life? The question becomes still more troubling when we recognize how little freedom people have for study and reflection once they graduate from college and their available energies get channeled into jobs and family. If an investigation of the here and now never happens in a course we teach, then it probably won't happen at all.

A third obstacle is specialization: the trepidation of nonspecialists when it comes to teaching materials outside their expertise, along with the resentment of specialists at the spectacle of dilettantes getting the details wrong. True, specialization has succeeded, as we can see from the financial power of the research university. But the rapid decay of public culture, which depends on broad-based general knowledge, tells a very different story. In the early modern world, books and ideas made democracy possible, but that achievement seems unlikely to survive in a world of hyperspecialists where ordinary people feel unqualified to voice their views about global climate change or women's rights because they lack appropriate credentials. Of course it's even worse when our fellow citizens feel entitled to sound off in the absence of any knowledge. This book is based on the belief that general knowledge is real and should be taught, especially in courses on writing. The different areas of knowledge in our time hang together coherently because they constellate around a shared but often invisible center that might be called the cultural commons:

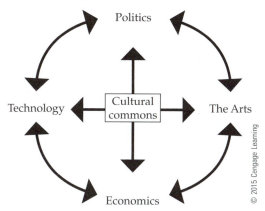

Of course, future Web designers might read *Wired*; future business people might pore over *Business Week*; aspiring directors of museums are going to look over the pages of *ArtForum*. But as for reading outside one's future *métier*, that's a far less likely scenario, especially now, when the humanities have been pushed to the margins. The one place within the university—and perhaps within our whole culture—where connective thinking has the freedom to restore the sense of a coherent world might be English 101, the humble first-year writing class taken by most undergraduates. No matter how English 101 might look to faculty and students, it may be the one remaining course whose concern is nearly universal: not this or that specific knowledge but the way that meaning itself gets made and then communicated. And precisely because the explosive growth of knowledge has produced an explosive growth of ignorance, learning how to make meaning would appear to be more important than ever.

Yet even in English 101, change is impeded by the past's dead weight and by the idea that students starting college are incapable of wading through twenty pages from *The Atlantic* or the *New York Times Magazine*. And this attitude persists even though tenth graders somehow find a way to cope with the challenges of Shakespeare's plays, and even though the students in English 101 might be doing physics that same term or reading Max Weber for some other class. This book imagines students differently—as prepared for complex material if they are supported by the proper scaffolding. It sees teachers too in a different light, as public intellectuals well qualified to introduce the world of living ideas, which is, after all, the only world that really matters.

What does exploring the world of ideas entail? How do we learn to do it? The same way we learn to do any activity—by practice. Not even the most careful study of the laws of physics can replace hours spent wobbling and falling as one tries to get the feel for how to ride a bike without training wheels. Similarly, no amount of outlining or rote work with the five paragraph essay can prepare students for the challenge of making connections between what they've read and what they know, think they know, or would like to know. To learn how to engage with complexity, writers need to practice bringing together ideas with realms of experience that the department-based model of higher education keeps separate. And that's where this reader comes in: we've designed it to help students spend the semester practicing connective thinking. The readings change from edition to edition, but the central goal of the reader remains the same: to practice connecting until it becomes clear what it means to use writing as a way of thinking new thoughts.

The Introduction, "Reading and Writing About the New Humanities," provides students with specific advice about how to read creatively, make synthetic links among the texts, and develop an argument. New sequenced assignments at the end of the book offer faculty and students questions they can use to forge connections between essays and then position their own emerging ideas in the conversation.

Nearly half of the readings are new to this edition. New readings from across the disciplines include excerpts from ten important books published in the last three years: Leslie Bell's *Hard to Get: Twenty-Something Women and the Paradox of Sexual Freedom*; Cathy Davidson's *Now You See It: How Technology and Brain Science Will Transform Schools and Business for the 21st Century*; Barbara Fredrickson's *Love 2.0: How Our Supreme Emotion Affects Everything We Feel, Think, Do, and Become*; Karen Ho's *Liquidated: An Ethnography of Wall Street*; Maggie Nelson's *The Art of Cruelty: A Reckoning*; Andrew Solomon's *Far from the Tree: Parents, Children, and the Search for Identity*; Joseph Stiglitz's *The Price of Inequality: How Today's Divided Society Endangers Our Future*; Sherry Turkle's *Alone Together: Why We Expect More from Technology and Less from Each Other*; Ethan Watters's *Crazy Like Us: The Globalization of the American Psyche*; and Tim Wu's *The Master Switch: The Rise and Fall of Information Empires*. We also include Jonathan Lethem's "The Ecstasy of Influence: A Plagiarism," first published in *Harper's*, and Michael Moss's "The Extraordinary Science of Addictive Junk Food," which appeared in *The New York Times Magazine*.

Special thanks go to colleagues in the School of Arts and Sciences Writing Program at Rutgers: Lynda Dexheimer, Michael Goeller, Regina Masiello, and

Alessandra Sperling. We are also indebted to our excellent editors, Karen Mauk and Kate Derrick. To friends and colleagues across the country who have contributed to this enterprise, we would like to offer our heartfelt thanks for responding to questionnaires and helping us determine the shape of this book over its five editions:

Kara Poe Alexander, Baylor University; Dan Bauer, Georgia College and State University; Tisha Bender, Rutgers University; Manuel Betancourt, Rutgers University; Jerry Bingham, Heartland Community College; Lynn Z. Bloom, University of Connecticut, Storrs; Barbara B. Booker, Pasco-Hernando Community College; Kirk Branch, Montana State University; John C. Brereton, University of Massachusetts, Boston; Susan E. Carlisle, Boston University; Kristi Costello, Binghamton University; Suzanne Diamond, Youngstown State University; Heather Dorn, Binghamton University; Hedda Fish, San Diego State University; Lisa Fluet, College of the Holy Cross; Maureen Fonts, University of Miami; Melora Giardetti, Simpson College; Elizabeth Gilmartin-Keating, Monmouth University; Andrew Green, University of Miami; Rachael Groner, Temple University; Jeffrey Gross, Christian Brothers University; Alfred E. Guy, Jr., Yale University; Andrew Haggerty, Broome Community College; Paul Hammond, Rutgers University; Susanmarie Harrington, University of Vermont; Brian Hayter, Grossmont College; Jessica Hedges, Rutgers University; Deborah H. Holdstein, Columbia College Chicago; Joanna Johnson, University of Miami; Deborah Kirkman, University of Kentucky; Bret Kofford, San Diego State University, Imperial Valley; Thomas C. Laughner, University of Notre Dame; Jennifer Lee, University of Pittsburgh; John Levine, University of California, Berkeley; Jenna Lewis, Rutgers University; Tara Lockhart, San Francisco State University; Gina L. Maranto, University of Miami; Trinyan Mariano, Florida State University; Stephen M. North, SUNY, Albany; Judith Gatton Prats, University of Kentucky; Brendan Prawdzik, Christian Brothers University; Glenda Pritchett, Quinnipiac University; Thomas Recchio, University of Connecticut; Gail Shivel, Florida International University; Jeremy Smyczek, University of North Carolina, Wilmington; Tony Spicer, Eastern Michigan University; Roberta J. Stagnaro, San Diego State University; Gordon P. Thomas, University of Idaho; Anna Tripp, California State University, Northridge; Mark Vareschi, University of Wisconsin-Madison; Anthony Viola, Marshall University; Paul Wise, University of Toledo; Paul Yeoh, Rutgers University; and Sue Zabowksi, University of Miami.

—Kurt Spellmeyer and Richard E. Miller

Reading and Writing About the New Humanities

This book probably differs from many you have encountered, at least those that you have encountered in school. Generally, the books taught in school tell students how or what to think, but ours has a different purpose. We wanted to put in your hands a book that would let you think for yourself, and do so while you read and write about some of the most important issues of our time. Environmental breakdown, rapid cultural change, the effects of electronic media on our ways of interacting—these are just a few of the issues we address.

The articles and essays collected here touch on subjects as diverse as the psychology of elephants and the practice of Tibetan meditation, but these subjects in and of themselves aren't the real point of the book. The real point is thinking, and we believe that thinking in our time needs to assume a new and more appropriate form. In the last 100 years our world has seen change more rapid and profound than it had witnessed in the previous thousand. From the media, we get daily reports on subjects our great-grandparents might have found absolutely incomprehensible: breakthroughs in nanotechnology; mergers of U.S. firms with partners overseas; the covert spread of weapons that could destroy humanity many times over; a new account of the universe in the first few seconds after the Big Bang; melting polar icecaps and rising seas; a growing gap between the poor and mega-rich, while the middle class slowly withers away. Such events are truly without precedent.

We need a new kind of thinking because we live in a world defined by possibilities, and possibilities go hand in hand with risk and unintended consequences. The globalized economy could lead to a future where poverty will become a distant memory, or the whole planet could be transformed into a sweatshop run by a One Percent indifferent to the suffering of ordinary people. The Web could produce a Renaissance of learning, or it could degrade all forms of communication, ushering in a new Dark Age of vulgarity and mass ignorance. Cultures long divided by geography might greet one another with open arms, or we could see a clash of civilizations that would unleash the worst instincts of everyone. Unlike the problems from your textbooks in school, the questions arising from events in our time don't have answers hidden in the teacher's edition. The best educated, most experienced people still can't predict with certainty how the next century will turn out. And even expertise is not good enough because the questions we face now are more complex than people anywhere have ever faced before. Globalization, to take one good example, is not just the concern of economists, or historians, or anthropologists. Instead, it is an issue for all of them together—and for everybody else as well. The degradation of the biosphere is not exclusively the concern of environmental science, but also a matter for political theory, sociology, and economics. The complexity and open-endedness of the big problems of our time require us to work hard to devise new understandings of ourselves and of the world. One purpose of this book is to provide a forum for these understandings to emerge.

Perhaps it may seem strange that we would entertain such lofty goals in a course designed for undergraduates. Surely the experts are better equipped than students just beginning their careers at college or the university. But this assumption might be unjustified. While the forms of expertise available today clearly have enormous value, most of the current academic disciplines were created more than a century ago, and the divisions of knowledge on which they are based reflect the needs of a very different day. In 1900, gas-powered cars were a new technology, while airplanes and radios had yet to be invented. Scientists still wrestled with the structure of the atom. The British Empire dominated three-fourths of the globe, and "culture" meant the traditions of Western Europe's elite, never more than one-tenth of one percent of the population of that region. In a certain sense, the current generation of college students and teachers needs to reinvent the university itself, not by replacing one department with another, but by forging broad connections across areas of knowledge that still remain in relative isolation. Forging these connections is the "new way of thinking" that we had in mind when we created this book.

NEW HUMANITIES FOR NEW TIMES:
THE SEARCH FOR COHERENCE

Probably some readers will be surprised by the absence of material from the traditional humanities: poems and plays, photographs of paintings and statues, excerpts from great works of philosophy such as Plato's *Republic* and Descartes's *Discourse on Method*. Clearly, no one should leave Aristotle, Shakespeare, or Toni Morrison unread. And anyone unfamiliar with Leonardo da Vinci, Frida Kahlo, Thelonious Monk, and Georgia O'Keeffe has missed a priceless opportunity. Yet this book grows out of our belief that the humanities today must reach further than in centuries past. Without consciously intending to, humanists might have contributed to the decline of their own influence. One could even argue their devotion to the past led them to neglect the future. Humanists have often been quite willing to leave real-world concerns to other fields, devoting themselves primarily to passive contemplation, aesthetic pleasure, and the production of criticism few people ever read. Consequently, outside the university many people see the humanities as entertainment or pretentiousness while putting business and technology on a pedestal as the only real truth.

If the humanities are going to survive, they must be understood in a new way: not as a particular area of knowledge but as the human dimension of *all* knowledge. Robotics and artificial intelligence may lie outside the boundaries of the old humanities, but they enter the purview of the New Humanities when we stop to ponder, as Sherry Turkle does, the cultural consequences of technologies that seemed tremendously exciting at first but now appear to make us more like our machines. Once we define the humanities this way—as the human dimension of all knowledge—it may come as a surprise to observe that some of today's foremost humanists work in disciplines quite far removed from English, History, and Philosophy. Oliver Sacks, one of the writers in this collection, is a world-renowned neurologist whose case histories have helped reveal the brain's deeper mysteries while humanizing patients who suffer from mental illnesses, cranial injuries, and cognitive disorders. Karen Ho is an anthropologist whose subject is the growing presence of Wall Street firms on Ivy League campuses. Barbara Fredrickson is a psychologist who studies the physiology behind what she calls our "supreme emotion"—love—with results some critics have described as "amazing."

The New Humanities, as represented by this book, enlarge the arena of human concern in other ways as well. They invite us to take academic knowledge beyond the confines of the university. In a certain sense, this operation requires that we all become our own teachers: we have to find in our own lives—our problems, values, dreams, goals, and commitments—an organizing principle that cannot be found in the curriculum. The great, unspoken secret of higher education is that the curriculum has no center: specialization makes sure of that. Historians write primarily for historians; literary critics for other critics. As we shuttle back and forth between these specialized disciplines, the only coherence we will ever find is the coherence we construct for ourselves. Under these conditions, the New Humanities can teach us a different way of using knowledge, a way of thinking that connects many different fields of study.

Specialized learning in the disciplines typically deals with the "how," but it often leaves unanswered the "why." There has never been a course called "Life 101," and given the persistence of specialization, such a course will probably never exist. But something important will be missing if we leave the "why" questions unexplored. Should we continue to pursue a technological utopia? Does modern science mean the end of religion? Is social inequality an acceptable price to pay for economic growth? Any attempt to answer these questions requires specialized knowledge, yet knowledge alone is not enough. Because a cogent, well-informed case can be made on either side of almost every issue, the source of our ultimate commitments has to be found in our own lives. The "why" questions shape these commitments because they address our most basic relations to other people and the world. In different ways, these questions ask us how we ourselves will choose to think and act. No expert can choose on our behalf, because no expert can live our lives for us or define what our experience should mean.

The coherence missing from the curriculum is not a quality of knowledge in itself. When it emerges, that coherence comes instead from our own creative activity. Again and again, we need to make connections that bridge the gaps between areas of knowledge, linking the formal learning we acquire to our personal experience. But even after we have created this coherence, it will still be incomplete because there is always something more to learn that remains unconnected. We might think of coherence, then, not as a goal we can finally reach but as an ideal worth pursuing throughout the course of our lives. Needless to say, cynicism and fragmentation are always options, too, and they require no special effort. One could easily live as though nothing and no one mattered, but in such a case, learning and living become exercises in futility. The New Humanities offer a better path.

KNOWLEDGE IN DEPTH AND KNOWLEDGE OF THE WORLD

As everybody understands, formal education has been carefully designed to keep the disciplines separate. In economics classes, we typically read economics; in history classes, we read history. This approach allows information to be conveyed in small, efficiently managed packages. We can divide, say, biology from chemistry, and then we can divide biology into vertebrate and invertebrate, and chemistry into organic and inorganic. We start with the general and move to the particular. Ideally, we learn in depth, with increasing mastery of details that become more and more refined. At the end of the semester, if everything goes well, we can distinguish between an ecosystem and a niche, a polymer and a plastic, a neo-Kantian and a neo-Hegelian. We can contrast Hawthorne's treatment of the outsider with Salinger's, or we can explain the debate about whether slavery or states' rights actually caused the Civil War.

Knowledge in depth is indispensable. But it can also produce a sense of disconnection, the impression that education is an empty ritual without real-world consequences beyond getting a grade or fulfilling a requirement. In the classroom, we learn to calculate sine and cosine without ever discovering how these calculations might be used and why they were invented. Searching for symbols in a poem or a short story becomes a mental exercise on par with doing a crossword puzzle. Instead of reflecting on why events have happened and how they get remembered and recorded, we refine our ability to recapitulate strings of dates and names. At its worst, learning in depth can produce a strange disconnect: the purpose of learning becomes learning itself, while activity in the real world seems increasingly remote. As students reach the final years of high school, they may grasp vaguely that they should have read *Hamlet,* be able to identify *The Declaration of Independence,* and explain how photosynthesis has influenced the shape of leaves, but in response to an actual tragedy—an environmental disaster or a war—they might feel unqualified to speak and completely at a loss about what to do.

College-level learning can offer an escape from this predicament by giving students greater freedom to choose what they will study, and in many cases the subjects they choose are closely related to their real-world goals. But even with this newfound freedom, the problem of disconnection crops up in other ways. After years of hard work, a student who has mastered electrical engineering may still leave college poorly informed about the global economy in which most engineers now do their work. Students well versed in Renaissance drama or the history of World War I could understand the past quite well but find the events of their own time impossible to explain. For some people, this problem of disconnection may arise long before they graduate. The student who sets out to memorize facts from, say, a social psychology text might find that these facts grow increasingly stale. Easily memorized one day, they are quickly forgotten the next. The risk of knowledge in depth is that we lose our sense of the larger world and we forget that a field like psychology, for all its current sophistication, began with tentative and somewhat clumsy questions about how the mind might work. Ironically, the more we treat an area of knowledge as a reality in itself, the less we may be able to understand and use what we have supposedly learned.

There is another kind of knowledge we create when we ask ourselves how our learning applies to the world outside the classroom. This line of questioning is more complex than it might seem initially because the larger world is never simply waiting there for us. All knowledge starts with parts and fragments, even our knowledge of the private lives we know in most detail. To each of us, our private life may seem complete, just as a field like psychology can seem to explain everything once we are immersed in its methods and facts. But this sense of completeness is an illusion produced by the limits of our perspective. Beyond the reach of what we know here and now, nothing seems to matter. We begin to get a glimpse of the larger world only when we shift our focus from one reality to another: only then can we become aware of the holes in our prior certainties, and only then are we able to think in new and revealing ways. This movement from the known to the unknown is the essence of all learning; indeed, the most successful learners are generally those who have developed the highest tolerance for not knowing—those who continue to question and explore issues beyond their own areas of specialization, entertaining alternatives that others might find unimaginable.

Knowledge itself can be defined in many ways: as a quantity of information, as technical expertise, as cultivated taste, as a special kind of self-awareness. Various as these definitions might appear, they share an underlying commonality. Whatever form knowledge eventually takes, it always emerges from a process we might describe as **connecting**. The eighteenth-century English scientist Sir Isaac Newton, who first understood the relations between force, mass, and acceleration, might have been inspired in his scientific work by his deeply held religious convictions about the rational perfection of God and His Creation. Many other notable thinkers have also found inspiration through connection. Roughly 200 years after Newton's discoveries sparked a scientific revolution, a young lawyer born in India, Mohandas K. Gandhi, drew on Henry David Thoreau's *Civil Disobedience*, written in support of abolitionists just before the Civil War, to launch a campaign of passive resistance against the racist government of South Africa. Two years before Gandhi spent his first term in jail as a political prisoner, a French artist and intellectual, Marcel Duchamp, shocked the art world with a painting—*Nude Descending a Staircase*—inspired by scientific photographs of athletes in motion. Whether we are talking about physics or political systems, epidemiology or art, knowledge by its very nature brings together disparate worlds of thought and action.

Creative Reading I: The Prospective View

The selections in this book are intended for creative reading. Our assumption is that the humanities should do more than preserve the past or let professors flaunt their brilliance. After all, studies have consistently shown that people retain little of what they are taught unless they put that knowledge to use. At its best, higher learning can offer beginners the chance to practice the same activities that more accomplished thinkers engage in: beyond receiving knowledge, beginners too should have a hand in its creation. The articles and book chapters collected here offer many occasions of that kind. It's true that the selections pose challenges—sometimes because they are long and complex, sometimes because they draw on specialized fields, and sometimes because they open up unusual perspectives. But those challenges are also opportunities: they ask the reader to become an active co-creator with the writer.

The phrase "creative reading" might sound strange. Almost every college and university has a program in creative writing, but creative reading programs don't exist. It's not hard to understand why: many people think of reading as nothing more than passively internalizing words on a page. Yet reading is always more complex than the common sense view would suggest. Like a conversation or dialogue, reading requires us to engage in an active back-and-forth that calls on our attentiveness, imagination, patience, and receptivity. Just as the participants in a conversation have to imagine what the other people think, what they expect to hear, and what they might say next, so readers need to see themselves as involved in a kind of dialogue, moving back and forth from textual details to a sense of the larger whole. And just as we can't know where a conversation is going until it's actually over, so reading transports us to a place we can never entirely predict.

When we try to understand a difficult text like the ones collected here, we won't get far by following along, word by word and detail by detail. As we read we also need to ask ourselves what the writer's larger point might be and how each small step contributes to the unfolding of the entire argument. When

Karen Armstrong starts "Homo religiosus" with a description of the way it feels to descend into the caverns of Lascaux, few of us might be able to foresee the direction her ideas will take. But we can begin with a **prospective view**, a guess at the argument that might lie ahead. Reading further we could be surprised to find that the cave paintings of Lascaux get left behind as we move from Stone Age shamanism to the rise of the world religions we are familiar with today. Actually, a dramatic shift like this—from cave paintings to theology—is quite typical of complex thought, and skillful readers are the ones who know how to keep revising their prospective views as they move ahead. Working with a complex text means continuing the dialogue until we reach an understanding that seems to include everything we've learned.

One way to test your understanding of a text after you have finished reading is to look for key words or ideas and ask how they fit with everything else. Here for example is a question we ask in the "Questions for Making Connections within the Reading" that follow the Armstrong selection:

> Re-read the chapter and carefully note the many differences between religion then and religion now. Next go back and look for the continuities. In spite of the differences, would you say that much of the Paleolithic legacy survives to this day? Can we conclude that religion has become more mature and sophisticated, or is it possible that we have lost touch with what religion actually represents?

A question like this is designed to find out how well you have managed to create a comprehensive understanding of the text. Unless you test your understanding in this way, you might assume that simply having read the words automatically confers a working knowledge when in reality what you really know might be quite limited. Each time you extend your prospective view by looking carefully at a text's details, you draw closer to the kind of mastery that accomplished readers can achieve.

Creative Reading II: Interpretation and the Retrospective View

The fact that reading goes on all the time should not lead us to overlook just how complicated it can get. The act of reading starts with nothing more than ink marks on a page, and those marks cannot tell us anything in and of themselves. But when you read with a prospective view, you are actually creating a text that exists only after you have done the work. The reader's job, however, does not end there. Even after reading with a prospective view has created a coherent text, the **meaning** of that text still remains unclear because what we call "meaning" actually depends on the connections we make within the text or between one text and another. Meaning is a product of interpretation, and interpretation demands from us another form of creative reading: the search for a **retrospective view**. If "prospective" means "looking forward," "retrospective" means "looking back." The most basic form of interpretation starts when we isolate one part of the text—even if it's only a sentence—and use it as a frame or window through which we can take a second, retrospective look at the entire document.

Consider, for example, the first sentence of Jonathan Lethem's controversial essay, "The Ecstasy of Influence: A Plagiarism." That first sentence is not Lethem's at all. Instead, he identifies it as the work of the poet and Anglican preacher John Donne, writing in the seventeenth century: "All mankind is of one author, and is one volume." Everything that follows in Lethem's argument can be interpreted in the light of Donne's claim that mankind is indeed "one author," not many isolated individuals whose creations belong exclusively to them. Bob Dylan's "thefts" from popular movies, Shakespeare, and F. Scott Fitzgerald; episodes of *The Simpsons* that draw on *The Flintstones* and *The Honeymooners*; Walt Disney's earliest Mickey Mouse cartoon, which borrows from actor/director Buster Keaton's classic silent film *Steamboat Bill*—all of these examples can be used to support the truth of Donne's observation.

If we try to explain what Lethem meant by writing "The Ecstasy of Influence," we could simply say that he wanted to show that creative people often borrow from each other. But his examples push that insight much farther. Not only do creative people borrow, but they also appear to steal in ways that often seem to violate conventional morality. And yet, what if Donne is right and all of us are ultimately "one author"? Wouldn't that mean that we are free to use everybody's work as our own? If we reread Lethem's essay in the light of the Donne quotation, we might see the stories Lethem tells in a more positive fashion: less as examples of stealing and more as evidence of a generosity implicit in all human relations. If we really are all one author, then the work of every individual becomes a kind of gift to everybody else. Using Donne for our retrospective view, we might conclude that creativity always involves what universities condemn as plagiarism. Far from trying to stamp out intellectual dishonesty, we could see the persistence of "theft" as proof we are interconnected in a way that makes private property impossible when it comes to the life of the mind. Explicitly, Lethem ventures no such claim, but we could use the passage from Donne to maintain that plagiarism is a creative act when we use the words of others to say something new.

Creative Reading III: Connective Thinking and the Search for a Shared Horizon

The simplest form of interpretation links one part of the text to other parts—linking the Donne passage, for example, to Bob Dylan's lyrics. But what about connections to other texts? These connections are especially important because no one's world is entirely defined by the perspective or "horizon" of any single text alone. Indeed, there is far more to creativity than Lethem's essay can fully express, however complex and many-layered it might be. Because no one lives in a one-text world, the truths we learn from "The Ecstasy of Influence" cannot be confined to the pages of that essay. As soon as we read something in another class, or we engage in conversations with our friends, all sorts of new connections will begin to compete for our attention. The different texts we encounter might come from worlds of experience far removed from ours, but once they have entered into our own lives, we need to bring them together in a way that creates a shared horizon, a greater, more inclusive coherence.

One great tragedy of formal education is that it often works against this shared horizon by promoting imitative thinking: we learn to reproduce information made and organized by someone else. Imitative thinking presupposes the sufficiency of knowledge in its present state, and it preserves the separateness of different texts and differing realities. But this separateness cannot be maintained except at the cost of a greater incoherence. Maybe the lecture in English today contradicted a point made yesterday in anthropology class. Or perhaps an article you are asked to read describes an aspect of the social world in a way that you consider incomplete, biased, or flatly incorrect. On occasions like these, when we come face-to-face with the limitations of knowledge, imitative thinking cannot help us. Instead we are obliged to think connectively—to think *across texts* rather than thinking only from inside them.

Connective thinking calls for another kind of interpretation. Instead of starting with one part of a text and using it as a window to review the rest, we can use it as a window to begin a retrospective reading of another writer's work. We might start again with the Donne passage Lethem quotes: "All mankind is of one author, and is one volume." Then, with this sentence, we could take a second look at Joseph Stiglitz's argument in "Rent Seeking and the Making of an Unequal Society." At first glance these two texts might appear as completely unrelated as any two could be. The first deals with uses that creative people make of work done by others, the second with the growth of inequality in the United States. And yet when we start to read retrospectively, a shared horizon can emerge. The easiest way to search for that horizon would be to find a passage from Stiglitz that makes a point central to his argument. One passage describes the failure of our current political system to redistribute the nation's wealth to benefit the whole society:

> We have a political system that gives inordinate power to those at the
> top, and they have used that power not only to limit the extent of
> redistribution but also to shape the rules of the game in their favor and
> to extract from the public large "gifts." Economists have a word for
> these activities: they call them rent seeking, getting income not as a
> reward [for] creating wealth but by grabbing a larger share of the wealth
> that would otherwise have been produced without their effort....
> Those at the top have learned how to suck out money from the rest
> in ways the rest are hardly aware of.

Clearly, this passage has nothing to do with Bob Dylan's lyrics or *The Simpsons*. But it still says something important about our obligations to other human beings. Although Stiglitz never suggests, as Donne does, that everything we do belongs to everyone else, he still seems to argue that the good of each person depends in some manner on the good of all. Lethem's argument for the "cultural commons" has no explicit parallel in Stiglitz's argument, yet Stiglitz's argument still implies that wealth belongs to the whole society, and that inequality is basically unjust because it overlooks this fact. Lethem never uses the word "redistribution," a key term in Stiglitz's analysis, yet "The Ecstasy of Influence" might be read as a call for the continuous redistribution of words, images, and ideas. If Stiglitz wants both a free market and a strong government to save working Americans from ruin, Lethem also argues for a "market" as well as a "gift economy."

These connections between Lethem and Stiglitz certainly do not exhaust the possibilities, and we will find many more connections by rereading other passages. Eventually, as we work through these new connections, we might begin to discover that a larger point has begun to emerge—such as the conclusion that free markets depend on high levels of equality. An overarching point like this one seldom arises right away. For a nerve-wracking interval, the individual connections might appear disjointed, even contradictory, but then, suddenly, a larger view may present itself—like the pattern in a Persian carpet we unroll a few inches at a time.

Of course some passages in Stiglitz might not connect in a fruitful way to Lethem. Initially, a connection might look promising, but then we could discover that it leads to a dead end. It's possible to spend many frustrating hours following connections that go nowhere. But this is precisely what thinking involves: forging new connections where none exist now. Imitation means letting others do that work and sitting back to admire the results; creativity means taking risks. Some of the risks we take will truly surprise us with their spectacular results, while others may prove quite disappointing. Both risk and failure, on occasion, are the price of creative reading—the price of discovery.

Some people are convinced that creativity cannot be taught at all, but we believe that it can be taught and learned by asking readers to make connections between texts that might appear unrelated at first glance. Many of the questions you will find in this book seem to push hard in that direction. One question, for example, asks you to work out the connections between Charles Siebert's report on the fate of elephants in Africa and Barbara Fredrickson's discussion of the complex biology that underlies our experience of love. Attempts by preservationists to rescue a species may seem worlds away from the science behind our intimate lives, but we are asking you to undertake what all creativity involves—venturing beyond the familiar.

Prospective Writing

Imitative thinking goes hand in hand with writing to tell—writing for the purpose of demonstrating a command of existing knowledge. In American schools, the classic example of writing to tell is the venerable book report. Like imitative thinking, writing to tell has its appropriate place. Connective thinking calls, however, for a different approach that might be described as prospective writing. Just as you can read prospectively, looking for a larger coherence behind all the individual details, so you can write without knowing from the start where your ideas will lead. A good example of writing of this kind is "The Mind's Eye," by Oliver Sacks. Because Sacks is a neurologist, an Oxford-trained physician as well as a professor of medicine—we might have expected him to begin with some of the answers he has found in his four decades of research. Instead he sets out with a question that sounds startling in its simplicity: "to what extent are we … shaped, predetermined, by our brains, and to what extent do we shape our own brains?" In attempting to think through this question, Sacks might have drawn on research by other specialists in fields like chemistry, genetics, and neuroanatomy. He might have taped electrodes to the heads of volunteers or studied their brains with an MRI machine. These are all certainly legitimate ways of responding to the question, but the sources Sacks prefers to use are the first person narratives written by people who have gone blind but then adapted to the loss of sight in a variety of creative ways.

Perhaps the question that Sacks poses—Do our brains shape us, or do we shape our brains?—has followed him from the earliest years of his career as a scientist. Or perhaps he framed the question only after reading the books mentioned in his essay. But no matter how his project began, what seems certain is that these accounts called into doubt much that Sacks had once assumed about the development of the brain. On the one hand, his training led him to suppose that the tasks assigned to the regions of the brain were unalterable after childhood. On the other hand, the accounts he read strongly suggested to him that our brains can rebuild themselves—that our brains are capable of major change throughout adult life. We cannot know exactly what inspired Sacks, but surely one powerful motive was the profound discontinuity between his old assumptions and the new evidence. Facing that discontinuity, Sacks was prepared to take a risk—to put his old assumptions to the test.

From time immemorial, teachers of English have told their students to begin the task of writing only when they clearly know what they intend to say. But these instructions have always expressed more fantasy than truth. Typically, a thesis or argument will remain fairly vague until we have done a great deal of prospective writing. Discontinuities lead us to the search for a shared horizon, and from this shared horizon new questions come. Then, provided we are willing to push far enough, a coherent thesis will begin to emerge, not all at once in a grand sweep but with one insight building on the next. At some point, these insights will cohere—the pattern in the carpet once again. Retrospectively we can recognize the direction of our thoughts, a direction writing itself has revealed. We write, stop, and assess where our writing has gone. Only then are we ready to revise, and to convey our discoveries to others in the form of a well-crafted presentation.

In order for an author like Sacks to become a source for our own writing, we need to start with a question that his work leaves unresolved, at least partially. If human brains are inherently as flexible as he suggests, then why do people generally seem so similar in their outlooks and behavior? Could it be that education, not biology, has made us all the same? If in the future we abolish formal schooling, would our mental lives become much less uniform than they appear to be now? Of course, each of us is free to conclude that our basic human nature will never change regardless of alterations in our brains, and in that case we might choose to brush aside the implications of Sacks's ideas. But these ideas might nudge us to rethink a number of our presuppositions. If events are capable of changing our brains, then perhaps we are doing serious damage when we spend countless hours glued to glowing screens or tweeting about our last meal. Do we need, instead, to care for our mental health as thoughtfully as we care for our bodies through diet and exercise? While we explore questions like this one, we might also draw on Martha Stout's discussion of the way the brain responds to psychological trauma. Or we might make some fruitful connections to Robert Thurman's ideas about the pursuit of wisdom. Ultimately, through prospective writing, we start to develop a thesis of our own.

Developing a Thesis: From Prospective to Retrospective Writing

A thesis is not exactly an argument in the ordinary sense of the word. In everyday speech, the term *argument* suggests an adversarial stance: with great vehemence we might argue for, or against, online education of the kind that Cathy Davidson describes. "Making an argument" tends to mean deciding ahead of time what you think and then looking for "support" to back up your points. There is, however, another way. Instead of simply taking sides in an existing controversy, each of us can move beyond such debates, which are often hackneyed and overly simplistic, in order to say something genuinely new. To do so is to imagine ourselves in a different light, not as combatants but as engaged participants in a conversation. Even if we read a writer with distaste, what matters most are the questions raised, not the answers given. Precisely because the search for a thesis starts with some degree of uncertainty, it demands a willingness on our part to suspend judgment and pursue ideas wherever they might lead. Remember, however, that this pursuit does not require our complete assent or unwavering commitment. We can always entertain and explore ideas we will eventually reject.

The writing process closely parallels the process of reading. Once readers create an understanding of the text through prospective reading, they can go on to view it retrospectively in the search for meaning. Much the same holds true for writing in its different stages. We might consider the first few drafts to be essentially prospective. As we explore possible connections and see how they unfold, we will notice that the process has carried us in unforeseen directions, some highly productive and some cul-de-sacs. But a later stage in the process requires that we move from a preliminary draft, replete with loose ends and promising connections, to become the interpreter of the work we've done. Retrospective writing is interpretive because it tries to tease out the implicit meaning, which it develops further and refines. If the first drafts are exploratory, the final draft is meant to present the writer's discoveries in a way that will conform to the reader's expectations. A thesis statement, logical organization, transitions, and well-structured paragraphs are all tools at our disposal for an effective public presentation.

Let's suppose we start writing with the idea that Fredrickson's "positivity resonance," the sense of rapport two people sometimes feel in each other's company, is an experience we can always trust. But when we turn to Michael Moss's account of the way the food industry has used psychological research to manipulate our behavior, our initial trust in resonance might begin to seem less persuasive than it did. And then we face a question we may not have foreseen, one that Fredrickson never entertains: when does resonance cross the line into something like addiction? Instead of treating this change in our position as a failure or a lapse, we should appreciate its value as a genuine discovery, which we could achieve only after a great deal of hard work. When revising we should not try to conceal the evidence of such a redirection in our thinking. By trying to erase the steps that led us to confusion, we can fail to show our audience the great discovery we have actually made. The strongest writing doesn't simply argue a point but also leads the reader through a thinking process.

The genre most familiar to students starting college is the "five paragraph essay" they learn to compose throughout their high school years. The first paragraph should present the main idea. Three body paragraphs should elaborate, and the final paragraph should sum up the main idea yet again. This format was designed to give beginners some control over a process that can become overwhelming with its sheer complexity. But this virtue is also the greatest defect of the five paragraph model. None of the selections in *The New Humanities Reader* look remotely like the kind of essay students write while they are in high school. Not only do most of the selections connect with many areas of knowledge at once, but they also offer thinking far more layered and nuanced than the high school format could allow. Instead of pounding home a single idea, they guide the reader through a journey of the mind that typically has many twists and turns, that takes two steps forward and one step back, that entertains alternative possibilities and, at times, answers criticisms. Instead of suppressing complexity, the writers here embrace it as the source of a deeper understanding. In your own writing you can learn to do the same.

THE SPIRIT OF THE NEW HUMANITIES

Because we can learn from everything, no one should fear making mistakes. We should never forget that the greatest thinkers of every age have often been refuted later, whereas ordinary people have sometimes lived more wisely than they were given credit for. Not so long ago, the best-educated Europeans believed that all celestial bodies beyond the moon were eternal and changeless.

Scholars taught that matter in every form could be reduced to the basic elements of earth, air, fire, and water. Medical experts sternly warned against the perils of regular bathing and eating whole grains. In sexual reproduction, men were supposed to contribute the blueprint, while women provided the raw material. One could spend a lifetime enumerating the follies that have passed for knowledge. And when we pause to consider such a checkered history, we might decide that education is itself a folly.

But maybe not. Instead of expecting knowledge to be true once and for all, we might try to see it as pragmatic and provisional, always subject to revision given further evidence or new circumstances. In our society today, the sciences may offer the best example of this experimentalist attitude, but some philosophers and artists of every generation have also refused the twin consolations of dogmatism and disillusionment. In the years ahead, our society will face many challenges—environmental, social, cultural, economic and political—that are sure to seem overwhelming. Given the high level of uncertainty that has become a constant feature of our lives, people may be drawn to ideologies that promise truths exempt from all revision and insulated from the challenges of diversity. If this book does nothing else, we hope that it will offer an alternative more compatible with the values espoused by the readings we have chosen: trust in the world and trust in ourselves.

QUESTIONS FOR READING

1. "Reading and Writing About the New Humanities" makes this claim on the very first page: "We need a new kind of thinking because we live in a world defined by possibilities, and possibilities go hand in hand with risk and unintended consequences." How do "possibilities" define the life of our times, and what role does "possibility" play in these detailed accounts of reading and writing? As you reread each section, ask yourself about the place of possibility in teaching and learning. How does an approach that stresses possibility differ from one that privileges strict rules, fixed methods, and pre-ordained answers?

2. Reading and writing are often taught as highly predictable activities. Supposedly, when we read, we follow word by word until we have transferred the writer's thoughts from his or her mind to ours. When we write, we should have a clear argument that we ought to outline before we compose. But "Reading and Writing About the New Humanities" takes a different view. It represents reading and writing as complex activities. Readers are not passive receivers, after all, but actively help to create what they read. And writing is a process of discovery that can lead to insights we seldom have when we first sit down to write. Not only are reading and writing more complex than many people assume but both involve moments of real uncertainty. Using this introduction as your guide, consider the role that

uncertainty plays in the acts of reading and writing. Should we try to avoid uncertainty, or is the experience somehow liberating? What is the relation between uncertainty and the learning process?

3.　When people write, they often have in mind what is called an "implied reader." The implied reader for the Harry Potter books might be someone who likes fantasy, mystery, and adventure. The implied reader for the *Financial Times* is probably an investor. Using specific evidence from "Reading and Writing About the New Humanities," create a detailed portrait of the implied reader of this book. Does this implied reader coincide with the normal image of "the student"? Does it coincide with what we ordinarily think of as a "consumer," "an informed citizen," an "individualist"? Feel free to choose the term that best describes the implied reader of this book, and then explain how you have reached that conclusion.

QUESTIONS FOR WRITING

1.　The term *creative writing* seldom gets applied to the prose that students are required to grind out for their high school essays on *Great Expectations* or for term papers about the Civil War. *Creative writing* is usually reserved for the poems, plays, and fiction students read and sometimes write outside of class, far from the judgments of teachers and the pressure to get good grades. This way of thinking is not inaccurate. It reflects a cultural commonplace: the humanities supposedly provide a time-out for the freedom of imagination, while the other disciplines deal with difficult real-world concerns. The problem with this way of thinking is that it implicitly assumes creative writing cannot be factual or conceptually dense. And it assumes that writing about the real world has to be a boring, empty routine. In what ways does "Reading and Writing About the New Humanities" reject the conventional division between the creative and the real world? In what ways does it challenge the idea that creativity is spontaneous, subjective, and disconnected from realities?

2.　We invite you to use this introduction to frame the first essay you read in the course. Whichever selection your instructor assigns, write an essay that explores moments where you see the essay's author engaged in creative reading and/or connective thinking. Are there other kinds of reading and thinking evident in the selected essay, kinds deserving of other adjectives? How do you know when creative reading has occurred? Is the evidence there on the page or is it in the eye of the beholder?

3.　We make much of the limits of the five-paragraph essay in our introduction. It's a pretty easy target, actually, and none of the essays collected here fit that mold. Consider the organization of the first essay you've been assigned. How is its organization connected to the meaning of the piece? Which organizational decision would you say is the most important one made by the author?

KAREN ARMSTRONG

In 1981, Karen Armstrong published *Through the Narrow Gate,* a controversial account of her experience as a Sister of the Society of the Holy Child Jesus, a Roman Catholic order. Armstrong left the convent and the Church in 1972, "wearied by religion" and "worn out by years of struggle," and then spent the intervening years pursuing a doctorate in literature and teaching at an English girls' school. Although her first book was a milestone, Armstrong has described her life's real turning point as a series of trips she made to Jerusalem beginning in 1982. Shocked by Israel's invasion of Lebanon and also by the Palestinians' intifada, Armstrong found herself questioning just how accurately most Westerners—herself included—understood the lives and beliefs of Muslims in the Middle East.

Convinced that the West was "posing as a tolerant and compassionate society and yet passing judgments from a position of extreme ignorance and irrationality," Armstrong set out to help rectify cross-cultural misperceptions and religious misunderstandings. She has written a number of books that explore relations among Judaism, Christianity, and Islam, including *Holy War: The Crusades and Their Impact on Today's World* (1991); *Mohammed: A Biography of the Prophet* (1992); and *Islam: A Short History* (2000). She has also written a biography, *Buddha* (2001), and *The Battle for God* (2000), an account of the rise of fundamentalism in modern societies.

The selection that follows comes from *The Case for God* (2009), in which Armstrong, a self-described "freelance monotheist," responds to the writings of New Atheists Richard Dawkins, Daniel C. Dennett, Sam Harris, Victor J. Stenger, and Christopher Hitchens. Armstrong makes the case that their view of religion has been shaped by the very fundamentalism they reject. Dawkins, for example, assumes that religion rests on faith in "a superhuman, supernatural intelligence who deliberately designed and created the universe and everything in it." Today this view of God is accepted by hundreds of millions of believers, yet Armstrong argues that in earlier times, religion was understood quite differently—as *mythos,* a

Biographical information and opening quotations are taken from http://www.islamfortoday.com/karenarmstrong.htm; the middle quotation is from www.washington-report.org/backissues/0293/9302038.htm. The quotation from Richard Dawkins appears on p. 304 of *The Case for God.* The final quotation is drawn from http://speakingoffaith.publicradio.org/programs/armstrong/transcript.shtml.

symbolic language meant to transform our consciousness and our ways of being. As she told an interviewer in 2008, she sees religion as "poetry":

> Now a poet spends a great deal of time listening to his unconscious, and slowly calling up a poem word by word, phrase by phrase, until something beautiful is brought forth, we hope, into the world that changes people's perceptions. And we respond to a poem emotionally. And I think we should take as great a care when we write our theology as we would if we were writing such a poem ... because I do see religion as a kind of art form.

Homo religiosus

When the guide switches off his flashlight in the underground caverns of Lascaux in the Dordogne, the effect is overwhelming. "The senses suddenly are wiped out," one visitor recalled, "the millennia drop away ... You were never in darker darkness in your life. It was—I don't know, just a complete knockout. You don't know whether you are looking north, south, east, or west. All orientation is gone, and you are in a darkness that never saw the sun." Normal daylight consciousness extinguished, you feel a "timeless dissociation from every concern and requirement of the upper world that you have left behind."[1] Before reaching the first of the caves decorated by our Palaeolithic ancestors in the Stone Age, seventeen thousand years ago, visitors have to stumble for some eighty feet down a sloping tunnel, sixty-five feet below ground level, penetrating ever more deeply into the bowels of the earth. Then the guide suddenly turns the beam of his flashlight onto the ceiling, and the painted animals seem to emerge from the depths of the rock. A strange beast with gravid belly and long pointed horns walks behind a line of wild cattle, horses, deer, and bulls that seem simultaneously in motion and at rest.

In all there are about six hundred frescoes and fifteen hundred engravings in the Lascaux labyrinth. There is a powerful bellowing black stag, a leaping cow, and a procession of horses moving in the opposite direction. At the entrance to another long passage known as the Nave, a frieze of elegant deer has been painted above a rocky ledge so that they appear to be swimming. We see these images far more clearly than the Palaeolithic artists did, since they had to work by the light of small flickering lamps, perched precariously on scaffolding that has left holes in the surface of the wall. They often painted new pictures over old images, even though there was ample space nearby. It seems that location was crucial and that, for reasons we cannot fathom, some places were deemed more suitable than others. The subject matter was also governed by rules that we can never hope to understand. The artists selected only a few of the species known to them, and there are no pictures of the reindeer on which they relied for food.[2] Animals are consistently paired—oxen and bison with horses, bison with mammoths—in combinations that would not occur in real life.[3] Lascaux is not unique. There are about three hundred decorated caves in this region of southern France and northern Spain. In some the artwork is more elementary, but in all these caverns the imagery and layout are basically the same. The earliest site, at Grotte Chauvet, dates from about 30,000 BCE, a time when *Homo sapiens* seems to have undergone an abrupt evolutionary change in this locality. There was a dramatic rise in population, which may have resulted in social tension. Some historians believe that the cave art records a "corpus of socially constructed rituals ... for conflict control ... pictorially encoded for storage and transmission through generations."[4] But the paintings also express an intensely aesthetic appreciation of the natural world. Here we have the earliest known evidence of an ideological system, which remained in place for some twenty thousand years, after which the caves fell into disuse in about 9000 BCE.[5]

It is now generally agreed that these labyrinths were sacred places for the performance of some kind of ritual. Some historians have argued that their purpose was purely pragmatic, but their upkeep alone would have required an immense amount of unproductive labor. Some of these sites were so deep that it took hours to reach their innermost core. Visiting the caves was dangerous, exhausting, uneconomical, and time-consuming. The general consensus is that the caves were sanctuaries and that, as in any temple, their iconography reflected a vision that was radically different from that of the outside world.[6] We do not build temples like this in the modern West. Our worldview is predominantly rational, and we think more easily in concepts than images. We find it hard enough to decode the symbolism of a medieval cathedral such as the one in Chartres, so these Palaeolithic shrines offer an almost insurmountable challenge.

But there are a few clues to aid our understanding. A remarkable picture, dated to about 12,000 BCE, in a cave at Lascaux known as the Crypt because it is even deeper than the other caverns, depicts a large bison that has been eviscerated by a spear thrust through its hindquarters. Lying in front of the wounded beast is a man, drawn in a far more rudimentary style than the animals, with arms outstretched, phallus erect, and wearing what seems to be a bird mask; his staff, which lies on the ground nearby, is also topped by a bird's head. This seems to be an illustration of a well-known legend and could have been the founding myth of the sanctuary. The same scene appears on an engraved reindeer horn at nearby Villars and on a sculpted block in a cliff shelter at Roc de Sers near Limoges, which is five thousand years older than the Lascaux painting.[7] Fifty-five similar images in the other caves and three more Palaeolithic rock drawings in Africa have been found, all showing men confronting animals in a state of trance with upraised arms.[8] They are probably shamans.

We know that shamanism developed in Africa and Europe during the Palaeolithic period and that it spread to Siberia and thence to America and Australia, where the shaman is still the chief religious practitioner among the indigenous hunting peoples. Even though they have inevitably been influenced by neighboring civilizations, many of the original structures of these societies, which were arrested at a stage similar to that of the Palaeolithic, remained intact until the late nineteenth century.[9] Today there is a remarkable continuity in the descriptions of the shaman's ecstatic flight all the way from Siberia, through the Americas to Tierra del Fuego:[10] he swoons during a public stance and believes that he flies through the air to consult the gods about the location of game. In these traditional societies, hunters do not feel that the species are distinct or permanent categories: men can become animals and animals human. Shamans have bird and animal guardians and can converse with the beasts that are revered as messengers of higher powers.[11] The shaman's vision gives meaning to the hunting and killing of animals on which these societies depend.

The hunters feel profoundly uneasy about slaughtering the beasts, who are their friends and patrons, and to assuage this anxiety, they surround the hunt with taboos and prohibitions. They say that long ago the animals made a covenant with humankind and now a god known as the Animal Master regularly sends flocks from the lower world to be killed on the hunting plains, because the hunters promised to perform the rites that will give them posthumous life. Hunters often abstain from sex before an expedition, hunt in a state of ritual purity, and feel a deep empathy with their prey. In the Kalahari Desert, where wood is scarce, the Bushmen have to rely on light weapons that can only graze the skin, so they anoint their arrows with a lethal poison that kills the animal very slowly. A tribesman has to remain with his victim, crying when it cries and participating symbolically in its death throes. Other tribes identify with their prey by donning animal costumes. After stripping the meat from the bones, some reconstruct their kill by laying out its skeleton and pelt; others bury these inedible remains, symbolically restoring the beast to the netherworld from which it came.[12]

The hunters of the Palaeolithic age may have had a similar worldview. Some of the myths and rites they devised appear to have survived in the traditions of later, literate cultures. Animal sacrifice, for example, the central rite of nearly every religious system in antiquity, preserved prehistoric hunting ceremonies and continued to honor a beast that gave its life for the sake of humankind.[13] One of the functions of ritual is to evoke an anxiety in such a way that the community is forced to confront and control it. From the very beginning, it seems, religious life was rooted in acknowledgment of the tragic fact that life depends upon the destruction of other creatures.

The Palaeolithic caves may have been the scene of similar rites. Some of the paintings include dancing men dressed as animals. The Bushmen say that their own rock paintings depict "the world behind this one that we see with our eyes," which the shamans visit during their mystical flights.[14] They smear the walls of the caves with the blood, excrement, and fat of their kill in order to restore it, symbolically, to the earth; animal blood and fat were ingredients of the Palaeolithic paints, and the act of painting itself could have been a ritual of restoration.[15] The images may depict the eternal, archetypal animals that take temporary physical form in the upper world.[16] All ancient religion was based on what has been called the perennial philosophy, because it was present in some form in so many premodern cultures. It sees every single person, object, or experience as a replica of a reality in a sacred world that is more effective and enduring than our own.[17] When an Australian Aborigine hunts his prey, he feels wholly at one with First Hunter, caught up in a richer and more potent reality that makes him feel fully alive and complete.[18] Maybe the hunters of Lascaux re-enacted the archetypal hunt in the caves amid these paintings of the eternal hunting ground before they left their tribe to embark on the perilous quest for food.[19]

We can, of course, only speculate. Some scholars believe that these caverns were likely to have been used for the initiation ceremonies that marked the adolescent boy's rite of passage from childhood to maturity. This type of initiation was crucial in ancient religion and is still practiced in traditional societies today.[20] When they reach puberty, boys are taken from their mothers and put through frightening ordeals that transform them into men. The tribe cannot afford the luxury of allowing an adolescent to "find himself" Western-style; he has to relinquish the dependency of infancy and assume the burdens of adulthood overnight. To this end, boys are incarcerated in tombs, buried in the earth, informed that they are about to be eaten by a monster, flogged, circumcised, and tattooed. If the initiation is properly conducted, a youth will be forced to reach for inner resources that he did not know he possessed. Psychologists tell us that the terror of such an experience causes a regressive disorganization of the personality that, if skillfully handled, can lead to a constructive reorganization of the young man's powers. He has faced death, come out the other side, and is now psychologically prepared to risk his life for his people.

But the purpose of the ritual is not simply to turn him into an efficient killing machine; rather, it is to train him to kill in the sacred manner. A boy is usually introduced to the more esoteric mythology of his tribe during his initiation. He first hears about the Animal Master, the covenant, the magnanimity of the beasts, and the rituals that will restore his life while he is undergoing these traumatic rites. In these extraordinary circumstances, separated from everything familiar, he is pushed into a new state of consciousness that enables him to appreciate the profound bond that links hunter and prey in their common struggle for survival. This is not the kind of knowledge we acquire by purely logical deliberations, but is akin to the understanding derived from art. A poem, a play, or, indeed, a great painting has the power to change our perception in ways that we may not be able to explain logically but that seem incontestably true. We find that things that appear distinct to the rational eye are in some way profoundly connected or that a perfectly commonplace object—a chair, a sunflower, or a pair of boots—has numinous significance. Art involves our emotions, but if it is to be more than a superficial epiphany, this new insight must go deeper than feelings that are, by their very nature, ephemeral.

If the historians are right about the function of the Lascaux caves, religion and art were inseparable from the very beginning. Like art, religion is an attempt to construct meaning in the face of the relentless pain and injustice of life. As meaning-seeking creatures, men and women fall very easily into despair. They have created religions and works of art to help them find value in their lives, despite all the dispiriting evidence to the contrary. The initiation experience also shows that a myth, like that of the Animal Master, derives much of its meaning from the ritualized context in which it is imparted.[21] It may not be empirically true, it may defy the laws of logic, but a good myth will tell us something valuable about the human predicament. Like any work of art, a myth will make no sense unless we open ourselves to it wholeheartedly and allow it to change us. If we hold ourselves aloof, it will remain opaque, incomprehensible, and even ridiculous.

Religion is hard work. Its insights are not self-evident and have to be cultivated in the same way as an appreciation of art, music, or poetry must be developed. The intense effort required is especially evident in the underground labyrinth of Trois Frères at Ariège in the Pyrenees. Doctor Herbert Kuhn, who visited the site in 1926, twelve years after its discovery, described the frightening experience of crawling through the tunnel—scarcely a foot high in some places—that leads to the heart of this magnificent Palaeolithic sanctuary. "I felt as though I were creeping through a coffin," he recalled. "My heart is pounding and it is difficult to breathe. It is terrible to have the roof so close to one's head." He could hear the other members of his party groaning as they struggled through the darkness, and when they finally arrived in the vast underground hall, it felt "like a redemption."[22] They found themselves gazing at a wall covered in spectacular engravings: mammoths, bison, wild horses, wolverines, and musk oxen; darts flying everywhere; blood spurting from the mouths of the bears; and a human figure clad in animal skin playing a flute. Dominating the scene was a large painted figure, half man, half beast, who fixed his huge, penetrating eyes on the visitors. Was this the Animal Master? Or did this hybrid creature symbolize the underlying unity of animal and human, natural and divine?

A boy would not be expected to "believe" in the Animal Master before he entered the caves. But at the culmination of his ordeal, this image would have made a powerful impression; for hours he had, perhaps, fought his way through nearly a mile of convoluted passages to the accompaniment of "songs, cries, noises or mysterious objects thrown from no one knows where," special effects that would have been "easy to arrange in such a place."[23] In archaic thinking, there is no concept of the supernatural, no huge gulf separating human and divine. If a priest donned the sacred regalia of an animal pelt to impersonate the Animal Master, he became a temporary manifestation of that divine power.[24] These rituals were not the expression of a "belief" that had to be accepted in blind faith. As the German scholar Walter Burkert explains, it is pointless to look for an idea or doctrine *behind* a rite. In the premodern world, ritual was not the product of religious ideas; on the contrary, these ideas were the product of ritual.[25] *Homo religiosus* is pragmatic in this sense only; if a ritual no longer evokes a profound conviction of life's ultimate value, he simply abandons it. But for twenty thousand years, the hunters of the region continued to thread their way through the dangerous pathways of Trois Frères in order to bring their mythology—whatever it was—to life. They must have found the effort worthwhile or they would, without a backward glance, have given it up.

Religion was not something tacked on to the human condition, an optional extra imposed on people by unscrupulous priests. The desire to cultivate a sense of the transcendent may be *the* defining human characteristic. In about 9000 BCE, when human beings developed agriculture and were no longer dependent on animal meat, the old hunting rites lost some of their appeal and people ceased to visit the caves. But they did not discard religion altogether. Instead they developed a new set of myths and rituals based on the fecundity of the soil that filled the men and women of the Neolithic age with religious awe.[26] Tilling the fields became a ritual that replaced the hunt, and the nurturing Earth took the place of the Animal Master. Before the modern period, most men and women were naturally inclined to religion and they were prepared to work at it. Today many of us are no longer willing to make this effort, so the old myths seem arbitrary, remote, and incredible.

Like art, the truths of religion require the disciplined cultivation of a different mode of consciousness. The cave experience always began with the disorientation of utter darkness, which annihilated normal habits of mind. Human beings are so constituted that periodically they seek out *ekstasis,* a "stepping outside" the norm. Today people who no longer find it in a religious setting resort to other outlets: music, dance, art, sex, drugs, or sport. We make a point of seeking out these experiences that touch us deeply within and lift us momentarily beyond ourselves. At such times, we feel that we inhabit our humanity more fully than usual and experience an enhancement of being.

Lascaux may seem impossibly distant from modern religious practice, but we cannot understand either the nature of the religious quest or our current religious predicament unless we appreciate the spirituality that emerged quite early in the history of *Homo religiosus* and continued to animate the major confessional traditions until the early modern period, when an entirely different kind of religiosity emerged in the West during the seventeenth century. To do that we must examine a number of core principles that will be of fundamental importance to our story.

The first concerns the nature of the ultimate reality—later called God, Nirvana, Brahman, or Dao. In a rocky overhang at Laussel, near Lascaux, there is a small stone relief that is seventeen thousand years old and was created at about the same time as the earliest of the nearby cave paintings. It depicts a woman holding a curved bison's horn above her head so that it immediately suggests the rising, crescent moon; her right hand lies on her pregnancy. By this time, people had begun to observe the phases of the moon for practical purposes, but their religion had little or nothing to do with this protoscientific observation of the physical cosmos.[27] Instead, material reality was symbolic of an unseen dimension of existence. The little Venus of Laussel already suggests an association between the moon, the female cycle, and human reproduction. In many parts of the world, the moon was linked symbolically with a number of apparently unrelated phenomena: women, water, vegetation, serpents, and fertility. What they all have in common is the regenerative power of life that is continually able to renew itself. Everything could so easily lapse into nothingness, yet each year after the death of winter, trees sprout new leaves, the moon wanes but always waxes brilliantly once more, and the serpent, a universal symbol of initiation, sloughs off its old withered skin and comes forth gleaming and fresh.[28] The female also manifested this inexhaustible power. Ancient hunters revered a goddess known as the Great Mother. In large stone reliefs at Çatalhüyük in Turkey, she is shown giving birth, flanked by boars' skulls and bulls' horns—relics of a successful hunt. While hunters and animals died in the grim struggle for survival, the female was endlessly productive of new life.[29]

Perhaps these ancient societies were trying to express their sense of what the German philosopher Martin Heidegger (1899–1976) called "Being," a fundamental energy that supports and animates everything that exists. Being is transcendent. You could not see, touch, or hear it but could only watch it at work in the people, objects, and natural forces around you. From the documents of later Neolithic and pastoral societies, we know that Being rather than *a* being was revered as the ultimate sacred power. It was impossible to define or describe because Being is all-encompassing and our minds are only equipped to deal with particular beings, which can merely participate in it in a restricted manner. But certain objects became eloquent symbols of the power of Being, which sustained and shone through them with particular clarity. A stone or a rock (frequent symbols of the sacred) expressed the stability and durability of Being; the moon, its power of endless renewal; the sky, its towering transcendence, ubiquity, and universality.[30] None of these symbols was worshipped for and in itself. People did not bow down and worship a rock *tout court;* the rock was simply a focus that directed their attention to the mysterious essence of life. Being bound all things together; humans, animals, plants, insects, stars, and birds all shared the divine life that sustained the entire cosmos. We know, for example, that the ancient Aryan tribes, who had lived on the Caucasian steppes since about 4500 BCE, revered an invisible, impersonal force within themselves and all other natural phenomena. Everything was a manifestation of this all-pervading "Spirit" (Sanskrit: *manya*).[31]

There was, therefore, no belief in a single supreme being in the ancient world. Any such creature could only be *a* being—bigger and better than anything else, perhaps, but still a finite, incomplete reality. People felt it natural to imagine a race of spiritual beings of a higher nature than themselves that they called "gods." There were, after all, many unseen forces at work in the world—wind, heat, emotion, and air—that were often identified with the various deities. The Aryan god Agni, for example, *was* the fire that had transformed human life, and as a personalized god symbolized the deep affinity people felt with these sacred forces. The Aryans called their gods "the shining ones" *(devas)* because Spirit shone through them more brightly than through mortal creatures, but these gods had no control over the world: they were not omniscient and were obliged, like everything else, to submit to the transcendent order that kept everything in existence, set the stars on their courses, made the seasons follow each other, and compelled the seas to remain within bounds.[32]

By the tenth century BCE, when some of the Aryans had settled in the Indian subcontinent, they gave a new name to the ultimate reality. Brahman was the unseen principle that enabled all things to grow and flourish. It was a power that was higher, deeper, and more fundamental than the gods. Because it transcended the limitations of personality, it would be entirely inappropriate to pray to Brahman or expect it to answer your prayers. Brahman was the sacred energy that held all the disparate elements of the world together and prevented it from falling apart. Brahman had an infinitely greater degree of reality than mortal creatures, whose lives were limited by ignorance, sickness, pain, and death.[33] You could never define Brahman because language refers only to individual beings and Brahman was "the All"; it was everything that existed, as well as the inner meaning of all existence.

Even though human beings could not think about the Brahman, they had intimations of it in the hymns of the Rig Veda, the most important of the Aryan scriptures. Unlike the hunters of Lascaux, the Aryans do not seem to have thought readily in images. One of their chief symbols of the divine was sound, whose power and intangible quality seemed a particularly apt embodiment of the all-pervasive Brahman. When the priest chanted the Vedic hymns, the music filled the air and entered the consciousness of the congregation so that they felt surrounded by and infused with divinity. These hymns, revealed to ancient "seers" (rishis), did not speak of doctrines that the faithful were obliged to believe, but referred to the old myths in an allusive, riddling fashion because the truth they were trying to convey could not be contained in a neatly logical presentation. Their beauty shocked the audience into a state of awe, wonder, fear, and delight. They had to puzzle out the underlying significance of these paradoxical poems that yoked together apparently unrelated things, just as the hidden Brahman pulled the disparate elements of the universe into a coherent whole.[34]

During the tenth century, the Brahmin priests developed the Brahmodya competition, which would become a model of authentic religious discourse.[35] The contestants began by going on a retreat in the forest, where they performed spiritual exercises, such as fasting and breath control, that concentrated their minds and induced a different type of consciousness. Then the contest could begin. Its goal was to find a verbal formula to define the Brahman, in the process pushing language as far as it could go, until it finally broke down and people became vividly aware of the ineffable, the other. The challenger asked an enigmatic question, and his opponent had to reply in a way that was apt but equally inscrutable. The winner was the contestant who reduced his opponents to silence—and in that moment of silence, when language revealed its inadequacy, the Brahman was present; it became manifest only in the stunning realization of the impotence of speech.

The ultimate reality was not a personalized god, therefore, but a transcendent mystery that could never be plumbed. The Chinese called it the Dao, the fundamental "Way" of the cosmos. Because it comprised the whole of reality, the Dao had no qualities, no form; it could be experienced but never seen; it was not a god; it predated heaven and earth and was beyond divinity. You could not say anything about the Dao, because it transcended ordinary categories: it was more ancient than antiquity and yet it was not old; because it went far beyond any form of "existence" known to humans, it was neither being nor nonbeing.[36] It contained all the myriad patterns, forms, and potential that made the world the way it was and guided the endless flux of change and becoming that we see all around us. It existed at a point where all the distinctions that characterize our normal modes of thought became irrelevant.

In the Middle East, the region in which the Western monotheisms would develop, there was a similar notion of the ultimate. In Mesopotamia, the Akkadian word for "divinity" was *ilam,* a radiant power that transcended any particular deity. The gods were not the source of *ilam* but, like everything else, could only reflect it. The chief characteristic of this "divinity" was *ellu* ("holiness"), a word that had connotations of "brightness," "purity," and "luminosity." The gods were called the "holy ones" because their symbolic stories, effigies, and cults evoked the radiance of *ellu* within their worshippers. The people of Israel called their patronal deity, the "holy one" of Israel, Elohim, a Hebrew variant on *ellu* that summed up everything that the divine could mean for human beings. But holiness was not confined to the gods. Anything that came into contact with divinity could become holy too: a priest, a king, or a temple—even the sacred utensils of the cult. In the Middle East, people would have found it far too constricting to limit *ilam* to a single god; instead, they imagined a Divine Assembly, a council of gods of many different ranks, who worked together to sustain the cosmos and expressed the multifaceted complexity of the sacred.[37]

People felt a yearning for the absolute, intuited its presence all around them, and went to great lengths to cultivate their sense of this transcendence in creative rituals. But they also felt estranged from it. Almost every culture has developed a myth of a lost paradise from which men and women were ejected at the beginning of time. It expressed an inchoate conviction that life was not *meant* to be so fragmented, hard, and full of pain. There *must* have been a time when people had enjoyed a greater share in the fullness of being and had not been subject to sorrow, disease, bereavement, loneliness, old age, and death. This nostalgia informed the cult of "sacred geography," one of the oldest and most universal religious ideas. Certain places that stood out in some way from the norm—like the labyrinthine caverns of the Dordogne—seemed to speak of "something else."[38] The sacred place was one of the earliest and most ubiquitous symbols of the divine. It was a sacred "center" that brought heaven and earth together and where the divine potency seemed particularly effective.

A popular image, found in many cultures, imagined this fructifying, sacred energy welling up like a spring from these focal places and flowing, in four sacred rivers, to the four quarters of the earth. People would settle only in sites where the sacred had once become manifest because they wanted to live as closely as possible to the wellsprings of being and become as whole and complete as they had been before they were ejected from paradise.

This brings us to the second principle of premodern religion. Religious discourse was not intended to be understood literally because it was only possible to speak about a reality that transcended language in symbolic terms. The story of the lost paradise was a myth, not a factual account of a historical event. People were not expected to "believe" it in the abstract; like any *mythos,* it depended upon the rituals associated with the cult of a particular holy place to make what it signified a reality in the lives of participants.

The same applies to the creation myth that was central to ancient religion and has now become controversial in the Western world because the Genesis story seems to clash with modern science. But until the early modern period, nobody read a cosmology as a literal account of the origins of life. In the ancient world, it was inspired by an acute sense of the contingency and frailty of existence. Why had anything come into being at all, when there could so easily have been nothing? There has never been a simple or even a possible answer to this question, but people continue to ask it, pushing their minds to the limit of what we can know. One of the earliest and most universal of the ancient cosmologies is particularly instructive to us today. It was thought that one of the gods, known as the "High God" or "Sky God" because he dwelt in the farthest reaches of the heavens, had single-handedly created heaven and earth.[39] The Aryans called him Dyaeus Pitr, the Chinese Tian ("Heaven"), the Arabians Allah ("*the* God"), and the Syrians El Elyon ("Most High God"). But the High God proved to be an unviable deity, and his myth was jettisoned.

It suffered from an internal contradiction. How could a mere being—even such a lofty one—be responsible for being itself? As if in response to this objection, people tried to elevate the High God to a special plane. He was considered too exalted for an ordinary cult: no sacrifices were performed in his honor; he had no priests, no temples, and virtually no mythology of his own. People called on him in an emergency, but otherwise he scarcely ever impinged on their daily lives. Reduced to a mere explanation—to what would later be called First Cause or Prime Mover—he became *Deus otiosus,* a "useless" or "superfluous" deity, and gradually faded from the consciousness of his people. In most mythologies, the High God is often depicted as a passive, helpless figure; unable to control events, he retreats to the periphery of the pantheon and finally fades away. Today some of the indigenous peoples—Pygmies, Aboriginal Australians, and Fuegians—also speak of a High God who created heaven and earth, but, they tell anthropologists, he has died or disappeared; he "no longer cares" and "has gone far away from us."[40]

No god can survive unless he or she is actualized by the practical activity of ritual, and people often turn against gods who fail to deliver. The High God is often mythologically deposed, sometimes violently, by a younger generation of more dynamic deities—gods of storm, grain, or war—who symbolized relevant, important realities. In Greek *mythos,* the High God Uranus ("Heaven") was brutally castrated by his son Kronos. Later Kronos himself was overthrown by his own son Zeus, head of the younger gods, who lived more accessibly on Mount Olympus. In our own day, the God of the monotheistic tradition has often degenerated into a High God. The rites and practices that once made him a persuasive symbol of the sacred are no longer effective, and people have stopped participating in them. He has therefore become *otiosus,* an etiolated reality who for all intents and purposes has indeed died or "gone away."

In the ancient world, the High God myth was replaced by more relevant creation stories that were never regarded as factual. As one of the later hymns of the Rig Veda insists, nobody—not even the highest *deva*—could explain how something had issued from nothing.[41] A good creation myth did not describe an event in the distant past but told people something essential about the present. It reminded them that things often had to get worse before they got better, that creativity demanded self-sacrifice and heroic struggle, and that everybody had to work hard to preserve the energies of the cosmos and establish society on a sound foundation. A creation story was primarily therapeutic. People wanted to tap into the massive implosion of energy that had—somehow—brought the world we know into being, so they would recite a creation myth when they were in need of an infusion of sacred potency: during a political crisis, at a sickbed, or when they were building a new house. The creation myth was often re-enacted during the New Year ceremonies, when the old year was ebbing away. Nobody felt obliged to "believe" in a particular cosmology; indeed, each culture usually had several creation stories, each of which had its own lesson to impart, and people thought nothing of making up a new one if their circumstances changed.

Once people had abandoned the myth of the High God, there was no concept of creation "out of nothing" (*ex nihilo*) in the ancient world. A god could only assist a creative process that was already well under way. In the tenth century, another Indian *rishi* suggested that the world had been set in motion by a primordial sacrifice—something that made sense in India, where new vegetation was often seen to sprout from a rotting tree so that it was not unnatural to think of death resulting in new life. The *rishi* imagined the Purusha ("Person"), the first, archetypal human being, striding of his own free will to the place of sacrifice and allowing the gods to put him to death; thence everything—animals, horses, cattle, heaven, earth, sun, moon, and even some of the gods—emerged from his corpse.[42] This *mythos* encapsulated an important truth: we are at our most creative when we do not cling to our selfhood but are prepared to give ourselves away.

The cosmology was not influenced by current scientific speculation because it was exploring the interior rather than the external world. The priests of Mesopotamia undertook the first successful astronomical observations, noting that the seven celestial bodies they sighted—later known as Sun, Moon, Mercury, Venus, Mars, Jupiter, and Saturn—moved in an apparently circular path through the constellations. But the chief inspiration behind their creation myth was their pioneering town planning.[43] The first cities had been established in Sumer in the Fertile Crescent in about 3500 BCE; it was an enterprise that required enormous courage and perseverance, as time and time again, the mud-brick buildings were swept away by the flooding of the Tigris and the Euphrates. Constantly it seemed that the Sumerians' fragile urban civilization would sink back into the old rural barbarism, so the city needed a regular infusion of sacred energy. And yet it seemed such an extraordinary achievement that the city was extolled as a holy place. Babylon was the "Gate of the gods" (*Babi-lani*), where heaven and earth could meet; it re-created the lost paradise, and the ziggurat, or temple tower, of Esagila replicated the cosmic mountain or the sacred tree, which the first men and women had climbed to meet their gods.[44]

It is difficult to understand the creation story in Genesis without reference to the Mesopotamian creation hymn known from its opening words as the *Enuma Elish*. This poem begins by describing the evolution of the gods from primordial sacred matter and their subsequent creation of heaven and earth, but it is also a meditation on contemporary Mesopotamia. The raw material of the universe, from which the gods emerge, is a sloppy, undefined substance—very like the silty soil of the region. The first gods—Tiamat, the primal Ocean; Apsu, the "Abyss"; and Mummu, "Womb" of chaos—were inseparable from the elements and shared the inertia of aboriginal barbarism and the formlessness of chaos: "When sweet and bitter mingled together, no reed was plaited, no rushes muddied the water, the gods were nameless, natureless, futureless."[45] But new gods emerged, each pair more distinct than the last, culminating in the splendid Marduk, the Sun God and the most developed specimen of the divine species. But Marduk could not establish the cosmos until he had overcome the sluggish torpor of Tiamat in a tremendous battle. Finally he stood astride Tiamat's massive carcass, split her in two to make heaven and earth, and created the first man by mixing the blood of one of the defeated gods with a handful of dust. After this triumph, the gods could build the city of Babylon and establish the ritual "from which the universe receives its structure, the hidden world is made plain, and the gods assigned their places."[46]

There was no ontological gulf separating these gods from the rest of the cosmos; everything had emerged from the same sacred stuff. All beings shared the same predicament and had to participate in a ceaseless battle against the destructive lethargy of chaos. There were similar tales in neighboring Syria, where Baal, god of storm and life-giving rain, had to fight the sea dragon Lotan, symbol of chaos, Yam, the primal sea, and Mot, god of sterility, in order to establish civilized life.[47] The Israelites also told stories of their god Yahweh slaying sea monsters to order the cosmos.[48] In Babylon, the *Enuma Elish* was chanted on the fourth day of the New Year festival in Esagila, a re-enactment that symbolically continued the process Marduk had begun and that activated this sacred energy. There was a ritualized mock battle and a saturnalia that re-created the lawlessness of chaos. In archaic spirituality, a symbolic return to the formless "nothingness" of the beginning was indispensable to any new creation.[49] It was possible to move forward only if you had the courage to let go of the present, unsatisfactory state of affairs, sink back into the potent confusion of the beginning, and begin again.

As life became more settled, people had the leisure to develop a more interior spirituality. The Indian Aryans, always in the vanguard of religious change, pioneered this trend, achieving the groundbreaking discovery that the Brahman, being itself, was also the ground of the human psyche. The transcendent was neither external nor alien to humanity, but the two were inextricably connected. This insight would become central to the religious quest in all the major traditions. In the early Upanishads, composed in the seventh century BCE, the search for this sacred Self (*atman*) became central to Vedic spirituality. The Upanishadic sages did not ask their disciples to "believe" this but put them through an initiation whereby they discovered it for themselves in a series of spiritual exercises that made them look at the world differently. This practically acquired knowledge brought with it a joyous liberation from fear and anxiety.

We have a precious glimpse of the way this initiation was carried out in the Chandogya Upanishad. Here the great sage Uddalaka Aruni slowly and patiently brings this saving insight to birth within his son Shvetaketu and has him perform a series of tasks. In the most famous of these experiments, Shvetaketu had to leave a lump of salt in a beaker of water overnight and found, of course, that even though the salt had dissolved, the water still tasted salty. "You, of course, did not see it there, son," Uddalaka pointed out, "yet it was always right there." So too was the invisible Brahman, essence and inner self of the entire world. "And you are *that,* Shvetaketu."[50] Like the salt, the Brahman could not be seen but was manifest in every single living thing. It was the subtle essence in the tiny banyan seed, from which a giant tree would grow, yet when Shvetaketu dissected the seed, he could not see anything at all. The Brahman was also the sap in every part of the tree that gave it life, and yet it could never be pinned down or analyzed.[51] All things shared the same essence, but most people did not realize this. They imagined they were unique and special and clung to these particularities—often with extreme anxiety and expenditure of effort. But in reality these qualities were no more durable than rivers that flowed into the same sea. Once they had merged, they became "just the ocean," and no longer asserted their individuality by insisting "I am that river," "I am this river." "In exactly the same way, son," Uddalaka persisted, "when all these creatures reach the Existent, they are not aware that: 'We are reaching the Existent.'" Whether they were tigers, wolves, or gnats, they all merged into Brahman. To hold on to the mundane self, therefore, was a delusion that led inescapably to pain, frustration, and confusion, which one could escape only by acquiring the deep, liberating knowledge that the Brahman was their atman, the truest thing about them.[52]

The Upanishadic sages were among the first to articulate another of the universal principles of religion—one that had already been touched upon in the Purusha myth. The truths of religion are accessible only when you are prepared to get rid of the selfishness, greed, and self-preoccupation that, perhaps inevitably, are ingrained in our thoughts and behavior but are also the source of so much of our pain. The Greeks would call this process *kenosis,* "emptying." Once you gave up the nervous craving to promote yourself, denigrate others, draw attention to your unique and special qualities, and ensure that you were first in the pecking order, you experienced an immense peace. The first Upanishads were written at a time when the Aryan communities were in the early stages of urbanization; *logos* had enabled them to master their environment. But the sages reminded them that there were some things—old age, sickness, and death—that they could not control; things—such as their essential self—that lay beyond their intellectual grasp. When, as a result of carefully crafted spiritual exercises, people learned not only to accept but to embrace this unknowing, they found that they experienced a sense of release.

The sages began to explore the complexities of the human psyche with remarkable sophistication; they had discovered the unconscious long before Freud. But the atman, the deepest core of their personality, eluded them. Precisely *because* it was identical with the Brahman, it was indefinable. The atman had nothing to do with our normal psycho-mental states and bore no resemblance to anything in our ordinary experience, so you could speak of it only in negative terms. As the seventh-century sage Yajnavalkya explained: "About this Self [atman] one can only say 'not … not' [neti … neti]."[53]

> You can't see the Seer who does the seeing. You can't hear the Hearer who does the hearing; you can't think with the Thinker who does the thinking; and you can't perceive the Perceiver who does the perceiving. This Self within the All [Brahman] is this *atman* of yours.[54]

Like the Brahmodya, any discussion of the atman in the Upanishads always ended in silence, the numinous acknowledgment that the ultimate reality was beyond the competence of language.

Authentic religious discourse could not lead to clear, distinct, and empirically verified truth. Like the Brahman, the atman was "ungraspable." You could define something only when you saw it as separate from yourself. But "when the Whole [Brahman] has become a person's very self, then who is there for him to see and by what means? Who is there for me to think of and by what means?"[55] But if you learned to "realize" the truth that your most authentic "Self was identical with Brahman, you understood that it too was "beyond hunger and thirst, sorrow and delusion, old age and death."[56] You could not achieve this insight by rational logic. You had to acquire the knack of thinking outside the ordinary "lowercase" self, and like any craft or skill, this required long, hard, dedicated practice.

One of the principal technologies that enabled people to achieve this self-forgetfulness was yoga.[57] Unlike the yoga practiced in Western gyms today, it was not an aerobic exercise but a systematic breakdown of instinctive behavior and normal thought patterns. It was mentally demanding and, initially, physically painful. The yogin had to do the opposite of what came naturally. He sat so still that he seemed more like a plant or a statue than a human being; he controlled his respiration, one of the most automatic and essential of our physical functions, until he acquired the ability to exist for long periods without breathing at all. He learned to silence the thoughts that coursed through his mind and concentrate "on one point" for hours at a time. If he persevered, he found that he achieved a dissolution of ordinary consciousness that extracted the "I" from his thinking.

To this day, yogins find that these disciplines, which have measurable physical and neurological effects, evoke a sense of calm, harmony, and equanimity that is comparable to the effect of music. There is a feeling of expansiveness and bliss, which yogins regard as entirely natural, possible for anybody who has the talent and application. As the "I" disappears, the most humdrum objects reveal wholly unexpected qualities since they are no longer viewed through the distorting filter of one's own egotistic needs and desires. When she meditated on the teachings of her guru, a yogin did not simply accept them notionally but experienced them so vividly that her knowledge was, as the texts say, "direct"; bypassing the logical processes like any practically acquired skill, it had become part of her inner world.[58]

But yoga also had an ethical dimension. A beginner was not allowed to perform a single yogic exercise until he had completed an intensive moral program. Top of the list of its requirements was *ahimsa,* "nonviolence." A yogin must not swat a mosquito, make an irritable gesture, or speak unkindly to others but should maintain constant affability to all, even the most annoying monk in the community. Until his guru was satisfied that this had become second nature, a yogin could not even sit in the yogic position. A great deal of the aggression, frustration, hostility, and rage that mars our peace of mind is the result of thwarted egotism, but when the aspiring yogin became proficient in this selfless equanimity, the texts tell us that he would experience "indescribable joy."[59] Their experience of yoga led the sages to devise a new creation myth. In the beginning, there was only a single Person, who looked around him and discovered that he was alone. In this way, he became aware of himself and cried: "Here I am!" Thus the "I," the ego principle, was born. Immediately the Person became afraid, because we instinctively feel that we must protect the fragile ego from anything that threatens it, but when the Person remembered that because he was alone, there was no such threat, his fear left him. But he was lonely, so he split his body in two to create a man and a woman, who together gave birth to every single being in the cosmos "down to the very ants." And the Person realized that even though he was no longer alone, there was still nothing to fear. Was he not identical with Brahman, the All? He was one with all the things that he had made; indeed, he was himself his own creation.[60] He had even created the gods, who were essentially a part of himself.[61]

Even now, if a man knows "I am *brahman*" in this way, he becomes this whole world. Not even the gods are able to prevent it, for he becomes their very self [atman]. So when a man venerates another deity, thinking, "He is one, and I am another," he does not understand.[62] This insight, Yajnavalkya explained, brought with it a joy comparable to that of sexual intercourse, when one loses all sense of duality and is "oblivious to everything within or without."[63] But you would not have this experience unless you had performed the yogic exercises. Other traditions would also find that these fundamental principles were indispensable: Buddhism, Jainism, Confucianism, and Daoism, as well as the three monotheistic faiths of Judaism, Christianity, and Islam. Each had its own unique genius and distinctive vision, each its peculiar flaws. But on these central principles they would all agree. Religion was not a notional matter. The Buddha, for example, had little time for theological speculation. One of his monks was a philosopher manqué and, instead of getting on with his yoga, constantly pestered the Buddha about metaphysical questions: Was there a god? Had the world been created in time or had it always existed? The Buddha told him that he was like a man who had been shot with a poisoned arrow and refused medical treatment until he had discovered the name of his assailant and what village he came from. He would die before he got this perfectly useless information. What difference would it make to discover that a god had created the world? Pain, hatred, grief, and sorrow would still exist. These issues were fascinating, but the Buddha refused to discuss them because they were irrelevant: "My disciples, they will not help you, they are not useful in the quest for holiness; they do not lead to peace and to the direct knowledge of Nirvana."[64]

The Buddha always refused to define Nirvana, because it could not be understood notionally and would be inexplicable to anybody who did not undertake his practical regimen of meditation and compassion. But anybody who did commit him- or herself to the Buddhist way of life could attain Nirvana, which was an entirely natural state.[65] Sometimes, however, Buddhists would speak of Nirvana using the same kind of imagery as monotheists use for God: it was the "Truth," the "Other Shore," "Peace," the "Everlasting," and "the Beyond." Nirvana was a still center that gave meaning to life, an oasis of calm, and a source of strength that you discovered in the depths of your own being. In purely mundane terms, it was "nothing," because it corresponded to no reality that we could recognize in our ego-dominated existence. But those who had managed to find this sacred peace discovered that they lived an immeasurably richer life.[66] There was no question of "believing" in the existence of Nirvana or taking it "on faith." The Buddha had no time for abstract doctrinal formulations divorced from action. Indeed, to accept a dogma on somebody else's authority was what he called "unskillful" or "unhelpful" (*akusala*). It could not lead to enlightenment because it amounted to an abdication of personal responsibility. Faith meant trust that Nirvana existed and a determination to realize it by every practical means in one's power.

Nirvana was the natural result of a life lived according to the Buddha's doctrine *of anatta* ("no self"), which was not simply a metaphysical principle but, like all his teachings, a program of action. *Anatta* required Buddhists to *behave* day by day, hour by hour, as though the self did not exist. Thoughts of "self" not only led to "unhelpful" (*akusala*) preoccupation with "me" and "mine," but also to envy, hatred of rivals, conceit, pride, cruelty, and—when the self felt under threat—violence. As a monk became expert in cultivating this dispassion, he no longer interjected his ego into passing mental states but learned to regard his fears and desires as transient and remote phenomena. He was then ripe for enlightenment: "His greed fades away, and once his cravings disappear, he experiences the release of the mind."[67] The texts indicate that when the Buddha's first disciples heard about *anatta,* their hearts were filled with joy and they immediately experienced Nirvana. To live beyond the reach of hatred, greed, and anxieties about our status proved to be a profound relief.

By far the best way of achieving *anatta* was compassion, the ability to *feel with* the other, which required that one dethrone the self from the center of one's world and put another there. Compassion would become the central practice of the religious quest. One of the first people to make it crystal clear that holiness was inseparable from altruism was the Chinese sage Confucius (551–479 BCE). He preferred not to speak about the divine because it lay beyond the competence of language, and theological chatter was a distraction from the real business of religion.[68] He used to say: "My Way has one thread that runs right through it." There were no abstruse metaphysics; everything always came back to the importance of treating others with absolute respect.[69] It was epitomized in the Golden Rule, which, he said, his disciples should practice "all day and every day":[70] "Never do to others what you would not like them to do to you."[71] They should look into their own hearts, discover what gave them pain, and then refuse under any circumstance whatsoever to inflict that pain on anybody else.

Religion was a matter of doing rather than thinking. The traditional rituals of China enabled an individual to burnish and refine his humanity so that he became a *junzi,* a "mature person." A *junzi* was not born but crafted; he had to work on himself as a sculptor shaped a rough stone and made it a thing of beauty. "How can I achieve this?" asked Yan Hui, Confucius's most talented disciple. It was simple, Confucius replied: "Curb your ego and surrender to ritual (*li*)."[72] A *junzi* must submit every detail of his life to the ancient rites of consideration and respect for others. This was the answer to China's political problems: "If a ruler could curb his ego and submit to *li* for a single day, everyone under Heaven would respond to his goodness."[73]

The practice of the Golden Rule "all day and every day" would bring human beings into the state that Confucius called *ren,* a word that would later be described as "benevolence" but that Confucius himself refused to define because it could be understood only by somebody who had acquired it. He preferred to remain silent about what lay at the end of the religious journey. The practice of *ren* was an end in itself; it was itself the transcendence you sought. Yan Hui expressed this beautifully when he spoke of the endless struggle to achieve *ren* "with a deep sigh."

> The more I strain my gaze towards it, the higher it soars. The deeper
> I bore down into it, the harder it becomes. I see it in front, but suddenly
> it is behind. Step by step, the Master skil[l]fully lures one on. He has
> broadened me with culture, restrained me with ritual. Even if I wanted
> to stop, I could not. Just when I feel that I have exhausted every
> resource, something seems to rise up, standing over me sharp and clear.
> Yet though I long to pursue it, I can find no way of getting to it at all.[74]

Living a compassionate, empathetic life took Yan Hui beyond himself, giving him momentary glimpses of a sacred reality that was not unlike the "God" worshipped by monotheists. It was both immanent and transcendent: it welled up from within but was also experienced as an external presence "standing over me sharp and clear."

Religion as defined by the great sages of India, China, and the Middle East was not a notional activity but a practical one; it did not require belief in a set of doctrines but rather hard, disciplined work, without which any religious teaching remained opaque and incredible. The ultimate reality was not a Supreme Being—an idea that was quite alien to the religious sensibility of antiquity; it was an all-encompassing, wholly transcendent reality that lay beyond neat doctrinal formulations. So religious discourse should not attempt to impart clear information about the divine but should lead to an appreciation of the limits of language and understanding. The ultimate was not alien to human beings but inseparable from our humanity. It could not be accessed by rational, discursive thought but required a carefully cultivated state of mind and the abnegation of selfishness.

NOTES

1. Joseph Campbell, *Primitive Mythology: The Masks of God,* rev. ed. (New York, 1988), p. 305; Joseph Campbell with Bill Moyers, *The Power of Myth* (New York, 1988), p. 79.
2. André Leroi-Gourhan, *Treasures of Prehistoric Art* (New York, n.d.), p. 112. This rules out the suggestion that the paintings were simply a form of hunting magic.
3. Ibid., p. 118.
4. John E. Pfeiffer, *The Creative Explosion* (New York, 1982), p. viii.
5. André Leroi-Gourhan, *Les religions préhistorique: Paléolithique* (Paris, 1964), pp. 83–84; Mircea Eliade, *A History of Religious Ideas,* 3 vols., trans. Willard R. Trask (Chicago and London, 1978, 1982, 1985), 1:16.

6. Joseph Campbell, *Historical Atlas of World Mythologies*, 2 vols. (New York, 1988), 1,1:58.

7. Ibid., 1,1:65.

8. Leo Frobenius, *Kulturgeschichte Africas* (Zurich, 1933), pp. 131–32; Campbell, *Primitive Mythology*, p. 300.

9. Mircea Eliade, *History of Religious Ideas*, 1:24.

10. Joseph Campbell with Bill Moyers, *Power of Myth*, pp. 85–87.

11. Ibid., pp. 72–79; *Historical Atlas*, 1,1:48–49; Mircea Eliade, *History of Religious Ideas*, 1:7–8.

12. Walter Burkert, *Homo Necans: The Anthropology of Ancient Greek Sacrificial Ritual and Myth*, trans. Peter Bing (Berkeley, Los Angeles, and London, 1983), pp. 16–22.

13. Walter Burkert, *Structure and History in Greek Mythology and Ritual* (Berkeley, Los Angeles, and London, 1980), pp. 54–56; Walter Burkert, *Homo Necans*, pp. 42–45.

14. Joseph Campbell, *Historical Atlas*, 1, 2:xiii.

15. Ibid., 1,1:93.

16. Joseph Campbell, *Primitive Mythology*, p. 66.

17. Mircea Eliade, *The Myth of the Eternal Return, or Cosmos and History*, trans. Willard R. Trask (Princeton, N.J., 1954), pp. 1–34.

18. Huston Smith, *The World's Religions*, rev. ed. (New York, 1991), p. 367.

19. Mircea Eliade, *History of Religious Ideas*, 1:17.

20. Mircea Eliade, *Birth and Rebirth: The Religious Meanings of Initiation in Human Cultures* (New York, 1958); Mircea Eliade, *Myths, Dreams and Mysteries: The Encounter between Contemporary Faiths and Archaic Realities*, trans. Philip Mairet (London, 1960), pp. 194–226; Joseph Campbell with Bill Moyers, *Power of Myth*, pp. 81–85.

21. Mircea Eliade, *Myths, Dreams*, p. 225.

22. Herbert Kuhn, *Auf den Spuren des Eiszeitmenscken* (Wiesbaden, 1953), pp. 88–89; Joseph Campbell, *Primitive Mythology*, pp. 307–8.

23. Abbé Henri Breuil, *Four Hundred Centuries of Cave Art* (Montignac, France, 1952), pp. 170–71.

24. Joseph Campbell, *Primitive Mythology*, p. 311.

25. Walter Burkert, *Homo Necans*, pp. 27–34.

26. Mircea Eliade, *Patterns in Comparative Religion*, trans. Rosemary Sheed (London, 1958), pp. 331–43.

27. Alexander Marshack, "Lunar Notations on Upper Palaeolithic Remains," *Scientia* 146 (1964).

28. Mircea Eliade, *Patterns in Comparative Religion*, pp. 146–85.

29. Walter Burkert, *Homo Necans*, pp. 78–82.

30. Mircea Eliade, *Patterns in Comparative Religion*, pp. 1–124, 216–39.

31. Mary Boyce, *Zoroastrians: Their Religious Beliefs and Practices*, 2nd ed. (London and New York, 2001), p. 2; Peter Clark, *Zoroastrians: An Introduction to an Ancient Faith* (Brighton and Portland, Ore., 1998), p. 18.

32. Mary Boyce, *Zoroastrians*, pp. 9–11.

33. Jan Gonda, *Change and Continuity in Indian Religion* (The Hague, 1965), p. 200; Louis Renou, "Sur la notion de *brahman*," *Journal Asiatique* 237 (1949).

34. Louis Renou, *Religions of Ancient India* (London, 1953), pp. 10, 16–18; Michael Witzel, "Vedas and Upanishads" in Gavin Flood, ed., *The Blackwell Companion to Hinduism* (Oxford, 2003), pp. 70–71.

35. J. C. Heesterman, *The Inner Conflict of Tradition: Essays in Indian Ritual, Kingship and Society* (Chicago and London, 1985), pp. 70–72, 126.

36. Zhuangzi, *The Book of Zhuangzi*, 6:29–31.

37. Mark S. Smith, *The Origins of Biblical Monotheism: Israel's Polytheistic Background and the Ugaritic Texts* (New York and London, 2001), pp. 41–79.

38. Mircea Eliade, *Patterns in Comparative Religion*, pp. 367–88; Mircea Eliade, *The Sacred and the Profane: The Nature of Religion*, trans. Willard R. Trask (New York, 1959), pp. 50–54, 64; Mircea Eliade, *Images and Symbols: Studies in Religious Symbolism*, trans. Philip Mairet (Princeton, N.J., 1991), pp. 37–56.

39. Mircea Eliade, *Patterns in Comparative Religion*, pp. 38–63; Mircea Eliade, *Myths, Dreams*, pp. 172–78; Wilhelm Schmidt, *The Origin of the Idea of God* (New York, 1912), passim.

40. Mircea Eliade, *The Sacred and the Profane*, pp. 120–25.

41. Rig Veda 10.129.

42. Rig Veda 10.90.

43. Gwendolyn Leick, *Mesopotamia: The Invention of the City* (London, 2001), p. 268.

44. Thorkild Jacobsen, "The Cosmos as State," In H. and H. A. Frankfort, eds., *The Intellectual Adventure of Ancient Man: An Essay on the Speculative Thought in the Ancient Near East* (Chicago, 1946), pp. 186–97.

45. "The Babylonian Creation" 1.1 in N. K. Sanders, trans. and ed., *Poems of Heaven and Hell from Ancient Mesopotamia* (London, 1971).

46. *Enuma Elish* 6.19, In Sanders, *Poems of Heaven and Hell*.

47. E. O. James, *The Ancient Gods* (London, 1960), pp. 87–90.

48. Psalms 89:10–13; 93:1–4; Isaiah 27:1; Job 7:12; 9:8; 26:12; 38:7.

49. Mircea Eliade, *Myths, Dreams*, pp. 80–81.

50. Chandogya Upanishad (CU) 6.13; my italics. All quotations from the Upanishads are from Patrick Olivelle, trans. and ed., *Upanisads* (Oxford and New York, 1996).

51. CU 6.11–12.

52. CU 6.10.

53. Brhadaranyaka Upanishad (BU) 4.5.15.

54. BU 3.4.

55. BU 4.5.13–15.

56. BU 3.5.1.

57. Mircea Eliade, *Yoga, Immortality and Freedom*, trans. Willard R. Trask (New York, 1958).

58. Women participated in Upanishadic spirituality and, later, in Buddhist practice.

59. Patanjali, Yoga Sutra 2.42, in Eliade, *Yoga*, p. 52.

60. BU 1.4.1–5.

61. BU 1.4.6.

62. BU 1.4.10.

63. BU 4.3.21.

64. Samyutta Nikaya 53:31. The quotations from the Pali Canon of Buddhist scriptures are my own version of the texts cited.

65. Sutta-Nipata 43:1–44.

66. Majjima Nikaya 29.

67. *Vinaya:* Mahavagga 1.6.

68. Confucius, Analects 17.19. Unless otherwise stated, quotations from the Analects are taken from Arthur Waley, trans. and ed., *The Analects of Confucius* (New York, 1992).

69. Analects 4.15.

70. Analects 15.23.

71. Ibid.

72. Analects 12.1. Translation suggested by Benjamin I. Schwartz, *The World of Thought in Ancient China* (Cambridge, Mass., and London, 1985), p. 77.

73. Ibid.

74. Analects 9.10.

QUESTIONS FOR MAKING CONNECTIONS
WITHIN THE READING

1. In "Homo religiosus," Armstrong takes us back to the roots of religion in the Paleolithic era. The portrait she paints might surprise many readers. "In archaic thinking," she argues, "there [was] no concept of the supernatural, no huge gulf separating human and divine." There was "no belief in a single supreme being," and indeed belief itself was beside the point because religion was openly understood as a myth, not a literal truth. Reread the chapter and carefully note the many differences between religion then and religion now. Next, go back and look for the continuities. In spite of the differences, would you say that much of the Paleolithic legacy survives to this day? Can we conclude that religion has become more mature and sophisticated, or is it possible that we have lost touch with what religion actually represents? Where does Armstrong herself seem to stand on this final question?

2. Whether we are looking at the Middle East, ancient China, or the culture of Aryan peoples who came off the steppes and settled in India, Armstrong insists that religion was "a matter of doing rather than thinking." But what exactly does she mean by "doing"? What kinds of activities might religion have entailed in ancient times? Start with the ancient shamans whose activities are hinted at by the frescoes at Chauvet, and then follow the historical thread until you reach Heidegger. Clearly, religious activities are meant to enhance ordinary life, but at the same time they appear to involve forms of behavior that are quite distinct from everyday existence. How do the mundane and the sacred interact in the history of religious "doing"?

3. One central concern of "Homo religiosus" is the self in its connections to the universe as a whole. Even though religion in our time is quite commonly understood in terms of a personal relationship with God, Armstrong emphasizes the importance of what the ancient Greeks called *ekstasis,* a "stepping outside the norm," and *kenosis,* the "emptying" of the self. In what way does self-emptying connect the individual with the "sacred energy" of the universe? How might the experience of "nothingness" make people more alive and creative? What gets lost, in Armstrong's view, when we imagine the "ultimate reality" as a "Supreme Being"?

QUESTIONS FOR WRITING

1. According to Armstrong, "All ancient religion was based on what has been called the perennial philosophy, because it was present in some form in so many premodern cultures." To support this claim she looks at religion among such disparate groups as the Australian Aborigines, the ancient Aryans and Chinese, the peoples of the Middle East, and the ancient Greeks. While their belief systems can appear quite dissimilar today, Armstrong points to underlying commonalities. For example, just as the Aryans thought of their gods as *devas* or shining ones, so the forerunners of the Abrahamic faiths—Judaism, Christianity, and Islam—used the world *ilam,* meaning "radiant power," to describe their own deities. What are the implications of these parallels? Have we put so great an emphasis on the differences that we have lost touch with the greater unity? What factors might explain the emphasis on such differences?

2. One theme of Armstrong's recent work has been the distinction between two forms of knowing that she calls *logos* and *mythos. Logos* describes a kind of truth that strives for objectivity through the use of critical reason, while *mythos* describes a truth whose purpose is to overcome our subjective sense of separateness from the world and other living beings. Though past societies understood the distinction between the two, Armstrong contends that in our time both skeptics and religious people treat *mythos* as a set of objective claims. After reading "Homo religiosus," would you say that *mythos* should have a place in our lives today? Is it really possible for us to keep *mythos* separate from *logos*? How might the two become confused, and what dangers might rise from confusing them?

QUESTIONS FOR MAKING CONNECTIONS
BETWEEN READINGS

1. What might Armstrong have to say about our relationship with technology as it is described by Sherry Turkle in Selections from *Alone Together: Why We Expect More from Technology and Less from Each Other?* One place

to start in developing your response might be this passage from "Homo religiosus":

> Human beings are so constituted that periodically they seek out *ekstasis,* a "stepping outside" the norm. Today people who no longer find [*ekstasis*] in a religious setting resort to other outlets: music, dance, art, sex, drugs, or sport. We make a point of seeking out these experiences that touch us deeply within and lift us momentarily beyond ourselves. At such times, we feel that we inhabit our humanity more fully than usual and experience an enhancement of being.

Can our attitude toward technology be defined as *religious* in Armstrong's sense of the word? Think about the popular notion of the *singularity*—does that qualify as religious? Does our current technology "lift us ... beyond ourselves" and allow us to "inhabit our humanity more fully"? Or, by contrast, does our reliance on technology amount to an inversion of *ekstasis,* a contraction rather than an opening? Have machines taken the place of the animals that once figured in our rituals and mysteries? If we are no longer connecting to nature, what are we connecting to?

2. Armstrong sees religion as "matter of doing" rather than a matter of allegiance to unchanging beliefs. Reread her chapter and carefully note the many different forms of "doing" she explores, from ritual sacrifice to yoga. In what sense might we understand premodern religion as a form of psychotherapy of the kind practiced today by Martha Stout, author of "When I Woke Up Tuesday Morning, It Was Friday"? Were religious practices possibly designed to overcome dissociated states and the pathologies that they cause? Or does religion actually encourage dissociation? If the answer to this last question is yes, what might be the purpose of turning away from the here and now, at least temporarily?

LESLIE BELL

WOMEN'S SEXUALITY HAS become a fault line where values collide with particular force. One widely cited article that appeared in *the New York Times* (2008) described a debate between two Harvard students, Janie Fredell, a leader of the campus abstinence movement, and Lena Chen, a popular blogger on sex. Afterward, Fredell explained to the *Times* reporter, "It takes a strong woman to be abstinent, and that's the sort of woman I want to be." But Chen's rationale for the opposite—an active sexual life—was similar in its emphasis on strength. "For me," Chen said, "being a strong woman means not being ashamed that I like to have sex." Since the debate, books critical of the so-called hookup culture have become national bestsellers. The title of Donna Freitas's book says it all: *The End of Sex: How Hookup Culture Is Leaving a Generation Unhappy, Sexually Unfulfilled, and Confused About Intimacy*. But other writers, like Hanna Rosin, take the opposing view: "Single young women in their sexual prime ... are for the first time in history more successful, on average, than the single young men around them. They are more likely to have a college degree and, in aggregate, they make more money. What makes this remarkable development possible is not just the pill or legal abortion but the whole new landscape of sexual freedom."

Into this debate comes Leslie C. Bell's *Hard to Get: Twenty-Something Women and the Paradox of Sexual Freedom*, from which the following selection comes. While celebrating women's sexuality and the crucial role it plays in their psychological development, Bell also recognizes the paradox implicit in this new freedom. To pursue the same sexual fulfillments as men is to risk shaming or exploitation, but seeking sexual intimacy in conventional relationships often means that women are expected to subordinate their aspirations to those of their male partners. Bell suggests, however, that women have many more alternatives. Celibacy and hooking up are not the only options, nor do women have to choose between intimacy and a career. Drawing on psychoanalytic tradition, Bell argues that women need to free themselves from the dynamic of "splitting"—the black-and-white thinking that closes down the possibility of living in a truly liberating way.

Bell received a B.A. from Swarthmore College, an M.S.W. from the Smith College School for Social Work, and a Ph.D. in psychoanalytic sociology from the

Reprinted from HARD TO GET: TWENTY-SOMETHING WOMEN AND THE PARADOX OF SEXUAL FREEDOM, by permission of the University of California Press. Copyright © 2013 by Leslie C. Bell.

Quotations of Fredell and Chen are from Randall Patterson, "Students of Virginity," *New York Times Magazine*, March 30, 2008. The quotation from Hanna Rosin is taken from "Boys on the Side," *The Atlantic*, August 22, 2012. <http://www.theatlantic.com/magazine/archive/2012/09/boys-on-the-side/309062/> Biographical information is from http://www.lesliecbell.com/n-the-side/309062/sample-page/.

University of California, Berkeley. She maintains a private practice as a psychotherapist, and has taught courses on women's development, gender inequality, and sexuality at U.C. Berkeley and at the Women's Therapy Center in the city of Berkeley, where she also mentors graduate students. Bell has served as a fellow for the Woodrow Wilson Foundation, the Social Science Research Council, the American Psychoanalytic Association, and the Robert Stoller Foundation.

Selections from Hard to Get: Twenty-Something Women and the Paradox of Sexual Freedom

Excited yet embarrassed, Claudia, a twenty-eight-year-old postdoctoral researcher, told me about a one-night stand she'd had the night before our interview. I listened as she described the encounter: the fun of flirting with the man at a concert, the excitement and nervousness when it was still unclear what would happen, and the pleasure of being touched by someone she found so attractive. But I noticed that her pleasure gave way to worry that her strong sexual desires might get her into trouble. "I wish I weren't so horny, so I didn't need to go out and get it so much. I wish I could take a pill to kill my desire," she confided. Claudia felt some shame about her sexual desires and feared others might label her a "ho" for acting on them. She imagined that her Mexican Catholic family would be horrified if they knew about the number of sexual partners she'd had, that they would be devastated and disappointed that their daughter had not become the woman they raised her to be: a good girl who would marry her first boyfriend.[1] At the same time, the strength of her sexual desires sometimes frightened her, and she feared that men might find them overwhelming. Claudia also worried that being in a relationship would mean a loss of her identity, as she had witnessed her mother sacrifice her own dreams and adventurous spirit to be a wife and parent. Consequently, Claudia had not settled down, and she felt baffled at how difficult it had been to develop successful relationships with men. She had doggedly pursued her career goals as an academic and felt accomplished in that arena, but wondered why she hadn't had as much success in relationships.

At every turn and from every angle, Claudia was uncomfortable with the dimensions of her sexuality. Claudia, like many twenty-something women, was not playing hard to get. But good sex and relationships were proving elusive.

This is not the outcome Claudia's feminist foremothers dreamed of for her. Today's young women are supposed to be liberated from old edicts about sex and love. Their twenties ought to be a decade of freedom and exploration. But in interviews and in my psychotherapy practice with young women, I have found them to be more confused than ever about not only *how* to get what they want, but *what* they want.

Did Claudia want a relationship? Maybe, but not too serious a relationship; she didn't want to be held back from pursuing her goals. Did she want casual sex? Maybe, but only if she could feel safe enough. Did she want to have regular orgasms? Yes, but she was afraid of losing too much control....

Young women who are college-educated and childless are part of a new generation that has a longer time for self-exploration than did earlier generations of women. For many women, the twenties are no longer a time principally devoted to either partnership or children. They have more freedom than women a few generations ago would have imagined possible. This period would seem to be ripe with possibilities for sexual and relationship satisfaction.[2]

I take a look at this new in-between period of early adulthood for twenty-somethings and how it offers women a mixed bag: opportunities, to be sure, but also retrograde messages about their identities as sexual beings, partners, and future mothers. And while they have plenty of training in how to be successful and in control of their careers, young women have little help or training, apart from the self-help aisle in their local bookstore, in how to manage these freedoms, mixed messages, and their own desires to get what they want from sex and love....

THE PARADOX OF SEXUAL FREEDOM

This in-between period of early adulthood provides a window into the social, cultural, and economic changes that have been afoot for the past five decades.[3] And twenty-something women bear the imprint of those changes. For these resourceful women, sex and relationships really can occur independent of marriage and reproduction in their twenties. The current average age of first sexual intercourse for girls is seventeen, leaving ten years of sexual and relationship activity before the current average age of marriage at twenty-seven. These women don't think twice about cohabiting with a partner, or about delaying marriage until their own careers are on track.

In formulating this study, I thought that these women would describe this time in their lives as one in which they were relatively free from social restrictions and proscriptions on sexuality and relationships, but through my research and my psychotherapy practice, I discovered a different story. Instead of feeling free, twenty-something women are weighed down by vying cultural notions about the kind of sex and relationships they should be having in their twenties. Be assertive, but not aggressive. Be feminine, but not too passive. Be sexually adventurous, but don't alienate men with your sexual prowess. Be honest and open, but don't overwhelm someone with too much personal information. They are taught to seek out a companionate relationship of equals. But at the same time they are instructed by increasingly popular arguments from the burgeoning field of evolutionary psychology about irreconcilable differences between men and women. Meanwhile, they spend their twenties hearing gloomy forecasts about their chances of marriage if they don't marry before thirty, and their chances of conceiving a baby if they don't get pregnant before thirty-five. Given the discordant nature of these prescriptions, it's no wonder that the women I interviewed and counsel struggle to square these contradictory messages with their own individual experiences.

With relationships, women hear that they ought to use their twenties to "live it up" and not necessarily to be serious about relationships. Indeed, they ought not care very much about relationships, and shouldn't be devastated when relationships don't work out. Hearing advice across the self-help spectrum—from *The Rules,* which admonishes them to pretend to be independent to get into a relationship, to *He's Just Not That into You,* which entreats them to stop being so needy and get on with their lives after a breakup—young women often struggle to admit that they need anyone, but it's particularly difficult to say that they need a man. At the same time, they are enjoined to remember that partnership and marriage are just around the corner, when they turn thirty, so the dating and experimentation of their twenties must result in a relationship, and must come to an end. At that point, books such as *Marry Him* advise that they find someone who is "good enough" and hold on to him for dear life.[4]

This is a confusing set of messages with high stakes. If the goal is still marriage, what should young women do with all of their training in not needing anyone? What kind of a marriage should they hope for? It's difficult to square their experiences in their twenties with marriage, which inevitably involves need, compromise, dependence, and vulnerability.

When it comes to sex, women hear that they ought to spend their twenties being sexually experimental, but only to a point. There is a fine line between being experimental and being a slut. Their peers, television shows such as *Sex and the City,* and movies seem to encourage sexual experimentation. And they may find advice about sexual positions to try in *Glamour* or *Cosmopolitan* magazines. But at the same time, books, such as *Unhooked* and *A Return to Modesty,* advise them to return to courtship practices from the early 1900s.[5] And real women, not those in magazines, books, and movies, often contend with messages from their families, religions, and partners that they ought not to be sexually assertive, or sexually active at all.

These contradictory directives leave young women in a bind, and without much help in figuring out what they actually want. Every piece of "modern" advice about maintaining independence and using their twenties to explore and experiment sexually is layered over a piece of "old-fashioned" advice about getting married before it's "too late," not being too assertive or passionate in sex, and not being too sexually experienced.

These confusing messages are in contrast to the clear and helpful direction young women in the twenty-first century receive about how to succeed academically and professionally. Parents, educational institutions, workplaces, companies, and countless nonprofit organizations have focused on empowering girls and women to get ahead in fields and endeavors where they had lagged behind for generations. This training has often focused on developing a sense of control and mastery, and these efforts have largely succeeded. Today more women attend college than do men, and women make up close to half of all law and medical school graduates, although their entry into the highest echelons of these professions is still limited.[6] But the skills twenty-something women have developed in getting ahead educationally and professionally have not translated well into getting what they want and need in sex and relationships....

SPLITTING

In seeking to understand how women respond to the freedoms, opportunities, and accompanying confusion, uncertainty, and anxiety of their twenties, I turned to psychoanalytic theory. From my viewpoint as a psychotherapist, I found that psychoanalytic insights could help us to understand how people respond to anxiety, and how and why people may report wanting something and yet seem to thwart themselves in their efforts to get that thing. Freud and other early psychoanalytic theorists have been rightly critiqued for focusing on men, assuming heterosexuality, depriving mothers of subjectivity, and having a biological determinist bent. At the same time, I (and many other feminists) have found psychoanalytic theory to be one of the most effective tools we possess to account for how women and men, sometimes unwittingly, perpetuate gender inequality. Psychoanalytic theories help us to understand why women, with the best and clearest of intentions, may unconsciously undermine their ability to reach their goals.[7]

The contradictions and uncertainties that characterize today's young women's lives lead many of them to systematically employ certain unconscious defenses to resolve their internal conflicts and anxiety, often to their detriment. I contend that splitting—a tendency to think in either/or patterns and to insist that one cannot feel two seemingly contradictory desires at once—has become a widespread sociological phenomenon among young women. This process has become a means for women to reconcile the disconcertingly uneven progress of their psychological, economic, and emotional lives in the twenty-first century.

Psychoanalytically oriented psychotherapists employ the notion of splitting, sometimes referred to as dualistic or binary thinking, widely in their work with patients, although it's fallen out of favor in the field of cultural anthropology, where it is associated with the structuralism of Claude Lévi-Strauss. Splitting continues to be a helpful concept in clinical work because it describes the defensive processes of so many patients, including many of the women with whom I spoke. These are neither total nor absolute splits in the grand narrative sense of the term—splits between black and white or masculine and feminine that undergird the foundations of society—but multiple splits that people invoke at different times and in various situations to manage anxiety and to defend against uncertainty. I therefore discuss multiple and shifting psychological and social splits as a way to make sense of the lived experiences of twenty-something women as they navigate sex and relationships.

I argue that splitting came to predominate among many of the women with whom I spoke, not because they were in any way pathological, but because of the unsettled nature of this new in-between period of early adulthood for women, and the uncertainty and anxiety that accompany it.[8] Confused about freedom and what it is to be a woman today, young women often split their social and psychological options—into independence, strength, safety, and control versus relatedness, vulnerability, need, and desire—as though they're mutually exclusive and not equally important to human development.[9] Despite all the advances of women over the past fifty years, these experiences are frequently split into masculine and feminine ones, with the masculine being overvalued socially and psychologically. In modern western culture, autonomy and all that accompany it are much more highly valued than are interdependence and all that accompany it. Splitting leads some women to assume that they cannot be strong and autonomous when they are interdependent with others, vulnerable, and intimate. Vulnerability, needs, desires, and intimacy, then, often become new taboos for young women—experiences to be avoided rather than embraced.

It's no wonder that splitting is often young women's preferred method to make sense of the dizzying array of freedoms before them. A group of people trying to be autonomous and successful at work, and to have love and sex lives in which they express their vulnerability, need, and desire, is groundbreaking and historically unprecedented. This new in-between developmental period brings these two life spheres together at a time when neither is yet firmly established. But splitting makes young women feel that their options are limited as opposed to expansive.

STRATEGIES OF DESIRE

I argue that the women I spoke with employed *strategies of desire* to solve the problems at hand—problems of desire, autonomy, agency, intimacy, and safety—in a new in-between developmental period in which the rules aren't clear. These strategies of desire were sometimes conscious, sometimes unconscious, and women developed varying ones based on the cultural tools available to them, their psychological tendencies, their family backgrounds, and their relationship experiences. They were after—albeit with different degrees of internal conflict—sexual experiences, relationship experiences, safety, and control. This notion of a strategy helps describe the ways in which these women both had agency and were limited by the cultural notions available to them.[10]

In my research and clinical practice, I've found that the women to whom I've spoken have tended to employ strategies of desire clustered in three types. These strategies are based on the degree of conflict over sexual and relational desires that women are able to tolerate. My three archetypes—those of the Sexual Woman, the Relational Woman, and the Desiring Woman—are ways to interpret broad sets of behavior. Of course, they flatten out individual experiences to a degree, but they provide a broad paradigm for understanding how contemporary women cope with a confusing and sometimes conflicting set of beliefs and behaviors.

Women mobilized defensive strategies of the Sexual Woman and the Relational Woman when they were unable to tolerate the degree of internal conflict and anxiety that they felt over sexual and relational desires.[11] Both archetypes defensively split their desires, leaving them frustrated in their ability to get what they want.

Women who had little conflict over sexual desire and a high degree of conflict over relational desire used the strategies of desire of the Sexual Woman.[12] These women had benefited from the increased sexual freedom that characterized their childhood, adolescence, and twenties, and they succeeded in developing comfort with their sexual desires. Revealing sexual desire did not fill them with fear and dread and did not threaten their identity or sense of self. However, they feared losing their identities and independence through being in an intimate relationship. So they felt conflicted about having and letting somebody in on their relational desire.[13] For many women, these strategies reflected a split between a strong and independent identity and a relationship. They used strategies that allowed the expression of sexual desire but preserved their identities and independence from the perceived threat of relationships.

For example, one of my informants, twenty-nine-year-old Jayanthi, delighted in defying her Indian parents' expectations by sleeping with as many men as she could in her early twenties. She enjoyed sex a great deal, and over the course of her twenties learned how to regularly have an orgasm. But Jayanthi also derived pleasure from being able to attract men and turn them on, and from the control that she felt in not getting emotionally attached to men even when they may have felt attached to her. As she moved into her late twenties, though, she was left with a nagging desire for something more intimate and lasting than a mere sexual encounter. But she worried about losing control, and losing herself, in intimate relationships with men. Women such as Jayanthi represent a new take on the dilemma of female desire: at ease with sexual desire, but ill at ease with desire for a relationship.

Women who had little conflict over relational desire but a high degree of conflict over sexual desire gravitated toward the strategies of desire of the Relational Woman.[14] These women were comfortable feeling and expressing their desire for relationships but feared that either a man or a relationship couldn't withstand their strong sexual desire. They felt conflicted about having and expressing sexual desire and so gave it up. Unlike good girls of yesteryear, women who employed strategies of the Relational Woman had felt and understood the power of sexual desire. It was for this reason that they avoided it. They worried that asserting their sexual desires might overwhelm the men (or women, although this was more rare) with whom they wanted to be in relationships. Or they worried that their strong sexual desire might be incompatible with a stable relationship. These women then developed strategies of desire that inhibited their desires for sex. They illustrate the problem of splitting sexual desire from safety and stability in relationships.

For example, twenty-eight-year-old Alicia might, at first glance, have looked like a good girl of old. She delayed sex until after college, acted demurely, and was only subtly flirtatious with men, and she wanted more than anything to be part of a traditional family. Alicia also felt inhibited from expressing her sexual desires to men and was more comfortable with being passive in sex than she was with initiating sex. But Alicia, unlike a prototypical good girl, knew what she wanted from sex and actively fantasized about it. She didn't, however, share those desires with the men with whom she was in relationships. She worried that her sexual desires would be incompatible with the kind of committed relationship that she wanted, so she held herself back from expressing them.

Women who could tolerate the conflicts they felt over sexual and relational desire made use of the productive strategies of desire of the Desiring Women. These women used their conflicts to inform how they could pursue their desires; they were comfortable with and expressed their desires for sex and a relationship....[15]

The Bad Girl

Jayanthi

One of the apparent advantages of being a bad girl is that it's supposed to be fun. Being a bad girl may be a bad deal in other respects—it gains a woman social condemnation and ostracism, and leads to others' assumptions of limitless availability for sex; the list goes on. But at least it should be fun. There can be pleasure in defying others' expectations, breaking the rules, and upsetting tradition. And there can be pleasure in having no messy emotional consequences, no attachments, no settling down, and no guilt about sex. There is also appeal in the drama and excitement of having crazy stories to tell and creating a history for oneself, especially if one's history previously has been defined by others' expectations of what a woman should be and do.

However, I found that the real-life experience of being the bad girl was often not so much fun. Instead, this approach sometimes left the women I studied feeling unhappy and numb. Particularly for women with fragile senses of self, the bad-girl strategy seemed to provide a strong identity. At the same time, it ostensibly protected women from losing track of their identities in a relationship by never investing in one emotionally. But rather than feeling strong and protected, some bad girls were left feeling alone and vulnerable.

Jayanthi, a twenty-nine-year-old second-generation Indian American woman born in 1974, spent her early twenties rebelling against her upper-middle-class, traditional but moderately religious Hindu family, doing everything she could to be "bad" in their eyes.[16] Jayanthi spent years casually hooking up with men, and she enjoyed some of it, but often felt "played" and used by them. She would then retreat from men and sex and be a "goody-goody girl" who toyed with her parents' offers of an arranged marriage. But eventually she'd swing back to being bad.

Having lots of sex felt like both a way to rebel against her parents and a way to assert her sense of herself as a strong woman. But while the sex helped Jayanthi to define herself in opposition to a stereotypical good girl, she didn't get much pleasure or a solid sense of herself out of it. She felt more confused than ever about whether she was good or bad, Indian or American. And even as she eventually figured some things out about how to have an orgasm, Jayanthi confided anxiously that she worried about losing herself in relationships with men. She imagined that in a relationship, she'd get swept up into her partner's world and lose track of her identity and things that mattered to her.

I heard this fear of losing track of their identities again and again from women in their twenties. Self-help books call out to them to "focus on yourself," "make yourself happy," and not to "lose yourself in a relationship." But without a solid and reliable identity, these intonations rang hollow for women such as Jayanthi. This [section of my argument] explores why Jayanthi so feared that she would be subsumed in a relationship with a man. Why did a woman with such passionate interests of her own fear that she would lose track of herself and her desires in a relationship?

TENTATIVE IDENTITY

Jayanthi, a dancer and teacher who was tiny in stature, spoke very quickly and seemed to have boundless energy. Her enthusiasm for life, for dance, and for political causes was palpable, and she expressed strong opinions about the things in life that mattered to her. I was surprised, then, when Jayanthi confessed that she worried about being overwhelmed by a relationship, concerned that she'd quickly lose her own identity in the other person. It was difficult to square her fear of disappearing into someone else with the forceful personality before me. I came to learn that Jayanthi's strength felt very tentative to her, and was not something that she could count on when faced with the prospect of close emotional and physical ties with a man.

Jayanthi's early sexual experiences profoundly shaped her expectations of men and their trustworthiness. She had her first kiss and sexual experience in college at eighteen, and it was passionate and fun. They didn't have intercourse, but experimented with almost everything else. It turned out, however, that Jayanthi had greater expectations of a relationship than the man did. She later felt the man had "played" her—he was dating other women, and she was disgusted and put off by that. In that first experience, she felt devastated and too emotionally involved. She vowed not to be played by a man again. So to avoid being either played or too involved, Jayanthi spent the next decade bouncing back and forth between being good and being bad. In both cases, she distanced herself from the men she was involved with, either physically or emotionally. While being a good girl, Jayanthi remained both physically and emotionally removed from men. And while being a bad girl, Jayanthi was physically close to but emotionally distant from men.

When employing the good-girl strategy, Jayanthi entertained her parents' offers to find a suitable Indian partner for her. On a few occasions, she met men whose families her parents knew as a way to anchor herself amid the "craziness." Or she would troll listings on Indian matchmaking websites, consoling herself that she might find some clarity and certainty about the entirety of her life if she had a secure partner who met her parents' and community's expectations of her. "When I got confused, I would freak out and feel, 'I need to settle down. I need to find a partner, and I'm not seeing anybody now, so I better do it my parents' way, through family friends or meeting people online,'... It was like, you marry somebody and that problem of what you're gonna do with your life disappears." Being a good girl gave Jayanthi some clarity and purpose, but it didn't feel like an identity of her own.

THE BAD-GIRL STRATEGY

Being a bad girl, on the other hand, gave Jayanthi a strong sense of identity. Particularly for women from families with traditional ideas and teachings about sex (for example, some immigrant families and conservative religious families), being a bad girl can enable them to feel independent and "bad-ass," and to separate from the parents and traditions that may have felt restrictive to them while they were growing up. Tired of being a good girl who met all her parents' and community's expectations, Jayanthi began casually hooking up with men after college, often meeting several in one night.

> I was twenty-one and hadn't had that many experiences in intimacy, didn't know what it's about, really. I was still a virgin, I went to a women's college. I'm my mom and dad's ideal child—what is that? Fuck the standards, fuck the expectations of what I'm supposed to be. I'm just gonna break them. So I just broke them. So I ended up really going crazy.... I was just like, "I don't want to be the poster child, so the other extreme is this." It was like the Virgin Mary or the ho. And I was going to the other side. And I just didn't like that. And I was like, "Okay, I'm not gonna do this anymore." I'd try not to do it and then it'd be the other extreme. I wouldn't find anybody meaningful. I'd try not to associate with that group of people, and then I'd be having a really, really sheltered life again and I'd be like, "Fuck this, I don't want to do this," and I'd go and freak out again.

She was aware now that she had been feeling insecure at the time, and that she had been seeking out attention and affection. She reflected that she loved part of it, but also felt lucky for not having gotten STDs and not having been raped or killed (although, as we learn later ... she was in the process of redefining a specific encounter as rape, one in which she "kind of gave my body without giving my mind; I didn't really want it to happen"). At the time she had longed for a sexual history, for stories that would make her feel real and alive.

[At the time I was] in one box or another box, and in both ways I had censorship. I was censored on this really sheltered side 'cause it was limiting what I wanted to do. And when I was doing everything, I was censoring myself, 'cause I didn't know what … I wanted. I kind of knew what I wanted, but I wasn't able to really express that. I wasn't able to really say no. I wasn't able to be honest to myself, [to say,] "Jay, what are you doing to yourself?" … I would just give in. So both sides had censorship. Both sides had limitations, and [on] both sides I felt I was being trapped in some way. So I felt like, "God, this is shit, this is terrible." So basically what happened was … by the beginning of '98 I realized I was being played by a lot of different guys. I was being manipulated. I was given fake affection. I was silencing myself. I was putting myself in hard situations, dangerous ones, risky ones, not even pleasurable situations at times. But it wasn't all bad. Otherwise I wouldn't have continued on with it. I also liked the drama, I liked the excitement, I liked the fact I was having stories, I liked being bad. And then there were some people I actually loved having sex with and I loved the intimacy with. So it all came in a package. I don't want it to come across as all negative. Otherwise it makes no sense as to why I stayed there and did it, okay?

When I asked how she made sense of it at the time, she replied:

What I was thinking at the time was, "I'm liberating myself, this is liberation, I'm getting myself out. I've been repressed for so long, and I'm just gonna let it out, I don't care." So that's what it was … I look back and I'm like, "Damn, I should have cared a little more about protection." But at the time I was like, "I don't care, I've been so repressed, this is all about letting it out." That's what was going on at the time … "I want to party, I want to meet people, I want to hook up, I want to have stories, I want to have a history." I didn't have a history, so I wanted to create a history. I don't want to be naïve.[17]

Jayanthi worked hard to give herself a history that differed from her family's expectations—she needed sexual experiences and crazy stories about sexual exploits to create that history. Prior to her crazy time, she felt herself to be meeting all her parents' expectations of a good Indian girl. She went to a women's college, was not sexually promiscuous, did traditional Indian dance, and cooked Indian food. Releasing herself from the repression she felt as her parents' daughter allowed her to feel more her own woman.

The bad-girl strategy also appealed to Jayanthi because prior to college, she hadn't felt attractive. Growing up in a predominantly white town in the Southwest, she found that the attractive and popular girls were always white, and Jayanthi felt that boys didn't find her pretty. On top of not feeling desirable because she was Indian American, Jayanthi felt sheltered by her parents, who would not allow her to date. Embracing the bad-girl strategy highlighted for Jayanthi the degree to which she actually was considered desirable and attractive.

Being a bad girl allowed Jayanthi to control her identity, rather than having it controlled by either her family or the men she encountered. With American men, Jayanthi had felt stereotyped as naïve, passive, innocent, shy, submissive, and virginal because she was an Indian woman. Indian men also expected her to be a nice, virginal girl whom they could bring home to their families. By having extensive sexual experiences, Jayanthi could feel herself to be different from these stereotypes.

Being her own woman in charge of her identity, however, didn't automatically translate into her enjoying sex. Jayanthi never had orgasms during the "sexual frenzy" time: "I didn't really express much desire, I just took whatever was given. It wasn't about how I liked it. No one had any interest in making me come, and I had no interest in coming 'cause it wasn't even about me." She also says that 30 percent of the time, she had sex because she felt obligated to do so.

A turning point in Jayanthi's bad-girl era came one night in India. It was only recently that she was able to recount fully this experience.

I used to go and dance at this one club a lot. There was this one African person there, 'cause a lot of West Africans, East Africans come do some studies in India 'cause it's cheaper for them. So there was this one, I think he was from Sudan. He—I forget his name. He was kind of cute. I was like, "I don't mind fooling around with him." And I didn't have a car, so had to depend on these guys to take me home. I wouldn't sleep at my place 'cause my mom was so mad at me at the time for doing all this. She was just like, "If you're gonna do it, you have to come back in the morning. I'm not gonna open up the gate for you." So I'd have to sleep at other people's places. So I decided one night, he asked me to come home with him. I was like, "Sure, I'll come home with you." But he stayed with three other African roommates. So we get home around five in the morning after dancing at the club. Me and him are fooling around, then we start talking, and we have sex, and I'm okay with it. Not that I really want to have sex with him, but whatever, I'll do it. Then we went to take a shower. He stepped out for a minute, and then his friend came in and took a shower with me, finished up with me. And I didn't know what to do. 'Cause, again, I'm in this unknown place. I don't want to be like, "What the fuck are you doing? Get the fuck out!" I didn't know what to do. I was like, "I guess I'll have to be cool with it, have to pretend like I'm cool with having a shower with his friend." After the shower with his friend, his friend wanted to have sex with me. And I think I had sex with him too. And then he was lying down with me for ten minutes and then he got up. I was lying there [thinking], "Oh, my God, I need to get home." I didn't know what to do. Then his other roommate came in, and he wanted me to have sex with him. I didn't have sex with him. I just kind of gave him oral sex, which I didn't really want to do. By this time, I was like, "This is so crazy." And then the fourth guy came in. By then I was like, "I'm not doing anything." I just got up and was like, "I'm just gonna go home. Can one of you help me get a taxi or something to get home?" I still had to be nice to them 'cause I needed their help to get a taxi. That's the powerlessness I felt.... It was only recently, literally recently,

Leslie, that I thought back on it, and I was like, "Oh, my God, that actually happened to me. Oh, my God, what was that about?"

She had now come to understand and describe this experience as a disturbing version of sexual exploitation. Earlier it had felt like another in a series of crazy antics—something that was annoying, but not exploitative and devastating. Jayanthi now felt saddened and disturbed by the experience, angry at the men who pressured her to have sex with them, shocked that they could be such "assholes," and sad that she felt so starved for attention that she allowed herself to be in such a vulnerable position. Over the course of the interviews, she reflected that perhaps she reacted against such experiences of exploitation by later using men as sex objects and playing them.

After this experience, Jayanthi's strategy shifted from being a bad girl who was "up for anything" to being a bad girl who was in control. She began to use men for sex and became the player herself, by which she meant being a smooth talker, acting and talking as though she cared about the men with whom she was involved. But when playing men, she was just after sex and had no intention of becoming emotionally involved. She felt that she had been played by men earlier, but from those experiences she herself learned how to play, so she began juggling people and having sex with multiple partners without becoming emotionally involved. She used men for sex and dumped them when they became too serious or emotionally engaged. And she successfully avoided being hurt herself by steering clear of any emotional connection to the men she slept with. One of the ways in which she remained untouched emotionally was by hooking up primarily with African American men. These men became a solution and a part of her strategy—they weren't white men, who oversexualized her, and they weren't Indian American men, who undersexualized her. But they also weren't "relationship material," according to her family or herself, so this strategy "protected" her from the possibility of developing an emotional connection with the men.

The Good Girl

Alicia

Despite its limited charms, being a "good" girl ought at least to protect women from harm of various kinds. If young women follow the rules for being good, it seems that they should emerge from college and their twenties unscathed by the emotional and physical damage that afflicts women who explore and experiment with sexuality.

Alicia was a very good girl. A twenty-eight-year-old Hispanic woman raised by her Catholic grandparents, Alicia didn't have sex until after college, and then protected herself from unplanned pregnancies, which were common in her working-class family. When she finally did have sex, in committed relationships, being a good girl didn't protect Alicia from STDs—she contracted gonorrhea from one partner and genital warts from another.[18] Nor did being a good girl ensure that Alicia had satisfying and committed relationships. Alicia was frustrated that she'd ostensibly done the right thing but still ended up with two STDs, and without a lasting relationship.

This [section] explores why Alicia, who worked so hard to protect herself from harm and the dangers of pregnancy, was so profoundly hurt by partners. How did a woman who escorted her friends to Planned Parenthood as a teenager wind up having so much trouble keeping herself safe?

GOOD-GIRL REBEL

Alicia became a good girl as a way out. A way out of poverty. A way out of teen pregnancy. A way out of conforming to low expectations. To be a good girl in her working-class Hispanic family was, ironically, to be a rebel. Particularly for women from impoverished and working-class backgrounds, being a good girl is often a mark of distinction from their peers, many of whom are sexually active early but don't use birth control and so sometimes become parents as teenagers. Being a good girl gave Alicia an alternative to the well-worn path of teen pregnancy, sexual exploitation by older men, and dropping out of school that many of her peers had followed. Women such as Alicia, who are determined, as she said, "not to become a statistic," may delay sex "because no form of birth control is 100 percent effective." Following the good-girl strategy buys some poor and working-class girls the time for education and development that middle-class and upper-middle-class girls claim as their birthright. And being a good girl did work for Alicia as a strategy to get an education, get out of poverty, and separate from her family of origin.[19] Being a good girl, for Alicia, was only partly about delaying sex. It also involved doing the right things academically and socially.

Spunky might be the word to describe Alicia, a petite and pretty businesswoman with spiky salt-and-pepper hair, although it doesn't fully capture her mix of strength, humor, and sadness. Born in 1975, she was funny and warm, combining sarcasm with a dose of sweetness so that she didn't come off as harsh or embittered. She described herself this way: "I'm a good little girl. However, I do have my mind and my mouth, and I use them."

In some ways Alicia's family molded her into being a good girl—as noted, she was raised Catholic, and her father [forbade] her from dating in high school. But at the same time that her family encouraged her use of the good-girl strategy, Alicia also adopted it as a way to separate herself from them, to prove that she was different from them by not becoming a teen mom or a high-school dropout. So during high school Alicia didn't date at all. And during college she dated a bit, but never for longer than a few months. Many girls in the same circumstances, including her cousins, asserted themselves through rebellion by having sex early. Alicia's rebellion was to succeed academically and to be different from her family.

In Alicia's family, sex was either bad—she would end up a "ho" like other girls in the neighborhood if she had sex, or pregnant like her cousins—or it was the good and unspoken part of romance with a man that would lead to a relationship and marriage. Alicia recalled that her family addressed sex obliquely, never directly: "It sounded like this great thing, this indirect great thing: 'You're going to find a man who's going to respect you,'" and sex would then follow naturally. Alicia did not learn about the mechanics of sex from her family, nor did she learn a great deal from her Catholic school. Most of her information came from friends. She was determined not to be "irresponsible," as she saw several of her friends being—having unprotected sex, becoming pregnant, or contracting STDs.

Alicia's choice of partners was another way in which she rebelled against her family. Her primary relationships were with African American men of whom her family didn't approve. She described wishing there were "eligible" men from her own culture, but found it difficult to meet "educated Hispanic men." There are indeed more college-educated Latina women than there are college-educated Latino men in the United States, but educated African American women also often bemoan the lack of eligible, educated African American men.[20] And yet Alicia seemed to find educated African American men easily. She felt that they were able to bridge the two worlds she inhabited—they often had an understanding of the neighborhood and inner-city culture in which she grew up, they knew what it was like to feel like an outsider, and they had access to and valued education. At the same time that they understood her and the world she came from, they served to further distance her from her family of origin.

Although Alicia's grandparents raised her, she also sought out other parental figures in friends' parents, teachers, and people for whom she babysat. While she professed gratitude to her grandparents for having raised her, she felt alienated from them because of her ambitions and their acceptance of her abusive father. She avidly sought role models outside her family, and was determined not to repeat her family's patterns: early marriage and pregnancy, lack of education, low income, lack of "culture," alcohol and drug abuse, physical and sexual abuse, lack of "responsibility" and "respectability."

The families and women Alicia did want to model herself after as a child were Caucasian and middle or upper-middle class, and their race and class were important parts of what made them different from her and her family. The person she most wanted to emulate was a "lovely woman" with "beautiful green eyes" and blonde hair for whom she babysat. For Alicia, she was the epitome of a lady. She drank milk with her tea. She spoke in a very educated and correct manner. She dressed nicely, sometimes wearing scarves. Her house was tastefully decorated, with pictures each in their own frame and not stuck in the corner of existing frames, as they were in Alicia's home. She was a great hostess and knew how to make people feel comfortable and welcome. And she had a loving relationship with her husband.

Another woman Alicia admired deeply was the mother of her childhood friend Christine. The mother came from a white working-class background and worked hard to build a successful family and life. At the same time that she provided a good life for her three children, she was also generous to those less fortunate than she. She opened her home and family to Alicia, who spent a lot of time with them. Alicia told a poignant story of the kind of devotion this woman had to her husband and children, which Alicia wished she herself had experienced.

> At times I used to think, "Your mother's a slave to your father, Christine." And she'd say, "No, that's just how you do it." I remember her waking up at four in the morning to pack his lunch 'cause he didn't want her to pack it the night before, 'cause it wasn't as fresh. Deirdre [the mother] would get up and pack his lunch, make coffee, and they would sit on the couch. I remember being asleep in Christine's bedroom, hearing them have their coffee in the morning and him saying, "Well, momma, I gotta go to work now." And she'd say, "Okay." And I remember waking up to that … [soft, slow], so it [teary, she pauses and whispers] … that's what I wanted. And when I have a husband, that's what I want.… I wanted to be in Christine's family so bad. And to have a mother who cared, and who was there when she was sick. And to have a dad and a mom to go camping and have fun on the weekend.

The stability, structure, and love of a traditional family seemed to afford all of the experiences Alicia herself lacked in her upbringing. A traditional family became the solution to the problem of instability in Alicia's mind. And being a good girl was the strategy Alicia adopted to enable her to have a traditional family. By being a good girl, she would acquire a good man who would treat her well, want to marry her, and build a "respectable" life with her.

Through her receipt of scholarships to private schools beginning in elementary school, Alicia managed to assume middle-class values about education and opportunity (e.g., that education is a valuable investment and worth delaying pregnancy for).[21] Alicia willed and worked her way out of her working-class background through academic accomplishment and abstinence.

ESCAPE FROM THE PAST

By being a good girl, Alicia wasn't only escaping her working-class background. She was also trying to protect herself from the dangers of men to whom she was close, who early on proved themselves undeserving of her trust.

I heard less about Alicia's family and their role in her life than I did from most women with whom I spoke. Alicia seemed determined to convey, to others and to herself, the degree to which she had gotten over her family's impact on her. She wanted to have a sense of control over her life, and minimizing her family's perceived influence on her was one strategy to do so. Her parents divorced when she was four years old due to her father's physical abuse of her mother and his drug abuse. Her mother raised Alicia and her brother as a single mom for one year. And then "she dropped us off for an overnight stay at my grandparents and she never came to pick us up. Now she did come when it was convenient for her, when she needed kids in tow for work functions or family functions on her side." Alicia's father lived in the house with her, her brother, and her grandparents, but Alicia did not consider him her parent.

> My paternal grandparents raised us. My father was in the household, although he was pretty much not employed at times. [He was] alcoholic. I knew he was my father and he lived in this house, but I didn't understand why he did the things he did. As I grew older, I feared him. As I grew older, I … saw who he was and knew I didn't want to be that. Now we don't talk, and we haven't spoken to one another since probably '93.… Because I believe when people act certain ways and do things to children, they lose their parental rights. And at times he touched me, he kissed me, he put guns to my head. And after that I said, "I can't no more." … So I've chosen not to speak to him, chosen not to deal with him, However, when I go to my grandparents' house, because the parasite still lives there, I see him. He'll walk out of the room, he'll go in the backyard, he'll go in the bedroom and close the door. We don't talk.

As a preadolescent child, Alicia was kissed and touched sexually by her father. She was loathe to discuss his behavior's impact on her development, although she knew it to be profound. She sought to cut him out of her life and therefore minimize his current impact on her.

Alicia's early sexual experiences reinforced the notion that men she was close to were dangerous and would hurt her. Her first intercourse was a date rape with someone she saw briefly after college when she was twenty-one. She said no and told the man to get off her, but he persisted and had sex with her, and they stayed the night together in bed, with him kissing her good-bye in the morning. Even at the time we spoke, she did not think about having been raped, although she knew that technically she had been. After the rape, she did not want to be intimate with or touch anyone for a very long time. She was not scared of sex, but as she said, she "had no desire to have a penis near [her] vaginal area." While fluent in Spanish, Alicia still did not know the Spanish words for sexual body parts. In discussing the rape, this was the one time in our conversations that she used the word *vagina* and not "downstairs" or "down there"; in this one clinical and angry description, she used the word itself. She understood this trauma as not unlike the rest of her life, which had been difficult. Her mantra was "You gotta move on. Get up, go forward, come on." Alicia willed herself not to be defined by this experience and did not consider the rape her "first time" having sex. She thought of herself as a virgin until she first had consensual intercourse at age twenty-five.

Alicia was able to be a good girl but still play with sexuality with men to whom she wasn't close. She could be quite flirtatious, and was particularly bold with someone she knew she would never see again. She was very comfortable flirting, particularly when she knew someone found her appealing and attractive. She enjoyed knowing that she looked good and took pleasure in it. She did not feel threatened at work by her sexuality, as did other women with whom I spoke. They worried about being sexualized by coworkers in ways that were defining and limiting. But Alicia actually enjoyed flirting at work when she knew it was safe. She recounted an incident with a man at work whom she knew to be looking down her blouse. During meetings she would purposefully drop things and make sure he saw her pick them up, or tease him by touching his leg under the table. When it came to men she was not close to, Alicia was able to play with her attractiveness and sexuality in a way that was unique among the women with whom I spoke. This seemed safer to her than sexually focused interactions with men to whom she was close. The more distant a man, the safer he felt to her.

NOTES

1. Throughout the book, I use the terms that the women themselves used to describe their own race, ethnicity, or sexual orientation. Claudia described herself as Mexican, while Alicia (another interviewee) described herself as Hispanic, and still other respondents described themselves as Latina.

2. Whether the twenties constitute a new developmental period is under rigorous debate both in the field of psychology, where a developmental period must have distinctive developmental tasks and challenges that set it apart from other periods, and in the culture at large. In 2010, the *New York Times* recently ran a cover story in its Sunday magazine on twenty-somethings and the particular struggles they face (R.M. Henig, "What Is It about 20-Somethings?" *New York Times Magazine*, August 18, 2010). J.J. Arnett, a psychologist, is the chief proponent of the notion that the twenties constitute a distinctive life stage—"emerging adulthood" is what he terms it (*Emerging Adulthood. The Winding Road from the Late Teens through the Twenties* [Oxford: Oxford University Press, 2006]). See also R. Settersten and B. Ray, *Not Quite Adults: Why 20-Somethings Are Choosing a Slower Path to Adulthood, and Why It's Good for Everyone* (New York: Bantam, 2010); and K. Hymowitz, *Manning Up: How the Rise of Women Has Turned Men into Boys* (New York: Basic Books, 2011). I am less concerned with whether the twenties now constitute an official developmental stage than I am with the unique struggles that twenty-something women contend with, given the particular opportunities, limitations, and message they face.

3. Sociology has paid scant attention to adult development, perhaps because it seems such an individual and not a social phenomenon. And yet some sociological theorists have noted the importance of generational experiences to development at both an individual and a group level. See, for example, K. Mannheim, "The Problem of Generations," in his *Essays on the Sociology of Knowledge* (London: Routledge, 1972 [1952]), 276–320; and N. Chodorow, "Born into a World at War: Listening for Affect and Personal Meaning." *American Imago* 59, no. 3 (2002): 297–315. Individual development, while seemingly a psychological matter, is also a sociological matter when it takes a new form among groups of people subject to similar social influences. And experiences of sexuality, which are both profoundly personal and inevitably socially influenced, cannot be understood without studying individuals in depth.

4. E. Fein and S. Schneider, *The Rules: Time-Tested Secrets for Capturing the Heart of Mr. Right* (New York: Grand Central Publishing, 1996); G. Behrendt and L. Tuccillo, *He's Just Not That into You: The No Excuses Truth to Understanding Guys* (New York: Gallery, 2009); L. Gottlieb, *Marry Him: The Case for Settling for Mr. Good Enough* (New York: Dutton Adult, 2010).

5. L. S. Stepp, *Unhooked: How Young Women Pursue Sex, Delay Love, and Lose at Both* (New York: Riverhead Books, 2007); W. Shalit, *A Return to Modesty: Discovering the Lost Virtue* (New York: Touchstone, 2000).

6. Despite all these efforts and advances, there is still a clear ceiling in many fields beyond which most women do not advance. In 2006, only 23 percent of U.S. college presidents were women (American Council on Education, *The American College President, 2007 Edition* [Washington, DC: American Council on Education, 2007]). In 2010, only 16.6 percent of representatives in the House of Representatives and 17 percent of U.S. senators were women. Also, in 2010, only fifteen heads of Fortune 500 companies were women. Additionally, women continue to earn less than men (R. Drago and C. Williams, *The Gender Wage Gap: 2009* [Washington DC: Institute for Women's Policy Research, 2009]).

7. Freud's initial foray into psychoanalysis began with his trying to help women who suffered from hysteria. Through his work with them, he developed the notion of the unconscious to account for the manifestation of physical symptoms such as paralysis, shortness of breath, tics, and loss of sense of smell when there was nothing physically wrong with the women (J. Breuer and S. Freud, 1953 [1895], "Studies on Hysteria," in *The Standard Edition of the Complete Psychological Works of Sigmund Freud*, vol. 2 [London: Hogarth Press], 1–319). These women were previously assumed to be incurable, or, if curable, then only by medical science. Freud believed there to be meaning in the symptoms the young women manifested. Along with his colleague Breuer and one of Breuer's patients, Anna O., Freud came upon the "talking cure." After trying hypnosis and other techniques, Freud, Breuer, and their patients used talking to trace symptoms back to their origins, which sometimes led to the elimination of the symptoms when fully understood and accounted for. They found that, from the point of view of a person's unconscious fantasies or beliefs, there is meaning in symptoms that may appear to be crazy and irrational. An unconscious part of the mind reflects desires, wishes, and fantasies that are not conscious to us in our waking lives but which inform the ways that we think, act, and feel. Physical symptoms can be traced to meaningful experiences that caused such profound inner conflict that women developed the symptoms to manage the conflict. For example, one patient could not tolerate the anger and resentment that she felt over having to tend her dying father. Another patient could not tolerate the shame and anger that she felt at having been sexually abused by her father's friend. They both developed physical symptoms rather than consciously experiencing personally and socially unacceptable feelings.

8. See A. Swidler, *Talk of Love: How Culture Matters* (Chicago: University of Chicago Press, 2001), in which she describes unsettled times as situations "when new strategies of action are being developed and tried out" (89). See also B. D. Whitehead, *Why There Are No Good Men Left: The Romantic Plight of the New Single Woman* (New York: Broadway, 2002), in which she chronicles this unsettled time. While she focuses chiefly on the absence of men for highly educated women, she also makes the point that while highly educated women are trained for professional success, they are not trained for dating and marriage in this new time.

9. For a discussion of the ways in which danger has always been a powerful disincentive for women to be sexually free, see C. Vance, ed., *Pleasure and Danger Exploring Female Sexuality*, 1st ed. (Boston: Routledge, 1984). In it various authors argue that, throughout the ages, danger has been a reason for women to avoid sex, be wary of

it, and be careful about it. And several authors in the volume argue that danger threatens not just physical safety, but emotional safety as well.

10. Hochschild introduces the notion of gender strategy in *The Second Shift* as a "plan of action through which a person tries to solve the problems at hand, given the cultural notions of gender at play" (15). Swidler also uses the concept of strategies in *Talk of Love* to discuss the ways that individuals mobilize the cultural resources available to them to solve life's difficulties. She argues that culture powerfully influences social action by shaping the selves, skills, and worldviews out of which people can build life strategies. A.C. Wilkins, in her *Wannabes, Goths, and Christians: The Boundaries of Sex, Style, and Status* (Chicago: University of Chicago Press, 2008), argues that the various groups of young people she studied mobilized various strategies depending upon the cultural projects they were engaged in to develop, express, and live their identities.

11. While sociologists recognize the ways in which strategies are not entirely consciously formulated, sociologists do not generally use the concept of unconscious defenses to understand or elaborate individuals' use of strategies. For an exception to this, see *The Second Shift*, in which Hochschild points to something like a defense in describing the myths that families develop to cover the mismatch between what they believe and what they actually do regarding the second shift.

12. Thirty percent of my respondents (n = 6) used strategies of the Sexual Woman.

13. Settersten and Ray, in *Not Quite Adults*, found similar feelings among twenty-something women whom they researched: "Wary is probably the best word to describe her and most of her peers' feelings towards marriage—wary of compromise, wary of giving up one's individuality, wary of missing out on something better" (84).

14. Twenty-five percent of my respondents (n = 5) used strategies of the Relational Woman.

15. Forty-five percent of my respondents (n = 9) used strategies of the Desiring Woman.

16. While race and ethnicity shaped the ways in which my respondents' sexuality was received by others, they did not markedly influence my respondents' experiences of sexuality in any systematic way. That is, while race and ethnicity were factors in my respondents' sexual development, they did not cause my respondents to differ from one another according to race. This may be due to my relatively small sample size, or to self-selection, education, and class trumping race and ethnicity; or to my respondents' common experience of college. Throughout the book, then, I discuss the influence of race and ethnicity on each particular woman and each woman's particular experience of sexualized or desexualized representations of women in the racial or ethnic group to which they belong.

17. A. Levy documents the rise of what she terms "raunch culture" in *Female Chauvinist Pigs: Women and the Rise of Raunch Culture* (New York: Free Press, 2006). She charts the rise in pressure on young women to adopt a stance of being a female chauvinist pig. But, she argues, in doing so they essentially open themselves up to being used by men. The rise of raunch culture, she argues, makes it acceptable and even required that young, liberated women make themselves into "liberated" objects of desire.

18. H. Brückner and P. Bearman ("After the Promise: The STD Consequences of Adolescent Virginity Pledges," *Journal of Adolescent Health* 36 [2005]: 271–78) find that communities with high rates of abstinence pledging among teens also have high

rates of STDs. This could be because more teens pledge in communities where they perceive more danger from sex (in which case the pledge is doing some good), or it could be because fewer people in these communities use condoms when they break the pledge.

19. See J. Bettie, *Women without Class: Girls, Race, and Identity* (Berkeley: University of California Press, 2003), for an excellent account of how most working-class Latina girls grow into working-class lives, which is what Alicia was working so hard to avoid.

20. According to a 2007 report from the National Center for Education Statistics (*Status and Trends in the Education of Racial and Ethnic Minorities, NCES 2007–0039* [Washington, DC: U.S. Department of Education, 2007]), black women received twice as many associate's, bachelor's, and postsecondary degrees as their male counterparts between 2003 and 2004 (67 percent versus 33 percent)—a larger disparity between genders than in any other racial group. In 2001, Hispanic women were awarded 60 percent of associate's and bachelor's degrees conferred to Hispanic undergraduates, and Hispanic men only 40 percent. Similarly, and only slightly less dramatically, in 2001, white women were awarded 57 percent of associate's and bachelor's degrees conferred on white undergraduates, and white men only 43 percent (National Center for Education Statistics, *Gender Differences in Participation and Completion of Undergraduate Education and How They Have Changed over Time* [Washington, DC: U.S. Department of Education, 2005]).

21. Legal scholars N. Cahn and J. Carbone ("Red Families v. Blue Families," *GWU Legal Studies Research Paper* 343 [August 16, 2007]) identify what they term "the new middle-class morality," which involves delaying family formation until the late twenties or early thirties. This new morality correlates more closely to blue-state demographic patterns, and presumably Alicia's childhood, spent in Northern California, a model of blue-state demographic patterns, influenced her determination to delay family formation.

QUESTIONS FOR MAKING CONNECTIONS
WITHIN THE READING

1. In an overview of her methodology as a researcher, Bell offers this observation: "women's experiences of sexuality are often complicated by violence and coercion," factors which made it essential for Bell to create an atmosphere of "trust and safety" when she interviewed her subjects. How do the stories of both Jayanthi and Alicia exemplify this opposition between violence/coercion and safety/trust? What specific forms of violence/coercion do these two women face, and where do they look for safety/trust? Are trust and safety essential for personal growth? How about violence and coercion—is it necessary to experience these as well?

2. A key term in Bell's argument is *splitting*, which she borrows from the discourse of psychoanalysis. What is splitting and how does it help women to cope with the anxieties produced by the contradictions they face? What problems does splitting eventually create? Do you see evidence of splitting in Bell's accounts of Jayanthi and Alicia? On the basis of their stories, would

you say that splitting is encouraged by our society? Do "good girls" and "bad girls" really exist, and why might these stark oppositions remain such enduring fixtures of the way people think about women's lives?

3. *Freedom* is a pivotal word in Bell's discussion of women's lives, but she never actually defines or explains the term. On the basis of this selection, describe the different forms of freedom that might be available to women in our time. In what ways do social and cultural norms complicate or undermine the legal freedoms women now enjoy—the freedom, for example, to explore sexuality outside of marriage? What is the relation between freedom and tradition, and between freedom and desire? Is freedom possible without desire, and can desire have the ultimate effect of undermining freedom? Is freedom possible without structures and constraints, and when do structures and constraints make freedom unattainable? Be sure to consider potential differences between women's lives and men's.

QUESTIONS FOR WRITING

1. Bell is both a sociologist and a therapist. Like all sociologists she investigates structures that are intersubjective—shared, that is, by everyone in a society. At the same time, as a therapist she is concerned with what seems to be unique in the lives of individual women. To what degree does Bell's research suggest that our subjective dilemmas are produced by our inter-subjective environment—by social structures that exist before we are even born? To what degree do we have the subjective freedom to resist or adapt our lives in response to what we learn as individuals? Will there always be a tension between your life as an individual and the codes and values of society?

2. Is sexuality the real issue in debates about women and their sexual lives? And if it is, why does the subject appear to play a much smaller part in the dis-cussion of men's lives? What other issues or concerns might lie behind the heated public discussions of women's sexuality? Could it be that identity itself is a cultural flash point? What evidence do you see in Bell's analysis to support the claim that the controversy over hookup culture and women's sexual activity is actually about their struggles to define themselves and create their own lives rather than internalizing social expectations? When writers call for a return to the morality of the past, are they really arguing for a return to the social relations that gave men unquestioned superiority?

QUESTIONS FOR MAKING CONNECTIONS BETWEEN READINGS

1. Barbara Fredrickson in Selections from *Love 2.0: How Our Supreme Emotion Affects Everything We Feel, Think, Do, and Become* approaches her topic

from a point of view that she describes as scientific. She encourages her readers to give greater credence to the findings of brain science than to attitudes that have their roots in tradition, literature, the arts, and the popular media. Her confidence in empirical research is so strong that she is even willing to concede that she loves her husband of many years only, strictly speaking, when the two of them share "positivity resonance." By contrast, Bell's subject is sexuality, not love, and her method differs from Fredrickson's in important ways. Bell asks her readers to think about their sexuality less as an empirical fact than as a cultural construction—a set of conventional behaviors they are free to change. What is gained by thinking about love and sex in Bell's way, as arbitrary and open to revision, and what advantages might come with seeing it through Fredrickson's eyes as a product of biology instead?

2. Bell creates a helpful typology to define the strategies women use in dealing with themselves and others: the Sexual Woman, the Relational Woman, and the Desiring Woman. For Bell, the ideal is the Desiring Woman, the one who can learn from contradictions between her own desires and society's scripts. The Desiring Woman might be said to become the creator of her own identity. Typologies, a common tool of social scientists, can be used to think about many different aspects of our lives—including the lives of men. Look, for example, at Susan Faludi's descriptions of cadets at The Citadel. Try to develop a typology that will help readers to understand how the cadets have coped, or failed to cope, with the social pressures they face. You might think, for example, about how the cadets deal with their conflicted attitudes toward women. Does Faludi's evidence suggest that anyone at The Citadel manages to find the balance Bell applauds, a balance between inner needs and the demands of social life? Or do all the cadets remain trapped in the dynamic of *splitting*?

CATHY DAVIDSON

REMARKABLY, CATHY N. DAVIDSON occupies two distinguished faculty chairs at Duke University, but reputation never stands in her way when it comes to taking controversial positions. Over the last decade she has become one of the most impassioned advocates of the electronic media—which, she argues, have the potential to transform our ways of thinking more radically than any invention since the printing press. At a time when many observers mourn the demise of the book, Davidson argues that we need to embrace the possibilities of the Web: an explosive growth of new knowledge, nearly immediate access, and an unprecedented freedom in the shaping of information itself. She urges that this spirit of creativity should extend beyond the screen to the schools, which she sees as backward looking at a time when educators finally have the tools to end a spirit-crushing uniformity. Far from pushing the arts and humanities into obsolescence, the new technologies could provide the means for everyone to participate in the making of culture.

Not everyone agrees, however, with Davidson about the new media. In a review for the online journal *Slate*, Annie Paul Murphy accuses her of capitulating to the hype about the wonders of the Web:

> [Davidson] is easily moved to rapture and to dismay, propelled by an enthusiasm for anything new and digital and by an almost allergic aversion to any practices or artifacts from the pre-Internet era. Nor does she have much use for people born before 1980. The inhabitants and the knowledge of the past are merely obstacles to be trampled in the headlong rush toward an interactive, connected, collaborative future. This future, as Davidson imagines it, is one in which games replace books, online collaboration replaces individual effort, and "crowdsourced" verdicts replace expertise.

Other critics of the Web, if not of Davidson herself, argue that it has undermined our ability to read carefully by teaching us to "skim" instead of pausing to reflect. Whatever readers might ultimately decide about these criticisms, Davidson has had the integrity to put her ideas into practice. From 1998 to 2006 she served as Vice

Provost for Interdisciplinary Studies at Duke University and helped to create ISIS, Duke's highly successful program in Information Science and Information Studies. While a vice provost at Duke she created quite a stir when her university, in partnership with Apple, Inc., distributed free iPods to all incoming students. In spite of the scandal, or perhaps because of it, President Obama nominated Davidson to a six-year term on the National Council on the Humanities. The following selection comes from Davidson's new book *Now You See It: How Technology and Brain Science Will Transform Schools and Business for the 21st Century* (2011).

Project Classroom Makeover

The *Newsweek* cover story proclaimed, "iPod, Therefore I Am."

On MTV News, it was "Dude, I just got a free iPod!"

Peter Jennings smirked at the ABC-TV news audience, "Shakespeare on the iPod? Calculus on the iPod!"

The online academic publication *Inside Higher Ed* worried for our reputation. How would Duke University "deal with the perception that one of the country's finest institutions—with selective admissions, a robust enrollment, and a plush endowment—would stoop to a publicity ploy"?

And *The Duke Chronicle* was apoplectic: "The University seems intent on transforming the iPod into an academic device, when the simple fact of the matter is that iPods are made to listen to music. It is an unnecessarily expensive toy that does not become an academic tool simply because it is thrown into a classroom."[1]

What had these pundits so riled up? In 2003, we at Duke were approached by Apple about becoming one of six "Apple Digital Campuses." Each campus would choose a technology that Apple was then developing and would propose a campus wide use for it. It would be a partnership of business and education, exploratory in all ways. One university selected Apple PowerBooks loaded with iLife digital audio and video production software. Another chose e-portfolios, online workspaces where students could develop multimedia projects together and then archive them. Another selected audio software for creating audio archives and other infrastructure. What landed us in hot water was that, at Duke, instead of any of these, we chose a flashy new music-listening gadget that young people loved but that baffled most adults: iPods.

In 2003, the iPod did not have a single known educational app, nor did it seem to fall into that staid, stolid, overpriced, and top-down category known as IT, or instructional technology. Gigantic billboards had sprung up everywhere showing young people dancing, their silhouettes wild against brilliant bright backgrounds. What could possibly be educational about iPods? No one was thinking about their learning potential because they were so clearly about young users, not about IT administrators. That's why they intrigued us.

Our thinking was that educators had to begin taking seriously the fact that incoming students were born after the information age was in full swing. They were the last entering class who, as a group, would remember the before and after of the Internet. If they were born roughly in 1985 or so, they would have been entering grade school around the time that Tim Berners-Lee was inventing the protocols for the World Wide Web. These kids had grown up searching for information online. They had grown up socializing online, too, playing games with their friends online and, of course, sharing music files online. Categories and distinctions that an earlier generation of students would have observed in school and at home, between knowledge making and play, came bundled in a new way for this first generation of kids who, in their informal learning, were blurring that boundary. Their schools hadn't changed much, but at home, online, they were already information searchers. They had learned by googling. What if instead of telling them what they should know, we asked them? What if we continued the lesson of the Internet itself and let them lead us into a new, exploratory way of learning in order to see if this self-directed way might mean something when it came to education? What if we assumed that their experiences online had already patterned their brains to a different kind of intellectual experimentation—and what if we let them show us where the pedagogical results of such an experiment might lead?

From the way most schools operated in 2003—from preschool to graduate schools—you wouldn't have had much of an idea that the Internet had ever been invented. It was as if young people were still going to the library to look in the *Encyclopedia Britannica* for knowledge, under the watchful eye of the friendly local librarian. Schools of education were still training teachers without regard for the opportunities and potential of a generation of kids who, from preschool on, had been transfixed by digital media.

The opportunity seemed to be staring us in the face. At home, five-year olds were playing Pokémon every chance they could, exchanging the cards at preschool with their pals, and then designing tools online to customize their characters and even writing elementary code to streamline their game play. They were memorizing hundreds of character names and roles and mastering a nine-year-old reading level just to play, but teacher training on every level was still text-based. It was as if schools were based on a kind of "hunt-and-peck" literacy, whereas kids were learning through searching, surfing, and browsing the Web. They were playing games in 3-D multimedia, learning to read and write not through schoolbooks but as they played games online and then traded their Pokémon cards with their friends.

When Duke announced that we would be giving a free iPod to every member of the entering first-year class, there were no conditions. We simply asked students to dream up learning applications for this cool little white device with the adorable earbuds, and we invited them to pitch their ideas to the faculty. If one of their profs decided to use iPods in a course, the prof, too, would receive a free Duke-branded iPod and so would all the students in the class (whether they were first-years or not). We would not control the result. This was an educational experiment without a syllabus. No lesson plan. No assessment matrix rigged to show that our investment had been a wise one.... After all, as we knew from the science of attention, to direct attention in one way precluded all the other ways. So we asked our basic questions in as broad and open-ended a way possible: *Are there interesting learning applications for this device that is taking over young America as a source of entertainment?* And then the most revolutionary question of all: *What do you students have to tell us about learning in a digital age?*

If it were a reality show, you might call it Project Classroom Makeover. It was a little wild, a little wicked, exactly what you have to do to create a calculated exercise in disruption, distraction, and difference: a lesson in institutional unlearning, in breaking our own patterns and trying to understand more of the intellectual habits of a new generation of students and providing a unique space where those new talents might flourish. Instead of teaching, we hoped to learn. We wanted to tap into a wellspring of knowledge young people brought to college from their own informal learning outside of school. We didn't know what would happen, but we had faith that the students would come up with something interesting. Or not. We couldn't deny that failure was also a possibility.

At the time, I was vice provost for interdisciplinary studies at Duke, a position equivalent to what in industry would be the R & D (research and development) person, and I was among those responsible for cooking up the iPod experiment and figuring out how it could work in the most interesting ways.[2] We wanted to stir up some of the assumptions in traditional higher education. We didn't count on causing the uproar that we did. We assumed some of our fellow educators would raise an eyebrow, but we didn't imagine an educational innovation would land us on the cover of *Newsweek*. Usually, if education is on the cover, it's another grim national report on how we are falling behind in the global brain race. Come to think of it, that *is* what the *Newsweek* cover story was about! Like Socrates before us, Duke was leading youth astray, tugging them down the slippery slope to perdition by thin, white vinyl iPod cords.

We were inverting the traditional roles of teacher and learner, the fundamental principle in education: hierarchy based on credentials. The authority principle, based on top-down expertise, is the foundation of formal education, from kindergarten playgroups to advanced graduate courses. At least since the GI Bill that followed World War II, and the rapid expansion at that time of the public university system, a college degree has been the entry card to middle-class, white-collar achievement. Not graduating from high school and lacking a college degree has constituted failure, and education has constructed its objectives backward from that (negative) goal, in some cities all the way down to competition for the right private nursery school.

What this means for young people who come to an elite private university is that they have taken one of a number of specific routes to get there. One way is to test to get into the best preschools so you can go to the best private grammar schools so you can be admitted to the most elite boarding schools so you can be competitive at the Ivies or an elite school outside the Ivies like Stanford or Duke. Another way is through public schools, a lifetime of determined and focused study, getting A's and even A+ grades in every class, always taking the most difficult courses, earning perfect scores on tests, and doing lots of extracurricular work, too. These students have been focused toward educational achievement their entire lives.[3] We wondered what these astonishing young overachievers would do if given the chance not to follow the rules but to make them.

IN THE WORLD OF TECHNOLOGY, *crowdsourcing* means inviting a group to collaborate on a solution to a problem, but that term didn't yet exist in 2003 when we conducted the iPod experiment. It was coined by Jeff Howe of *Wired* magazine in 2006 to refer to the widespread Internet practice of posting an open call requesting help in completing some task, ranging from writing code (that's how the open source code that powers the Mozilla browser was written) to creating a winning logo (such as the "Birdie" design of Twitter, which cost a total of six bucks).[4] Crowdsourcing is "outsourcing" to the "crowd," and it works best when you observe three nonhierarchical principles. First, the fundamental principle of all crowdsourcing is that difference and diversity—not expertise and uniformity—solves problems. Second, if you predict the result in any way, if you try to force a solution, you limit the participation and therefore the likelihood of success. And third, the community most served by the solution should be chiefly involved in the process of finding it.

In the iPod experiment, we were crowdsourcing educational innovation for a digital age to our incoming students. We were walking the walk. Crowdsourced thinking is very different from credentialing, or relying on top-down expertise. If anything, crowdsourcing is suspicious of expertise, because the more expert we are, the more likely we are to be limited in what we even conceive to be the problem, let alone the answer. While formal education typically teaches hierarchies of what's worth paying attention to, crowdsourcing works differently, in that it assumes that no one of us individually is smarter than all of us collectively. No matter how expert we are, no matter how brilliant, we can improve, we can learn, by sharing insights and working together collectively.

Once the pieces were in place, we decided to take our educational experiment one step further. By giving the iPods to the first-year students, we ended up with a lot of angry sophomores, juniors, and seniors. They'd paid hefty private-university tuitions too! So we relented and said *any* student could have a free iPod—just so long as she convinced a prof to require one for a course and came up with a learning app in that course.

Does that sound sneaky? Far be it from me to say that we *planned* this, but once the upperclassmen coveted the iPods, once they'd begun to protest enviously and vehemently, those iPods suddenly tripled and quadrupled in perceived value: Everyone wanted one.

If "Shakespeare on the iPod" is the smirking setup, here's the punch line: Within one year, we had distributed more free iPods to students in forty-eight separate "iPod courses" than we had given without strings to the 1,650 entering first-year students.

That was vindicating enough, but it wasn't all. The real treasure trove was to be found in the students' innovations. Working together, and often alongside their profs, they came up with far more learning apps for their iPods than anyone—even at Apple—had dreamed possible. No one has ever accused Steve Jobs of not being cagey, and Apple's Digital Campus strategy was an R & D winner. The company's flagship technology now had an active lab of students creating new apps for it. There was also plenty of publicity for the iPod as a potential learning tool—the teenagers of America should all thank us for making it easier to pitch the purchase to their parents. In the first year of the iPod experiment, Duke students came up with dozens of stunning new ways to learn. Most predictable were uses whereby students downloaded audio archives relevant to their courses—Nobel Prize acceptance speeches by physicists and poets, the McCarthy hearings, famous trials, congressional debates, or readings by T. S. Eliot or Toni Morrison, or Thomas Edison's famous recitation of "Mary Had a Little Lamb"—one of the first sound recordings ever made. Almost instantly students figured out that they could also record lectures on their iPods and listen at their leisure. Classes from Spanish 101 to Introduction to Jazz to organic chemistry could be taped and listened to anywhere. You didn't have to go to the library or the language lab to study. You could listen to assignments on the bus, at the gym, while out on a run—and everyone did. Because everyone had the device, sound suddenly had a new educational role in our text- and visuals-dominated classroom culture.

Some version of this convenient form of listening was possible with that radical eighties technology, the Sony Walkman. But the Walkman connected to radio and to tapes, not to the World Wide Web, with its infinite amount of information ready for downloading.

Interconnection was the part the students grasped before any of us did. Students who had grown up connected digitally gravitated to ways that the iPod could be used for *collective* learning. They turned the iPods into social media and networked their learning in ways we did not anticipate. In the School of the Environment, with the encouragement of Professor Marie Lynn Miranda, one class interviewed families in a North Carolina community concerned with lead paint in their homes and schools. Each student would upload the day's interviews to a course Web site, and any other student could download and comment on the interviews. At the end of the course, they combined their interviews, edited them digitally, and created an audio documentary that aired on local and regional radio stations and all over the Web.[5]

Some med students realized that there was an audio library of all the possible heart arrhythmias, but no way to access it in a real-time health exam. They came up with a way to put a stethoscope in one ear, using very simple signal-tracking technology to match what they were hearing in the patient's chest to the cataloged conditions. The implications of this original use were obvious, and soon students studying to be doctors and nurses were "operationalizing" such techniques for the diagnostic use of doctors in rural North Carolina and Africa. Dr. Martha Adams, a senior administrator at the Duke School of Medicine, grasped how revolutionary it was to be able to make state-of-the-art medical research available to those far outside major research centers, and to also make it possible for doctors elsewhere to report on health problems and patterns they were observing in their own communities, thus advancing medical research in both directions. Soon she was working with the National Institutes of Health and leading a national outreach iPod initiative. Once again, attention was being focused in multiple directions at once, not just on outcomes but on process and on interaction, the mirroring happening (as it must, definitionally) in both directions.

In the music department, composing students uploaded compositions to their iPods so their fellow students could listen and critique. Music performance students inserted their voices or their instruments into duets or choruses or orchestras. You could listen to how you sounded as first chair in the flute section of a famous philharmonic orchestra. Students in Duke's engineering department had a field day mangling and dissecting their iPods to study (hack, some would say) everything from Apple's ultrasecret computer code to the physical properties of the famous white plastic exterior of the original iPods.

And they began exploring apps, developing applications that could be added to the iPod's repertoire of abilities without Apple having to give away its proprietary code. In other words, the iPod could still remain an iPod with its own distinctive characteristics, but it could change and morph as new features were added and new capabilities emerged, including some developed by users. To me, this was a conceptual breakthrough: that a commercial product might also be susceptible to consumer customization, a way of extending the infinitely changeable open-source properties of the Internet itself to a product with a far more fixed, finite identity. It was a hybrid of old and new thinking. If that isn't a metaphor for attention in the digital age, I don't know what is.

By the end of our first experimental year, Duke was part of a new movement to transform the iPod from a listening device into an interactive broadcasting device. We were proud to host the world's first-ever academic "podcasting" conference early in 2005. I recently found one of our announcements for the conference and was amused to see those quotation marks around *podcasting*. No one was quite sure even what to call this new phenomenon, in which you could record a lecture, upload it to a Web site, and then anyone anywhere in the world could download it. Shakespeare on an iPod? Absolutely. And that lecture on Shakespeare delivered in the Allen Building at Duke could later be listened to by a student riding a bus in Bangkok or Brasilia. That may not seem revolutionary now. It is hard to remember way back then, in the distant past of the Internet, before iPhones and netbooks, before MySpace and Facebook, and a full two years before YouTube was invented with its motto to "Broadcast Yourself."

The first podcasting conference drew standing-room-only attendance. It was sponsored by one of the first programs I'd spearheaded at Duke, something (another hybrid) called Information Science + Information Studies, or ISIS for short—artists and computer scientists, social scientists and engineers, and everyone in between in a new configuration. Lots of news media crowded into the auditorium at the Center for Interdisciplinary Engineering, Medicine, and Applied Science to witness the event. In a short span, the message had changed from "How could anyone possibly think this device could be used for learning?" to "This device facilitates sophisticated academic research and has the potential to make that learning instantly available to anyone in the world—for free."

The conceptual breakthrough of podcasting was access. It was expensive buying all those iPods, but the result was a breakthrough in education far beyond Duke, one whose purpose was to make a world of information cheaper to access than it ever had been before. With very little outlay, you had the potential of transmitting anything you heard, anywhere: You could download anything you heard worldwide. Not prerecorded programs made by professionals but content created and uploaded by anyone, ready for downloading— and for remixing and uploading again. When we launched the iPod experiment, no one expected that someday there would be an iTunes U (formed in 2007) with over 350,000 lectures and other educational audio and video files compiled by universities, libraries, and museums all around the world and available for download.

Duke took a lot of heat for being a "rich, privileged institution" that could afford this frivolity, but a revolution in the democratization of knowledge is not frivolous, especially considering that, once customized, an individual mobile device is actually an inexpensive computer. Several years after the Duke experiment, in the fall of 2008, Culbreth Middle School, a public school in nearby Chapel Hill, North Carolina, created its own iPod program for an experimental group of staff and students. They chose the iPod instead of a more traditional laptop because of "the mobility of the device in one's pocket with instant access to information and apps."[6] In January 2010, seventh graders were encouraged to explore the different ways their iPods could be used to keep them informed in the wake of the disastrous earthquake that brought destruction to Haiti. They used iPods to gather measurements of earthquake magnitude and related information, including demographic data, humanitarian assistance updates, local Haitian news podcasts, and historical information on Haitian culture and politics. The device also performed Creole-language translation. Students were even able to maintain up-to-date communication with a local graduate student who was in Haiti at the time and was badly injured in the earthquake. They used their iPods to educate themselves about a terrible disaster far away and produced their own podcasts from the information they gleaned. The experiment left little doubt that in the event of an emergency closer to home, students would be able to contribute their new knowledge to disaster-relief and fund-raising efforts locally.

The iPod experiment was not an investment in technology. It was an investment in a new form of attention, one that didn't require the student to always face forward, learn from on high, memorize what was already a given, or accept knowledge as something predetermined and passively absorbed. It was also an investment in student-led curiosity, whose object was not a hunk of white plastic, but the very nature of interactivity, crowdsourcing, customizing, and inspired inquiry-driven problem solving. At our most ambitious, we hoped to change the one-directional model of attention that has formed the twentieth-century classroom.[7]

THIS IPOD EXPERIMENT WAS A start at finding a new learning paradigm of formal education for the digital era. As we have [learned], an infant's neural pathways are being sheared and shaped along with his values and his behavior in constant interaction with the people around him who exert influence over his life. The iPod experiment was an acknowledgment that the brain is, above all, interactive, that it selects, repeats, and mirrors, always, constantly, in complex interactions with the world. The experiment was also an acknowledgment that the chief mode of informal learning for a new generation of students had been changed by the World Wide Web. It was an attempt to put the new science of attention together with the new digital technology that both demanded and, in some ways, helped produce it.

I'm not going to argue that the *interactive* task of surfing is better or worse than the reception model that dominated mass education in the twentieth century. "Better" and "worse" don't make a lot of sense to me. But there's a difference and, as we have seen, difference is what we pay attention to. Said another way, we concentrate in a different way when we are making the connections, when we are clicking and browsing, than when we are watching (as in a TV show or movie) or listening or even reading a book. Indisputably, the imagination is engaged in making connections in all of those forms, as it is in anything we experience. It is engaged in a different way when we ourselves are making the connections, when we're browsing from one to another link that interests us and draws our attention. We don't need a "better or worse" because we have both, and both are potentially rich and fascinating cognitive activities. But the relative newness of the surfing/searching experience drove our interest in the potential of the iPod experiment; in 2003, educators already knew how to mine traditional media, but we had not yet figured out how to harness the new forms of attention students who had grown up surfing the Web were mastering. The Web does not prescribe a clear, linear pathway through the content. There is no one way to move along a straight-and-narrow road from beginning to end.

The formal education most of us experienced—and which we now often think of when we picture a classroom—is based on giving premium value to expertise, specialization, and hierarchy. It prepared us for success in the twentieth century, when those things mattered above all. Yet what form of education is required in the information age, when what matters has grown very different? What form of education is required in a world of social networking, crowdsourcing, customizing, and user-generated content; a world of searching and browsing, where the largest-ever encyclopedia is created not by experts but by volunteers around the world—as is the world's second most popular Web browser (Mozilla's Firefox), the world's most massive online multiplayer game (World of Warcraft, with over 11 million subscribers a month), and all the social networking and communication sites, from MySpace and Facebook to Twitter?

Another way of asking the question is: How do we make over the twentieth-century classroom to take advantage of all the remarkable digital benefits of the twenty-first century?

The iPod experiment was a start, but to get a sense of just how big a task we face, it's useful to have a sense of how schools came to be the way they are, shaped by the values of a very different world.

Do you remember the classic story by Washington Irving, "The Legend of Sleepy Hollow"? It was written in 1820 and features a parody of the pompous schoolmaster in the form of Ichabod Crane, a homely, gawky, and self-satisfied pedant who is confident in his role as a dispenser of knowledge. He knows what does and does not constitute knowledge worth having and is equally sure that students must be drilled in that knowledge and tested to make sure they measure up. If you blindfolded Ichabod Crane, spun him around, and set him down in a twenty-first-century classroom, he would be baffled by electricity, dumbfounded by moving images, confused by the computers and cell phones, but he'd know exactly where to stand, and he'd know exactly where he stood.

It's shocking to think of how much the world has changed since the horse-and-buggy days of Sleepy Hollow and how little has changed within the traditional classroom in America. On March 10, 2010, the National Governors Association and the Council of Chief State School Officers even called for "sweeping new school standards that could lead to students across the country using the same math and English textbooks and taking the same tests, replacing a patchwork of state and local systems in an attempt to raise student achievement nationwide."[8] Ichabod Crane lives!

What in the world is going on? In the past in America, times of enormous innovation in the rest of society, including in technology and in industry, have also been times of tremendous innovation in education. What has happened to us? Rather than thinking of ways we can be preparing our students for their future, we seem determined to prepare them for our past.

Literally. The current passion for national standards is reminiscent of the conversations on education at our country's beginnings, back in 1787, the year the U.S. Constitution was adopted. Technology was changing the world then, too. At the time of the signing of the Constitution, the new invention of steam-powered presses, coupled with the invention of machine-made ink and paper, made for mass printing of cheap books and newspapers, putting print into the hands of middle-class readers for the first time in human history. The new institution of the circulating library made books available even to the working poor. Books proliferated; newspapers sprang up everywhere. And that's when a cry for standards and public education was born in America, in response to a new democratic government that needed informed citizens and new technologies of print that made books and newspapers widely available.

Thomas Jefferson himself advocated that America had to launch a "crusade against ignorance" if the nation was to survive as an independent representative democracy.[9] By 1791, when the Bill of Rights was added to the U.S. Constitution, seven states were making provisions for public education. There was not yet anything like an "educational system" in the United States, though. Education was attended to unevenly by local, regional, state, and private institutions, some secular, some sectarian, an inheritance that continues to this day in the form of state-controlled educational policy, local and regional school boards, and other decentralized means of oversight.

Horace Mann, whose name can be found over the entrance of many public schools in America, was the first great champion of national educational reform. The son of a farmer of limited means, Mann clawed his way to an education, earning money by braiding straw to pay the local tuitions for the elementary schools he attended for only six weeks at a time, leaving the rest of his time free to help with family farming operations. He enrolled at Brown University at age twenty, graduated in three years as valedictorian of the class of 1819, and dedicated himself to the creation of the "common schools," which after around 1840 became the predecessor of a free, publicly supported education system.

The common schools were scheduled around the agriculture year so farm kids could attend too. The schools were open to both boys and girls, regardless of class, although several states explicitly forbade the attendance of nonwhite children. The schools were locally controlled, with the kind of local politics governing curriculum and textbook assignments then that we see now in the state-by-state regulation of education, even after our "national educational policy" has been adopted.

Mandatory, compulsory public schooling developed over the course of the last half of the nineteenth century and got its full wind at the turn into the twentieth century as part of America's process of industrialization. Public education was seen as the most efficient way to train potential workers for labor in the newly urbanized factories. Teaching them control, socializing them for the mechanized, routinized labor of the factory was all part of the educational imperative of the day. Whether meant to calm the supposedly unruly immigrant populace coming to American shores or to urbanize farmers freshly arriving in the city, education was designed to train unskilled workers to new tasks that required a special, dedicated form of attention. School was thought to be the right training ground for discipline and uniformity. Kids started attending school at the same age, passed through a carefully graduated system, and were tested systematically on a standardized curriculum, with subjects that were taught in time blocks throughout the day. In ways large and small, the process mimicked the forms of specialized labor on the assembly line, as well as the divisions of labor (from the CEO down to the manual laborers) in the factory itself.

Many features now common in twenty-first-century public education began as an accommodation to the new industrial model of the world ushered in during the last part of the nineteenth century. With machines that needed to run on schedule and an assembly line that required human precision and efficiency, schools began to place a great emphasis on time and timeliness. Curriculum, too, was directed toward focusing on a task, including the mastery of a specified syllabus of required learning. "Efficiency" was the byword of the day, in the world of work and in the world of school. Learning to pay attention as directed—through rote memorization and mastery of facts—was important, and schools even developed forms of rapid-fire question-and-answer, such as the spelling bee or the math bee. This was a new skill, different from the elite models of question-and-answer based on the Socratic method; the agrarian model of problem solving, in which one is responsible for spotting a problem and solving it (whether a wilted corn tassel or an injured horse); and the apprenticeship model of the guild wherein one learned a craft by imitating the skills of a master. An assembly line is far more regular and regulated. One person's tardiness, no matter how good the excuse, can destroy everyone else's productivity on the line. Mandatory and compulsory schooling for children was seen as a way of teaching basic knowledge—including the basic knowledge of tasks, obedience, hierarchy, and schedules. The school bell became a symbol of public education in the industrial era.[10]

So did specialization. With the advent of the assembly line, work became segmented. A worker didn't perform a whole job but one discrete task and then passed the job on to the next person and the next and so forth down the assembly line. The ideal of labor efficiency displaced the ideal of artisanship, with increased attention paid to the speed and accuracy of one kind of contribution to a larger industrial process. Focused attention to a task became the ideal form of attention, so different from, for example, the farmer on his horse scanning his land for anything that might look out of place or simply in need of care.

By 1900, state and regional schools were becoming the norm, replacing locally managed ones, and by 1918, every state had passed laws mandating children to attend elementary school or more. A concession was made to Catholics in that they could create a separate, parochial school system that would also meet these state regulations, another legacy that comes down to the present in the form of "faith-based schools."

During the first six decades of the twentieth century, as America ascended to the position of a world power, the rhetoric of education followed suit, with an increasing emphasis on producing leaders. While the nineteenth-century common schools had focused on elementary education, the twentieth-century focus was increasingly on the institution of high school, including improving graduation rates. In 1900, approximately 15 percent of the U.S. population received a high school diploma, a number that increased to around 50 percent by 1950.

After World War II, there was a rapid expansion of both high schools and higher education, invigorated after 1957 when the Russians surprised the world by launching *Sputnik,* the first man-made object ever to orbit the earth. As America competed against Russian science in the Cold War, policy makers placed more and more emphasis on educational attainment. Many economists argue that America's economic growth through the 1960s was fueled by this educational expansion.

Robert Schwartz, dean of the Harvard Graduate School of Education, notes that since the last quarter of the twentieth century, the pattern of educational expansion that has characterized the United States from the Revolutionary War forward has changed.[11] Since 1975, American educational attainment has leveled off or even dropped while there has been a dramatic increase in the number of jobs requiring exploratory, creative problem solving typically encouraged by postsecondary education. We are seeing the first signs that our education system is slipping in comparison to our needs.

The current high school graduation rate is roughly the same as it was in 1975, approximately 75 percent. Our graduation rate from four-year colleges is

28 percent, also roughly the same as it was thirty-five years ago. That this has even remained consistent in the face of all that has changed in the last thirty-five years is remarkable enough, a credit to both the drive and quality of American students and the patchwork, piecemeal reforms we've used to hold the system together. Yet while we've been holding steady, other countries have made rapid gains. Whereas in the 1960s we ranked first in the proportion of adults with high school degrees, we now rank thirteenth on the list of the thirty countries surveyed by the Organisation for Economic Co-operation and Development (OECD), an organization that coordinates statistics from market-based democracies to promote growth. By contrast, South Korea has moved from twenty-seventh place on that list to our old number one spot.

Most troubling is what happened from 1995 to 2005. During this one decade, the United States dropped from second to fifteenth place in college completion rates among OECD nations. For the wealthiest and most powerful nation on earth to rank fifteenth is nothing short of a national disgrace. This is especially the case, given that our system of education *presumes* college preparation is the ideal, even in environments where most kids are not going on to college. By that standard, we are failing.

It's not that we cared about education before 1975 but don't today. Our heart is not the problem. Look at the numbers. The Swiss are the only people on earth who spend more per child on public education than Americans. According to OECD, we spend over $11,000 per year per child on public education. That's more than double the rate of South Korea. Education spending accounts for more than 7 percent of our GDP.[12] However, the OECD statistics show that our graduation rates now are roughly on a par with those of Turkey and Mexico, not nations to which we like to compare ourselves by other indicators of our power or success.[13]

It is little wonder that educators and parents are constantly reacting to the comparative, global numbers with ever more strident calls for standards. The problem, however, is the confusion of "high standards" with "standardization." Our national educational policy depends on standardized tests, but it is not at all clear that preparing students to achieve high test scores is equivalent to setting a high standard for what and how kids should know and learn.

The real issue isn't that our schools are too challenging. It's the opposite. Among the top quartile of high school students, the most frequent complaint and cause of disaffection from schooling is boredom and lack of rigor. That also happens to be true among the lowest group, for whom low expectations lead to low motivation.[14] Kids aren't failing because school is too hard but because it doesn't interest them. It doesn't capture their attention.

Relevance has been proved to be a crucial factor for keeping students in high school, especially mid- and lower-level students. Tie what kids learn in school to what they can use in their homes, their families, and their neighborhood—and vice versa—and not surprisingly, that relevance kicks their likelihood of staying in school up a few notches. Because in the United States (but not in many countries with higher college attendance), going to college requires money for tuition, our emphasis on college as the grail of secondary education only rubs in its inaccessibility (its irrelevance) to lower-income kids—a fact that contributes to high school dropouts. Finally, for all groups, and especially for students in the lowest-achieving group, relationships with teachers and counselors who believe in them and support them (often against peer, familial, or cultural pressure) is a determining factor in remaining in school. These key factors for educational success—rigor, relevance, and relationships—have been dubbed the new three *Rs,* with student-teacher ratio being particularly important. Small class size has been proved to be one of the single most significant factors in kids' staying in and succeeding in school. Twenty seems to be the magic number.[15] Even on a neurological level, brain researchers have shown that kids improve with directed, special attention to their own skills and interests, the opposite of our move toward standardization.[16]

The biggest problem we face now is the increasing mismatch between traditional curricular standards of content-based instruction and the new forms of thinking required by our digital, distributed workplace. At any level—blue collar or white collar—those jobs requiring "routine thinking skills" are increasingly performed by machine or outsourced to nations with a lower standard of living than the United States. Yet virtually all of contemporary American education is still based on the outmoded model of college prep that prepares students for middle management and factory jobs that, because of global rearrangements in labor markets, in large part no longer exist.

We've all seen industrial jobs for manual laborers dwindle in the United States and other First World economies, either taken over by machines or outsourced abroad to workers who are unprotected by unions or fair labor laws. The same is now the case for routinized white-collar office jobs. In exploitative "digital sweatshops" all around the world, workers at minimal wages can do everything from preparing your tax return to playing your online strategy games for you, so your avatar can be staging raids while you are on the trading floor or in your executive office on Wall Street.

To be prepared for jobs that have a real future in the digital economy, one needs an emphasis on creative thinking, at all levels. By this I mean the kind of thinking that cannot be computerized and automated. This creative thinking requires attention to surprise, anomaly, difference, and disruption, and an ability to switch focus, depending on what individual, unpredictable problems might arise. Perhaps surprisingly, these noncomputational jobs, impervious to automation, occur at all levels across the blue-collar and white-collar spectrum. Many of these jobs require highly specialized and dexterous problem-solving abilities or interpersonal skills—but do not require a college degree.

We were criticized for the iPod experiment. Many treated it as if it were an extravagance, superfluous to real learning and real education. But the iPod experiment exemplifies a form of inquiry-based problem solving wherein solutions are not known in advance and cannot be more successfully outsourced to either a computer or to a Third World laborer who performs repetitive tasks over and over in horrific conditions at minimal wages. The new global economics of work (whatever one thinks about it politically) is not likely to change, and so we must. And that change begins with schooling. Learning to think in multiple ways, with multiple partners, with a dexterity that cannot be comput-erized or outsourced, is no longer a luxury but a necessity. Given the altered shape of global labor, the seemingly daring iPod experiment turns out actually to be, in the long run, a highly pragmatic educational model.

PART OF OUR FAILURE RATE in contemporary education can be blamed on the one-size-fits-all model of standards that evolved over the course of the twentieth century; as we narrow the spectrum of skills that we test in schools, more and more kids who have skills outside that spectrum will be labeled as failures. As what counts as learning is increasingly standardized and limited, increasing numbers of students learn in ways that are not measured by those standards. This is the lesson of attention blindness yet again: If you measure narrowly, you see results just as narrowly. In other words, the more standardized our assessment, the more kids fail. Their failure is then diagnosed as a learning disability or a disorder. But they are failing when assessed by a standard that has almost nothing to do with how they learn online or—more important—what skills they need in a digital age.

The mismatch is just wrong. It's as if we're still turning out assembly-line kids on an assembly-line model in an infinitely more varied and variable custom-izing, remixed, mashable, user-generated, crowdsourced world. As long as we define their success by a unified set of standards, we will continue to miss their gifts, we will not challenge their skills, and, in the end, we will lose them from our schools just as, implicitly, we have lost interest in them.

We need far more inquiry-based opportunities for our kids. It doesn't have to be as expensive or as radical as the iPod experiment. The world is full of pro-blems to solve that cost little except imagination, relevant learning, and careful guidance by a teacher with the wisdom to *not control* every outcome or to think that the best way to measure is by keeping each kid on the same page of the same book at the same time.

I recently visited a middle school where one girl with green- and blue-striped hair, creatively and eccentrically dyed, sat against the wall, remote from the other kids, as drawn into herself as she could possibly be without disappear-ing, looking for all the world like the kid who will never hear anything. When I, a stranger, came into the classroom, some of the other kids fussed over my unex-pected appearance there, and my *difference*: One girl admired my purple leather jacket, another asked if I was an artist, because I was wearing a black turtleneck and skinny black pants. One boy asked about the image of an electric fan on my long, illustrated scarf from South Africa, and a waggish little boy hummed, with perfect pitch, "Who's That Lady?" when he saw me in his classroom. When I asked how in the world a twelve-year-old knew the Isley Brothers, he said snap-pily, "The Swiffer commercial." There was a lot of buzz in the class about the visitor, in other words. The green-haired girl in the corner slowly shifted her gaze in my direction, gave the smallest upward movement at the corner of her lips before returning to her frown and letting her eyes move back to outer space again, away from the strange visitor, determinedly *not there*.

I thought of a blog post I'd read earlier that week by the prolific business writer Seth Godin, creator of the popular user-generated community Web site

Squidoo. Godin's post was called "What You Can Learn from a Lousy Teacher," and his list of what you can learn from the teacher you cannot please included: "Grades are an illusion, your passion and insight are reality; your work is worth more than mere congruence to an answer key; persistence in the face of a skeptical authority figure is a powerful ability; fitting in is a short-term strategy, standing out pays off in the long run; and if you care enough about work to be criticized, you've learned enough for today."[17] This remote young woman against the wall didn't look defeated by school. There was something *resolute* in her. I could sense that she had, somehow, taken in intuitively the kinds of lessons Godin was preaching, even if it would take her another decade to fully realize what, in her body language, she was already showing she'd absorbed.

She stayed that way, barely making eye contact with the teacher or any other students, until drawings begun during the previous class were handed around to be worked on again. The transformation I witnessed then was so rapid and thorough that I thought of what Pygmalion must have seen the first time his statue came to life. She went from being still, glassy-eyed, self-contained, and entirely not-present to a concentrated, focused, dedicated bundle of intensity. She still didn't interact with the other kids, but all eyes were on her as she began her day's work on a highly detailed line drawing she was executing. Unlike the bustle at the other tables in the room, there was a silence around her, with the kids practically tiptoeing into the circle of her aura to watch, not speaking to her or to one another, then moving away. I was dying to see her drawing but even more interested in the compact energy she'd created around herself and the other kids, generated from the passion of her drawing. Rather than interrupt that magic, I moved away.

Later in the day, I saw her waiting for her ride home, in the homeroom period at the end of the day, and again the sullen remoteness of I-am-not-here returned After all the kids had gone, I asked her teacher to tell me about her. She'd been diagnosed as profoundly learning disabled, with attention deficit disorder. Her parents sent her to this magnet arts school after she had failed elsewhere. At home, the only thing she seemed to enjoy doing was doodling, but her elementary school had laid off its art teachers, sacrificed to educational cutbacks and the fact that, in our standardized forms of testing, there is no EOG (end-of-grade exam) for art. Art is therefore an add-on that many public schools cannot afford. It was only at the new school that her skills as an artist were recognized. She quickly went from the class failure to the class artist. She mastered the editing tools on the class computer and transferred her imagination and creativity there, too, much to the admiration of her classmates.

I think again about what learning disabilities signify for kids today. In the *Diagnostic and Statistical Manual of Mental Disorders* (the infamous DSM), attention deficit disorder is characterized by distractibility, frequent switching from one activity to another, boredom with a task after just a brief time trying to execute it, and difficulty organizing and completing a task or in focusing on a task in which one is not interested. That last phrase is key. ADD almost never applies to *all* activities, only those in which the child is not interested. This isn't a disability (a fixed biological or cognitive condition) but a disposition (susceptible to change depending on the environment). Keep the kids interested and ADD goes away.

The girl with the green hair has special skills that show up nowhere on her compulsory EOG state tests, on which she continues to score poorly. "Your work is worth more than mere congruence to an answer key." This girl's talents don't count on those tests, and yet she has a special and valued ability that cannot be replaced by a computer program. The problem is that her fate is to a large extent controlled by her performance on the EOG tests, and unless the adults in her life—teachers and parents—are resolute in shepherding her along a path where her talents are valued, they may ultimately wind up undeveloped.

I identified with this girl. When I was in school, my talents had been math and writing, and there was a teacher, Miss Schmidt, who saw those gifts, despite my abysmal test scores, despite the fact that we had to memorize the preamble to the Constitution and the Gettysburg Address to graduate from eighth grade and I just couldn't. I tried and failed over and over many times, staying after school, trying to say it out loud and failing again. Miss Schmidt was feeling certain that I wasn't really trying but just being "obstinate." Then, during one of our painful after-class sessions, she had a hunch. She offered me the opportunity to write an essay instead, one essay about each brief text I was failing to memorize. I stayed up all night working on this and returned the next day with my project. My scrawl filled every page in a small spiral binder—*two hundred* pages.

I remember her eyes widening as she took this smudgy, worn binder from my hand. She looked through it in disbelief and bewilderment as she turned over pages and pages of my barely readable handwriting. There were even footnotes. "You still don't have them memorized, do you?" Miss Schmidt asked. I shook my head. After a moment, she got out the special state certification and, beside my name, put the check mark I needed to graduate from middle school. I'd passed.

Sometimes you learn from the good teachers too. It's not easy to be a good teacher all the time. The girl with the green hair was lucky to find one who honored her talent. Before I left his classroom, I told him, if he thought it appropriate, to let the girl know that the visitor, that professor from Duke University, had noticed her beautiful artwork and admired it. I told him, if he thought it appropriate, to let the girl know that, when the visitor was her age, her hair was purple.

As MATTHEW B. CRAWFORD ARGUES in *Shop Class as Soulcraft*, his eloquent study of the importance of making and fixing things, our national standards for secondary schools miss kids like this young lady. Our schools are geared, implicitly and explicitly, to be college preparatory. They are weighted toward a twentieth-century, white-collar, middle-management economy.[18] Our standardized education not only bores kids but prepares them for jobs that no longer exist as they once did. Attention blindness again. Our one-size-fits-all educational model focuses steadily and intently on the past.

The space age was America's educational glory moment, when we occupied the number one spot. At that moment, there was a splendid flowering of many kinds of educational theory, including progressive theories, free schools, Montessori schools, science and technology schools, new math, old math, and on and on. It was thought that we were facing a brave new world of science for, after all, incomprehensibly, men had walked on the moon. Education took that fervor to its heart, blossoming, experimenting with innovations as bold and expansive as the solar system itself.

Now, in a digital age, we can communicate and learn in ways not even imagined by Neil Armstrong and Buzz Aldrin walking for the first time on the face of the moon: "One small step for man, one giant leap for mankind." Yet our educational vision has shrunk to the tiny bubble of a multiple-choice exam. Our dreams of new standards of knowledge have shrunk to the right or wrong answer, chosen not among infinitely variable possibilities but among A, B, C, D, and, perhaps, none of the above.

I hate this kind of education. I'm prejudiced, I admit it. So don't ask me. Ask any adult. Ask yourself. What was the most formative experience of your life in school? I suspect your answer isn't "I scored in the 94th percentile on my fifth-grade end-of-grade compulsory exam." Whenever I ask this question, invariably I hear a story of a great teacher who had faith, who inspired and challenged someone to do more than she ever thought was possible before.

Ichabod Crane may nod approval at our current national educational policy. It may seem familiar to him and right. For those of us who remember what inspired us, what commanded our attention, there was always something experimental and daring, there was always something more.

Some of the best teaching I ever witnessed did not happen courtesy of the Internet. It was many years ago, in rural Alberta, Canada. Inez Davidson, the mother of my first husband, Ted, began her teaching career at eighteen, teaching in a one-room schoolhouse in Pincher Creek, a coal-mining town in the Canadian Rockies. She rode half-wild horses to school each morning, alone in the dark and the cold through grizzly country, "putting miles on them," as she would say, before they could be sold to local ranchers as well-trained working horses. Inez was maybe five feet tall, but no one messed with her, ever.

Ted's father was a rancher in the town of Mountain View when he married Inez. Mountain View is as pretty as its name, a gorgeous ranching community in the foothills of the Rockies. The Davidson homestead looked out upon Chief Mountain, the sacred mountain of the Blackfoot and Blood Indian tribes. The area was made up mostly of Native peoples and Mormons or adamant ex-Mormons like the Davidsons, plus elk, moose, black bear, grizzlies, mountain lions, and so forth. Two hundred people in two hundred square miles. The area was poor, too. Rural electrification only came to Alberta in the late 1950s. Even in the 1970s and 1980s, when I was there, the kitchen had a stove that also burned wood (for when the electricity went out), and the entire house had only two additional propane heaters. This was *Canada*, in the foothills of the Rocky Mountains. In winter, it was sometimes 20 or 40 degrees below zero. The hallways and bathrooms and bedrooms were unheated. There was an outhouse for when the plumbing was overtaxed. It was a lot for a gal from Chicago to take in.

My mother-in-law taught in the three-room schoolhouse in Mountain View. For many years, there were more former residents of Mountain View with PhDs, MDs, or law degrees than from any other town in Alberta besides the two major cities in the province, Edmonton and Calgary. By the time I came on the scene, graduate students earning their degrees in education departments in the province were coming to Mountain View to find out what was happening there, that such a backwater was sending students not only to college but well beyond.

Mrs. Davidson, as she was called, was a main reason for this educational success story. How did she do it? First, she got in a lot of trouble, every year, with the school superintendent because she refused, ever, to teach to a test. She covered what the province demanded of third, fourth, and fifth graders and far more, but she always did it her way, as a challenge, a game, an interactive and communal learning activity. She made learning fun—and she was tough.

She was very skeptical of the concept of learning disabilities. She taught long after the normal retirement age and began to see kids coming to school who were more hyperactive than she'd seen in her earlier career and was convinced that part of the reason was environmental and part behavioral. She was concerned about both food additives and contaminants in the air and drinking water even in cattle country, where the water supply was tainted by runoff from oil and smelting plants far away. She was also shocked at how parents were driving kids to school instead of having them walk or ride horses in; these were forms of physical exercise she believed were important to kids' health, well-being, and concentration in the classroom. She loathed it when she saw kids medicated as a remedy for their learning disabilities, and was much more interested in all the subtle and obvious ways kids learned—and learned differently.

She insisted that everyone had a unique way of learning and believed that to be true of the smartest students as well as the academically weakest. She took pride in finding challenges that inspired kids who had clear cognitive restrictions or physical ones, and defied anyone to bring her a kid she couldn't teach. Rodney, a close friend to all the Davidson boys, was a brilliant athlete but very poor in school. Reading was hard and math unbearable. He couldn't conceptualize arithmetic on any level and used his fingers to count even the simplest arithmetic. Other teachers wrote him off as "slow." Mrs. Davidson bought him an abacus and had him research all the sophisticated things the ancient Egyptians could calculate on one. She then taught him to use the different parts of each of his ten fingers as if they were beads on an abacus. He could put his hands under the table and, without anyone seeing, do "rapid calculation" instantly. He did so as a kid, acing math tests, and he did so as an adult, gaining a reputation for uncanny speed and accuracy in the brawny, take-no-prisoners arena of the cattle auctions. Rodney was no one's fool.

Two of Inez Davidson's best teaching tricks involved games. One was that, on every Friday, she would divide up the kids, the fifth graders on one side of the room, the little kids—third and fourth graders—on the other. Whatever they had learned that week would be the subject of the Friday contests. The first part of the day would be spent with the previous week's winners figuring out what kind of competition they would make. They would devise the rules and explain them to the other group. The competition would then require one group testing the other on the answers to various problems in all the different areas they had studied that week.

Mrs. Davidson would serve as the referee. The little kids worked hard to beat the older kids, who of course had their honor to defend, and each team tried to ask harder and harder questions to stump the other. Once Mrs. Davidson felt that the week's work had been covered, she would declare a winning team. The winning group could head out to the playground fifteen minutes early while the losers sat there an *interminable* fifteen minutes—nine hundred seconds!—getting a head start on next week's contest. Some weeks, though, they had so much fun scheming on the hard questions they'd ask the following week that Mrs. Davidson would have to point to the clock to remind them that study hall was over and that it was time to go outside to the schoolyard to play with their friends.

Sometimes they had an hour of these competitions on Friday, sometimes two hours. The other teachers grumbled that Mrs. Davidson's kids got away with murder. Ted, who had his mother as a teacher for all three years because there wasn't anyone else in Mountain View, ended up winning a full scholarship to the University of Chicago, where he tested out of virtually all of his first- and second-year college courses. Not bad for a kid from a cow town in the Canadian Rockies.

Mrs. Davidson taught her kids to dream. Every year, there would be some new, ambitious project with a theme that would unfold over the course of the year. One year, the project was for each child to find a pen pal in another town called Mountain View somewhere in the world. There was only one map in the school, so a first step was to take an enormous piece of newsprint, cover the map, and spend days and days tracing out all the countries on their own map. Then, each child went to the library, which held far fewer books for the entire school than my study holds today, and they each started reading about all the countries in the world, looking for other Mountain Views. They would then mark their particular Mountain View on the hand-drawn map tacked up in the schoolroom. They had to think of ways to communicate with kids in these other Mountain Views. Since this was a Mormon area, there were families who had been on missions to other parts of the world, so that was the obvious way to make contacts, but this was a contest, and ingenuity was rewarded.

One kid remembered that Hang Sang, the elderly Chinese man who ran the local general store, the only store in town, had come over to Canada to work on the railroad, as had so many Chinese immigrants. Taciturn, with a thick accent, Mr. Sang was amused and delighted when one child suddenly wanted help writing a letter—in Chinese. The kid had somehow found out about a town called Mountain View in China. That was the child who won the contest, and long after the contest was over, he spent time with Mr. Sang, talking to him in the back of his store.

But of course they all won. The globe became smaller through the connections they made, and their town became larger. They learned geography and anthropology and foreign languages too. The project lasted not just one full year but many years, and some kids visited those other Mountain Views when they grew up. To this day, I don't drive through a town named Mountain View (there are a lot of them in the world, actually) without wondering if one of Mrs. Davidson's kids sent a letter there and, through the connection made, was inspired to go on, later, to become a professor or a doctor or a veterinarian.

None of what happened in Mrs. Davidson's classroom in Mountain View, Alberta, Canada, depended upon an iPod. None of it required the Internet. But the Internet requires this kind of interactive, motivated, inspired, and curious form of learning. The key here is that Mrs. Davidson's classroom was not really divided up into "subjects" so much as it was into problems, puzzles, brain teasers, challenges, games, word problems, and intellectual obstacle courses, many of which require kids working together toward a solution. What counts is the little kids showing, with pride, that they are every bit as smart as the big kids and the big kids showing, with pride, that they are king, and all of them understanding (although they'd fight you rather than admit it) that they need one another to learn and to dream.

Like the iPod experiment, what this classroom story shows is that kids want to learn and can propel themselves to all kinds of learning as long as there is a payoff, not in what is won or achieved in statistical terms, but what is won and achieved inside, in the sense of self-confidence and competence. Learning, in this sense, is skill and will, an earned conviction that, faced with a challenge ahead, this past achievement will get one through. You can count on your ability to learn, and nowhere is that more important than when what you've learned in the past no longer suffices for the future. That is the glistening paradox of great education: It is not about answering test questions. It is about knowing that, when tested by the most grueling challenges ahead, you have the capacity to learn what is required to succeed.

It is in this sense that unlearning is a skill as vital as learning. It is a skill you have to acquire, too. Unlearning requires that you take an inventory of your changed situation, that you take an inventory of your current repertoire of skills, and that you have the confidence to see your shortcomings and repair them. Without confidence in your ability to learn something new, it is almost impossible to see what you have to change in order to succeed against a new challenge. Lacking confidence in your ability to change, it's much easier to blame the changed situation—typically, new technologies—and then dig in your heels, raising a bulwark against the new. Confidence in your ability to learn *is* confidence in your ability to unlearn, to switch assumptions or methods or partnerships in order to do better. This is true not only for you, as an individual, but for whole institutions.

That's what those kids in a tiny town in rural Alberta learned as fourth and fifth graders pitted against the sixth graders (and vice versa). Mrs. Davidson had to fight the school superintendent every year. Her kids all knew that, too. They knew that she'd put herself on the line for their learning; she'd stand up to anybody, including the superintendent, on their behalf. She dared him, year after year, to fire her. In a different era, he might have, but every year, there'd be the ritual dressing down in his office. I was never in the room with them, but I have a feeling that it wasn't Mrs. Davidson who left feeling chastised.

Put those kids in a lecture hall, give them a standardized curriculum with standardized forms of measuring achievement and ability, and they learn a different lesson. They might well master what they are supposed to learn, but that's not education. When you think of learning as something external to yourself, learning becomes a levy—*an assessment, not an asset.* The assessment no longer matters after the schooling stops. The asset is a resource one draws on for a lifetime.

How can the lessons of this woman's extraordinary classroom be put to use? The model of learning in Mrs. Davidson's classes is probably as old as human history. It is the game. As in a game, there are parameters, what you need to know in order to succeed within the game's rules and requirements, subject matter, or methods. There is a specific target or goal, and you compete with others and against others to win. The real winner, always, is you, not because you earned the trophy but because you learned the inestimable skill of responding to a challenge.

NOTES

1. These are all quoted and the experiment is discussed in James Todd, "The iPod Idea: Wired for Scholarship," *Duke Magazine* 91, no. 5, Sept.–Oct. 2005.

2. The iPod experiment would never have happened without approval and funding of this forward-looking initiative, for which credit goes to my colleagues Tracy Futhey, Vice President for Information Technology, and Provost Peter Lange.

3. On values formation and the blind spots it leaves, see Barbara Herrnstein Smith, *Contingencies of Value: Alternate Perspectives for Critical Theory* (Cambridge, MA: Harvard University Press, 1988).

4. Jeff Howe, *Crowdsourcing: Why the Power of the Crowd Is Driving the Future of Business* (New York: Crown, 2008).

5. Professor Marie Lynn Miranda is a pioneer in using new technologies to help shape community activism on environmental policy. Her Web site is: http://fds.duke.edu /db/Nicholas/esp/faculty/mmiranda (accessed May 6, 2010).

6. Maria Magher, "iPod Gets Top Marks: Culbreth Middle School Is the First in the State to Require Device," *Chapel Hill News*, Mar. 14, 2010.

7. I have written about this at length with my HASTAC cofounder, David Theo Goldberg, in a research report that was first put up on the Web for comment from anyone who wished to offer it, then published in a research report based on colloquia we held all over the country, *The Future of Learning Institutions in a Digital Age* (Cambridge, MA: MIT Press, 2009). The expanded book form of this project is Cathy N. Davidson and David Theo Goldberg, *The Future of Thinking: Learning Institutions in a Digital Age* (Cambridge, MA: MIT Press, 2010).

8. "States Push for Nationalized Educational Standard," *US. and World News*, CBS Interactive, Mar. 10, 2010.

9. The classic studies of American education include Lawrence Cremin, *American Education: The National Experience* (New York: HarperCollins, 1980); Carl Kaestle, *Pillars of the Republic: Common Schools and American Society, 1780–1860* (New York: Hill & Wang, 1983); and Michael Katz, *Reconstructing American Education* (Cambridge, MA: Harvard University Press, 1987).

10. See Alvin Toffler and Heidi Toffler, *Revolutionary Wealth: How It Will Be Created and How It Will Change Our Lives* (New York: Knopf, 2006): 357–62.

11. Robert Schwartz "The American High School in Context," paper delivered to Sino-U.S. Seminar on Diversity in High School, Mar. 23, 2009. This is the single most concise survey and set of statistics I have found anywhere, and one remarkably free of the polemics and politics (left or right) that confuse many of the statistics. This debt to him is not just for this wise assessment and sorting of the numbers but for his distinguished career of contribution to national educational policy since the Carter administration.

12. These are official figures from the Organisation for Economic Co-operation and Development (OECD), an international organization of thirty countries "committed to democracy and the market economy."

13. Ibid.

14. Special thanks to tweeter Michael Josefowicz, a retired printer who tweets as ToughLoveforX, for this clarifying distinction between *standards* and *standardization*. Schwartz's essay discusses the surveys of why students drop out of school.

15. On class size and academic performance, see foundational work in, for example, Glen E. Robinson and James H. Wittebols, *Class Size Research: A Related Cluster Analysis for Decision-Making.* (Arlington, VA: Education Research Service, 1986); Jeremy D. Finn, *Class Size and Students at Risk: What Is Known? What is Next?* (Washington, DC: U.S. Department of Education, Office of Educational Research and Improvement, National Institute on the Education of At-Risk Students, 1998); and Gene V. Glass, Leonard S. Cahen, Mary L. Smith, and Nikola N. Filby, *School Class Size: Research and Policy* (Beverly Hills, CA: Sage, 1982).

16. See William R. Dagged and Paul David Nussbaum, "How Brain Research Relates to Rigor, Relevance and Relationships." See also Peter S. Eriksson, Ekaterina Perfilieva, Thomas Bjork-Eriksson, Ann-Marie Alborn, Claes Nordborg, Daniel A. Peterson, and Fred H. Gage, "Neurogenesis in the Adult Human Hippocampus," *Nature Medicine* 4 (1998): 1313–17. There is a prolific body of research and policy statements on the "new three Rs"–including other xRs, such as responsibility, representing, relating, and so forth. See, for example, Clifford Adelman, *Principal Indicators of Student Academic Histories in Postsecondary Education, 1972–2000* (Washington, DC: US Department of Education, Institute of Education Sciences, 2004); and Anthony P. Carnevale and Donna M. Desrochers, *Connecting Education Standards and Employment: Course-Taking Patterns of Young Workers* (Washington, DC: Achieve Inc., 2002).

17. Seth Godin, "What You Can Learn from a Lousy Teacher," http://sethgodin.typepad.com/seths_blog/2010/03/what-you-can-learn-from-a-lousy-teacher.html (accessed Mar. 20, 2010).

18. Matthew B. Crawford, *Shop Class as Soulcraft: An Inquiry into the Value of Work* (New York: Penguin, 2009).

QUESTIONS FOR MAKING CONNECTIONS
WITHIN THE READING

1. Do you recognize yourself in Davidson's portrayal of the "first generation of kids" to grow up with the Internet? Do you regard yourself and other people your age as *information seekers*? Have the schools that you attended prior to college ignored the potential of the Internet, as Davidson suggests? If most students are adept at finding information via the Web, does it make sense for schools and universities to focus on skills they already have? Have you found that in terms of *quality*, however you wish to define it, the information furnished by the Web can hold its own with other sources, such as books and lectures? Have you found Facebook and Twitter to be effective forms of knowledge delivery?

2. Davidson argues that crowdsourcing has advantages over authority as an organizing principle for education. What forms of social interaction does crowdsourcing involve, and what are its potential strengths as well as its potential liabilities? What forms of interaction are implied by the authority principle? In what ways might the growth of standardized testing reflect the basic values of a system premised on authority? In what ways do crowdsourcing and collaboration offer alternatives to the standardization that Davidson inveighs against? Could crowdsourcing, and the Web in general, inadvertently produce standardization of another kind?

3. It is possible to argue that Davidson sees the new technology—like the free iPods gifted to the students at Duke—as a means to an end rather than an end in itself. What end(s) does she want students to pursue? What, in other words, are her political or cultural objectives? Based on the selection, would you say that Davidson wants to nudge us toward a more egalitarian way of life? What assumptions does she appear to make about ordinary people? Does she see creativity as exceptional? How about intelligence? Does she view failure as socially produced—that is, as forced upon learners by the educational system itself?

QUESTIONS FOR WRITING

1. In the widely read essay "Is Google Making Us Stupid," Nicholas Carr blames the Web for shortening our attention spans and training us to race through online information without stopping to reflect carefully on its meaning or its implications. "Once," Carr writes, "I was a scuba diver in the sea of words. Now I zip along the surface like a guy on a Jet Ski." Does the Web indeed promote "shallowness" in our use of information, and how might Davidson respond to the charge that it is making us less thoughtful? Are the activities she describes, such as inventing new apps, conducive to reflection? How does the experience of surfing the Web differ from reading

a novel? How does it differ from watching TV? Is interpreting a novel or poem a more active process than surfing the Web?

2. What is Davidson's philosophy of education? What does she believe should be its most important goals, and which aspects of contemporary schooling does she regard as detrimental? How has Davidson's experience of "difference" influenced her attitudes toward learning, and how were those attitudes shaped by the example of her mother-in-law, Inez Davidson? How might Davidson respond to Annie Paul Murphy's charge that her program for reform disregards past cultural achievements: "the inhabitants and the knowledge of the past are merely obstacles to be trampled in the headlong rush toward an interactive, connected, collaborative future"? What is the value of the past in Davidson's philosophy?

QUESTIONS FOR MAKING CONNECTIONS
BETWEEN READINGS

1. In what ways might the new technology celebrated by Davidson pose a challenge to the ideology of "smartness" that Ho describes? How might the Internet help undermine a prestige-based hierarchy that *smartness* reinforces? If everyone has access to high status knowledge and can use it in creative ways, what impacts might such a change have on higher education—and on social life in general? Conversely, how might Ho's research complicate Davidson's egalitarian plans because, as Ho suggests, hierarchy is deeply entrenched in higher education? If Davidson were teaching at a less prestigious university than Duke, would her iPod program have generated the same degree of controversy? Does her optimism inadvertently reflect her own privileged situation within an elite institution?

2. The Internet-savvy "kids" whom Davidson lauds and wants professors to learn from are roughly the same people Twenge describes in "An Army of One: Me." Will Davidson's call for a nonhierarchical and student-centered education succeed if the students have been socialized into narcissism, as Twenge alleges? Does the Web actually promote the uncritical self-absorption of "generation me," or might it represent an antidote? Do the social media make people more social, or do they actually encourage psychological isolation? Does the Internet itself promote the idea that everyone will be exceptional if they just develop self-esteem? How might Davidson respond to Twenge's argument?

SUSAN FALUDI

PULITZER PRIZE–WINNING journalist Susan Faludi first became interested in writing about feminism in the fifth grade, when she polled her classmates to determine their feelings about the Vietnam War and legalized abortion. In the furor that followed Faludi's release of data showing her peers' liberal attitudes, Faludi came to realize, as she put it in an interview, "the power that you could have as a feminist writer. Not being the loudest person on the block, not being one who regularly interrupted in class or caused a scene, I discovered that through writing I could make my views heard, and I could actually create change."

The daughter of a Hungarian immigrant who survived the Holocaust, Faludi was raised in Queens and attended Harvard, where she studied literature and American history. After graduating in 1981, Faludi worked for a number of newspapers, including the *New York Times* and the *Wall Street Journal*, before devoting her time to writing *Backlash: The Undeclared War Against American Women* (1991), a study of the media's assault on feminism. The following year, *Backlash* won the National Book Critics Circle Award for general nonfiction and made Faludi into a household name. She appeared on the cover of *Time* magazine with Gloria Steinem and, almost overnight, became a national spokesperson on women's rights and the future of feminism.

While doing research for *Backlash*, Faludi began to wonder why the men who opposed women's progress were so angry. In setting out to understand this anger, she interviewed men's groups, sex workers in the pornography industry, union members, the unemployed, and other disenfranchised males. As part of this project "The Naked Citadel" describes an all-male military academy after it mistakenly admitted one young woman, an account later included in Faludi's second book, *Stiffed: The Betrayal of the American Man* (1999). Although now twenty years old, the story told in "The Naked Citadel" might be more relevant than ever. According to the Pentagon's own figures, 26,000 servicewomen and men were victims of sexual harassment or assault in 2012. Faludi's most recent book, *The Terror Dream: Fear and Fantasy in Post-9/11 America* (2007), returns to the issues of gender and aggression. While "The Naked Citadel" explores anti-feminist attitudes in a time of peace, *The Terror Dream* charts the difficulties facing feminism in a time of war. Faludi concludes in this book that the terrorist attacks

Quotations come from Brian Lamb's interview with Susan Faludi on Booknotes, October 25, 1992 <http://www.booknotes.org/transcripts/10096.htm> and Kate Melloy's interview with Susan Faludi, "Feminist Author Susan Faludi Preaches Male Inclusion" <http://www.kollegeville.com/kampus/faludi.htm>.

on September 11, 2001 have created further challenges for feminism by ushering in an era of hysterical insistence on traditional roles for men and women: the men are summoned to protect, while the women must be passively defended. In spite of this predicament, Faludi holds out hope for a society where men and women can work together cooperatively and on equal footing. But she also believes that "[t]o revive a genuine feminism, we must disconnect feminism from the individual pursuit of happiness and reconnect it with the individual desire for social responsibility: the basic human need and joy to be part of a larger, meaningful struggle, which engages the entire society."

The Naked Citadel

Along the edges of the quad, in the gutters, the freshman cadets were squaring their corners. The "knobs," as they are called for their nearly hairless doorknob pates, aren't allowed to step on the lawn of the broad parade ground, which is trimmed close, as if to match their shorn heads. Keeping off the grass is one of many prohibitions that obtain at The Citadel, a public military college on Charleston's Ashley River. Another is the rule that so many of the cadets say brought them to this Moorish-style, gated campus: Girls keep out.

The campus has a dreamy, flattened quality, with its primary colors, checkerboard courtyards, and storybook-castle barracks. It feels more like an architect's rendering of a campus—almost preternaturally clean, orderly, antiseptic—than the messy real thing. I stood at the far end of the quad, at the academic hall's front steps, and watched the cadets make their herky-jerky perpendicular turns as they drew closer for the first day of class. They walked by stiffly, their faces heat-blotched and vulnerable, and as they passed each in turn shifted his eyes downward. I followed one line of boys into a classroom, a Western Civ class—except, of course, they weren't really boys at all. These were college men, manly recruits to an elite military college whose virile exploits were mythicized in best-selling novels by Calder Willingham and Pat Conroy, both Citadel alumni. So why did I expect their voices to crack when they spoke for the first time? Partly, it was the grammar-schoolish taking of attendance, compulsory at The Citadel. Multiple absences can lead to "tours," hours of marching back and forth in the courtyard with a pinless rifle over one shoulder; or to "cons," confinement to one's room.

But mostly it was the young men themselves, with their doughy faces and twitching limbs, who gave me the urge to babysit. Despite their enrollment in a college long considered "the big bad macho school" (as a former R.O.T.C. commander, Major General Robert E. Wagner, once put it), the cadets lacked the swagger and knowingness of big men on campus. They perched tentatively on their chairs, their hands arranged in a dutiful clasp on their desktops, as if they were expecting a ruler slap to the knuckles. A few dared to glance over at the female visitor, but whenever they made eye contact they averted their gaze and color stained their cheeks.

"As many of you probably know," their teacher said, "this was almost the day the first woman joined The Citadel." The cadets continued to study their polished shoes. "How do you, in fact, feel about whether women should be allowed to attend?"

Silence reigned. Maybe the cadets felt the question put them in an awkward spot. Not only was their teacher in favor of admitting women to The Citadel's Corps of Cadets, the teacher *was* a woman. Indeed, Professor Jane Bishop seemed to be in the strange situation of calling in an air strike on her own position. It was the first day of fall classes in the 1993–94 academic year at The Citadel, and she was broaching the question of the hour. But this incongruity wasn't limited to her classroom. From the moment I stepped onto the school's campus, I had been struck by an unexpected circumstance: though an all-male institution—an institution, moreover, whose singular mission was "making men"—The Citadel was by no means free of women. Female teachers were improving cadets' minds, female administrators were keeping their records, and an all-female (and all-black) staff served the meals in the mess hall. There was also the fact that female students made up seventy-seven percent of the enrollment of the evening school, and many other female students attended summer school with the cadets. What about them? Of course, summer school and evening school aren't part of the military college proper. Cadets don't attend the evening school; and as Major Rick Mill, The Citadel's public-relations director, notes, those cadets who attend the summer school "aren't wearing their uniforms."

Today they were, and so was their teacher. All permanent instructors, regardless of their sex (about fifteen percent are women), wear uniforms as part of their required affiliation with a largely ceremonial outfit once known as the South Carolina Unorganized Militia, and still called by the unfortunate acronym SCUM. Bishop wore hers with what seemed like a deliberate air of disarray.

The cadets' uniforms were considerably tidier—testament to the efficacy of the famous cadet shirt tuck, a maneuver akin to hospital-corners bedmaking and so exacting a cadet cannot perform it without assistance. Even so, the gray cadet uniform, with the big black stripe down the side of the pants and the nametag above the left breast, is the sort more often seen on high-school band members than on fighting soldiers.

"Remember," Bishop prodded them, "speech is free in the classroom."

At last, a cadet unclasped and raised a hand. "Well, I'd have no problem with her in the day program, but she can't join the Corps."

"She," as everyone there knew, was Shannon Faulkner, the woman who had challenged the school's hundred-and-fifty-year-old all-male policy by omitting reference to her sex from her application and winning acceptance to the Corps of Cadets earlier that year—acceptance that was rescinded once the administrators discovered their error. Faulkner's attempt to gain entrance then shifted from the admissions office to the courts. She was allowed under court order to attend day classes during the spring semester of 1994, the first woman to do so. On July 22nd, a United States District Court ruled that The Citadel must admit Faulkner into the Corps of Cadets proper; three weeks later, the Fourth United States Circuit Court of Appeals granted The Citadel a stay pending appeal.

Yet why shouldn't she be permitted into the Corps, Bishop pressed. One of her students recited the fitness requirement—forty-five pushups and fifty-five sit-ups in two-minute sets, and a two-mile run in sixteen minutes. But the administration made passing the fitness test a requirement for graduation only *after* Shannon Faulkner filed suit. An alumnus recounted in court that many upperclassmen he knew who had failed the test skipped the punitive morning run and "sat around and ate doughnuts." Another of Bishop's students cited the shaved-head rule. But this, too, seemed a minor point. A woman cadet could conceivably get a buzz cut. Sinéad O'Connor had done it, Bishop pointed out, without undue injury to her career. And, anyway, after freshman year the men no longer get their heads shaved. Other deprivations of freshman year were invoked: having to "brace" on demand—that is, assume a stance in which a knob stands very erect and tucks in his chin until it puckers up like a rooster's wattle—and having to greet every upperclassman's bellowed command and rebuke with "Sir, yes sir!" or "Sir, no sir!" or "Sir, no excuse sir!" But women, obviously, aren't incapable of obeisance; one might even say they have a long history of it.

Weighing heaviest on the cadets' minds, it turned out, was the preservation of the all-male communal bathroom. The sharing of the stall-less showers and stall-less toilets is "at the heart of the Citadel experience," according to more than one cadet. The men bathe as a group; they walk to the shower down the open galleries, in full view of the courtyard below, and do so, one cadet said, in "nothing but our bathrobes" or "even without any clothes." Another cadet said, "I know it sounds trivial, but all of us in one shower, it's like we're all one, we're all the same, and—I don't know—you feel like you're exposed, but you feel safe. You know these guys are going to be your friends for life." His voice trailed off. "I just can't explain it but when they take that away, it's over. This place will be ruined."

"If women come here, they'll have to put up window shades in all the rooms," a cadet said. "Think of all the windows in the barracks. That could be eight thousand, nine thousand dollars. You've got to look at the costs."

At the end of the hour, the cadets filed out and resumed their double-time jog along the gutters—and their place in the "fourth-class system." This "system" is a nine-month regimen of small and large indignities intended to "strip" each young recruit of his original identity and remold him into the "Whole Man," a vaguely defined ideal, half Christian soldier, half Dale Carnegie junior executive. As a knob explained it to me, "We're all suffering together. It's how we bond." Another knob said, "It's a strange analogy, but it's almost like a P.O.W. camp."

One cadet dawdled, glancing nervously around, then sidled up to me. He spoke in a near whisper, and what he had to say had nothing to do with lavatory

Freshmen are in the "fourth-class system," a regimen to "strip" each recruit of his identity and remold him into the "Whole Man." Illustration by Mark Zingarelli, originally published in *The New Yorker*. © Mark Zingarelli/House of Zing

etiquette or military tradition. "The great majority of the guys here are very misogynistic," he said. "All they talk about is how girls are pigs and sluts."

I asked him to explain at greater length. He agonized. "I have to keep quiet," he said, but he finally agreed to meet me later, in an out-of-the-way spot on the upper floor of the student-activities center. He rejoined his classmates with that distinctive knob march, "the march of the puppets," as a professor described it to me later. It was a gait caused in some cases, I was told, by the most conscientious cadets' efforts to keep their shirts perfectly straight with the help of garters—one end of the garter clipped to the shirttail, the other end to the socks.

As I waited for my cadet informant, I decided to kill an hour on the vast parade ground, where the Corps of Cadets marches every Friday afternoon in full dress uniforms, and where, according to an old school brochure, "manhood meets mastery." This is a paramilitary display, not a military one. Despite the regalia and officer ranks, and despite its notoriously fierce military discipline ("To discipline is to teach" is the motto emblazoned on one of the school's books of regulations), this is a military academy by self-designation only. Unlike the federal service academies—West Point, Annapolis, the Air Force Academy—The Citadel has no connection with the United States Armed Forces (other than its R.O.T.C. program and its employment of some active and retired officers). Its grounds are adorned with dusty and decommissioned military hardware—a Sherman tank, a submarine's torpedo-loading hatch, a Phantom jet named Annette, two cannons named Betsy and Lizzie. In most cases, the weapons, including the pinless M-14s the cadets carry, are inoperative. The mouths of the various cannons are stuffed with cement—all except those of Betsy and Lizzie, which are fired during parades, but carefully aimed high enough so that their powder does not dust the crenellated barracks. The overall effect is that of a theme park for post–Cold War kids.

The hokeyness and childlike innocence of the scene—the stage-prop artillery, the toy-soldier clip-clop of the cadets as they squared their corners—were endearing, in a Lost Boys sort of way, and I strolled over to the student-activities center for my rendezvous with my cadet informant thinking that The Citadel's version of martial culture was not so menacing after all. The cadet was not in evidence. I spent the next thirty minutes prowling the halls, which were lined with portraits of stern-faced "generals" (I couldn't tell which were United States military and which were scum), and examining ads on the student bulletin board for items like "Save the Males" bumper stickers. I tried to reach the cadet's room by phone—women aren't admitted into the barracks—but he was not there. A bit thoughtlessly, I left a message with an upperclassman and headed toward town.

At my hotel, the receptionist handed me a message from my vanished cadet. "Please, don't ever call here again!" it read. The phone clerk peered at me curiously. "Sorry about that exclamation mark, but he seemed quite distraught," she said. "His voice was shaking."

What brought a young man to an all-male preserve in the last decade of the twentieth century, anyway? What was going on outside the academy gates that impelled thousands of boys, Southern and Northern alike (about a fifth of its student body of about two thousand are Yankees), to seek refuge behind a pair of corroding cannons?

"The forces arrayed against us," an attorney named Robert Patterson declared in a February, 1994, court hearing, consider his military academy to be "some big-game animal to be hunted down, tracked, caught, badgered, and killed so that some lawyer or some organization can go back up and hang a trophy on a wall in an office." Patterson was defending not The Citadel but the Virginia Military Institute, which is the only other public military academy in the United States that does not admit women, and which was involved in a similar sex-discrimination suit. (Three months later, Patterson, a V.M.I. alumnus, returned to court to defend The Citadel.) "I will say this, Your Honor," he went on. "This quest by these people constitutes the longest and most expensive publicly financed safari in the annals of big-game hunting."

The Citadel's administration has fought the female hunters with a legal arsenal of nearly a million dollars and with dour, tight-lipped determination, which has only increased with time. The Citadel's president, Claudius Elmer (Bud) Watts III, who is a retired Air Force lieutenant general and a second-generation Citadel alumnus, views Shannon Faulkner's legal efforts as an enemy invasion, placing his young troops "under attack." "The Citadel is in this to the end," he pronounced at a press conference held in the spring of 1994 on the parade ground, his feet planted between Betsy and Lizzie, his uniform decked with ribbons, and his chin tucked in, as is his custom, as if in a permanent brace position.

Later, in his living room, surrounded by coffee-table books on football, Watts told me firmly, "You cannot put a male and a female on that same playing field," though he couldn't say exactly why. Of his own Citadel years he conceded, "I've not the foggiest notion if it would have been different" had women attended. He was just glad there were no female cadets then; otherwise, he said, the cadets would have faced "a different form of intimidation—not wanting to be embarrassed in front of a girl."

Faulkner has been opposed not only by many Citadel staff and alumni but—at least, publicly—by almost all the current cadets. They say that her presence in the Corps would absolutely destroy a basic quality of their experience as Citadel men. She would be what one Citadel defender called in his court deposition "a toxic kind of virus." Tellingly, even before the United States District Court judge enjoined The Citadel to admit Faulkner to the Corps of Cadets for the fall of 1994, and before the injunction was set aside, the administration announced its selection of her living quarters: the infirmary.

Cadets cite a number of reasons that women would have a deleterious effect on the Corps of Cadets, and the reasons are repeated so often as to be easily predictable, though their expression can be novel. "Studies show—I can't cite them, but studies show that males learn better when females aren't there," one cadet explained to me (a curious sentiment at a school where a knob motto about grades is "2.0 and Go"). "If a girl was here, I'd be concerned not to look foolish. If you're a shy student, you won't be as inhibited." Another cadet said, "See, you don't have to impress them here. You're free." From a third: "Where does it end?

Will we have unisex bathrooms?" But among the reasons most frequently heard for repelling Faulkner at the gate is this: "She would be destroying a long and proud tradition."

The masculine traditions of West Point and Annapolis were also closely guarded by their male denizens, but the resistance to women joining their ranks was nowhere near as fierce and filled with doomsday rhetoric as The Citadel's efforts to repel feminine interlopers. At Norwich University, a private military college in Northfield, Vermont, that voluntarily opened its barracks to women in 1974, two years before the federal service academies, the administration actually made an effort to recruit and accommodate women. "There was no storm of protest," said a Norwich spokeswoman, Judy Clauson. But then, "it was a time when there were so many rules that were being loosened." The Air Force veteran Linnea Westberg, who was one of the eight women in Norwich's first coed class, recalled, of her integration into its corps, that "ninety-five percent of the male cadets were fine, especially the freshmen, who didn't know any different." Westberg said she was baffled by the intensity of The Citadel's opposition to women in its corps. "It's hard for me to believe it's still an issue."

"The Citadel is a living museum to the way things used to be," John Drennan, a Citadel graduate and a public defender in Charleston, told me one day during The Citadel's legal proceedings. But how, exactly, did things use to be? The cadets and the alumni of the school, along with those protesting against its exclusionary policies, envision its military tradition above all. And The Citadel once did have a strong military aspect: it was formed as an arsenal in 1822 in response to a slave revolt purportedly planned by the freed Charleston slave Denmark Vesey, which, though it was foiled, aroused widespread alarm in the region. Yet twenty years later the guns and the gold braid became mere adornment as The Citadel turned into an industrial school of domestic and practical skills. Union troops shut down The Citadel at the end of the Civil War, but it was reinvented and reopened in 1882, after the Union's Reconstruction officials had thoroughly stripped the school of all military muscle. Its new mission was to reinvigorate the masculinity of the South by showing its men how to compete with the business and industrial skills of the Yankee carpetbaggers, who were believed to be much better prepared than the sons of Dixie to enter the Darwinian fray of modern commerce. John Peyre Thomas, who ran The Citadel from 1882 to 1885, wrote of the need to teach spoiled plantation boys the rudiments of self-reliance. "It must be admitted that the institution of African slavery, in many respects, affected injuriously the white youth of the South," he wrote. "Reared from infancy to manhood with servants at his command to bring his water, brush his shoes, saddle his horse, and, in fine, to minister to his personal wants, the average Southern boy grew up in some points of character dependent, and lazy, and inefficient. He was found, too, wanting in those habits of order and system that come from the necessity, in man, to economize time and labor."

What makes the school's Reconstruction-era mission important is that in so many ways it remains current; the masculine and industrial culture of our age and that of the conquered South may have more in common than we care to imagine. Again, we are at a psychic and economic crisis point for manhood. And, again, the gun issues hide the butter issues: the bombast masks a deep insecurity about employment and usefulness in a world where gentleman soldiers are an anachronism and a graduate with gentleman's Cs may find himself busing tables at Wendy's.

The uncertain prospects of Citadel graduates are worsened by military downsizing. Only about a third of recent graduates entered the military—a figure that has fallen steeply since the mid-seventies, when half of The Citadel's graduating class routinely took a service commission. News of Shannon Faulkner's court case competed in the Charleston *Post & Courier* with news of the shutting down of the local shipyards and decommissionings from the local military installations.

The night before the closing arguments in Faulkner's suit, I had dinner at the on-campus home of Philippe and Linda Ross, who have both taught at The Citadel. Philippe, the head of the Biology Department, had just completed his first round of moonlighting as a "retraining" instructor at the Charleston Naval Shipyard. He had been prepping laid-off nuclear engineers to enter one of the few growth industries in the area—toxic-waste management. Facing a room filled with desperate men each day had been a dispiriting experience, he said. He recalled the plea of a middle-aged engineer, thrust out of the service after twenty-six years: "All I want to do is work." Linda Ross, who was then teaching psychology at The Citadel, looked across the table with a pained expression. "That whole idea that if a young man went to college he could make a decent living and buy a house, and maybe even a boat, just does not hold anymore," she said softly. "There's a Citadel graduate working as a cashier at the grocery store. And the one thing these young men felt they could count on was that if things got hard they could always go into the military. No more. And they are bitter and angry."

In the fall of 1991, Michael Lake, a freshman, decided to leave The Citadel. He had undergone weeks of bruising encounters with upperclassmen—encounters that included being knocked down with a rifle butt and beaten in the dark by a pack of cadets. Incidents of hazing became so violent that, in a school where publicly criticizing the alma mater is virtually an act of treason, several athletes told their stories to *Sports Illustrated*. Much of the violence was aimed at star freshman athletes: a member of the cycling team was forced to hang by his fingers over a sword poised two inches below his testicles; a place-kicker had his head dunked in water twenty times until he was unconscious; a linebacker was forced to swallow his chewing tobacco and tormented until, he said later, "I was unable even to speak clearly in my classes." It was a time when the Churchill Society, a literary club reportedly containing a white-supremacist faction, was organized on campus. It was a time when the local chapter of the National Association for the Advancement of Colored People urged a federal investigation into a pair of racial incidents on the school's campus: the appearance of a noose over the bed of a black freshman who had earlier refused to sing "Dixie," and the shooting and wounding of a black cadet by a sniper who was never identified. (A few years earlier, upperclassmen wearing Klan-like costumes left a charred paper cross in the room of a black cadet.) And it was a time when a leader of the Junior Sword Drill, a unit of cadet sword-bearers, leaped off a five-foot dresser onto the head of a prostrate cadet, then left him in a pool of blood in a barracks hall. According to one cadet, a lacrosse-team member returning from an away game at three in the morning stumbled upon the victim's unconscious body, his face split open, jaw and nose broken, mouth a jack-o'-lantern of missing teeth.

One night, at about 2 A.M., high-ranking cadets trapped a raccoon in the barracks and began to stab it with a knife. Beau Turner, a student at the school, was awakened by the young men's yelling. "My roommate and I went out there to try and stop it," Turner recalled, "but we were too late." Accounts of the episode vary. In a widely circulated version (which was referred to in a faculty member's testimony), the cadets chanted, "Kill the bitch! Kill the bitch!" as they tortured the raccoon to death.

In October 1993, two upperclassmen burst into the room of two freshmen and reportedly kneed them in the genitals, pulled out some of their chest hair, and beat them up. They were arrested on charges of assault and battery, and agreed to a program of counseling and community service, which would wipe clean their records. They withdrew from The Citadel, in lieu of expulsion, the spokesman Major Rick Mill said.

One of the offending cadets, Adrian Baer, told me that he and the other accused sophomore, Jeremy Leckie, did indeed come back from drinking, burst into the knobs' room after 10 P.M., and "repeatedly struck them in the chest and stomach" and bruised one of them in the face, but he denied having kicked them in the groin and yanked out chest hair. He said that what he did was common procedure—and no different from the "motivational" treatment he had received as a knob at the hands of a senior who came into *his* room. They entered the freshmen's room, Baer explained, because they viewed one of the occupants as "a problem" knob who "needed some extra motivation." Baer elaborated: "His pinkie on his right hand wouldn't completely close when he went to salute. He caught a lot of heat for that, of course, because it's a military school; it's important to salute properly." The strict rule that upperclassmen not fraternize with knobs, he said, meant that they couldn't simply counsel the freshman kindly. "If we just sat down and said, 'Listen, guy, we have a little problem,' that would be fraternization. And more important, knobs would lose respect for upperclassmen. It's a lot of denial on the part of officials at The Citadel about hazing," Baer said. "They don't want to believe it goes on." Leckie's father, Timothy Rinaldi, said that while he believed his son "was definitely in the wrong," he felt The Citadel's fourth-class system bred such behavior. "They help build this monster," he said of The Citadel. "The monster gets up off the table and starts walking through town—and now Dr. Frankenstein wants to shoot it."

Needless to say, not every cadet embraces the climate of cruelty; the nocturnal maulings likely frighten as many cadets as they enthrall. But the group mentality that pervades The Citadel assures that any desire on the part of a cadet to speak out about the mounting violence will usually be squelched by the threat of ostracism and shame. While group rule typifies many institutions, military and civilian, that place a premium on conformity, the power and authoritarianism of the peer group at The Citadel is exceptional because the college gives a handful of older students leave to "govern" the others as they see fit. (A lone officer provided by the military, who sleeps in a wing off one of the dorms, seldom interferes.) This is a situation that, over the years, an occasional school official has challenged, without success. A former assistant commandant for discipline, Army Lieutenant Colonel T. Nugent Courvoisie, recalled that he "begged" the school's president back in the sixties to place more military officers—and ones who were more mature—in the barracks, but his appeals went unheeded. Discipline and punishment in the dorms is in the hands of the student-run regimental command, and ascendancy in this hierarchy is not always predicated on compassion for one's fellow man. In consequence, the tyranny of the few buys the silence of the many.

This unofficial pact of silence could, of course, be challenged by the Citadel officialdom. On a number of occasions over the past three decades—most recently when some particularly brutal incidents found their way into the media—The Citadel has commissioned "studies." But when the administration does go on the offensive, its animus is primarily directed not at miscreant cadets but at the "unfair" media, which are "victimizing" the institution by publicizing the bad behavior of its boys.

In recent years, enough bad news leaked out locally to become a public-relations nightmare, and the school appointed a committee of Citadel loyalists to assess the situation. Even the loyalists concluded, in a January 1992 report, that the practice of physical abuse of freshmen, along with food and sleep deprivation, had gotten out of hand. As a result, Major Mill told me, The Citadel ordered upperclassmen to stop using pushups as a "disciplinary tool" on individual cadets. "That was the most important one" of the reforms prompted by the report, Mill said. Other reforms were adopted: for example, freshmen would no longer be compelled to deliver mail to upperclassmen after their evening study hours, thus reducing opportunities for hazing; freshmen would—at least officially—no longer be compelled to "brace" in the mess hall. At the same time, the report declared that it "wholeheartedly endorses the concept of the fourth-class system," which it called "essential to the attainment of college objectives and the development of the Citadel man."

Institutions that boast of their insularity, whether convents or military academies, are commonly pictured in the public imagination as static, unchanging abstractions, isolated from the ebb and flow of current events. But these edifices are rarely as otherworldly as their guardians might wish; indeed, in the case of The Citadel, its bricked-off culture has functioned more as a barometer of national anxieties than as a garrison against them. The militaristic tendencies within the Corps seem to vary inversely with the esteem in which the American soldier is held in the larger society. In times when the nation has been caught up in a socially acceptable conflict, one in which its soldiers return as heroes greeted by tickertape parades, The Citadel has loosened its militaristic harness, or even removed it altogether. Thus, during perhaps the most acceptable war in American history, the Second World War, the fourth-class system of knob humiliation was all but discontinued. Upperclassmen couldn't even order a knob to brace. The changes began largely in response to the demands of the real military for soldiers they could use in a modern war. "The War Department and the Navy Department were asking R.O.T.C. to do less drilling, more calculus," Jamie Moore, a professor of history at The Citadel and a former member of the United States Army's Historical Advisory Committee, told me. "The Citadel dismantled its fourth-class system because it was getting in the way of their military training." The changes didn't seem to interfere with the school's production of Whole Men; on the contrary, an extraordinary percentage of The Citadel's most distinguished graduates come from these years, among them United States Senator Ernest (Fritz) Hollings; Alvah Chapman, Jr., the former chief executive of Knight-Ridder; and South Carolina's former governor John C. West.

The kinder, gentler culture of the Second World War–era Citadel survived well into the next decade. Although a new fourth-class system was soon established, it remained relatively benign. "We didn't have the yelling we have today," Colonel Harvey Dick, class of '53 and now a member of The Citadel's governing body, recalled. "They didn't even shave the freshmen's heads."

The postwar years also brought the admission of women to the summer program, and without the hand-wringing provoked by Shannon Faulkner's application. "WOMEN INVADE CITADEL CLASSES FIRST TIME IN SCHOOL'S HISTORY," the Charleston daily noted back on page 16 of its June 21, 1949, edition. "Most male students took the advent of the 'amazons' in their stride," the paper reported cheerfully. "Only the younger ones seemed at all uneasy. Professors and instructors were downright glad to see women in their classes."

The Vietnam War, needless to say, did not inspire the same mood of relaxation on campus. "The fourth-class system was very physical," Wallace West, the admissions director who was an undergraduate at The Citadel during the Vietnam War years, said. "When I was there, there was no true emphasis on academics, or on positive leadership. It was who could be worked to physical exhaustion." Alumni from those years recounted being beaten with sticks, coat hangers, and rifle butts. That was, of course, the era that inspired Pat Conroy's novel *The Lords of Discipline,* a tale of horrific hazing, directed with special virulence against the school's first African-American cadet. "They just tortured us," Conroy recalled from his home in Beaufort, South Carolina. "It taught me the exact kind of man I didn't want to be," he added.

In 1968, the administration appointed a committee to investigate the violence. The committee issued a report that, like its 1992 successor, concluded "there have been significant and extensive abuses to the [fourth-class] system." And, with its strong recommendation that hazing result in expulsion, the report seemed to promise a more pacific future on campus.

In the past decade and a half, however, the record of violence and cruelty at The Citadel has attracted increasing notice, even as the armed forces have been racked by downsizing and scandal. The Citadel president during much of this era, Major General James A. Grimsley, Jr., declined to discuss this or any other aspect of campus life during his tenure. "I don't do interviews," he said. "Thank you for calling, young lady." He then hung up. Others have been less reticent.

Thirteen years before Vice-Admiral James B. Stockdale consented to be Ross Perot's running mate, he took on what turned out to be an even more thankless task: fighting brutal forms of hazing at The Citadel. In 1979, Stockdale, who had graduated from Annapolis, was chosen to be The Citadel's president because of his status as a genuine military hero: he had survived eight years as a P.O.W. in Vietnam. This hero failed to see the point of manufactured adversity. In an afterword to the book *In Love and War,* a collaboration between Stockdale and his wife, Sybil, he wrote that there was "something mean and out of control about the regime I had just inherited."

On his first day in the president's office, Stockdale opened a desk drawer and discovered "what turned out to be Pandora's box," he wrote. "From the top down, what was written on the papers I took out of the desk drawers—and conversations with some of their authors—was enough to break anybody's heart." Among them was a letter from an infuriated father who wanted to know what had happened to his son "to change him from a levelheaded, optimistic, aggressive individual to a fatigued, irrational, confused and bitter one." He also found copies of memos from The Citadel's staff physician complaining repeatedly of (as Stockdale recalled) "excessive hospitalization"—such as the case of a knob who had suffered intestinal bleeding and was later brought back to the infirmary, having been exercised to unconsciousness. Stockdale sought to reform the system, but he was stymied at every turn. He clashed with The Citadel's powerful Board of Visitors, an eleven-member committee of alumni that sets school policy. The Board of Visitors overruled his expulsion of a senior cadet who had reportedly been threatening freshmen with a pistol. A year into his presidency, Stockdale submitted his resignation. After he left, the board reinstated an avenging friend of the senior cadet who, according to Stockdale, had attempted to break into his house one evening. (The then chairman of the Board of Visitors maintains that the cadet was drunk and looking for the barracks.)

"They thought they were helping people into manhood," Stockdale recalled, from a more serene post in Palo Alto, California, where he is a scholar at Stanford's Hoover Institution on War, Revolution, and Peace. "But they had no idea what that meant—or who they were."

After Watts became president, in 1989, some faculty members began to observe a creeping militarization imposed by the administration upon the Corps's already drill-heavy regimen. Four special military days were added to the academic year. At the beginning of one semester, President Watts held a faculty meeting in a room above the mess hall. "Watts had these soldiers standing around the room with their hands behind them," Gardel Feurtado, a political-science professor and one of only two African-American professors, recalled. Watts, he said, lectured the faculty for about three hours. "He didn't talk about academics or educational goals. He just talked about cadets' training, and he showed us a film of it," Feurtado told me. According to Feurtado, Watts told the faculty to line up in groups behind the soldiers for a tour of the barracks.

"I said, 'Enough of this,' and I started to walk out. And this soldier stopped me and said, 'Where do you think you're going, sir?' and I said, 'You do realize that I am not in the military?'" Feurtado had to push by him to leave.

When Michael Lake looked back on the
abuse he suffered during his abbreviated knob
year of '91, he could now see before him, like
the emergence of invisible ink on what appeared
to be a blank piece of paper, the faint outlines of
another struggle. What he saw was a submerged
gender battle, a bitter but definitely fixed contest
between the sexes, concealed from view by the
fact that men played both parts. The beaten
knobs were the women, "stripped" and humiliated, and the predatory upperclassmen were the
men, who bullied and pillaged. If they couldn't
re-create a male-dominant society in the real
world, they could restage the drama by casting
male knobs in all the subservient feminine roles.

Illustration by Mark Zingarelli,
originally published in *The New
Yorker.* © Mark Zingarelli/House
of Zing

"They called you a 'pussy' all the time," Lake recalled. "Or a 'fucking little
girl.'" It started the very first day they had their heads shaved, when the upperclassmen stood around and taunted. "Oh, you going to get your little girlie locks
cut off?" When they learned that Lake would be playing soccer that fall, their
first response was "What is that, a girl's sport?" Another former cadet said that
he had withstood "continual abuse," until he found himself thinking about
jumping out the fourth-story window of the barracks—and quit. He reported
an experience similar to Lake's. Virtually every taunt equated him with a
woman: whenever he showed fear, they would say, "You look like you're having an abortion," or "Are you menstruating?" The knobs even experienced a
version of domestic violence. The upperclassmen, this cadet recalled, "would
go out and get drunk and they would come home and haze, and you just
hoped they didn't come into your room."

"According to the Citadel creed of the cadet," Lake said, "women are
objects, they're things that you can do with whatever you want to." In order
to maintain this world-view, the campus has to be free of women whose status
might challenge it—a policy that, of course, is rarely enunciated. The acknowledged policy is that women are to be kept at a distance so they can be
"respected" as ladies. Several months before Faulkner's lawsuit came to trial,
I was sitting in the less than Spartan air-conditioned quarters of the senior regimental commander, Norman Doucet, the highest-ranking cadet, who commanded the barracks. Doucet, who was to be The Citadel's star witness at the
Faulkner trial, was explaining to me how excluding women had enhanced his
gentlemanly perception of the opposite sex. "The absence of women makes us
understand them better," Doucet said. "In an aesthetic kind of way, we appreciate them more—because they are not there."

Women at less of a remove fare less well. In The Citadel's great chain of
being, the "waitees"—as many students call that all-black, all-female mess-hall
staff—rate as the bottom link. Some upperclassmen have patted them on their
rear ends, tried to trip them as they pass the tables, or hurled food at their
retreating backs. Cadets have summoned them with "Come here, bitch," or

addressed one who dropped a plate or forgot an order as "you stupid whore." The pages of the *Brigadier,* the school's newspaper, bear witness to the cadets' contempt for these women. Gary Brown, now the editor-in-chief of the *Brigadier,* once advised fellow-cadets to beware of "waitee" food contamination—"the germ-filled hands, the hair follicles, and other unknown horrors." Not only was he dismayed by "wavy little follicles in my food" but he found the women insufficiently obedient. "Duty is certainly not the sublimest word in the Waitee language," he wrote. In a letter to the editor, Jason S. Pausman, class of '94, urged fellow-cadets to demand "waitees without chronic diseases that involve sneezing, coughing or wiping of body parts ... The reality is simple, we CANNOT sit by and let the waitees of this school control us."

Some women faculty members report similarly resentful responses to their presence, despite—or because of—their positions of authority. Angry messages on a professor's door are one tactic. When Jane Bishop recently posted on her office door a photocopy of a *New York Times* editorial supporting women's admission to the Corps of Cadets, she found it annotated with heated rejoinders in a matter of days. "Dr. Bishop, you are a prime example of why women should not be allowed here," one scribble read. Another comment: "Women will destroy the world."

The Citadel men's approach to women seems to toggle between extremes of gentility and fury. "First, they will be charming to the women to get their way," Linda Ross said. "But if that doesn't work they don't know any other way. So then they will get angry." It's a pattern that is particularly evident in some cadets' reaction to younger faculty women.

December Green joined The Citadel's Political Science Department in 1988, the first woman that the department had ever hired for a tenure-track position. She was twenty-six and attractive—"someone the cadets might fantasize about," a colleague recalled. They were less enchanted, however, by her left-leaning politics. She soon found herself getting obscene phone calls in the middle of the night. Then obscenities began appearing on her office door. "Pussy" is the one that sticks in her mind.

Though Green's work at The Citadel was highly praised—she received an award for teaching, research, and service—she said that no one in the administration tried to stop her when she left in 1992 in despair over her inability to contain the cadets' fury. Nor, apparently, had anyone responded to her appeals to correct the situation. "A lot of terrible things happened to me there," Green, who is now teaching in Ohio, said, reluctant to revisit them. The hostility ranged from glowering group stares in the hallway to death threats—some of which appeared on the cadets' teacher-evaluation forms. The male faculty offered little support. Green recalls the department chairman instructing her to "be more maternal toward the students" when a cadet lodged a complaint about her (she had challenged his essay in which he praised apartheid). And a professor who stood by one day while his students harassed her and another woman informed her, "You get what you provoke."

Green said she eventually had to get an unlisted number to stop the obscene calls, and also moved, in part out of fear of the cadets' vengeance. The last straw,

The legendary Citadel elder known as the Boo, who oversaw racial integration at The Citadel in the sixties, says, "With women, there's going to be sexual harassment." His wife, Margaret, counters, "Oh, honey, those cadets are harassing each other right now." "That's different," he says. "That's standard operating procedure." Illustration by Mark Zingarelli, originally published in *The New Yorker*. © Mark Zingarelli/House of Zing

however, came when she submitted the written threats she had received to her chairman, who passed them on to the dean of undergraduate studies, in hopes of remedial action. The dean, she said, did nothing for some months, and then, after she inquired, said he had "misplaced" the offending documents.

The dean, Colonel Isaac (Spike) Metts, Jr., told me he didn't recall saying he misplaced the documents but "I might have said it's not on my desk at that time and I don't know where it is." He added that Green was a "very valuable" professor. "I don't know what else we could've done," Metts said. In any event, soon after submitting the threatening notes to the dean, Green gave up. At her exit interview, she recalled, President Watts told her he didn't understand why she had been upset by the cadet harassment. "It's just a bunch of kid stuff," another male colleague said. (Lewis Spearman, the assistant to the president, said that, because of federal privacy law, Watts would have no response to Green's version of events.)

The remaining category of women that cadets have to deal with is "the dates," as the young women they socialize with are generally called. (There are no wives; Citadel policy forbids cadets to marry, and violators are expelled.) In some respects, these young women are the greatest challenge to the cadet's sense of gender hierarchy. While the "waitees" can be cast as household servants and the female teachers as surrogate mothers, the dates are more difficult to place. Young women their age are often college students, with the same aspirations as the cadets, or even greater ones. The cadets deal with young women's rising ambitions in a number of ways. One is simply to date high-school girls, an option selected by a number of cadets. Another strategy, facilitated by The Citadel, is to cast the young women who are invited on campus into the homecoming-queen mold. The college holds a Miss Citadel contest each year, and Anne Poole, whose husband, Roger, is the vice-president of academic affairs and the dean of the college, has sat on the judging panel. Each cadet company elects a young woman mascot from a photograph competition, and their faces appear in the yearbook.

The school also sends its young men to an in-house etiquette-training seminar, in which the Citadel "hostess," a pleasant woman in her forties named Susan Bowers, gives them a lecture on how "to act gentlemanly with the girls." She arms cadets with *The Art of Good Taste,* a do's-and-don'ts manual with a chapter entitled "Helping the Ladies." The guidebook outlines the "correct way of offering an arm to a lady ... to help her down the steps," and the best method for assisting "a lady in distress." (The example of distress provided involves an elderly woman trying to open a door when her arms are full of shopping bags.) Such pointers are illustrated with pictures of fifties-style coeds sporting Barbie-doll hair flips and clinging to the arms of their cadets, who are escorting them to "the Hop." The manual's preface states emphatically, "At all times [ladies] must be sheltered and protected not only from the elements and physical harm but also from embarrassment, crudity, or coarseness of any sort."

Susan Bowers explained the duties of her office: "At the beginning of the year, we do 'situation cards' for the freshmen. And we'll bring in cheerleaders and use them as props.... We show cadets how to go through the receiving line, how to introduce your date, and what to say to them. In the past, we didn't have the cheerleaders to use, so they dressed up some of the guys as girls." Bowers said she felt bad for the cadets, who often come to her seeking maternal consolation. "They are very timid—afraid, almost," she said. "They are so lost, and they need a shoulder."

The Art of Good Taste is silent on the subject of proper etiquette toward women who require neither deference nor rescue. And, as Linda Ross observed, when the gentlemanly approach fails them, cadets seem to have only one fallback—aggression. Numerous cadets spoke to me of classmates who claimed to have "knocked around" uncompliant girlfriends. Some of those classmates, no doubt, were embellishing to impress a male audience, but not always. "I know lots of stories where cadets are violent toward women," a 1991 Citadel graduate named Ron Vergnolle said. He had witnessed cadets hitting their girl-friends at a number of Citadel parties—and observed one party incident in which two cadets held down a young woman while a third drunken cadet leaned over and vomited on her. Vergnolle, a magna cum laude graduate of the Citadel class of '91, recounted several such stories to me, and added that bragging about humiliating an ex-girlfriend is a common practice—and the more outrageous the humiliation, the better the story, as far as many cadets are concerned. Two such cadet storytellers, for example, proudly spread the word of their exploits on Dog Day, a big outdoor party sponsored by The Citadel's senior class. The two cadets told about the time they became enraged with their dates, followed them to the Portosans, and, after the women had entered, pushed the latrines over so they landed on the doors, trapping the occupants. The cadets left them there. Another cadet told Vergnolle that he had tacked a live hamster to a young woman's door. There was also the cadet who boasted widely that, as vengeance against an uncooperative young woman, he smashed the head of her cat against a window as she watched in horror. "The cat story," Vergnolle noted, "that was this guy's calling card."

Something of these attitudes shows up even in the ditties the cadets chant during their daily runs. Many of the chants are the usual military "jodies," well known for their misogynistic lyrics. But some are vintage Citadel and include lyrics about gouging out a woman's eyes, lopping off body parts, and evisceration. A cadence remembered by one Citadel cadet, sung to the tune of "The Candy Man," begins, "Who can take two jumper cables/Clip 'em to her tit/ Turn on the battery and watch the bitch twitch." Another verse starts with "Who can take an ice pick ..." and so on.

The day after last Thanksgiving, the phone rang at one-thirty in the morning in the home of Sandy and Ed Faulkner in Powdersville, South Carolina, a tiny community on the outskirts of Greenville. The caller was a neighbor. They had better come outside, he said—a car had been circling their block. Sandy and Ed, the parents of Shannon Faulkner, went out on their front lawn and looked around. At first, they saw nothing. Then, as they turned back to the house, they saw that across the white porch columns and along the siding of the house, painted in gigantic and what Sandy later recalled as "blood-red" letters, were the words, "Bitch," "Dyke," "Whore," and "Lesbo." Ed got up again at 6 A.M. and, armed with a bucket of white paint, hurried to conceal the message from his daughter.

A few days after the judge ordered The Citadel to admit Faulkner to the Corps of Cadets, morning rush-hour drivers in Charleston passed by a huge portable sign that read "Die Shannon." At least this threat wasn't home delivered. In the past year, instances of vandalism and harassment have mounted at the Faulkner home. Someone crawled under the house and opened the emergency exhaust valve on the water heater. The gas tank on Sandy's car was pried open. Someone driving a Ford Bronco mowed down the mailbox. Another motorist "did figure-eights through my flower bed," Sandy said. "This year, I didn't even plant flowers because I knew they would just tear them up." And someone with access to Southern Bell's voice-mail system managed, twice, to tap into their voice mail and change their greeting, both times to a recording featuring rap lyrics about a "bitch" with a "big butt." Callers phoned in the middle of the night with threatening messages. Sandy called the county sheriffs department about the vandalism, but in Anderson County, which has been home to many Citadel graduates, the deputy who arrived was not particularly helpful. He told them, Sandy recalled, "Well, if you're going to mess with The Citadel, you're just going to have to expect that."

Every trial has its rare moments of clarity, when the bramble of admissibility arguments and technicalities is cut away and we see the actual issue in dispute. One such moment came toward the end of the Faulkner-Citadel trial, when Alexander Astin, the director of the Higher Education Research Institute at the University of California at Los Angeles, took the stand. Astin, who is widely viewed as a leading surveyor of college-student performance and attitudes, found no negative effects on male students in nineteen all-male colleges he had studied which had gone coeducational.

"Can you tell me what kind of woman you would think would want to attend a coeducational Citadel?" Robert Patterson, the Citadel attorney who had previously represented V.M.I., asked Astin, his voice full of unflattering insinuation about the kind of woman he imagined her to be.

ASTIN: I suppose the same as the kind of men who want to go there.

PATTERSON: Would it be a woman that would not be all that different from men?

ASTIN: Yes.

To Patterson, this was a triumphant moment, and he closed on it: he had forced the government's witness to admit that a woman like Shannon Faulkner would have to be a mannish aberration from her gender. But in fact Astin's testimony expressed the precise point that the plaintiff's side had been trying to make all along, and that The Citadel strenuously resisted: that the sexes were, in the end, not all that different.

"I was considered the bitch of the band," Shannon Faulkner said, without embarrassment, of her four years in her high school's marching band—just stating a fact. She was lounging on the couch in her parents' living room, comfortable in an old T-shirt and shorts, one leg swung over an arm of the couch. "That's because I was the one who was mean and got it done." The phone rang, for the millionth time—another media call. "I'm not giving statements to the press right now," she said efficiently into the phone and hung up. She did not apologize for her brusqueness, as I was half expecting her to do, after she put down the receiver. There is nothing of the good girl about her. Not that she is disagreeable; Shannon Faulkner just doesn't see the point in false deference. "I never let anyone push me around, male or female," Faulkner said, and that fact had been exasperatingly obvious to reporters who covered the trial: they found that all the wheedling and cheap flatteries that usually prompt subjects to say more than they should didn't work with Faulkner.

One could scrounge around in Faulkner's childhood for the key to what made her take on The Citadel. You could say that it was because she was born six weeks premature, and her fierce struggle to live forged a "survivor." You could cite her memory that as a small child she preferred playing outside with the boys to playing with certain girls whom she deemed "too prissy." You could point to her sports career in high school and junior high: she lettered in softball for four years and kept stats for three of the schools' four basketball teams. You could note her ability to juggle tasks: she edited the yearbook, wrote for the school paper, and graduated with a 3.48 grade-point average. And you could certainly credit the sturdy backbone and outspokenness of both her mother and her maternal grandmother; this is a family where the women talk and the men keep a low profile. Her father, Ed, owns a small fence-building business. At thirty, a few years after Shannon's birth, Sandy returned to college to get her degree, a double major in psychology and education, and became a high-school teacher of psychology, sociology, United States history, and minority cultures. When a male professor had complained about certain "older women" in his class who asked "too many questions," Sandy hurled one of her wedge-heeled sandals at him. "I said, 'I'm paying for this class, and don't you ever tell me what I can ask.'" Shannon's maternal grandmother, sixty-seven-year-old Evelyn Richey, was orphaned at six and worked most of her life in textile factories, where, she noted, "women could do the job and men got the pay." Of her granddaughter's suit she said, "Women have got to come ahead. I say, let's get on with the show."

But there's little point in a detailed inspection of family history because there's no real mystery here. What is most striking about Shannon herself is that she's not particularly unusual. She reads novels by Tom Clancy and John Grisham, has worked in a local day-care center, is partial to places like Bennigan's. She wants a college education so she can support herself and have a career as a teacher or a journalist—she hasn't yet decided which. She might do a stint in the military, she might not. She is in many ways representative of the average striving lower-middle-class teenage girl, circa 1994, who intends to better herself and does not intend to achieve that betterment through a man—in fact, she has not for a moment entertained such a possibility.

Throughout the trial, cadets and Citadel alumni spoke of a feminist plot: she is "a pawn" of the National Organization for Women, or—a theory repeatedly posited to me by cadets—"Her mother put her up to it." Two Citadel alumni asked me in all seriousness if feminist organizations were paying Shannon Faulkner to take the stand. In truth, Shannon makes an unlikely feminist poster girl. She prefers to call herself "an individualist" and seems almost indifferent to feminist affairs; when I mentioned Gloria Steinem's name once in conversation, Shannon asked me, "Who's that?" After the judge issued his decision to admit her to the Corps, she told the *New York Times* that she didn't consider the ruling a victory "just for women"—only a confirmation of her belief that if you want something, "go for it." Shannon Faulkner's determination to enter The Citadel's Corps of Cadets was fuelled not so much by a desire to trailblaze as by a sense of amazement and indignation that this trail was barricaded in the first place. She had never, she told the court, encountered such a roadblock in all her nineteen years—a remark that perhaps only a young woman of her fortunate generation could make without perjuring herself.

Shannon Faulkner got the idea of attending The Citadel back in December of 1992. She was taking a preparatory education course at Wren High School, the local public school. Mike Hazel, the teacher, passed out articles for them to read and discuss, and Faulkner picked the article in *Sports Illustrated* about hazing at The Citadel. "It was almost as accidental as Rosa Parks," Hazel recalled. "I just held up *Sports Illustrated* and asked, 'Who wants to do this?'"

Faulkner told me she'd selected the article because "I had missed that issue." During the ensuing discussion, the class wandered off the subject of hazing and onto the question of what, exactly, a public state institution was doing barring women from its classrooms. After a while, Faulkner got up and went down to the counselor's office and returned with an application form from The Citadel. "I said, 'Hey, it doesn't even say 'Male/Female,'" she recalled. While she was sitting in class, she filled it out. "I didn't really make a big to-do about it."

Two weeks after Faulkner received her acceptance letter, The Citadel got word she was a woman and revoked her admission, and in August of 1993 she went off to spend a semester at the University of South Carolina at Spartanburg while the courts thrashed out the next move. As the lawyers filed papers, The Citadel's defenders delivered their own increasingly agitated personal beliefs to the plaintiff herself. Faulkner worked evenings as a waitress in a local bar called Chiefs Wings and Firewater until the nightly tirades from the many drunk Citadel-graduate customers got to be too much. Actually, Faulkner said, she wouldn't have quit if some of her male college friends hadn't felt the need to defend her honor. "I didn't want them getting hurt," she said. Her manner of dealing with the Citadel crowd was more good-humored. One day at the bar, she recalled, "a guy came up to me. 'Are you Shannon Faulkner?' he asked, and I said, 'Why?'—very casual. Then he got real huffy-puffy, madder and madder." Finally, she said, he stuck his ring in her face, then slammed his hand down on the table. "You will never wear *that!*" he yelled. Shannon saw him a few times in the bar after that, scowling at her from a far table. To lighten the mood, she once had the bartender send him a beer. He wouldn't drink it.

"I never show my true emotions in public," Shannon said. "I consider that weak." She can laugh at the cadets' threats, even when they turn ugly, because she doesn't see the reason for all the fuss. Whenever she is asked to sign the latest T-shirt inspired by the controversy, which depicts a group of male bulldogs (The Citadel's mascot) in cadet uniforms and one female bulldog in a red dress, above the caption "1,952 Bulldogs and 1 Bitch," Faulkner told me, "I always sign under the 'Bitch' part."

The first day that Shannon Faulkner attended classes, in January 1994, the cadets who had lined up by the academic building told the media the same thing over and over. "We were trained to be gentlemen, and that's what we'll be." But in Shannon's first class, biology, all three cadets assigned to sit in her row changed their seats. The teacher, Philippe Ross, had to threaten to mark them absent to get them to return to their places. (More than twenty unexcused absences a semester is grounds for failure.) Shortly thereafter, a rumor began to circulate that Faulkner was using a fake I.D. in the local bars. This summer, talk of a plot against Faulkner surfaced—to frame her, perhaps by planting drugs in her belongings. The threat seemed real enough for Faulkner to quit her summer job, in the Charleston area, and return home.

The *Brigadier's* column "Scarlet Pimpernel" took up the anti-Shannon cause with a vengeance. The columnist dubbed her "the divine bovine," likening her to a plastic revolving cow at a nearby mall (the mounting of which is a cadet tradition). The "Pimpernel" comments on an incident that occurred on

Faulkner's first day were particularly memorable. An African-American cadet named Von Mickle dared to shake her hand in front of the media and say, "It's time for women," and compared the exclusion of women to that of blacks. For this lone act, he was not only physically threatened by classmates but derided in the "Pimpernel." "The PIMP doth long to tame the PLASTIC COW on this most wondrous of nights," the anonymous author wrote, with the column's usual antique-English flourishes and coded references. "But it seems that we will have a live specimen, a home grown DAIRY QUEEN from the stables of Powdersville. Perhaps NON DICKLE will be the first to saddle up. He is DIVINE BOVINE's best friend after all."

More disturbing were cadet writings on Faulkner that were not for public consumption. Tom Lucas, a graduate student in The Citadel's evening program, told me about some "very harsh" graffiti that he'd found all over one of the men's rooms in The Citadel's academic building. The inscription that most stuck in his mind: "Let her in—then fuck her to death."

On the whole, The Citadel administrators to whom I spoke were defensive, evasive, or dismissive of the cadets' hostile words and deeds toward Faulkner. When I asked Citadel officials to respond to reports of barracks violence, harassment of women on staff, or verbal abuse of Faulkner, the responses were dismaying. Cases of violence and abuse were "aberrations"; cadets who spoke up were either "troublemakers" or "mama's boys"; and each complaint by a female faculty member was deemed a "private personnel matter" that could not be discussed further.

Certainly the administrators and trustees themselves are less than enthusiastic about Faulkner's arrival. William F. Prioleau, Jr., until recently a member of the Board of Visitors, implied on a radio talk show that abortions would go up as a result of the female invasion, as he claimed had happened at West Point. Meanwhile, in The Citadel's Math Department, all that was going up as a result of Shannon Faulkner's presence was the grade-point average. Faulkner's highest mark at the semester's end was in calculus, where she earned an A (prompting a surprised Dean Poole to comment to her that she was "certainly not the stereotypical woman"). The Math Department has in recent years invited A students to an annual party. But rather than include Faulkner, the department limited the guest list to math majors. Math professor David Trautman, who was in charge of invitations to the party, explained in an e-mail message to colleagues, "Her presence would put a damper on the evening."

Linda Ross, then a professor at The Citadel, was speaking one day with a seventy-six-year-old alumnus, and the talk turned to Faulkner's lawsuit. He asked her if she thought it possible that this young woman might prevail. "Well, it's probably an inevitable turning of the tide," Ross said, shrugging. To her amazement, the alumnus began to cry.

"I have the worst chance in society of getting a job, because I'm a white male," William H. Barnes, the senior platoon leader, shouted at me over the din in The Citadel's mess hall, a din created by the upperclassmen's tradition of berating knobs at mealtime. "And that's the major difference between me and my father." In a society where, at least since the Second World War, surpassing one's father has been an expected benchmark of American manhood, Barnes's point is a plangent one. But it's hard to say which Citadel generation is more undone by the loss of white male privilege—the young men who will never partake of a dreamed world of masculine advantage or the older men who are seeing that lived world split apart, shattered.

"I was in Vietnam in '63, and I'll defy you or Shannon or anyone else to hike through the rice paddies," the usually genial Colonel Harvey Dick, sixty-seven, a Board of Visitors member, an ex-marine, and an Army lieutenant colonel, was practically shouting from his recliner armchair in his Charleston home. He popped a Tums in his mouth. "There's just no way you can do that.... You can't pick up a ninety-five-pound projectile. There are certain things out there that are differences." On the wall above his head were seven bayonets. He was wearing his blue Citadel T-shirt, which matched the Citadel mementos that overwhelmed his den—Citadel mugs, hats, footballs, ceramic bulldogs. It was a room known in the Dick household as "Harvey's 'I Love Me' Room." Dick treated it as his command post—whenever the phone rang, he whipped it off the cradle and barked "Colonel Dick!"—but what he was commanding was unclear; he retired in 1993 from a sixteen-year stint as The Citadel's assistant commandant. Still, he at least knew that he was once in charge, that he once enjoyed lifetime job security as a career military man. This was something his son couldn't say: Harvey Dick II, a nuclear pipe fitter, had recently been laid off at the Charleston Naval Shipyard.

Colonel Dick wanted it known that he wasn't "one of those male-chauvinist pigs"; in fact, he believes that women are smarter than men. "Women used to let the men dominate," he said. "Maybe we need a male movement, since evidently we're coming out second on everything." He slipped another Tums from an almost empty roll. The sun was dropping as we spoke, and shadows fell across the Citadel hats and figurines in his room. "Go back and look at your Greek and Roman empires and why they fell," he said.

His wife cleared her throat. "This doesn't have anything to do with male-female," she said.

"I see a decline in this great nation of ours," Dick said. He crossed his arms and stared into the gathering darkness of the late summer afternoon. After a while, he said, "I guess I sound like a buffoon."

Unlike the cadets, the older male Citadel officials often have to face dissent from wives or daughters whose views and professional aspirations or accomplishments challenge their stand on women's proper place. Lewis Spearman, the assistant to the president, recently remarried, and his wife is a feminist paralegal who is now getting her master's degree in psychology. She says she engaged for more than a year in "shriekfests" with him over the Shannon Faulkner question before she halfheartedly came around to The Citadel party line on barring women. And, while the wife of Dean Poole may have sat on the Miss Citadel judging panel, their daughter, Mindy, had loftier ambitions. Despite the fact that she suffered from cystic fibrosis, she was an ardent skier, horseback rider, and college athlete, rising at 5 A.M. daily with her crew-team members at the University of Virginia. And, despite a double lung transplant during her junior year, she graduated in 1991 with honors and won a graduate fellowship. "She was an outstanding young lady," Poole said. "I was very proud of her." His eyes clouding over at the memory, he recalled that she had made him promise to take her to the big Corps Day parade on The Citadel's sesquicentennial. The day the father and daughter were to attend the parade was the day she died. "Sort of an interesting footnote," he said, wiping at his moist eyes. What if she had wanted to go to The Citadel? Well, actually, Poole said, she had talked about it. If she had persisted he would have tried to change her mind, he said, but he added, "I would never have stopped her from doing something she wanted to do."

One of the biggest spousal battles over Shannon Faulkner is waged nightly at the home of a man who might seem the least likely figure at The Citadel to wind up with a feminist wife. Probably The Citadel's most legendary elder, thanks to Pat Conroy's thinly veiled and admiring portrait of him in *The Lords of Discipline,* is Lieutenant Colonel T. Nugent Courvoisie, who, as an assistant commandant in the sixties, oversaw the admission of the first African-American cadet to The Citadel. A gravelly voiced and cigar-chomping tender tyrant, Courvoisie—or the Boo, as he is known, for obscure reasons—was a fixture at the school for more than two decades. There are two Citadel scholarships in his family name, and his visage peers down from two portraits on campus.

A courtly man, and still dapper at seventy-seven, the Boo, who has since given up cigars, insisted on picking me up at my hotel and driving me to his home, though I had a rental car sitting in the parking lot. On the drive over, he ticked off the differences between the sexes that he believed made it impossible for The Citadel to admit women—differences such as that "the average female is not as proficient athletically as the average male." When we were settled in the living room, the Boo on his recliner and his second wife, Margaret, who is also seventy-seven, in a straight-back chair, the subject of Shannon Faulkner was revisited. The first words out of Margaret's mouth were "The Citadel wants to chop the head off women." A low growl emanated from the Boo's corner. He lowered the recliner a notch. "We don't talk about it here," Margaret said—an obvious untruth. "We haven't come to blows yet, but—"

The Boo interrupted, "I have the correct view."

She retorted, "No one has the *correct* view." She turned and addressed me. "You have to understand him," she said of her husband of nine years. "This is a man who went to military prep schools and a church that was male-dominated, naturally."

The Boo interrupted. "J.C. picked twelve *men* as his disciples," he said.

Margaret rolled her eyes. "See? He even takes it into the church—and he's on such familiar ground with Christ he calls him J.C."

The Boo said, "J.C. never picked a woman, except his mother."

Margaret said, "Oh God, see, this is why we don't go into it."

But, as usual, go into it they did. As the words got batted back and forth, with Margaret doing most of the batting, the Boo levered his recliner progressively lower, until all I could see of him were the soles of his shoes.

MARGARET: You had plenty of good women soldiers in Saudi Arabia.

BOO: Plenty of pregnant ones....

MARGARET: What, do you think [the cadets] didn't get girls pregnant before? There've been plenty of abortions. And I know of a number of cases that, by the time [a cadet] graduated, there were four or five kids.

BOO: That's an exaggeration. Maybe two or three ... With women, there's going to be sexual harassment.

MARGARET: Oh, honey, those cadets are harassing each other right now, all the time.

BOO: That's different. That's standard operating procedure.

In the nineteen-sixties, Margaret worked in the library at The Citadel, where she would often see Charles Foster, the first African-American cadet (who died a few years ago), alone at one of the library desks. "He would just come to the library and sit there a lot. It's hard to be the only one, to be the groundbreaker. That's why I admire this girl."

Boo's voice boomed from the depths of his recliner: "But there's no need for her. She's ruining a good thing."

Margaret gave a mock groan. "This is the last vestige of male bastionship," she said, "and it's going to kill 'em when it crumbles." Boo raised his chair halfway back up and considered Margaret. "She has a good mind," he told me after a while.

Margaret smiled. "I'm a new experience for him. He's always been military. People didn't disagree with him."

The Boo showed the way upstairs, to the attic, where he has his own "Citadel room"—a collection of Citadel memorabilia vaster than but almost identical to Dick's. Around the house, there were sketches of Boo at various points in his Citadel career. He told me that, before he retired, the cadets commissioned a portrait of him that hangs in Jenkins Hall. "Man, I looked good in that," he said. "Like a man. A leader."

Margaret didn't think so. "No, it was horrible," she said. "It didn't look like you."

"If Shannon were in my class, I'd be fired by March for sexual harassment," Colonel James Rembert, an English professor, was saying as we headed toward his classroom. He had a ramrod bearing and a certain resemblance to Ted Turner (who, it happens, sent all three of his sons to The Citadel—Beau Turner among them—and donated twenty-five million dollars to the school earlier this year). The Colonel identifies himself as one of "the last white Remberts" in South Carolina, the Remberts being a Huguenot family of sufficiently ancient lineage to gain him admission to the St. John's Hunting Club of South Carolina—an all-male society chaired by a Citadel alumnus. Rembert, who has a Cambridge University doctorate and wrote a book on Jonathan Swift, said he preferred the company of men, in leisure and in learning. "I've dealt with young men all my life," he went on. "I know how to play with them. I have the freedom here to imply things I couldn't with women. I don't want to have to watch what I say."

The literary work under discussion that day was *Beowulf,* and the cadets agreed that it was all about "brotherhood loyalty" and, in the words of one student, "the most important characteristics of a man—glory and eternal fame." Then they turned to their papers on the topic.

"Mr. Rice," Rembert said in mock horror. "You turned in a single-spaced paper." This was a no-no. Rembert instructed him to take a pencil and "pen-e-trate"—Rembert drew the syllables out—the paper with the point. He shook his head. "What a pansy!" Rembert said. "Can't catch, can't throw, can't write." Another student was chastised for the use of the passive voice. "Never use the passive voice—it leads to effeminacy and homosexuality," Rembert told the class. "So next time you use the passive voice I'm going to make you lift up your limp wrist." Literary pointers concluded, Rembert floated the subject of Shannon Faulkner. The usual objections were raised. But then the class wandered into more interesting territory, provoked by a cadet's comment that "she would change the relationship between the men here." Just what is the nature of that relationship?

"When we are in the showers, it's very intimate," a senior cadet said. "We're one mass, naked together, and it makes us closer.... You're shaved, you're naked, you're afraid together. You can cry." Robert Butcher, another senior, said that the men take care of each classmate. "They'll help dress him, tuck in his shirt, shine his shoes." "You mean like a mother-child relationship?" I asked.

"That *is* what it is," another cadet said. "It's a family, even the way we eat—family style." A fourth cadet said, "Maybe it's a Freudian thing, but males feel more affection with each other when women are not around. Maybe we're all homosexuals."

The class groaned. "Speak for yourself, buddy," a number of cadets said, almost in a chorus.

Rembert said, "With no women, we can hug each other. There's nothing so nurturing as an infantry platoon."

The hooted-down cadet weighed in again: "When I used to wrestle in high school, we had this great tradition. Right before the game, the coach, he'd slap us really hard on the butt."

Rembert, a onetime paratrooper, said he and his skydiving buddies did that, too, right before they jumped. "First man out gets a pat right there."

Over lunch, Rembert returned to the theme of manly nurturance among Citadel men. "We hug each other," he said. One of his colleagues "always kisses me on the cheek," he went on. "It's like a true marriage. There's an affectionate intimacy that you will find between cadets. With this security they can, without being defensive, project tenderness to each other."

Months later, I was sitting in court watching Norman Doucet, the cadet regimental commander, testify. He was showing the judge a video of the Citadel experience and explaining the various scenes. First we were shown "one of the

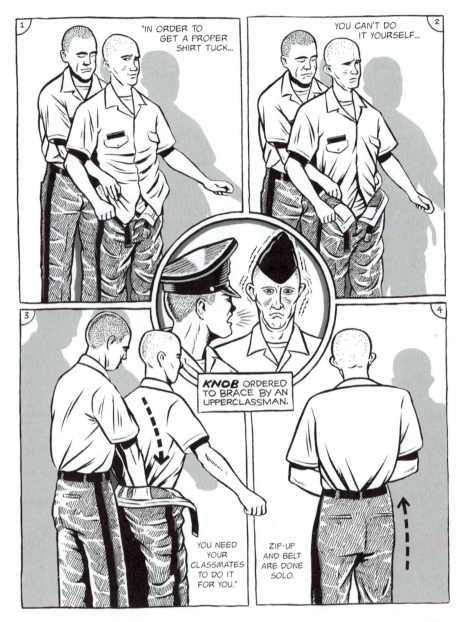

Dependency is a main theme in cadet relationships. Colonel James Rembert says that the cadets' intimate bond is "like a true marriage." Illustration by Mark Zingarelli, originally published in *The New Yorker*. © Mark Zingarelli/House of Zing

great parts" of a knob's first day—the mothers looking weepy at the gate as their sons were led away. Doucet lingered over the head-shaving scene. "This is what does it, right here," he said. "Mothers can't even tell their sons apart after this." Thus shielded from the prying maternal eye, the cadets began their new life, and the video action shifted to a typical day in the life of the Corps. But the editing made it a day as heavy on early-morning domestic chores as it was on martial activity. Much of the film was devoted to housekeeping: scenes of cadets making beds, dressing each other, sweeping, taking out the trash, all of which Doucet described as "like some kind of a ballet or a dance that's going on." This is a dance where the most important moves took place before the show, in the dressing room. "What they are doing here is the Citadel shirt tuck," Doucet said. The tuck requires that a cadet unzip his pants halfway and fold down his waistband, then stand still while his helper approaches him from the back, puts his arms around the cadet's waist, pulls the loose shirt material firmly to the back, jams it as far down in the pants as he can, and then pulls the cadet's pants up. "If you watch closely right here, this is what the fourth-class system is all about," Doucet continued. "In order to get a proper shirt tuck, you can't do it yourself—you need your classmates to do it for you. There's really a lot of dependence upon your classmates." But, as Doucet's account suggested, cadets can experience that dependence only in concealment, away from mothers, away from all women.

When a Citadel attorney asked Doucet why female cadets would pose a problem on the campus, the only issue he raised was the humiliation that cadets feel if women observe the cadets' on-campus interactions. He spoke of the shame that knobs feel when, on occasion, a woman happened to be on the parade ground while upperclassmen were disciplining them. The cadets observing in the courtroom nodded in agreement.

It may seem almost paradoxical that the fourth-class system should be so solicitous of the emotional vulnerability of its wards—the same wards it subjects to such rigors. And yet the making of Whole Men evidently requires an initial stage of infantilization. Indeed, the objective of recapitulating childhood development is plainly spelled out in The Citadel's yearbook, known as "the Sphinx." The 1990 "Sphinx" explained, "As a freshman enters, he begins to release his childhood and takes the first steps to becoming a 'Citadel Man.'... As a 'knob,' every aspect of life is taught, a new way to walk.... Knobs are told how, where, and when to walk." Reentrance into manhood for the toddling knobs occurs on Recognition Day, when the upperclassmen force the knobs to do calisthenics until they drop, then gently lift up their charges and nurse them with cups of water. At that moment, for the first time in nine months, the older cadets call the knobs by their first names and embrace them.

The relationship between knobs and upperclassmen following Recognition Day, as they are integrated into the Corps, shifts from maternal to matrimonial. The yearbooks of the last several years picture Citadel men spending a lot of time embracing and kissing. Of course, this impulse, when it is captured on film, is always carefully disarmed with a jokey caption.

One afternoon, a group of cadets recounted for me the campus's many "nudity rituals," as they jokingly called them. There's "Senior Rip-Off Day," a spring rite in which three hundred seniors literally rip each other's clothes off, burn them in a bonfire, and hug and wrestle on the ground. There's "Nude Platoon," in which a group of juniors, unclad except for their cross-webbing, run around the quad yelling, "We love the Nude Platoon!" And there's the birthday ritual, in which the birthday boy is stripped, tied to a chair, and covered with shaving cream, while his groin is coated in liquid shoe polish.

During the fall semester before graduation, the seniors receive their "band of gold" (as it is called) in the Ring Ceremony. The chaplain blesses each class ring. (Receiving the ring, which I was constantly reminded is "the biggest class ring of any college," is a near-sacrament, and the yearbooks are filled with pictures of young men holding up their rings in fervor, as if clutching a crucifix before a vampire.) Then each senior walks through a ten-foot replica of the class ring with his mother on one arm and his "date" on the other. In a sort of reverse marriage ceremony, the mother gives the cadet away. Mother and date accompany him through the towering ring; then he kisses Mother farewell and marches under the arched swords of the Junior Sword Drill, a new bride of the Corps. Several cadets and alumni told me that when a Citadel graduate marries, it is a tradition to slide the class ring over the wedding band. Indeed, I saw such an ordering of priorities on the fingers of a number of Citadel men in the courtroom.

In the late-twentieth-century setting of The Citadel, in a time when extreme insecurity and confusion about masculinity's standing run rampant, the Corps of Cadets once again seeks to obscure a domestic male paradise with an intensifying of virile showmanship and violence. The result is a ruthless intimacy, in which physical abuse stands in for physical affection, and every display of affection must be counterbalanced by a display of sadism. Knobs told me that they were forced to run through the showers while the upperclassmen "guards" knocked the soap out of their hands and, when the knobs leaned over to retrieve it the upperclassmen would unzip their pants and yell, "Don't pick it up, don't pick it up! We'll use you like we used those girls!" A former Citadel Halloween tradition of upperclassmen dressing up—mostly in diapers and women's clothes—and collecting candy treats from knobs, has given way to "tricks" of considerable violence. (One upperclassman told me of cadets who knocked dressers over on candy-dispensing cadets and then walked on top of them.) The administration tried, unsuccessfully, to put a stop to the whole affair; too many freshmen were getting injured. And the playful pat on the butt that served to usher cadets into the brotherhood has degenerated into more invasive acts. According to a recent graduate, one company of cadets recently devised a regimen in which the older cadets tested sophomores nightly with increasingly painful treatments—beatings and stompings and so forth. The process, which they dubbed "Bananarama," culminated on a night in which an unpeeled banana was produced—and shoved into a cadet's anus.

Given this precarious dynamic, it is not surprising that in the past few years at The Citadel social rage has been directed toward any men who were perceived to be gay. Several young men who were suspected of homosexual inclinations were hounded out of the school. One cadet, Herbert Parker, who said that he was falsely accused of having a sexual encounter with a male janitor, recalled a year of total isolation—cadets refused to sit near him in the mess hall or in classes—and terror: incessant threatening phone calls and death threats. The cadets and the administration—which had responded to the report of his encounter by sending out a campus-security police car with lights flashing to question him—acted "like I had murdered someone."

The scapegoating reached such brutal proportions that the counseling center recently set up a sort of group-therapy session for the targeted young men, who are known as It, as in the game of tag.

One evening after the trial, I went over to the Treehouse, a "mixed" bar in Charleston, with an upstairs gay bar and nightly drag shows on the weekends. My intention was to ask about cadet violence against gay men. I presumed that on a campus where every second epithet was "faggot" such hate crimes were all but inevitable. There were indeed a few such cases, I learned, but the circumstances were different from what I had imagined. Nor were those cases the essence of my findings that evening.

"The proper terminology for The Citadel," a customer at the bar named Chris said, "is The Closet." Up and down the bar, heads bobbed in agreement. "They love faggots like me." What he meant by "like me," however, was not that he was gay. That night, he looked like a male model—sleek black hair and a handsome, chiseled face. But on the nights he was dressed for a performance he could pass for a woman. Arching an eyebrow, Chris said, "The cadets go for the drag queens."

Chris's observation was echoed in ensuing conversations in the bar. There are thousands of cadets, presumably, who have not dated drag queens, but in two visits to the Treehouse I could find only two drag queens, out of maybe a dozen, who did not tell me of dating a cadet—and that was only because these two found Citadel men "too emotional." Cadets can also occasionally be dangerous, Chris told me. "You can get the ones who are violent. They think they want it, then afterwards they turn on you, like you made them do it." Nonetheless, a drag queen who called himself Holly had been happily involved with a cadet for three years now. Marissa, another drag queen, the reigning "Miss Treehouse 1993–94," had gone out with one cadet, broken up, and was now in the throes of a budding romance with another. A third drag queen, who asked to be identified as Tiffany, was known to be a favorite of cadets.

As Chris and I were talking that first night, a drag queen called Lownie wandered in and settled on a bar stool. Lownie delighted in the Corps of Cadets pageantry—especially the Friday dress parades. "The parades are a big thing with the queers in Charleston," he said. "We'll have a cocktail party and go over and watch the boys. It's a very Southern-'lady' thing to do." Years ago, Lownie had been a student at the College of Charleston when he met *his* Citadel lover, and they had begun covert assignations—communicating through notes slipped in little-used books in the Citadel library. The only drawback, Lownie said, was dealing with his lover's constant emotional anxiety over making the grade at The Citadel. He was, in fact, a model macho cadet: a Junior Sword Drill member, a regimental officer, and a "hang king," who could dangle interminably from a closet rack by his fingertips. Lownie, who found such records more amusing than impressive, grinned, and said, "I used to make him wear his shako"—The Citadel's military cap—"when we were having sex. It's manhood at its most."

Lownie said he could begin to fathom his cadet's intense attachment to The Citadel—an emotion that he likened to a love affair—because he himself had spent four years in the Air Force. "The day-to-day aspect of being in a military environment is that you run around in a little bit of clothing and you are being judged as to how good a man you are by doing women's work—pressing pants, sewing, polishing shoes. You are a *better* man if you have mastery of womanly arts.... The camaraderie doesn't get any stronger than when you are in the barracks, sitting around at the end of the day in your briefs and T's and dogtags—like a bunch of hausfraus, talking and gossiping." The military stage set offers a false front and a welcome trapdoor—an escape hatch from the social burdens of traditional masculinity. Behind the martial backdrop, Lownie said, "you don't have to be a breadwinner. You don't have to be a leader. You can play back seat. It's a great relief. You can act like a human being and not have to act like a man."

"You know what the [cadet] I'm seeing now said to me?" Tiffany said. We were sitting in the dressing room a couple of hours before the night's performance, and as Tiffany spoke he peered into an elaborate mirror set illuminated with miniature movie-star lights, applying layer after layer of mascara and eyeliner with expert precision. "He said, 'You're more of a woman than a woman is.' And that's an exact quote." Tiffany stood up and struck a Southern belle pose by way of illustration. "I overexemplify everything a female is—my breasts, my hair, the way I hold myself." And who could better complete the hoopskirts picture than a fantasy gentleman in uniform?

Marissa, Miss Treehouse, looked up from his labors, painting row after row of fake nails with pink polish. "I love how they wear their caps slung low so you can't quite see their eyes," he said. "It's like all of us are female illusionists and they are male illusionists. A man in a uniform is a kind of dream."

Tiffany said, "For Halloween, you know what my cadet boyfriend wanted to dress as? A cadet."

The dressing-room scene before me, of a group of men tenderly helping each other get ready for the evening—an elaborate process of pinning and binding and stuffing—was not very different, in its way, from the footage in Norman Doucet's video of the cadets tucking in each other's shirts. As the drag queens conversed, they tossed stockings and Ace bandages and cosmetic bags back and forth. "Has anyone seen my mascara wand?" "O.K., who has the blush?" There was a homey comfort that reminded me of slumber parties when I was a girl, where we would put big pink spongy rollers in each other's hair and screech with laughter at the results. And suddenly it became obvious to me what was generating that void, that yearning, in the cadets' lives—and maybe in the lives of many American men. What was going on here was play—a kind of freedom and spontaneity that, in this culture, only women are permitted.

No wonder men found their Citadels, their Treehouses, where the rules of gender could be bent or escaped. For the drag queens of the Treehouse, the distinctions between the sexes are a goof, to be endlessly manipulated with fun-house-mirror glee. For cadets, despite the play set of The Citadel and the dress-up braids and ribbons, the guarding of their Treehouse is a dead-serious business. Still, undercover at The Citadel, the cadets have managed to create for themselves a world in which they get half the equation that Lownie described: they can "act like human beings" in the safety of the daily domestic life of the barracks. But, in return, the institution demands that they never cease to "act like a man"—a man of cold and rigid bearing, a man no more male than Tiffany's Southern belle is female, a man that no one, humanly, can be. That they must defend their inner humanity with outer brutality may say as much about the world outside The Citadel walls as about the world within them. The cadets feel called to defend those walls. Never mind that their true ideal may not be the vaunted one of martial masculinity, just as their true enemy is not Shannon Faulkner. The cadets at The Citadel feel that something about their life and routine is worthy on its merits and is endangered from without. And in that they may be right.

QUESTIONS FOR MAKING CONNECTIONS
WITHIN THE READING

1. In "The Naked Citadel," Susan Faludi provides a series of vignettes that describe life at the military school. Why does she present the vignettes in the order she does? Why does she start her article in Jane Bishop's classroom? Why does she then move to the courtroom? Make a chart that tracks the organization of Faludi's essay. What is the argument that Faludi is making by telling these vignettes in this order?

2. The sociologist Erving Goffman coined the term *total institutions* to describe places that become almost entirely self-enclosed and self-referential in their values and behaviors. Goffman's principal example was the mental asylum. Can we describe The Citadel accurately as a total institution? Are its values the product of its isolation, or does Faludi's account furnish evidence that the attitudes holding sway in The Citadel persist outside the institution as well? Is The Citadel just an aberration, or does it tell us certain truths about our own society?

3. Faludi offers this overview of The Citadel:

   > In the late-twentieth-century setting of The Citadel, in a time when extreme insecurity and confusion about masculinity's standing run rampant, the Corps of Cadets once again seeks to obscure a domestic male paradise with an intensifying of virile showmanship and violence. The result is a ruthless intimacy, in which physical abuse stands in for physical affection, and every display of affection must be counterbalanced by a display of sadism.

   On the basis of the evidence Faludi provides, is this a fair assessment of the culture of The Citadel? What evidence confirms this assessment? What evidence might be said to complicate or even contradict it? What other explanations might we offer for events at The Citadel? Does masculinity have to occupy the central place in our analysis, or might other factors be more important?

QUESTIONS FOR WRITING

1. In what sense is Susan Faludi a feminist? If we define a feminist as someone who is specifically concerned with defending the rights of women, does she qualify? Does she regard the rights of women as practically or theoretically distinct from the rights of men? How about the needs and aspirations of women? Are these fundamentally different from the needs and aspirations of men? Does Faludi see men as "oppressors of women"? Does she imply that our society systematically empowers men while systematically disempowering women, or does disempowerment cross gender lines?

2. The *Naked Citadel* might be described as a case study of the relations between sexuality and social structures. In what ways do social structures shape sexuality at The Citadel? Does Faludi's account call into question the belief in a single, natural form of male sexual expression? Is the problem with The Citadel that natural sexuality has been perverted by linking it to relations of power? Can sexuality and power ever be separated?

QUESTIONS FOR MAKING CONNECTIONS
BETWEEN READINGS

1. In "Immune to Reality," Daniel Gilbert sets out to create a theory of happiness, one that explains why humans, in general, are so unprepared to predict what things and accomplishments will lead to happiness. Does Gilbert's theory shed new light on the choices and the actions of the cadets at The Citadel? How would Gilbert's explanation for the cadets' behavior reinforce, extend, or contradict Faludi's understanding? Write an essay about the degree to which happiness, as Gilbert defines it, plays a role in education inside and outside The Citadel.

2. In "When I Woke Up Tuesday Morning, It Was Friday," from *The Myth of Sanity*, Martha Stout explores the psychological dynamics of dissociation. According to Stout, the experience of trauma "changes the brain itself." Under conditions of extreme pain or distress, the brain becomes unable to organize experience "usefully" or to integrate new experience with other, prior memories. Does it seem possible that dissociation plays a role in the training of cadets at The Citadel? What circumstantial evidence can you find to support this claim, or to dispute it? Does Stout's account of dissociation help to explain why so few cadets rebel against the treatment they receive? Is it possible that certain institutions use dissociation intentionally to weaken bonds sustained by affection and shared values? How might our society protect itself against the use of dissociation as a political instrument?

BARBARA FREDRICKSON

AT THE END of the 1938 film *The Wizard of Oz*, Dorothy Gale receives some sage advice about the importance of love. "A heart is not measured," the wizard says, "by how much you love but how much you are loved by others." These words echo notions expressed by countless writers long before the MGM studio was born. "Love is not love," William Shakespeare wrote, which "alters when it alteration finds ... O no! It is an ever-fixed mark." But what exactly is this *love*? Is it an experience or is it an emotion? Does it change constantly or should it remain "ever-fixed," as Shakespeare says? Advice about love is so prevalent that we can easily overlook its vagueness, sentimentality, and inherent contradictions.

Psychologist Barbara Lee Fredrickson, author of the book *Love 2.0: How Our Supreme Emotion Affects Everything We Feel, Think, Do, and Become*, has no doubt that love is real, but she has tried to bring scientific rigor to the tangled discourse on the topic. Her recent writing about love might be seen as an extension of her earlier research in the field of positive psychology, a branch of psychology focused on positive emotions as opposed to the disorders studied by previous researchers. Fredrickson's work on positive emotions culminated in what she describes as the "broaden-and-build theory," which suggests that positive emotions lead people to become more curious, outgoing, and creative. As she argues in an article from *American Psychologist* (2005), positive emotions probably evolved to improve our ancestors' odds for "survival and reproduction."

After completing her first book, *Positivity*, Fredrickson was quick to recognize one limitation of her argument: even if we know that positivity helps, how can those trapped by negative thinking ever change their habits of mind? How, in other words, can we apply the findings of positivity research? Toward an answer to these questions, Fredrickson's more recent studies focus on forms of human interaction that actively encourage positivity. Among these forms of interaction, Fredrickson sees love as the most important because it takes place in the "micro-moments" of our "resonance" with others: "Just as your body was designed to extract oxygen from the Earth's atmosphere, and nutrients from the foods you ingest, your body was designed to love." For the first time, research demonstrates that love can change our biochemistry and even the expression of our DNA. But perhaps the most important implications are to be found in our social lives rather than in our biology. If love, for example, plays an essential role in our neural processing, why does society often seem to reflect our worst tendencies, not our best? If we are naturally hardwired to love, why does love sometimes seem hard to find?

Selections from Love 2.0: How Our Supreme Emotion Affects Everything We Feel, Think, Do, and Become

LOVE, OUR SUPREME EMOTION

> The Eskimos had fifty-two names for snow because it was important to them: There ought to be as many for love.
>
> —MARGARET ATWOOD

Longing. You know the feeling. It's that ache of sensing that something vital is missing from your life; a deep thirst for more. More meaning, more connection, more energy—more *something.* Longing is that feeling that courses through your body just before you decide that you're restless, lonely, or unhappy.

Longing like this is not just another mental state. It's deeply physical. Your body craves some essential nutrient that it's not getting, yet you can't quite put your finger on what it is. Sometimes you can numb this ache with a deep dive into work, gossip, television, or gaming. More often than not, though, these and other attempts to fill the aching void are merely temporary distractions. The longing doesn't let up. It trails you like a shadow, insistently, making distractions all the more appealing. And distractions abound—that second or third glass of wine, that stream of texts and tweets, that couch and remote control.

Odds are, food is abundant in your life. And clean drinking water is as close as the nearest faucet and virtually limitless. You have access to reasonably clean air and adequate shelter. Those basic needs have long been met. What you long for now is far more intangible.

What you long for is love. Whether you're single or not, whether you spend your days largely in isolation or steadily surrounded by the buzz of conversation, love is the essential nutrient that your cells crave: true positivity-charged connection with other living beings.

Love, as it turns out, nourishes your body the way the right balance of sunlight, nutrient-rich soil, and water nourishes plants and allows them to flourish. The more you experience it, the more you open up and grow, becoming wiser and more attuned, more resilient and effective, happier and healthier. You grow spiritually as well, better able to see, feel, and appreciate the deep interconnections that inexplicably tie you to others, that embed you within the grand fabric of life.

Just as your body was designed to extract oxygen from the earth's atmosphere, and nutrients from the foods you ingest, your body was designed to love. Love—like taking a deep breath or eating an orange when you're depleted and thirsty—not only feels great but is also life-giving, an indispensable source of energy, sustenance, and health.

When I compare love to oxygen and food, I'm not just taking poetic license. I'm drawing on science: new science that illuminates for the first time how love, and its absence, fundamentally alters the biochemicals in which your body is steeped. They, in turn, can alter the very ways your DNA gets expressed within your cells. The love you do or do not experience today may quite literally change key aspects of your cellular architecture next season and next year—cells that affect your physical health, your vitality, and your overall well-being. In these ways and more, just as your supplies of clean air and nutritious food forecast how long you'll walk this earth—and whether you'll thrive or just get by—so does your supply of love.

It's Not What You Think

To absorb what the new science of love has to offer, you'll need to step back from "love" as you may now know it. Forget about the love that you typically hear on the radio, the one that's centered on desire and yearns for touch from a new squeeze. Set aside the take on love your family might have offered you, one that requires that you love your relatives unconditionally, regardless of whether their actions disturb you, or their aloofness leaves you cold. I'm even asking you to set aside your view of love as a special bond or relationship, be it with your spouse, partner, or soul mate. And if you've come to view love as a commitment, promise, or pledge, through marriage or any other loyalty ritual, prepare for an about-face. I need you to step back from all of your preconceptions and consider an upgrade. *Love 2.0* offers a different perspective—your body's perspective.

If you were asked today, by a roving reporter or an inquisitive dinner party guest, to provide your own definition of love, your answer would likely reflect a mishmash of shared cultural messages and your own deeply personal experiences with intimacy. However compelling your answer, I'd wager that your body has its own—quite different—definition of love. That's what this book is about. Love is not sexual desire or the blood-ties of kinship. Nor is it a special bond or commitment. Sure enough, love is closely related to each of these important concepts. Yet none, I will argue, capture the true meaning of love as your body experiences it.

The vision of love that I offer here will require a radical shift, a departure from what you've come to believe. It's time to upgrade your view of love. Love is not a category of relationships. Nor is it something "out there" that you can fall into, or—years later—out of. Seeing love as a special bond is extraordinarily common, albeit misleading. A bond like this can endure for years—even a lifetime with proper commitment and effort. And having at least one close relationship like this is vital to your health and happiness, to be sure. Even so, that special bond and the commitments people often build around it are better taken as the *products* of love—the results of the many smaller moments in which love infuses you—rather than as love per se. When you equate love with intimate relationships, love can seem confusing. At times it feels great, while at other times it hurts like hell. At times it lifts you up with grand dreams for your future and at other times oppresses you with shame about your inadequacies, or guilt about your past actions. When you limit your view of love to relationships or commitment, love becomes a complex and bewildering thicket of emotions, expectations, and insecurities. Yet when you redirect your eyes toward your body's definition of love, a clear path emerges that cuts through that thicket and leads you to a better life.

There's still more ground to clear. I need to ask you to disengage from some of your most cherished beliefs about love as well: the notions that love is exclusive, lasting, and unconditional. These deeply held beliefs are often more wish than reality in people's lives. They capture people's daydreams about the love-of-their-life whom they've yet to meet. Love, as your body defines it, is not exclusive, not something to be reserved for your soul mate, your inner circle, your kin, or your so-called *loved ones*. Love's reach turns out to be far wider than we're typically coaxed to imagine. Even so, love's timescale is far shorter than we typically think. Love, as you'll see, is not lasting. It's actually far more fleeting than most of us would care to acknowledge. On the upside, though, love is forever renewable. And perhaps most challenging of all, love is not unconditional. It doesn't emerge no matter what, regardless of conditions. To the contrary, you'll see that the love your body craves is exquisitely sensitive to contextual cues. It obeys preconditions. Yet once you understand those preconditions, you can find love countless times each day.

It's difficult to speak of love in scientific terms, I've found, because listeners have so many preexisting and strong beliefs about it. Many of these beliefs reflect our shared cultural heritage, like all those proliferating songs and movies that equate love with infatuation or sexual desire, or with stories that end happily ever after, or even the realistic marriage ceremonies that celebrate love as an exclusive bond and commitment. Other beliefs about love are deeply personal. They reflect your own unique life history, with its interpersonal triumphs and scars, lessons about intimacy learned and not yet learned. Left unaddressed, these preconceptions can derail any serious intellectual discussion of love. They may even keep you from soaking up the full implications of the new findings on it....

LOVE'S BIOLOGY

The soul must always stand ajar, ready to welcome the ecstatic experience.

—EMILY DICKINSON

It's all too tempting, especially in Western culture, to take your body to be a noun, a thing. Sure, it's a living thing, but still, like other concrete things that you can see and touch, you typically describe your body with reference to its stable physical properties, like your height, your weight, your skin tone, your apparent age, and the like. A photo works well to convey these attributes. You recognize, of course, that five years from now, today's photo will seem a bit outdated. By then, your body's physical properties might shift a bit—you might, for instance, become a little shorter, a little heavier, a little paler, or look a little older. Still, you're comfortable with the idea that your body remains pretty much the same from day to day. It has constancy.

Yet constancy, ancient Eastern philosophies warn, is an illusion, a trick of the mind. Impermanence is the rule—constant change, the only constancy. True for all things, this is especially true for living things, which, by definition, change or adapt as needed in response to changes in context. Just as plants turn toward the sun and track its arc from dawn to dusk, your own heart alters its activity with each postural shift, each new emotion, even each breath you take. Seen in this light, your body is more verb than noun: It shifts, cascades, and pulsates; it connects and builds; it erodes and flushes. Mere photographs fail to capture these nonstop and mostly unseen churning dynamics. Instead, you need movies. Increasingly, scientists work to capture these and other dynamic changes as they unfurl within living, breathing, and interacting bodies. True, scientists need to understand form as well as function, anatomy as well as physiology, nouns as well as verbs. Yet when it comes to love, verbs rule. Positivity resonance lies in the action, the doing, the connecting. It wells up, like a wave forming in the ocean, and then dissipates, like that same wave, after its crash. To fully appreciate love's biology, you'll need to train your eye to see this ever-shifting ebb and flow.

Taking cues from what leading neuroscientist Stephen Porges calls the *social engagement system*, I describe love's biology as a system, a whole comprised of several interacting parts. You can think of love, or positivity resonance, as one of the more complex and recurrent *scenes* nested within the *act* of your day, which is in turn nested within the *play* of your life. As with any scene in a play, the drama of love has its own cast of characters. Here I turn the spotlight on three main biological characters: your brain; one particular hormone, oxytocin, which circulates throughout your brain and body; and your vagus nerve, the tenth cranial nerve that runs from deep within your brain stem down to your heart, lungs, and other internal organs. Other characters step onto the biological stage to deliver their own lines, to be sure, but these three are primary players in love's biology.

Although always on stage, these main characters deliver their lines quietly, most often fully outside of your conscious awareness. As you move through your day, these biological characters—your brain, your oxytocin, and your vagus nerve—are ever responsive to set changes. As you interact with one person after another, they gently nudge you to attend to these others more closely and forge connections when possible. They shape your motives and behaviors in subtle ways, yet ultimately, their actions serve to strengthen your relationships and knit you in closer to the social fabric of life. In the sections that follow, I'll shine the spotlight on each of these three main characters in turn, to help you see how each forges and supports those life-giving moments of positivity resonance for which your body thirsts.

Love on the Brain

When you and another truly connect, love reverberates between you. In the very moment that you experience positivity resonance, your brain syncs up with the other person's brain. Within each moment of love, you and the other are on the same wavelength. As your respective brain waves mirror one another, each of you—moment by moment—changes the other's mind.

… How do you know it really happens? You can't see this brain synchrony surface in real time after all. What you'd need is some way to peer inside two people's heads while they chatted so that you could tell whether their respective brain activity really does march along in time together. This would tell you whether they really "click." Only with this sort of X-ray vision could you decide whether love is better described as a solo act—an emotion contained within the boundaries of the person feeling it—or a duet or ensemble, performed by a duo or group. That sort of X-ray vision sounds like science fiction.

Yet turning science fiction into science fact is what scientists and engineers love most. Breakthrough work by neuroscientist Uri Hasson, of Princeton University, has done just that. He and his team have found ways to measure multiple brains connecting through conversation. The obstacles they faced to do this were large. First, brain scanners are loud machines—no place to carry on actual conversations. Second, they're also extraordinarily expensive, both to buy and to use. Almost all brain imaging studies thus scan just one person's brain at a time. Yet with clever engineering and clever experimental logistics, Hasson's team cleared both obstacles. They created a custom optic microphone that canceled out the noise of the scanner without distorting the delicate brain signals his team sought to capture. The logistics feat was to mimic a natural conversation by pulling it apart in time.

Suppose, for a moment, you were stranded at the airport last week. Your plane to Miami was delayed for hours. Bored with your reading and web-browsing, you got to talking to another stranded passenger, a lively young college student on her way home for break. You'd been chatting back and forth for a while, every so often, meeting eyes and sharing smiles. The conversation was very natural, like you were friends already. Somehow or another, she got to telling you about her crazy high school prom experience. In great detail, she launched into how she happened to have two dates to the same prom; how she ended up having only five minutes to get dressed and ready for the prom after a full day of scuba diving; how, on her way to after-prom festivities, she crashed her boyfriend's car in the wee hours of the morning; and then how she completely lucked out of getting ticketed (or arrested!) by the officer who witnessed her accident. She's a good storyteller: You hung on her every word. Fifteen minutes melted away as she shared all the twists and turns of her hapless prom night. It's clear, too, that you both enjoyed the chance to connect, rather than read, while you waited for your plane together.

Okay, now it's time for a set change: Instead of in an airport terminal, this conversation actually unfolded in a brain imaging lab at Princeton University. And instead of you sitting side by side with your impromptu friend, Hasson's team actually invited her to visit the lab weeks ago, and they audio-recorded her entire prom story while scanning her brain's activity with functional magnetic resonance imaging (fMRI). You're here lying in the scanner today, listening to her story over fancy headphones, while Hasson's team records your own brain activity. After you get out of the scanner, they ask you to report on what you heard in as much detail as possible. This takes a while; hers was a long, circuitous story after all.

Hasson's team later looked at the extent to which your brain activity mirrored hers. They painstakingly matched up each specific brain area across the two of you, time-locked your respective scans, and looked for "coupling," or the degree to which your brains lit up in synchrony with each other, matched in both space and time.

It turns out that the brain coupling evident between you two is surprisingly widespread. In other words, speaking with and listening to the human voice appear to activate much of the exact same brain activity at pretty much the same time. Keep in mind that—despite your new friend's gift for storytelling—this was still a pretty artificial conversation. Isolated inside the brain scanner across different days, you never actually got to see each other's gestures, meet each other's eyes, or even take turns speaking. You only listened to her voice over headphones. The brain coupling that would emerge in real time with the full and animated dialogue that could well spring up between the two of you if you were in fact seated side by side in the airplane terminal is likely to be far more extensive. Yet hearing someone's voice offers an important channel of sensory and temporal connection, because voice can convey so much emotion. By contrast, consider how little brain coupling would emerge if the connection between the two of you were to be further reduced, for instance, if you only read her story, at your own pacing and presumed intonations, or only heard *about* her story, as in my thumbnail depiction of it a few paragraphs back.

Forget the idea of a few isolated mirror neurons. So-called mirror neurons refer to a microscopic brain area that Italian neurophysiologists found to "light up" both when a monkey reaches for a banana and when that same monkey sees a person reach for a banana. The discovery of mirror neurons was a huge breakthrough because it told us that taking some action and seeing someone else take that same action are far more alike than previously thought. This means that when you know something—like why that person who just walked into your office is smiling—you know it because your brain and body simulate being in that person's shoes, in their skin. Your knowing is not just abstract and conceptual; it's embodied and physical. Yet it seems now that the concept of isolated mirror neurons was just the tip of the unseen and enormous iceberg. What Hasson and his team uncovered was far more extensive neuronal coupling than previously imagined. Far from being isolated to one or two brain areas, really "clicking" with someone else appears to be a whole brain dance in a fully mirrored room. The reflections between the two of you are that penetrating and widespread.

It turns out that you weren't the only one listening to your new friend's prom story. Hasson's team invited ten other people to have their brains scanned while listening to the very same audio-recording of her story that you heard. Whereas you listened attentively to everything she said, others didn't so much. Those differences showed up clearly when you were each asked to recount her story afterward. By tallying up the matches between her original, impromptu prom story and each listener's retelling of it, Hasson's team rank-ordered the whole set of listeners by how well they understood the story. Those differences in comprehension reflect the success or failure of communication—how thoroughly information from her brain was transferred to your brain, and to the brains of the other listeners. Strikingly, Hasson's team discovered that the degree of success in communication predicted the degree of brain coupling between speaker and listener, and did so in surprising ways.

Most of the time, across most brain areas, listeners' brains mirrored the speaker's brain after a short time lag, around one to three seconds later. It only makes sense, after all, that the speaker leads this dance, since the story is hers and she chooses her words before you and the others hear them. In other cases, though, this neural pas de deux between speaker and listener showed hardly any lag at all—the respective changes in brain activity were virtually synchronized. Your particular case was different, however. Recall that you were the one who grasped your new friend's story better than anybody. You hung on every word and picked up every detail of it, even the seemingly inconsequential ones. Your more complete grasp of her story went hand in hand with something truly remarkable: Your brain activity actually *anticipated* her brain activity by a few seconds in several cortical areas. Excellent communication, it thus seems, doesn't simply involve following along very closely. It also involves forecasting. Once you were in sync and on the same page with your new friend, enjoying her and her story, you could even anticipate what she'd say next, or how she'd say it. Your brain could anticipate her brain's next move.

Brain coupling, Hasson argues, is the means by which we understand each other. He goes even further to claim that communication—a true meeting of the minds—is a single act, performed by two brains. Considering the positivity resonance of love, what I find most fascinating about these findings is that a key brain area that showed coupling in Hasson's speaker-listener study was the insula, an area linked with conscious feeling states. Evidence for synchrony in two people's insulae suggests that in good communication, two individuals come to feel a single, shared emotion as well, one that is distributed across their two brains.

Indeed, in other work, Hasson and colleagues have shown that people's brains come particularly into sync during emotional moments. Neural coupling, then—really understanding someone else—becomes all the more likely when you share the same emotion. Even more so than ordinary communication, a micro-moment of love is a single act, performed by two brains. Shared emotions, brain synchrony, and mutual understanding emerge together. And mutual understanding is just steps away from mutual care. Once two people understand each other—really "get" each other in any given moment—the benevolent concerns and actions of mutual care can flow forth unimpeded.

As you move through your day, quite naturally you move in and out of different scenes. Each scene, of course, has its own script. For perhaps most of your day, you're pretty much caught up in your own thoughts and plans, oblivious to the presence or feelings of anyone nearby. Your brain, in such moments, is doing its own thing. But in those rarer moments when you truly connect with someone else over positivity—by sharing a smile, a laugh, a common passion, or an engaging story—you become attuned, with genuine care and concern for the other. You empathize with what they're going through, as your two brains sync up and act as one, as a unified team.

Neural coupling like this is a biological manifestation of oneness. Laboratory studies have already shown that when positive emotions course through you, your awareness expands from your habitual focus on "me" to a more generous focus on "we." When you're feeling bad—afraid, anxious, or angry—even your best friend can seem pretty remote or separate from you. The same goes for when you're feeling nothing in particular. Not so, when you're feeling good. Under the influence of positive emotions, your sense of self actually expands to include others to greater degrees. Your best friend, in these lighthearted moments, simply seems like a bigger part of you.

Hasson's work suggests that when you share your positive emotions with others, when you experience positivity resonance together with this sense of expansion, it's also deeply physical, evident in your brain. The emotional understanding of true empathy recruits coinciding brain activity in both you and the person of your focus. Another telling brain imaging study, this one conducted by scientists in Taipei, Taiwan, illustrates self-other overlap at the neuronal level. Imagine for a moment being a participant in this study. While you are in the fMRI brain scanner, the researchers show you a number of short, animated scenes and ask you to picture yourself in these scenes. Some of these scenes depict painful events, like dropping something heavy on your toe or getting your fingers pinched in a closing door. What the brain images show is that, compared to imagining neutral, nonpainful situations, imagining yourself in these painful situations lights up the well-known network of brain areas associated with pain processing, including the insula, that area linked with conscious feeling states. When you are later asked to imagine these same painful events happening to a loved one—your spouse, your best friend, or your child, for instance—these same brain areas light up. By and large, then, your loved one's pain *is* your pain. By contrast, when you imagine these painful events happening to complete strangers, a different pattern of activation emerges altogether, one that shows little activation in the insula and more activation in areas linked with distinguishing and distancing yourself from others, and actively inhibiting or regulating emotions, as if to prevent their pain from becoming your pain. At the level of brain activity during imagined pain, you and your beloved are virtually indistinguishable.

Whereas the Taipei research team defined love to be a lasting loving relationship (what, for clarity's sake, I call a bond), the work from Hasson's team at Princeton tells me that neural synchrony and overlap can also unfold between you and a complete stranger—if you let it. Positivity resonance between brains, as it turns out, requires only connection, not the intimacy or shared history that comes with a special bond. Even so, the distinctions revealed in the Taipei study, between imagining your loved one's pain and imagining a stranger's pain, underscore that stifled emotions and guarded personal boundaries, while at times necessary and fully appropriate, can also function as obstacles to positivity resonance. As we'll see in the next section, your attunement to various opportunities for positive connection with others is supported not just by neural synchrony, but by the hormone oxytocin as well.

Biochemistries in Love

Oxytocin, which is nicknamed by some the "cuddle hormone" or the "love hormone," is actually more properly identified as a neuropeptide because it acts not just within your body but also within your brain. Oxytocin has long been known to play a key role in social bonding and attachment. Clear evidence of this first emerged from experiments with a monogamous breed of prairie voles: Oxytocin, when dripped into one animal's brain in the presence of the opposite sex, creates in that animal a long-lasting preference to remain together with the other, cuddled up side by side, behavior taken as evidence that oxytocin sparked the formation of a powerful social bond between them. In humans, oxytocin surges during sexual intercourse for both men and women, and, for women, during childbirth and lactation, pivotal interpersonal moments that stand to forge new social bonds or cement existing ones. The natural blasts of oxytocin during such moments are so large and powerful that for many years they all but blinded scientists to the more subtle ebb and flow of oxytocin during more typical day-to-day activities, like playing with your kids, getting to know your new neighbor, or striking a deal with a new business partner. Technical obstacles also needed to be cleared. Decades after oxytocin's role in monogamous prairie voles had been amply charted, scientists studying human biochemistry still struggled to find ways to reliably and noninvasively measure and manipulate oxytocin during natural behavior. Scientific understanding of oxytocin's role in your everyday social life could not advance without more practical research tools at hand.

Dramatic new evidence of oxytocin's power to shape your social life first surfaced in Europe, where laws permitted the use of a synthetic form of oxytocin, available as a nasal spray, for investigational purposes. Among the first of these studies was one in which 128 men from Zurich played the so-called trust game with real monetary outcomes on the line. At random, these men were assigned to either the role of "investor" or the role of "trustee," and each was given an equivalent pot of starting funds. Investors made the first move in the game. They could give some, all, or none of their allocated funds to the trustee. During the transfer of funds, the experimenter tripled their investment while letting the trustee know how much the investors had originally transferred. Trustees made the next move. They could give some, all, or none of their new allotment of funds (the investors' tripled investment plus their own original allocation) back to investors. The structure of the game puts investors, but not trustees, at risk. If an investor chose to entrust the other guy with his investment, he risked receiving nothing in return if the trustee chose to selfishly keep the entire monetary gain for himself. But if the trustee was fair, they could each double their money.

Prior to playing this trust game, using a double-blind research design, participants received either oxytocin or an inert placebo by nasal spray. The effect of this single intranasal blast of oxytocin on the outcome of the trust game was dramatic: The number of investors who trusted their entire allotment to their trustee more than doubled. Interestingly, related research using this same trust game showed that the mere act of being entrusted with another person's money raises the trustee's naturally occurring levels of oxytocin, and that the greater the trustee's oxytocin rise, the more of his recent windfall he sacrificed back to the investor. The neuropeptide oxytocin, then, steers the actions of both the investor and the trustee, shaping both trust and reciprocity. These findings suggest that through synchronous oxytocin surges, trust and cooperation can quickly become mutual.

Since the original study on oxytocin and the trust game was published in *Nature* in 2005, variations on it have abounded. We now know, for instance, that oxytocin doesn't simply make people more trusting with money, it also makes them far more trusting—a whopping 44 percent more trusting—with confidential information about themselves. Interestingly, the simple act of sharing an important secret from your life with someone you just met increases your naturally circulating levels of oxytocin, which in turn raises your confidence that you can trust that person to guard your privacy. Thankfully, we also know that oxytocin does not induce trust indiscriminately, making people gullible and therefore open to exploitation. The effects of oxytocin on trust turn out to be quite sensitive to interpersonal cues, like those subtle signs that tip you off that another may be the gambling type or irresponsible in other ways. Rest assured, then, if oxytocin spray were to be aerated through your workplace ventilation system, you'd still maintain your shrewd attunement to subtle signs that suggest whether someone is worthy of your trust or not.

Researchers have since moved on to examine the effects of oxytocin on people's sensitivities to the subtle social cues that signal whether or not trust is warranted. From this work, I can tell you that, under the influence of oxytocin, you attend more to people's eyes and become specifically more attuned to their smiles, especially subtle ones. Perhaps because of the closer attention you pay to peoples' smiles and eyes, you become a better judge of their feelings and view people on the whole as more attractive and trustworthy. You also become particularly sensitized to environmental cues linked to positive social connections—for instance, to words like *love* and *kissing*. Researchers who have combined the use of oxytocin nasal spray (versus placebo) with brain imaging have also learned that oxytocin modulates the activity of your amygdala, the subcortical structure deep within your brain linked to emotional processing. Specifically, under the influence of a single blast of oxytocin nasal spray, the parts of your amygdala that tune in to threats are muted, whereas the parts that tune in to positive social opportunities are amplified. Reflecting these negativity-dampening effects, a single shot of oxytocin can also help you glide through stressful social situations, like giving an impromptu speech or discussing a conflict-ridden topic with your spouse. If you were to face these difficulties under the influence of oxytocin, studies suggest, you'd have less cortisol, the so-called stress hormone, coursing through you, and you'd behave more positively, both verbally, by disclosing your feelings, and nonverbally, by making more eye contact and friendly gestures. Related research shows that behaving kindly in these ways also raises your naturally occurring levels of oxytocin, which in turn curbs stress-induced rises in heart rate and blood pressure, reduces feelings of depression, and increases your pain thresholds.

More generally, oxytocin has been cast as a lead character in the mammalian *calm-and-connect* response, a distinct cascade of brain and body responses best contrasted to the far more familiar *fight-or-flight* response. Let's face it, meeting new people can be a little scary at times. Think back to what it was like for you on your first day at a new school or in a new job. You're suddenly thrown in with people you'd never heard of before. Even if a new person seems friendly, it's hard to know his true motives. Will he help you? Or will he instead take advantage of you in one way or another? Human greed, after all, runs rampant and can yield all manner of exploitation. Oxytocin appears both to *calm* fears that might steer you away from interacting with strangers and also to sharpen your skills for *connection*. As I've mentioned, though, oxytocin is far from blind. It indeed heightens your attunement to cues that signal whether others are sincere or not. Through eye contact and close attention to all manner of smiles—and the embodied simulations such visual intake triggers—your gut instincts about whom to trust and whom not to trust become more reliable. Rather than avoid all new people out of fear and suspicion, oxytocin helps you pick up on cues that signal another person's goodwill and guides you to approach them with your own. Because all people need social connections, not just to reproduce, but to survive and thrive in this world, oxytocin has been dubbed "the great facilitator of life."

It, too, can jump the gap between people such that someone else's oxytocin flow can trigger your own. A biochemical synchrony can then emerge that supports mutual engagement, care, and responsiveness.

The clearest evidence that oxytocin rises and falls in synchrony between people comes from studies of infants and their parents. When an infant and a parent—either mom or dad—interact, sometimes they are truly captivated by each other, and other times not. When an infant and parent do click, their coordinated motions and emotions show lots of mutual positive engagement. Picture moms or dads showering their baby with kisses, tickling their baby's tiny fingers and toes, smiling at their baby, and speaking to him or her in that high-pitched, singsong tone that scientists call *motherese*. These parents are superattentive. As they tickle and coo they're also closely tracking their baby's face for signs that their delight is mutual. In step with their parent's affectionate antics, these attentive babies babble, coo, smile, and giggle. Positivity resonates back and forth between them. Micro-moments of love blossom.

Of course, not every infant-parent interaction is so rosy. Some pairs show little mutual engagement. Some moms and dads rarely make eye contact with their infants and emit precious little positivity, either verbally or nonverbally. These pairs are simply less attuned to each other, less connected. And in those rare moments when they are engaged, the vibe that joins them is distinctly more negative. They connect over mutual distress or indifference, rather than over mutual affection.

It turns out that positive behavioral synchrony—the degree to which an infant and a parent (through eye contact and affectionate touch) laugh, smile, and coo together—goes hand in hand with oxytocin synchrony. Researchers have measured oxytocin levels in the saliva of dads, moms, and infants both before and after a videotaped, face-to-face parent-infant interaction. For infant-parent pairs who show mutual positive engagement, oxytocin levels also come into sync. Without such engagement, however, no oxytocin synchrony emerges.

Positivity resonance, then, can be viewed as the doorway through which the exquisitely attuned biochemical tendencies of one generation influence those of the next generation to form lasting, often lifelong bonds. Knowing, too, that oxytocin can ebb and flow in unison among non-kin—even among brand-new acquaintances just learning to trust each other—micro-moments of love, of positivity resonance, can also be viewed as the doorways through which caring and compassionate communities are forged. Love, we know, builds lasting resources. Oxytocin, studies show, swings the hammer.

This core tenet of my broaden-and-build theory—that love builds lasting resources—finds support in a fascinating program of research on ... rodents. It turns out that rat moms and their newborn pups show a form of positive engagement and synchrony analogous to that of human parents with their infants. Sensitive parenting in a rat mom, however, is conveyed by her attentively licking and grooming her newborn pups. When a rat mom licks and grooms her pup, it increases the pup's sensitivity to oxytocin, as indicated, for instance, by the number of oxytocin receptors deep within the pup's amygdala, as well as within other subcortical brain regions. Sure enough, these well-groomed—or I dare say well-*loved*—rat pups grow up to have calmer demeanors; they're less skittish, more curious. The researchers can be certain that it's the experiences of loving connection that determine the brain and behavioral profiles of the next generation (that is, their oxytocin receptors and calm demeanors)—and not simply shared genes—because cross-fostering studies show the same patterns of results. That is, even when a rat mom raises a newborn pup that is not her own, her maternal attention still forecasts that pup's brain sensitivity to oxytocin and whether it grows up to be anxious or calm.

Touring Vagus

Who you are today is also shaped by the third biological character that I want you to meet: your tenth cranial nerve. This key conduit connects your brain to your body and is also called your vagus nerve (sounds like Vegas, as in Las Vegas). It emerges from your brain stem deep within your skull and, although it makes multiple stops at your various internal organs, perhaps most significantly it connects your brain to your heart. You already know that your heart rate shoots up when you feel insulted or threatened—registering the ancestral fight-or-flight response—but you may not know that it's your vagus nerve that eventually soothes your racing heart, by orchestrating (together with oxytocin) the equally ancestral calm-and-connect response.

Keeping in mind that love *is* connection, you should know that your vagus nerve is a biological asset that supports and coordinates your experiences of love. Completely outside of your awareness, your vagus nerve stimulates tiny facial muscles that better enable you to make eye contact and synchronize your facial expressions with another person. It even adjusts the minuscule muscles of your middle ear so you can better track the other person's voice against any background noise. In these exquisitely subtle yet consequential ways, your vagus nerve increases the odds that the two of you will connect, upping your chances for positivity resonance.

Scientists can measure the strength of your vagus nerve—your biological aptitude for love—simply by tracking your heart rate in conjunction with your breathing rate. Specifically, I can look at the degree to which your heart rate, as tracked by sensors placed on your lowest ribs, is patterned by your breathing rate, as revealed by an expandable bellows that encircles your rib cage. This pattern is called *vagal tone*. Like muscle tone, the higher your vagal tone, the better.

In addition to putting the brakes on the big jumps in your heart rate that may be caused by stress, fear, or exertion, your vagus nerve also increases the routine efficiency of your heart, beat by beat, or more precisely, breath by breath. The human heart rate tends to run fairly high, as if we're always on guard for the next danger that might be hidden around the corner. When you're breathing in, a fast heart rate is an efficient heart rate. After all, each successive heartbeat during an in-breath circulates more freshly oxygenated blood throughout your brain and body. Yet when you're breathing out, a fast heart rate is not all that helpful because your supply of freshly oxygenated blood is waning. Here again, your vagus nerve steps in to help out. It can very gently apply the brake on your heart while you exhale, slowing your heart rate down a small degree. In turn your vagus nerve can gently let up on the brake while you inhale, letting your naturally high heart rate resume to grab all the oxygenated blood that it can get. This creates a subtle yet healthy pattern of cardiac arrhythmia: Your heart rate speeds up a bit when you inhale and slows down a bit when you exhale. This is the pattern that reflects your vagal tone, the strength or condition of your vagus nerve. It characterizes the nimbleness with which your primitive, nonconscious brain holds the reins on your galloping heart.

I give you this quick tour of vagus because this conduit within you, between your brain and your heart, has a story to tell about how attuned you are to sources of love in your midst. It even makes a quiet prediction about what illnesses may beset you and how long you're likely to live. Your biological propensities for love and health are intimately intertwined. Measured at rest, vagal tone also tends to be extraordinarily stable over time. For most people, it remains roughly the same year after year, rhythmically channeling them toward loneliness or social prosperity, sickness or health.

That's because people with higher vagal tone, science has shown, are more flexible across a whole host of domains—physical, mental, and social. They simply adapt better to their ever-shifting circumstances, albeit completely at non-conscious levels. Physically, they regulate their internal bodily processes more efficiently, like their glucose levels and inflammation. Mentally, they're better able to regulate their attention and emotions, even their behavior. Socially, they're especially skillful in navigating interpersonal interactions and in forging positive connections with others. By definition, then, they experience more micro-moments of love. It's as though the agility of the conduit between their brains and hearts—as reflected in their high vagal tone—allows them to be exquisitely agile, attuned, and flexible as they navigate the ups and downs of day-to-day life and social exchanges. High vagal tone, then, can be taken as high loving potential. Indeed, this is what doctoral student Bethany Kok and I have found: Compared to people with lower vagal tone, those with higher vagal tone experience more love in their daily lives, more moments of positivity resonance.

You might now be wondering whether you're one of the lucky ones blessed with high vagal tone. If you are, that's great. Yet even if you're not advantaged with high vagal tone today, the latest science gives plenty of reason for hope. Just as you can build muscle tone through regular physical exercises, you can build vagal tone…. The key, once again, is the power of love.

My students and I work together in what I call the PEP Lab, or the Positive Emotions and Psychophysiology Laboratory. Not long ago, we conducted an experiment on the effects of learning the ancient mind-training practice of loving-kindness meditation. Our study participants visited the PEP Lab at the University of North Carolina one by one, and we measured their vagal tone while they sat and relaxed for a few minutes. At the end of this initial laboratory testing session, we instructed participants how to log on to the study website each evening to record their emotions and social connections of the day. A few weeks later, by random assignment, we determined which participants would learn loving-kindness meditation and which would not. All would continue to monitor their day-to-day emotions and social connections using our study website. Months later, weeks after the meditation workshop ended, one by one we invited all participants back to the PEP Lab, where we again measured their vagal tone under the same resting conditions as before….

[It] was those study participants who had been assigned at random to learn loving-kindness meditation who changed the most. They devoted scarcely more than an hour of their time each week to the practice. Yet within a matter of months, completely unbeknownst to them, their vagus nerves began to respond more readily to the rhythms of their breathing, emitting more of that healthy arrhythmia that is the fingerprint of high vagal tone. Breath by breath—loving moment by loving moment—their capacity for positivity resonance matured. Moreover, through painstaking statistical analyses, we pinpointed that those who experienced the most frequent positivity resonance in connection with others showed the biggest increases in vagal tone. Love literally made people healthier.

Upward Spirals Unleashed

It's time now to step back from isolated scientific findings and take in the big picture. Recall that your body's positivity resonance operates within a much larger system. Along with love and all the other positive emotions, this system also includes your enduring resources—your physical health, your social bonds, your personality traits, and your resilience. Having assets like these certainly makes life easier, and more satisfying. In addition, though, such resources also serve as booster shots that increase the frequency and intensity of your micro-moments of positivity resonance. Love built those resources in you, and those resources in turn boost your experiences of love. This is not a simple case of cause and effect. The causal arrow instead runs in both directions at once, creating the dynamic and reciprocal causality that drives self-sustaining trajectories of growth. Through love, you become a better version of yourself. And as your better self, you experience love more readily. It is in this dance between your enduring resources and your micro-moments of love that life-giving upward spirals are born.

... By learning how to self-generate love, you can raise your vagal tone. And with higher vagal tone, your attention and actions become more agile, more attuned to the people in your midst. You become better able to forge the interpersonal connections that give rise to positivity resonance. Through vagal tone, then, love begets love.

Likewise, evidence suggests that positivity resonance raises your oxytocin levels. And under the influence of oxytocin, you grow calmer, more attuned to others, friendlier, and more open. Here, too, your skills for forging connections sharpen, which increases your ability to cultivate positivity resonance. Through oxytocin as well then, love begets love.

Recall, too, that positive connections with others create neural coupling, or synchronous brain activity between people. With repetition, positivity resonance also produces structural changes in the brain, for instance, rendering the threat-detecting amygdala more sensitive to the calming influence of oxytocin. While much of the work on neuroplasticity—the brain's capacity to change with experience—comes from research on nonhuman animals, tantalizing evidence has also recently emerged from studies of humans. Becoming a parent, for instance, not only opens the door for parent-infant positivity resonance but also appears to usher in structural changes in brain regions that facilitate positivity resonance. This research shows how love reroutes the neural wiring of your brain, making it more likely that you'll have healthy habits and healthy social bonds in the future. Through brain plasticity, too, then, love begets love.

Plasticity, or openness to change, characterizes your body's cells as well. New cells are born within you all the time. Even now, as you take time to read this book, new cells are coming online within you, taking their predetermined place within the massive orchestra of communication and mutual influence that you call your body. Yet not everything about the birth of your new cells is scripted in advance by your DNA. Some aspects are open to contextual influences signaled by the changing biochemicals that course through you. If you feel lonely and disconnected from others, for instance, your circulating levels of the stress hormone cortisol will rise. Your cortisol levels, in turn, signal your immune system to alter the way your genes are expressed in your next-generation white blood cells, specifically making them less sensitive to cortisol. When this happens, studies show, your inflammatory response becomes more chronic, less responsive to cues that a crisis situation has subsided. This is how, over time, chronic feelings of loneliness can weaken people's immune systems and open the door to inflammation-based chronic illnesses, like cardiovascular disease and arthritis. The data go further to suggest that *feeling* isolated or unconnected to others does more bodily damage than *actual* isolation, suggesting that painful emotions drive the bodily systems that in turn steer you toward dire health outcomes. By tracking how your emotions—and the biochemical changes they trigger—alter gene expression within your immune system, the tools of molecular biology now show how a lack of love compromises your immunity and your health.

Even so, there is ample reason for hope. In countless social exchanges each day, your potential to alleviate loneliness with love is enormous. Your biology, as we have seen in this chapter, enacts your experiences of love. Even so, you have more control over your biology than you realize. Once you grasp the pathways and common obstacles to love, you gain a measure of control over the biochemicals that bathe your cells. To a considerable extent, you orchestrate the messages that your cells hear, the messages that tell your cells whether to grow toward health or toward illness. My collaborators and I are just beginning to chart the ways that oxytocin and other ingredients that make up love's biochemistry trigger healthy changes in gene expression that may foster physical and mental well-being. Also through the plasticity of your cells, we hypothesize, love begets love.

All of love's unseen biological transformations—in your brain rhythms, your blood stream, your vagus nerve, and your cells—in turn ready you to become even more attuned to love, better equipped, biologically, to cultivate moments of positivity resonance with others. This latent biological upward spiral is a powerful force: Love can affect you so deeply that it reshapes you from the inside out and by doing so alters your destiny for further loving moments. With each micro-moment of love, then, you climb another rung on the spiraling ladder that lifts you up to your higher ground, to richer and more compassionate social relationships, to greater resilience and wisdom, and to better physical health.

NOTES

106 **The Eskimos had fifty-two names for snow:** Margaret Atwood (1972). *Surfacing*. New York: Simon and Schuster.

108 **having at least one close relationship like this is vital to your health and happiness, to be sure:** James S. House, Karl R. Landis, and Debra Umberson (1988). "Social relationships and health." *Science* 241(4865): 540–45. See also Ed Diener and Martin E. P. Seligman (2002). "Very happy people." *Psychological Science* 13(l): 81–84.

109 **The soul must always stand ajar, ready to welcome the ecstatic experience:** Emily Dickinson (1960). *The Complete Poems of Emily Dickinson*. Edited by Thomas Johnson. Boston: Little Brown.

109 *the social engagement system:* Stephen W. Porges (2003). "Social engagement and attachment: A phylogenetic perspective." *Annals of the New York Academy of Sciences* 1008: 31–47.

111 **the degree to which your brains lit up in synchrony with each other, matched in both space and time:** Greg J. Stephens, Lauren J. Silbert, and Uri Hasson (2010). "Speaker-listener neural coupling underlies successful communication." *Proceedings of the National Academy of Sciences (USA)* 107(32): 14425–30. See also Uri Hasson (2010). "I can make your brain look like mine." *Harvard Business Review*, December.

111 **voice can convey so much emotion:** Klaus R. Scherer, Tom Johnstone, and Gudrun Klasmeyer (2009). "Vocal expression of emotion." In *Handbook of Affective Sciences*, edited by Richard J. Davidson, Klaus R. Scherer, and Hill H. Goldsmith, pp. 433–56. New York: Oxford University Press; and Jo-Anne Bachorowski and Michael J. Owren (2008). "Vocal expressions of emotion." In *The Handbook of Emotions*, 3rd ed., edited by Michael Lewis, Jeanette M. Haviland-Jones, and Lisa Feldman Barrett, pp. 196–210.

112 **Your knowing is not just abstract and conceptual; it's embodied and physical:** Paula N. Niedenthal, Martial Mermillod, Marcus Maringer, and Ursula Hess (2010). "The Simulation of Smiles (SIMS) model: Embodied stimulation and the meaning of facial expressions." *Behavioral and Brain Sciences* 33(6): 417–80.

112 **Brain coupling, Hasson argues, is the means by which we understand each other:** You might be wondering how Hasson and his team can be so sure they've captured communication, a true transfer of information from one brain to another, and not simply matched responses to listening to the same sounds, like hearing your own voice, or the incomprehensible dialogue from a foreign-language film. They ruled this out by having listeners also hear a story in Russian (which none of them understood). In that case, virtually no neural coupling emerged.

112 **a single act, performed by two brains:** Hasson (2010), p. 1.

112 **the insula, an area linked with conscious feeling states:** A. D. (Bud) Craig (2009). "How do you feel—now? The anterior insula and human awareness." *Nature Reviews Neuroscience* 10: 59–70.

113 **people's brains come particularly into sync during emotional moments:** Uri Hasson, Yuval Nir, Ifat Levy, Galit Fuhrmann, and Rafael Malach (2004). "Intersubject synchronization of cortical activity during natural vision." *Science* 303: 1634–40.

113 **your awareness expands from your habitual focus on "me" to a more generous focus on "we":** This is work I described in my first book, *Positivity* (2009). See especially chapter 4.

114 **as if to prevent their pain from becoming your pain:** Yawei Cheng, Chenyi Chen, Ching-Po Lin, Kun-Hsien Chou, and Jean Decety (2010). "Love hurts: An fMRI study." *Neuroimage* 51: 923–29. See also work by Mary Helen Immordino-Yang, Andrea McColl, Hanna Damasio, and Antonio Damasio (2009). "Neural correlates of admiration and compassion." *Proceedings of the National Academy of Sciences (USA)* 106(19): 8021–26.

114 **stifled emotions … can also function as obstacles to positivity resonance:** For support for this idea, see work by Iris Mauss and colleagues. It suggests that stifled positivity erodes social connection and thereby limits well-being. Iris B. Mauss, Amanda J. Shallcross, Allison S. Troy, Oliver P. John, Emilio Ferrer, Frank H. Wilhelm, and James J. Gross (2011). "Don't hide your happiness! Positive emotion dissociation, social connectedness, and psychological functioning." *Journal of Personality and Social Psychology* 100(4): 738–48.

114 **oxytocin sparked the formation of a powerful social bond between them:** Jessie R. Williams, Thomas R. Insel, Carroll R. Harbaugh, and C. Sue Carter (1994). "Oxytocin administered centrally facilitates formation of partner preference in female prairie voles (microtus ochrogaster)." *Journal of Neuroendocrinology* 6: 247–50. See also work by Mary M. Cho, A. Courtney DeVries, Jessie R. Williams, and C. Sue Carter (1999). "The effects of oxytocin and vasopressin on partner preferences in male and female prairie voles (microtus ochrogaster)." *Behavioral Neuroscience* 113(5): 1071–79.

114 **oxytocin surges during sexual intercourse:** Marie S. Carmichael, Richard Humbert, Jean Dixon, Glenn Palmisano, Walter Greenleaf, and Julian M. Davidson (1987). "Plasma oxytocin increases in the human sexual response." *Journal of Clinical Endocrinology and Metabolism* 64(1): 27–31.

114 **a synthetic form of oxytocin, available as a nasal spray, for investigational purposes:** Synthetic oxytocin has now been approved for limited investigational use within the United States by the U.S. Federal Drug Administration.

115 **a double-blind research design:** This is the gold standard in human science: Neither the researchers nor the participants are aware of who receives which nasal spray—the spray with the drug or the chemically inert spray that serves as the placebo control.

115 **trusted their entire allotment to their trustee more than doubled:** Michael Kosfeld, Markus Heinrichs, Paul J. Zak, Urs Fischbacher, and Ernst Fehr (2005). "Oxytocin increases trust in humans." *Nature* 435(2): 673–76.

115 **the mere act of being entrusted with another person's money raises the trustee's naturally occurring levels of oxytocin, and that the greater the trustee's oxytocin rise, the more of his recent windfall he sacrificed back to the investor:** Paul J. Zak, Robert Kurzban, and William T. Matzner (2005). "Oxytocin is associated with human trustworthiness." *Hormones and Behavior* 48: 522–27. Interestingly, the effect of being trusted on circulating oxytocin and monetary sacrifice is far higher if trustees have just had a shoulder massage. See Vera B. Morhenn, Jang Woo Park, Elisabeth Piper, and Paul J. Zak (2008). "Monetary sacrifice among strangers is mediated by endogenous oxytocin release after physical contact." *Evolution and Human Behavior* 29: 375–83.

115 **more trusting—a whopping 44 percent more trusting—with confidential information about themselves:** Moira Mikolajczak, Nicolas Pinon, Anthony Lane, Philippe de Timary, and Olivier Luminet (2010). "Oxytocin not only increases trust when money is at stake, but also when confidential information is in the balance." *Biological Psychology* 85: 182–84.

115 **sharing an important secret from your life with someone you just met increases your naturally circulating levels of oxytocin:** Szabolcs Keri and Imre Kiss (2011). "Oxytocin response in a trust game and habituation of arousal." *Physiology and Behavior* 102: 221–24. The effect of telling secrets on oxytocin holds unless you are diagnosed with schizophrenia; see Szabolcs Keri, Imre Kiss, and Oguz Keleman (2009). "Sharing secrets: Oxytocin and trust in schizophrenia." *Social Neuroscience* 4(4): 287–93.

115 **The effects of oxytocin on trust turn out to be quite sensitive to interpersonal cues:** Moiri Mikolajczak, James J. Gross, Anthony Lane, Olivier Corneille, Philippe de Timary, and Olivier Luminet (2010). "Oxytocin makes people trusting, not gullible." *Psychological Science* 21(8): 1072–74. Likewise, oxytocin seems to especially promote trust with in-group members; see Carsten K. W. De Dreu, Lidred L. Greer, Gerben A. Van Kleef, Shaul Shalvi, and Michel J. J. Handgraaf (2010). "Oxytocin promotes human ethnocentrism." *Proceedings of the National Academy of Sciences (USA)* 108(4): 1262–66.

115 **under the influence of oxytocin, you attend more to people's eyes:** Adam J. Guastella, Philip B. Mitchell, and Mark R. Dadds (2008). "Oxytocin increases gaze to the eye region of human faces." *Biological Psychiatry* 63: 3–5.

115 **more attuned to their smiles, especially subtle ones:** Abigail A. Marsh, Henry H. Yu, Daniel S. Pine, and R. J. R. Blair (2010). "Oxytocin improves specific recognition of positive facial expressions." *Psychopharmacology* 209: 225–32.

115 **a better judge of their feelings:** Gregor Domes, Markus Heinrichs, Andre Michel, Christoph Berger, and Sabine C. Herpertz (2007). "Oxytocin improves 'mind-reading' in humans." *Biological Psychiatry* 61: 731–33.

115 **view people on the whole as more attractive and trustworthy:** Angeliki Theodoridou, Angela C. Rowe, Ian S. Penton-Voak, and Peter J. Rogers (2009). "Oxytocin and social perception: Oxytocin increases perceived facial trustworthiness and attractiveness." *Hormones and Behavior* 56: 128–132.

115 **particularly sensitized to environmental cues linked to positive social connections—for instance, to words like** *love and kissing:* Christian Unkelback, Adam J. Guastella, and Joseph P. Forgas (2008). "Oxytocin selectively facilitates recognition of positive sex and relationship words." *Psychological Science* 19(11): 1092–94.

116 **the parts of your amygdala that tune in to threats are muted, whereas the parts that tune in to positive social opportunities are amplified:** Matthias Gamer, Bartosz Zurowski, and Christian Buchel (2010). "Different amygdala subregions mediate valence-related and attentional effects of oxytocin in humans." *Proceedings of the National Academy of Sciences (USA)* 107(20): 9400–9405. See also: Peter Kirsch, Christine Esslinger, Qiang Chen, et al. (2005). "Oxytocin modulates neural circuitry for social cognition and fear in humans." *Journal of Neuroscience* 25(49): 11489–93; and Predrag Petrovic, Raffael Kalisch, Tania Singer, and Raymond J. Dolan (2008). "Oxytocin attenuates affective evaluations of conditioned faces and amygdale activity." *Journal of Neuroscience* 28(26): 6607–15.

116 **If you were to face these difficulties under the influence of oxytocin, studies suggest:** Beate Ditzen, Marcel Schaer, Barbara Gabriel, et al. (2009). "Intranasal oxytocin increases positive communication and reduces cortisol levels during couple conflict." *Biological Psychiatry* 65: 728–731. See also work by Markus Heinrichs, Thomas Baumgartner, Clemens Kirschbaum, and Ulrike Ehlert (2003). "Social support and oxytocin interact to suppress cortisol and subjective responses to psychosocial stress." *Biological Psychiatry* 54: 1389–98.

116 **behaving kindly in these ways also raises your naturally occurring levels of oxytocin, which in turn curbs stress-induced rises in heart rate and blood pressure:** Julianne Holt-Lunstad, Wendy A. Birmingham, and Kathleen Light (2008). "Influence of a 'warm touch' support enhancement intervention among married couples on ambulatory blood pressure, oxytocin, alpha amylase, and corti-sol." *Psychosomatic Medicine* 70: 976–85. See also forthcoming experimental work by Stephanie L. Brown, early versions of which she presented in a talk at the Society for Experimental Social Psychology meeting in October 2011 entitled "Prosocial behavior and health: Towards a biological model of a caregiving system."

116 **reduces feelings of depression, and increases your pain thresholds:** Kerstin Uvnäs-Moberg, E. Bjorkstrand, Viveka Hillegaart, and S. Ahlenius (1999). "Oxytocin as a possible mediator of SSRI-induced antidepressant effects." *Psychopharmacology* 142(1): 95–101. See also work by Maria Petersson, Pawel Alster, Thomas Lundeberg, and Kerstin Uvnäs-Moberg (1996). "Oxytocin increases nociceptive thresholds in a long-term perspective in female and male rats." *Neuroscience Letters* 212(2): 87–90.

116 **the mammalian *calm-and-connect* response:** Kerstin Uvnäs-Moberg, Ingemar Arn, and David Magnusson (2005). "The psychobiology of emotion: The role of the oxytocinergic system." *International Journal of Behavioral Medicine* 12(2): 59–65. See also Kerstin Uvnäs-Moberg's 2003 book written for a general audience, *The Oxytocin Factor: Tapping the Hormone of Calm, Love and Healing.* New York: Perseus.

116 **Human greed, after all, runs rampant and can yield all manner of exploitation:** Compelling new insights on the nature of greed can be drawn from new experimental research on social class. See work by Paul K. Piff, Daniel M. Stancato, Stephané Côté, Rodolfo Mendoza-Denton, and Dacher Keltner (2012). "Higher social class predicts increased unethical behavior." *Proceedings of the National Academy of Sciences (USA)* 109(11): 4086–91.

116 **Oxytocin appears both to calm fears that might steer you away from interacting with strangers and also to sharpen your skills for *connection:*** Anne Campbell (2009). "Oxytocin and human social behavior." *Personality and Social Psychological Review* 14(3): 281–95.

116 **your gut instincts about whom to trust and whom not to trust become more reliable:** Niedenthal et al. (2010).

116 **oxytocin has been dubbed "the great facilitator of life":** Heon-Jin Lee, Abbe H. Macbeth, Jerome H. Pagani, and W. Scott Young, III (2009). "Oxytocin: The great facilitator of life." *Progress in Neurobiology* 88(2): 127–51.

117 **Without such engagement, however, no oxytocin synchrony emerges:** Ruth Feldman, Ilanit Gordon, and Orna Zagoory-Sharon (2010). "The cross-generation transmission of oxytocin in humans." *Hormones and Behavior* 58: 669–76.

117 **When a rat mom licks and grooms her pup, it increases the pup's sensitivity to oxytocin:** Frances A. Champagne, Ian C. G. Weaver, Josie Diorio, Sergiy

Dymov, Moshe Szyf, and Michael J. Meaney (2006). "Maternal care associated with methylation of the estrogen receptor-α1b promoter and estrogen receptor-α1b expression in the medial preoptic area of female off-spring." *Endocrinology* 147(6): 2909–15.

118 **your vagus nerve increases the odds that the two of you will connect:** Porges (2003).

119 **regulate their internal bodily processes more efficiently, like their glucose levels and inflammation:** Julian F. Thayer and Esther Sternberg (2006). "Beyond heart rate variability: Vagal regulation of allostatic systems." *Annals of the New York Academy of Sciences* 1088: 361–72.

119 **better able to regulate their attention and emotions, even their behavior:** Stephen W. Porges, Jane A. Doussard-Roosevelt, and Ajit Maiti (1994), "Vagal tone and the physiological regulation of emotion." *Monographs of the Society for Research in Child Development* 59(2/3): 167–86.

119 **especially skillful in navigating interpersonal interactions and in forging positive connections with others:** Kok and Fredrickson (2010).

119 **those with higher vagal tone experience more love in their daily lives, more moments of positivity resonance:** Kok and Fredrickson (2010).

120 **their vagus nerves began to respond more readily to the rhythms of their breathing, emitting more of that healthy arrhythmia that is the fingerprint of high vagal tone:** Kok, et al. (in press).

120 **Having assets like these certainly makes life easier, and more satisfying:** Michael A. Cohn, Barbara L. Fredrickson, Stephanie L. Brown, et al. (2009). "Happiness unpacked: Positive emotions increase life satisfaction by building resilience." *Emotion* 9(3): 361–68.

120 **appears to usher in structural changes in brain regions that facilitate positivity resonance:** Pil Young Kim (2009). "The interplay of brain and experience in parental love." *Dissertation Abstracts International: Section B: The Sciences and Engineering* 70(6-B): 3810.

121 **your inflammatory response becomes more chronic, less responsive to cues that a crises situation has subsided:** Steve W. Cole (2009). "Social regulation of human gene expression." *Current Directions in Psychological Science* 18(3): 132–37.

121 *feeling* **isolated or unconnected to others does more bodily damage than** *actual* **isolation:** Steve W. Cole, Louise C. Hawkley, Jesusa M. Arevalo, et al. (2007). "Social regulation of gene expression in human leukocytes." *Genomic Biology* 8: R189.

121 **you orchestrate the messages that your cells hear, the messages that tell your cells whether to grow toward health or toward illness:** Of course, other forces are at work as well. You do not hold sole responsibility (or blame) for your health or illness via the emotions you experience. In other words, please do not use this science to blame those who suffer from illnesses for their own fate. For a sharp critique of how science can be misused in this manner, see Barbara Ehrenreich (2009). *Bright-Sided: How the Relentless Promotion of Positive Thinking Has Undermined America.* New York: Metropolitan Books.

121 **just beginning to chart the ways that oxytocin and other ingredients that make up love's biochemistry trigger healthy changes in gene expression:** In ongoing research funded by the U.S. National Institutes of Health (R01NR012899)

I've teamed up with Steve W. Cole, director of UCLA's Social Genomics Core Laboratory, to examine how learning loving-kindness meditation may alter people's patterns of gene expression. We are especially interested in changes that may occur in the cells that regulate inflammatory processes in the immune system.

QUESTIONS FOR MAKING CONNECTIONS
WITHIN THE READING

1. Fredrickson, a psychologist, claims to reveal the "true meaning of love as your body experiences it." What does she imply by distinguishing between your body and you? Are you identical to your body, and how do you normally think about your body's relation to yourself? How does the body's experience differ from the experience of the mind? In Fredrickson's account of love, what role does the body play? When Fredrickson instructs you to "set aside the take on love your family might have offered you" and to suspend the "view of love as a special bond or relationship," does she mean that such views of love are incorrect, or does she simply want us to approach the subject from a different angle?

2. Since the time of Plato, Western thinkers have been fascinated—and frustrated—by the relations between the mind and the body. The body was described as material—made of matter—whereas the mind was immaterial, supposedly *pure thought*. Does Fredrickson see body and mind as separate? Does her account suggest that emotions like love would exist at all without the body? If thoughts and feelings are impossible without the existence of the body, then what is the mind? Does Fredrickson suggest that our mental lives are completely determined by our biology, or do we have some degree of freedom?

3. What is gained by thinking about "love's biology" as a "system"? How is the body involved in the operation of this system? In what ways are other people part of the system? How much of the experience of love involves consciousness and how much happens below the threshold of our conscious minds? What are the implications of this research for our thinking about the nature of the self? Does the self exist only by virtue of its relations to others in a system of some kind? What other systems can you think of, and how might they be compared to the one that creates the experience of love?

QUESTIONS FOR WRITING

1. A long tradition in many cultures represents suffering as redemptive. Suffering is believed to instill greater patience, endurance, and strength of will. To what degree does Fredrickson take issue with this view, at least implicitly? How can positive emotions, even if they are sometimes subtle and brief,

help us become more flexible, attuned to others and creative? If positive emotions can have the powerful effects that Fredrickson describes, why has suffering enjoyed such prestige as a path to truth? Could it be the case that many of our traditional ideas about love as a form of self-sacrifice are bound up with a mistaken view of suffering as redemptive?

2. If love is, as Fredrickson affirms, the "supreme" emotion, why do people frequently behave in a manner that seems very far removed from "positivity resonance"? Instead of speculating broadly, look back over the selection for clues: where does Fredrickson's account reveal potential vulnerabilities in the system? For example, Uri Hasson's work suggests that just as people can share positive emotions, they can transmit negative emotions as well. Because positivity is not guaranteed by our biology, Fredrickson's essay might be seen as an argument for a special kind of mental hygiene. If we understand our emotions more fully, can we live more happily? Can we change the world beyond ourselves by trying to be happier?

QUESTIONS FOR MAKING CONNECTIONS
BETWEEN READINGS

1. In his essay "Wisdom," Robert Thurman argues that the existence of the self is only temporary and conditioned by its surroundings. "Realizing your selflessness," he writes, "does not mean that you become a nobody, it means that you become the type of somebody who is a viable, useful somebody, not a rigid, fixated, I'm-the-center-of-the-universe, isolated from others somebody. You become the type of somebody who is over the idea of a conceptually fixed and self-created 'self.'" Would Fredrickson agree that we are basically selfless? How does positivity resonance change our relations to others, and could it be said to take us beyond the limits of ourselves? Does love make us more "fixed" or more fluid? What can we learn about ourselves from the fact that love, according to Fredrickson, is not just one of the many positive emotions we experience from time to time but has a special status as "our supreme emotion"?

2. Oliver Sacks in "The Mind's Eye," sets out to explore the relations between our minds and our brains. As he asks, "To what extent are we—our experiences, our reactions—shaped, predestined, by our brains, and to what extent do we shape our own brains? Does the mind run the brain or the brain the mind?" How might Fredrickson answer these questions? Clearly, the experience of love involves the brain in complex ways, but would Fredrickson reach the conclusion that our conscious lives are largely predetermined by our brain's activity? Does she agree that our conscious choices can change our cognitive habits, as they do in the case of the blind men and women Sacks writes about? Is it possible for us to consciously cultivate greater "positivity"?

DANIEL GILBERT

HISTORICALLY, THE STUDY of human psychology has tended to emphasize the negative. Scholars and practitioners of mental health focused on the mysteries of schizophrenia, depression, and other forms of psychological distress. In recent years, however, an interdisciplinary cohort of psychologists and other researchers have directed their attention to what turns out to be an equally misunderstood area: human happiness.

Among the leaders of this movement—sometimes called "positive psychology," or, more informally, "happiness studies"—is Daniel Gilbert, a professor of social psychology at Harvard University. Gilbert pioneered the field of affective forecasting, or the study of the way that people try to predict their future emotional states based on their current situation. In fact, these predictions are often incorrect. Having dropped out of high school to travel and write science fiction, Gilbert is well suited to explore the role that the unexpected can play in our search for happiness. While living in Denver, Colorado, Gilbert tried to enroll in a creative writing course at a local community college. Turned away because the class was over enrolled, he decided to take the only open course: psychology. Realizing that psychology "wasn't about crazy people" but "about all of us," Gilbert "stumbled" onto the path that brought him to the present.

In his international bestseller *Stumbling on Happiness* (2006), Gilbert argues that people suffer from "illusions of prospection." Through his experimental research, he learned of a remarkable discrepancy: even though few people believe they can predict what the future will bring, many more are convinced they can foresee how they will feel when the future arrives. Yet our predictions are often subject to a high degree of "impact bias," which leads us to overestimate just how intense our feelings will be, whether they are negative or positive.

The chapter from *Stumbling on Happiness* included here, "Immune to Reality," offers just some of Gilbert's counterintuitive discoveries. For example, we meet experimental subjects who fail to predict their level of happiness just minutes into the future. While we might not be surprised by their inability to make these predictions, we probably remain confident that we understand ourselves well enough to avoid the same mistakes. Gilbert also explains the

Quotations are drawn from an interview conducted by Dave Weich of Powell's books at <http://www.powells.com/blog/interviews/daniel-gilbert-stumbles-onto-something-big-by-dave/>.

operations of the "psychological immune system," which protects us when we suffer wrenching setbacks but not when we try to cope with minor ones, imparting a surprising complacency in the face of significant blows but often leaving us quite helpless when we deal with trivial irritations. Gilbert's conclusions challenge the conventional ways we understand our mental well-being by showing just how poorly these conventions reflect the reality of our emotional lives. Through their work, Gilbert and the other champions of happiness studies are seeking to reshape how we go about the "pursuit of happiness."

Immune to Reality

Upon my back, to defend my belly; upon my wit, to defend my wiles; upon my secrecy, to defend mine honesty; my mask, to defend my beauty.

—SHAKESPEARE, *THE HISTORY OF TROILUS AND CRESSIDA*

Albert Einstein may have been the greatest genius of the twentieth century, but few people know that he came *this* close to losing that distinction to a horse. Wilhelm von Osten was a retired schoolteacher who in 1891 claimed that his stallion, whom he called Clever Hans, could answer questions about current events, mathematics, and a host of other topics by tapping the ground with his foreleg. For instance, when Osten would ask Clever Hans to add three and five, the horse would wait until his master had finished asking the question, tap eight times, then stop. Sometimes, instead of *asking* a question, Osten would write it on a card and hold it up for Clever Hans to read, and the horse seemed to understand written language every bit as well as it understood speech. Clever Hans didn't get *every* question right, of course, but he did much better than anyone else with hooves, and his public performances were so impressive that he soon became the toast of Berlin. But in 1904 the director of the Berlin Psychological Institute sent his student, Oskar Pfungst, to look into the matter more carefully, and Pfungst noticed that Clever Hans was much more likely to give the wrong answer when Osten was standing in back of the horse than in front of it, or when Osten himself did not know the answer to the question the horse had been asked. In a series of experiments, Pfungst was able to show that Clever Hans could indeed read—but that what he could read was Osten's body language. When Osten bent slightly, Clever Hans would start tapping, and when Osten straightened up, or tilted his head a bit, or faintly raised an eyebrow,

Clever Hans would stop. In other words, Osten was signaling Clever Hans to start and stop tapping at just the right moments to create the illusion of horse sense.

Clever Hans was no genius, but Osten was no fraud. Indeed, he'd spent years patiently talking to his horse about mathematics and world affairs, and he was genuinely shocked and dismayed to learn that he had been fooling himself, as well as everyone else. The deception was elaborate and effective, but it was perpetrated unconsciously, and in this Osten was not unique. When we expose ourselves to favorable facts, notice and remember favorable facts, and hold favorable facts to a fairly low standard of proof, we are generally no more aware of our subterfuge than Osten was of his. We may refer to the processes by which the psychological immune system does its job as "tactics" or "strategies," but these terms—with their inevitable connotations of planning and deliberation—should not cause us to think of people as manipulative schemers who are consciously *trying* to generate positive views of their own experience. On the contrary, research suggests that people are *typically unaware* of the reasons why they are doing what they are doing,[1] but when asked for a reason, they readily supply one.[2] For example, when volunteers watch a computer screen on which words appear for just a few milliseconds, they are unaware of seeing the words and are unable to guess which words they saw. But they are influenced by them. When the word *hostile* is flashed, volunteers judge others negatively.[3] When the word *elderly* is flashed, volunteers walk slowly.[4] When the word *stupid* is flashed, volunteers perform poorly on tests.[5] When these volunteers are later asked to explain *why* they judged, walked, or scored the way they did, two things happen: First, they don't know, and second, they do not say, "I don't know." Instead, their brains quickly consider the facts of which they *are* aware ("I walked slowly") and draw the same kinds of plausible but mistaken inferences about themselves that an observer would probably draw about them ("I'm tired").[6]

When we cook facts, we are similarly unaware of why we are doing it, and this turns out to be a good thing, because *deliberate* attempts to generate positive views ("There must be *something* good about bankruptcy, and I'm not leaving this chair until I discover it") contain the seeds of their own destruction. Volunteers in one study listened to Stravinsky's *Rite of Spring*.[7] Some were told to listen to the music, and others were told to listen to the music while consciously trying to be happy. At the end of the interlude, the volunteers who had tried to be happy were in a *worse* mood than were the volunteers who had simply listened to the music. Why? Two reasons. First, we may be able deliberately to generate positive views of our own experiences if we close our eyes, sit very still, and do nothing else,[8] but research suggests that if we become even slightly distracted, these deliberate attempts tend to backfire and we end up feeling worse than we did before.[9] Second, deliberate attempts to cook the facts are so transparent that they make us feel cheap. Sure, we *want* to believe that we're better off without the fiancée who left us standing at the altar, and we *will* feel better as soon as we begin to discover facts that support this conclusion ("She was never really right for me, was she, Mom?"), but the process by which we discover those facts must *feel* like a discovery and not like a snow job. If we *see* ourselves cooking the facts ("If I phrase the question just this way and ask nobody but Mom, I stand a pretty good chance of having my favored conclusion confirmed"), then the jig is up and *self-deluded* joins *jilted* in our list of pitiful qualities. For positive views to be credible, they must be based on facts that we believe we have come upon honestly. We accomplish this by unconsciously cooking the facts and then consciously consuming them. The diner is in the dining room, but the chef is in the basement. The benefit of all this unconscious cookery is that it works, but the cost is that it makes us strangers to ourselves. Let me show you how.

LOOKING FORWARD TO LOOKING BACKWARD

To my knowledge, no one has ever done a systematic study of people who've been left standing at the altar by a cold-footed fiancé. But I'm willing to bet a good bottle of wine that if you rounded up a healthy sample of almost brides and nearly grooms and asked them whether they would describe the incident as "the worst thing that ever happened to me" or "the best thing that ever happened to me," more would endorse the latter description than the former. And I'll bet an entire *case* of that wine that if you found a sample of people who'd never been through this experience and asked them to predict which of all their possible future experiences they are most likely to look back on as "the best thing that ever happened to me," not one of them will list "getting jilted." Like so many things, getting jilted is more painful in prospect and more rosy in retrospect. When we contemplate being hung out to dry this way, we naturally generate the most dreadful possible view of the experience; but once we've actually *been* heartbroken and humiliated in front of our family, friends, and florists, our brains begin shopping for a less dreadful view—and as we've seen, the human brain is one smart shopper. However, because our brains do their shopping unconsciously, we tend not to realize they will do it at all; hence, we blithely assume that the dreadful view we have when we look forward to the event is the dreadful view we'll have when we look back on it. In short, we do not realize that our views will change because we are normally unaware of the processes that change them.

This fact can make it quite difficult to predict one's emotional future. In one study, volunteers were given the opportunity to apply for a good-paying job that involved nothing more than tasting ice cream and making up funny names for it.[10] The application procedure required the volunteer to undergo an on-camera interview. Some of the volunteers were told that their interview would be seen by a judge who had sole discretionary authority to decide whether they would be hired (judge group). Other volunteers were told that their interview would be seen by a jury whose members would vote to decide whether the volunteer should be hired (jury group). Volunteers in the jury group were told that as long as one juror voted for them, they would get the job—and thus the only circumstance under which they would *not* get the job was if the jury voted unanimously against them. All of the volunteers then underwent an interview, and

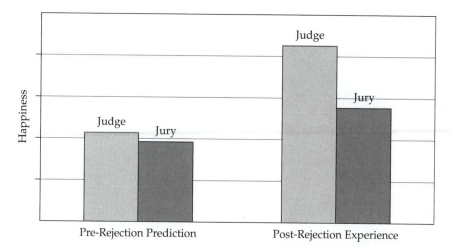

FIGURE Volunteers were happier when they were rejected by a capricious judge than by a unanimous jury (*bars on right*). But they could not foresee this moment before it happened (*bars on left*).

all predicted how they would feel if they didn't get the job. A few minutes later, the researcher came into the room and explained apologetically that after careful deliberation, the judge or jury had decided that the volunteer just wasn't quite right for the job. The researcher then asked the volunteers to report how they felt.

The results of the study are shown in the figure above. As the bars on the left show, volunteers in the two groups expected to feel equally unhappy. After all, rejection is a major whack on the nose, and we expect it to hurt whether the whacker is a judge, a jury, or a gang of Orthodox rabbis. And yet, as the bars on the right show, the whacks hurt more when they were administered by a jury than by a judge. Why? Well, just imagine that you've applied for a job as a swimsuit model, which requires that you don something skimpy and parade back and forth in front of some gimlet-eyed twit in a three-dollar suit. If the twit looked you over, shook his head, and said, "Sorry, but you're not model material," you'd probably feel bad. For a minute or two. But this is the sort of interpersonal rejection that everyone experiences from time to time, and after a few minutes, most of us get over it and go on with our lives. We do this quickly because our psychological immune systems have no trouble finding ways to exploit the ambiguity of this experience and soften its sting: "The guy wasn't paying attention to my extraordinary pivot," or "He's one of those weirdos who prefers height to weight," or "I'm supposed to take fashion advice from a guy with a suit like *that?*"

But now imagine that you've just modeled the skimpy thing for a whole roomful of people—some men, some women, some old, some young—and they all look you over and shake their heads in unison. You'd probably feel bad. Truly bad. Humiliated, hurt, and confused. You'd probably hurry offstage with a warm feeling in your ears, a tight feeling in your throat, and a wet feeling in your eyes. Being rejected by a large and diverse group of people is a demoralizing experience because it is so thoroughly unambiguous, and hence it is difficult for the psychological immune system to find a way to think about it that is both positive and credible. It's easy to blame failure on the eccentricities of a judge, but it's much more difficult to blame failure on the eccentricities of a unanimous jury. Claims such as "a synchronized mass blink caused ninety-four people to miss my pivot at precisely the same moment" are just not credible. Similarly, volunteers in this study found it easier to blame their rejection on an idiosyncratic judge than on a panel of jurors, which is why they felt worse when they were rejected by a jury.

Now, all this may seem painfully obvious to you as you contemplate the results of this study from the comfort of your sofa, but allow me to suggest that it is painfully obvious only after someone has taken pains to point it out to you. Indeed, if it were really painfully obvious, then why were a bunch of smart volunteers *unable to predict that it would happen just a few minutes before it did*? Why didn't the volunteers realize that they would have more success blaming a judge than a jury? Because when volunteers were asked to predict their emotional reactions to rejection, they imagined its sharp sting. Period. They did not go on to imagine how their brains might try to relieve that sting. Because they were unaware that they would alleviate their suffering by blaming those who caused it, it never occurred to them that they would be more successful if a single person were to blame rather than an entire group. Other studies have confirmed this general finding. For example, people *expect* to feel equally bad when a tragic accident is the result of human negligence as when it is the result of dumb luck, but they *actually* feel worse when luck is dumb and no one is blameworthy.[11]

Ignorance of our psychological immune systems causes us to mispredict the circumstances under which we will blame others, but it also causes us to mispredict the circumstances under which we will blame ourselves.[12] Who can forget the scene at the end of the 1942 film *Casablanca* in which Humphrey Bogart and Ingrid Bergman are standing on the tarmac as she tries to decide whether to stay in Casablanca with the man she loves or board the plane and leave with her husband? Bogey turns to Bergman and says: "Inside we both know you belong with Victor. You're part of his work, the thing that keeps him going. If that plane leaves the ground and you're not with him, you'll regret it. Maybe not today. Maybe not tomorrow. But soon and for the rest of your life."[13]

This thin slice of melodrama is among the most memorable scenes in the history of cinema—not because it is particularly well acted or particularly well written but because most of us have stood on that same runway from time to time. Our most consequential choices—whether to marry, have children, buy a house, enter a profession, move abroad—are often shaped by how we imagine our future regrets ("Oh no, I forgot to have a baby!"). Regret is an emotion we feel when we blame ourselves for unfortunate outcomes that might have been prevented had we only behaved differently in the past, and because that emotion is decidedly unpleasant, our behavior in the present is often designed to preclude it.[14] Indeed, most of us have elaborate theories about when and why people feel regret, and these theories allow us to avoid the experience. For instance, we expect to feel more regret when we learn about alternatives to our choices than when we don't,[15] when we accept bad advice than when we reject good advice,[16] when our bad choices are unusual rather than conventional,[17] and when we fail by a narrow margin rather than by a wide margin.[18]

But sometimes these theories are wrong. Consider this scenario. You own shares in Company A. During the past year you considered switching to stock in Company B but decided against it. You now find that you would have been better off by $1,200 if you had switched to the stock of Company B. You also owned shares in Company C. During the past year you switched to stock in Company D. You now find out that you'd have been better off by $1,200 if you kept your stock in Company C. Which error causes you more regret? Studies show that about nine out of ten people expect to feel more regret when they foolishly switch stocks than when they foolishly fail to switch stocks, because most people think they will regret foolish actions more than foolish inactions.[19] But studies also show that nine out of ten people are wrong. Indeed, in the long run, people of every age and in every walk of life seem to regret *not* having done things much more than they regret things they *did*, which is why the most popular regrets include not going to college, not grasping profitable business opportunities, and not spending enough time with family and friends.[20]

But why do people regret inactions more than actions? One reason is that the psychological immune system has a more difficult time manufacturing positive and credible views of inactions than of actions.[21] When our action causes us to accept a marriage proposal from someone who later becomes an axe murderer, we can console ourselves by thinking of all the things we learned from the experience ("Collecting hatchets is not a healthy hobby"). But when our inaction causes us to reject a marriage proposal from someone who later becomes a movie star, we can't console ourselves by thinking of all the things we learned from the experience because ... well, there wasn't one. The irony is all too clear: Because we do not realize that our psychological immune systems can rationalize an excess of courage more easily than an excess of cowardice, we hedge our bets when we should blunder forward. As students of the silver screen recall, Bogart's admonition about future regret led Bergman to board the plane and fly away with her husband. Had she stayed with Bogey in Casablanca, she would probably have felt just fine. Not right away, perhaps, but soon, and for the rest of her life.

LITTLE TRIGGERS

Civilized people have learned the hard way that a handful of iniquitous individuals can often cause more death and destruction than an invading army. If an enemy were to launch hundreds of airplanes and missiles against the United States, the odds are that none would reach its target because an offensive strike of that magnitude would trigger America's defensive systems, which are presumably adequate to quash the threat. On the other hand, were an enemy to launch seven guys with baggy pants and baseball caps, those men might well reach their targets and detonate bombs, release toxins, or fly hijacked airplanes into tall buildings. Terrorism is a strategy based on the idea that the best offense is the one that fails to trigger the best defense, and small-scale incursions are less likely to set off the alarm bells than are large-scale assaults. Although it is possible to design a defensive system that counters even the smallest threat (e.g., electrified borders, a travel ban, electronic surveillance, random searches), such systems are extraordinarily costly, in terms of both the resources required to run them and the number of false alarms they produce. A system like that would be an exercise in overkill. To be effective, a defensive system must respond to threats; but to be practical, it must respond only to threats that exceed some *critical threshold*—which means that threats that fall short of the critical threshold may have a destructive potential that belies their diminutive size. Unlike large threats, small threats can sneak in under the radar.

The Intensity Trigger

The psychological immune system is a defensive system, and it obeys this same principle. When experiences make us feel sufficiently unhappy, the psychological immune system cooks facts and shifts blame in order to offer us a more positive view. But it doesn't do this *every* time we feel the slightest tingle of sadness, jealousy, anger, or frustration. Failed marriages and lost jobs are the kinds of large-scale assaults on our happiness that trigger our psychological defenses, but these defenses are not triggered by broken pencils, stubbed toes, or slow elevators. Broken pencils may be annoying, but they do not pose a grave threat to our psychological well-being and hence do not trigger our psychological defenses. The paradoxical consequence of this fact is that it is sometimes more difficult to achieve a positive view of a *bad* experience than of a *very bad* experience.

For example, volunteers in one study were students who were invited to join an extracurricular club whose initiation ritual required that they receive three electric shocks.[22] Some of the volunteers had a truly dreadful experience because the shocks they received were quite severe (severe-initiation group), and others had a slightly unpleasant experience because the shocks they received were relatively mild (mild-initiation group). Although you might expect people to dislike anything associated with physical pain, the volunteers in the severe-initiation group actually liked the club more. Because these volunteers suffered greatly, the intensity of their suffering triggered their defensive systems, which immediately began working to help them achieve a credible and positive view of their experience. It isn't easy to find such a view, but it can be done. For example, physical suffering is bad ("Oh my God, that *really* hurt!"), but it isn't *entirely* bad if the thing one suffers for is extremely valuable ("But I'm joining a *very* elite group of *very* special people."). Indeed, research shows that when people are given electric shocks, they actually feel *less pain* when they believe they are suffering for something of great value.[23] The intense shocks were unpleasant enough to trigger the volunteers' psychological defenses, but the mild shocks were not, hence the volunteers valued the club most when its initiation was most painful.[24] If you've managed to forgive your spouse for some egregious transgression but still find yourself miffed about the dent in the garage door or the trail of dirty socks on the staircase, then you have experienced this paradox.

Intense suffering triggers the very processes that eradicate it, while mild suffering does not, and this counterintuitive fact can make it difficult for us to predict our emotional futures. For example, would it be worse if your best friend insulted you or insulted your cousin? As much as you may like your cousin, it's a pretty good bet that you like yourself more, hence you probably think that it would be worse if the epithet were hurled your way. And you're right. It *would* be worse. At first. But if intense suffering triggers the psychological immune system and mild suffering does not, then over time you should be more likely to generate a positive view of an insult that was directed at you ("Felicia called me a pea-brain ... boy, she can really crack me up sometimes") than one that was directed at your cousin ("Felicia called Cousin Dwayne a pea-brain ... I mean, she's *right*, of course, but it wasn't very nice of her to say"). The irony is that you may ultimately feel better when you are the *victim* of an insult than when you are a *bystander* to it.

This possibility was tested in a study in which two volunteers took a personality test and then *one* of them received feedback from a psychologist.[25] The feedback was professional, detailed, and unrelentingly negative. For example, it contained statements such as "You have few qualities that distinguish you from others," and "People like you primarily because you don't threaten their competence." Both of the volunteers read the feedback and then reported how much they liked the psychologist who had written it. Ironically, the volunteer who was the *victim* of the negative feedback liked the psychologist *more* than did the volunteer who was merely a *bystander* to it. Why? Because bystanders were miffed ("Man, that was a really crummy thing to do to the other volunteer."), but they were not devastated, hence their psychological immune systems did nothing to ameliorate their mildly negative feelings. But victims *were* devastated ("Yikes, I'm a certified loser!"), hence their brains quickly went shopping for a positive view of the experience ("But now that I think of it, that test could only provide a small glimpse into my very complex personality, so I rather doubt it means much.") Now here's the important finding: when a new group of volunteers was asked to *predict* how much they would like the psychologist, they predicted that they would like the psychologist *less* if they were victims than if they were bystanders. Apparently, people are not aware of the fact that their defenses are more likely to be triggered by intense rather than mild suffering, thus they mispredict their own emotional reactions to misfortunes of different sizes.

The Inescapability Trigger

Intense suffering is one factor that can trigger our defenses and thus influence our experiences in ways we don't anticipate. But there are others. For example, why do we forgive our siblings for behavior we would never tolerate in a friend? Why aren't we disturbed when the president does something that would have kept us from voting for him had he done it before the election? Why do we overlook an employee's chronic tardiness but refuse to hire a job seeker who is two minutes late for the interview? One possibility is that blood is thicker than water, flags were made to be rallied around, and first impressions matter most. But another possibility is that we are more likely to look for and find a positive view of the things we're *stuck with* than of the things we're not.[26] Friends come and go, and changing candidates is as easy as changing socks. But siblings and presidents are *ours*, for better or for worse, and there's not much we can do about it once they've been born or elected. When the experience we are having is not the experience we want to be having, our first reaction is to go out and have a different one, which is why we return unsatisfactory rental cars, check out of bad hotels, and stop hanging around with people who pick their noses in public. It is only when we cannot change the experience that we look for ways to change our view of the experience, which is why we love the clunker in the driveway, the shabby cabin that's been in the family for years, and Uncle Sheldon despite his predilection for nasal spelunking. We find silver linings only when we must, which is why people experience an increase in happiness when genetic tests reveal that they don't have a dangerous genetic defect, or when the tests reveal that they do have a dangerous genetic defect, but not when the tests are inconclusive.[27] We just can't make the best of a fate until it is inescapably, inevitably, and irrevocably ours.

Inescapable, inevitable, and irrevocable circumstances trigger the psychological immune system, but, as with the intensity of suffering, people do not always recognize that this will happen. For example, college students in one study signed up for a course in black-and-white photography.[28] Each student took a dozen photographs of people and places that were personally meaningful, then reported for a private lesson. In these lessons, the teacher spent an hour or two showing students how to print their two best photographs. When the prints were dry and ready, the teacher said that the student could keep one of the photographs but that the other would be kept on file as an example of student work. Some students (inescapable group) were told that once they had chosen a photograph to take home, they would not be allowed to change their minds. Other students (escapable group) were told that once they had chosen a photograph to take home, they would have several days to change their minds—and if they did, the teacher would gladly swap the photograph they'd taken home for the one they'd left behind. Students made their choices and took one of their photographs home. Several days later, the students responded to a survey asking them (among other things) how much they liked their photographs. The results showed that students in the escapable group liked their photograph *less* than did students in the inescapable group. Interestingly, when a new group of students was asked to *predict* how much they would like their photographs if they were or were not given the opportunity to change their minds, these students predicted that escapability would have no influence whatsoever on their satisfaction with the photograph. Apparently, inescapable circumstances trigger the psychological defenses that enable us to achieve positive views of those circumstances, but we do not anticipate that this will happen.

Our failure to anticipate that inescapability will trigger our psychological immune systems (hence promote our happiness and satisfaction) can cause us to make some painful mistakes. For example, when a new group of photography students was asked whether they would prefer to have or not to have the opportunity to change their minds about which photograph to keep, the vast majority preferred to have that opportunity—that is, the vast majority of students preferred to enroll in a photography course in which they would ultimately be dissatisfied with the photograph they produced. Why would anyone prefer less satisfaction to more? No one does, of course, but most people do seem to prefer more freedom to less. Indeed, when our freedom to make up our minds—or to change our minds once we've made them up—is threatened, we experience a strong impulse to re-assert it,[29] which is why retailers sometimes threaten your freedom to own their products with claims such as "Limited stock" or "You must order by midnight tonight."[30] Our fetish for freedom leads us to patronize expensive department stores that allow us to return merchandise rather than attend auctions that don't, to lease cars at a dramatic markup rather than buying them at a bargain, and so on.

Most of us will pay a premium today for the opportunity to change our minds tomorrow, and sometimes it makes sense to do so. A few days spent test-driving a little red roadster tells us a lot about what it might be like to own one, thus it is sometimes wise to pay a modest premium for a contract that includes a short refund period. But if keeping our options open has benefits, it also has costs. Little red roadsters are naturally cramped, and while the committed owner will find positive ways to view that fact ("Wow! It feels like a fighter jet!"), the buyer whose contract includes an escape clause may not ("This car is so tiny. Maybe I should return it."). Committed owners attend to a car's virtues and overlook its flaws, thus cooking the facts to produce a banquet of satisfaction, but the buyer for whom escape is still possible (and whose defenses have not yet been triggered) is likely to evaluate the new car more critically, paying special attention to its imperfections as she tries to decide whether to keep it. The costs and benefits of freedom are clear—but alas, they are not equally clear: We have no trouble anticipating the advantages that freedom may provide, but we seem blind to the joys it can undermine.[31]

EXPLAINING AWAY

If you've ever puked your guts out shortly after eating chili con carne and found yourself unable to eat it again for years, you have a pretty good idea of what it's like to be a fruit fly. No, fruit flies don't eat chili, and no, fruit flies don't puke. But they do associate their best and worst experiences with the circumstances that accompanied and preceded them, which allows them to seek or avoid those circumstances in the future. Expose a fruit fly to the odor of tennis shoes, give it a very tiny electric shock, and for the rest of its very tiny life it will avoid places that smell tennis-shoey. The ability to associate pleasure or pain with its circumstances is so vitally important that nature has installed that ability in every one of her creatures, from *Drosophila melanogaster* to Ivan Pavlov.

But if that ability is necessary for creatures like us, it certainly isn't sufficient because the kind of learning it enables is far too limited. If an organism can do no more than associate particular experiences with particular circumstances, then it can learn only a very small lesson, namely, to seek or avoid those particular circumstances in the future. A well-timed shock may teach a fruit fly to avoid the tennis-shoe smell, but it won't teach it to avoid the smell of snowshoes, ballet slippers, Manolo Blahniks, or a scientist armed with a miniature stun gun. To maximize our pleasures and minimize our pains, we must be able to associate our experiences with the circumstances that produced them, but we must also be able to *explain* how and why those circumstances produced the experiences they did. If we feel nauseous after a few turns on the Ferris wheel and our explanation involves poor equilibrium, then we avoid Ferris wheels in the future—just as a fruit fly would. But unlike a fruit fly, we also avoid some things that are *not* associated with our nauseating experience (such as bungee jumping and sailboats) and we do *not* avoid some things that *are* associated with our nauseating experience (such as hurdy-gurdy music and clowns). Unlike a mere association, an explanation allows us to identify particular aspects of a circumstance (spinning) as the *cause* of our experience, and other aspects (music) as irrelevant. In so doing, we learn more from our upchucks than a fruit fly ever could.

Explanations allow us to make full use of our experiences, but they also change the nature of those experiences. As we have seen, when experiences are unpleasant, we quickly move to explain them in ways that make us feel better ("I didn't get the job because the judge was biased against people who barf on Ferris wheels."). And indeed, studies show that the mere act of explaining an unpleasant event can help to defang it. For example, simply writing about a trauma—such as the death of a loved one or a physical assault—can lead to surprising improvements in both subjective well-being and physical health (e.g., fewer visits to the physician and improved production of viral antibodies).[32] What's more, the people who experience the greatest benefit from these writing exercises are those whose writing contains an *explanation* of the trauma.[33]

But just as explanations ameliorate the impact of *unpleasant* events, so too do they ameliorate the impact of *pleasant* events. For example, college students volunteered for a study in which they believed they were interacting in an online chat room with students from other universities.[34] In fact, they were actually interacting with a sophisticated computer program that simulated the presence of other students. After the simulated students had provided the real student with information about themselves ("Hi, I'm Eva, and I like to do volunteer work."), the researcher pretended to ask the simulated students to decide which of the people in the chat room they liked most, to write a paragraph explaining why, and then to send it to that person. In just a few minutes, something remarkable happened: the real student received e-mail messages from *every one* of the simulated students indicating that they liked the real student best! For example, one simulated message read: "I just felt that something clicked between us when I read your answers. It's too bad we're not at the same school!" Another read: "You stood out as the one I would like the most. I was especially interested in the way you described your interests and values." A third read: "I wish I could talk with you directly because ... I'd ask you if you like being around water (I love water-skiing) and if you like Italian food (it's my favorite)."

Now, here's the catch: Some real students (informed group) received e-mail that allowed them to know *which* simulated student wrote each of the messages, and other real students (uninformed group) received e-mail messages that had been stripped of that identifying information. In other words, every real student received exactly the same e-mail messages indicating that they had won the hearts and minds of all the simulated people in the chat room, but only real students in the informed group knew *which* simulated individual had written each of the messages. Hence, real students in the informed group were able to generate explanations for their good fortune ("Eva appreciates my values because we're both involved with Habitat for Humanity, and it makes sense that Catarina would mention Italian food."), whereas real students in the uninformed group were not ("Someone appreciates my values.... I wonder who? And why would anyone mention Italian food?"). The researchers measured how happy the real students were immediately after receiving these messages and then again fifteen minutes later. Although real students in both groups were initially delighted to have been chosen as everyone's best friend, only the real students in the uninformed group remained delighted fifteen minutes later. If you've ever had a secret admirer, then you understand why real students in the uninformed group remained on cloud nine while real students in the informed group quickly descended to clouds two through five.

Unexplained events have two qualities that amplify and extend their emotional impact. First, they strike us as rare and unusual.[35] If I told you that my brother, my sister, and I were all born on the same day, you'd probably consider that a rare and unusual occurrence. Once I explained that we were triplets, you'd find it considerably less so. In fact, just about *any* explanation I offered ("By *same day* I meant we were all born on a Thursday" or "We were all delivered by cesarean section, so Mom and Dad timed our births for maximum tax benefits") would tend to reduce the amazingness of the coincidence and make the event seem more probable. Explanations allow us to understand how and why an event happened, which immediately allows us to see how and why it might happen again. Indeed, whenever we say that something *can't* happen—for example, mind reading or levitation or a law that limits the power of incumbents—we usually just mean that we'd have no way to explain it if it did. Unexplained events seem rare, and rare events naturally have a greater emotional impact than common events do. We are awed by a solar eclipse but merely impressed by a sunset despite the fact that the latter is by far the more spectacular visual treat.

The second reason why unexplained events have a disproportionate emotional impact is that we are especially likely to keep thinking about them. People spontaneously try to explain events,[36] and studies show that when people do not complete the things they set out to do, they are especially likely to think about and remember their unfinished business.[37] Once we explain an event, we can fold it up like freshly washed laundry, put it away in memory's drawer, and move on to the next one; but if an event defies explanation, it becomes a *mystery* or a *conundrum*—and if there's one thing we all know about mysterious conundrums, it is that they generally refuse to stay in the back of our minds. Filmmakers and novelists often capitalize on this fact by fitting their narratives with mysterious endings, and research shows that people are, in fact, more likely to keep thinking about a movie when they can't explain what happened to the main character. And if they *liked* the movie, this morsel of mystery causes them to remain happy longer.[38]

Explanation robs events of their emotional impact because it makes them seem likely and allows us to stop thinking about them. Oddly enough, an explanation doesn't actually have to *explain* anything to have these effects—it merely needs to *seem* as though it does. For instance, in one study, a researcher approached college students in the university library, handed them one of two cards with a dollar coin attached, then walked away. You'd probably agree that this is a curious event that begs for explanation. Both cards stated that the researcher was a member of the "Smile Society," which was devoted to "random acts of kindness." But one card also contained two extra phrases: "Who are we?" and "Why do we do this?" These empty phrases didn't really provide any new information, of course, but they made students *feel* as though the curious event had been explained ("Aha, *now* I understand why they gave me a dollar!"). About five minutes later, a different researcher approached the student and claimed to be doing a class project on "community thoughts and feelings." The researcher asked the student to complete some survey questions, one of which was "How positive or negative are you feeling right now?" The results showed that those students who had received a card with the pseudo-explanatory phrases felt less happy than those who had received a card without them. Apparently, even a fake explanation can cause us to tuck an event away and move along to the next one.

Uncertainty can preserve and prolong our happiness, thus we might expect people to cherish it. In fact, the opposite is generally the case. When a new group of students was asked which of the two cards [offering a free dollar] would make them happier, 75-percent chose the one with the meaningless explanation. Similarly, when a group of students was asked whether they would prefer to know or not know which of the simulated students had written each of the glowing reports in the online chat-room study, 100-percent chose to know. In both cases, students chose certainty over uncertainty and clarity over mystery—despite the fact that in both cases clarity and certainty had been shown to diminish happiness. The poet John Keats noted that whereas great authors are "capable of being in uncertainties, mysteries, doubts, without any irritable reaching after fact and reason," the rest of us are "incapable of remaining content with half-knowledge."[39] Our relentless desire to explain everything that happens may well distinguish us from fruit flies, but it can also kill our buzz.

ONWARD

The eye and the brain are conspirators, and like most conspiracies, theirs is negotiated behind closed doors, in the back room, outside of our awareness. Because we do not realize that we have generated a positive view of our current experience, we do not realize that we will do so again in the future. Not only does our naïveté cause us to overestimate the intensity and duration of our distress in the face of future adversity, but it also leads us to take actions that may undermine the conspiracy. We are more likely to generate a positive and credible view of an action than an inaction, of a painful experience than of an annoying experience, of an unpleasant situation that we cannot escape than of one we can. And yet, we rarely choose action over inaction, pain over annoyance, and commitment over freedom. The processes by which we generate positive views are many: we pay more attention to favorable information, we surround ourselves with those who provide it, and we accept it uncritically. These tendencies make it easy for us to explain unpleasant experiences in ways that exonerate us and make us feel better. The price we pay for our irrepressible explanatory urge is that we often spoil our most pleasant experiences by making good sense of them.

NOTES

The notes contain references to the scientific research that supports the claims I make in the text. Occasionally they contain some extra information that may be of interest but that is not essential to the argument. If you don't care about sources, aren't interested in nonessentials, and are annoyed by books that make you flip back and forth all the time, then be assured that the only important note in [this chapter] is this one.

1. T. D. Wilson, *Strangers to Ourselves: Discovering the Adaptive Unconscious* (Cambridge, Mass.: Harvard University Press, 2002); and J. A. Bargh and T. L. Chartrand, "The Unbearable Automaticity of Being," *American Psychologist* 54: 462–79 (1999).

2. R. E. Nisbett and T. D. Wilson, "Telling More Than We Can Know: Verbal Reports on Mental Processes," *Psychological Review* 84: 231–59 (1977); D. J. Bem, "Self-Perception Theory," in *Advances in Experimental Social Psychology*, ed. L. Berkowitz, vol. 6 (New York: Academic Press, 1972), 1–62; M. S. Gazzaniga, *The Social Brain* (New York: Basic Books, 1985); and D. M. Wegner, *The Illusion of Conscious Will* (Cambridge, Mass.: MIT Press, 2003).

3. E. T. Higgings, W. S. Rholes, and C. R. Jones, "Category Accessibility and Impression Formation," *Journal of Experimental Social Psychology* 13: 141–54 (1977).

4. J. Bargh, M. Chen, and L. Burrows, "Automaticity of Social Behavior: Direct Effects of Trait Construct and Stereotype Activation on Action," *Journal of Personality and Social Psychology* 71: 230–44 (1996).

5. A. Dijksterhuis and A. van Knippenberg, "The Relation Between Perception and Behavior, or How to Win a Game of Trivial Pursuit," *Journal of Personality and Social Psychology* 74: 865–77 (1998).

6. Nisbett and Wilson, "Telling More Than We Can Know."

7. J. W. Schooler, D. Ariely, and G. Loewenstein, "The Pursuit and Assessment of Happiness Can Be Self-Defeating," in *The Psychology of Economic Decisions: Rationality and Well-Being*, eds. I. Brocas and J. Carillo, vol. 1 (Oxford: Oxford University Press, 2003).

8. K. N. Ochsner et al., "Rethinking Feelings: An fMRI Study of the Cognitive Regulation of Emotion," *Journal of Cognitive Neuroscience* 14: 1215–29 (2002).

9. D. M. Wegner, R. Erber, and S. Zanakos, "Ironic Processes in the Mental Control of Mood and Mood-Related Thought," *Journal of Personality and Social Psychology* 65: 1093–104 (1993); and D. M. Wegner, A. Broome, and S. J. Blumberg, "Ironic Effects of Trying to Relax Under Stress," *Behaviour Research and Therapy* 35: 11–21 (1997).

10. D. T. Gilbert et al., "Immune Neglect: A Source of Durability Bias in Affective Forecasting," *Journal of Personality and Social Psychology* 75: 617–38 (1998).

11. Ibid.

12. D. T. Gilbert et al., "Looking Forward to Looking Backward: The Misprediction of Regret," *Psychological Science* 15: 346–50 (2004).

13. M. Curtiz, *Casablanca*, Warner Bros., 1942.

14. T. Gilovich and V. H. Medvec, "The Experience of Regret: What, When, and Why," *Psychological Review* 102: 379–95 (1995); N. Roese, *If Only: How to Turn Regret into Opportunity* (New York: Random House 2004); G. Loomes and R. Sugden, "Regret Theory: An Alternative Theory of Rational Choice Under Uncertainty," *Economic Journal* 92: 805–24 (1982); and D. Bell, "Regret in Decision Making Under Uncertainty," *Operations Research* 20: 961–81 (1982).

15. I. Ritov and J. Baron, "Outcome Knowledge, Regret, and Omission Bias," *Organizational Behavior and Human Decision Processes* 64: 119–27 (1995); I. Ritov and J. Baron, "Probability of Regret: Anticipation of Uncertainty Resolution in Choice: Outcome Knowledge, Regret, and Omission Bias," *Organizational Behavior and Human Decision Processes* 66: 228–36 (1996); and M. Zeelenberg, "Anticipated Regret, Expected Feedback and Behavioral Decision Making," *Journal of Behavioral Decision Making* 12: 93–106 (1999).

16. M. T. Crawford et al., "Reactance, Compliance, and Anticipated Regret," *Journal of Experimental Social Psychology* 38: 56–63 (2002).

17. I. Simonson, "The Influence of Anticipating Regret and Responsibility on Purchase Decisions," *Journal of Consumer Research* 19: 105–18 (1992).

18. V. H. Medvec, S. F. Madey, and T. Gilovich, "When Less Is More: Counterfactual Thinking and Satisfaction Among Olympic Medalists," *Journal of Personality and Social Psychology* 69: 603–10 (1995); and D. Kahneman and A. Tversky, "Variants of Uncertainty," *Cognition* 11: 143–57 (1982).

19. D. Kahneman and A. Tversky, "The Psychology of Preferences," *Scientific American* 246: 160–73 (1982).

20. Gilovich and Medvec, "The Experience of Regret."

21. T. Gilovich, V. H. Medvec, and S. Chen, "Omission, Commission, and Dissonance Reduction: Overcoming Regret in the Monty Hall Problem," *Personality and Social Psychology Bulletin* 21: 182–90 (1995).

22. H. B. Gerard and G. C. Mathewson, "The Effects of Severity of Initiation on Liking for a Group: A Replication," *Journal of Experimental Social Psychology* 2: 278–87 (1966).

23. P. G. Zimbardo, "Control of Pain Motivation by Cognitive Dissonance," *Science* 151: 217–19 (1966).

24. See also E. Aronson and J. Mills, "The Effect of Severity of Initiation on Liking for a Group," *Journal of Abnormal and Social Psychology* 59: 177–81 (1958); J. L. Freedman, "Long-Term Behavioral Effects of Cognitive Dissonance," *Journal of Experimental Social*

Psychology 1: 145–55 (1965); D. R. Shaffer and C. Hendrick, "Effects of Actual Effort and Anticipated Effort on Task Enhancement," *Journal of Experimental Social Psychology* 7: 435–47 (1971); H. R. Arkes and C. Blumer, "The Psychology of Sunk Cost," *Organizational Behavior and Human Decision Processes* 35: 124–40 (1985); and J. T. Jost et al., "Social Inequality and the Reduction of Ideological Dissonance on Behalf of the System: Evidence of Enhanced System Justification Among the Disadvantaged," *European Journal of Social Psychology* 33: 13–36 (2003).

25. D. T. Gilbert et al., "The Peculiar Longevity of Things Not So Bad," *Psychological Science* 15: 14–19 (2004).

26. D. Frey et al., "Re-evaluation of Decision Alternatives Dependent upon the Reversibility of a Decision and the Passage of Time," *European Journal of Social Psychology* 14: 447–50 (1984); and D. Frey, "Reversible and Irreversible Decisions: Preference for Consonant Information as a Function of Attractiveness of Decision Alternatives," *Personality and Social Psychology Bulletin* 7: 621–26 (1981).

27. S. Wiggins et al., "The Psychological Consequences of Predictive Testing for Huntington's Disease," *New England Journal of Medicine* 327: 1401–5 (1992).

28. D. T. Gilbert and J. E. J. Ebert, "Decisions and Revisions: The Affective Forecasting of Changeable Outcomes," *Journal of Personality and Social Psychology* 82: 503–14 (2002).

29. J. W. Brehm, *A Theory of Psychological Reactance* (New York: Academic Press, 1966).

30. R. B. Cialdini, *Influence: Science and Practice* (Glenview, Ill.: Scott, Foresman, 1985).

31. S. S. Iyengar and M. R. Lepper, "When Choice Is Demotivating: Can One Desire Too Much of a Good Thing?" *Journal of Personality and Social Psychology* 79: 995–1006 (2000); and B. Schwartz, "Self-Determination: The Tyranny of Freedom," *American Psychologist* 55: 79–88 (2000).

32. J. W. Pennebaker, "Writing About Emotional Experiences as a Therapeutic Process," *Psychological Science* 8: 162–66 (1997).

33. J. W. Pennebaker, T. J. Mayne, and M. E. Francis, "Linguistic Predictors of Adaptive Bereavement," *Journal of Personality and Social Psychology* 72: 863–71 (1997).

34. T. D. Wilson et al., "The Pleasures of Uncertainty: Prolonging Positive Moods in Ways People Do Not Anticipate," *Journal of Personality and Social Psychology* 88: 5–21 (2005).

35. B. Fischoff, "Hindsight ≠ foresight: The Effects of Outcome Knowledge on Judgment Under Uncertainty," *Journal of Experimental Psychology: Human Perception and Performance* 1: 288–99 (1975); and C. A. Anderson, M. R. Lepper, and L. Ross, "Perseverance of Social Theories: The Role of Explanation in the Persistence of Discredited Information," *Journal of Personality and Social Psychology* 39: 1037–49 (1980).

36. B. Weiner, "'Spontaneous' Causal Thinking," *Psychological Bulletin* 97: 74–84 (1985); and R. R. Hassin, J. A. Bargh, and J. S. Uleman, "Spontaneous Causal Inferences," *Journal of Experimental Social Psychology* 38: 515–22 (2002).

37. B. Zeigarnik, "Das Behalten erledigter und unerledigter Handlungen," *Psychologische Forschung* 9: 1–85 (1927); and G. W. Boguslavsky, "Interruption and Learning," *Psychological Review* 58: 248–55 (1951).

38. Wilson et al., "Pleasures of Uncertainty."

39. J. Keats, letter to Richard Woodhouse, 27 October 1881, in *Selected Poems and Letters by John Keats*, ed. D. Bush (Boston: Houghton Mifflin, 1959).

QUESTIONS FOR MAKING CONNECTIONS
WITHIN THE READING

1. Throughout "Immune to Reality," Gilbert describes mental operations using terms from everyday life: the brain is "one smart shopper"; our brains are "conspirators"; once we come up with an explanation, "we can fold it up like freshly washed laundry, put it away in memory's drawer, and move on to the next one." Obviously, Gilbert is seeking to make his thoughts about human psychology readily accessible, but what exactly is he trying to convey with these descriptions? As you reread the essay, generate a list of the most significant images and analogies Gilbert uses to describe mental operations. What does this list tell you about Gilbert's theory of mind?

2. On the basis of the experiments and studies Gilbert presents, would you say that happiness is fundamentally an illusion? Or is it the *pursuit* of happiness that deserves to be reconsidered? If happiness is not something that we can pursue consciously, then how do we go about becoming happy? Should we be pursuing something other than happiness?

3. What is the meaning of "reality" at the end of Gilbert's discussion of our "psychological immune system"? What exactly is it that this system is designed to protect us from? Is the psychological immune system analogous to our biological immune system, or does it operate according to a different logic? Is the reality from which this system protects us ultimately an illusion? Or are psychological realities fundamentally different from material realities?

QUESTIONS FOR WRITING

1. The Declaration of Independence proclaims that "all men" are "endowed by their Creator with certain unalienable Rights," among them "Life, Liberty and the pursuit of Happiness." What are the *political* implications of the research indicating that the pursuit of happiness is often misdirected because people typically fail to recognize the conditions that will really make them happy? Does Gilbert's work suggest that Thomas Jefferson's thinking in the Declaration was based on a false assumption? Can any government responsibly claim to make happiness available?

2. What are the *economic* implications of Gilbert's argument? If people began to choose "action over inaction, pain over annoyance, and commitment over freedom," would the consumer economy survive? That is, is consumerism dependent upon our collective ignorance about the path to happiness, or is the hope that one's life will be improved by increased purchasing power itself a path to happiness? Is trying to be happy with what one has a form of action or inaction? If Gilbert is right that "explanation robs events of their emotional impact," what role does explanation play in consumer economy? Is a healthy economy dependent upon consumers who are well informed or consumers who are "immune to reality"?

QUESTIONS FOR MAKING CONNECTIONS
BETWEEN READINGS

1. In "Son," Andrew Solomon writes about the experience of both children and parents who are challenged by the dissonance between what they expect from the future and what they actually get. Children feel trapped by parental expectations, and parents sometimes see their dreams destroyed by the adults their children become. In what ways do Solomon's reflections both confirm and complicate Gilbert's claims about the ways we "stumble" into happiness? Although Gilbert often makes a convincing case for the limitations of our ability to foresee the real sources of our happiness, he has less to say about our role in finding happiness at last. Do we really "stumble" into happiness, or is happiness an achievement that requires creativity on our part? Does Solomon himself get to happiness more or less by accident, or does it require him to actively become the author of his own life?

2. What are the connections between the quest for happiness as Gilbert describes it and the cultivation of wisdom that Robert Thurman outlines? Is the Buddhist experience of nothingness a way of freeing people from the hot states in which we overestimate our own capacity to find satisfaction through changes in external conditions? Or is the notion of wisdom itself an example of the kind of unconscious fact cooking Gilbert describes, which generates happiness only if it feels "like a discovery and not like a snow job"? Is there a way to determine, finally, if another person is happy or wise? Can one even know oneself with certainty if Gilbert is correct? How about if Thurman is correct?

◆◆◆

MALCOLM GLADWELL

HOW DO CULTURES change, and is it possible to control and direct cultural change? These are some of the questions that interest Malcolm Gladwell, author of the best-selling books *The Tipping Point: How Little Things Can Make a Big Difference* (2000), *Blink: The Power of Thinking Without Thinking* (2005), *Outliers: The Story of Success* (2008), and *What the Dog Saw and Other Adventures* (2009). Gladwell first became interested in the notion that ideas might spread through culture like a virus while he was covering the AIDS epidemic for the *Washington Post*. In epidemiology, the "tipping point" is the moment when a virus reaches critical mass; AIDS, as Gladwell learned while doing his research, reached its tipping point in 1982, "when it went from a rare disease affecting a few gay men to a worldwide epidemic." Fascinated by this medical fact, Gladwell found himself wondering whether it also applied to the social world. Is there a specific point where a fad becomes a fashion frenzy, or where delinquency and mischief turn into a crime wave? At what point might repetition lead to change?

The Tipping Point is the result of Gladwell's effort to understand why some ideas catch on and spread like wildfire while others fail to attract widespread attention and wither on the vine. Drawing on psychology, sociology, and epidemiology, Gladwell examines events as diverse as Paul Revere's ride, the success of *Sesame Street* and *Blue's Clues*, and the precipitous decline in the crime rate in New York City, which is discussed in "The Power of Context," the chapter included here. Working across these wide-ranging examples, Gladwell develops an all-encompassing model of how cultural change occurs, a model that highlights the influential role that context plays in shaping and guiding human acts and intentions.

Gladwell returns to the importance of context from a different direction in a later book, *Outliers: The Story of Success*. There he investigates the forces behind the achievements of figures like Bill Gates, Mozart, and the Beatles. Even though many Americans believe that success follows from hard work and genetics, Gladwell paints a much more complicated picture that includes not only practice and education but also social circumstances, timing, culture, and a great deal of luck. A helping hand is often decisive: we might be talented, brilliant, and ambitious, but no one ever makes it to the top without many different kinds of support.

Quotations come from Q&A with Malcolm at <http://www.gladwell.com/tippingpoint/> and interview by Toby Lester, *The Atlantic Unbound* <http://www.theatlantic.com/unbound/interviews/ba2000-03-29.htm>.

Gladwell was born in England, grew up in Canada, and graduated with a degree in history from the University of Toronto in 1984. After spending over a decade as a science writer and New York bureau chief for the *Washington Post*, he joined the staff of the *New Yorker* in 1996. In 2007, he received the American Sociological Association's first Award for Excellence in the Reporting of Social Issues. Gladwell sees himself as "a kind of translator between the academic and nonacademic worlds." As he puts it, "There's just all sorts of fantastic stuff out there, but there's not nearly enough time and attention paid to that act of translation. Most people leave college in their early twenties, and that ends their exposure to the academic world. To me that's a tragedy."

The Power of Context

Bernie Goetz and the Rise and Fall of New York City Crime

1. On December 22, 1984, the Saturday before Christmas, Bernhard Goetz left his apartment in Manhattan's Greenwich Village and walked to the IRT subway station at Fourteenth Street and Seventh Avenue. He was a slender man in his late thirties, with sandy-colored hair and glasses, dressed that day in jeans and a windbreaker. At the station, he boarded the number two downtown express train and sat down next to four young black men. There were about twenty people in the car, but most sat at the other end, avoiding the four teenagers, because they were, as eyewitnesses would say later, "horsing around" and "acting rowdy." Goetz seemed oblivious. "How are ya?" one of the four, Troy Canty, said to Goetz, as he walked in. Canty was lying almost prone on one of the subway benches. Canty and another of the teenagers, Barry Allen, walked up to Goetz and asked him for five dollars. A third youth, James Ramseur, gestured toward a suspicious-looking bulge in his pocket, as if he had a gun in there.

"What do you want?" Goetz asked.

"Give me five dollars," Canty repeated.

Goetz looked up and, as he would say later, saw that Canty's "eyes were shiny, and he was enjoying himself.... He had a big smile on his face," and somehow that smile and those eyes set him off. Goetz reached into his pocket and pulled out a chrome-plated, five-shot Smith and Wesson .38, firing at each of the four youths in turn. As the fourth member of the group, Darrell Cabey, lay screaming on the ground, Goetz walked over to him and said, "You seem all right. Here's another," before firing a fifth bullet into Cabey's spinal cord and paralyzing him for life.

In the tumult, someone pulled the emergency brake. The other passengers ran into the next car, except for two women who remained riveted in panic. "Are you all right?" Goetz asked the first, politely. Yes, she said. The second woman was lying on the floor. She wanted Goetz to think she was dead. "Are you all right?" Goetz asked her, twice. She nodded yes. The conductor, now on the scene, asked Goetz if he was a police officer.

"No," said Goetz. "I don't know why I did it." Pause. "They tried to rip me off."

The conductor asked Goetz for his gun. Goetz declined. He walked through the doorway at the front of the car, unhooked the safety chain, and jumped down onto the tracks, disappearing into the dark of the tunnel.

In the days that followed, the shooting on the IRT caused a national sensation. The four youths all turned out to have criminal records. Cabey had been arrested previously for armed robbery, Canty for theft. Three of them had screwdrivers in their pockets. They seemed the embodiment of the kind of young thug feared by nearly all urban-dwellers, and the mysterious gunman who shot them down seemed like an avenging angel. The tabloids dubbed Goetz the "Subway Vigilante" and the "Death Wish Shooter." On radio call-in shows and in the streets, he was treated as a hero, a man who had fulfilled the secret fantasy of every New Yorker who had ever been mugged or intimidated or assaulted on the subway. On New Year's Eve, a week after the shooting, Goetz turned himself in to a police station in New Hampshire. Upon his extradition to New York City, the *New York Post* ran two pictures on its front page: one of Goetz, handcuffed and head bowed, being led into custody, and one of Troy Canty—black, defiant, eyes hooded, arms folded—being released from the hospital. The headline read, "Led Away in Cuffs While Wounded Mugger Walks to Freedom." When the case came to trial, Goetz was easily acquitted on charges of assault and attempted murder. Outside Goetz's apartment building, on the evening of the verdict, there was a raucous, impromptu street party.

2. The Goetz case has become a symbol of a particular, dark moment in New York City history, the moment when the city's crime problem reached epidemic proportions. During the 1980s, New York City averaged well over 2,000 murders and 600,000 serious felonies a year. Underground, on the subways, conditions could only be described as chaotic. Before Bernie Goetz boarded the number two train that day, he would have waited on a dimly lit platform, surrounded on all sides by dark, damp, graffiti-covered walls. Chances are his train was late, because in 1984 there was a fire somewhere on the New York system every day and a derailment every other week. Pictures of the crime scene, taken by police, show that the car Goetz sat in was filthy, its floor littered with trash, and the walls and ceiling thick with graffiti, but that wasn't unusual because in 1984 every one of the 6,000 cars in the Transit Authority fleet, with the exception of the midtown shuttle, was covered with graffiti—top to bottom, inside and out. In the winter, the cars were cold because few were adequately heated. In the summer, the cars were stiflingly hot because none were air-conditioned. Today, the number two train accelerates to over 40 miles an hour as it rumbles toward the Chambers Street express stop. But it's doubtful Goetz's train went that fast. In 1984, there were 500 "red tape" areas on the system—places where track damage had made it unsafe for trains to go more than 15 miles per hour. Fare-beating was so commonplace that it was costing the Transit Authority as much as $150 million in lost revenue annually. There were about 15,000 felonies on the system a year—a number that would hit 20,000 a year by the end of the decade—and harassment of riders by panhandlers and petty criminals was so pervasive that ridership of the trains had sunk to its lowest level in the history of the subway system. William Bratton, who was later to be a key figure in New York's successful fight against violent crime, writes in his autobiography of riding the New York subways in the 1980s after living in Boston for years and being stunned at what he saw:

> After waiting in a seemingly endless line to buy a token, I tried to put a coin into a turnstile, and found it had been purposely jammed. Unable to pay the fare to get into the system, we had to enter through a slam gate being held open by a scruffy-looking character with his hand out; having disabled the turnstiles, he was now demanding that riders give him their tokens. Meanwhile, one of his cohorts had his mouth on the coin slots, sucking out the jammed coins and leaving his slobber. Most people were too intimidated to take these guys on: Here, take the damned token, what do I care? Other citizens were going over, under, around, or through the stiles for free. It was like going into the transit version of Dante's *Inferno*.

This was New York City in the 1980s, a city in the grip of one of the worst crime epidemics in its history. But then, suddenly and without warning, the epidemic tipped. From a high in 1990, the crime rate went into precipitous decline. Murders dropped by two-thirds. Felonies were cut in half. Other cities saw their crime drop in the same period. But in no place did the level of violence fall farther or faster. On the subways, by the end of the decade, there were 75-percent fewer felonies than there had been at the decade's start. In 1996, when Goetz went to trial a second time, as the defendant in a civil suit brought by Darrell Cabey, the case was all but ignored by the press, and Goetz himself seemed almost an anachronism. At a time when New York had become the safest big city in the country, it seemed hard to remember precisely what it was that Goetz had once symbolized. It was simply inconceivable that someone could pull a gun on someone else on the subway and be called a hero for it.

3. During the 1990s violent crime declined across the United States for a number of fairly straightforward reasons. The illegal trade in crack cocaine, which had spawned a great deal of violence among gangs and drug dealers, began to decline. The economy's dramatic recovery meant that many people who might have been lured into crime got legitimate jobs instead, and the general aging of the population meant that there were fewer people in the age range—males between eighteen and twenty-four—that is responsible for the majority of all violence. The question of why crime declined in New York City, however, is a little more complicated. In the period when the New York epidemic tipped down, the city's economy hadn't improved. It was still stagnant. In fact, the city's poorest neighborhoods had just been hit hard by the welfare cuts of the early 1990s. The waning of the crack cocaine epidemic in New York was clearly a factor, but then again, it had been in steady decline well before crime dipped. As for the aging of the population, because of heavy immigration to New York in the 1980s, the city was getting younger in the 1990s, not older. In any case, all of these trends are long-term changes that one would expect to have gradual effects. In New York the decline was anything but gradual. Something else clearly played a role in reversing New York's crime epidemic.

The most intriguing candidate for that "something else" is called the Broken Windows Theory. Broken Windows was the brainchild of the criminologists James Q. Wilson and George Kelling. Wilson and Kelling argued that crime is the inevitable result of disorder. If a window is broken and left unrepaired, people walking by will conclude that no one cares and no one is in charge. Soon, more windows will be broken, and the sense of anarchy will spread from the building to the street on which it faces, sending a signal that anything goes. In a city, relatively minor problems like graffiti, public disorder, and aggressive panhandling, they write, are all the equivalent of broken windows, invitations to more serious crimes:

> Muggers and robbers, whether opportunistic or professional, believe they reduce their chances of being caught or even identified if they operate on streets where potential victims are already intimidated by prevailing conditions. If the neighborhood cannot keep a bothersome panhandler from annoying passersby, the thief may reason, it is even less likely to call the police to identify a potential mugger or to interfere if the mugging actually takes place.

This is an epidemic theory of crime. It says that crime is contagious—just as a fashion trend is contagious—that it can start with a broken window and spread to an entire community. The Tipping Point in this epidemic, though, isn't a particular kind of person.... It's something physical like graffiti. The impetus to engage in a certain kind of behavior is not coming from a certain kind of person but from a feature of the environment.

In the mid-1980s Kelling was hired by the New York Transit Authority as a consultant, and he urged them to put the Broken Windows Theory into practice. They obliged, bringing in a new subway director by the name of David Gunn to oversee a multibillion-dollar rebuilding of the subway system. Many subway advocates, at the time, told Gunn not to worry about graffiti, to focus on the larger questions of crime and subway reliability, and it seemed like reasonable advice. Worrying about graffiti at a time when the entire system was close to collapse seems as pointless as scrubbing the decks of the *Titanic* as it headed toward the icebergs. But Gunn insisted. "The graffiti was symbolic of the collapse of the system," he says. "When you looked at the process of rebuilding the organization and morale, you had to win the battle against graffiti. Without winning that battle, all the management reforms and physical changes just weren't going to happen. We were about to put out new trains that were worth about ten million bucks apiece, and unless we did something to protect them, we knew just what would happen. They would last one day and then they would be vandalized."

Gunn drew up a new management structure and a precise set of goals and timetables aimed at cleaning the system line by line, train by train. He started with the number seven train that connects Queens to midtown Manhattan, and began experimenting with new techniques to clean off the paint. On stainless-steel cars, solvents were used. On the painted cars, the graffiti were simply painted over. Gunn made it a rule that there should be no retreat, that once a car was "reclaimed" it should never be allowed to be vandalized again. "We were religious about it," Gunn said. At the end of the number one line in the Bronx, where the trains stop before turning around and going back to Manhattan, Gunn set up a cleaning station. If a car came in with graffiti, the graffiti had to be removed during the changeover, or the car was removed from service. "Dirty" cars, which hadn't yet been cleansed of graffiti, were never to be mixed with "clean" cars. The idea was to send an unambiguous message to the vandals themselves.

"We had a yard up in Harlem on 135th Street where the trains would lay up overnight," Gunn said. "The kids would come the first night and paint the side of the train white. Then they would come the next night, after it was dry, and draw the outline. Then they would come the third night and color it in. It was a three-day job. We knew the kids would be working on one of the dirty trains, and what we would do is wait for them to finish their mural. Then we'd walk over with rollers and paint it over. The kids would be in tears, but we'd just be going up and down, up and down. It was a message to them. If you want to spend three nights of your time vandalizing a train, fine. But it's never going to see the light of day."

Gunn's graffiti cleanup took from 1984 to 1990. At that point, the Transit Authority hired William Bratton to head the transit police, and the second stage of the reclamation of the subway system began. Bratton was, like Gunn, a disciple of Broken Windows. He describes Kelling, in fact, as his intellectual mentor, and so his first step as police chief was as seemingly quixotic as Gunn's. With felonies—serious crimes—on the subway system at an all-time high, Bratton decided to crack down on fare-beating. Why? Because he believed that, like graffiti, fare-beating could be a signal, a small expression of disorder that invited much more serious crimes. An estimated 170,000 people a day were entering the system, by one route or another, without paying a token. Some were kids, who simply jumped over the turnstiles. Others would lean backward on the turnstiles and force their way through. And once one or two or three people began cheating the system, other people—who might never otherwise have considered evading the law—would join in, reasoning that if some people weren't going to pay, they shouldn't either, and the problem would snowball. The problem was exacerbated by the fact fare-beating was not easy to fight. Because there was only $1.25 at stake, the transit police didn't feel it was worth their time to pursue it, particularly when there were plenty of more serious crimes happening down on the platform and in the trains.

Bratton is a colorful, charismatic man, a born leader, and he quickly made his presence felt. His wife stayed behind in Boston, so he was free to work long hours, and he would roam the city on the subway at night, getting a sense of what the problems were and how best to fight them. First, he picked stations where fare-beating was the biggest problem and put as many as ten policemen in plainclothes at the turnstiles. The team would nab fare-beaters one by one, handcuff them, and leave them standing, in a daisy chain, on the platform until they had a "full catch." The idea was to signal, as publicly as possible, that the transit police were now serious about cracking down on fare-beaters. Previously, police officers had been wary of pursuing fare-beaters because the arrest, the trip to the station house, the filling out of necessary forms, and the waiting for those forms to be processed took an entire day—all for a crime that usually merited no more than a slap on the wrist. Bratton retrofitted a city bus and turned it into a rolling station house, with its own fax machines, phones, holding pen, and fingerprinting facilities. Soon the turnaround time on an arrest was down to an hour. Bratton also insisted that a check be run on all those arrested. Sure enough, one out of seven arrestees had an outstanding warrant for a previous crime, and one out of twenty was carrying a weapon of some sort. Suddenly it wasn't hard to convince police officers that tackling fare-beating made sense. "For the cops it was a bonanza," Bratton writes. "Every arrest was like opening a box of Cracker Jack. What kind of toy am I going to get? Got a gun? Got a knife? Got a warrant? Do we have a murderer here?... After a while the bad guys wised up and began to leave their weapons home and pay their fares." Under Bratton, the number of ejections from subway stations—for drunkenness or improper behavior—tripled within his first few months in office. Arrests for misdemeanors, for the kind of minor offenses that had gone unnoticed in the past, went up fivefold between 1990 and 1994. Bratton turned the transit police into an organization focused on the smallest infractions, on the details of life underground.

After the election of Rudolph Giuliani as mayor of New York in 1994, Bratton was appointed head of the New York City Police Department, and he applied the same strategies to the city at large. He instructed his officers to crack down on quality-of-life crimes: on the "squeegee men" who came up to drivers at New York City intersections and demanded money for washing car windows, for example, and on all the other above-ground equivalents of turnstile-jumping and graffiti. "Previous police administration had been handcuffed by restrictions," Bratton says. "We took the handcuffs off. We stepped up enforcement of the laws against public drunkenness and public urination and arrested repeat violators, including those who threw empty bottles on the street or were involved in even relatively minor damage to property.... If you peed in the street, you were going to jail." When crime began to fall in the city—as quickly and dramatically as it had in the subways—Bratton and Giuliani pointed to the same cause. Minor, seemingly insignificant quality-of-life crimes, they said, were Tipping Points for violent crime.

Broken Windows Theory and the Power of Context are one and the same. They are both based on the premise that an epidemic can be reversed, can be tipped, by tinkering with the smallest details of the immediate environment. This is, if you think about it, quite a radical idea. Think back, for instance, to the encounter between Bernie Goetz and those four youths on the subway: Allen, Ramseur, Cabey, and Canty. At least two of them, according to some reports, appear to have been on drugs at the time of the incident. They all came from the Claremont Village housing project in one of the worst parts of the South Bronx. Cabey was, at the time, under indictment for armed robbery. Canty had a prior felony arrest for possession of stolen property. Allen had been previously arrested for attempted assault. Allen, Canty, and Ramseur also all had misdemeanor convictions, ranging from criminal mischief to petty larceny. Two years after the Goetz shooting, Ramseur was sentenced to twenty-five years in prison for rape, robbery, sodomy, sexual abuse, assault, criminal use of a firearm, and possession of stolen property. It's hard to be surprised when people like this wind up in the middle of a violent incident.

Then there's Goetz. He did something that is completely anomalous. White professionals do not, as a rule, shoot young black men on the subway. But if you look closely at who he was, he fits the stereotype of the kind of person who ends up in violent situations. His father was a strict disciplinarian with a harsh temper, and Goetz was often the focus of his father's rage. At school, he was the one teased by classmates, the last one picked for school games, a lonely child who would often leave school in tears. He worked, after graduating from college, for Westinghouse, building nuclear submarines. But he didn't last long. He was constantly clashing with his superiors over what he saw as shoddy practices and corner-cutting, and sometimes broke company and union rules by doing work that he was contractually forbidden to do. He took an apartment on Fourteenth Street in Manhattan, near Sixth Avenue, on a stretch of city block that was then heavy with homelessness and drug dealing. One of the doormen in the building, with whom Goetz was close, was beaten badly by muggers. Goetz became obsessed with cleaning up the neighborhood. He complained endlessly about a vacant newsstand near his building, which was used by vagrants as a trash bin and stank of urine. One night, mysteriously, it burned down, and the next day Goetz was out on the street sweeping away the debris. Once at a community meeting, he said, to the shock of others in the room, "The only way we're going to clean up this street is to get rid of the spics and niggers." In 1981, Goetz was mugged by three black youths as he entered the Canal Street station one afternoon. He ran out of the station with the three of them in pursuit. They grabbed the electronics equipment he was carrying, beat him, and threw him up against a plate-glass door, leaving him with permanent damage to his chest. With the help of an off-duty sanitation worker, Goetz managed to subdue one of his three attackers. But the experience left him embittered. He had to spend six hours in the station house, talking to police, while his assailant was released after two hours and charged, in the end, with only a misdemeanor. He applied to the city for a gun permit. He was turned down. In September 1984, his father died. Three months later, he sat down next to four black youths on the subway and started shooting.

Here, in short, was a man with an authority problem, with a strong sense that the system wasn't working, who had been the recent target of humiliation. Lillian Rubin, Goetz's biographer, writes that his choice to live on Fourteenth Street could hardly have been an accident. "For Bernie," she writes, "there seems to be something seductive about the setting. Precisely because of its deficits and discomforts, it provided him with a comprehensible target for the rage that lives inside him. By focusing it on the external world, he need not deal with his internal one. He rails about the dirt, the noise, the drunks, the crime, the pushers, the junkies. And all with good reason." Goetz's bullets, Rubin concludes, were "aimed at targets that existed as much in his past as in the present."

If you think of what happened on the number two train this way, the shooting begins to feel inevitable. Four hoodlums confront a man with apparent psychological problems. That the shooting took place on the subway seems incidental. Goetz would have shot those four kids if he had been sitting in a Burger King. Most of the formal explanations we use for criminal behavior follow along the same logic. Psychiatrists talk about criminals as people with stunted psychological development, people who have had pathological relationships with their parents, who lack adequate role models. There is a relatively new literature that talks about genes that may or may not dispose certain individuals to crime. On the popular side, there are endless numbers of books by conservatives talking about crime as a consequence of moral failure—of communities and schools and parents who no longer raise children with a respect for right and wrong. All of those theories are essentially ways of saying that the criminal is a personality type—a personality type distinguished by an insensitivity to the norms of normal society. People with stunted psychological development don't understand how to conduct healthy relationships. People with genetic predispositions to violence fly off the handle when normal people keep their cool. People who aren't taught right from wrong are oblivious to what is and what is not appropriate behavior. People who grow up poor, fatherless, and buffeted by racism don't have the same commitment to social norms as those from healthy middle-class homes. Bernie Goetz and those four thugs on the subway were, in this sense, prisoners of their own, dysfunctional world.

But what do Broken Windows and the Power of Context suggest? Exactly the opposite. They say that the criminal—far from being someone who acts for fundamental, intrinsic reasons and who lives in his own world—is actually someone acutely sensitive to his environment, who is alert to all kinds of cues, and who is prompted to commit crimes based on his perception of the world around him. That is an incredibly radical—and in some sense unbelievable—idea. There is an even more radical dimension here. The Power of Context is an environmental argument. It says that behavior is a function of social context. But it is a very strange kind of environmentalism. In the 1960s, liberals made a similar kind of argument, but when they talked about the importance of environment they were talking about the importance of fundamental social factors: crime, they said, was the result of social injustice, of structural economic inequities, of unemployment, of racism, of decades of institutional and social neglect, so that if you wanted to stop crime you had to undertake some fairly heroic steps. But the

Power of Context says that what really matters is little things. The Power of Context says that the showdown on the subway between Bernie Goetz and those four youths had very little to do, in the end, with the tangled psychological pathology of Goetz, and very little as well to do with the background and poverty of the four youths who accosted him, and everything to do with the message sent by the graffiti on the walls and the disorder at the turnstiles. The Power of Context says you don't have to solve the big problems to solve crime. You can prevent crimes just by scrubbing off graffiti and arresting fare-beaters.... This is what I meant when I called the Power of Context a radical theory. Giuliani and Bratton—far from being conservatives, as they are commonly identified— actually represent on the question of crime the most extreme liberal position imaginable, a position so extreme that it is almost impossible to accept. How can it be that what was going on in Bernie Goetz's head doesn't matter? And if it is really true that it doesn't matter, why is that fact so hard to believe?

4. [Elsewhere] I talked about two seemingly counterintuitive aspects of persuasion. One was the study that showed how people who watched Peter Jennings on ABC were more likely to vote Republican than people who watched either Tom Brokaw or Dan Rather because, in some unconscious way, Jennings was able to signal his affection for Republican candidates. The second study showed how people who were charismatic could—without saying anything and with the briefest of exposures—infect others with their emotions. The implications of those two studies go to the heart of the Law of the Few, because they suggest that what we think of as inner states—preferences and emotions—are actually powerfully and imperceptibly influenced by seemingly inconsequential personal influences, by a newscaster we watch for a few minutes a day or by someone we sit next to, in silence, in a two-minute experiment. The essence of the Power of Context is that the same thing is true for certain kinds of environments—that in ways that we don't necessarily appreciate, our inner states are the result of our outer circumstances. The field of psychology is rich with experiments that demonstrate this fact.

In the early 1970s, a group of social scientists at Stanford University, led by Philip Zimbardo, decided to create a mock prison in the basement of the university's psychology building. They took a thirty-five-foot section of corridor and created a cell block with a prefabricated wall. Three small, six-by-nine-foot cells were created from laboratory rooms and given steel-barred, black-painted doors. A closet was turned into a solitary confinement cell. The group then advertised in the local papers for volunteers, men who would agree to participate in the experiment. Seventy-five people applied, and from those Zimbardo and his colleagues picked the twenty-one who appeared the most normal and healthy on psychological tests. Half of the group were chosen, at random, to be guards, and were given uniforms and dark glasses and told that their responsibility was to keep order in the prison. The other half were told that they were to be prisoners. Zimbardo got the Palo Alto Police Department to "arrest" the prisoners in their homes, cuff them, bring them to the station house, charge them with a fictitious crime, fingerprint them, then blindfold them and bring them to the prison Psychology Department basement. Then they were stripped and given a prison uniform to wear, with a number on the front and back that was to serve as their only means of identification for the duration of their incarceration.

The purpose of the experiment was to try to find out why prisons are such nasty places. Was it because prisons are full of nasty people, or was it because prisons are such nasty environments that they make people nasty? In the answer to that question is obviously the answer to the question posed by Bernie Goetz and the subway cleanup, which is how much influence does immediate environment have on the way people behave? What Zimbardo found out shocked him. The guards, some of whom had previously identified themselves as pacifists, fell quickly into the role of hard-bitten disciplinarians. The first night they woke up the prisoners at two in the morning and made them do push-ups, line up against the wall, and perform other arbitrary tasks. On the morning of the second day, the prisoners rebelled. They ripped off their numbers and barricaded themselves in their cells. The guards responded by stripping them, spraying them with fire extinguishers, and throwing the leader of the rebellion into solitary confinement. "There were times when we were pretty abusive, getting right in their faces and yelling at them," one guard remembers. "It was part of the whole atmosphere of terror." As the experiment progressed, the guards got systematically crueler and more sadistic. "What we were unprepared for was the intensity of the change and the speed at which it happened," Zimbardo says. The guards were making the prisoners say to one another they loved each other, and making them march down the hallway, in handcuffs, with paper bags over their heads. "It was completely the opposite from the way I conduct myself now," another guard remembers. "I think I was positively creative in terms of my mental cruelty." After thirty-six hours, one prisoner began to get hysterical, and had to be released. Four more then had to be released because of "extreme emotional depression, crying, rage, and acute anxiety." Zimbardo had originally intended to have the experiment run for two weeks. He called it off after six days. "I realize now," one prisoner said after the experiment was over, "that no matter how together I thought I was inside my head, my prisoner behavior was often less under my control than I realized." Another said: "I began to feel that I was losing my identity, that the person I call _____, the person who volunteered to get me into this prison (because it was a prison to me, it still is a prison to me, I don't regard it as an experiment or a simulation ...) was distant from me, was remote, until finally I wasn't that person. I was 416. I was really my number and 416 was really going to have to decide what to do."

Zimbardo's conclusion was that there are specific situations so powerful that they can overwhelm our inherent predispositions. The key word here is "situation." Zimbardo isn't talking about environment, about the major external influences on all of our lives. He's not denying that how we are raised by our parents affects who we are, or that the kinds of schools we went to, the friends we have, or the neighborhoods we live in affect our behavior. All of these things are undoubtedly important. Nor is he denying that our genes play a role in determining who we are. Most psychologists believe that nature—genetics—accounts for about half of the reason why we tend to act the way we do. His point is simply that there are certain times and places and conditions when much of that can be swept away, that there are instances where you can take normal people from good schools and happy families and good neighborhoods and powerfully affect their behavior merely by changing the immediate details of their situation....

The mistake we make in thinking of character as something unified and all-encompassing is very similar to a kind of blind spot in the way we process information. Psychologists call this tendency the Fundamental Attribution Error (FAE), which is a fancy way of saying that when it comes to interpreting other people's behavior, human beings invariably make the mistake of overestimating the importance of fundamental character traits and underestimating the importance of the situation and context. We will always reach for a "dispositional" explanation for events, as opposed to a contextual explanation. In one experiment, for instance, a group of people are told to watch two sets of similarly talented basketball players, the first of whom are shooting baskets in a well-lighted gym and the second of whom are shooting baskets in a badly lighted gym (and obviously missing a lot of shots). Then they are asked to judge how good the players were. The players in the well-lighted gym were considered superior. In another example, a group of people are brought in for an experiment and told they are going to play a quiz game. They are paired off and they draw lots. One person gets a card that says he or she is going to be the "Contestant." The other is told he or she is going to be the "Questioner." The Questioner is then asked to draw up a list of ten "challenging but not impossible" questions based on areas of particular interest or expertise, so someone who is into Ukrainian folk music might come up with a series of questions based on Ukrainian folk music. The questions are posed to the Contestant, and after the quiz is over, both parties are asked to estimate the level of general knowledge of the other. Invariably, the Contestants rate the Questioners as being a lot smarter than they themselves are.

You can do these kinds of experiments a thousand different ways and the answer almost always comes out the same way. This happens even when you give people a clear and immediate environmental explanation of the behavior they are being asked to evaluate: that the gym, in the first case, has few lights on; that the Contestant is being asked to answer the most impossibly biased and rigged set of questions. In the end, this doesn't make much difference. There is something in all of us that makes us instinctively want to explain the world around us in terms of people's essential attributes: he's a better basketball player, that person is smarter than I am.

We do this because ... we are a lot more attuned to personal cues than contextual cues. The FAE also makes the world a much simpler and more understandable place... The psychologist Walter Mischel argues that the human mind has a kind of "reducing valve" that "creates and maintains the perception of continuity even in the face of perpetual observed changes in actual behavior." He writes:

> When we observe a woman who seems hostile and fiercely independent some of the time but passive, dependent and feminine on other occasions, our reducing valve usually makes us choose between the two

syndromes. We decide that one pattern is in the service of the other, or that both are in the service of a third motive. She must be a really castrating lady with a façade of passivity—or perhaps she is a warm, passive-dependent woman with a surface defense of aggressiveness. But perhaps nature is bigger than our concepts and it is possible for the lady to be a hostile, fiercely independent, passive, dependent, feminine, aggressive, warm, castrating person all-in-one. Of course which of these she is at any particular moment would not be random or capricious—it would depend on who she is with, when, how, and much, much more. But each of these aspects of her self may be a quite genuine and real aspect of her total being.

Character, then, isn't what we think it is or, rather, what we want it to be. It isn't a stable, easily identifiable set of closely related traits, and it only seems that way because of a glitch in the way our brains are organized. Character is more like a bundle of habits and tendencies and interests, loosely bound together and dependent, at certain times, on circumstance and context. The reason that most of us seem to have a consistent character is that most of us are really good at controlling our environment.

5. Some years ago two Princeton University psychologists, John Darley and Daniel Batson, decided to conduct a study inspired by the biblical story of the Good Samaritan. As you may recall, that story, from the New Testament Gospel of Luke, tells of a traveler who has been beaten and robbed and left for dead by the side of the road from Jerusalem to Jericho. Both a priest and a Levite—worthy, pious men—came upon the man but did not stop, "passing by on the other side." The only man to help was a Samaritan—the member of a despised minority—who "went up to him and bound up his wounds" and took him to an inn. Darley and Batson decided to replicate that study at the Princeton Theological Seminary. This was an experiment very much in the tradition of the FAE, and it is an important demonstration of how the Power of Context has implications for the way we think about social epidemics of all kinds, not just violent crime.

Darley and Batson met with a group of seminarians, individually, and asked each one to prepare a short, extemporaneous talk on a given biblical theme, then walk over to a nearby building to present it. Along the way to the presentation, each student ran into a man slumped in an alley, head down, eyes closed, coughing and groaning. The question was, who would stop and help? Darley and Batson introduced three variables into the experiment, to make its results more meaningful. First, before the experiment even started, they gave the students a questionnaire about why they had chosen to study theology. Did they see religion as a means of personal and spiritual fulfillment? Or were they looking for a practical tool for finding meaning in everyday life? Then they varied the subject of the theme the students were asked to talk about. Some were asked to speak on the relevance of the professional clergy to the religious vocation. Others were given the parable of the Good Samaritan. Finally, the instructions given by the experimenters to each student varied as well. In some of the cases, as he sent the students on their way, the experimenter would look at his watch and say, "Oh, you're late. They were expecting you a few minutes ago. We'd better get moving." In other cases, he would say, "It will be a few minutes before they're ready for you, but you might as well head over now."

If you ask people to predict which seminarians played the Good Samaritan (and subsequent studies have done just this), their answers are highly consistent. They almost all say that the students who entered the ministry to help people and those reminded of the importance of compassion by having just read the parable of the Good Samaritan will be the most likely to stop. Most of us, I think, would agree with those conclusions. In fact, neither of those factors made any difference. "It is hard to think of a context in which norms concerning helping those in distress are more salient than for a person thinking about the Good Samaritan, and yet it did not significantly increase helping behavior," Darley and Batson concluded. "Indeed, on several occasions, a seminary student going to give his talk on the parable of the Good Samaritan literally stepped over the victim as he hurried on his way." The only thing that really mattered was whether the student was in a rush. Of the group that was, 10-percent stopped to help. Of the group who knew they had a few minutes to spare, 63-percent stopped.

What this study is suggesting, in other words, is that the convictions of your heart and the actual contents of your thoughts are less important, in the end, in guiding your actions than the immediate context of your behavior. The words "Oh, you're late" had the effect of making someone who was ordinarily compassionate into someone who was indifferent to suffering—of turning someone, in that particular moment, into a different person. Epidemics are, at their root, about this very process of transformation. When we are trying to make an idea or attitude or product tip, we're trying to change our audience in some small yet critical respect: we're trying to infect them, sweep them up in our epidemic, convert them from hostility to acceptance. That can be done through the influence of special kinds of people, people of extraordinary personal connection. That's the Law of the Few. It can be done by changing the content of communication, by making a message so memorable that it sticks in someone's mind and compels them to action. That is the Stickiness Factor. I think that both of those laws make intuitive sense. But we need to remember that small changes in context can be just as important in tipping epidemics, even though that fact appears to violate some of our most deeply held assumptions about human nature.

This does not mean that our inner psychological states and personal histories are not important in explaining our behavior. An enormous percentage of those who engage in violent acts, for example, have some kind of psychiatric disorder or come from deeply disturbed backgrounds. But there is a world of difference between being inclined toward violence and actually committing a violent act. A crime is a relatively rare and aberrant event. For a crime to be committed, something extra, something additional, has to happen to tip a troubled person toward violence, and what the Power of Context is saying is that those Tipping Points may be as simple and trivial as everyday signs of disorder like graffiti and farebeating. The implications of this idea are enormous. The previous notion that disposition is everything—that the cause of violent behavior is always "sociopathic personality" or "deficient superego" or the inability to delay gratification or some evil in the genes—is, in the end, the most passive and reactive of ideas about crime. It says that once you catch a criminal you can try to help him get better—give him Prozac, put him in therapy, try to rehabilitate him—but there is very little you can do to prevent crime from happening in the first place.

Once you understand that context matters, however, that specific and relatively small elements in the environment can serve as Tipping Points, that defeatism is turned upside down. Environmental Tipping Points are things that we can change: we can fix broken windows and clean up graffiti and change the signals that invite crime in the first place. Crime can be more than understood. It can be prevented. There is a broader dimension to this. Judith Harris has convincingly argued that peer influence and community influence are more important than family influence in determining how children turn out. Studies of juvenile delinquency and high school drop-out rates, for example, demonstrate that a child is better off in a good neighborhood and a troubled family than he or she is in a troubled neighborhood and a good family. We spend so much time celebrating the importance and power of family influence that it may seem, at first blush, that this can't be true. But in reality it is no more than an obvious and common-sensical extension of the Power of Context, because it says simply that children are powerfully shaped by their external environment, that the features of our immediate social and physical world—the streets we walk down, the people we encounter—play a huge role in shaping who we are and how we act. It isn't just serious criminal behavior, in the end, that is sensitive to environmental cues, it is all behavior. Weird as it sounds, if you add up the meaning of the Stanford prison experiment and the New York subway experiment, they suggest that it is possible to be a better person on a clean street or in a clean subway than in one littered with trash and graffiti.

"In a situation like this, you're in a combat situation," Goetz told his neighbor Myra Friedman, in an anguished telephone call just days after the shooting. "You're not thinking in a normal way. Your memory isn't even working normally. You are so hyped up. Your vision actually changes. Your field of view changes. Your capabilities change. What you are capable of changes." He acted, Goetz went on, "viciously and savagely.... If you corner a rat and you are about to butcher it, okay? The way I responded was viciously and savagely, just like that, like a rat."

Of course he did. He was in a rat hole.

QUESTIONS FOR MAKING CONNECTIONS
WITHIN THE READING

1. "The Power of Context" is one of the middle chapters in Malcolm Gladwell's book *The Tipping Point: How Little Things Can Make a Big Difference*. In "The Power of Context," Gladwell refers to the three principles that govern what he calls the epidemic transmission of an idea: the Law of the Few, the Stickiness Factor, and the Power of Context. He provides thumbnail

sketches of the first two principles in this chapter, along with an elaboration of the Power of Context. What is the *Law of the Few*? What is the *Stickiness Factor*? How much can you piece together about the first two principles from what Gladwell presents in "The Power of Context"?

2. Gladwell states that the "Broken Windows Theory and the Power of Context are one and the same." What is the "Broken Windows Theory" of crime? How would one go about testing this theory? What other theories are available to explain the cause of crime? Why does it matter which theory one accepts? What real-world consequences followed from the application of a theory in the case of crime prevention in New York? What if some other theory had been applied?

3. Why is it a mistake to think of "character as something unified and all-encompassing"? If we accept the alternative, that character is fragmented and situation specific, what follows? How is Gladwell's argument meant to change its readers' understanding of criminals and their behavior? What about law-abiding citizens and their behavior?

QUESTIONS FOR WRITING

1. Toward the end of "The Power of Context," Gladwell asserts that his discussion of the relationship between criminal activity and local context has implications that "are enormous." Gladwell leaves it to his readers to spell out these implications. How would our social structure, our criminal system, our modes of education have to change if we abandoned what Gladwell terms our "most passive and reactive of ideas about crime"?

2. Gladwell argues that "small changes in context" can play a major role in determining whether an idea takes off or disappears without a trace. This fact, he goes on, "appears to violate some of our most deeply held assumptions about human nature." What does "human nature" mean, if one accepts the argument Gladwell makes in "The Power of Context"? Is it possible to create any form of human behavior just by manipulating the contextual background? Does Gladwell's view suggest that humans are more free than previously thought, or that their behavior is more fully determined than previously thought?

QUESTIONS FOR MAKING CONNECTIONS
BETWEEN READINGS

1. Drawing on Darley and Batson's Good Samaritan study, Gladwell finds evidence that "the convictions of your heart and the actual contents of your thoughts are less important, in the end, in guiding your actions than the

immediate context of your behavior." The challenge here is defining what counts as one's "immediate context." Does the generation you belong to count as an immediate context? Explore this possibility and its implications by turning to Jean Twenge's description of the characteristics and qualities of Generation Me. What relationship, if any, is there between the influence of membership in a generation and the power of context, as Gladwell describes it?

2. In *The Naked Citadel*, Susan Faludi provides a rich description of life in an alternate social structure—the military academy. Does Malcolm Gladwell's account help to explain why Shannon Faulkner wasn't welcomed into the academy? Did Faulkner's appearance cause the academy to "tip"? Does Gladwell's theory have any predictive value? That is, could it tell us, ahead of time, whether the academy would be transformed by being required to admit women?

KAREN HO

As KAREN HO's writing demonstrates, finance and education now intersect in a way few outsiders know much about: some of America's most powerful and prestigious universities have close ties with Wall Street firms. In 2007, the year before the recession began, more than half of Harvard's graduates chose careers in business or a related field. Two years later, thirty-six percent of Princeton's most recent graduates took a job in finance. Although the percentages have recently declined, the ties between the Ivy League and "the Street" have disturbing implications for the future of higher education in the United States.

For a long time colleges and universities played a special social role because the diversity of the curriculum reflected the rich development of culture over many centuries. History, literature, foreign languages, math and science, anthropology, sociology, psychology—these and other academic disciplines have given many generations of students the opportunity to broaden their minds while preparing them for their future work in a wide variety of fields. But now this ideal of higher education as an exploration of possibilities has come under intense pressure from the influence of "financialization." A number of observers have looked critically at this recent turn, but Karen Ho's writing is unique for several reasons. For one thing, the time she spent working on Wall Street gives her an insider's eye, but she is also an anthropologist who believes the Street has created a distinctive outlook that threatens to remake the whole society in its narrowing image:

> Wall Street shapes not just the stock market but also the very nature of employment and what kinds of workers are valued [everywhere]....
> The kind of worker they imagine is a worker like themselves. A worker who is constantly retraining, a worker who is constantly networked, a worker whose skill set is very interchangeable, a worker who thinks of downsizing as a challenge—a worker who thrives on this. This becomes the prototype, but in many ways that's quite removed from the daily lives of most American workers.

On Wall Street, rapid change and high risk hold the key to personal success, but for many other Americans, values of this kind have undermined their security and

Excerpts from LIQUIDATED, by Karen Ho, pp. 1–38 and 39–72. Copyright, 2009, Duke University Press. All rights reserved. Republished by permission of the copyright holder. www.dukeupress.edu

Figures on Harvard, Princeton students come from Catherine Rampell, "Out of Harvard and into Finance," *New York Times* December 11, 2011. The quotation comes from Barbara Kiviat, "An Anthropologist on What's Wrong with Wall Street," *Time*, July 22, 2009.

quality of life. If Ho is correct, then Americans need to rediscover or invent values of a different, more democratic kind. But where will this search for new values take place? Traditionally, such alternatives have come from colleges and universities. What will happen to the United States, however, if these institutions too are captured by the "ideology" of finance?

Biographies of Hegemony

When I began to conduct fieldwork in 1998 and 1999, delving into the network of contacts, coworkers, and friends I developed at Stanford, Princeton, and Bankers Trust (BT), it struck me how often my informants ranked and distinguished themselves according to their "smartness." The term seemed fundamental to the Wall Street lexicon. My informants proclaimed that the smartest people in the world came to work there; Wall Street, in their view, had created probably the most elite work-society ever to be assembled on the globe. Almost all the front-office workers that I encountered emphasized how smart their coworkers were, how "deep the talent" was at their particular bank, how if one just hired "the smartest people," then everything else fell into place. Chris Logan and Nicolas Bern, recent Princeton graduates working at BT and Merrill Lynch respectively, explained that from their relatively fresh perspective, what was most culturally unique about Wall Street was the experience of being surrounded by, as Bern put it, the "smartest and most ambitious people." Logan added that the three qualities of success on Wall Street are to be "smart, hardworking, and aggressive. Everything else is considered tangential." According to Kate Miller, a Spelman College graduate and former analyst at Morgan Stanley, interviewees are typically told they will be working with "the brightest people in the world. These are the greatest minds of the century."

Such sentiments were not confined to eager young analysts or investment banking representatives talking up their industry to overawed recruits. Julio Muñoz, who received his MBA from Harvard and was an associate in investment banking at Donaldson, Lufkin and Jenrette (DLJ), a prestigious boutique investment bank which has since been bought out by Credit Suisse First Boston (CSFB), claimed that the most distinguishing features of investment banks are their smartness and exclusivity:

> People are really smart. They really don't hire any—the hiring standards are pretty good. That's one thing they really focused on doing, and that differentiates investment banking from other working environments in that they really do target the experienced individuals with good academic background.... [This] really brings to the investment banks a very

elite society—somebody in society that had the means to study in X universities. If you really narrowed down the universities where the investment banks recruit, your number probably will not exceed fifteen to twenty universities.

Similarly, John Carlton, a senior managing director at BT who had worked at multiple investment banks such as Kidder Peabody and CSFB, stated that the key characteristics of Wall Street investment bankers are their smartness, aggressiveness, and self-confidence: "There is always a premium on having smart people ... so, it is highly competitive. What happens is that a lot of people say, 'Look, some of the best and brightest people are going to Wall Street. I'm pretty smart myself; I should go [there] as well. And, by the way, I get paid very well.'" Remarking on how hedge funds attract the most brilliant minds from investment banks, Robert Hopkins, a vice president of mergers and acquisitions at Lehman Brothers, exclaimed, "We are talking about the smartest people in the world. We are! They are the smartest people in the world. If you [the average investor or the average corporation] don't know anything, why wouldn't you invest with the smartest people in the world? They must know what they are doing."[1]

The "culture of smartness" is central to understanding Wall Street's financial agency, how investment bankers are personally and institutionally empowered to enact their worldviews, export their practices, and serve as models for far-reaching socioeconomic change. On Wall Street, "smartness" means much more than individual intelligence; it conveys a naturalized and generic sense of "impressiveness," of elite, pinnacle status and expertise, which is used to signify, even prove, investment bankers' worthiness as advisors to corporate America and leaders of the global financial markets. To be considered "smart" on Wall Street is to be implicated in a web of situated practices and ideologies, coproduced through the interactions of multiple institutions, processes, and American culture at large, which confer authority and legitimacy on high finance and contribute to the sector's vast influence. The culture of smartness is not simply a quality of Wall Street, but a currency, a driving force productive of both profit accumulation and global prowess.

The key criterion of smartness is an ability to "wow" the clients—generally speaking, the top executives of Fortune 500 companies. In this sense, although technical skill and business savvy also help to constitute smartness on Wall Street, they are often considered secondary, learnable "on the job." "The best," "the greatest," and "the brightest" minds in the world are sorted and recognized through a credentialing process that is crucially bolstered by image and performance. In other words, smartness must be represented and reinforced by a specific appearance and bodily technique that dominantly signals that impressiveness; not surprisingly, such characteristics as being impeccably and smartly dressed, dashing appearance, mental and physical quickness, aggressiveness, and vigor reference the default upperclassness, maleness, whiteness, and heteronormativity of ideal investment bankers. Here I focus mainly on the specific elitism that is the key valence of smartness....

What allows investment bankers to claim smartness, what defines and legitimates them as smart in the first place, and what particular kind of smartness is being deployed? Where these questions become especially clear is during the process of investment banker identity and social formation: the recruiting, training, and orientation of freshly minted college graduates and MBAs, their initiation into the world of Wall Street. Here it is possible to discern, in starkest relief, Wall Street's cultural values in action, particularly the construction and maintenance of the hegemonic elitism that produces "expert" knowledge of financial markets. Through the continual praxis of recruitment and orientation, the Street enacts and regenerates the very foundations of its legitimacy.

Through the process of recruitment and orientation, investment banks define their notion of both what it takes and what it means to be a successful subject in an age of global capital. To play the role of "master of the universe" requires not only especially strong doses of self-confidence and institutional legitimation, but also a particular set of beliefs regarding Wall Street's role in the world and one's own role on Wall Street. Investment bankers, trained to view financial markets and corporate America through particular, highly ideological lenses, are also imbued with a sense of their own personal exemplariness as agents of *and models for* socioeconomic change—a sense that must be embodied, believed in, and continually "pumped up." In approaching the question of how investment bankers become empowered to advise and influence the direction of corporations in the United States and globally vis à vis their personal trajectories, qualities, connections, associations, and identities, I make the case for the importance of the biographical and the institutional in enacting global capitalist change. The building blocks of dominant capitalist practices are also personal and cultural; people's experiences, their university and career tracking and choices, are constitutive of capitalist hegemony; and the financial is cultural through and through.

In particular, I focus on the construction of "the smart investment banker": a member of an extended "family" network of elite university alumni and a living symbol of know-how and global agency. Their impressiveness and financial influence are further cemented and proven by surviving brutally intense hard work and an insecure job environment, which in turn allows them to internalize the merit of their analyses and recommendations. Through the institutional culture of Wall Street broadly conceived—where job experiences and workplace incentives map onto elite biographies—investment bankers not only imbibe a particular ideology of shareholder value and spread it across corporate America, but they are also pushed to refashion and reconstruct the working lives of millions in the image of their own.

By investigating investment bankers, as individuals and as collective agents of change, I do not assume a priori that "the market" always already exercises power, but rather that the particular biographies, experiences, and practices of investment bankers, who are both empowered and constrained by their cultural and institutional locations, create social change and financial hegemony on a daily basis. Just as "it is through the 'small stories' that one can begin to unravel and challenge homogenizing discourses embedded within concepts such as globalization, 'the' market, and 'the' state," it is possible to decenter the market as an abstract agent and powerful force by demonstrating that it is only through the small and the everyday that we can understand the creation of hegemony in all its particularity and contextuality. Otherwise, we risk privileging, homogenizing, or taking for granted the metanarratives of the market, the big stories (Crossa 2005, 29; S. 170).

RECRUITMENT

I first entered the cultural world of investment banks through the herculean recruiting efforts that Wall Street undertakes at the most elite universities. Despite my own ambivalence and feelings of mystification about Wall Street as an anthropology graduate student, this direct link—the pipeline between Princeton University and investment banks—enabled my very access to each step of the recruiting process, not to mention the field site itself. Wall Street, in a sense, came to me. Although I hardly recognized it at the time, Wall Street's ubiquity on campus, as well as the intensity of undergraduate interest in investment banking, meant that merely being a student at Princeton allowed, in a sense, automatic participant observation of this world. After fieldwork, I returned to Princeton to write the dissertation, thinking I would be getting away from Wall Street, retreating to an ivory-tower refuge in order to do some serious thinking and writing. Instead, it was more like reentering the belly of the beast. I was a graduate advisor at an undergraduate resident hall. Two weeks into the job, taking a walk after dinner I crossed paths with an undergraduate crowd (two of whom lived in my residence hall) headed toward Nassau Hall. Before I knew it, they had steered me into a Merrill Lynch presentation! The masses of students converging on these recruitment presentations and information sessions are akin to the campus traffic generated by the gatherings and dispersals of concert crowds. Already a veteran of the actual recruitment process back in 1996, now, almost four years later, after campus recruiting had even further intensified as a result of the bull market, I found myself participating in countless dining hall discussions about investment banking, attending still more presentations, and reading endless investment banking advertisements, updates, news, and opinion pieces in the pages of the *Daily Princetonian*. In 2000, I also had access on a regular basis to many of Wall Street's cultural representations and practices at Harvard University because my younger sister was an undergraduate there at the time. She introduced me to friends going through the recruiting process and kept me continually updated on how many of her acquaintances had suddenly, in their senior year, found their true calling as Wall Street investment bankers or management consultants. As many of my previous investment banking informants were also Harvard graduates, I have been able to make detailed observations of Wall Street's interactions with two elite universities.

More so than even the other Ivy League schools, Harvard and Princeton are the "prime recruiting ground for all of the most prestigious Wall Street, management consulting and other types of firms that offer the most sought after jobs.... The Princeton badge is a powerful currency that buys access" (Karseras 2006). As many of my informants have elaborated, "If you go to Harvard, Yale, or Princeton, there are really only two career fields presented: banking and consulting" (Duboff 2005). This shocking narrowness was verified throughout my time at Princeton and on Wall Street: I found not only that most bankers came from a few elite institutions, but also that most undergraduate and even many graduate students assumed that the only "suitable" destinations for life after Princeton— the only sectors offering a truly "Princeton-like job"—were, first, investment banking, and second, management consulting.[2] With its extensive alumni network and juggernaut recruitment machine, Wall Street is the "de facto home away from Princeton for recent graduates, many of whom continue living together even as they take on new responsibilities and lifestyles" (Hall 2005).

As perhaps the most important feeder school to Wall Street, Princeton sends astounding numbers of recruits into financial services in general, and in particular investment banking. According to the Office of Career Services, 30 percent of the class of 2001, 37 percent of the class of 2003, and 40 percent of the class of 2005 and 2006 entered financial services after graduation (Chan 2001; Creed 2003; Easton 2006; Henn 2001). Whereas from 2000 to 2005, 470 Princeton students pursued law or medical degrees, "520 Princeton students—about 40 percent of Princeton students choosing fulltime jobs directly after graduation—decided to work in the financial services sector," amounting to the largest percentage in a single industry (Hall 2005). At Harvard University, which rivals Princeton as the primary producer of Wall Street recruits, investment banking (as well as management consulting) also provides the majority of jobs for its students upon graduation (Lerer 1997). According to Harvard's Office of Career Services, in 2005, close to half of Harvard students go through "the recruiting process to vie for investment banking and consulting jobs" (Huber 2006).

As Devon Peterson, an undergraduate writing for the *Daily Princetonian*, observed in 2002, "It's been common knowledge that many of [Princeton's] undergraduates join the financial realm every year, creating a kind of lighthearted, self-deprecating joke about Philosophy majors becoming I-bankers and once hopeful novelists heading to Wall Street" (Peterson 2002). How do so many undergraduates who enter these institutions without any prior knowledge of investment banking, who once aspired to become, say writers or teachers, "realize" by the time they graduate that they have always wanted to go to Wall Street? How do these talented and well-connected students, with access to a wide range of possible futures, come to believe that investment banking is one of the *only* prestigious job options available post graduation? I argue that such changes in life courses and the attendant discursive transformations must be unpacked in order to understand the particular worldviews, cultural associations, and orientations the recruiting process demands and calls into being.

The forces that push these college students toward investment banking are obviously multiple: the particular college environment, the strength of alumni and peer networks, the cultural linking of success and smartness with Wall Street, the hierarchical narrowing of career options and what constitutes prestige, to name a few. Perhaps the most self-evident reason for Wall Street's recruiting monopoly is simply that its presence dominates campus life: recruiters visit the university virtually every week, even on weekends; they show up in the greatest numbers at career forums, panel discussions, and social events; their advertisements for information sessions "meet and greets," and free drinks and hors d'oeuvres dominate the campus newspapers daily; their company literature and application forms are easily accessible, either at campus locations or online.

The recruiting process saturates almost every aspect of campus life from the very first day of the academic year. Investment banks and consulting firms dominate the early fall career fairs, setting the terms for what constitutes a successful career (and what it looks like), and monopolize the attention of the student body by showing up with the most polish, fanfare, and numbers. They hand out the best goodie bags, the most titillating magnet sets, mugs, Frisbees, water bottles, caps, and t-shirts, and in a matter of days, thousands of students become walking advertisements as their logos disperse into campus life. At the 2006 Princeton Career Fair, 60 of the 104 firms represented were in financial services or consulting (Rampell 2006). At the 2003 Harvard Career Forum, more than half of the close to one hundred firms in attendance were in investment banking, general finance, and consulting (Urken and Habib 2003). Marketed as general career exploration meant to attract a diversity of students and pathways, these forums actually constitute "recruitment on a grand scale" for the investment banking and consulting industries *(Harvard Crimson* 1995). This early and intense branding of Wall Street careers as the symbol of arrival, the equating of investment banking with "career" in general, serves to narrow students' notions of success and gives the impression that for graduates, there's nothing else out there besides investment banking and consulting (N. Guyer 2003).

Taufiq Rahim, a *Daily Princetonian* columnist, wrote of what he called the "hunting season": "They're here. I can see them. I can smell them. They're in my inbox. They're in my mailbox. They're on my voicemail. They're outside my door. They're on campus, and they smell blood.... They're the investment banks, the consulting firms: McKinsey, Goldman Sachs, Bain and Company, Merrill Lynch" (Rahim 2003). Below I reproduce Goldman Sachs's "Recruitment Calendar" for Harvard undergraduates at the millennium (see Table 1). The recruitment schedule is painstakingly detailed, demonstrating the active pursuit of Harvard students: they will not fall through the cracks. As the director of Princeton's Career Services cautioned students about Wall Street recruiters: "They come after you. If you're hiding under the bed and you don't want to talk anymore, they'll come and get you" (Shapira 1998).

On the day of the recruitment presentation (and most investment banks usually have multiple campus events, as separate divisions will have their own presentations and interview timelines), a given bank's representatives descend in droves to central campus locations, usually the fanciest business hotel near campus. For Princeton, bankers will charter a bus, a few limos, and even some taxis to drive a group of thirty to fifty investment bankers, research analysts, and traders (usually alumni who will also serve as recruiters) from New York City to the Nassau Inn at Princeton. The same goes for Harvard. Elaborate recruitment presentations are held at the Charles Hotel in Cambridge or the Faculty Club; dozens of recent Harvard graduates and seasoned alumni currently working on Wall Street fill the rooms. Including recent hires from Harvard and Princeton allows potential recruits to witness former classmates as smart and successful, as having made the transition from undergraduate life onto the Wall Street fast track.

The very first Wall Street recruitment event I ever attended, in 1995 as a graduate student still contemplating research on Wall Street, was a session presented by Goldman Sachs, widely known among potential employees as the

T A B L E 1   Goldman Sachs Recruitment Schedule at Harvard University, 2000–2001.

Division	Date	Event
Firmwide	September 6, 2000	Thirteenth Annual Women's Leadership Conference Panel Discussion, 10:00–11:30 A.M.
Firmwide	September 14, 2000	HSA Business Leadership Dinner The Charles Hotel, 6:00–8:00 P.M.
Firmwide	September 27, 2000	Resume Writing Workshop Office of Career Services, 12:00–3:00 P.M.
Firmwide	September 27, 2000	Firmwide Information Session The Charles Hotel 6:00–8:00 P.M.
Investment Management	October 2, 2000	Divisional Presentation The Charles Hotel, 6:30–8:00 P.M.
Investment Banking	October 3, 2000	Divisional Presentation The Charles Hotel, 6:30–8:00 P.M.
Equities	October 5, 2000	Divisional Presentation Faculty Club, 8:00–9:30 P.M.
Firmwide	October 11, 2000	HSA Career Week Panel Discussion on "My Career"
Firmwide	October 13, 2000	Career Forum Gordon Track and Tennis Center
Sales and Trading	October 16, 2000	Divisional Presentation The Charles Hotel, 6:30–8:00 P.M.
All Divisions	October 19, 2000	Resume Drop
Corporate Treasury	October 25, 2000	Resume Drop (open)
Corporate Treasury	October 27, 2000	2 Open Full-time Analyst Interview Schedules
Firmwide	October 30, 2000	Minority Event (tentative)
Fixed Income, Currency & Commodities	October 30, 2000	Resume Drop (open)
Fixed Income, Currency & Commodities	November 1, 2000	1.5 Closed Full-Time Analyst Interview Schedules 1.5 Open Full-Time Analyst Interview Schedules
Investment Banking	November 2, 2000	3 Closed Full-Time Analyst Interview Schedules
Equities	November 3, 2000	3 Closed Full-Time Analyst Interview Schedules
Investment Research	November 9, 2000	2 Closed Full-Time Analyst Interview Schedules (1 Schedule for London)
Investment Management	November 9, 2000	2 Closed Full-Time Analyst Interview Schedules
Firmwide	December 4, 2000	Women's Event (tentative)

TABLE 1 **Continued**

Division	Date	Event
Firmwide	December 14, 2000	Resume Drop for Spring
The Hull Group	January 30, 2001	1 Closed Full-Time Analyst Interview Schedule
Equities	February 2, 2001	3 Closed Full-Time Analyst Interview Schedules
Fixed Income Research and Strategy	February 7, 2001	1 Closed Full-Time Analyst Interview Schedule
Fixed Income, Currency & Commodities	February 7, 2001	1.5 Closed Full-Time Analyst Interview Schedules 1.5 Open Summer Analyst Interview Schedules
Investment Banking	February 7, 2001	3 Closed Full-Time Analyst Interview Schedules
Investment Management	February 8, 2001	1 Closed Full-Time Analyst Interview Schedule 2 Closed Summer Analyst Interview Schedules
Equities	February 9, 2001	3 Closed Full-Time Analyst Interview Schedules
Investment Research	February 13, 2001	1 Closed Full-Time Analyst Interview Schedule
Investment Banking Training and Professional Development	February 21, 2001	1 Closed Full-Time Analyst Interview Schedule 1 Closed Summer Analyst Interview Schedule
Firmwide	TBD	IPO Case Study in conjunction with the Office of Career Services

most prestigious and exclusive investment bank on Wall Street. Arriving a little late at Princeton township's hallowed Nassau Inn, I was greeted by a sea of charcoal gray, navy, and black business suits. There must have been over 150 well-coiffed and starched, professionally driven undergraduates crowding the hotel's ballroom to hear a panel of sixteen Goldman Sachs executives, mostly Princeton grads. Apprehension and eagerness pervaded the room: this was not a time for socializing but rather for competitive vying for "face time" and searing first impressions with the recruiters. Instead of saying hello to friends, juniors and seniors surveyed the room and sought to get on their marks. As the only graduate student in the room, (as far as I could tell), awkwardly attempting to both observe and participate in the recruiting process, not to mention the fact that I was dressed in an old pair of slightly wrinkled gray slacks and a denim vest (of all things), I felt completely out of place.

The lights soon darkened for an introductory slide and video presentation. It was a recorded narration with sweeping views of Manhattan and fast-moving visuals of the globe, suit-clad workers traveling or walking briskly to corporate towers, and sharp-dressed bankers videoconferencing or huddled up in teams with their sleeves rolled up. The narrator explained that a Wall Street career was all about "dealing with change." "The world is going to continue to change faster and faster, so we need people like you." When the lights came on, we turned our attention to the panel. I counted eight white men, five white women, one Latino man, one South Asian woman, and one black man. A relatively older white man, a managing director (Princeton class of '82), began to speak in a tone of pride: "We are a Princeton family. I met my wife here. Princeton students make the best analysts, which is why we recruit heavily here." The other speakers who were recent graduates introduced themselves by naming the schools they had attended: Harvard, Williams, Harvard, Princeton, Wharton, Princeton, Princeton, Princeton. "I'm from the University of Chicago," said the south Asian woman wryly. "I'm not quite as bright as everyone else." The Princetonian managing director then got down to business. "The two-year program will go by in a flash. Your learning and growth curve will be exponential. You will get actual interaction with clients. You are part of the team at our firm; the last thing you should be doing is photocopying. We hire ten people to do that, and that's all they do. We need your intelligence." It quickly became apparent that this was the evening's guiding theme. "So why should you work here?" asked the recent white male alumnus from Harvard. "Because if you hang out with dumb people, you'll learn dumb things. In investment banking, the people are very smart; that's why they got the job. It's very fast, very challenging, and they'll teach as quickly as you can learn." Some speakers emphasized the access to power offered by a Goldman Sachs position. "Our analysts can go anywhere in the world," said one of the white male vice presidents who is an alumnus from Wharton. "We've got Hong Kong, we've got Sydney, we've got London." He returned, inevitably, to the presentation's central motif; with an admiring gaze at the audience, he exclaimed, "You are all so smart!" Finally, the Princetonian managing director got up and announced, "Let's break up, go to the Nassau Inn Tap Room; drinks are on us!" The swarm of undergraduates then beelined toward the panelists, eager for face time with actual Goldman Sachs executives while I was still lingering in my seat. Determined to join the fray, I surveyed the scene and realized that every investment banker was already surrounded by two to three semi-circle layers of undergraduates: as the first layer moved to impress and receive the business card of the banker holding court, the second layer would quickly move into "face-time" position. The only room in the crowd for me was actually behind the speaker's back where there was no waiting line! In that position, I mainly observed throughout the night, and the only person who turned around to talk to me was the young South Asian American analyst from the University of Chicago, and I held on dearly to her business card as a sign of my initiation into this grueling process.

During subsequent recruitment presentations, I experienced much of the same: well-suited alumnae declaring, "We only hire superstars," "We are only hiring from five different schools," "You are the cream of the crop." In these sessions, I was stuck by how proclamations of elitism (through "world-class" universities, the discourses of smartness and globalization) seemed foundational to the very core of how investment bankers see themselves, the world, and their place in it. Representing a world of "collective smartness" and exclusivity seemed fundamentally connected not only to the criteria for becoming an investment banker but also to the very nature of what they do. What precisely were the links between elitism and the enactments of their financial expertise and global dreams, between Wall Street's claims to smartness and their promises of global prowess? Motivated in large part by these compelling presentations, I decided that to understand these grandiose, even mystifying, pronouncements, I had to get a job on Wall Street. I took a leave of absence from graduate school to participate "for real" in this process.

The "vigorous college recruiting season" is usually capped off with elaborate "sell days" to encourage seniors to accept the job. Such perks include "ski trips to Utah and dinners at Lahiere's" (Princeton's four-star restaurant) (Easton 2006; Shapira 1998). Every junior and senior that I interviewed spoke about the allure of recruiting, the constant wining and dining, the fancy spreads at upscale hotels and clubs. According to the *Daily Princetonian* staff writer Alice Easton:

> After months of dressing up in suits and ties, making their way to New York or the Nassau Inn and trying to impress panels of interviewers with their technical and social skills, juniors applying for summer internships in finance and consulting can now reap the benefits of their work: elaborate "sell days" to convince them to accept the job…. "They paid for two nights at a fancy hotel in New York…. They rented out a museum and had a cocktail party, and then rented out the VIP room in a nightclub in Soho."… The company later sent him chocolates in the mail…. [They showed recruits] a whole lifestyle. (Easton 2006)

The obvious implication is that if Harvard and Princeton students join these firms, then in a few years, they too can have it all.

During one of my visits to Harvard University to see my sister in 2000, I sat down with Kendra Lin, a premed student who was not planning to go into investment banking but wanted to understand "what the hype was all about" and possessed a genuine curiosity about why her classmates were so obsessed with Wall Street. In addition to attending the various career forums and participating formally in the recruiting process by signing up with the Office of Career Services (OCS), many Harvard students also participate in immersion programs to educate them about Wall Street and management consulting. Therefore, at the time, at the onset of recruiting season, Harvard Student Agencies, in collaboration with Harvard Business School and leading investment banks and management consulting firms, sponsored the Harvard Business Leadership Program (BLP), a week of recruitment, training, socializing, and general orientation to Wall Street financial institutions, management consulting, and general business practices. Being chosen to participate in BLP was itself a competitive process to search for "business leaders," and as the president of various student associations, Lin made the cut.

Describing her impressions of the BLP events, Lin said that the speakers who made the greatest impression were the representatives of Goldman Sachs. "They're this really elite investment bank that advises many leaders in corporate America on their mergers and acquisitions and securities offerings. They talked about how they managed the privatizations of the largest corporations in China and Spain, to name a few." While some of the non-investment-banking financial firms and smaller start-up corporations (who were in the minority) appeared "homely" to Lin, firms like J. P. Morgan and Goldman Sachs and management consulting groups like Boston Consulting Group "looked very accomplished" and "thought very highly of themselves." As a result, all the Harvard students flocked to talk to them. During the cocktail and dinner hour after the presentations, investment banks proclaimed that Harvard produced the most stellar recruits. Lin talked at length about her favorable impression of Goldman Sachs:

> I really enjoyed Goldman—as a side note, all of these firms are really talented in recruiting students. They make Harvard students feel like they are the cream of the crop. We have the best minds. This image of the Harvard student runs thick through recruiters and through people at the business school. I have heard this many times over the course of the week: that Harvard students are the best business people because you can give them any problem and they will be the ones to come up with the solution most quickly.... I left his speech believing that Goldman is the Harvard of all investment banks, but they all sure know how to sell themselves well.

Goldman Sachs, as Lin described, worked very hard to position itself as an extension of Harvard and, in doing so, confirmed Harvard as the progenitor of the best.

According to Lin, investment bankers emphasized how they "had the perfect life." One executive talked about how "he lives in the burbs, has a minivan, a dog, and two kids. Seriously! His wife graduated from Pritzker [the University of Chicago's business school] and is now a Harvard Medical School professor, and he is a rich VP." After hearing Lin's initial impressions on Wall Street recruiting presentations, I asked her what she thought about her week-long experience with BLP—the dinners, the socials, the business school case studies. What did she like and dislike?

KL: It's all a schmooze fest. You have to schmooze your recruiters. You have to master rounds of interviews followed by more schmoozing, and then once you get there, you have to "live the lifestyle" of a business person. Be social, drink, go to parties, and schmooze some more. Also ... there is no commitment really to social change.

KH: Interesting observations. How did you realize just from this week, so early on, that people have to "live the lifestyle"? How were you clued into this point?

KL: I think it was the set up of the whole BLP that first clued me in to that: I mean, they cater *all* of our meals, our dinners are all at the Charles hotel, and they are quite extravagant for a bunch of college kids. Hey, I love duck and sushi! Before we go into the hotel for dinner, there is a social hour where they serve juice and soda, and that's where it hit me. Basically you see all these students huddled around the bankers and consultants and kissing their ass. Everyone's all dressed up—it's a different culture. Put that together with stereotypes of businessmen from movies, you see that it really is pretty much like that.

This conflation of elite universities with investment banking and "the perfect lifestyle" is crucial to the recruitment process, reproducing as it does the ambience of Wall Street cocktail parties, where investment bankers "schmooze clients" in lavish, impeccably catered settings. These norms are enacted for and demonstrated to students, and like Lin, they immediately pick up on the importance of performing "smartness," not to mention how Wall Street business success is premised on pedigree, competitive consumption, and heteronormativity.

Not surprisingly, Wall Street's intense focus and persistence at Princeton, Harvard, and a few other campuses have repercussions for student culture. Newspapers and dorms overflow with debates about the pros and cons of investment banking work life, excited discussions of what investment bankers "actually do," and romanticized tales of high-roller life in Manhattan. Students begin to see "i-banking" as a "mysterious, glamorous and relatively undefined world" (Hall 2005). A glance at the campus publications at Princeton and Harvard demonstrates what amounts to a communal obsession, with constant news and opinion articles on "recruiting insanity," "avoiding the i-banking shadow," "schmoozing at Nassau Inn," "defending the indefensible career," "the dangerous allure of recruiting," "aspiring Gordon Gekkos," "new recruits," "future financiers flock to a Darwinian fete," "banking on pain," "i-banking ire," "how investment banking consumed my life," and "is there more to life than investment banking?" Heated campus panel discussions debate the relative merits of banking and consulting, as panelists (firm representatives, usually former students) face off with a cost-benefit analysis of the two career choices and use the platform to further recruit students to their side. It is hardly surprising, then, that the much-mythologized field of investment banking often presents itself as the solution to anxieties about postgraduation life.

Although most of my recruitment participation was with undergraduates (as I myself went through the college analyst recruitment program), the process for elite business schools for the recruitment of MBAS for associate positions (one level higher than analyst) has similar components. For the most part, many graduate students at prestigious business schools, such as Harvard Business School (HBS), Wharton, Sloan (MIT Business School), Columbia Business School, and so forth, have had financial experience. Most have worked as analysts at investment banks or in management consulting firms; those who do not have a financial background have plenty of opportunity to study finance as a "concentration" in business schools. All MBAs are literally bombarded by recruitment presentations and information sessions sponsored by their school's own student finance clubs and associations as well as Wall Street investment banks themselves.

Starting the first year, MBA students realize that to work on Wall Street after graduating from the two-year masters program, they must intern on Wall Street their first summer and receive a job offer thirteen weeks into the internship. As Bill Hayes, a recent MIT Sloan alumnus and an associate at Goldman Sachs, described the process in 2001:

> Within a month of school starting, everyone starts coming. Hotel pre-sentations; meet and greets. They invite you out for drinks in the effort to get the best and brightest to apply. The bulge bracket firms don't have to sell themselves (the smaller banks do) since all the students gravitate toward them. I guess only they can afford it. They'll have a reception, and you have to meet people and hope you make some sort of connection. For Merrill, I went to a presentation, sent in my resume, and they called. Goldman came in with a whole crew of Wharton alumni, and then went to HBS afterwards. At the same time this is all happening, we have smaller events where the school Finance Club has receptions with bankers from top firms, where half of the MBA class shows up, or these clubs have information "learning" sessions like "Investment Banking 101" and "Day on the Job," which is a smaller setting, and you hope to make a contact with a recent grad to give you an "in." You have to send follow-up e-mails and thank-you's to every contact. Our Finance Club also organized mock interviews, resume workshops, and "trips to Wall Street" where anyone can go and visit all the banks. I met with Morgan and Goldman and Lehman. You go to their offices and try to distinguish yourself.... They only hire from these elite schools because they are already prefiltered. It makes you feel good; you've already been nominated. Bankers will say, "You might ask why we ask about GPA and test scores. Because we've done the correlation between top GPA and test scores from top schools and performance in the organization, and we know you will succeed."

Wall Street saturation of business school life is certainly equal to that of the general university population. The difference is that elite MBA programs explicitly represent themselves as channels to and of Wall Street; they are not emphasizing a general liberal arts education. Students often enter these institutions precisely to get a job in finance, and just a few months into the scramble for a job at top Wall Street investment banks, the first-round interview slots are full.

For MBAs, the selling of "the perfect lifestyle" is, on the one hand, expected and taken for granted, and on the other, understood as ironic, as most MBAs, having worked on Wall Street as college graduates, have experienced their "lifestyle" as simultaneously grueling and exploitative. What is more seductive is the forecasting of elite social networking and Wall Street influence over corporate America. Such an anointing was unmistakable at the Harvard Business School Women's Panel, an event catered for young professional women to network and apply to business schools, sponsored by Harvard Business School and held at Citigroup's Headquarters in New York City in 1999. Although designed as an open career forum, the HBS alumnae panelists talked almost exclusively about finance and management consulting: "For HBS women, 30 percent go into consulting and about 40 percent go into finance and investment banking." "Banking internships come pretty quickly into the process. You receive one-on-one counseling before your internship decision. Recruiters are there pretty early." What struck me the most was panelist Jordan Thompson's parallel between Harvard and Wall Street: "I've never been to so many black tie parties. I was invited to so many parties and you see that people bring their intensity, enthusiasm, and ambitions as much in their work as in their social lives. I organized pub nights and cross-section mixes. When you are social chair at HBS, you have a certain carte blanche to talk to and call up the CEOs of companies." What Thompson experienced as social chair of her class mirrored the Wall Street's relationship with corporate America. Wall Street, armed with HBS graduates, has "carte blanche" to advise CEOs on the latest deals and expectations.

THE CROSS-POLLINATION OF ELITISM

They are declared to be "the best and the brightest." They quickly become used to the respect, status, and impressive nods from peers, parental figures, job prospectors, and society at large. Those most enamored of, or dependent on, their putative membership in "the cream of the crop" seek ways to maintain and continue the high status to which they have become accustomed, especially as graduation looms near. As Devon Peterson, an undergraduate writer for the *Daily Princetonian*, observed about the "the allures and drawbacks of elite jobs": "For four years we have enjoyed being the most elite college-aged kids in one of the most elite, unilaterally powerful nations ever to exist.... These banking firms provide us with a way to maintain our elite status in society by providing avenues to wealth and power that other professions do not" (Peterson 2002). Peterson's reference to himself as being at the pinnacle of power is a crucial window into the identity formation of bankers-to-be. Dafna Hochman, an undergraduate writer for the *Harvard Crimson*, similarly recognizes, not only the central importance of being the best, as defined by prestige, status, and smartness, to Harvard students, but also that what gives Wall Street crucial competitive advantage in recruiting is its acute understanding of this phenomena. Wall Streeters are able to sell themselves so effectively because they know what attracts these students: it is also precisely what investment banks themselves seek. Hochman (1999) observes, "The business world is obviously desperate to milk our minds, youth, creativity and work ethic. And they have correctly assessed what it takes to attract us: appear competitive, prestigious, and upwardly mobile.... They know that four years ago, we wanted the absolute best. We did not settle for number three or four on the college rankings. They prey on our desire to find the 'Harvard' of everything: activities, summer jobs, relationships and now careers."

Elite Students and Life after Graduation

Implicit in this transformation from undergraduate to investment banker is Wall Street's notion that if students do not choose Wall Street postgraduation, they are somehow "less smart," as smartness is defined by continued aggressive striving to perpetuate elite status. The cultivation of a particular kind of banker and the privileging of an elite norm, insidiously racialized, are nowhere better illustrated than with this event in Kate Miller's work life. In 1997, Miller, former analyst at Morgan Stanley, was one of its first recruits from a historically black college. In the following narrative describing her experience with a senior manager, Miller further demonstrates that what constitutes "smartness" is explicitly dependent on school pedigree as well as race.

> Well, there were a couple of officers that were known for being really good guys and being fair to people of color. And it was very interesting because I was in Word Processing [an actual floor of the bank where all the documents investment banks use to pitch deals are professionally printed]. I was trying to work on a document with some of the assistants there, and a principal [equivalent to senior vice president] came into Word Processing and was talking about his experiences recruiting that year. And he turned to me, well, he was saying to another analyst, "Well, you know, I just really have problems with the idea of us recruiting at historically black colleges. I mean, I know people say that the students that attend those schools are smart enough to attend Harvard and Stanford and get into these great institutions, but actually choose to attend the black college. Well, I have a problem with that. If they're that smart, and they're turning down one of the top institutions in the country, then I think that shows poor judgment, and we should really rethink whether or not these are the type of people that we want working at our company." He said this so that I overheard, and I guess he had assumed that I had gone to an Ivy League school because he then sort of turned to me and said, "Well, what do you think, Kate?" And I said, "Well, I went to a black college; I went to Spelman." And he just sort of looked at me and realized he made an incredible mistake and just said, "Well, I guess I lost my case. I guess you proved your point against me." So I just sort of shrugged my shoulders. Well, what do you say? You've been there for five months. You never really worked with the guy. It's not like you two have a rapport. But it was awkward, especially to think that this was one of the cool guys who really thought that it was important to increase diversity within the company.

By virtue of "choosing" Spelman College, Miller demonstrated a lack of judgment; she was not only quantitatively "less smart" because she chose not to attend Harvard or Stanford, but she was also more provincial, less global. The complete equating of smartness with these institutions, the identification of historically white colleges as global, universal institutions, as well as the wholesale erasure of the white upper-class male privilege embedded in these universities are part and parcel of how excellence is understood. Central to Wall Street's construction of its own superiority is the corollary assumption that other corporations and industries are "less than"—less smart, less efficient, less competitive, less global, less hardworking—and thus less likely to survive the demands of global capitalism unless they restructure their cultural values and practices according to the standards of Wall Street. In a meritocratic feedback loop, their growing influence itself becomes further evidence that they are, in fact, "the smartest."

It is important to pause here to acknowledge that many of these students are of course quite aware of how the culture of smartness, as coproduced by elite universities, students, and Wall Street, capitalizes on, monopolizes, and narrows students' interests. Katherine Reilly, an undergraduate *Daily Princetonian* columnist, asked her fellow students to find "the courage to buck a system that has served us so well": "We should not let our type-A drive for success, money, or power or our fear of ending up outside the realm of 'acceptable' Princeton accomplishment dictate what we do with our lives" (Reilly 2003). Similarly, Dafna Hochman indicted Harvard for portraying the Wall Street recruiting process as every student's career process: this conflation "reflects Harvard's subtle and not so subtle attempts to challenge our values, delude our personal goals and to generally morph our diverse interests and talents into its ideal type of a respectable alum" (Hochman 1999). Fellow undergraduate *Harvard Crimson* writer Matthew Siegel wondered, "Could it be at all possible that the culture of success at Harvard drives people to skip right over the most important part of cognition—getting to know themselves and what they want and need—and instead, sends them straight into the outstretched arms of J. P. Morgan's H.R. department?" (Siegel 2003). Interestingly enough, his answer to why investment banking has so seduced Harvard undergraduates does not centrally implicate investment banking as the culprit: "It's not about investment banking. It is about the possibility that with all our running around trying to impress everyone all the time, it becomes hard to know what we really want" (Siegel 2003). Many students recognize the monopolistic hold that banking and consulting have on their future aspirations and that the very act of participating in recruiting precludes the questioning of "our place and privilege in the world" because the desire to hold on to privilege is naturalized vis à vis recruiting (Suleiman 1998). It is one thing if one's goal in life is to make "multi-million-dollar corporations even richer" or if one "cannot be happy unless you work for Goldman," but the crux of the problem is that students hardly question or ponder what they might truly be passionate about, much less the contradictions of their own privilege (Graham-Felsen 2003). Instead, these students more than likely continue with "the absurd impression that there is only one thing to do next year," that is, resort to the already-laid-out "typical Princeton job," the next step toward continued upward mobility, the surefire sign that one truly is the best and the brightest (Suleiman 1998).

Certainly, the pinnacle of meritocracy is necessarily precarious: it is shot through with class, race, and gender hierarchies; with the constant and anxious performance of smartness; and with a prestigious branding so dependent on the singularity of the apex that it cannot help but degrade. The fact that American culture, as Katherine Newman presciently pointed out long ago, has virtually no cultural repertoire that helps make sense of downward mobility for the middle class is perhaps doubly true for the elite, for whom expanding or diverging from the narrow path of status maintenance is understood and experienced as slippage or corrosion (Newman 1999). Where to find Harvard after Harvard? The push to replicate is excruciatingly intense. As Devon Peterson (2002) observed: "Perhaps most difficult to overcome is the naturally difficult task of giving up social status and an elite way of life."

"Wall Street University": Kinship Networks and Elite Extension

Wall Street and elite universities work together to foster and exploit this need to "find the next Harvard," in the process creating a symbiotic relationship that furthers each institution's dreams, goals, and practices. Wall Street has enjoyed long-standing historical ties with status-heavy Ivy League universities, ties that have produced generations of financiers and advisors to American industry. Since the 1980s, at precisely the time that Wall Street worked to solidify its expert influence over most U.S. corporations, these historical ties have been transformed into massive feeder relationships. Investment banks have naturalized themselves as the primary destinations for elite graduates as part of a program to consolidate and justify Wall Street's domination of corporate America, regardless of the "quality" of advice. In addition, over the past twenty-five years, student anxieties over preserving their elite status have increased, making Wall Street, at least until mid-2008, a much more attractive possibility than before. These developments, I argue, have converged to create a culture of "survival of the smartest."

Wall Street did not begin to recruit in droves at elite East Coast schools until the early 1980s. Throughout the mid-twentieth century, elite university graduates interested in business careers looked to management training programs with industrial, aerospace, or chemical corporations, rather than Wall Street firms (*Harvard Crimson* 1963; Wilentz 1975). For decades, general, "open" recruiting was not a standard practice for most businesses: Ivy League graduates relied on family wealth and networks, entered graduate school, or were approached via the "old boys' network" for financial or industrial fast-track grooming; and most Ivy League faculty, determined to perpetuate the ivory tower model, were "outraged by recruiting" (Beniger 1967). At Harvard in the 1950s, Wall Street financiers recruited a relatively small number of men directly from the well-established residential houses at Harvard College by holding small panels and conferences in intimate settings such as the Lowell House common room and the Eliot House dining hall (*Harvard Crimson* 1953, 1957). These efforts were small-scale as interest in the securities markets had plummeted after the Great Depression, and Wall Street was not necessarily the first choice for dynamic, ambitious college graduates. Furthermore, Wall Street and many other businesses searched for managers from business schools, not undergraduate programs (Masters 1986). In general, because of economic stability in the postwar era for the upper-middle and upper classes, the postgraduation job search lacked the anxiety so often associated with it later. Most elite graduates had "job futures so well established that they never have to go seek" recruiting (Wilentz 1975). Remarking on a "trend" toward "working right after college," *Harvard Crimson* writer Jeffrey Senger (1984) reported that it was not until 1984 that a majority of Harvard, Yale and Princeton graduates sought jobs after graduation; in 1974, only one-third, and in 1959, only one-tenth. For example, with surprisingly little angst, the *Harvard Crimson*, in an article headlined "The Jobless Class of '72," said that "by choice or by chance, over half of the Class of 1972 found themselves with nowhere to go and nothing to do after graduation." The culprit was not so much economic hard times as the fact that "students who were planning on business careers were unwilling to make long-term commitments" and that those going to graduate schools "also wanted to take a breather from the academic regimen" (Bennett 1972). It is also important to remember that campus culture in the Vietnam Era was much more hostile to big business in general than in subsequent years, as evidenced (for example) by student protests against napalm manufacturer Dow Chemical Corporation's attempt to recruit at Harvard in 1967 (Beniger 1967).

As Wall Street investment banks profited exorbitantly from their increasing influence over corporate America in the 1980s, they began to recruit at elite universities on a grand scale, creating the two-year analyst programs for the express purpose of targeting undergraduates directly out of college. This new cadre of workers, no longer handpicked through small-scale networks of family, friends, and close business associates, was legitimated by placing even greater cachet on the universities where they were recruited. In place of the elite, individualized family of men came the elite "Princeton" or "Harvard" family, which relied on a new variant of kinship based on alumni rather than "old boys'" networks. Recall my own initiation into "the Princeton family" in my very first recruitment presentation in 1995 when a Goldman Sachs managing director and Princeton alumnus addressed the audience as "the Princeton family" to establish both connection with "us" and to delineate an elite selectivity—just as not everyone can be a student at Princeton, investment banking is not a profession in which all can participate. "Princeton alumnae make the best analysts." That women and minorities were not explicitly excluded in this process was a crucial part of this new ideology of meritocracy.

What made this central glue of elite-institution-alumni stick to Wall Street despite the possible dilution of elitism caused by this extension of exclusivity to all alumni, ostensibly, was the formation of a generic culture of "the best" which pervaded and extended from, say, Wharton to Wall Street. By attracting masses of elite university alumni to Wall Street, investment banks and universities coproduce an extension and transferal of elitism via what I call a human kinship bridge. For example, in 2004, when Goldman Sachs CEO Hank Paulson gave a keynote speech to Wharton MBA students, the first point he made "after stating

Goldman Sachs's $23 billion in revenue in 2004" was "the importance his firm places on 'hiring and retaining the best people' in order to maintain a 'culture of excellence'." Paulson then emphasized the strong, intimate relationship his firm has with Wharton, "saying that more people were hired from the University to work at Goldman Sachs in 2004 than from any other school in the country" (Siegal 2005).

When a Harvard or Princeton education is seen as the normative "baseline" pedigree it becomes ordinary as well as collective, encompassing, even universal. Wall Street smartness is, in a sense, "generic," and it is precisely this notion of elitism so pervasive as to be commonplace, smartness so sweeping as to become generic, that reinforces Wall Street's claims of extraordinariness. Specifically, the assumption is that everyone on Wall Street is smart and comes from Princeton or Harvard; as such, this smartness generically applies to *all members of this class* or kind in a way that is naturalized and comprehensively descriptive of this entire group of workers. The notion of Wall Street smartness is so ingrained that it does not have to be emphasized as "special" or qualified; as such, smartness is not a "brand name" or external label, but a blanket, sweeping generalization about all investment bankers. Wall Street's generic smartness is so comprehensive as to connote a global application to all members. Of course, while Princeton and Harvard are pinnacle "brand names," their generic status on Wall Street further attests to how special the accumulation of merit is at investment banks.

The kinship of generically smart investment bankers guarantees the extension and reinforcement of all the social particularities of those universities' positions in American culture, while simultaneously rendering invisible its normative, unmarked privilege. Marked investment bankers, who usually strive to be generically kin (and generically smart), feel the brunt of these contradictions daily. Kate Miller observed that she "never felt like more of a black woman with all of the negative stereotypes attached than I did when I was working at Morgan Stanley." She chose not to pursue a career in investment banking (or was discouraged from doing so), so her narratives illustrate a certain level of what might be called alienation from Wall Street culture and values. She described her initial experiences this way:

> I felt like the first thing people saw when they looked at me was not a bright person who had been admitted to the analyst class but a black woman. And most of the people that I worked with really had very little exposure to other races. I'm sure some of the men had very little exposure to women on a professional basis. Even though the industry has made a lot of strides to be more inclusive of women, I still think that white male officers prefer to work with white male analysts.

This pattern of exclusion, where white male vice presidents pick white male analysts to be on their team, where Yale graduates seek to work with other Yale graduates, greatly influenced Miller's opportunity to work on "higher profile" deals and to make connections with potential mentors. Many first-year analysts get to know senior-level bankers through various formal and informal alma mater networking events. Miller poignantly observed, "If you're an analyst from Dartmouth and there are fifteen managing directors who also went to Dartmouth, then you get to know those fifteen managing directors. Well, Spelman College grad, guess what? There are no MDs, VPs, even associates that graduated from Spelman." Given that smartness and membership in a financial kin network that drives business and social opportunities are intimately dependent on both elite institutions and one's closeness to the unmarked, generic norm, Miller's various identities as a black woman from Spelman renders her less smart, less kin, and by extension, less of an investment banker.

Creating Pinnacle Status and Generic Smartness

Solidifying Wall Street as "the" extension of hyperelite universities requires the convergence of student aspirations, cultural pressures of elite upward mobility, Wall Street reframing of alumni kinship, and its marketing and monopoly of the recruitment process. In this section, I demonstrate one concrete way in which these entanglements of elitism are "operationalized" by even further narrowing the space at the top such that the most coveted investment banks and the "most" prestigious universities are not only associated singularly with each other but also distinguished from (and desired more than) the "regularly" prestigious ones. I argue that by painstakingly differentiating and creating hierarchies between and within elite universities through the recruitment process, investment bankers further intertwine their identities with the most elite universities, create demand for their jobs and institutions, and solidify their association with smartness.

As I have described, the two universities from which the prestigious Wall Street investment banks most actively recruit all students without restriction to major or department are Harvard and Princeton. It turns out that recruitment at other elite universities is not approached in a similar manner. For example, although investment banks also widely recruit at Yale, often included with Harvard and Princeton as one of the "top three" schools for banking or consulting, Yale, however, lags behind the other two in its reputation on Wall Street. According to one Yale alumnus who works on Wall Street, "because investment bankers perceive hostility" from many students at Yale, "they concentrate their recruitment energies at Princeton and Harvard.... They're looking to hire a larger portion of students from Harvard and Princeton, despite the fact that the number of applicants from each school is relatively similar" (Tanenbaum 2005). Yale is perceived by many of my investment banker informants to be more "liberal and 'artsy'," less free-market oriented in a sense, and perhaps even tainted by New Haven, a largely working-class, majority African American city. Instead of recruiting universally at Yale, as happens at Harvard and Princeton, banks might require Yale students to demonstrate their quantitative ability, by, say, majoring in economics or undergoing a financial internship (Engler 2006).[3]

A similar phenomenon occurs at the University of Pennsylvania. There, again, investment banks do not recruit as actively from the general undergraduate population as a whole, although undergraduates and graduates from Penn's renowned Wharton School of Business are among the most highly sought-after recruits. "Some college seniors said it was difficult to find investment banking and consulting opportunities without a Wharton pedigree. It's harder to [secure financial jobs] if you are in the College" (Miley 2000). "Wharton may be the reason big-name investment banks are attracted to … Penn." In 2005, over half of Wharton graduates went into investment banking (Steinbery 2006). Similar to Yale, non-Wharton undergraduates at Penn report that they need to demonstrate technical or financial expertise in order to attract Wall Street investment banks.

By contrast, investment banking recruiters at Princeton and Harvard explicitly express how they *do not care* if undergraduates are trained in finance because a skilled background or already-acquired technical expertise is *not* really what they are looking for. As Gia Moron, a media and recruiting spokesperson at Goldman Sachs, told *The Harvard Crimson*, "We have found that financial know-how is easy to teach—in fact, training is an important part of a new hire's orientation—but the skills that the most successful candidates possess are beyond teaching: Energy, a history of excellence and achievement, leadership and interpersonal skills are some of the stand-outs" (Ho 2003). According to a Princeton undergraduate, Kate Daviau ('06), "They understand that interns come in knowing basically nothing—but if you're smart and personable, it's worth it to them to hire you." The *Daily Princetonian* writer Catherine Rampell observed that from all her interactions with potential Wall Street employees during her years at Princeton, most do not even know what "financial services" is. "Most are going into finance because they haven't figured out what else they could do," yet "finance employers are seeking them out, telling them they're qualified for finance" no matter what their training, major, or department—as long as they are from Princeton. "They bombard us with food, mail, Princeton alumni connection, and they keep telling us we're qualified, we're perfectly qualified even though we've never 'held a real job' " (Rampell 2006).

This open-ended, "generic" recruitment at Princeton and Harvard not only naturalizes the students there as "the best," the elite among the elite, but also sheds light on what actually constitutes smartness for Wall Street. Being the best and the brightest, especially for college graduates, does not mean possessing actual technical skills, a background in finance, or even a specific aptitude for banking. Instead, Princeton and Harvard recruits bring to the table just the right mix of general qualities and associations: they are not too technical or geeky (MIT), not too liberal (Yale), not too far away (Stanford), and their universities carry more historical prestige than the remaining Ivies (Brown, Columbia, Cornell, Dartmouth, University of Pennsylvania). Possessed of a combination of traditional cachet, class standing, and pedigree, they can show prima facie evidence of their "excellence" by virtue of their schools' (presumably) exclusive selection processes; and they demonstrate a constant striving for further "excellence" by virtue of their participation in the intense process of recruiting and their evident desire for a high-status, upper-crust lifestyle.

NOTES

1. Certainly, this idea has currency beyond Wall Street, though I would argue that, as evidenced by Bethany McLean's and Peter Elkind's *The Smartest Guys in the Room* (2003) on the Enron executives and Wall Street advisors, these financiers are so convinced of their own brilliance that they created illusory businesses for short-term stock price appreciation while scamming small investors and their own employees. The culture of smartness is particularly heralded, utilized, and valued in finance capital as productive of spectacular profit accumulation and global dominance.

2. Management consulting is considered a professional service where consulting firms advise corporate America on such "strategic" matters as entering a new business, streamlining existing departments, restructuring and downsizing, outsourcing, and so forth. Projects might include figuring out how to increase a company's market share, how to exit a certain business, where to move and relocate a particular division. At elite universities, becoming a management consulting analyst for some of the top consulting firms such as McKinsey and Bain is almost as highly sought after as investment banking, though not quite as prestigious or lucrative. The fact that one of the most popular debates on Harvard's and Princeton's campuses are panel sessions entitled "Investment Banking vs. Consulting" is evidence, not only of the production of narrow career "choices," but also of the limiting of what constitutes an acceptable job after graduation. That there are heated debates and panel discussions on campus about whether or not to choose "investment banking or consulting" (not to mention the fact that literally hundreds of students pack auditoriums to hear this topic) is a culturally specific phenomenon. Usually, panelists composed of firm representatives (usually former students) face off about the pros and cons of the two career choices, and use the platform to further recruit students to their "side." Discussion usually ranges from talk of compensation and the "caliber of people" to work hours and the amount of "strategic" responsibility an entry-level employee can have over corporate America. In a *Harvard Crimson* opinion piece, "Avoiding a Path to Nowhere," J. Mehta, a Harvard undergraduate, called attention to this oddness, in a sense, as well as the narrowness of such a debate. He writes, "I-banking and consulting. Consulting and I-banking. I-banking vs. consulting. What more could be on a Harvard senior's mind?" He continues, "We are caught in a vicious cycle, in which the brightest and most ambitious enter fields that most solidify the social status quo—blazing a path to nowhere in which the next generation of equally smart and energetic Harvard graduates are bound to follow" (Mehta 1998).

3. Yale numbers are significantly lower that that of Princeton and Harvard. According to their recruitment office, "30 percent of Yale students chose jobs in non-profits, 30 percent go to graduate or professional school, and 40 percent choose corporate careers in finance, consulting, publishing, communications, manufacturing, even brewing" (Tanenbaum 2005). A survey by the Office of Institutional Research showed that ordinarily around 20 percent of Yale students enter finance, but only 13 percent did in 2002 with the financial downturn (Pryor 2006).

REFERENCES

Beniger, James. 1967. "Smithies, Walzer, and Peretz Discuss the Five R's: Recruitment, ROTC, Ranking, Research, and Relationship." *Harvard Crimson*, 11 November, www.thecrimson.com (accessed 11 May 2007).

Bennett, Amanda. 1972. "The Jobless Class of '72." *Harvard Crimson*, 16 December, www.thecrimson.com (accessed 11 May 2007).

Chan, Kai. 2001. "A Cacophony of Career Choices." *Daily Princetonian*, 13 February, www.dailyprincetonian.com (accessed 27 February 2007).

Creed, Jesse. 2003. "Students Face Weak Job Market despite Improvements." *Daily Princetonian*, 26 September, www.dailyprincetonian.com (accessed 27 February 2007).

Crossa, Veronica. 2005. "Converting the 'Small Stories' into 'Big' Ones: A Response to Susan Smith's 'States, Markets and an Ethic of Care'." *Political Geography* 24, 29–34.

Duboff, Josh. 2005. "Six College Students Create Job-Search Site." *Yale Daily News*, 11 February, www.yaledailynews.com (accessed 19 March 2007).

Easton, Alice. 2006. "Firms Lure Students with Extravagance." *Daily Princetonian*, 13 March, www.dailyprincetonian.com (accessed 27 February 2007).

Engler, Steve. 2006. "Don't Let Job Frenzy Overwhelm Your Life." *Yale Daily News*, 18 October, www.yaledailynews.com (accessed 19 March 2007).

Guyer, Nora. 2003. "There Is More to Life Than I-Banking." *Harvard Crimson*, 28 April, www.thecrimson.com (accessed 27 February 2007).

Hall, Cailey. 2005. "Wall Street: Paradise Found?" *Daily Princetonian*, 25 September, www.dailyprincetonian.com (accessed 27 February 2007).

Harvard Crimson. 1953. "Finance Industry Needs Graduates, Businessmen Say." 25 February, www.thecrimson.com (accessed 11 May 2007).

Henn, Brian. 2001. "Fewer Jobs in Financial Services Worry Class of '02." *Daily Princetonian*, 9 November, www.dailyprincetonian.com (accessed 27 February 2007).

Ho, Margaret. 2003. "Campus Recruiting Rates Inch Upward." *Harvard Crimson*, 26 September, www.thecrimson.com (accessed 27 February 2007).

Hochman, Dafna V. 1999. "Recruiting Your Career." *Harvard Crimson*, 15 October, www.thecrimson.com (accessed 27 February 2007).

Huber, H. Max. 2006. "Careers 'R Us: Online Recruiting Isn't Just for Aspiring Gordon Gekkos Anymore." *Harvard Crimson*, 5 October, www.thecrimson.com (accessed 27 February 2007).

Karseras, Hugh. 2006. "Starting Out on the Right Foot." *Daily Princetonian*, 21 November, www.dailyprincetonian.com (accessed 27 February 2007).

Mehta, Jal D. 1998. "Avoiding a Path to Nowhere." *Harvard Crimson*, 16 October, www.theharvardcrimson.com (accessed 27 February 2007).

Miley, Marissa. 2000. "Career Fair Provides Exposure for Students and Companies." *Daily Pennsylvanian*, 9 October, www.dailypennsylvanian.com (accessed 27 February 2007).

Newman, Katherine 1999. Falling from Grace: Downward Mobility in the Age of Affluence. Berkeley: University of California Press.

Peterson, Devon. 2002. "Careers at Princeton: The Allure and Drawbacks of Elite Jobs." *Daily Princetonian*, 16 October, www.dailyprincetonian.com (accessed 27 February 2007).

Pryor, Christina. 2006. "Future I-bankers Face Grueling Interview Cycle." *Yale Daily News*, 1 November, www.yaledailynews.com (accessed 19 March 2007).

Rahim, Taufiq. 2003. "Recruiting Insanity." *Daily Princetonian*, 15 October, www.dailyprincetonian.com (accessed 27 February 2007).

Rampell, Catherine. 2006. "In the Nation's Financial Service." *Daily Princetonian*, 6 October, www.dailyprincetonian.com (accessed 27 February 2007).

Reilly, Katherine. 2003. "Courage to Buck a System That Has Served Us So Well." *Daily Princetonian*, 23 April, www.dailyprincetonian.com (accessed 27 February 2007).

Senger, Jeffrey. 1984. "A Stampede to the Work Place." *Harvard Crimson*, 7 June, www.thecrimson.com (accessed 11 May 2007).

Shapira, Ian. 1998. "Companies Use Aggressive Tactics to Bolster Employee Recruitment." *Daily Princetonian*, 19 February, www.dailyprincetonian.com (accessed 27 February 2007).

Siegel, Matthew L. 2003. "Dress for Success: The I-Banker Has No Clothes." *Harvard Crimson*, 20 October, www.thecrimson.com (accessed 27 February 2007).

Smith, Susan J. 2005. "States, Markets and an Ethic of Care." *Political Geography* 24, 1–20.

Tanenbaum, Jessica. 2005. "I-Banking for Dummies." *Yale Daily News*, 6 October, www.yaledailynews.com (accessed 19 March 2007).

Wilentz, Amy. 1975. "The Class, Leaving." *Harvard Crimson*, 12 June, www.thecrimson.com (accessed 11 May 2007).

QUESTIONS FOR MAKING CONNECTIONS
WITHIN THE READING

1. Ho points out that a future in finance has not always been the preferred goal of students at Harvard and other elite universities. Before the 1980's, she writes, "Ivy League graduates relied on family wealth and networks … for financial or industrial fast-track grooming." How do the values of Ivy League students seem to have changed over time? What factors might explain how Wall Street became so pervasive a presence in the lives of Ivy League undergraduates? How might the growing influence of finance on university campuses reflect changes in the larger culture?

2. Why does Ho see "smartness" as an "ideology" and not an empirical fact? Clearly, many students come to the Ivies with excellent grades, well-developed skills, and broad-based general knowledge, but does "smartness" actually refer to qualities like these? Or does "smartness" signify something more complex? How does "smartness" help to create a sense of group solidarity and exclusiveness, and in what ways might it accentuate the students' fears about not fitting in? If students like Princeton's Katherine Reilly understand that "smartness" exerts pressure on people to embrace a narrow set of expectations, why does hers remain the minority view?

3. One of Ho's most important terms is *hegemony*, which refers to the use of culture rather than force as an instrument of domination (political, social, or economic). How does the elite educational system create hegemony, and who, exactly, dominates whom? Does the hegemony that Ho describes

reach beyond the university? Is the university itself dominated by *the Street*? Within the system of hegemony, should we see all Ivy League students as equal? Are all being groomed for membership in the elite? Or do we find within the Ivy League itself a division between the future elite and those destined to become subordinate?

QUESTIONS FOR WRITING

1. When Ho describes investment bankers, she often uses the word *power*. For example, she writes, "I do not assume a priori [automatically] that 'the market' always already exercises power, but rather that the particular biographies, experiences, and practices of investment bankers, who are both empowered and constrained by their cultural and institutional locations, create social change and financial hegemony on a daily basis." Should we think of power as something possessed by individuals or groups, or does it have to be created and sustained by the actions of the powerful? How does Wall Street use the Ivy Leagues to create its power? Why is it necessary for financiers to recruit so relentlessly? Is the presence of Wall Street on campus a sign of its strength or its weakness?

2. Using the evidence that Ho provides, can we say that Wall Street qualifies as a true meritocracy—that is, an elite system whose success has been achieved by virtue of ability, strength of character, and hard work? Or, conversely, do investment bankers represent an example of unearned privilege? One measure of a meritocracy is the degree to which its members are required to compete in order to gain entry into the ranks of the elite. Are the Ivy Leaguers recruited by Wall Street subjected to rigorous competition, or would you say they have been protected from competing by the process of recruitment? What other evidence can you provide to support the case for meritocracy, or the case for special privilege?

QUESTIONS FOR MAKING CONNECTIONS
BETWEEN READINGS

1. In "Immune to Reality," Daniel Gilbert makes the claim that people are surprisingly inept at predicting what will make them happy in the future. Gilbert argues that we stumble into happiness because it turns up inadvertently, and he suggests that our conscious intentions to realize long-held dreams are just as likely to end in frustration as in felicity. What might Gilbert say to the students recruited by the investment banking firms? Even if those students had read Gilbert (who teaches at Harvard, by the way), would they be likely to step off the fast track to "success"? If they

understood Gilbert's argument but still persisted in careers on the Street, what motives might explain their choice?

2. In what ways might the ideology of "smartness" contribute to the growing inequality that Joseph Stiglitz examines in "Rent Seeking and the Making of an Unequal Society"? As you develop your response, you might pay particular attention to his distinction between the supposed "geniuses of business" like Steve Jobs and Mark Zuckerberg, and the "giant" Stiglitz celebrates, Tim Berners-Lee, inventor of the World Wide Web, who could have become a billionaire but instead chose to make his idea freely available. Would it be fair to say that the recruitment programs in the Ivy League are designed to create a culture of rent-seeking? And does the existence of this culture complicate Stiglitz's call for systemic reform? How might the ideology of "smartness" work against the prospects for greater equality?

STEVEN JOHNSON

STEVEN JOHNSON, THE founder and editor of one of the Web's earliest magazines, *Feed*, is the author of many books, including *Emergence: The Connected Lives of Ants, Brains, Cities, and Software* (2001), from which "The Myth of the Ant Queen" is drawn; *Mind Wide Open: Your Brain and the Neuroscience of Everyday Life* (2004); *Everything Bad Is Good for You: How Today's Popular Culture Is Actually Making Us Smarter* (2005); and *The Invention of Air: A Story of Science, Faith, Revolution, and the Birth of America* (2009).

Johnson's preoccupation in all these books, most controversially in *Everything Bad Is Good for You*, is with reconceiving the nature of intelligence. Although it is common to think of intelligence as located in the individual—the outstanding student, the creative genius, the scientist at work in his lab—Johnson proposes that intelligence is not an attribute of individuals at all, but a property that emerges out of a system working as a whole. To illustrate this new view of intelligence, Johnson looks at complex systems like ant colonies, cities, and software programs, and he argues that in these contexts intelligence emerges in the absence of any central form of leadership or authority. The intelligence of the whole is created by individual agents—ants, people, "subroutines"—following what Johnson terms "local rules." By showing how decentralized, adaptive, self-organizing systems use lower-level thinking to solve higher-order problems, Johnson asks his readers to see the advent of the Internet not simply as an extension of human intelligence but also as a new frontier where the very nature of human intelligence is being transformed, one hyperlink at a time.

Johnson acknowledges the difficulties involved in imagining intelligence along these lines. When filmmakers try to depict artificial intelligence, for example, they envision a future where cyborgs look and think just like ordinary humans. Johnson predicts, however, that when there is a breakthrough in the effort to create artificial intelligence (AI), the result "won't quite look like human intelligence. It'll have other properties in it, and it may be hard for us to pick up on the fact that it is intelligent because our criteria [are] different."

Johnson's most recent book *Future Perfect: The Case for Progress in a Networked Age* (2012) asks readers to consider how the Web might be used to address our society's most urgent challenges. His proposal deviates from classic liberalism, with its faith in activist government, but also from the libertarian spirit popular among many Internet entrepreneurs. Instead, Johnson identifies himself as a "peer progressive" who is convinced that "peer networks" represent a new and more democratic way of organizing our collective creativity.

The Myth of the Ant Queen

It's early fall in Palo Alto, and Deborah Gordon and I are sitting in her office in Stanford's Gilbert Biological Sciences building, where she spends three-quarters of the year studying behavioral ecology. The other quarter is spent doing fieldwork with the native harvester ants of the American Southwest, and when we meet, her face still retains the hint of a tan from her last excursion to the Arizona desert.

I've come here to learn more about the collective intelligence of ant colonies. Gordon, dressed neatly in a white shirt, cheerfully entertains a few borderline-philosophical questions on group behavior and complex systems, but I can tell she's hankering to start with a hands-on display. After a few minutes of casual rumination, she bolts up out of her chair. "Why don't we start with me showing you the ants that we have here," she says. "And then we can talk about what it all means."

She ushers me into a sepulchral room across the hallway, where three long tables are lined up side by side. The initial impression is that of an underpopulated and sterilized pool hall, until I get close enough to one of the tables to make out the miniature civilization that lives within each of them. Closer to a Habitrail than your traditional idea of an ant farm, Gordon's contraptions house an intricate network of plastic tubes connecting a dozen or so plastic boxes, each lined with moist plaster and coated with a thin layer of dirt.

"We cover the nests with red plastic because some species of ants don't see red light," Gordon explains. "That seems to be true of this species, too." For a second, I'm not sure what she means by "this species"—and then my eyes adjust to the scene, and I realize with a start that the dirt coating the plastic boxes is, in fact, thousands of harvester ants, crammed so tightly into their quarters that I had originally mistaken them for an undifferentiated mass. A second later, I can see that the whole simulated colony is wonderfully alive, the clusters of ants pulsing steadily with movement. The tubing and cramped conditions and surging crowds bring one thought immediately to mind: the New York subway system, rush hour.

At the heart of Gordon's work is a mystery about how ant colonies develop, a mystery that has implications extending far beyond the parched earth of the Arizona desert to our cities, our brains, our immune systems—and increasingly, our technology. Gordon's work focuses on the connection between the microbehavior of individual ants and the overall behavior of the colonies themselves, and part of that research involves tracking the life cycles of individual colonies, following them year after year as they scour the desert floor for food, competing with other colonies for territory, and—once a year—mating with them. She is a student, in other words, of a particular kind of emergent, self-organizing system.

Dig up a colony of native harvester ants and you'll almost invariably find that the queen is missing. To track down the colony's matriarch, you need to examine the bottom of the hole you've just dug to excavate the colony: you'll find a narrow, almost invisible passageway that leads another two feet underground, to a tiny vestibule burrowed out of the earth. There you will find the queen. She will have been secreted there by a handful of ladies-in-waiting at the first sign of disturbance. That passageway, in other words, is an emergency escape hatch, not unlike a fallout shelter buried deep below the West Wing.

But despite the Secret Service–like behavior, and the regal nomenclature, there's nothing hierarchical about the way an ant colony does its thinking. "Although *queen* is a term that reminds us of human political systems," Gordon explains, "the queen is not an authority figure. She lays eggs and is fed and cared for by the workers. She does not decide which worker does what. In a harvester ant colony, many feet of intricate tunnels and chambers and thousands of ants separate the queen, surrounded by interior workers, from the ants working outside the nest and using only the chambers near the surface. It would be physically impossible for the queen to direct every worker's decision about which task to perform and when." The harvester ants that carry the queen off to her escape hatch do so not because they've been ordered to by their leader; they do it because the queen ant is responsible for giving birth to all the members of the colony, and so it's in the colony's best interest—and the colony's gene pool—to keep the queen safe. Their genes instruct them to protect their mother, the same way their genes instruct them to forage for food. In other words, the matriarch doesn't train her servants to protect her, evolution does.

Popular culture trades in Stalinist ant stereotypes—witness the authoritarian colony regime in the animated film *Antz*—but in fact, colonies are the exact opposite of command economies. While they are capable of remarkably coordinated feats of task allocation, there are no Five-Year Plans in the ant kingdom. The colonies that Gordon studies display some of nature's most mesmerizing decentralized behavior: intelligence and personality and learning that emerges from the bottom up.

I'm still gazing into the latticework of plastic tubing when Gordon directs my attention to the two expansive white boards attached to the main colony space, one stacked on top of the other and connected by a ramp. (Imagine a two-story parking garage built next to a subway stop.) A handful of ants meander across each plank, some porting crumblike objects on their backs, others apparently just out for a stroll. If this is the Central Park of Gordon's ant metropolis, I think, it must be a workday.

Gordon gestures to the near corner of the top board, four inches from the ramp to the lower level, where a pile of strangely textured dust—littered with tiny shells and husks—presses neatly against the wall. "That's the midden," she says. "It's the town garbage dump." She points to three ants marching up the ramp, each barely visible beneath a comically oversize shell. "These ants are on midden duty: they take the trash that's left over from the food they've collected—in this case, the seeds from stalk grass—and deposit it in the midden pile."

Gordon takes two quick steps down to the other side of the table, at the far end away from the ramp. She points to what looks like another pile of dust. "And this is the cemetery." I look again, startled. She's right: hundreds of ant carcasses are piled atop one another, all carefully wedged against the table's corner. It looks brutal, and yet also strangely methodical.

I know enough about colony behavior to nod in amazement. "So they've somehow collectively decided to utilize these two areas as trash heap and cemetery," I say. No individual ant defined those areas, no central planner zoned one area for trash, the other for the dead. "It just sort of happened, right?"

Gordon smiles, and it's clear that I've missed something. "It's better than that," she says. "Look at what actually happened here: they've built the cemetery at exactly the point that's furthest away from the colony. And the midden is even more interesting: they've put it at precisely the point that maximizes its distance from both the colony *and* the cemetery. It's like there's a rule they're following: put the dead ants as far away as possible, and put the midden as far away as possible without putting it near the dead ants."

I have to take a few seconds to do the geometry myself, and sure enough, the ants have got it right. I find myself laughing out loud at the thought: it's as though they've solved one of those spatial math tests that appear on standardized tests, conjuring up a solution that's perfectly tailored to their environment, a solution that might easily stump an eight-year-old human. The question is, who's doing the conjuring?

It's a question with a long and august history, one that is scarcely limited to the collective behavior of ant colonies. We know the answer now because we have developed powerful tools for thinking about—and modeling—the emergent intelligence of self-organizing systems, but that answer was not always so clear. We know now that systems like ant colonies don't have real leaders, that the very idea of an ant "queen" is misleading. But the desire to find pacemakers in such systems has always been powerful—in both the group behavior of the social insects, and in the collective human behavior that creates a living city.

Records exist of a Roman fort dating back to A.D. 76 situated at the confluence of the Medlock and Irwell Rivers, on the northwestern edge of modern England, about 150 miles from London. Settlements persisted there for three centuries, before dying out with the rest of the empire around A.D. 400. Historians believe that the site was unoccupied for half a millennium, until a town called Manchester began to take shape there, the name derived from the Roman settlement Mamucium—Latin for "place of the breastlike hill."

Manchester subsisted through most of the millennium as a nondescript northern-England borough: granted a charter in 1301, the town established a college in the early 1400s, but remained secondary to the neighboring town of Salford for hundreds of years. In the 1600s, the Manchester region became a node for the wool trade, its merchants shipping goods to the Continent via the great ports of London. It was impossible to see it at the time, but Manchester—and indeed the entire Lancashire region—had planted itself at the very center of a technological and commercial revolution that would irrevocably alter the future of the planet. Manchester lay at the confluence of several world-historical rivers: the nascent industrial technologies of steam-powered looms; the banking system of commercial London; the global markets and labor pools of the British Empire. The story of that convergence has been told many times, and the debate over its consequences continues to this day. But beyond the epic effects that it had on the global economy, the industrial takeoff that occurred in Manchester between 1700 and 1850 also created a new kind of city, one that literally exploded into existence.

The statistics on population growth alone capture the force of that explosion: a 1773 estimate had 24,000 people living in Manchester; the first official census in 1801 found 70,000. By the midpoint of the century, there were more than 250,000 people in the city proper—a tenfold increase in only seventy-five years. That growth rate was as unprecedented and as violent as the steam engines themselves. In a real sense, the city grew too fast for the authorities to keep up with it. For five hundred years, Manchester had technically been considered a "manor," which meant, in the eyes of the law, it was run like a feudal estate, with no local government to speak of—no city planners, police, or public health authorities. Manchester didn't even send representatives to Parliament until 1832, and it wasn't incorporated for another six years. By the early 1840s, the newly formed borough council finally began to institute public health reforms and urban planning, but the British government didn't officially recognize Manchester as a city until 1853. This constitutes one of the great ironies of the Industrial Revolution, and it captures just how dramatic the rate of change really was: the city that most defined the future of urban life for the first half of the nineteenth century didn't legally become a city until the great explosion had run its course.

The result of that discontinuity was arguably the least planned and most chaotic city in the six-thousand-year history of urban settlements. Noisy, polluted, massively overcrowded, Manchester attracted a steady stream of intellectuals and public figures in the 1830s, traveling north to the industrial magnet in search of the modern world's future. One by one, they returned with stories of abject squalor and sensory overload, their words straining to convey the immensity and uniqueness of the experience. "What I have seen has disgusted and astonished me beyond all measure," Dickens wrote after a visit in the fall of 1838. "I mean to strike the heaviest blow in my power for these unfortunate creatures." Appointed to command the northern districts in the late 1830s, Major General Charles James Napier wrote: "Manchester is the chimney of the world. Rich rascals, poor rogues, drunken raga-muffins and prostitutes form the moral.... What a place! The entrance to hell, realized." De Tocqueville visited Lancashire in 1835 and described the landscape in language that would be echoed throughout the next two centuries: "From this foul drain the greatest stream of human industry flows out to fertilize the whole world. From this filthy sewer pure gold flows. Here humanity attains its most complete development and its most brutish; here civilization works its miracles, and civilized man is turned back almost into a savage."

But Manchester's most celebrated and influential documentarian was a young man named Friedrich Engels, who arrived in 1842 to help oversee the family cotton plant there, and to witness firsthand the engines of history bringing the working class closer to self-awareness. While Engels was very much on the payroll of his father's firm, Ermen and Engels, by the time he arrived in Manchester he was also under the sway of the radical politics associated with the Young Hegelian school. He had befriended Karl Marx a few years before and had been encouraged to visit Manchester by the socialist Moses Hess, whom he'd met in early 1842. His three years in England were thus a kind of scouting mission for the revolution, financed by the capitalist class. The book that Engels eventually wrote, *The Condition of the Working Class in England,* remains to this day one of the classic tracts of urban history and stands as the definitive account of nineteenth-century Manchester life in all its tumult and dynamism. Dickens, Carlyle, and Disraeli had all attempted to capture Manchester in its epic wildness, but their efforts were outpaced by a twenty-four-year-old from Prussia.

But *The Condition* is not, as might be expected, purely a document of Manchester's industrial chaos, a story of all that is solid melting into air, to borrow a phrase Engels's comrade would write several years later. In the midst of the city's insanity, Engels's eye is drawn to a strange kind of order, in a wonderful passage where he leads the reader on a walking tour of the industrial capital, a tour that reveals a kind of politics built into the very topography of the city's streets. It captures Engels's acute powers of observation, but I quote from it at length because it captures something else as well—how difficult it is to think in models of self-organization, to imagine a world without pacemakers.

> The town itself is peculiarly built, so that someone can live in it for years and travel into it and out of it daily without ever coming into contact with a working-class quarter or even with workers—so long, that is to say, as one confines himself to his business affairs or to strolling about for pleasure. This comes about mainly in the circumstances that through an unconscious, tacit agreement as much as through conscious, explicit intention, the working-class districts are most sharply separated from the parts of the city reserved for the middle class....
>
> I know perfectly well that this deceitful manner of building is more or less common to all big cities. I know as well that shopkeepers must in the nature of the business take premises on the main thoroughfares. I know in such streets there are more good houses than bad ones, and that the value of land is higher in their immediate vicinity than in neighborhoods that lie at a distance from them. But at the same time I have never come across so systematic a seclusion of the working class from the main streets as in Manchester. I have never elsewhere seen a concealment of such fine sensibility of everything that might offend the eyes and nerves of the middle classes. And yet it is precisely Manchester that has been built less according to a plan and less within the limitations of official regulations—and indeed more through accident—than any other town. Still ... I cannot help feeling that the liberal industrialists, the Manchester "bigwigs," are not so altogether innocent of this bashful style of building.

You can almost hear the contradictions thundering against each other in this passage, like the "dark satanic mills" of Manchester itself. The city has built a *cordon sanitaire* to separate the industrialists from the squalor they have unleashed on the world, concealing the demoralization of Manchester's working-class districts—and yet that disappearing act comes into the world without "conscious, explicit intention." The city seems artfully planned to hide its atrocities, and yet it "has been built less according to a plan" than any city in history. As Steven Marcus puts it, in his history of the young Engels's sojourn in Manchester, "The point to be taken is that this astonishing and outrageous arrangement cannot fully be understood as the result of a plot, or even a deliberate design, although those in whose interests it works also control it. It is indeed too huge and too complex a state of organized affairs ever to have been *thought up* in advance, to have preexisted as an idea."

Those broad, glittering avenues, in other words, suggest a Potemkin village without a Potemkin. That mix of order and anarchy is what we now call emergent behavior. Urban critics since Lewis Mumford and Jane Jacobs have known that cities have lives of their own, with neighborhoods clustering into place without any Robert Moses figure dictating the plan from above. But that understanding has entered the intellectual mainstream only in recent years—when Engels paced those Manchester streets in the 1840s, he was left groping blindly, trying to find a culprit for the city's fiendish organization, even as he acknowledged that the city was notoriously unplanned. Like most intellectual histories, the development of that new understanding—the sciences of complexity and self-organization—is a complicated, multithreaded tale, with many agents interacting over its duration. It is probably better to think of it as less a linear narrative and more an interconnected web, growing increasingly dense over the century and a half that separates us from Engels's first visit to Manchester.

Complexity is a word that has frequently appeared in critical accounts of metropolitan space, but there are really two kinds of complexity fundamental to the city, two experiences with very different implications for the individuals trying to make sense of them. There is, first, the more conventional sense of complexity as sensory overload, the city stretching the human nervous system to its very extremes, and in the process teaching it a new series of reflexes—and leading the way for a complementary series of aesthetic values, which develop out like a scab around the original wound. The German cultural critic Walter Benjamin writes in his unfinished masterpiece, *The Arcades Project:*

> Perhaps the daily sight of a moving crowd once presented the eye with a spectacle to which it first had to adapt.... [T]hen the assumption is not impossible that, having mastered this task, the eye welcomed opportunities to confirm its possession of its new ability. The method of impressionist painting, whereby the picture is assembled through a riot of flecks of color, would then be a reflection of experience with which the eye of a big-city dweller has become familiar.

There's a long tributary of nineteenth- and twentieth-century urban writing that leads into this passage, from the London chapters of Wordsworth's *Prelude* to the ambulatory musings of Joyce's *Dubliners:* the noise and the senselessness somehow transformed into an aesthetic experience. The crowd is something you throw yourself into, for the pure poetry of it all. But complexity is not solely a matter of sensory overload. There is also the sense of complexity as a self-organizing system—more Santa Fe Institute than Frankfurt School. This sort of complexity lives up one level: it describes the system of the city itself, and not its experiential reception by the city dweller. The city is complex because it overwhelms, yes, but also because it has a coherent personality, a personality that self-organizes out of millions of individual decisions, a global order built out of local interactions. This is the "systematic" complexity that Engels glimpsed on the boulevards of Manchester: not the overload and anarchy he documented elsewhere, but instead a strange kind of order, a pattern in the streets that furthered the political values of Manchester's elite without being deliberately planned by them. We know now from computer models and sociological studies—as well as from the studies of comparable systems generated by the social insects, such as Gordon's harvester ants—that larger patterns can emerge out of uncoordinated local actions. But for Engels and his contemporaries, those unplanned urban shapes must have seemed like a haunting. The city appeared to have a life of its own.

A hundred and fifty years later, the same techniques translated into the language of software ... trigger a similar reaction: the eerie sense of something life-like, something organic forming on the screen. Even those with sophisticated knowledge about self-organizing systems still find these shapes unnerving—in their mix of stability and change, in their capacity for open-ended learning. The impulse to build centralized models to explain that behavior remains almost as strong as it did in Engels's day. When we see repeated shapes and structure emerging out of apparent chaos, we can't help looking for pacemakers.

Understood in the most abstract sense, what Engels observed are *patterns* in the urban landscape, visible because they have a repeated structure that distinguishes them from the pure noise you might naturally associate with an unplanned city. They are patterns of human movement and decision-making that have been etched into the texture of city blocks, patterns that are then fed back to the Manchester residents themselves, altering their subsequent decisions. (In that sense, they are the very opposite of the traditional sense of urban complexity—they are signals emerging where you would otherwise expect only noise.) A city is a kind of pattern-amplifying machine: its neighborhoods are a way of measuring and expressing the repeated behavior of larger collectivities—capturing information about group behavior, and sharing that information with the group. Because those patterns are fed back to the community, small shifts in behavior can quickly escalate into larger movements: upscale shops dominate the main boulevards, while the working class remains clustered invisibly in the alleys and side streets; the artists live on the Left Bank, the investment bankers in the Eighth Arrondissement. You don't need regulations and city planners deliberately creating these structures. All you need are thousands of individuals and a few simple rules of interaction. The bright shop windows attract more bright shop windows and drive the impoverished toward the hidden core. There's no need for a Baron Haussmann in this world, just a few repeating patterns of movement, amplified into larger shapes that last for lifetimes: clusters, slums, neighborhoods.

Not all patterns are visible to every city dweller, though. The history of urbanism is also the story of more muted signs, built by the collective behavior of smaller groups and rarely detected by outsiders. Manchester harbors several such secret clusters, persisting over the course of many generations, like a "standing wave in front of a rock in a fast-moving stream." One of them lies just north of Victoria University, at a point where Oxford Road becomes Oxford Street. There are reports dating back to the mid-nineteenth century of men cruising other men on these blocks, looking for casual sex, more lasting relationships, or even just the camaraderie of shared identity at a time when that identity dared not speak its name. Some historians speculate that Wittgenstein visited these streets during his sojourn in Manchester in 1908. Nearly a hundred years later, the area has christened itself the Gay Village and actively promotes its coffee bars and boutiques as a must-see Manchester tourist destination, like Manhattan's Christopher Street and San Francisco's Castro. The pattern is now broadcast to a wider audience, but it has not lost its shape.

But even at a lower amplitude, that signal was still loud enough to attract the attention of another of Manchester's illustrious immigrants: the British polymath Alan Turing. As part of his heroic contribution to the war effort, Turing had been a student of mathematical patterns, designing the equations and the machines that cracked the "unbreakable" German code of the Enigma device. After a frustrating three-year stint at the National Physical Laboratory in London, Turing moved to Manchester in 1948 to help run the university's embryonic computing lab. It was in Manchester that Turing began to think about the problem of biological development in mathematical terms, leading the way to the "Morphogenesis" paper, published in 1952, that Evelyn Fox Keller would rediscover more than a decade later. Turing's war research had focused on detecting patterns lurking within the apparent chaos of code, but in his Manchester years, his mind gravitated toward a mirror image of the original code-breaking problem: how complex patterns could come into being by following simple rules. How does a seed know how to build a flower?

Turing's paper on morphogenesis—literally, "the beginning of shape"—turned out to be one of his seminal works, ranking up there with his more publicized papers and speculations: his work on Gödel's undecidability problem, the Turing Machine, the Turing Test—not to mention his contributions to the physical design of the modern digital computer. But the morphogenesis paper was only the beginning of a shape—a brilliant mind sensing the outlines of a new problem, but not fully grasping all its intricacies. If Turing had been granted another few decades to explore the powers of self-assembly—not to mention access to the number-crunching horsepower of non-vacuum-tube computers— it's not hard to imagine his mind greatly enhancing our subsequent understanding of emergent behavior. But the work on morphogenesis was tragically cut short by his death in 1954.

Alan Turing was most likely a casualty of the brutally homophobic laws of postwar Britain, but his death also intersected with those discreet patterns of life on Manchester's sidewalks. Turing had known about that stretch of Oxford Road since his arrival in Manchester; on occasion, he would drift down to the neighborhood, meeting other gay men—inviting some of them back to his flat for conversation, and presumably some sort of physical contact. In January of 1952, Turing met a young man named Arnold Murray on those streets, and the two embarked on a brief relationship that quickly turned sour. Murray—or a friend of Murray's—broke into Turing's house and stole a few items. Turing reported the theft to the police and, with his typical forthrightness, made no effort to conceal the affair with Murray when the police visited his flat. Homosexuality was a criminal offense according to British law, punishable by up to two years' imprisonment, and so the police promptly charged both Turing and Murray with "gross indecency."

On February 29, 1952, while the Manchester authorities were preparing their case against him, Turing finished the revisions to his morphogenesis paper, and he argued over its merits with Ilya Prigogine, the visiting Belgian chemist whose work on nonequilibrium thermodynamics would later win him a Nobel prize. In one day, Turing had completed the text that would help engender the discipline of biomathematics and inspire Keller and Segel's slime mold discoveries fifteen years later, and he had enjoyed a spirited exchange with the man who would eventually achieve world fame for his research into self-organizing systems. On that winter day in 1952, there was no mind on the face of the earth better prepared to wrestle with the mysteries of emergence than Alan Turing's. But the world outside that mind was conspiring to destroy it. That very morning, a local paper broke the story that the war-hero savant had been caught in an illicit affair with a nineteen-year-old boy.

Within a few months Turing had been convicted of the crime and placed on a humiliating estrogen treatment to "cure" him of his homosexuality. Hounded by the authorities and denied security clearance for the top-secret British computing projects he had been contributing to, Turing died two years later, an apparent suicide.

Turing's career had already collided several times with the developing web of emergence before those fateful years in Manchester. In the early forties, during the height of the war effort, he had spent several months at the legendary Bell Laboratories on Manhattan's West Street, working on a number of encryption schemes, including an effort to transmit heavily encoded wave forms that could be decoded as human speech with the use of a special key. Early in his visit to Bell Labs, Turing hit upon the idea of using another Bell invention, the Vocoder—later used by rock musicians such as Peter Frampton to combine the sounds of a guitar and the human voice—as a way of encrypting speech. (By early 1943, Turing's ideas had enabled the first secure voice transmission to cross the Atlantic, unintelligible to German eavesdroppers.) Bell Labs was the home base for another genius, Claude Shannon, who would go on to found the influential discipline of information theory, and whose work had explored the boundaries between noise and information. Shannon had been particularly intrigued by the potential for machines to detect and amplify patterns of information in noisy communication channels—a line of inquiry that promised obvious value to a telephone company, but could also save thousands of lives in a war effort that relied so heavily on the sending and breaking of codes. Shannon and Turing immediately recognized that they had been working along parallel tracks: they were both code-breakers by profession at that point, and in their attempts to build automated machines that could recognize patterns in audio signals or numerical sequences, they had both glimpsed a future populated by even more intelligence machines. Shannon and Turing passed many an extended lunchtime at the Bell Labs, trading ideas on an "electronic brain" that might be capable of humanlike feats of pattern recognition.

Turing had imagined his thinking machine primarily in terms of its logical possibilities, its ability to execute an infinite variety of computational routines. But Shannon pushed him to think of the machine as something closer to an actual human brain, capable of recognizing more nuanced patterns. One day over lunch at the lab, Turing exclaimed playfully to his colleagues, "Shannon wants to feed not just data to a brain, but *cultural* things! He wants to play music to it!" Musical notes were patterns, too, Shannon recognized, and if you could train an electronic brain to understand and respond to logical patterns of zeros and ones, then perhaps sometime in the future we could train our machines to appreciate the equivalent patterns of minor chord progressions and arpeggios. The idea seemed fanciful at the time—it was hard enough getting a machine to perform long division, much less savor Beethoven's Ninth. But the pattern recognition that Turing and Shannon envisioned for digital computers has, in recent years, become a central part of our cultural life, with machines both generating music for our entertainment and recommending new artists for us to enjoy. The connection between musical patterns and our neurological wiring would play a central role in one of the founding texts of modern artificial intelligence, Douglas Hofstadter's *Gödel, Escher, Bach*. Our computers still haven't developed a genuine ear for music, but if they ever do, their skill will date back to those lunchtime conversations between Shannon and Turing at Bell Labs. And that learning, too, will be a kind of emergence, a higher-level order forming out of relatively simple component parts.

Five years after his interactions with Turing, Shannon published a long essay in the *Bell System Technical Journal* that was quickly repackaged as a book called *The Mathematical Theory of Communication*. Dense with equations and arcane chapter titles such as "Discrete Noiseless Systems," the book managed to become something of a cult classic, and the discipline it spawned—information theory—had a profound impact on scientific and technological research that followed, on both a theoretical and practical level. *The Mathematical Theory of Communication* contained an elegant, layman's introduction to Shannon's theory, penned by the esteemed scientist Warren Weaver, who had early on grasped the significance of Shannon's work. Weaver had played a leading role in the Natural Sciences division of the Rockefeller Foundation since 1932, and when he retired in the late fifties, he composed a long report for the foundation, looking back at the scientific progress that had been achieved over the preceding quarter century. The occasion suggested a reflective look backward, but the document that Weaver produced (based loosely on a paper he had written for *American Scientist*) was far more prescient, more forward-looking. In many respects, it deserves to be thought of as the founding text of complexity theory—the point at which the study of complex systems began to think of itself as a unified field. Drawing upon research in molecular biology, genetics, physics, computer science, and Shannon's information theory, Weaver divided the last few centuries of scientific inquiry into three broad camps. First, the study of simple systems: two or three variable problems, such as the rotation of planets, or the connection between an electric current and its voltage and resistance. Second, problems of "disorganized complexity": problems characterized by millions or billions of variables that can only be approached by the methods of statistical mechanics and probability theory. These tools helped explain not only the behavior of molecules in a gas, or the patterns of heredity in a gene pool, but also helped life insurance companies turn a profit despite their limited knowledge about any individual human's future health. Thanks to Claude Shannon's work, the statistical approach also helped phone companies deliver more reliable and intelligible long-distance service.

But there was a third phase to this progression, and we were only beginning to understand. "This statistical method of dealing with disorganized complexity, so powerful an advance over the earlier two-variable methods, leaves a great field untouched," Weaver wrote. There was a middle region between two-variable equations and problems that involved billions of variables. Conventionally, this region involved a "moderate" number of variables, but the size of the system was in fact a secondary characteristic:

> Much more important than the mere number of variables is the fact that these variables are all interrelated.... These problems, as contrasted with the disorganized situations with which statistics can cope, *show the essential feature of organization*. We will therefore refer to this group of problems as those of *organized complexity*.

Think of these three categories of problems in terms of [a] billiards table analogy.... A two- or three-variable problem would be an ordinary billiards table, with balls bouncing off one another following simple rules: their velocities, the friction of the table. That would be an example of a "simple system"—and indeed, billiard balls are often used to illustrate basic laws of physics in high school textbooks. A system of disorganized complexity would be that same table enlarged to include a million balls, colliding with one another millions of times a second. Making predictions about the behavior of any individual ball in that mix would be difficult, but you could make some accurate predictions about the overall behavior of the table. Assuming there's enough energy in the system at the outset, the balls will spread to fill the entire table, like gas molecules in a container. It's complex because there are many interacting agents, but it's disorganized because they don't create any higher-level behavior other than broad statistical trends. Organized complexity, on the other hand, is like [a] motorized billiards table, where the balls follow specific rules and through their various interactions create a distinct macrobehavior, arranging themselves in a specific shape, or forming a specific pattern over time. That sort of behavior, for Weaver, suggested a problem of organized complexity, a problem that suddenly seemed omnipresent in nature once you started to look for it:

> What makes an evening primrose open when it does? Why does salt water fail to satisfy thirst? ... What is the description of aging in biochemical terms? ... What is a gene, and how does the original genetic constitution of a living organism express itself in the developed characteristics of the adult?
>
> All these are certainly complex problems. But they are not problems of disorganized complexity, to which statistical methods hold the key. They are all problems which involve dealing simultaneously with a sizable number of factors which are interrelated into an organic whole.

Tackling such problems required a new approach: "The great central concerns of the biologist ... are now being approached not only from *above,* with the broad view of the natural philosopher who scans the whole living world, but also from *underneath,* by the quantitative analyst who measures the underlying facts." This was a genuine shift in the paradigm of research, to use Thomas Kuhn's language—a revolution not so much in the interpretations that science built in its attempt to explain the world, but rather in the types of questions it asked. The paradigm shift was more than just a new mind-set, Weaver recognized; it was also a by-product of new tools that were appearing on the horizon. To solve the problems of organized complexity, you needed a machine capable of churning through thousands, if not millions, of calculations per second—a rate that would have been unimaginable for individual brains running the numbers with the limited calculating machines of the past few centuries. Because of his connection to the Bell Labs group, Weaver had seen early on the promise of digital computing, and he knew that the mysteries of organized complexity would be much easier to tackle once you could model the behavior in close-to-real time. For millennia, humans had used their skills at observation and classification to document the subtle anatomy of flowers, but for the first time they were perched on the brink of answering a more fundamental question, a question that had more to do with patterns developing over time than with static structure: why does an evening primrose open when it does? And how does a simple seed know how to make a primrose in the first place? ...

"Organized complexity" proved to be a constructive way of thinking ... but ... was it possible to model and explain the behavior of self-organizing systems using more rigorous methods? Could the developing technology of digital computing be usefully applied to this problem? Partially thanks to Shannon's work in the late forties, the biological sciences ... made a number of significant breakthroughs in understanding pattern recognition and feedback.... Shortly after his appointment to the Harvard faculty in 1956, the entomologist Edward O. Wilson convincingly proved that ants communicate with one another—and coordinate overall colony behavior—by recognizing patterns in pheromone trails left by fellow ants.... At the Free University of Brussels in the fifties, Ilya Prigogine was making steady advances in his understanding of nonequilibrium thermodynamics, environments where the laws of entropy are temporarily overcome, and higher-level order may spontaneously emerge out of underlying chaos. And at MIT's Lincoln Laboratory, a twenty-five-year-old researcher named Oliver Selfridge was experimenting with a model for teaching a computer how to learn.

There is a world of difference between a computer that passively receives the information you supply and a computer that actively learns on its own. The very first generation of computers such as ENIAC had processed information fed to them by their masters, and they had been capable of performing various calculations with that data, based on the instruction sets programmed into them. This was a startling enough development at a time when "computer" meant a person with a slide rule and an eraser. But even in those early days, the digital visionaries had imagined a machine capable of more open-ended learning. Turing and Shannon had argued over the future musical tastes of the "electronic brain" during lunch hour at Bell Labs, while their colleague Norbert Wiener had written a best-selling paean to the self-regulatory powers of feedback in his 1949 manifesto *Cybernetics*.

"Mostly my participation in all of this is a matter of good luck for me," Selfridge says today, sitting in his cramped, windowless MIT office. Born in England, Selfridge enrolled at Harvard at the age of fifteen and started his doctorate three years later at MIT, where Norbert Wiener was his dissertation adviser. As a precocious twenty-one-year-old, Selfridge suggested a few corrections to a paper that his mentor had published on heart flutters, corrections that Wiener graciously acknowledged in the opening pages of *Cybernetics*. "I think I now have the honor of being one of the few living people mentioned in that book," Selfridge says, laughing.

After a sojourn working on military control projects in New Jersey, Selfridge returned to MIT in the mid-fifties. His return coincided with an explosion of interest in artificial intelligence (AI), a development that introduced him to a then-junior fellow at Harvard named Marvin Minsky. "My concerns in AI," Selfridge says now, "were not so much the actual processing as they were in how systems change, how they evolve—in a word, how they learn." Exploring the possibilities of machine learning brought Selfridge back to memories of his own education in England. "At school in England I had read John Milton's *Paradise Lost*," he says, "and I'd been struck by the image of Pandemonium—it's Greek for 'all the demons.' Then after my second son, Peter, was born, I went over *Paradise Lost* again, and the shrieking of the demons awoke something in me." The pattern recognizer in Selfridge's brain had hit upon a way of teaching a computer to recognize patterns.

"We are proposing here a model of a process which we claim can adaptively improve itself to handle certain pattern-recognition problems which cannot be adequately specified in advance." These were the first words Selfridge delivered at a symposium in late 1958, held at the very same National Physical Laboratory from which Turing had escaped a decade before. Selfridge's presentation had the memorable title "Pandemonium: A Paradigm for Learning," and while it had little impact outside the nascent computer-science community, the ideas Selfridge outlined that day would eventually become part of our everyday life—each time we enter a name in our Palm Pilots or use voice-recognition software to ask for information over the phone. Pandemonium, as Selfridge outlined it in his talk, was not so much a specific piece of software as it was a way of approaching a problem. The problem was an ambitious one, given the limited computational resources of the day: how to teach a computer to recognize patterns that were ill-defined or erratic, like the sound waves that comprise spoken language.

The brilliance of Selfridge's new paradigm lay in the fact that it relied on a distributed, bottom-up intelligence, and not a unified, top-down one. Rather than build a single smart program, Selfridge created a swarm of limited miniprograms, which he called demons. "The idea was, we have a bunch of these demons shrieking up the hierarchy," he explains. "Lower-level demons shrieking to higher-level demons shrieking to higher ones."

To understand what that "shrieking" means, imagine a system with twenty-six individual demons, each trained to recognize a letter of the alphabet. The pool of demons is shown a series of words, and each demon "votes" as to whether each letter displayed represents its chosen letter. If the first letter is *a*, the *a*-recognizing demon reports that it is highly likely that it has recognized a match. Because of the similarities in shape, the *o*-recognizer might report a possible match, while the *b*-recognizer would emphatically declare that the letter wasn't intelligible to it. All the letter-recognizing demons would report to a master demon, who would tally up the votes for each letter and choose the demon that expressed the highest confidence. Then the software would move on to the next letter in the sequence, and the process would begin again. At the end of the transmission, the master demon would have a working interpretation of the text that had been transmitted, based on the assembled votes of the demon democracy.

Of course, the accuracy of that interpretation depended on the accuracy of the letter recognizers. If you were trying to teach a computer how to read, it was cheating to assume from the outset that you could find twenty-six accurate letter recognizers. Selfridge was after a larger goal: how do you teach a machine to recognize letters—or vowel sounds, minor chords, fingerprints—in the first place? The answer involved adding another layer of demons, and a feedback mechanism whereby the various demon guesses could be graded. This lower level was populated by even less sophisticated miniprograms, trained only to recognize raw physical shapes (or sounds, in the case of Morse code or spoken language). Some demons recognized parallel lines, others perpendicular ones. Some demons looked for circles, others for dots. None of these shapes were associated with any particular letter; these bottom-dwelling demons were like two-year-old children—capable of reporting on the shapes they witnessed, but not perceiving them as letters or words.

Using these minimally equipped demons, the system could be trained to recognize letters, without "knowing" anything about the alphabet in advance. The recipe was relatively simple: present the letter *b* to the bottom-level demons, and see which ones respond, and which ones don't. In the case of the letter *b*, the vertical-line recognizers might respond, along with the circle recognizers. Those lower-level demons would report to a letter-recognizer one step higher in the chain. Based on the information gathered from its lieutenants, that recognizer would make a guess as to the letter's identity. Those guesses are then "graded" by the software. If the guess is wrong, the software learns to dissociate those particular lieutenants from the letter in question; if the guess happens to be right, it *strengthens* the connection between the lieutenants and the letter.

The results are close to random at first, but if you repeat the process a thousand times, or ten thousand, the system learns to associate specific assemblies of shape-recognizers with specific letters and soon enough is capable of translating entire sentences with remarkable accuracy. The system doesn't come with any predefined conceptions about the shapes of letters—you train the system to associate letters with specific shapes in the grading phase. (This is why handwriting-recognition software can adapt to so many different types of penmanship, but *can't* adapt to penmanship that changes day to day.) That mix of random beginnings organizing into more complicated results reminded Selfridge of another process, whose own underlying code was just then being deciphered in the form of DNA. "The scheme sketched is really a natural selection on the processing demons," Selfridge explained. "If they serve a useful function they survive and perhaps are even the source for other subdemons who are themselves judged on their merits. It is perfectly reasonable to conceive of this taking place on a broader scale.... [I]nstead of having but one Pandemonium we might have some crowd of them, all fairly similarly constructed, and employ natural selection on the crowd of them."

The system Selfridge described—with its bottom-up learning, and its evaluating feedback loops—belongs in the history books as the first practical description of an emergent software program. The world now swarms with millions of his demons.

QUESTIONS FOR MAKING CONNECTIONS
WITHIN THE READING

1. Do you accept Johnson's analogy between the behavior of harvester ants and the emergence of cities like Manchester? Does Johnson mean that instinct guides human builders in much the same way as it guides the ants? Does he mean that in both cases an order has emerged entirely by accident? Or does he mean that there is something about "systems" in general—ant colonies as well as sprawling conurbations—that makes them self-organizing? What exactly is a self-organizing system, and how do both the ant colony and the city qualify as equally appropriate examples? How does each system organize itself?

2. The idea of self-organizing systems might seem to suggest that order automatically and smoothly arises as ants and human beings go about their private business. Can Manchester in the nineteenth century, when Napier, Dickens, and Engels each observed it, be described as orderly? Was there an order behind the apparent disorder? How can we distinguish between a self-organizing system and results that are produced entirely by chance?

3. One could say that there are three different parts to "The Myth of the Ant Queen." The first deals with the colony of harvester ants. The second deals with the city of Manchester. The third deals with the emergence of complexity theory. In what ways are these three parts connected? Why doesn't Johnson make the connections more explicit—why does he leave them for the reader to work out? Could the structure of his chapter in some way reflect the nature of his argument about self-organization?

QUESTIONS FOR WRITING

1. What role does intelligence play in self-organizing systems? This question might be more complex than it seems at first because intelligence may exist on multiple levels. The intelligence demonstrated by an ant colony may be much greater than the intelligence of an individual ant. On any particular day during the 1880s, life in Manchester must have seemed to many people very close to absolute chaos, but could it be said that the city as a whole possessed a certain intelligence? Does Johnson mean to suggest that the ideas and aspirations of individuals do not matter? Are we, from the standpoint of complexity theory, intelligent beings? What is intelligence, anyway?

2. Families, communities, schools, religious groups, circles of friends, political parties, public service organizations—all of these qualify as social institutions, and there are many others. Choose one institution and, drawing on Johnson's chapter, decide whether it qualifies as truly self-organizing. If it does not, can you imagine how it might be reorganized in a bottom-up fashion? In what ways do our customs and traditions encourage or discourage self-organization? What do you conclude from the importance of kings, presidents, generals, CEOs, bosses, coaches, principals, and other leaders in our culture?

QUESTIONS FOR MAKING CONNECTIONS
BETWEEN READINGS

1. Johnson's purpose in writing "The Myth of the Ant Queen" is to teach us to see complex systems in a new and decentered way that is, he suggests, more consistent with the way nature really works. Instead of trying to identify structures of leadership or basic laws and rules, we need to understand the principle of self-organization, which creates order from the ground up instead of from the top down. In his discussion of the rise of the city of Manchester, Johnson implies that self-organization will produce the optimum results. But what would Joseph Stiglitz say about Johnson's proposition? Would he agree that self-organization always leads to the best results,

or does he think that the consequences can be quite destructive? What might Stiglitz say to Johnson about the limitations and dangers of decentralized economies?

2. At first glance, Robert Thurman's claim that we have no permanent or essential self may seem like sheer nonsense, since, clearly, each of us is a self or has one. But does "the self," as we call it, actually represent a self-organizing system, more like an ant colony than a single ant, or more like a city than a single neighborhood? As you work through this question, you should move beyond the two texts to consider your own experience. Are you always the same person from one moment to the next? To what degree is your identity at any particular time shaped by your interactions with others? Can you accurately predict what you will be like ten years from now? Ten months? Ten days?

JONATHAN LETHEM

CRITICS OFTEN USE the word *prolific* to describe Jonathan Lethem. He has published nine novels, five collections of stories, two essay volumes, a novella, and a comic book. But a better word for him might be *protean*. In the religion of the ancient Greeks, Proteus was a god of the sea who presided over unexpected change, a power that gave him the ability to alter his shape whenever humans tried to compel him to foretell events. Like the mythical Proteus, Lethem is a shape-shifter whose work threads across boundaries of all kinds—the boundaries between detective fiction, for example, and the "serious" literature of ideas. What Lethem has written about New York might be said to encapsulate his view of both life and art:

> To live in Manhattan is to be persistently amazed at the worlds squirreled inside one another, like those lines of television cable and fresh water and steam heat and outgoing sewage and telephone wire and whatever else which cohabit in the same intestinal holes that pavement-demolishing workmen periodically wrench open.... We only pretend to live on something as orderly as a grid.

For Lethem, the writer's task is to look beneath the reassuring surface. He believes the truth is seldom found by stopping with the obvious or respecting conventions. Indeed, he sees the act of writing as fundamentally promiscuous.

Perhaps it is not at all surprising that Lethem would have some unexpected ideas about what it means to be creative. Normally we think of creativity as the ability to say or do something completely original, but the isolation implied by this belief strikes Lethem as unappealing. Instead, he celebrates what he calls the "ecstasy of influence." If we wish, we can treat words, ideas, and images as somebody's private property, but we can also view them as available for everyone to use. Nothing, he suggests, is totally original: everything is bound up with everything else, if not on the surface, then underneath, like the "lines of television cable and fresh water" hidden by the "grid." Once we give up the idea of the private ownership of culture, writing and thinking take on a new life, as acts of generosity that place us in debt to everyone who has made our creativity possible.

Quotation comes from Michiko Kakutani, "One by One, Narratives Reflecting Life's Mosaic," *New York Times*, January 8, 2008.

Lethem's argument is powerful, and many writers, artists, and scientists have experienced the *ecstasy* he describes. But where does that leave the writing done in the university itself? Most universities impose harsh penalties on plagiarists, the people who use the words of others without attribution—that is, without an acknowledgment of someone's prior ownership. Indeed, your own college or university might expel students found guilty of cheating. Where does cheating start and creativity stop?

The Ecstasy of Influence: A Plagiarism

All mankind is of one author, and is one volume; when one man dies, one chapter is not torn out of the book, but translated into a better language; and every chapter must be so translated....

—JOHN DONNE

Love and Theft

Consider this tale: a cultivated man of middle age looks back on the story of an *amour fou,* one beginning when, traveling abroad, he takes a room as a lodger. The moment he sees the daughter of the house, he is lost. She is a preteen, whose charms instantly enslave him. Heedless of her age, he becomes intimate with her. In the end she dies, and the narrator—marked by her forever—remains alone. The name of the girl supplies the title of the story: *Lolita.*

The author of the story I've described, Heinz von Lichberg, published his tale of Lolita in 1916, forty years before Vladimir Nabokov's novel. Lichberg later became a prominent journalist in the Nazi era, and his youthful works faded from view. Did Nabokov, who remained in Berlin until 1937, adopt Lichberg's tale consciously? Or did the earlier tale exist for Nabokov as a hidden, unacknowledged memory? The history of literature is not without examples of this phenomenon, called cryptomnesia. Another hypothesis is that Nabokov, knowing Lichberg's tale perfectly well, had set himself to that art of quotation that Thomas Mann, himself a master of it, called "higher cribbing." Literature has always been a crucible in which familiar themes are continually recast. Little of what we admire in Nabokov's *Lolita* is to be found in its predecessor; the former is in no way deducible from the latter. Still: did Nabokov consciously borrow and quote?

"When you live outside the law, you have to eliminate dishonesty." The line comes from Don Siegel's 1958 film noir, *The Lineup,* written by Stirling

Silliphant. The film still haunts revival houses, likely thanks to Eli Wallach's blazing portrayal of a sociopathic hit man and to Siegel's long, sturdy auteurist career. Yet what were those words worth—to Siegel, or Silliphant, or their audience—in 1958? And again: what was the line worth when Bob Dylan heard it (presumably in some Greenwich Village repertory cinema), cleaned it up a little, and inserted it into "Absolutely Sweet Marie"? What are they worth now, to the culture at large?

Appropriation has always played a key role in Dylan's music. The songwriter has grabbed not only from a panoply of vintage Hollywood films but from Shakespeare and F. Scott Fitzgerald and Junichi Saga's *Confessions of a Yakuza.* He also nabbed the title of Eric Lott's study of minstrelsy for his 2001 album *Love and Theft.* One imagines Dylan liked the general resonance of the title, in which emotional misdemeanors stalk the sweetness of love, as they do so often in Dylan's songs. Lott's title is, of course, itself a riff on Leslie Fiedler's *Love and Death in the American Novel,* which famously identifies the literary motif of the interdependence of a white man and a dark man, like Huck and Jim or Ishmael and Queequeg—a series of nested references to Dylan's own appropriating, minstrel-boy self. Dylan's art offers a paradox: while it famously urges us not to look back, it also encodes a knowledge of past sources that might otherwise have little home in contemporary culture, like the Civil War poetry of the Confederate bard Henry Timrod, resuscitated in lyrics on Dylan's newest record, *Modern Times.* Dylan's originality and his appropriations are as one.

The same might be said of *all* art. I realized this forcefully when one day I went looking for the John Donne passage quoted above. I know the lines, I confess, not from a college course but from the movie version of *84, Charing Cross Road* with Anthony Hopkins and Anne Bancroft. I checked out *84, Charing Cross Road* from the library in the hope of finding the Donne passage, but it wasn't in the book. It's alluded to in the play that was adapted from the book, but it isn't reprinted. So I rented the movie again, and there was the passage, read in voice-over by Anthony Hopkins but without attribution. Unfortunately, the line was also abridged so that, when I finally turned to the Web, I found myself searching for the line "all mankind is of one volume" instead of "all mankind is of one author, and is one volume."

My Internet search was initially no more successful than my library search. I had thought that summoning books from the vasty deep was a matter of a few keystrokes, but when I visited the website of the Yale library, I found that most of its books don't yet exist as computer text. As a last-ditch effort I searched the seemingly more obscure phrase "every chapter must be so translated." The passage I wanted finally came to me, as it turns out, not as part of a scholarly library collection but simply because someone who loves Donne had posted it on his homepage. The lines I sought were from Meditation 17 in *Devotions upon Emergent Occasions,* which happens to be the most famous thing Donne ever wrote, containing as it does the line "never send to know for whom the bell tolls; it tolls for thee." My search had led me from a movie to a book to a play to a website and back to a book. Then again, those words may be as famous as they are only because Hemingway lifted them for his book title.

Literature has been in a plundered, fragmentary state for a long time. When I was thirteen I purchased an anthology of Beat writing. Immediately, and to my very great excitement, I discovered one William S. Burroughs, author of something called *Naked Lunch,* excerpted there in all its coruscating brilliance. Burroughs was then as radical a literary man as the world had to offer. Nothing, in all my experience of literature since, has ever had as strong an effect on my sense of the sheer possibilities of writing. Later, attempting to understand this impact, I discovered that Burroughs had incorporated snippets of other writers' texts into his work, an action I knew my teachers would have called plagiarism. Some of these borrowings had been lifted from American science fiction of the Forties and Fifties, adding a secondary shock of recognition for me. By then I knew that this "cut-up method," as Burroughs called it, was central to whatever he thought he was doing, and that he quite literally believed it to be akin to magic. When he wrote about his process, the hairs on my neck stood up, so palpable was the excitement. Burroughs was interrogating the universe with scissors and a paste pot, and the least imitative of authors was no plagiarist at all.

Contamination Anxiety

In 1941, on his front porch, Muddy Waters recorded a song for the folklorist Alan Lomax. After singing the song, which he told Lomax was entitled "Country Blues," Waters described how he came to write it. "I made it on about the eighth of October '38," Waters said. "I was fixin' a puncture on a car. I had been mistreated by a girl. I just felt blue, and the song fell into my mind and it come to me just like that and I started singing." Then Lomax, who knew of the Robert Johnson recording called "Walkin' Blues," asked Waters if there were any other songs that used the same tune. "There's been some blues played like that," Waters replied. "This song comes from the cotton field and a boy once put a record out—Robert Johnson. He put it out as named 'Walkin' Blues.' I heard the tune before I heard it on the record. I learned it from Son House." In nearly one breath, Waters offers five accounts: his own active authorship: he "made it" on a specific date. Then the "passive" explanation: "it come to me just like that." After Lomax raises the question of influence, Waters, without shame, misgivings, or trepidation, says that he heard a version by Johnson, but that his mentor, Son House, taught it to him. In the middle of that complex genealogy, Waters declares that "this song comes from the cotton field."

Blues and jazz musicians have long been enabled by a kind of "open source" culture, in which pre-existing melodic fragments and larger musical frameworks are freely reworked. Technology has only multiplied the possibilities; musicians have gained the power to *duplicate* sounds literally rather than simply approximate them through allusion. In Seventies Jamaica, King Tubby and Lee "Scratch" Perry deconstructed recorded music, using astonishingly primitive pre-digital hardware, creating what they called "versions." The recombinant nature of their means of production quickly spread to DJs in New York and London. Today an endless, gloriously impure, and fundamentally social process generates countless hours of music.

Visual, sound, and text collage—which for many centuries were relatively fugitive traditions (a cento here, a folk pastiche there)—became explosively central to a series of movements in the twentieth century: futurism, cubism, Dada, musique concrète, situationism, pop art, and appropriationism. In fact, collage, the common denominator in that list, might be called *the* art form of the twentieth century, never mind the twenty-first. But forget, for the moment, chronologies, schools, or even centuries. As examples accumulate—Igor Stravinsky's music and Daniel Johnston's, Francis Bacon's paintings and Henry Darger's, the novels of the Oulipo group and of Hannah Crafts (the author who pillaged Dickens's *Bleak House* to write *The Bondwoman's Narrative*), as well as cherished texts that become troubling to their admirers after the discovery of their "plagiarized" elements, like Richard Condon's novels or Martin Luther King Jr.'s sermons—it becomes apparent that appropriation, mimicry, quotation, allusion, and sublimated collaboration consist of a kind of sine qua non of the creative act, cutting across all forms and genres in the realm of cultural production.

In a courtroom scene from *The Simpsons* that has since entered into the television canon, an argument over the ownership of the animated characters Itchy and Scratchy rapidly escalates into an existential debate on the very nature of cartoons. "Animation is built on plagiarism!" declares the show's hot-tempered cartoon-producer-within-a-cartoon, Roger Meyers Jr. "You take away our right to steal ideas, where are they going to come from?" If nostalgic cartoonists had never borrowed from *Fritz the Cat*, there would be no *Ren & Stimpy Show*; without the Rankin/Bass and Charlie Brown Christmas specials, there would be no *South Park*; and without *The Flintstones*—more or less *The Honeymooners* in cartoon loincloths—*The Simpsons* would cease to exist. If those don't strike you as essential losses, then consider the remarkable series of "plagiarisms" that links Ovid's "Pyramus and Thisbe" with Shakespeare's *Romeo and Juliet* and Leonard Bernstein's *West Side Story,* or Shakespeare's description of Cleopatra, copied nearly verbatim from Plutarch's life of Mark Antony and also later nicked by T. S. Eliot for *The Waste Land*. If these are examples of plagiarism, then we want more plagiarism.

Most artists are brought to their vocation when their own nascent gifts are awakened by the work of a master. That is to say, most artists are converted to art by art itself. Finding one's voice isn't just an emptying and purifying oneself of the words of others but an adopting and embracing of filiations, communities, and discourses. Inspiration could be called inhaling the memory of an act never experienced. Invention, it must be humbly admitted, does not consist in creating out of void but out of chaos. Any artist knows these truths, no matter how deeply he or she submerges that knowing.

What happens when an allusion goes unrecognized? A closer look at *The Waste Land* may help make this point. The body of Eliot's poem is a vertiginous mélange of quotation, allusion, and "original" writing. When Eliot alludes to Edmund Spenser's "Prothalamion" with the line "Sweet Thames, run softly, till I end my song," what of readers to whom the poem, never one of Spenser's most popular, is unfamiliar? (Indeed, the Spenser is now known largely because of Eliot's use of it.) Two responses are possible: grant the line to Eliot, or later discover the source and understand the line as plagiarism. Eliot evidenced no small anxiety about these matters; the notes he so carefully added to *The Waste Land* can be read as a symptom of modernism's contamination anxiety. Taken from this angle, what exactly is postmodernism, except modernism without the anxiety?

Surrounded by Signs

The surrealists believed that objects in the world possess a certain but unspecifiable intensity that had been dulled by everyday use and utility. They meant to reanimate this dormant intensity, to bring their minds once again into close contact with the matter that made up their world. André Breton's maxim "Beautiful as the chance encounter of a sewing machine and an umbrella on an operating table" is an expression of the belief that simply placing objects in an unexpected context reinvigorates their mysterious qualities.

This "crisis" the surrealists identified was being simultaneously diagnosed by others. Martin Heidegger held that the essence of modernity was found in a certain technological orientation he called "enframing." This tendency encourages us to see the objects in our world only in terms of how they can serve us or be used by us. The task he identified was to find ways to resituate ourselves vis-à-vis these "objects," so that we may see them as "things" pulled into relief against the ground of their functionality. Heidegger believed that art had the great potential to reveal the "thingness" of objects.

The surrealists understood that photography and cinema could carry out this reanimating process automatically; the process of framing objects in a lens was often enough to create the charge they sought. Describing the effect, Walter Benjamin drew a comparison between the photographic apparatus and Freud's psychoanalytic methods. Just as Freud's theories "isolated and made analyzable things which had heretofore floated along unnoticed in the broad stream of perception," the photographic apparatus focuses on "hidden details of familiar objects," revealing "entirely new structural formations of the subject."

It's worth noting, then, that early in the history of photography a series of judicial decisions could well have changed the course of that art: courts were asked whether the photographer, amateur or professional, required permission before he could capture and print an image. Was the photographer *stealing* from the person or building whose photograph he shot, pirating something of private and certifiable value? Those early decisions went in favor of the pirates. Just as Walt Disney could take inspiration from Buster Keaton's *Steamboat Bill, Jr.,* the Brothers Grimm, or the existence of real mice, the photographer should be free to capture an image without compensating the source. The world that meets our eye through the lens of a camera was judged to be, with minor exceptions, a sort of public commons, where a cat may look at a king.

Novelists may glance at the stuff of the world too, but we sometimes get called to task for it. For those whose ganglia were formed pre-TV, the mimetic deployment of pop-culture icons seems at best an annoying tic and at worst a dangerous vapidity that compromises fiction's seriousness by dating it out of the

Platonic Always, where it ought to reside. In a graduate workshop I briefly passed through, a certain gray eminence tried to convince us that a literary story should always eschew "any feature which serves to date it" because "serious fiction must be Timeless." When we protested that, in his own well-known work, characters moved about electrically lit rooms, drove cars, and spoke not Anglo-Saxon but postwar English—and further, that fiction he'd himself ratified as great, such as Dickens, was liberally strewn with innately topical, commercial, and timebound references—he impatiently amended his proscription to those explicit references that would date a story in the "frivolous Now." When pressed, he said of course he meant the "trendy mass-popular-media" reference. Here, trans-generational discourse broke down.

I was born in 1964; I grew up watching Captain Kangaroo, moon landings, zillions of TV ads, the Banana Splits, *M*A*S*H,* and *The Mary Tyler Moore Show.* I was born with words in my mouth—"Band-Aid," "Q-tip," "Xerox"—object-names as fixed and eternal in my logosphere as "taxicab" and "toothbrush." The world is a home littered with pop-culture products and their emblems. I also came of age swamped by parodies that stood for originals yet mysterious to me—I knew Monkees before Beatles, Belmondo before Bogart, and "remember" the movie *Summer of '42* from a *Mad* magazine satire, though I've still never seen the film itself. I'm not alone in having been born backward into an incoherent realm of texts, products, and images, the commercial and cultural environment with which we've both supplemented and blotted out our natural world. I can no more claim it as "mine" than the sidewalks and forests of the world, yet I do dwell in it, and for me to stand a chance as either artist or citizen, I'd probably better be permitted to name it.

Consider Walker Percy's *The Moviegoer:*

> Other people, so I have read, treasure memorable moments in their lives: the time one climbed the Parthenon at sunrise, the summer night one met a lonely girl in Central Park and achieved with her a sweet and natural relationship, as they say in books. I too once met a girl in Central Park, but it is not much to remember. What I remember is the time John Wayne killed three men with a carbine as he was falling to the dusty street in *Stagecoach,* and the time the kitten found Orson Welles in the doorway in *The Third Man.*

Today, when we can eat Tex-Mex with chopsticks while listening to reggae and watching a YouTube rebroadcast of the Berlin Wall's fall—i.e., when damn near *everything* presents itself as familiar—it's not a surprise that some of today's most ambitious art is going about trying to *make the familiar strange.* In so doing, in reimagining what human life might truly be like over there across the chasms of illusion, mediation, demographics, marketing, imago, and appearance, artists are paradoxically trying to restore what's taken for "real" to three whole dimensions, to reconstruct a univocally round world out of disparate streams of flat sights.

Whatever charge of tastelessness or trademark violation may be attached to the artistic appropriation of the media environment in which we swim, the alternative—to flinch, or tiptoe away into some ivory tower of irrelevance—is far worse. We're surrounded by signs; our imperative is to ignore none of them.

Usemonopoly

The idea that culture can be property—*intellectual* property—is used to justify everything from attempts to force the Girl Scouts to pay royalties for singing songs around campfires to the infringement suit brought by the estate of Margaret Mitchell against the publishers of Alice Randall's *The Wind Done Gone*. Corporations like Celera Genomics have filed for patents for human genes, while the Recording Industry Association of America has sued music downloaders for copyright infringement, reaching out-of-court settlements for thousands of dollars with defendants as young as twelve. ASCAP bleeds fees from shop owners who play background music in their stores; students and scholars are shamed from placing texts facedown on photocopy machines. At the same time, copyright is revered by most established writers and artists as a birthright and bulwark, the source of nurture for their infinitely fragile practices in a rapacious world. Plagiarism and piracy, after all, are the monsters we working artists are taught to dread, as they roam the woods surrounding our tiny preserves of regard and remuneration.

A time is marked not so much by ideas that are argued about as by ideas that are taken for granted. The character of an era hangs upon what needs no defense. In this regard, few of us question the contemporary construction of copyright. It is taken as a law, both in the sense of a universally recognizable moral absolute, like the law against murder, and as naturally inherent in our world, like the law of gravity. In fact, it is neither. Rather, copyright is an ongoing social negotiation, tenuously forged, endlessly revised, and imperfect in its every incarnation.

Thomas Jefferson, for one, considered copyright a necessary evil: he favored providing just enough incentive to create, nothing more, and thereafter allowing ideas to flow freely, as nature intended. His conception of copyright was enshrined in the Constitution, which gives Congress the authority to "promote the Progress of Science and useful Arts, by securing for limited Times to Authors and Inventors the exclusive Right to their respective Writings and Discoveries." This was a balancing act between creators and society as a whole; second comers might do a much better job than the originator with the original idea.

But Jefferson's vision has not fared well, has in fact been steadily eroded by those who view the culture as a market in which everything of value should be owned by someone or other. The distinctive feature of modern American copyright law is its almost limitless bloating—its expansion in both scope and duration. With no registration requirement, every creative act in a tangible medium is now subject to copyright protection: your email to your child or your child's finger painting, both are automatically protected. The first Congress to grant copyright gave authors an initial term of fourteen years, which could be renewed for another fourteen if the author still lived. The current term is the life of the author plus seventy years. It's only a slight exaggeration to say that each time Mickey Mouse is about to fall into the public domain, the mouse's copyright term is extended.

Even as the law becomes more restrictive, technology is exposing those restrictions as bizarre and arbitrary. When old laws fixed on reproduction as the compensable (or actionable) unit, it wasn't because there was anything fundamentally invasive of an author's rights in the making of a copy. Rather it was because copies were once easy to find and count, so they made a useful benchmark for deciding when an owner's rights had been invaded. In the contemporary world, though, the act of "copying" is in no meaningful sense equivalent to an infringement—we make a copy every time we accept an emailed text, or send or forward one—and is impossible anymore to regulate or even describe.

At the movies, my entertainment is sometimes lately preceded by a dire trailer, produced by the lobbying group called the Motion Picture Association of America, in which the purchasing of a bootleg copy of a Hollywood film is compared to the theft of a car or a handbag—and, as the bullying supertitles remind us, "You wouldn't steal a handbag!" This conflation forms an incitement to quit thinking. If I were to tell you that pirating DVDs or downloading music is in no way different from loaning a friend a book, my own arguments would be as ethically bankrupt as the MPAA's. The truth lies somewhere in the vast gray area between these two overstated positions. For a car or a handbag, once stolen, no longer is available to its owner, while the appropriation of an article of "intellectual property" leaves the original untouched. As Jefferson wrote, "He who receives an idea from me, receives instruction himself without lessening mine; as he who lights his taper at mine, receives light without darkening me."

Yet industries of cultural capital, who profit not from creating but from distributing, see the sale of culture as a zero-sum game. The piano-roll publishers fear the record companies, who fear the cassette-tape manufacturers, who fear the online vendors, who fear whoever else is next in line to profit most quickly from the intangible and infinitely reproducible fruits of an artist's labor. It has been the same in every industry and with every technological innovation. Jack Valenti, speaking for the MPAA: "I say to you that the VCR is to the American film producer and the American public as the Boston Strangler is to the woman home alone."

Thinking clearly sometimes requires unbraiding our language. The word "copyright" may eventually seem as dubious in its embedded purposes as "family values," "globalization," and, sure, "intellectual property." Copyright is a "right" in no absolute sense; it is a government-granted monopoly on the use of creative results. So let's try calling it that—not a right but a *monopoly on use,* a "usemonopoly"—and then consider how the rapacious expansion of monopoly rights has always been counter to the public interest, no matter if it is Andrew Carnegie controlling the price of steel or Walt Disney managing the fate of his mouse. Whether the monopolizing beneficiary is a living artist or some artist's heirs or some corporation's shareholders, the loser is the community, including living artists who might make splendid use of a healthy public domain.

The Beauty of Second Use

A few years ago someone brought me a strange gift, purchased at MoMA's downtown design store: a copy of my own first novel, *Gun, With Occasional Music,* expertly cut into the contours of a pistol. The object was the work of Robert The, an artist whose specialty is the reincarnation of everyday materials. I regard my first book as an old friend, one who never fails to remind me of the spirit with which I entered into this game of art and commerce—that to be allowed to insert the materials of my imagination onto the shelves of bookstores and into the minds of readers (if only a handful) was a wild privilege. I was paid $6,000 for three years of writing, but at the time I'd have happily published the results for nothing. Now my old friend had come home in a new form, one I was unlikely to have imagined for it myself. The gun-book wasn't readable, exactly, but I couldn't take offense at that. The fertile spirit of stray connection this appropriated object conveyed back to me— the strange beauty of its second use—was a reward for being a published writer I could never have fathomed in advance. And the world makes room for both my novel and Robert The's gun-book. There's no need to choose between the two.

In the first life of creative property, if the creator is lucky, the content is sold. After the commercial life has ended, our tradition supports a second life as well. A newspaper is delivered to a doorstep, and the next day wraps fish or builds an archive. Most books fall out of print after one year, yet even within that period they can be sold in used bookstores and stored in libraries, quoted in reviews, parodied in magazines, described in conversations, and plundered for costumes for kids to wear on Halloween. The demarcation between various possible uses is beautifully graded and hard to define, the more so as artifacts distill into and repercuss through the realm of culture into which they've been entered, the more so as they engage the receptive minds for whom they were presumably intended.

Active reading is an impertinent raid on the literary preserve. Readers are like nomads, poaching their way across fields they do not own—artists are no more able to control the imaginations of their audiences than the culture industry is able to control second uses of its artifacts. In the children's classic *The Velveteen Rabbit,* the old Skin Horse offers the Rabbit a lecture on the practice of textual poaching. The value of a new toy lies not in its material qualities (not "having things that buzz inside you and a stick-out handle"), the Skin Horse explains, but rather in how the toy is used. "Real isn't how you are made…. It's a thing that happens to you. When a child loves you for a long, long time, not just to play with, but REALLY loves you, then you become Real." The Rabbit is fearful, recognizing that consumer goods don't become "real" without being actively reworked: "Does it hurt?" Reassuring him, the Skin Horse says: "It doesn't happen all at once…. You become. It takes a long time…. Generally, by the time you are Real, most of your hair has been loved off, and your eyes drop out and you get loose in the joints and very shabby." Seen from the perspective of the toymaker, the Velveteen Rabbit's loose joints and missing eyes represent vandalism, signs of misuse and rough treatment; for others, these are marks of its loving use.

Artists and their surrogates who fall into the trap of seeking recompense for every possible second use end up attacking their own best audience members for the crime of exalting and enshrining their work. The Recording Industry Association of America prosecuting their own record-buying public makes as little sense as the novelists who bristle at autographing used copies of their books for collectors. And artists, or their heirs, who fall into the trap of attacking the collagists and satirists and digital samplers of their work are attacking the next generation of creators for the crime of being influenced, for the crime of responding with the same mixture of intoxication, resentment, lust, and glee that characterizes all artistic successors. By doing so they make the world smaller, betraying what seems to me the primary motivation for participating in the world of culture in the first place: to make the world larger.

Source Hypocrisy, or, Disnial

The Walt Disney Company has drawn an astonishing catalogue from the work of others: *Snow White and the Seven Dwarfs, Fantasia, Pinocchio, Dumbo, Bambi, Song of the South, Cinderella, Alice in Wonderland, Robin Hood, Peter Pan, Lady and the Tramp, Mulan, Sleeping Beauty, The Sword in the Stone, The Jungle Book,* and, alas, *Treasure Planet,* a legacy of cultural sampling that Shakespeare, or De La Soul, could get behind. Yet Disney's protectorate of lobbyists has policed the resulting cache of cultural materials as vigilantly as if it were Fort Knox—threatening legal action, for instance, against the artist Dennis Oppenheim for the use of Disney characters in a sculpture, and prohibiting the scholar Holly Crawford from using any Disney-related images—including artwork by Lichtenstein, Warhol, Oldenburg, and others—in her monograph *Attached to the Mouse: Disney and Contemporary Art.*

This peculiar and specific act—the enclosure of commonwealth culture for the benefit of a sole or corporate owner—is close kin to what could be called *imperial plagiarism,* the free use of Third World or "primitive" artworks and styles by more privileged (and better-paid) artists. Think of Picasso's *Les Demoiselles d'Avignon,* or some of the albums of Paul Simon or David Byrne: even without violating copyright, those creators have sometimes come in for a certain skepticism when the extent of their outsourcing became evident. And, as when Led Zeppelin found themselves sued for back royalties by the bluesman Willie Dixon, the act can occasionally be an expensive one. *To live outside the law, you must be honest:* perhaps it was this, in part, that spurred David Byrne and Brian Eno to recently launch a "remix" website, where anyone can download easily disassembled versions of two songs from *My Life in the Bush of Ghosts,* an album reliant on vernacular speech sampled from a host of sources. Perhaps it also explains why Bob Dylan has never refused a request for a sample.

Kenneth Koch once said, "I'm a writer who likes to be influenced." It was a charming confession, and a rare one. For so many artists, the act of creativity is intended as a Napoleonic imposition of one's uniqueness upon the universe—*après moi le déluge* of copycats! And for every James Joyce or Woody Guthrie or Martin Luther King Jr., or Walt Disney, who gathered a constellation of voices in his work, there may seem to be some corporation or literary estate eager to stopper the bottle: cultural debts flow in, but they don't flow out. We might call this tendency "source hypocrisy." Or we could name it after the most pernicious source hypocrites of all time: Disnial.

You Can't Steal a Gift

My reader may, understandably, be on the verge of crying, "Communist!" A large, diverse society cannot survive without property; a large, diverse, and modern society cannot flourish without some form of intellectual property. But it takes little reflection to grasp that there is ample value that the term "property" doesn't capture. And works of art exist simultaneously in two economies, a market economy and a *gift economy*.

The cardinal difference between gift and commodity exchange is that a gift establishes a feeling-bond between two people, whereas the sale of a commodity leaves no necessary connection. I go into a hardware store, pay the man for a hacksaw blade, and walk out. I may never see him again. The disconnectedness is, in fact, a virtue of the commodity mode. We don't want to be bothered, and if the clerk always wants to chat about the family, I'll shop elsewhere. I just want a hacksaw blade. But a gift makes a connection. There are many examples, the candy or cigarette offered to a stranger who shares a seat on the plane, the few words that indicate goodwill between passengers on the late-night bus. These tokens establish the simplest bonds of social life, but the model they offer may be extended to the most complicated of unions—marriage, parenthood, mentorship. If a value is placed on these (often essentially unequal) exchanges, they degenerate into something else.

Yet one of the more difficult things to comprehend is that the gift economies—like those that sustain open-source software—coexist so naturally with the market. It is precisely this doubleness in art practices that we must identify, ratify, and enshrine in our lives as participants in culture, either as "producers" or "consumers." Art that matters to us—which moves the heart, or revives the soul, or delights the senses, or offers courage for living, however we choose to describe the experience—is received as a gift is received. Even if we've paid a fee at the door of the museum or concert hall, when we are touched by a work of art something comes to us that has nothing to do with the price. The daily commerce of our lives proceeds at its own constant level, but a gift conveys an uncommodifiable surplus of inspiration.

The way we treat a thing can change its nature, though. Religions often prohibit the sale of sacred objects, the implication being that their sanctity is lost if they are bought and sold. We consider it unacceptable to sell sex, babies, body organs, legal rights, and votes. The idea that something should never be commodified is generally known as *inalienability* or *unalienability*—a concept most famously expressed by Thomas Jefferson in the phrase "endowed by their Creator with certain unalienable Rights ..." A work of art seems to be a hardier breed; it can be sold in the market and still emerge a work of art. But if it is true that in the essential commerce of art a gift is carried by the work from the artist to his audience, if I am right to say that where there is no gift there is no art, then it may be possible to destroy a work of art by converting it into a pure commodity. I don't maintain that art can't be bought and sold, but that the gift portion of the work places a constraint upon our merchandising. This is the reason why even a really beautiful, ingenious, powerful ad (of which there are a lot) can never be any kind of real art: an ad has no status as gift; i.e., it's never really *for* the person it's directed at.

The power of a gift economy remains difficult for the empiricists of our market culture to understand. In our times, the rhetoric of the market presumes that everything should be and can be appropriately bought, sold, and owned—a tide of alienation lapping daily at the dwindling redoubt of the unalienable. In free-market theory, an intervention to halt propertization is considered "paternalistic," because it inhibits the free action of the citizen, now reposited as a "potential entrepreneur." Of course, in the real world, we know that child-rearing, family life, education, socialization, sexuality, political life, and many other basic human activities require insulation from market forces. In fact, paying for many of these things can ruin them. We may be willing to peek at *Who Wants to Marry a Multimillionaire* or an eBay auction of the ova of fashion models, but only to reassure ourselves that some things are still beneath our standards of dignity.

What's remarkable about gift economies is that they can flourish in the most unlikely places—in rundown neighborhoods, on the Internet, in scientific communities, and among members of Alcoholics Anonymous. A classic example is commercial blood systems, which generally produce blood supplies of lower safety, purity, and potency than volunteer systems. A gift economy may be superior when it comes to maintaining a group's commitment to certain extra-market values.

The Commons

Another way of understanding the presence of gift economies—which dwell like ghosts in the commercial machine—is in the sense of a *public commons*. A commons, of course, is anything like the streets over which we drive, the skies through which we pilot airplanes, or the public parks or beaches on which we dally. A commons belongs to everyone and no one, and its use is controlled only by common consent. A commons describes resources like the body of ancient music drawn on by composers and folk musicians alike, rather than the commodities, like "Happy Birthday to You," for which ASCAP, 114 years after it was written, continues to collect a fee. Einstein's theory of relativity is a commons. Writings in the public domain are a commons. Gossip about celebrities is a commons. The silence in a movie theater is a transitory commons, impossibly fragile, treasured by those who crave it, and constructed as a mutual gift by those who compose it.

The world of art and culture is a vast commons, one that is salted through with zones of utter commerce yet remains gloriously immune to any overall commodification. The closest resemblance is to the commons of a *language:* altered by every contributor, expanded by even the most passive user. That a language is a commons doesn't mean that the community owns it; rather it belongs *between* people, possessed by no one, not even by society as a whole.

Nearly any commons, though, can be encroached upon, partitioned, enclosed. The American commons include tangible assets such as public forests and minerals, intangible wealth such as copyrights and patents, critical infrastructures such as the Internet and government research, and cultural resources such as the broadcast airwaves and public spaces. They include resources we've paid for as taxpayers and inherited from previous generations. They're not just an inventory of marketable assets; they're social institutions and cultural traditions that define us as Americans and enliven us as human beings. Some invasions of the commons are sanctioned because we can no longer muster a spirited commitment to the public sector. The abuse goes unnoticed because the theft of the commons is seen in glimpses, not in panorama. We may occasionally see a former wetland paved; we may hear about the breakthrough cancer drug that tax dollars helped develop, the rights to which pharmaceutical companies acquired for a song. The larger movement goes too much unremarked. The notion of a *commons of cultural materials* goes more or less unnamed.

Honoring the commons is not a matter of moral exhortation. It is a practical necessity. We in Western society are going through a period of intensifying belief in private ownership, to the detriment of the public good. We have to remain constantly vigilant to prevent raids by those who would selfishly exploit our common heritage for their private gain. Such raids on our natural resources are not examples of enterprise and initiative. They are attempts to take from all the people just for the benefit of a few.

Undiscovered Public Knowledge

Artists and intellectuals despondent over the prospects for originality can take heart from a phenomenon identified about twenty years ago by Don Swanson, a library scientist at the University of Chicago. He called it "undiscovered public knowledge." Swanson showed that standing problems in medical research may be significantly addressed, perhaps even solved, simply by systematically survey-ing the scientific literature. Left to its own devices, research tends to become more specialized and abstracted from the real-world problems that motivated it and to which it remains relevant. This suggests that such a problem may be tack-led effectively not by commissioning more research but by assuming that most or all of the solution can already be found in various scientific journals, waiting to be assembled by someone willing to read across specialties. Swanson himself did this in the case of Raynaud's syndrome, a disease that causes the fingers of young women to become numb. His finding is especially striking—perhaps even scandalous—because it happened in the ever-expanding biomedical sciences.

Undiscovered public knowledge emboldens us to question the extreme claims to originality made in press releases and publishers' notices: Is an intellec-tual or creative offering truly novel, or have we just forgotten a worthy precur-sor? Does solving certain scientific problems really require massive additional funding, or could a computerized search engine, creatively deployed, do the same job more quickly and cheaply? Lastly, does our appetite for creative vitality require the violence and exasperation of another avant-garde, with its wearisome killing-the-father imperatives, or might we be better off ratifying *the ecstasy of influence*—and deepening our willingness to understand the commonality and timelessness of the methods and motifs available to artists?

Give All

A few years ago, the Film Society of Lincoln Center announced a retrospective of the works of Dariush Mehrjui, then a fresh enthusiasm of mine. Mehrjui is one of Iran's finest filmmakers, and the only one whose subject was personal relationships among the upper-middle-class intelligentsia. Needless to say, opportunities to view his films were—and remain—rare indeed. I headed uptown for one, an adaptation of J. D. Salinger's *Franny and Zooey,* titled *Pari,* only to discover at the door of the Walter Reade Theater that the screening had been canceled: its announcement had brought threat of a lawsuit down on the Film Society. True, these were Salinger's rights under the law. Yet why would he care that some obscure Iranian filmmaker had paid him homage with a meditation on his heroine? Would it have damaged his book or robbed him of some crucial remuneration had the screening been permitted? The fertile spirit of stray connection—one stretching across what is presently seen as the direst of international breaches—had in this case been snuffed out. The cold, undead hand of one of my childhood literary heroes had reached out from its New Hampshire redoubt to arrest my present-day curiosity.

A few assertions, then:

Any text that has infiltrated the common mind to the extent of *Gone With the Wind* or *Lolita* or *Ulysses* inexorably joins the language of culture. A map-turned-to-landscape, it has moved to a place beyond enclosure or control. The authors and their heirs should consider the subsequent parodies, refractions, quotations, and revisions an honor, or at least the price of a rare success.

A corporation that has imposed an inescapable notion—Mickey Mouse, Band-Aid—on the cultural language should pay a similar price.

The primary objective of copyright is not to reward the labor of authors but "to promote the Progress of Science and useful Arts." To this end, copyright assures authors the right to their original expression, but encourages others to build freely upon the ideas and information conveyed by a work. This result is neither unfair nor unfortunate.

Contemporary copyright, trademark, and patent law is presently corrupted. The case for perpetual copyright is a denial of the essential gift-aspect of the creative act. Arguments in its favor are as un-American as those for the repeal of the estate tax.

Art is sourced. Apprentices graze in the field of culture.

Digital sampling is an art method like any other, neutral in itself.

Despite hand-wringing at each technological turn—radio, the Internet—the future will be much like the past. Artists will sell some things but also give some things away. Change may be troubling for those who crave less ambiguity, but the life of an artist has never been filled with certainty.

The dream of a perfect systematic remuneration is nonsense. I pay rent with the price my words bring when published in glossy magazines and at the same moment offer them for almost nothing to impoverished literary quarterlies, or speak them for free into the air in a radio interview. So what are they worth? What would they be worth if some future Dylan worked them into a song? Should I care to make such a thing impossible?

Any text is woven entirely with citations, references, echoes, cultural languages, which cut across it through and through in a vast stereophony. The citations that go to make up a text are anonymous, untraceable, and yet *already read;* they are quotations without inverted commas. The kernel, the soul—let us go further and say the substance, the bulk, the actual and valuable material of all human utterances—is plagiarism. For substantially all ideas are secondhand, consciously and unconsciously drawn from a million outside sources, and daily used by the garnerer with a pride and satisfaction born of the superstition that he originated them; whereas there is not a rag of originality about them anywhere except the little discoloration they get from his mental and moral caliber and his temperament, and which is revealed in characteristics of phrasing. Old and new make the warp and woof of every moment. There is no thread that is not a twist of these two strands. By necessity, by proclivity, and by delight, we all quote. Neurological study has lately shown that memory, imagination, and consciousness itself is stitched, quilted, pastiched. If we cut-and-paste our selves, might we not forgive it of our artworks?

Artists and writers—and our advocates, our guilds and agents—too often subscribe to implicit claims of originality that do injury to these truths. And we too often, as hucksters and bean counters in the tiny enterprises of our selves, act to spite the gift portion of our privileged roles. People live differently who treat a portion of their wealth as a gift. If we devalue and obscure the gift-economy function of our art practices, we turn our works into nothing more than advertisements for themselves. We may console ourselves that our lust for subsidiary rights in virtual perpetuity is some heroic counter to rapacious corporate interests. But the truth is that with artists pulling on one side and corporations pulling on the other, the loser is the collective public imagination from which we were nourished in the first place, and whose existence as the ultimate repository of our offerings makes the work worth doing in the first place.

As a novelist, I'm a cork on the ocean of story, a leaf on a windy day. Pretty soon I'll be blown away. For the moment I'm grateful to be making a living, and so must ask that for a limited time (in the Thomas Jefferson sense) you please respect my small, treasured usemonopolies. Don't pirate my editions; do plunder my visions. The name of the game is Give All. You, reader, are welcome to my stories. They were never mine in the first place, but I gave them to you. If you have the inclination to pick them up, take them with my blessing.

KEY: I IS ANOTHER

This key to the preceding essay names the source of every line I stole, warped, and cobbled together as I "wrote" (except, alas, those sources I forgot along the way). First uses of a given author or speaker are highlighted in bold type. Nearly every sentence I culled I also revised, at least slightly—for necessities of space, in order to produce a more consistent tone, or simply because I felt like it.

Title

The phrase "the ecstasy of influence," which embeds a rebuking play on Harold Bloom's "anxiety of influence," is lifted from spoken remarks by Professor **Richard Dienst** of Rutgers.

Love and Theft

"… a cultivated man of middle age …" to "… hidden, unacknowledged memory?" These lines, with some adjustments for tone, belong to the **anonymous editor** or **assistant** who wrote the dust-flap copy of **Michael Maar's** *The Two Lolitas*. Of course, in my own experience, dust-flap copy is often a collaboration between author and editor. Perhaps this was also true for Maar.

"The history of literature …" to "… borrow and quote?" comes from Maar's book itself.

"Appropriation has always …" to "… Ishmael and Queequeg …" This paragraph makes a hash of remarks from an interview with **Eric Lott** conducted by **David McNair** and **Jayson Whitehead**, and incorporates both interviewers' and interviewee's observations. (The text-interview form can be seen as a commonly accepted form of multivocal writing. Most interviewers prime their subjects with remarks of their own—leading the witness, so to speak—and gently refine their subjects' statements in the final printed transcript.)

"I realized this …" to "… for a long time." The anecdote is cribbed, with an elision to avoid appropriating a dead grandmother, from **Jonathan Rosen**'s *The Talmud and the Internet*. I've never seen *84, Charing Cross Road,* nor searched the Web for a Donne quote. For me it was through Rosen to Donne, Hemingway, website, et al.

"When I was thirteen …" to "… no plagiarist at all." This is from **William Gibson**'s "God's Little Toys," in *Wired* magazine. My own first encounter with William Burroughs, also at age thirteen, was less epiphanic. Having grown up with a painter father who, during family visits to galleries or museums, approvingly noted collage and appropriation techniques in the visual arts (Picasso, Claes Oldenburg, Stuart Davis), I was gratified, but not surprised, to learn that literature could encompass the same methods.

Contamination Anxiety

"In 1941, on his front porch …" to "… 'this song comes from the cotton field.'" **Siva Vaidhyanathan**, *Copyrights and Copywrongs*.

"… enabled by a kind … freely reworked." **Kembrew McLeod**, *Freedom of Expression*. In *Owning Culture*, McLeod notes that, as he was writing, he

> happened to be listening to a lot of old country music, and in my casual listening I noticed that *six* country songs shared *exactly* the same vocal melody, including Hank Thompson's "Wild Side of Life," the Carter Family's "I'm Thinking Tonight of My Blue Eyes," Roy Acuff's "Great Speckled Bird," Kitty Wells's "It Wasn't God Who Made Honky Tonk Angels," Reno & Smiley's "I'm Using My Bible for a Roadmap," and Townes Van Zandt's "Heavenly Houseboat Blues."… In his extensively researched book, *Country: The Twisted Roots of Rock 'n' Roll,* Nick Tosches documents that the melody these songs share is both "ancient and British." There were no recorded lawsuits stemming from these appropriations.…

"… musicians have gained … through allusion." **Joanna Demers**, *Steal This Music*.

"In Seventies Jamaica …" to "… hours of music." Gibson.

"Visual, sound, and text collage …" to "… realm of cultural production." This plunders, rewrites, and amplifies paragraphs from McLeod's *Owning Culture*, except for the line about collage being the art form of the twentieth and twenty-first centuries, which I heard filmmaker **Craig Baldwin** say, in defense of sampling, in the trailer for a forthcoming documentary, *Copyright Criminals*.

"In a courtroom scene …" to "… would cease to exist." **Dave Itzkoff**, *New York Times*.

"… the remarkable series of 'plagiarisms' …" to "… we want more plagiarism." **Richard Posner**, combined from The Becker-Posner Blog and *The Atlantic Monthly*.

"Most artists are brought …" to "… by art itself." These words, and many more to follow, come from **Lewis Hyde**'s *The Gift*. Above any other book I've here plagiarized, I commend *The Gift* to your attention.

"Finding one's voice … filiations, communities, and discourses." Semanticist **George L. Dillon**, quoted in **Rebecca Moore Howard**'s "The New Abolitionism Comes to Plagiarism."

"Inspiration could be … act never experienced." **Ned Rorem**, found on several "great quotations" sites on the Internet.

"Invention, it must be humbly admitted … out of chaos." **Mary Shelley**, from her introduction to *Frankenstein*.

"What happens …" to "… contamination anxiety." **Kevin J. H. Dettmar**, from "The Illusion of Modernist Allusion and the Politics of Postmodern Plagiarism."

Surrounded By Signs

"The surrealists believed …" to the Walter Benjamin quote. **Christian Keathley**'s *Cinephilia and History, or the Wind in the Trees,* a book that treats fannish fetishism as the secret at the heart of film scholarship. Keathley notes, for instance, Joseph Cornell's surrealist-influenced 1936 film *Rose Hobart,* which simply records "the way in which Cornell himself watched the 1931 Hollywood potboiler *East of Borneo*, fascinated and distracted as he was by its B-grade star"—the star, of course, being Rose Hobart herself. This, I suppose, makes Cornell a sort of father to computer-enabled fan-creator re-workings of Hollywood product, like the version of George Lucas's *The Phantom Menace* from which the noxious Jar Jar Binks character was purged; both incorporate a viewer's subjective preferences into a revision of a filmmaker's work.

"… early in the history of photography" to "… without compensating the source." From *Free Culture,* by **Lawrence Lessig**, the greatest of public advocates for copyright reform, and the best source if you want to get radicalized in a hurry.

"For those whose ganglia …" to "… discourse broke down." From **David Foster Wallace**'s essay "E Unibus Pluram," reprinted in A *Supposedly Fun Thing I'll Never Do Again*. I have no idea who Wallace's "gray eminence" is or was.

I inserted the example of Dickens into the paragraph; he strikes me as over-looked in the lineage of authors of "brand-name" fiction.

"I was born … *Mary Tyler Moore Show*." These are the reminiscences of **Mark Hosler** from Negativland, a collaging musical collective that was sued by U2's record label for their appropriation of "I Still Haven't Found What I'm Looking For." Although I had to adjust the birth date, Hosler's cultural menu fits me like a glove.

"The world is a home … pop-culture products …" McLeod.

"Today, when we can eat …" to "… flat sights." Wallace.

"We're surrounded by signs, ignore none of them." This phrase, which I unfortunately rendered somewhat leaden with the word "imperative," comes from **Steve Erickson**'s novel *Our Ecstatic Days*.

Usemonopoly

"… everything from attempts …" to "defendants as young as twelve." **Robert Boynton**, *The New York Times Magazine,* "The Tyranny of Copyright?"

"A time is marked …" to "…what needs no defense." Lessig, this time from *The Future of Ideas*.

"Thomas Jefferson, for one …" to "'… respective Writings and Discoveries.'" Boynton.

"… second comers might do a much better job than the originator …" I found this phrase in Lessig, who is quoting Vaidhyanathan, who himself is char-acterizing a judgment written by **Learned Hand**.

"But Jefferson's vision … owned by someone or other." Boynton.

"The distinctive feature …" to "… term is extended." Lessig, again from *The Future of Ideas*.

"When old laws …" to "… had been invaded." **Jessica Litman**, *Digital Copyright*.

"'I say to you … woman home alone.'" I found the Valenti quote in Mcleod. Now fill in the blank: Jack Valenti is to the public domain as _____ is to _____.

The Beauty of Second Use

"In the first …" to "… builds an archive." Lessig.

"Most books … one year …" Lessig.

"Active reading is …" to "… do not own …" This is a mashup of **Henry Jenkins**, from his *Textual Poachers: Television Fans and Participatory Culture,* and **Michel de Certeau**, whom Jenkins quotes.

"In the children's classic …" to "… its loving use." Jenkins. (Incidentally, have the holders of the copyright to *The Velveteen Rabbit* had a close look at *Toy Story?* There could be a lawsuit there.)

Source Hypocrisy, or, Disnial

"The Walt Disney Company ... alas, *Treasure Planet* ..." Lessig.

"Imperial Plagiarism" is the title of an essay by **Marilyn Randall**.

"... spurred David Byrne ... *My Life in the Bush of Ghosts* ..." **Chris Dahlen**, *Pitchfork*—though in truth by the time I'd finished, his words were so utterly dissolved within my own that had I been an ordinary cutting-and-pasting journalist it never would have occurred to me to give Dahlen a citation. The effort of preserving another's distinctive phrases as I worked on this essay was sometimes beyond my capacities; this form of plagiarism was oddly hard work.

"Kenneth Koch ..." to "... *déluge* of copycats!" **Emily Nussbaum**, *The New York Times Book Review.*

You Can't Steal a Gift

"You can't steal a gift." Dizzy Gillespie, defending another player who'd been accused of poaching Charlie Parker's style: "You can't steal a gift. Bird gave the world his music, and if you can hear it you can have it."

"A large, diverse society ... intellectual property." Lessig.

"And works of art ..." to "... marriage, parenthood, mentorship." Hyde.

"Yet one ... so naturally with the market." **David Bollier**, *Silent Theft.*

"Art that matters ..." to "... bought and sold." Hyde.

"We consider it unacceptable ..." to "'... certain unalienable Rights ...'" Bollier, paraphrasing **Margaret Jane Radin**'s *Contested Commodities.*

"A work of art ..." to "... constraint upon our merchandising." Hyde.

"This is the reason ... person it's directed at." Wallace.

"The power of a gift ..." to "... certain extra-market values." Bollier, and also the sociologist Warren O. Hagstrom, whom Bollier is paraphrasing.

The Commons

"Einstein's theory ..." to "... public domain are a commons." Lessig.

"That a language is a commons ... society as a whole." **Michael Newton**, in the *London Review of Books,* reviewing a book called *Echolalias: On the Forgetting of Language* by **Daniel Heller-Roazen**. The paraphrases of book reviewers are another covert form of collaborative culture; as an avid reader of reviews, I know much about books I've never read. To quote Yann Martel on how he came to be accused of imperial plagiarism in his Booker-winning novel *Life of Pi,*

> Ten or so years ago, I read a review by John Updike in the *New York Times Review of Books* [sic]. It was of a novel by a Brazilian writer, Moacyr Scliar. I forget the title, and John Updike did worse: he clearly thought the book as a whole was forgettable. His review—one of those that makes you suspicious by being mostly descriptive ... oozed indifference. But one thing about it struck me: the premise.... Oh, the wondrous things I could do with this premise.

Unfortunately, no one was ever able to locate the Updike review in question.

"The American commons ..." to "... for a song." Bollier.

"Honoring the commons ..." to "... practical necessity." Bollier.

"We in Western ... public good." **John Sulston**, Nobel Prize–winner and co-mapper of the human genome.

"We have to remain ..." to "... benefit of a few." **Harry S Truman**, at the opening of the Everglades National Park. Although it may seem the height of presumption to rip off a president—I found claiming Truman's stolid advocacy as my own embarrassing in the extreme—I didn't rewrite him at all. As the poet Marianne Moore said, "If a thing had been said in the *best* way, how can you say it better?" Moore confessed her penchant for incorporating lines from others' work, explaining, "I have not yet been able to outgrow this hybrid method of composition."

Undiscovered Public Knowledge

"... intellectuals despondent ..." to "... quickly and cheaply?" **Steve Fuller**, *The Intellectual*. There's something of Borges in Fuller's insight here; the notion of a storehouse of knowledge waiting passively to be assembled by future users is suggestive of both "The Library of Babel" and "Kafka and his Precursors."

Give All

"... one of Iran's finest ..." to "... meditation on his heroine?" **Amy Taubin**, *Village Voice,* although it was me who was disappointed at the door of the Walter Reade Theater.

"The primary objective ..." to "... unfair nor unfortunate." **Sandra Day O'Connor**, 1991.

"... the future will be much like the past" to "... give some things away." Open-source film archivist **Rick Prelinger**, quoted in McLeod.

"Change may be troubling ... with certainty." McLeod.

"... woven entirely ..." to "... without inverted commas." **Roland Barthes**.

"The kernel, the soul ..." to "... characteristics of phrasing." **Mark Twain**, from a consoling letter to Helen Keller, who had suffered distressing accusations of plagiarism (!). In fact, her work included unconsciously memorized phrases; under Keller's particular circumstances, her writing could be understood as a kind of allegory of the "constructed" nature of artistic perception. I found the Twain quote in the aforementioned *Copyrights and Copywrongs,* by Siva Vaidhyanathan.

"Old and new ..." to "... we all quote." **Ralph Waldo Emerson**. These guys all sound alike!

"People live differently ... wealth as a gift." Hyde.

"... I'm a cork ..." to "... blown away." This is adapted from The Beach Boys song "'Til I Die," written by **Brian Wilson**. My own first adventure with song-lyric permissions came when I tried to have a character in my second novel quote the lyrics "There's a world where I can go and/Tell my secrets to/In my room/In my room." After learning the likely expense, at my editor's suggestion I replaced those with "You take the high road/I'll take the low road/I'll be in Scotland before you," a lyric in the public domain. This capitulation always bugged me, and in the subsequent British publication of the same book I restored the Brian Wilson lyric, without permission. *Ocean of Story* is the title of a collection of **Christina Stead**'s short fiction.

Saul Bellow, writing to a friend who'd taken offense at Bellow's fictional use of certain personal facts, said: "The name of the game is Give All. You are welcome to all my facts. You know them, I give them to you. If you have the strength to pick them up, take them with my blessing." I couldn't bring myself to retain Bellow's "strength," which seemed presumptuous in my new context, though it is surely the more elegant phrase. On the other hand, I was pleased to invite the suggestion that the gifts in question may actually be light and easily lifted.

Key to the Key

The notion of a collage text is, of course, not original to me. **Walter Benjamin**'s incomplete *Arcades Project* seemingly would have featured extensive interlaced quotations. Other precedents include **Graham Rawle**'s novel *Diary of an Amateur Photographer,* its text harvested from photography magazines, and **Eduardo Paolozzi**'s collage-novel *Kex,* cobbled from crime novels and newspaper clippings. Closer to home, my efforts owe a great deal to the recent essays of **David Shields**, in which diverse quotes are made to closely intertwine and reverberate, and to conversations with editor **Sean Howe** and archivist **Pamela Jackson**. Last year **David Edelstein**, in *New York* magazine, satirized the Kaavya Viswanathan plagiarism case by creating an almost completely plagiarized column denouncing her actions. Edelstein intended to demonstrate, through ironic example, how bricolage such as his own was ipso facto facile and unworthy. Although Viswanathan's version of "creative copying" was a pitiable one, I differ with Edelstein's conclusions.

The phrase *Je est un autre,* with its deliberately awkward syntax, belongs to **Arthur Rimbaud**. It has been translated both as "I is another" and "I is someone else," as in this excerpt from Rimbaud's letters:

> For *I* is someone else. If brass wakes up a trumpet, it is not its fault. To me this is obvious: I witness the unfolding of my own thought: I watch it, I listen to it: I make a stroke of the bow: the symphony begins to stir in the depths, or springs on to the stage.

> If the old fools had not discovered only the *false* significance of the Ego, we should not now be having to sweep away those millions of skeletons which, since time immemorial, have been piling up the fruits of their one-eyed intellects, and claiming to be, themselves, the authors!

QUESTIONS FOR MAKING CONNECTIONS
WITHIN THE READING

1. Discuss the relationship between the two economies that Lethem describes—the economy of the market and the economy of the gift. What is the role of property in the two economies, and what role do culture and the arts play in each? At first glance the two economies might appear to be antithetical, but Lethem suggests that the two of them can actually coexist. How is such coexistence possible, and in what ways might the two economies sustain and revitalize each other? How would the disappearance of the *public commons* damage the whole society? In what respects does private property depend on the health of the commons?

2. In your own words, explain the following passage: "A time is marked not so much by ideas that are argued about as by ideas that are taken for granted. The character of an era hangs upon what needs no defense. In this regard, few of us question the contemporary construction of copyright." How might it be possible that ideas which seem to require no defense are actually the most revealing ones? Why aren't the most discussed ideas the ones of greatest consequence? If the justness of the copyright appears to be self-evident, what can we conclude about the blindnesses of our own historical period? In what ways do our copyright laws reflect deeper anxieties about our relations to others? Does the common sense of our time prevent us from enjoying more creative lives?

3. Explain Lethem's point when he declares, "When damn near everything presents itself as familiar … it's not a surprise that some of today's most ambitious art is going about trying to make the familiar strange." What does Lethem mean when he claims that "everything presents itself as familiar"? And what might be involved in making the familiar strange? What effect does the familiar have on us, and what effect does strangeness have? How do the artists Lethem discusses make the familiar seem strange? How might taking the words of someone else and putting them to a new use illustrate the value of estrangement? Does Lethem himself manage to make the familiar strange, and why is doing so important to his argument?

QUESTIONS FOR WRITING

1. The anthropologist David Graeber has made the claim that all societies, even those that have developed sophisticated forms of private property, still observe an implicit communism on the level of basic human interactions. For example, if your father asks you for a wrench while he is repairing a faucet, you would not normally respond with the question, "What's in it for me?" If the word *communism* actually refers to the owning of things in common, does Lethem seem to accept the argument that something like

common ownership is required for the health of a society? In what ways might communism in this sense actually contribute to democracy as well as personal freedom? In what ways might the open source movement represent a rebellion against the dominant ways of thinking about property as fundamentally private?

2.   Does Lethem want students to cheat? When he writes that plagiarism is the soul of all human utterances, does he really mean it? Does he believe that you should feel free to learn from the *ideas* of others, while still respecting the principle of private ownership when it comes to *words*? Would he approve of your submitting a paper purchased from an Internet company? Would he approve of splicing into your next essay sentences or whole paragraphs taken from someone else's work, all without proper attribution? Does Lethem do the same thing himself? Is Lethem's argument *amoral*—that is, is it indifferent to ethical concerns? Is his view actually immoral—calculated to do harm? Or is Lethem trying to promote a different set of values? What might those values include?

QUESTIONS FOR MAKING CONNECTIONS
BETWEEN READINGS

1.   In what ways might the "ecstasy of influence" celebrated by Lethem qualify as a form of "love" in the sense explored by Barbara Fredrickson in *Love 2.0*? With its detailed attention to the brain, Fredrickson's argument might seem quite far removed from Lethem's literary concerns, but can biological science shed light on the process Lethem explores? Look, for example, at Fredrickson's discussion of "brain coupling":

> Communication—a true meeting of the minds—is a single act, performed by two brains. Considering the positivity resonance of love, what I find most fascinating about these findings is that a key brain area that showed coupling in [the] speaker-listener study was the insula, an area linked with conscious feeling states.

Does making someone else's language your own qualify as *brain coupling* too, and does it produce a change in your conscious emotional state? Can we think of sharing language as a form of *positivity resonance*? If love as Fredrickson defines it helps to expand the boundaries of the self, does the ecstasy of influence do the same?

2.   In his defense of the freedom to use culture creatively, Lethem levels criticism at a major player on the entertainment scene:

> The Walt Disney Company has drawn an astonishing catalogue from the work of others: *Snow White and the Seven Dwarfs, Fantasia, Pinocchio, Dumbo, Bambi, Song of the South, Cinderella, Alice in*

Wonderland, Robin Hood, Peter Pan, Lady and the Tramp, Mulan, Sleeping Beauty, The Sword in the Stone, The Jungle Book .... Yet Disney's protectorate of lobbyists has policed the resulting cache of cultural materials as vigilantly as if it were Fort Knox—threatening legal action.

As you explain and explore the reasoning behind Lethem's critique, consider Joseph Stiglitz's discussion of economic monopolies in "Rent Seeking and the Making of an Unequal Society." Is the Disney Company guilty of *rent seeking* in the sphere of culture? Does such behavior contribute to inequalities of access to cultural capital? Does Stiglitz want to bring open access to the economic sphere—access akin to the commons Lethem extols in the realm of culture? Or does Stiglitz argue for a change less sweeping in its scope?

BETH LOFFREDA

HOW DO THE media decide which stories to cover on any given day? And what gets left out when the stories that are chosen turn into three-minute segments on the nightly news or columns of print in the daily paper? These are some of the issues that Beth Loffreda takes up in *Losing Matt Shepard: Life and Politics in the Aftermath of Anti-Gay Murder*, her book-length study of how the residents of Wyoming responded when Shepard, a young gay student at the university in Laramie, was brutally beaten and left to die by the side of the road in the fall of 1998. Both an ethnographic study and a cultural critique, *Losing Matt Shepard* carefully explores the limits of the media's representation of the complexities of life in Wyoming after Shepard's highly publicized murder. In his review of *Losing Matt Shepard* for the *Lambda Book Report*, Malcolm Farley recommended that "[a]nyone who cares about the gay experience in America—or about America in general—should read Loffreda's fiercely intelligent account of the causes and consequences of Matt Shepard's murder."

Beth Loffreda is an associate professor of American Studies and Director of the Creative Writing Masters of Fine Arts Program at the University of Wyoming. Since the publication of *Losing Matt Shepard*, she has spoken widely on hate crimes legislation and the struggle for gay rights. She was also recognized as one of the University of Wyoming's most accomplished teachers in 2006, when she received the John P. Ellbogen Meritorious Classroom Teaching Award. Loffreda has published short fiction in *EPOCH* and *The Other Room*, and essays in *Postwestern Cultures: Literature, Theory, Space* (2007) and *West of 98: Living and Writing the New American West* (2011). Currently she is working on a collaborative project that deals with race and creative writing.

Asked by one interviewer about Laramie since Matt Shepard's murder, Loffreda said this in 2008: "[W]e have no new legislation devoted to protecting gay people in the state, no legislation against bias crimes; we have a university that still hasn't created domestic partner benefits despite years of effort, and is only just now beginning to consider a GLBT studies program." But in 2009 things began to change. Wyoming citizens elected their first openly gay state legislator, Cathy Connolly, a democrat and Laramie resident. Two years after Connolly's election, the University of Wyoming announced a new provision for domestic

Excerpt from LOSING MATT SHEPARD by Beth Loffreda. Copyright © 2000 Columbia University Press. Reprinted with permission of the publisher.

Biographical information is drawn from Beth Loffreda, *Losing Matt Shepard*. New York: Columbia University Press, 2000. Quotation from "'The Change Paragraph': A Post by Beth Loffreda," Columbia University Press blog, October 9th, 2008. <http://www.cupblog.org/?p=406>

partner benefits. And then in 2013, the Wyoming House considered a bill to legalize domestic partnerships for couples of the same sex. Even though the bill lost 35 to 24, its supporters saw the vote itself as an important first step.

Selections from Losing Matt Shepard

Life and Politics in the Aftermath of Anti-Gay Murder

Perhaps the first thing to know about Laramie, Wyoming, is that it is beautiful. On most days the high-altitude light is so precise and clear that Laramie appears some rarefied place without need of an atmosphere. We were having a stretch of days like that in early October 1998, as the news began to trickle in that a man had been found beaten somewhere on the edge of town. We'd later sort out the key facts: that Matt Shepard had encountered Russell Henderson and Aaron McKinney late Tuesday night in the Fireside Bar; that he'd left with them; that they had driven him in a pickup truck to the edge of town; that Henderson had tied him to a fence there and McKinney had beaten him viciously and repeatedly with a .357 Magnum; that they had taken his shoes and wallet and intended to rob his apartment but instead returned to town and got into a fight with two other young men, Jeremy Herrera and Emiliano Morales (McKinney clubbed Morales on the head with the same gun, still covered in Matt's blood; Herrera retaliated by striking McKinney's head with a heavy stick); that the police, responding to the altercation, picked up Henderson—McKinney had fled—and saw the gun, Matt's credit card, and his shoes in the truck but didn't yet know the fatal meaning of those objects; that after being released later that night, Henderson and his girlfriend, Chasity Pasley, and McKinney and his girlfriend, Kristen Price, began to hatch their false alibis; and that through all this Matt remained tied to the fence and wouldn't be found until Wednesday evening, after an entire night and most of a day had passed. We'd learn all that, and learn that Matt's sexuality was woven through all of it. Those facts reached us swiftly, but making sense of them took much longer.

Jim Osborn, a recent graduate of the university's education program, was the chair of the Lesbian, Gay, Bisexual, Transgender Association that October, a group that Matt, a freshman, had just recently joined. The LGBTA is the sole gay organization on campus and in Laramie itself. While students make up most of its membership, it welcomes university staff and townspeople as well, although only a few have joined. The group has been active since 1990; before that, another gay campus organization, Gays and Lesbians of Wyoming—GLOW—had an intermittent but vivid life in the 1970s and early 1980s.

Women typically outnumber men at LGBTA meetings, although not by a significant margin; altogether, attendance on any given night usually hovers between ten and twenty members. The group's email list, however, reaches far more. There's no single reason for that discrepancy; it most likely arises from a combination of factors, including the familiar reluctance of many college students to join groups and, more specifically in this case, the anxiety some gay or questioning students might feel attending a public meeting.

The LGBTA gathers weekly in a nondescript, carpeted seminar room on the second floor of the university union. It has no office space of its own. (When hundreds of letters arrived after Matt's murder, the group stored them in the corner of the Multicultural Resource Center downstairs.) Meetings are usually hourlong sessions, punctuated by bursts of laughter, during which the group plans upcoming events—speakers, dances, potlucks. The LGBTA juggles numerous, sometimes contradictory roles as it tries to be a public face for gay and lesbian issues on campus (organizing events, running panels about sexuality for many courses) and at the same time create a comfortable, safe space for socializing in a town without a gay bar or bookstore. It also serves as something of a gay news exchange, sharing information about what teachers might be supportive or not, what places in town and elsewhere might be safe or not, what's happening that might not show up in the campus paper, *The Branding Iron*.

That last role mattered on Tuesday, October 6th. As the members handled the last-minute details of Gay Awareness Week, scheduled to begin the following Monday, Jim Osborn warned the group to be careful. The week before, he had been harassed while walking across campus. A young man—Jim thinks he was probably a university student—had come up behind him, said, "You're one of those faggots, aren't you?" and thrown a punch. Jim is a big, strapping white man from northern Wyoming; he blocked the punch and hit his attacker. They then took off in opposite directions. Jim didn't report the attack to the police but did want to alert members of the LGBTA that it had happened. Matt was among those there to hear Jim's story. After the meeting, members of the group, including Matt and Jim, went out for coffee at the College Inn, something of a Tuesday-night LGBTA tradition. Jim remembers that Matt sat at the other end of a crowded table. It was the last Jim would see of him.

Jim can talk an eloquent blue streak and is something of an organizational genius—at LGBTA meetings I've listened to him recall the minutiae of university regulations and budget protocols as if they were fond personal memories. He also has a staggeringly large network of friends and acquaintances. On Thursday morning, he got an email from Tina Labrie, a friend of his and Matt's; she had introduced them in August, when Matt, new to Laramie, wanted to learn about the LGBTA. The message said that Matt had been found near death the evening before and was hospitalized in Fort Collins, Colorado. (Matt had initially been taken to Ivinson Memorial Hospital in Laramie and was then transferred to Poudre Valley Hospital's more sophisticated trauma unit. While Matt was being treated in the Ivinson Memorial ER, McKinney was a few curtains down, admitted earlier for the head wound he had received from Herrera; like Matt, McKinney would also be transferred to Poudre Valley.) Horrified, Jim phoned

Tina and learned that the police were trying to reconstruct Matt's whereabouts on Tuesday evening. When he called the Laramie Police to tell them what he knew, an officer informed him that Matt wasn't going to make it. Matt was suffering from hypothermia, and there was severe trauma to the brain stem. The officer told Jim that one side of Matt's head had been beaten in several inches and that the neurosurgeon was quite frankly surprised that he was still alive.

Bob Beck, news director for Wyoming Public Radio, also got word of the attack on Thursday. Beck has lived in Laramie since 1984; he's a tall, lanky midwesterner with a serious jones for Chicago Bulls basketball. On the radio he speaks in the sedated tones cultivated by NPR reporters everywhere, but in person he displays a vinegary wit and a likably aggravated demeanor. "It was a strange thing," he told me. "I teach a class, and one of my students called up and told me he needed to miss class that day because one of his friends had got beaten up very badly and was taken to the hospital in Fort Collins." That student was Phil Labrie, Tina's husband. Worried when they couldn't reach Matt, they had called the police on Wednesday, shortly after Matt was found, and learned what had happened. "[Phil] didn't tell me a lot of details because he said the cops had told him not to really tell anyone. But then he said I will know about it later and it will be a big story.... So I right away thought I better follow up on this immediately." He contacted the Albany County Sheriff's Office and learned that a press conference would be held later that day.

Beck attended the press conference that day—typically a routine exercise, but one that in this case would unexpectedly and profoundly shape public reaction to the attack. According to Beck, the sheriff

> indicated that there was a young man who had been very badly beaten, was on life support, had been taken to Poudre Valley Hospital. During the questioning, the sheriff at the time, Gary Puls, indicated that they thought he may have been beaten because he was gay. And when he described this situation to us he told us that [Shepard] was found by a mountain bike rider, tied to a fence like a scarecrow. My recollection is there was discussion of exactly what do you mean, "tied like a scarecrow," and I think every single one of us who were in the room got the impression certainly of being tied up spread-eagled, splayed out.

Matt hadn't actually been tied like a scarecrow; when he was approached first by the mountain biker, Aaron Kreifels, and then by Reggie Fluty, the sheriff's deputy who answered Kreifels's emergency call, Matt lay on his back, head propped against the fence, legs outstretched. His hands were lashed behind him and tied barely four inches off the ground to a fencepost. In dramatic and widely reported testimony, Fluty would later state that at first she thought Matt could have been no older than thirteen, he was so small (Matt was only five feet two inches, barely over one hundred pounds). And when she described Matt's brutally disfigured face, she said that the only spots not covered in blood were the tracks cleansed by his tears—an enduring image that continues to appear in essays, poetry, and songs dedicated to Shepard. It is most likely that Kreifels was the source of Puls's press-conference description. Kreifels told police and reporters that he at first thought Matt was a scarecrow flopped on the ground, maybe some kind of Halloween joke staged a few weeks early. No matter its provenance, the notion that Matt had been strung up in something akin to a crucifixion became the starting point for the reporting and reaction to come.

Beck says, "I know that's how we all reported it, and that was never corrected."[1] The vicious symbolism of that image, combined with Puls's early acknowledgment that the beating might have been an anti-gay hate crime, drew instant attention. Attending the press conference were the Associated Press, members of the Wyoming and Colorado media, Beck, and two friends of Matt, Walt Boulden and Alex Trout. According to press reports, Boulden and Trout, afraid that the attack might go unnoticed, had already begun to alert the media earlier that day. Boulden had had plans with Matt for Tuesday night; Matt had canceled and later, apparently, had decided to head off to the Fireside alone. Boulden was not shy about seizing the attack as a political opportunity, linking the assault to the Wyoming legislature's failure to pass a hate crimes bill: he told reporters that "they said nothing like that happens in Wyoming because someone is gay, but we've always known someone would have to get killed or beaten before they finally listened. I just can't believe it happened to someone I cared so much about." By Friday morning, when the police already had McKinney, Henderson, Price, and Pasley in custody (Beck says "the investigation was one of the better I've seen"), the media interest, spurred by Thursday's press conference, had increased exponentially.

At the same time, Laramie's gay residents were learning what had happened. Stephanie and Lisa, a lesbian couple active in the LGBTA, heard the news from Jim on Thursday evening. Lisa, a striking redhead and a good friend of Jim's, talked to him first: "He told me Matt had been beaten. And I said, well, shit, how badly? Is he okay? And Jim said no—he's in critical condition, had to be airlifted to Poudre Valley." Both Stephanie and Lisa knew Matt only slightly, although Stephanie had expected to have the chance to grow closer. She had just agreed to be Matt's mentor in a program the LGBTA was considering as a way to welcome new students to the gay community. Like Lisa, Steph has an edgy, witty charisma, but it deserted her that night, as she, Lisa, and Jim watched the first TV news reports. "There was this horrifying feeling that we were standing on the brink of learning something really, really awful," she says of that Thursday. "Like the part in the horror movie just before she opens the closet and finds the dead cat. It was that moment. For a day. And then we got the facts ... and everything started happening at this tremendous speed. The next day was the day the story broke. And there were newspaper reporters and cameras all over the place." Steph had called me early that Friday morning, spreading word of the attack and warning people associated with the LGBTA to watch their backs: "I can remember wanting to tell everybody, absolutely everybody, wanting to physically grab people by their lapels and make them listen."

An atmosphere of genuine shock permeated the university; most students and faculty I encountered that day wore stunned and distraught expressions that I imagine mirrored my own; they seemed absorbed simply in trying to understand how something so brutal could have happened within a short walk of their daily lives. Gay and lesbian members of the university that I spoke to felt a wrenching mix of fear and sadness; many, including Stephanie and Lisa, were also immediately and intensely angry. A number of students in my morning American Literature course, after a long discussion in which they sought answers for how to publicly express their repugnance for the crime, decided that the university's homecoming parade, coincidentally scheduled for the following morning, would be an ideal site for that response. Finding like-minded students in the United Multicultural Council, the LGBTA, and the student government, they began printing flyers, making hundreds of armbands, and arranging permits to join the parade.[2] Their unjaded eagerness to publicly involve themselves in the case contrasted sharply with the university administration's first official response, much of which had concerned itself with pointing out that the attack happened off campus and was committed by nonstudents.

On Friday afternoon—as Jim Osborn began to field what would eventually become an overwhelming flood of media requests for interviews—the four accused appeared in court for the first time. Bob Beck attended the initial appearance: "That's where you bring in the people, read them formal charges, and we then get their names, backgrounds—which is important for us." Beck had left for the courthouse a half hour early; initial appearances are typically held in a small room in the courthouse basement, and Beck thought it might be more full than usual. He was right. "It was sold out. It was wall-to-wall cameras." Residents of Laramie—professors and LGBTA members in particular—had also come to witness the proceedings. So many attended that the reading of the charges had to be delayed while everyone moved upstairs to the much larger district court. Beck remembers, "I went in—in fact it was so crowded I got shoved by where the jury box is located—and I stood behind the defendants when they came in. I got a really good look at everybody, and I was actually surprised at how young they looked, how scared they looked, and how little they were." Only Henderson, McKinney, and Chasity Pasley were charged that day; separate proceedings had been arranged for Kristen Price. Pasley wept throughout. She was someone Jim Osborn knew well and liked. She worked in the campus activities center and had helped Jim countless times when the LGBTA needed photocopying or assistance setting up for an event. "She was very supportive of the group," Jim says. Often when he saw her on a Wednesday, she'd ask, "Hey, how'd it go last night?" In the past, he had seen her wearing one of the group's "Straight But Not Narrow" buttons.

I was in the courtroom that afternoon and can remember the professional flatness with which the county judge, Robert Castor, read the charges aloud. Castor had arrived in the courtroom to find a cameraman sitting at the prosecution's table, an early symbol of the persistent media invasion, Bob Beck believes, that frustrated the court and the prosecutor, Cal Rerucha, and led them to sharply limit information about the case thereafter. Castor charged McKinney and Henderson with three identical counts of kidnapping, aggravated robbery, and attempted first-degree murder; Pasley he charged with a count of accessory after the fact to attempted first-degree murder (in addition to providing false alibis for their boyfriends, she and Price had also helped dispose of evidence, including Henderson's bloody clothing). After each count, Castor recited "the essential facts" supporting the charge, in what became a truly grim ritual of repetition. In language I've condensed from the court documents, the essential facts were these: "On or between October 6, 1998, and the early morning hours of October 7, 1998, Aaron McKinney and Russell Henderson met Matthew Shepard at the Fireside Bar, and after Mr. Shepard confided he was gay, the subjects deceived Mr. Shepard into leaving with them in their vehicle to a remote area near Sherman Hills subdivision in Albany County. En route to said location, Mr. Shepard was struck in the head with a pistol." (McKinney, we'd later learn, had apparently told Matt, "We're not gay, and you just got jacked," before striking him.) "Upon arrival at said location, both subjects tied their victim to a buck fence, robbed him, and tortured him, while beating him with the butt of a pistol. During the incident, the victim was begging for his life. The subjects then left the area, leaving the victim for dead." By the third time Castor read that Matt had begged for his life, the courtroom had become choked with sickness and grief. The true darkness of the crime had become impossible to flee.

The next morning—Saturday—began with the university's homecoming parade. As the parade kicked off, one hundred students, university employees, and townspeople lined up at the end of the long string of floats and marching bands. They had quietly gathered in the morning chill to protest the attack on Matt. The leaders of the march carried a yellow banner painted with green circles, symbols of peace chosen by the UMC. They were followed by a silent crowd wearing matching armbands and holding signs that read "No Hate Crimes in Wyoming," "Is This What Equality Feels Like?" and "Straight But Not Stupid." I walked a few yards from the front, watching Carly Laucomer, a university student holding the middle of the banner, field questions from reporters walking backward a single pace in front of her. Beside me, Cat, another university student, muttered that she wished the marchers weren't so sparse. Cat, like Carly, was then a student in my American Literature course, a smart young woman usually prepared to be disappointed by the world around her. Laramie surprised her. As the march moved west down Ivinson Avenue, spectators began to join, walking off sidewalks into the street. By the time the march reached downtown (where a giant second-story banner proclaimed, "Hate Is Not a Wyoming Value") and circled back toward campus, it had swelled beyond even Cat's demanding expectations; final estimates ranged from five to eight hundred participants. It didn't seem like much—just a bunch of people quietly walking—but it was a genuinely spontaneous, grassroots effort to protest the attack and express the community's profound dismay, and in that sense it was unforgettable.

A very different sort of tribute to Matt appeared in the Colorado State University homecoming parade the same day in the city of Fort Collins. As Matt lay in the hospital just a few miles away, a float in the parade carried a scarecrow draped in anti-gay epithets. While the papers were reluctant to report the full range of insults, I heard that the signs read "I'm Gay" and "Up My Ass." Colorado State University acted quickly to punish the sorority and fraternity responsible for the float (the censured students blamed vandalism committed by an unknown third party), but still it is worth pausing for a moment to consider the degree of dehumanization such an act required, how much those responsible must have felt, however fleetingly or unconsciously, that Matt was not a fellow human being, their age, with his future torn away from him. Fort Collins is home to a visible and energetic community of gay activists, and the float was widely denounced. Still, a week later Fort Collins would vote down, by nearly a two-to-one margin, City Ordinance 22, a proposal to expand the city's anti-discrimination statute to include protections for gays and lesbians.

Later that Saturday, a moment of silence for Matt was held before the University of Wyoming's football game; players wore the UMC's symbols on their helmets. And, impossibly, the media presence continued to grow. Bob Beck, juggling requests for interviews with his own reporting, was in the thick of it and felt a growing frustration at the sloppiness of what he saw around him. "Right away it was horrible. Part of that, in fairness, was that we didn't have all the information we needed. While the sheriff was very up front at first, next thing you know, nobody's talking." City officials, naturally unprepared (in a town with barely a murder a year) for the onslaught, focused their resources on the investigation and, angry that Laramie was being depicted as a hate crimes capital, began to restrict press access. But the media, especially the TV tabloids, Beck says, needed to turn things around quickly, and since they were getting stonewalled by the city and by many Laramie residents, "it seemed like the place they went to interview everybody was in bars. As we all know who are in the media, if you want to get somebody to be very glib, give you a few quick takes, you want to go to a bar. And you certainly are going to meet a segment of our population that will have more interesting things to say." I remember watching for footage of the Saturday morning march later that evening and seeing instead precisely the sort of bar interview Beck describes, a quick and dirty media tactic I heard many residents mock in the coming months.

Beck also remembers one of the first television news reports he saw: "It was this woman reporter outside the Fireside doing what we call a bridge, a stand-up: 'Hate: it's a common word in Wyoming.'" Beck couldn't believe it, but that mirrored precisely the assumptions of most of the media representatives he encountered that week. Journalists who interviewed him began with comments like, "Well, this kind of thing probably happens a lot up there," or, "You have that cowboy mentality in Wyoming, so this was bound to happen." Reporters criticized Laramie, he says, for not having a head trauma unit, not having gay bars, not pushing back homecoming. The tone of the questioning was hostile; Jim Osborn, speaking to journalists from locations as far-flung as Australia and the Netherlands, encountered it, too. Jim says the press he spoke to wanted to hear that this was a hateful, redneck town, that Wyoming was, in the inane rhyming of some commentators, "the hate state." But Jim insisted on what he considered accurate: "Nobody expects murder here—nobody. This is not a place where you kill your neighbor, and we see each other as neighbors. This is a good place."

But the crime, and Laramie, had already begun to take on a second life, a broadcast existence barely tethered to the truths of that night or this place, an existence nourished less by facts and far more by the hyperboles of tabloid emotion. Such a development should be unsurprising to even the most novice of cultural critics, yet to be in the middle of it, to watch rumor become myth, to see the story stitched out of repetition rather than investigation, was something else entirely. Beck told me, "Right away I saw pack journalism like I have not seen pack journalism in a while. It was really something. I remember going to the courthouse, and somebody would say, 'Hey I understand he got burned'— which wasn't true by the way—'where did he get burned?' And somebody would say, 'Oh, on his face,' and they're all taking notes, and they were sources for each other. They would never say where it came from or who had the information—it was just 'there were burns on his face.' " As Beck watched, the mistakes multiplied. One journalist would announce, " 'I did an interview with one of the deputies, and he told me this,' and they would all go with it; no one [else] went and interviewed the deputy. Now part of this is that the deputies and other officials weren't available to us … and the same stuff got continually reported." The lead investigator on the case, Sergeant Rob DeBree of the Sheriff's Office, held a press conference early on in an attempt to correct the errors, but, he told me, it didn't seem to make much of a difference—the media had become a closed loop, feeding off their own energies.

As the fall wore on, the distance between Laramie and its broadcast image would become unbridgeable. The court increasingly limited press access to the case and eventually, in the spring, issued a gag order. In response, the Wyoming Press Association wrangled with the court throughout that year over access to hearings and records, suggesting that the court model its treatment of the media on press access guidelines in the Timothy McVeigh trial. Beck assessed Wyoming Public Radio's own performance for me: "I'm not saying we didn't make any mistakes, because we probably did. But I finally got so weary of it I said, 'You know what? If we can't confirm it ourselves, we don't go with it.' It was just too wild."

As the weekend continued, vigils for Matt were held across the nation. By the end of the week, we'd heard word of vigils in Casper, Cheyenne, and Lander (Wyoming towns), Colorado, Idaho, Montana, Iowa, Arizona, Rhode Island, and Pennsylvania. A memorial in Los Angeles attracted an estimated five thousand participants; a "political funeral" in New York City that ended in civil disobedience and hundreds of arrests, about the same. Several hundred mourners lit candles at a vigil outside Poudre Valley Hospital, and a Web site set up by the hospital to give updates about Matt's condition eventually drew over 815,000 hits from around the world.

In Laramie, we held two vigils of our own Sunday night. Jim spoke at the first, held outside the St. Paul's Newman Catholic Center. Father Roger Schmit, the organizer of the event, had contacted him earlier that weekend and asked him to speak. Jim remembers, "I'm sitting here thinking, 'Catholic Church … this is not exactly the scene I want to get into.'" But the priest told him, Jim says, "This is such a powerful opportunity—people need to hear from you, and it will help them." Jim thought, "I want to hate him, I want to disagree with him, but I can't." Indeed, such bedfellows would become less strange in the coming months.

Matt's death triggered yearlong conversations in several Laramie churches; the Newman Center, the Episcopal church, and the Unitarian—Universalist Fellowship each began discussion groups devoted to questions of sexual orientation and religious doctrine. Father Schmit, the priest Jim regarded with such initial suspicion, would in particular become a vocal advocate for gay tolerance.

I attended that first vigil, which drew nearly one thousand people, a sizable fraction of Laramie's total population. As I crossed Grand Avenue, dodging traffic, the vigil already under way, I was struck by the size and murmurous intensity of the crowd. The speakers included friends of Matt, student leaders, and university officials. Father Schmit had also invited every religious leader in town but found many reluctant to come. The event was genuinely affecting and rightly given over to the desire, as Jim put it, to think of Matt "the person" and not the newly created symbol. While speakers did indeed condemn the homophobia that slid Matt from complicated human being to easy target, others, including Jim, also tried to rehumanize Matt by offering up small details—the nature of his smile, the clothes he liked to wear. The press was there, too, of course, and—perhaps inevitably under such circumstances—a faint odor of PR hung in the air. University president Phil Dubois told the assembled, "Nothing could match the sorrow and revulsion we feel for this attack on Matt. It is almost as sad, however, to see individuals and groups around the country react to this event by stereotyping an entire community, if not an entire state."

Stephanie sensed another trouble, a hypocrisy, at work that night:

> There was a tremendous outpouring of support—the vigils, the parade—and a lot of those people—not all of them, not even a substantial portion, but some of those people—if they had known that Matt was gay while he was alive, would have spit on him. But now it was a cause, and that made me upset. Not that I think you can't grieve over this because you're straight or anything like that, but I just questioned the sincerity of some people. And I grew to be very angry at the vigil Sunday night, because it was so like the one I had attended for Steve.

She meant Steve Heyman, a gay man who had been a psychology professor and LGBTA faculty adviser at the university. Heyman was found dead on November 1, 1993, on the edge of Route 70 in Denver. He appeared to have been tossed from a moving car. The case was never solved. To Stephanie, who had known and adored Heyman, the coincidence was unbearable. "It was the same candles, the same fucking hymns. I will never sing 'We are a gentle, angry people' again, because it doesn't change anything. And I'm not going to sing 'We are not afraid today deep in my heart' because I am afraid, and I will always be afraid, and that's what they want, that's why they kill us."

Driven by that anger, Stephanie spoke at the second vigil that night. Much smaller—perhaps one hundred people were in attendance—it was held on the edge of town, at the Unitarian Fellowship. People who went that night tell me it was different from the first. Instead of a lengthy list of official speakers, community members were invited to testify to their mourning, and to their experiences of anti-gay discrimination in Laramie. It was more intense, more ragged, more discomfiting. But both vigils held the same fragile promise of a changed Laramie, a town that—whether it much wanted to or not—would think hard and publicly and not in unison about the gay men and women in its midst, about their safety and comfort and rights.

Later that Sunday night, as the participants in that second vigil left for home, thought about the events of the day, and got ready for bed, Matt Shepard's blood pressure began to drop. He died in the early hours of Monday, October 12th. It was the first day of Gay Awareness Week at the University of Wyoming.

Monday, flags were flown at half-staff on the university campus. Later that week, in Casper, flags were lowered on the day of Matt's funeral to signal a "day of understanding." (According to local newspapers, Wyoming governor Jim Geringer was criticized by the Veterans of Foreign Wars for not following "proper flag etiquette.") That Monday eight hundred people gathered for a memorial service held on Prexy's Pasture, a patch of green in the middle of campus encircled by parking spaces and university buildings and anchored by a statue of "the university family," a happy heterosexual unit of father, mother, and child that one lesbian student, in a letter to the student newspaper, longingly imagined detonating. The memorial service was another exercise in what was becoming a familiar schizophrenia for Laramie residents. Even the layout of the event expressed it: speakers stood in a small clump ringed by sidewalk; spread beyond them was the far larger, shaggy-edged group of listeners. In between the two was an encampment of reporters, flourishing microphones and tape recorders, pivoting cameras back and forth, capturing clips of the speakers and reaction shots of the crowd. It was hard to see past the reporters to the event that had drawn us in the first place, and it was hard to know to a certainty whether we were all there simply to mourn Matt or to make sure that mourning was represented. Not that the second urge was itself necessarily a hypocrisy or a contradiction of the first. It was instead an early manifestation of Laramie's new double consciousness. We didn't simply live here anymore: we were something transmitted, watched, evaluated for symbolic resonance; something available for summary. I suspect a few people naturally sought that televised attention, felt authenticated and confirmed, even thrilled, by the opportunity to be representative; and others seized it, as Walt Boulden had, as a chance to articulate political goals that might otherwise go unheard. Mostly, though, it just pissed people off. As the memorial drew to a close, I walked past satellite vans and the professional autism of TV reporters practicing their opening lines and switching on their solemn expressions and talking to no one in particular.

I was on my way to the first event of Gay Awareness Week. Shortly after the memorial, Leslea Newman, scheduled long before the murder to give the keynote talk, spoke about her gay-themed children's books, which include the oft-censored *Heather Has Two Mommies*. The week's events would be held despite Matt's death, but attendance that evening hadn't necessarily swelled in response—there were maybe seventy folks scattered around in the darkened auditorium. Newman spoke with a bracing, funny, New York brusqueness that scuffed up the audience as she briskly detailed her skirmishes with religious conservatives, and she spoke as well of her sorrow over Matt and her friends' fearful pleading that she cancel her visit to Laramie. They weren't alone in feeling that anxiety; many of the members of the LGBTA were tensed for a backlash as they passed out pro-gay trinkets and "heterosexual questionnaires" at the "Straight But Not Narrow" table in the student union during Awareness Week. They knew the statistics: that anti-gay violence tends to rise sharply in the aftermath of a publicized bashing. But instead, as consoling letters and emails flooded the offices of *The Branding Iron*, the LGBTA, and Wyoming newspapers, supporters flocking to the union tables quickly ran through the association's supplies of buttons and stickers.

As the week dragged on, Laramie residents hung in their windows and cars flyers decrying hate provided by the Wyoming Grassroots Project (a year and a half later, you can still find a few examples around town, stubbornly hanging on). Yellow sashes fluttered from student backpacks; local businesses announced, on signs usually reserved for information about nightly rates, indoor pools, and bargain lunches, their dismay with the crime. The Comfort Inn: "Hate and Violence Are Not Our Way of Life." The University Inn: "Hate Is Not a Laramie Value." Arby's: "Hate and Violence Are Not Wyoming Values 5 Regulars $5.95." Obviously, those signs suggested a typically American arithmetic, promiscuously mixing moral and economic registers. Underneath the sentiment lingered a question: what will his death cost us? But it would be wrong, I think, to see all those gestures as merely cynical calculation, a self-interested weighing of current events against future tourism. We were trying to shape the media summary of Laramie all right, but we were also talking to each other, pained and wondering, through such signs.

Late Monday, about the same time as the Prexy's Pasture memorial, the charges against McKinney, Henderson, and Pasley were upgraded in a closed hearing to reflect Matt's death. Price's charge, the same as Pasley's—accessory after the fact to first-degree murder—was announced at her individual arraignment on Tuesday. In a *20/20* interview that week, Price offered her defense of McKinney and Henderson. She claimed Shepard approached McKinney and Henderson and "said that he was gay and wanted to get with Aaron and Russ." They intended, she said, "to teach a lesson to him not to come on to straight people"—as if torture and murder were reasonable responses to the supposed humiliation of overtures from a gay man. McKinney's father, speaking to the *Denver Post*, argued that no one would care about the crime if his son had killed a heterosexual, which struck me as not exactly on point, even as a media critique. Wyoming's Libertarian gubernatorial candidate (it was an election year) had his own unique twist: he told reporters, "If two gays beat and killed a cowboy, the story would have never been reported by the national media vultures."

Fred Phelps, a defrocked minister, leader of the tiny Kansas Westboro Baptist Church, and author of the Internet site GodHatesFags.com, announced that Monday that he intended to picket Matthew's funeral, scheduled for the coming Friday at St. Mark's Episcopal Church in Casper. His Web site also promised a visit to Laramie on October 19th, but in the end he didn't show. Phelps had made a name for himself in the 1990s as a virulently anti-gay activist, notorious for protesting at the funerals of AIDS victims. Never one to shy from media attention, Phelps faxed reporters images of the signs he and his followers intended to carry at the funeral: "Fag Matt in Hell," "God Hates Fags," "No Tears for Queers." On his Web site, Phelps wrote that "the parents of Matt Shepard did not bring him up in the nature and admonition of the Lord, or he would not have been trolling for perverted sex partners in a cheap Laramie bar." He also, to the bitter laughter of members of the LGBTA, deemed the University of Wyoming "very militantly pro-gay." "The militant homosexual agenda is vigorously pursued" at the university, he proclaimed. At the time of Phelps's statement, the university's equal employment and civil rights regulations did not include sexual orientation as a protected category, nor did the university offer insurance benefits to same-sex partners. President Dubois and the board of trustees, in response to Matt's death, eventually rectified the former failure in September 1999; the latter still remains true to this day. Apparently none of that mattered much in Phelps's estimation, and he would become a familiar figure in Laramie in the months to come.

The Westboro Church's announcement was only one manifestation of the murder's parallel national life, its transmutation into political and religious currency. Matt himself might have been dead, but his image was resurrected by Phelps as well as by his antagonists, and those resurrections, while not invariably hypocritical or grotesque, nevertheless struck me as always risky. Not because we shouldn't talk about Matt, about the murder, looking hard at the facts of it, as well as at its contexts. The risk, it seemed to me, lay in what his image was so often used for in the coming months—the rallying of quick and photogenic outrage, sundered from the hard, slow work for local justice.

On Wednesday, October 14th, the national gay organization the Human Rights Campaign held a candlelight vigil on the steps of the U.S. Capitol, noteworthy if only for the incongruity of an event that paired the likes of Ted Kennedy and Ellen DeGeneres. Jim Osborn was also there—Cathy Renna, a member of GLAAD (Gay and Lesbian Alliance Against Defamation), who had arrived in Laramie the previous weekend to monitor events for her organization, had asked Jim to participate and taken him to Washington. That night, DeGeneres declared that "this is what she was trying to stop" with her television sitcom *Ellen*. The proportions of that statement—the belief that a sitcom could breathe in the same sentence as the brutal vortex of murder—seemed out of kilter to say the least, but it is the age of celebrity politics, after all: Elton John would send flowers to Matt's funeral, Barbra Streisand would phone the Albany County Sheriff's office to demand quick action on the case, and Madonna would call up an assistant to UW president Dubois to complain about what had happened to Matt. Jim Osborn remembers standing next to Dan Butler, an actor on *Frasier*, during the vigil; later, he spotted Kristen Johnston (of *Third Rock from the Sun*) smoking backstage. Attended by numerous federal legislators, the vigil was skipped by Wyoming's two senators, who had announced their sorrow and condemned intolerance in press releases the previous day. The disconnect worked both ways: the Human Rights Campaign, for all its sustained rallying on the national level, never, according to Jim, sent a representative to Laramie until the following summer.

Back in Laramie, on the same day as the D.C. vigil, the university initiated a three-day series of teach-ins on "prejudice, intolerance, and violence" to begin, according to the announcement, "the healing process." The ideas expressed that day were valuable, the sympathies genuine, but I remember feeling overloaded by premature talk of closure. It may have seemed easy for straight mourners to move so quickly, but as Stephanie told me that week, she'd barely begun to realize the extent of her anger. In the face of that, the swiftness of the official move to "healing" seemed at best a well-intended deafness, and indeed, in their outrage by proxy, denunciations of hatred, and exhortations for tolerance, most of the speakers seemed to be talking implicitly and exclusively to straight members of the audience who already agreed.

Many professors on campus also made time in their classes that week to let their students talk about Matt; the university provided a list of teachers willing to facilitate such discussions if individual faculty were uncomfortable raising such an emotionally fraught issue. It was indeed, as Jim Osborn put it, a "teachable moment," and those conversations undoubtedly did real good. One student, who spoke to me on the condition I didn't use his name, told me that before Matt's death he "straight-up hated fags." It hadn't occurred to him that there actually were any gays or lesbians around (a surprisingly common assumption at the university, not to mention in Wyoming generally)—"fag" was a word handy mainly for demeaning other guys in his dorm for "being pussy" (a typical but still depressing conflation of slurs). After seeing students cry in one of his classes as they discussed Matt's death, he had what he called, with a defensive grin, a real breakthrough: he felt a little sick, he told me, that he had thought things about gays that the two killers had probably been thinking about Shepard.

It's impossible to quantify such changes in attitude, but clearly they were happening in many classrooms around campus. Those developments were heartening, but it would be wrong to imply that the changes were immediate or seismic; several students in the coming weeks would describe to me overhearing others saying Matt "got what he deserved." One woman told me that during a class devoted to discussing the murder, "There was a really ugly incident with a couple of guys in the back who were like 'I hate gays and I'm not changing my opinion.'" "People really think that way here," she finished with a resigned expression. In the coming year students and faculty checking out books on gay topics sometimes found them defaced, and in the spring of 1999 vandals defecated on the university's copies of *The Advocate*, a gay magazine.

It would be wrong, too, to imply that the faculty were perfectly equipped to handle the events of October. When Matt died, there was only one openly gay faculty member on the university campus—Cathy Connelly, a professor of sociology. Since her arrival in 1991, Professor Connelly had periodically taught graduate courses on gay and lesbian issues, but other than Connelly and the small Safe Zone diversity-training group, the university had few resources in place to respond to what had happened. Troubling as well were the reactions of more than one professor I spoke to that week, whose primary responses were to comment on their own uselessness, their own irrelevance—as scholars of obscure fields of inquiry—to such primal issues of life and death. Academics tend to be fairly skilled at self-lacerating narcissism, but it seemed to me at the time an appalling luxury, an indulgence in a kind of intellectual self-pity at a moment when the basic skills of education—critical thinking, articulation, self-reflection—could be so concretely valuable. I wondered about that, and I wondered, too, when we'd stop talking about how we felt and begin talking about what to do.

Not that public political gestures are always more meaningful than private, emotional ones. On October 15th, the day before Shepard's funeral, the U.S. House of Representatives approved a resolution condemning the murder. Sponsored by Wyoming's sole representative, Barbara Cubin, it struck me as an essentially empty gesture. The nonbinding resolution stated that the House would "do everything in its power" to fight intolerance, and Cubin herself announced that "our country must come together to condemn these types of brutal, nonsensical acts of violence. We cannot lie down, we cannot bury our heads, and we cannot sit on our hands." Stirring stuff, but she also told reporters that day that she opposes federal hate crimes legislation and suggested such things be left up to individual states. So much for "our country coming together." Cubin was not alone, of course, in her contradictory patriotic embrace of Matt; flags were lowered, resolutions passed, in a nation otherwise happy to express its loathing of gays by closeting them in the military, refusing them antidiscrimination protection in most cities and states, repressing their presence in school curricula, faculty, and clubs, and denouncing them in churches. Meanwhile, back in Wyoming that afternoon, a bewildered and frustrated Casper City Council grappled with more concrete resolutions than those that faced the United States Congress. At an emergency meeting to address Phelps's intended picketing of Matt's funeral, the council decided that protesters must stay at least fifty feet from the church. Casper's SWAT team and the Street Drug Unit would be in attendance outside St. Mark's. Streets would be closed nearby the church, the Casper *Star-Tribune* reported, to allow "media satellite vehicles to position themselves."

The funeral on Friday unfurled as a heavy, wet snow fell on Casper. The storm ripped down power lines, cutting electricity in and around Casper; hundreds of cottonwoods and elms lost their branches. Phelps and his handful of protesters (along with another anti-gay protester, W. N. Orwell of Enterprise, Texas) were penned inside black plastic barricades, taunting the huge crowd of mourners, which included strangers, gay and straight alike, drawn to the scene from Cheyenne, Denver, Laramie, and elsewhere. As Charles Levendosky put it a few days later in the *Star-Tribune*, "One thousand others from Wyoming and surrounding states flew or drove into Wyoming to mourn for Matt Shepard, the symbol." While a few mourners engaged in heated debate with the picketers—one carrying a sign reading "Get Back in Your Damn Closet"— most turned their backs to them, the umbrellas pulled out for the snow acting as a fortuitous blockade. To protect the Shepard family from hearing Phelps, the assembled crowd sang "Amazing Grace" to drown out his anti-gay preaching. (The family's loss would intensify that day—Shepard's great uncle suffered what would be a fatal heart attack in the church shortly before the service began.) The funeral inside St. Mark's remained restricted to friends and family of Matt, but a live audio feed carried the service to the First Presbyterian Church nearby. Outside St. Mark's, more mourners ("some wearing black leather," the *Star-Tribune* observed) listened to a KTWO radio broadcast of the service. At the funeral, Matt's cousin Ann Kirch, a minister in Poughkeepsie, New York, delivered the sermon. Emphasizing Matt's gentleness and desire "to help, to nurture, to bring joy to others," she echoed a statement made by Matt's father earlier in the day at a press conference outside city hall: "A person as caring and loving as our son Matt would be overwhelmed by what this incident has done to the hearts and souls of people around the world."

Three days later, the university held yet another memorial service. Around one thousand people heard songs by a multicultural chorus, psalms read by Geneva Perry of the university's Office of Minority Affairs, and statements by Tina Labrie, Jim Osborn, and Trudy McCraken, Laramie's mayor. Rounding out the service was university president Dubois, who made a passionate, personal plea for hate crimes legislation—the political issue that had already, only one week after his death, come to dominate discussions of Matt's murder. "No hate crime statute, even had it existed, would have saved Matt," Dubois read. "But Matt Shepard was not merely robbed, and kidnapped, and murdered. This was a crime of humiliation. This crime was all about being gay ... We must find a way to commemorate this awful week in a way that will say to the entire state and nation that we will not forget what happened here."

On Tuesday, October 20th, the Wyoming Lodging and Restaurant Association offered one such response to the nation by passing a resolution in favor of hate crimes legislation. The association was up front about its motivations: to curry favor among tourists who might seek recreation elsewhere. The director was quoted in the Casper *Star-Tribune*: "We want them to know this was an isolated case and could happen anywhere."

Could happen anywhere indeed. While that oft-repeated phrase was the quick defense offered by many who felt Laramie was being unfairly vilified, it also bumped up against an undeniable truth: in the late 1990s, homosexuality and vehement opposition to it were everywhere in American public culture and politics. Gays in the military, gays in the schools, gays in church, gays in marriage—the place of gay men and lesbians in American culture seemed to be debated in every way possible. For example, on October 14th, two days before Matt's funeral, the Supreme Court upheld a Cincinnati ordinance that denied gays and lesbians legal protection from discrimination in housing, employment, and other public accommodations. Later that autumn Ohio hosted a conference, organized by Focus on the Family, on how to prevent childhood homosexuality; one speaker there, John Paulk, became notorious during the summer of 1998 when he posed with his wife for national newspaper ads announcing that they were former homosexuals "cured" by their faith in God. About the same time the Supreme Court ruled on the city ordinance, the Roman Catholic Archdiocese of Cincinnati announced a deeply contradictory attempt to "reconcile church teachings that denounce homosexual sex as immoral but encourage the loving acceptance of gays." As long as they're celibate, that is—as long as they "live chaste lives." "Hate the sin, love the sinner"—that idea was invoked again and again in Laramie, in church congregations and letters to the editor. But it seems to me that in such visions sexuality slides so intimately close to identity itself that in the end such exhortations call for moral acrobatics requiring an impossible and fundamentally hypocritical kind of dexterity.

Religious justifications were everywhere, of course, in the attacks on homosexuality. Senate Majority Leader Trent Lott, in June 1998, said he learned from the Bible that "you should try to show them a way to deal with [homosexuality] just like alcohol ... or sex addiction ... or kleptomaniacs." Pat Robertson announced that "the acceptance of homosexuality is the last step in the decline of Gentile civilization." Bob Jones University in South Carolina instituted a rule banning gay alumni from returning to campus. The religious right boycotted Disney and American Airlines for having policies that refused to discriminate against gays and lesbians. Salt Lake City banned all student clubs rather than allow a gay-straight alliance to continue at one public high school. The Mormon Church donated roughly half a million dollars to supporters of Alaska's Proposition 2, an initiative banning same-sex marriage that succeeded in the fall of 1998. Bans on gay marriage would also pass in Hawaii, California, and West Virginia in the next year and a half. Vermont, with its legalization of gay "civil unions" early in 2000, would be one of the few bright spots.

That Matt's death occurred in the midst of such pervasive anxiety and upheaval might begin to explain why the nation paid attention, but it doesn't stretch very far—his was only one of thirty-three anti-gay murders that year, followed by, in the first months of 1999, a beheading in Virginia and a vicious beating in Georgia. Here in Laramie, we asked a version of that question, too: why Matt, when no one in the media seemed to take a second glance at the other truly awful recent murders we had the grim distinction of claiming? Why Matt, and not Daphne Sulk, a fifteen-year-old pregnant girl stabbed seventeen times and dumped in the snow far from town? Why Matt, and not Kristin Lamb, an eight-year-old Laramie girl who was kidnapped while visiting family elsewhere in Wyoming and then raped, murdered, and thrown in a landfill? Governor Geringer asked those very questions in an October 9th press release, and we asked them, too, in Laramie—in letters to the editor, in private conversation. But we didn't always mean the same thing. To some, the media attention to Matt seemed to imply that his death was somehow worse than the deaths of the two girls, and such an implication was genuinely offensive. To some, like Val Pexton, a graduate student in creative writing, it had something to do with the politics of gender: "What happened to [Lamb] was certainly as violent, as hateful, as horrible; and I guess one of my first thoughts was, if [Henderson and McKinney] had done that to a woman, would this have made it into the news outside of Laramie, outside of Wyoming?" And to some, like Jim Osborn, the comparison of Matt to Kristin and Daphne sometimes masked a hostility to gays: "They became incensed—why didn't Kristin Lamb get this kind of coverage, why didn't Daphne Sulk get this kind of coverage? That was the way people could lash out who very much wanted to say, fuck, it was just a gay guy. But they couldn't say it was just a gay guy, so they said, what about these two girls?"

In some ways, it's easy to understand why the media industry seized upon Matt, and why so many responded to the image it broadcast (Judy Shepard, Matt's mother, told *The Advocate* magazine in March 1999 that the family had received "about 10,000 letters and 70,000 emails," as well as gifts, stuffed animals, blankets, and food). Matt was young (and looked younger), small, attractive; he had been murdered in a particularly brutal fashion. The mistaken belief that he had been strung up on the fence provided a rich, obvious source of symbolism: religious leaders, journalists, and everyday people saw in it a haunting image of the Crucifixion, and at the memorial services and vigils for Matt here and else-where, that comparison was often drawn. And while Matt had not in reality been put on display in that fashion, the idea that he had been resonated deeply with America's bitter history of ritual, public violence against minorities—many, including *Time* magazine, compared the attack to a lynching. But Matt seemed to provide a source of intense, almost obsessive interest whose explanation lies well beyond these considerations. Perhaps it was merely the insistent repetition of his image in those early days. In the few snapshots that circulated in the press, Matt appeared boyish, pensive, sweet, charmingly vulnerable in oversized wool sweaters—a boy who still wore braces when he died, a boy who looked innocent of sex, a boy who died because he was gay but whose unthreatening image allowed his sexuality to remain an abstraction for many. In my darker moods, I wonder, too, if Matt invited such sympathy and political outrage precisely because he was dead—if, for many of the straight people who sincerely mourned his murder, he would nevertheless have been at best invisible while alive. To Jim Osborn, the explanation was less dark and more simple: Matt was "someone we can identify with. Matt was the boy next door. He looked like everybody's brother and everybody's neighbor. He looked like he could have been anyone's son."

"He was the nuclear son of the nuclear family." Jay, a Shoshone-Northern Arapahoe-Navajo American Indian born on the Wind River Reservation in the center of Wyoming, is talking to me about the limits of identification. "If that was me hung on the fence, they'd just say, oh, another drunk Indian. No one would have paid much attention." Jay is gay (he uses the Navajo term *nádleeh*—which he translates as "one who loves his own kind"—to describe him-self), and while he feels sympathy for Matt, he doesn't feel much kinship. To Jay, the reason why the nation seized upon Matt is just as simple as Jim Osborn's reason but radically different: to Jay, it was as if white, middle-class America finally had its own tragedy. His argument makes some undeniable sense: in a media culture consecrated to repetition, to the endless recopying of the supposed center of American life—white, moneyed, male—Matt did indeed fit the bill, did suit the recycled homogeneities of a still-myopic national culture. For Jay, the tremendous public outpouring of grief, no matter how sincere, remained essentially alienating. When I ask him how people he knows back on the reser-vation reacted to the murder, he sums up what he describes as a common response, which he himself shared: "Well, at least now one of them"—whites—"knows what we live through every day." Matt learned it, he says. "And one mother now knows, for a little while anyway, what our lives have always been." As he speaks, defiance, resignation, bitterness, and pride mingle in his voice. "Now people might know what our lives are like," what forms of violence—physical, political, cultural—native people experience in the still-hostile territories of the American West.

Jay's home on the reservation was without running water or electricity, but that never felt like deprivation or unusual circumstance to him—"It's just the way it was." When he was nine, Jay moved to Laramie with his family. They arrived after dark. "Laramie looked so beautiful—all these lights spread out—[it] seemed huge to me." He laughs as he describes how he has learned to love the materialism of life off the reservation—"I really, really like having things now," he admits in simultaneous mockery of himself and Anglo consumerism. When I ask him what white residents here don't know about their town, he replies that "Laramie's a nice town"—he likes life here fine—with a pointed caveat: "White people always say there's no bias in Laramie, no racism, but they just don't want to see." Jay has long black hair pulled back in a braid and a round, lived-in face; he's frequently mistaken for Hispanic. As a child, it didn't take him long to stumble across the racial fault lines he describes. In his first year in Laramie, as he walked home from school near the university campus, a college-aged man spit on him. And on the day we talked, a white woman hissed "spic" at Jay minutes before we met. A student at the university, Jay says there is a reason why the October vigils held for Matt were mostly attended by whites: when Matt died and then later, during the legal proceedings against Henderson and McKinney, Jay observes, "you never saw a minority alone on campus—they either left town, or stayed home, or walked in pairs or groups." They were, he and others say, afraid of a backlash—if "someone got killed for being gay, then someone might get killed for being black or Hispanic or native—that's how we felt." In Jay's opinion, the surprise and horror expressed at the vigils—not to mention simply attending them—was almost something of a white luxury: "They felt shock," Jay says, but "I wasn't shocked—I knew this was coming, since I was in high school, seeing the white and Hispanic kids fight. I knew sooner or later someone was going to die." To Jay, risk, the risk of visible difference, didn't seem all that unfamiliar.

Other minority students on campus confirm Jay's point, however melodramatic it might seem to some. Carina Evans, a young woman of Latino and African-American heritage, told me that when the minority community on campus heard that two Latino teenagers had also been attacked by Henderson and McKinney that night, "the immediate response was, oh my God, what about my safety? How safe am I here? And I think our way of dealing with it was just to not talk about it, because I think we figured the less we drew attention to ourselves, the less the chance that something else was going to happen. Which was a sorry response, but a lot of people left town, just did not feel safe, went away for the week or the weekend."[3] She and others thought, "I'm not going to make myself a target—I'm going to get out of here." No such retaliation was ever reported, but the fact that minority members of the community so feared its possibility that it felt logical to leave town—at the same time that so many white residents could unquestionably consider the attack an isolated incident—reveals something about the complexities of daily life in Laramie.

The divides that run through Jay's and Carina's lives became harder for many in Laramie to ignore in the aftermath of Matt's death. But it was nevertheless a town made defensive by such half-unearthed truths. "Hate is not a Wyoming value," residents kept telling each other, telling visitors, telling the press. "We really take care of each other here," a woman told me one day in a coffee shop, echoing a dearly held ethos I've heard from many in Laramie and that strikes me as generally true. That defensiveness intensified as it encountered the first, clumsy journalistic attempts to offer sociological explanations for the roots of Henderson and McKinney's violence, attempts that implied—to us here, anyway—that Laramie was to blame. Perhaps the most locally reviled version was an article written by Todd Lewan and Steven K. Paulson for the Associated Press that appeared in October, an occasionally persuasive attempt at class analysis hamstrung by bad facts and a love affair with the thuddingly clichéd symbolic density of the railroad tracks that cut through town. Here is their Laramie:

> On the east side is the University of Wyoming's ivy-clad main campus, where students drive sports cars or stroll and bike along oak-shaded sidewalks. On the opposite side of town, a bridge spans railroad tracks to another reality, of treeless trailer parks baking in the heavy sun, fenced-off half-acre lots, stray dogs picking for scraps among broken stoves, refrigerators, and junked pickups. Unlike the university students, youths on the west side have little in the way of entertainment: no malls, no organized dance troupes, no theater or playing fields.

Blowing holes in this picture is still a local sport, more than a year after the murder. Bob Beck, for example, takes fairly comprehensive aim at the story:

> They decided that the reason a murder like this happened was because those of us, including me, who live in west Laramie, the "other side of the tracks," are underprivileged, don't have benefits, all this stuff. Because we're over there, we're obviously looking to get even with the good side of the tracks and are going to commit a crime like this. [They] basically blamed the fact that some of us who live in west Laramie don't have a mall (meanwhile there isn't a mall on the east side either); so we don't have a mall, we don't have paved streets, apparently don't have trees. And this is the reason for all this violence? That was one of the most damaging stories in retrospect, because it got picked up by just about every major paper. A lot of people got their impressions of the case from that.

The list of mistakes could continue: Henderson and McKinney didn't even live in west Laramie; oaks rarely grow at seven thousand feet; and few university students drive fancy sports cars—more likely, like many of the students I've encountered, they're working fifteen to thirty hours a week to pay their tuition, maybe at the same Taco Bell where Henderson worked as a teenager. It's hard to choose, but my personal favorite is the anguished handwringing over west Laramie's lack of organized dance troupes. Organized dance troupes?

Plenty of folks I've spoken to volunteer that they live on the west side and are quick to say they're "not trash," that they like the rustic character of west

Laramie's unpaved streets, that they don't necessarily feel excluded from "Laramie proper," despite, for example, the west side's usual lack of representation on the city council. And I've found few residents who weren't offended by such shallow press characterizations of Laramie, who didn't argue that status doesn't matter much here, that Laramie is friendly and easygoing and safe, that most folks don't even bother to lock their doors. All their points of rebuttal are well taken, and indeed they're reasons why many love to live here. But nevertheless I think the eager rapidity with which so many of us rejected such examples of journalistic ineptitude masked at times a certain unease—and sometimes a hardworking amnesia—about the subtle realities of class, sexuality, and race here in Laramie. Those realities may be too complicated to sum up through the convenient shorthand of railroad tracks and trailer parks, but they still flow, hushed yet turbulent, beneath daily life in this town.

NOTES

1. Melanie Thernstrom's essay on the murder in the March 1999 issue of *Vanity Fair* notes that Matt was not strung up, but only in a parenthetical remark near the end of the piece, and the article itself has the title "The Crucifixion of Matthew Shepard." JoAnn Wypijewski's tough-minded essay "A Boy's Life," which appeared in the September 1999 issue of *Harper's Magazine*, was the first thorough demystification of this myth in the national media, but many people still believe it. For example, Melissa Etheridge's song "Scarecrow" on her 1999 album *Breakdown* relies on it, as well as on other early misstatements of fact, including the false report that Shepard had been burned by his killers.

2. While the United Multicultural Council did good work that day, and while some strong connections have been made between the UMC and the LGBTA since Matt's death, it would be wrong to imply that those ties have been built without friction. Carina Evans, a university student who worked in the Minority Affairs Office that year, observed that at the time some members of the "diversity clubs" represented by the UMC "would not deal with the gay issue. The United Multicultural Council had no representation from the LGBTA, had no representation of openly gay students—and I think that's not at all multicultural. But they don't want to handle that. It's not like they're hostile about it, but they just don't encourage it." The tension flows both ways: Jay, a gay American Indian now active in the UMC, told me that some gay students of color he knows are uncomfortable attending LGBTA meetings because they feel that some members are not sensitive to racial differences.

3. A Mexican-American student, Lindsey Gonzales, spoke to me as well about the attack on Morales and Herrera. Lindsey knew Morales quite well (they'd hung out together in the past). She thinks neither the media nor the public cared much about the attack on Morales and Herrera compared to Matt because "they didn't die." But if they had, she speculates, people probably wouldn't have cared much more. When I ask her why, she says she's not sure, but she speculates that racial prejudice is simply more "familiar," something with a longer and better-known history in America, whereas "we're all just getting used to" homosexuality right now, and "that made it a big deal."

QUESTIONS FOR MAKING CONNECTIONS
WITHIN THE READING

1. As Beth Loffreda works to unpack the significance of Matt Shepard's murder, she finds herself confronting a wide array of prejudices, not only about gays, but about Wyoming, the West, and Native Americans. Create a chart that details all of the prejudices that Loffreda uncovers. What are the relationships among these prejudices? Does Loffreda have any prejudices, or is her view unbiased?

2. In detailing the responses to Shepard's murder, Loffreda refers to many different individuals by name. Who are the most important people in the story that Loffreda has to tell? Which responses had more weight at the time of the murder? Which responses have the most weight with Loffreda? With you?

3. How is this selection from *Losing Matt Shepard* organized? Is it a series of observations or an argument? Does it build to a point? Does it have a structure? How does the structure that Loffreda has chosen influence what she has to say?

QUESTIONS FOR WRITING

1. One of Loffreda's arguments in *Losing Matt Shepard* is that Matt Shepard, the individual, got lost in the media frenzy that followed his murder. Part of the shock of Shepard's death, Loffreda reports, was "to watch rumor become myth, to see the story stitched out of repetition rather than investigation." If the media got Shepard's murder wrong, what are we to make of how and why they got it wrong? What would it take to provide "better coverage" of such tragedies? Are the print and visual media capable of providing nuanced understandings of unfolding events?

2. In describing how her colleagues at the University of Wyoming responded to Shepard's death, Loffreda records her own frustration at hearing teachers speak of their own "uselessness" and "irrelevance" in the face of such a tragedy. Such remarks struck Loffreda as "an appalling luxury, an indulgence in a kind of intellectual self-pity at a moment when the basic skills of education—critical thinking, articulation, self-reflection—could be so concretely valuable. I wondered about that, and I wondered, too, when we'd stop talking about how we felt and begin talking about what to do." What is it that teachers can or should do at such times? What role should secular institutions play in trying to shape the way their students see and understand the world?

QUESTIONS FOR MAKING CONNECTIONS
BETWEEN READINGS

1. This selection from *Losing Matt Shepard* closes with Loffreda's discussion of what she terms "the limits of identification," starting with her account of Jay, an American Indian student at the university. In a sense, Susan Faludi's *The Naked Citadel* could also be described as a piece centrally concerned with "the limits of identification"—including identification based on gender. What are the limits Loffreda has in mind, and what limits do you find at The Citadel? How are these limits discovered by people in both communities? Do you see evidence of change?

2. Beth Loffreda and Andrew Solomon both describe the experience of being gay in America, but Matt Shepard's journey of self-exploration was cut short by his murder in a community where many kinds of differences were still greeted with hostility. Use *Losing Matt Shepard* and *Son* to make an argument about the connection between cultural values and personal fulfillment. Does culture dictate who we become, or is there often a disconnect between individual needs and the cultural "scripts" or roles available to us—roles like manly man, womanly woman, straight male, lesbian, cheerleader, nerd, slacker, and so on? Does our development as individuals always require us to recognize the limitations of the cultural script? To what degree does our personal fulfillment depend on support from our larger society?

◆◆◆

MICHAEL MOSS

EVEN MORE THAN shelter and clothing, food occupies a special place in our lives. Needless to say, our existence would be unsustainable without it, but food is unique in another way: its appearance in the store, the campus cafeteria, or the restaurant down the street represents the work of countless people, most of whom we will never know. The food system, vast and enormously complex, ultimately operates on trust. But what happens when that trust is betrayed? This is the question journalist Michael Moss has set out to answer. In the course of his detailed investigation of the food industry, Moss learned that many corporations use the findings of contemporary science to create addictions that undermine the health of millions of Americans—while raking in enormous profits.

Investigative journalism of this kind is Moss's stock-in-trade. A winner of a Pulitzer Prize in 2010, he has written for the *Wall Street Journal,* the *Atlanta Journal-Constitution,* and *New York Newsday* before reporting for the *New York Times.* In 2006, three years into the U.S. occupation of Iraq, he brought to light a disturbing truth about the conduct of the war. A study done by the Pentagon—and later concealed—found that as many as 80 percent of the marines who died from upper body wounds could have survived if they had only been given extra protective armor. Simply by enlarging the existing plates, without adding new protection, the leadership would have prevented about a third of the fatal injuries. As early as 2003, Army General Richard A. Cody recognized the problem and made serious efforts to scale up production, but the ensuing missteps clearly showed a fatal lack of coordination between the Pentagon, the manufacturers, and their various suppliers.

Moss's reporting on the armor saved lives, and lives are at stake in his new book, *Salt Sugar Fat: How the Food Giants Hooked Us* (2013). Once again he acknowledges that certain people on the inside recognized a problem and set out to correct it. In the following selection, he recounts a meeting in 1999 where the head of Kraft Foods, Michael Mudd, warned his fellow CEOs that their industry was largely to blame for the obesity crisis. The failure of the industry to respond to his candid warning suggests that the problem cannot be understood by focusing on the ethical decisions of a few powerful individuals. Moss's

Body armor article: Michael Moss, "Pentagon Study Links Fatalities to Body Armor," *New York Times,* January 7, 2006. Reference to General Cody comes from Michael Moss, "Many Missteps Tied to Delay in Armor for Troops in Iraq," *New York Times,* March 7, 2005.

article strongly implies instead that real change requires us to start with the systemic nature of the threat to public health. Again and again the people Moss interviews are hardworking, intelligent men and women who have spent many years perfecting their expertise. But these same people often fail to think about the large-scale social implications of their work.

The Extraordinary Science of Addictive Junk Food

On the evening of April 8, 1999, a long line of Town Cars and taxis pulled up to the Minneapolis headquarters of Pillsbury and discharged 11 men who controlled America's largest food companies. Nestlé was in attendance, as were Kraft and Nabisco, General Mills and Procter & Gamble, Coca-Cola and Mars. Rivals any other day, the C.E.O.'s and company presidents had come together for a rare, private meeting. On the agenda was one item: the emerging obesity epidemic and how to deal with it. While the atmosphere was cordial, the men assembled were hardly friends. Their stature was defined by their skill in fighting one another for what they called "stomach share"—the amount of digestive space that any one company's brand can grab from the competition.

James Behnke, a 55-year-old executive at Pillsbury, greeted the men as they arrived. He was anxious but also hopeful about the plan that he and a few other food-company executives had devised to engage the C.E.O.'s on America's growing weight problem. "We were very concerned, and rightfully so, that obesity was becoming a major issue," Behnke recalled. "People were starting to talk about sugar taxes, and there was a lot of pressure on food companies." Getting the company chiefs in the same room to talk about anything, much less a sensitive issue like this, was a tricky business, so Behnke and his fellow organizers had scripted the meeting carefully, honing the message to its barest essentials. "C.E.O.'s in the food industry are typically not technical guys, and they're uncomfortable going to meetings where technical people talk in technical terms about technical things," Behnke said. "They don't want to be embarrassed. They don't want to make commitments. They want to maintain their aloofness and autonomy."

A chemist by training with a doctoral degree in food science, Behnke became Pillsbury's chief technical officer in 1979 and was instrumental in creating a long line of hit products, including microwaveable popcorn. He deeply admired Pillsbury but in recent years had grown troubled by pictures of obese children suffering from diabetes and the earliest signs of hypertension and heart disease. In the months leading up to the C.E.O. meeting, he was engaged in conversation with a group of food-science experts who were painting an increasingly grim picture of the public's ability to cope with the industry's formulations—from the body's fragile controls on overeating to the hidden power of some processed foods to make people feel hungrier still. It was time, he and a handful of others felt, to warn the C.E.O.'s that their companies may have gone too far in creating and marketing products that posed the greatest health concerns.

The discussion took place in Pillsbury's auditorium. The first speaker was a vice president of Kraft named Michael Mudd. "I very much appreciate this opportunity to talk to you about childhood obesity and the growing challenge it presents for us all," Mudd began. "Let me say right at the start, this is not an easy subject. There are no easy answers—for what the public health community must do to bring this problem under control or for what the industry should do as others seek to hold it accountable for what has happened. But this much is clear: For those of us who've looked hard at this issue, whether they're public health professionals or staff specialists in your own companies, we feel sure that the one thing we shouldn't do is nothing."

As he spoke, Mudd clicked through a deck of slides—114 in all—projected on a large screen behind him. The figures were staggering. More than half of American adults were now considered overweight, with nearly one-quarter of the adult population—40 million people—clinically defined as obese. Among children, the rates had more than doubled since 1980, and the number of kids considered obese had shot past 12 million. (This was still only 1999; the nation's obesity rates would climb much higher.) Food manufacturers were now being blamed for the problem from all sides—academia, the Centers for Disease Control and Prevention, the American Heart Association and the American Cancer Society. The secretary of agriculture, over whom the industry had long held sway, had recently called obesity a "national epidemic."

Mudd then did the unthinkable. He drew a connection to the last thing in the world the C.E.O.'s wanted linked to their products: cigarettes. First came a quote from a Yale University professor of psychology and public health, Kelly Brownell, who was an especially vocal proponent of the view that the processed-food industry should be seen as a public health menace: "As a culture, we've become upset by the tobacco companies advertising to children, but we sit idly by while the food companies do the very same thing. And we could make a claim that the toll taken on the public health by a poor diet rivals that taken by tobacco."

"If anyone in the food industry ever doubted there was a slippery slope out there," Mudd said, "I imagine they are beginning to experience a distinct sliding sensation right about now."

Mudd then presented the plan he and others had devised to address the obesity problem. Merely getting the executives to acknowledge some culpability was an important first step, he knew, so his plan would start off with a small but crucial move: the industry should use the expertise of scientists—its own and others—to gain a deeper understanding of what was driving Americans to overeat. Once this was achieved, the effort could unfold on several fronts. To be sure, there would be no getting around the role that packaged foods and drinks play in overconsumption. They would have to pull back on their use of salt, sugar and fat, perhaps by imposing industrywide limits. But it wasn't just a matter of these three ingredients; the schemes they used to advertise and market their products were critical, too. Mudd proposed creating a "code to guide the nutritional aspects of food marketing, especially to children."

"We are saying that the industry should make a sincere effort to be part of the solution," Mudd concluded. "And that by doing so, we can help to defuse the criticism that's building against us."

What happened next was not written down. But according to three participants, when Mudd stopped talking, the one C.E.O. whose recent exploits in the grocery store had awed the rest of the industry stood up to speak. His name was Stephen Sanger, and he was also the person—as head of General Mills—who had the most to lose when it came to dealing with obesity. Under his leadership, General Mills had overtaken not just the cereal aisle but other sections of the grocery store. The company's Yoplait brand had transformed traditional unsweetened breakfast yogurt into a veritable dessert. It now had twice as much sugar per serving as General Mills' marshmallow cereal Lucky Charms. And yet, because of yogurt's well-tended image as a wholesome snack, sales of Yoplait were soaring, with annual revenue topping $500 million. Emboldened by the success, the company's development wing pushed even harder, inventing a Yoplait variation that came in a squeezable tube—perfect for kids. They called it Go-Gurt and rolled it out nationally in the weeks before the C.E.O. meeting. (By year's end, it would hit $100 million in sales.)

According to the sources I spoke with, Sanger began by reminding the group that consumers were "fickle." (Sanger declined to be interviewed.) Sometimes they worried about sugar, other times fat. General Mills, he said, acted responsibly to both the public and shareholders by offering products to satisfy dieters and other concerned shoppers, from low sugar to added whole grains. But most often, he said, people bought what they liked, and they liked what tasted good. "Don't talk to me about nutrition," he reportedly said, taking on the voice of the typical consumer. "Talk to me about taste, and if this stuff tastes better, don't run around trying to sell stuff that doesn't taste good."

To react to the critics, Sanger said, would jeopardize the sanctity of the recipes that had made his products so successful. General Mills would not pull back. He would push his people onward, and he urged his peers to do the same. Sanger's response effectively ended the meeting.

"What can I say?" James Behnke told me years later. "It didn't work. These guys weren't as receptive as we thought they would be." Behnke chose his words deliberately. He wanted to be fair. "Sanger was trying to say, 'Look, we're not going to screw around with the company jewels here and change the formulations because a bunch of guys in white coats are worried about obesity.' "

The meeting was remarkable, first, for the insider admissions of guilt. But I was also struck by how prescient the organizers of the sit-down had been.

Today, one in three adults is considered clinically obese, along with one in five kids, and 24 million Americans are afflicted by type 2 diabetes, often caused by poor diet, with another 79 million people having pre-diabetes. Even gout, a painful form of arthritis once known as "the rich man's disease" for its associations with gluttony, now afflicts eight million Americans.

The public and the food companies have known for decades now—or at the very least since this meeting—that sugary, salty, fatty foods are not good for us in the quantities that we consume them. So why are the diabetes and obesity and hypertension numbers still spiraling out of control? It's not just a matter of poor willpower on the part of the consumer and a give-the-people-what-they-want attitude on the part of the food manufacturers. What I found, over four years of research and reporting, was a conscious effort—taking place in labs and marketing meetings and grocery-store aisles—to get people hooked on foods that are convenient and inexpensive. I talked to more than 300 people in or formerly employed by the processed-food industry, from scientists to marketers to C.E.O.'s. Some were willing whistle-blowers, while others spoke reluctantly when presented with some of the thousands of pages of secret memos that I obtained from inside the food industry's operations. What follows is a series of small case studies of a handful of characters whose work then, and perspective now, sheds light on how the foods are created and sold to people who, while not powerless, are extremely vulnerable to the intensity of these companies' industrial formulations and selling campaigns.

I. 'IN THIS FIELD, I'M A GAME CHANGER.'

John Lennon couldn't find it in England, so he had cases of it shipped from New York to fuel the "Imagine" sessions. The Beach Boys, ZZ Top and Cher all stipulated in their contract riders that it be put in their dressing rooms when they toured. Hillary Clinton asked for it when she traveled as first lady, and ever after her hotel suites were dutifully stocked.

What they all wanted was Dr Pepper, which until 2001 occupied a comfortable third-place spot in the soda aisle behind Coca-Cola and Pepsi. But then a flood of spinoffs from the two soda giants showed up on the shelves—lemons and limes, vanillas and coffees, raspberries and oranges, whites and blues and clears—what in food-industry lingo are known as "line extensions," and Dr Pepper started to lose its market share.

Responding to this pressure, Cadbury Schweppes created its first spin off, other than a diet version, in the soda's 115-year history, a bright red soda with a very un-Dr Pepper name: Red Fusion. "If we are to re-establish Dr Pepper back to its historic growth rates, we have to add more excitement," the company's president, Jack Kilduff, said. One particularly promising market, Kilduff pointed out, was the "rapidly growing Hispanic and African-American communities."

But consumers hated Red Fusion. "Dr Pepper is my all-time favorite drink, so I was curious about the Red Fusion," a California mother of three wrote on a blog to warn other Peppers away. "It's disgusting. Gagging. Never again."

Stung by the rejection, Cadbury Schweppes in 2004 turned to a food-industry legend named Howard Moskowitz. Moskowitz, who studied mathematics and holds a Ph.D. in experimental psychology from Harvard, runs a consulting firm in White Plains, where for more than three decades he has "optimized" a variety of products for Campbell Soup, General Foods, Kraft and PepsiCo. "I've optimized soups," Moskowitz told me. "I've optimized pizzas. I've optimized salad dressings and pickles. In this field, I'm a game changer."

In the process of product optimization, food engineers alter a litany of variables with the sole intent of finding the most perfect version (or versions) of a product. Ordinary consumers are paid to spend hours sitting in rooms where they touch, feel, sip, smell, swirl and taste whatever product is in question. Their opinions are dumped into a computer, and the data are sifted and sorted through a statistical method called conjoint analysis, which determines what features will be most attractive to consumers. Moskowitz likes to imagine that his computer is divided into silos, in which each of the attributes is stacked. But it's not simply a matter of comparing Color 23 with Color 24. In the most complicated projects, Color 23 must be combined with Syrup 11 and Packaging 6, and on and on, in seemingly infinite combinations. Even for jobs in which the only concern is taste and the variables are limited to the ingredients, endless charts and graphs will come spewing out of Moskowitz's computer. "The mathematical model maps out the ingredients to the sensory perceptions these ingredients create," he told me, "so I can just dial a new product. This is the engineering approach."

Moskowitz's work on Prego spaghetti sauce was memorialized in a 2004 presentation by the author Malcolm Gladwell at the TED conference in Monterey, Calif.: "After ... months and months, he had a mountain of data about how the American people feel about spaghetti sauce.... And sure enough, if you sit down and you analyze all this data on spaghetti sauce, you realize that all Americans fall into one of three groups. There are people who like their spaghetti sauce plain. There are people who like their spaghetti sauce spicy. And there are people who like it extra-chunky. And of those three facts, the third one was the most significant, because at the time, in the early 1980s, if you went to a supermarket, you would not find extra-chunky spaghetti sauce. And Prego turned to Howard, and they said, 'Are you telling me that one-third of Americans crave extra-chunky spaghetti sauce, and yet no one is servicing their needs?' And he said, 'Yes.' And Prego then went back and completely reformulated their spaghetti sauce and came out with a line of extra-chunky that immediately and completely took over the spaghetti-sauce business in this country.... That is Howard's gift to the American people.... He fundamentally changed the way the food industry thinks about making you happy."

Well, yes and no. One thing Gladwell didn't mention is that the food industry already knew some things about making people happy—and it started with sugar. Many of the Prego sauces—whether cheesy, chunky or light—have one feature in common: The largest ingredient, after tomatoes, is sugar. A mere half-cup of Prego Traditional, for instance, has the equivalent of more than two teaspoons of sugar, as much as two-plus Oreo cookies. It also delivers one-third of the sodium recommended for a majority of American adults for an entire day.

In making these sauces, Campbell supplied the ingredients, including the salt, sugar and, for some versions, fat, while Moskowitz supplied the optimization. "More is not necessarily better," Moskowitz wrote in his own account of the Prego project. "As the sensory intensity (say, of sweetness) increases, consumers first say that they like the product more, but eventually, with a middle level of sweetness, consumers like the product the most (this is their optimum, or 'bliss,' point)."

I first met Moskowitz on a crisp day in the spring of 2010 at the Harvard Club in Midtown Manhattan. As we talked, he made clear that while he has worked on numerous projects aimed at creating more healthful foods and insists the industry could be doing far more to curb obesity, he had no qualms about his own pioneering work on discovering what industry insiders now regularly refer to as "the bliss point" or any of the other systems that helped food companies create the greatest amount of crave. "There's no moral issue for me," he said. "I did the best science I could. I was struggling to survive and didn't have the luxury of being a moral creature. As a researcher, I was ahead of my time."

Moskowitz's path to mastering the bliss point began in earnest not at Harvard but a few months after graduation, 16 miles from Cambridge, in the town of Natick, where the U.S. Army hired him to work in its research labs. The military has long been in a peculiar bind when it comes to food: how to get soldiers to eat more rations when they are in the field. They know that over time, soldiers would gradually find their meals-ready-to-eat so boring that they would toss them away, half-eaten, and not get all the calories they needed. But what was causing this M.R.E.-fatigue was a mystery. "So I started asking soldiers how frequently they would like to eat this or that, trying to figure out which products they would find boring," Moskowitz said. The answers he got were inconsistent. "They liked flavorful foods like turkey tetrazzini, but only at first; they quickly grew tired of them. On the other hand, mundane foods like white bread would never get them too excited, but they could eat lots and lots of it without feeling they'd had enough."

This contradiction is known as "sensory-specific satiety." In lay terms, it is the tendency for big, distinct flavors to overwhelm the brain, which responds by depressing your desire to have more. Sensory-specific satiety also became a guiding principle for the processed-food industry. The biggest hits—be they Coca-Cola or Doritos—owe their success to complex formulas that pique the taste buds enough to be alluring but don't have a distinct, overriding single flavor that tells the brain to stop eating.

Thirty-two years after he began experimenting with the bliss point, Moskowitz got the call from Cadbury Schweppes asking him to create a good line extension for Dr Pepper. I spent an afternoon in his White Plains offices as he and his vice president for research, Michele Reisner, walked me through the Dr Pepper campaign. Cadbury wanted its new flavor to have cherry and vanilla on top of the basic Dr Pepper taste. Thus, there were three main components to play with. A sweet cherry flavoring, a sweet vanilla flavoring and a sweet syrup known as "Dr Pepper flavoring."

Finding the bliss point required the preparation of 61 subtly distinct formulas—31 for the regular version and 30 for diet. The formulas were then subjected to 3,904 tastings organized in Los Angeles, Dallas, Chicago and Philadelphia. The Dr Pepper tasters began working through their samples, resting five minutes between each sip to restore their taste buds. After each sample, they gave numerically ranked answers to a set of questions: How much did they like it overall? How strong is the taste? How do they feel about the taste? How would they describe the quality of this product? How likely would they be to purchase this product?

Moskowitz's data—compiled in a 135-page report for the soda maker—is tremendously fine-grained, showing how different people and groups of people feel about a strong vanilla taste versus weak, various aspects of aroma and the powerful sensory force that food scientists call "mouth feel." This is the way a product interacts with the mouth, as defined more specifically by a host of related sensations, from dryness to gumminess to moisture release. These are terms more familiar to sommeliers, but the mouth feel of soda and many other food items, especially those high in fat, is second only to the bliss point in its ability to predict how much craving a product will induce.

In addition to taste, the consumers were also tested on their response to color, which proved to be highly sensitive. "When we increased the level of the Dr Pepper flavoring, it gets darker and liking goes off," Reisner said. These preferences can also be cross-referenced by age, sex and race.

On Page 83 of the report, a thin blue line represents the amount of Dr Pepper flavoring needed to generate maximum appeal. The line is shaped like an upside-down U, just like the bliss-point curve that Moskowitz studied 30 years earlier in his Army lab. And at the top of the arc, there is not a single sweet spot but instead a sweet range, within which "bliss" was achievable. This meant that Cadbury could edge back on its key ingredient, the sugary Dr Pepper syrup, without falling out of the range and losing the bliss. Instead of using 2 milliliters of the flavoring, for instance, they could use 1.69 milliliters and achieve the same effect. The potential savings is merely a few percentage points, and it won't mean much to individual consumers who are counting calories or grams of sugar. But for Dr Pepper, it adds up to colossal savings. "That looks like nothing," Reisner said. "But it's a lot of money. A lot of money. Millions."

The soda that emerged from all of Moskowitz's variations became known as Cherry Vanilla Dr Pepper, and it proved successful beyond anything Cadbury imagined. In 2008, Cadbury split off its soft-drinks business, which included Snapple and 7-Up. The Dr Pepper Snapple Group has since been valued in excess of $11 billion.

II. 'LUNCHTIME IS ALL YOURS.'

Sometimes innovations within the food industry happen in the lab, with scientists dialing in specific ingredients to achieve the greatest allure. And sometimes, as in the case of Oscar Mayer's bologna crisis, the innovation involves putting old products in new packages.

The 1980s were tough times for Oscar Mayer. Red-meat consumption fell more than 10 percent as fat became synonymous with cholesterol, clogged arteries, heart attacks and strokes. Anxiety set in at the company's headquarters in Madison, Wis., where executives worried about their future and the pressure they faced from their new bosses at Philip Morris.

Bob Drane was the company's vice president for new business strategy and development when Oscar Mayer tapped him to try to find some way to reposition bologna and other troubled meats that were declining in popularity and sales. I met Drane at his home in Madison and went through the records he had kept on the birth of what would become much more than his solution to the company's meat problem. In 1985, when Drane began working on the project, his orders were to "figure out how to contemporize what we've got."

Drane's first move was to try to zero in not on what Americans felt about processed meat but on what Americans felt about lunch. He organized focus-group sessions with the people most responsible for buying bologna—mothers—and as they talked, he realized the most pressing issue for them was time. Working moms strove to provide healthful food, of course, but they spoke with real passion and at length about the morning crush, that nightmarish dash to get breakfast on the table and lunch packed and kids out the door. He summed up their remarks for me like this: "It's awful. I am scrambling around. My kids are asking me for stuff. I'm trying to get myself ready to go to the office. I go to pack these lunches, and I don't know what I've got." What the moms revealed to him, Drane said, was "a gold mine of disappointments and problems."

He assembled a team of about 15 people with varied skills, from design to food science to advertising, to create something completely new—a convenient prepackaged lunch that would have as its main building block the company's sliced bologna and ham. They wanted to add bread, naturally, because who ate bologna without it? But this presented a problem: There was no way bread could stay fresh for the two months their product needed to sit in warehouses or in grocery coolers. Crackers, however, could—so they added a handful of cracker rounds to the package. Using cheese was the next obvious move, given its increased presence in processed foods. But what kind of cheese would work? Natural Cheddar, which they started off with, crumbled and didn't slice very well, so they moved on to processed varieties, which could bend and be sliced and would last forever, or they could knock another two cents off per unit by using an even lesser product called "cheese food," which had lower scores than processed cheese in taste tests. The cost dilemma was solved when Oscar Mayer merged with Kraft in 1989 and the company didn't have to shop for cheese anymore; it got all the processed cheese it wanted from its new sister company, and at cost.

Drane's team moved into a nearby hotel, where they set out to find the right mix of components and container. They gathered around tables where bagfuls of meat, cheese, crackers and all sorts of wrapping material had been dumped, and they let their imaginations run. After snipping and taping their way through a host of failures, the model they fell back on was the American TV dinner—and after some brainstorming about names (Lunch Kits? Go-Packs? Fun Mealz?), Lunchables were born.

The trays flew off the grocery-store shelves. Sales hit a phenomenal $218 million in the first 12 months, more than anyone was prepared for. This only brought Drane his next crisis. The production costs were so high that they were losing money with each tray they produced. So Drane flew to New York, where he met with Philip Morris officials who promised to give him the money he needed to keep it going. "The hard thing is to figure out something that will sell," he was told. "You'll figure out how to get the cost right." Projected to lose $6 million in 1991, the trays instead broke even; the next year, they earned $8 million.

With production costs trimmed and profits coming in, the next question was how to expand the franchise, which they did by turning to one of the cardinal rules in processed food: When in doubt, add sugar. "Lunchables With Dessert is a logical extension," an Oscar Mayer official reported to Philip Morris executives in early 1991. The "target" remained the same as it was for regular Lunchables— "busy mothers" and "working women," ages 25 to 49—and the "enhanced taste" would attract shoppers who had grown bored with the current trays. A year later, the dessert Lunchable morphed into the Fun Pack, which would come with a Snickers bar, a package of M&M's or a Reese's Peanut Butter Cup, as well as a sugary drink. The Lunchables team started by using Kool-Aid and cola and then Capri Sun after Philip Morris added that drink to its stable of brands.

Eventually, a line of the trays, appropriately called Maxed Out, was released that had as many as nine grams of saturated fat, or nearly an entire day's recommended maximum for kids, with up to two-thirds of the max for sodium and 13 teaspoons of sugar.

When I asked Geoffrey Bible, former C.E.O. of Philip Morris, about this shift toward more salt, sugar and fat in meals for kids, he smiled and noted that even in its earliest incarnation, Lunchables was held up for criticism. "One article said something like, 'If you take Lunchables apart, the most healthy item in it is the napkin.'"

Well, they did have a good bit of fat, I offered. "You bet," he said. "Plus cookies."

The prevailing attitude among the company's food managers—through the 1990s, at least, before obesity became a more pressing concern—was one of supply and demand. "People could point to these things and say, 'They've got too much sugar, they've got too much salt,'" Bible said. "Well, that's what the consumer wants, and we're not putting a gun to their head to eat it. That's what they want. If we give them less, they'll buy less, and the competitor will get our market. So you're sort of trapped." (Bible would later press Kraft to reconsider its reliance on salt, sugar and fat.)

When it came to Lunchables, they did try to add more healthful ingredients. Back at the start, Drane experimented with fresh carrots but quickly gave up on that, since fresh components didn't work within the constraints of the processed-food system, which typically required weeks or months of transport and storage before the food arrived at the grocery store. Later, a low-fat version of the trays was developed, using meats and cheese and crackers that were formulated with less fat, but it tasted inferior, sold poorly and was quickly scrapped.

When I met with Kraft officials in 2011 to discuss their products and policies on nutrition, they had dropped the Maxed Out line and were trying to improve the nutritional profile of Lunchables through smaller, incremental changes that were less noticeable to consumers. Across the Lunchables line, they said they had reduced the salt, sugar and fat by about 10 percent, and new versions, featuring mandarin-orange and pineapple slices, were in development. These would be promoted as more healthful versions, with "fresh fruit," but their list of ingredients—containing upward of 70 items, with sucrose, corn syrup, high-fructose corn syrup and fruit concentrate all in the same tray—have been met with intense criticism from outside the industry.

One of the company's responses to criticism is that kids don't eat the Lunchables every day—on top of which, when it came to trying to feed them more healthful foods, kids themselves were unreliable. When their parents packed fresh carrots, apples and water, they couldn't be trusted to eat them. Once in school, they often trashed the healthful stuff in their brown bags to get right to the sweets.

This idea—that kids are in control—would become a key concept in the evolving marketing campaigns for the trays. In what would prove to be their greatest achievement of all, the Lunchables team would delve into adolescent psychology to discover that it wasn't the food in the trays that excited the kids; it was the feeling of power it brought to their lives. As Bob Eckert, then the C.E.O. of Kraft, put it in 1999: "Lunchables aren't about lunch. It's about kids being able to put together what they want to eat, anytime, anywhere."

Kraft's early Lunchables campaign targeted mothers. They might be too distracted by work to make a lunch, but they loved their kids enough to offer them this prepackaged gift. But as the focus swung toward kids, Saturday-morning cartoons started carrying an ad that offered a different message: "All day, you gotta do what they say," the ads said. "But lunchtime is all yours."

With this marketing strategy in place and pizza Lunchables—the crust in one compartment, the cheese, pepperoni and sauce in others—proving to be a runaway success, the entire world of fast food suddenly opened up for Kraft to pursue. They came out with a Mexican-themed Lunchables called Beef Taco Wraps; a Mini Burgers Lunchables; a Mini Hot Dog Lunchable, which also happened to provide a way for Oscar Mayer to sell its wieners. By 1999, pancakes—which included syrup, icing, Lifesavers candy and Tang, for a whopping 76 grams of sugar—and waffles were, for a time, part of the Lunchables franchise as well.

Annual sales kept climbing, past $500 million, past $800 million; at last count, including sales in Britain, they were approaching the $1 billion mark. Lunchables was more than a hit; it was now its own category. Eventually, more than 60 varieties of Lunchables and other brands of trays would show up in the grocery stores. In 2007, Kraft even tried a Lunchables Jr. for 3- to 5-year-olds.

In the trove of records that document the rise of the Lunchables and the sweeping change it brought to lunchtime habits, I came across a photograph of Bob Drane's daughter, which he had slipped into the Lunchables presentation he showed to food developers. The picture was taken on Monica Drane's wedding day in 1989, and she was standing outside the family's home in Madison, a beautiful bride in a white wedding dress, holding one of the brand-new yellow trays.

During the course of reporting, I finally had a chance to ask her about it. Was she really that much of a fan? "There must have been some in the fridge," she told me. "I probably just took one out before we went to the church. My mom had joked that it was really like their fourth child, my dad invested so much time and energy on it."

Monica Drane had three of her own children by the time we spoke, ages 10, 14 and 17. "I don't think my kids have ever eaten a Lunchable," she told me. "They know they exist and that Grandpa Bob invented them. But we eat very healthfully."

Drane himself paused only briefly when I asked him if, looking back, he was proud of creating the trays. "Lots of things are trade-offs," he said. "And I do believe it's easy to rationalize anything. In the end, I wish that the nutritional profile of the thing could have been better, but I don't view the entire project as anything but a positive contribution to people's lives."

Today Bob Drane is still talking to kids about what they like to eat, but his approach has changed. He volunteers with a nonprofit organization that seeks to build better communications between school kids and their parents, and right in the mix of their problems, alongside the academic struggles, is childhood obesity. Drane has also prepared a précis on the food industry that he used with medical students at the University of Wisconsin. And while he does not name his Lunchables in this document, and cites numerous causes for the obesity epidemic, he holds the entire industry accountable. "What do University of Wisconsin M.B.A.'s learn about how to succeed in marketing?" his presentation to the med students asks. "Discover what consumers want to buy and give it to them with both barrels. Sell more, keep your job! How do marketers often translate these 'rules' into action on food? Our limbic brains love sugar, fat, salt.... So formulate products to deliver these. Perhaps add low-cost ingredients to boost profit margins. Then 'supersize' to sell more.... And advertise/promote to lock in 'heavy users.' Plenty of guilt to go around here!"

III. 'IT'S CALLED VANISHING CALORIC DENSITY.'

At a symposium for nutrition scientists in Los Angeles on Feb. 15, 1985, a professor of pharmacology from Helsinki named Heikki Karppanen told the remarkable story of Finland's effort to address its salt habit. In the late 1970s, the Finns were consuming huge amounts of sodium, eating on average more than two teaspoons of salt a day. As a result, the country had developed significant issues with high blood pressure, and men in the eastern part of Finland had the highest rate of fatal cardiovascular disease in the world. Research showed that this plague was not just a quirk of genetics or a result of a sedentary lifestyle—it was also owing to processed foods. So when Finnish authorities moved to address the problem, they went right after the manufacturers. (The Finnish response worked. Every grocery item that was heavy in salt would come to be marked prominently with the warning "High Salt Content." By 2007, Finland's per capita consumption of salt had dropped by a third, and this shift—along with improved medical care—was accompanied by a 75 percent to 80 percent decline in the number of deaths from strokes and heart disease.)

Karppanen's presentation was met with applause, but one man in the crowd seemed particularly intrigued by the presentation, and as Karppanen left the stage, the man intercepted him and asked if they could talk more over dinner. Their conversation later that night was not at all what Karppanen was expecting. His host did indeed have an interest in salt, but from quite a different vantage point: the man's name was Robert I-San Lin, and from 1974 to 1982, he worked as the chief scientist for Frito-Lay, the nearly $3-billion-a-year manufacturer of Lay's, Doritos, Cheetos and Fritos.

Lin's time at Frito-Lay coincided with the first attacks by nutrition advocates on salty foods and the first calls for federal regulators to reclassify salt as a "risky" food additive, which could have subjected it to severe controls. No company took this threat more seriously—or more personally—than Frito-Lay, Lin explained to Karppanen over their dinner. Three years after he left Frito-Lay, he was still anguished over his inability to effectively change the company's recipes and practices.

By chance, I ran across a letter that Lin sent to Karppanen three weeks after that dinner, buried in some files to which I had gained access. Attached to the letter was a memo written when Lin was at Frito-Lay, which detailed some of the company's efforts in defending salt. I tracked Lin down in Irvine, Calif., where we spent several days going through the internal company memos, strategy papers and handwritten notes he had kept. The documents were evidence of the concern that Lin had for consumers and of the company's intent on using science not to address the health concerns but to thwart them. While at Frito-Lay, Lin and other company scientists spoke openly about the country's excessive consumption of sodium and the fact that, as Lin said to me on more than one occasion, "people get addicted to salt."

Not much had changed by 1986, except Frito-Lay found itself on a rare cold streak. The company had introduced a series of high-profile products that failed miserably. Toppels, a cracker with cheese topping; Stuffers, a shell with a variety of fillings; Rumbles, a bite-size granola snack—they all came and went in a blink, and the company took a $52 million hit. Around that time, the marketing team was joined by Dwight Riskey, an expert on cravings who had been a fellow at the Monell Chemical Senses Center in Philadelphia, where he was part of a team of scientists that found that people could beat their salt habits simply by refraining from salty foods long enough for their taste buds to return to a normal level of sensitivity. He had also done work on the bliss point, showing how a product's allure is contextual, shaped partly by the other foods a person is eating, and that it changes as people age. This seemed to help explain why Frito-Lay was having so much trouble selling new snacks. The largest single block of customers, the baby boomers, had begun hitting middle age. According to the research, this suggested that their liking for salty snacks—both in the concentration of salt and how much they ate—would be tapering off. Along with the rest of the snack-food industry, Frito-Lay anticipated lower sales because of an aging population, and marketing plans were adjusted to focus even more intently on younger consumers.

Except that snack sales didn't decline as everyone had projected, Frito-Lay's doomed product launches notwithstanding. Poring over data one day in his home office, trying to understand just who was consuming all the snack food, Riskey realized that he and his colleagues had been misreading things all along.

They had been measuring the snacking habits of different age groups and were seeing what they expected to see, that older consumers ate less than those in their 20s. But what they weren't measuring, Riskey realized, is how those snacking habits of the boomers compared to *themselves* when they were in their 20s. When he called up a new set of sales data and performed what's called a cohort study, following a single group over time, a far more encouraging picture—for Frito-Lay, anyway—emerged. The baby boomers were not eating fewer salty snacks as they aged. "In fact, as those people aged, their consumption of all those segments—the cookies, the crackers, the candy, the chips—was going up," Riskey said. "They were not only eating what they ate when they were younger, they were eating more of it." In fact, everyone in the country, on average, was eating more salty snacks than they used to. The rate of consumption was edging up about one-third of a pound every year, with the average intake of snacks like chips and cheese crackers pushing past 12 pounds a year.

Riskey had a theory about what caused this surge: Eating real meals had become a thing of the past. Baby boomers, especially, seemed to have greatly cut down on regular meals. They were skipping breakfast when they had early-morning meetings. They skipped lunch when they then needed to catch up on work because of those meetings. They skipped dinner when their kids stayed out late or grew up and moved out of the house. And when they skipped these meals, they replaced them with snacks. "We looked at this behavior, and said, 'Oh, my gosh, people were skipping meals right and left,'" Riskey told me. "It was amazing." This led to the next realization, that baby boomers did not represent "a category that is mature, with no growth. This is a category that has huge growth potential."

The food technicians stopped worrying about inventing new products and instead embraced the industry's most reliable method for getting consumers to buy more: the line extension. The classic Lay's potato chips were joined by Salt & Vinegar, Salt & Pepper and Cheddar & Sour Cream. They put out Chili-Cheese-flavored Fritos, and Cheetos were transformed into 21 varieties. Frito-Lay had a formidable research complex near Dallas, where nearly 500 chemists, psychologists and technicians conducted research that cost up to $30 million a year, and the science corps focused intense amounts of resources on questions of crunch, mouth feel and aroma for each of these items. Their tools included a $40,000 device that simulated a chewing mouth to test and perfect the chips, discovering things like the perfect break point: people like a chip that snaps with about four pounds of pressure per square inch.

To get a better feel for their work, I called on Steven Witherly, a food scientist who wrote a fascinating guide for industry insiders titled, "Why Humans Like Junk Food." I brought him two shopping bags filled with a variety of chips to taste. He zeroed right in on the Cheetos. "This," Witherly said, "is one of the most marvelously constructed foods on the planet, in terms of pure pleasure." He ticked off a dozen attributes of the Cheetos that make the brain say more. But the one he focused on most was the puff's uncanny ability to melt in the mouth. "It's called vanishing caloric density," Witherly said. "If something melts down quickly, your brain thinks that there's no calories in it ... you can just keep eating it forever."

As for their marketing troubles, in a March 2010 meeting, Frito-Lay executives hastened to tell their Wall Street investors that the 1.4 billion boomers worldwide weren't being neglected; they were redoubling their efforts to understand exactly what it was that boomers most wanted in a snack chip. Which was basically everything: great taste, maximum bliss but minimal guilt about health and more maturity than puffs. "They snack a lot," Frito-Lay's chief marketing officer, Ann Mukherjee, told the investors. "But what they're looking for is very different. They're looking for new experiences, real food experiences." Frito-Lay acquired Stacy's Pita Chip Company, which was started by a Massachusetts couple who made food-cart sandwiches and started serving pita chips to their customers in the mid-1990s. In Frito-Lay's hands, the pita chips averaged 270 milligrams of sodium—nearly one-fifth a whole day's recommended maximum for most American adults—and were a huge hit among boomers.

The Frito-Lay executives also spoke of the company's ongoing pursuit of a "designer sodium," which they hoped, in the near future, would take their sodium loads down by 40 percent. No need to worry about lost sales there, the company's C.E.O., Al Carey, assured their investors. The boomers would see less salt as the green light to snack like never before.

There's a paradox at work here. On the one hand, reduction of sodium in snack foods is commendable. On the other, these changes may well result in consumers eating more. "The big thing that will happen here is removing the barriers for boomers and giving them permission to snack," Carey said. The prospects for lower-salt snacks were so amazing, he added, that the company had set its sights on using the designer salt to conquer the toughest market of all for snacks: schools. He cited, for example, the school-food initiative championed by Bill Clinton and the American Heart Association, which is seeking to improve the nutrition of school food by limiting its load of salt, sugar and fat. "Imagine this," Carey said. "A potato chip that tastes great and qualifies for the Clinton-A.H.A. alliance for schools.... We think we have ways to do all of this on a potato chip, and imagine getting that product into schools, where children can have this product and grow up with it and feel good about eating it."

Carey's quote reminded me of something I read in the early stages of my reporting, a 24-page report prepared for Frito-Lay in 1957 by a psychologist named Ernest Dichter. The company's chips, he wrote, were not selling as well as they could for one simple reason: "While people like and enjoy potato chips, they feel guilty about liking them.... Unconsciously, people expect to be punished for 'letting themselves go' and enjoying them." Dichter listed seven "fears and resistances" to the chips: "You can't stop eating them; they're fattening; they're not good for you; they're greasy and messy to eat; they're too expensive; it's hard to store the leftovers; and they're bad for children." He spent the rest of his memo laying out his prescriptions, which in time would become widely used not just by Frito-Lay but also by the entire industry. Dichter suggested that Frito-Lay avoid using the word "fried" in referring to its chips and adopt instead the more healthful-sounding term "toasted." To counteract the "fear of letting oneself go," he suggested repacking the chips into smaller bags. "The more-anxious consumers, the ones who have the deepest fears about their capacity to control their appetite, will tend to sense the function of the new pack and select it," he said.

Dichter advised Frito-Lay to move its chips out of the realm of between-meals snacking and turn them into an ever-present item in the American diet. "The increased use of potato chips and other Lay's products as a part of the regular fare served by restaurants and sandwich bars should be encouraged in a concentrated way," Dichter said, citing a string of examples: "potato chips with soup, with fruit or vegetable juice appetizers; potato chips served as a vegetable on the main dish; potato chips with salad; potato chips with egg dishes for breakfast; potato chips with sandwich orders."

In 2011, *The New England Journal of Medicine* published a study that shed new light on America's weight gain. The subjects—120,877 women and men—were all professionals in the health field, and were likely to be more conscious about nutrition, so the findings might well understate the overall trend. Using data back to 1986, the researchers monitored everything the participants ate, as well as their physical activity and smoking. They found that every four years, the participants exercised less, watched TV more and gained an average of 3.35 pounds. The researchers parsed the data by the caloric content of the foods being eaten, and found the top contributors to weight gain included red meat and processed meats, sugar-sweetened beverages and potatoes, including mashed and French fries. But the largest weight-inducing food was the potato chip. The coating of salt, the fat content that rewards the brain with instant feelings of pleasure, the sugar that exists not as an additive but in the starch of the potato itself—all of this combines to make it the perfect addictive food. "The starch is readily absorbed," Eric Rimm, an associate professor of epidemiology and nutrition at the Harvard School of Public Health and one of the study's authors, told me. "More quickly even than a similar amount of sugar. The starch, in turn, causes the glucose levels in the blood to spike"—which can result in a craving for more.

If Americans snacked only occasionally, and in small amounts, this would not present the enormous problem that it does. But because so much money and effort has been invested over decades in engineering and then relentlessly selling these products, the effects are seemingly impossible to unwind. More than 30 years have passed since Robert Lin first tangled with Frito-Lay on the imperative of the company to deal with the formulation of its snacks, but as we sat at his dining-room table, sifting through his records, the feelings of regret still played on his face. In his view, three decades had been lost, time that he and a lot of other smart scientists could have spent searching for ways to ease the addiction to salt, sugar and fat. "I couldn't do much about it," he told me. "I feel so sorry for the public."

IV. 'THESE PEOPLE NEED A LOT OF THINGS, BUT THEY DON'T NEED A COKE.'

The growing attention Americans are paying to what they put into their mouths has touched off a new scramble by the processed-food companies to address health concerns. Pressed by the Obama administration and consumers, Kraft, Nestlé, Pepsi, Campbell and General Mills, among others, have begun to trim the loads of salt, sugar and fat in many products. And with consumer advocates pushing for more government intervention, Coca-Cola made headlines in January by releasing ads that promoted its bottled water and low-calorie drinks as a way to counter obesity. Predictably, the ads drew a new volley of scorn from critics who pointed to the company's continuing drive to sell sugary Coke.

One of the other executives I spoke with at length was Jeffrey Dunn, who, in 2001, at age 44, was directing more than half of Coca-Cola's $20 billion in annual sales as president and chief operating officer in both North and South America. In an effort to control as much market share as possible, Coke extended its aggressive marketing to especially poor or vulnerable areas of the U.S., like New Orleans—where people were drinking twice as much Coke as the national average—or Rome, Ga., where the per capita intake was nearly three Cokes a day. In Coke's headquarters in Atlanta, the biggest consumers were referred to as "heavy users." "The other model we use was called 'drinks and drinkers,' " Dunn said. "How many drinkers do I have? And how many drinks do they drink? If you lost one of those heavy users, if somebody just decided to stop drinking Coke, how many drinkers would you have to get, at low velocity, to make up for that heavy user? The answer is a lot. It's more efficient to get my existing users to drink more."

One of Dunn's lieutenants, Todd Putman, who worked at Coca-Cola from 1997 to 2001, said the goal became much larger than merely beating the rival brands; Coca-Cola strove to outsell every other thing people drank, including milk and water. The marketing division's efforts boiled down to one question, Putman said: "How can we drive more ounces into more bodies more often?" (In response to Putman's remarks, Coke said its goals have changed and that it now focuses on providing consumers with more low- or no-calorie products.)

In his capacity, Dunn was making frequent trips to Brazil, where the company had recently begun a push to increase consumption of Coke among the many Brazilians living in *favelas*. The company's strategy was to repackage Coke into smaller, more affordable 6.7-ounce bottles, just 20 cents each. Coke was not alone in seeing Brazil as a potential boon; Nestlé began deploying battalions of women to travel poor neighborhoods, hawking American-style processed foods door to door. But Coke was Dunn's concern, and on one trip, as he walked through one of the impoverished areas, he had an epiphany. "A voice in my head says, 'These people need a lot of things, but they don't need a Coke.' I almost threw up."

Dunn returned to Atlanta, determined to make some changes. He didn't want to abandon the soda business, but he did want to try to steer the company into a more healthful mode, and one of the things he pushed for was to stop marketing Coke in public schools. The independent companies that bottled Coke viewed his plans as reactionary. A director of one bottler wrote a letter to Coke's chief executive and board asking for Dunn's head. "He said what I had done was the worst thing he had seen in 50 years in the business," Dunn said. "Just to placate these crazy leftist school districts who were trying to keep people from having their Coke. He said I was an embarrassment to the company, and I should be fired." In February 2004, he was.

Dunn told me that talking about Coke's business today was by no means easy and, because he continues to work in the food business, not without risk.

"You really don't want them mad at you," he said. "And I don't mean that, like, I'm going to end up at the bottom of the bay. But they don't have a sense of humor when it comes to this stuff. They're a very, very aggressive company."

When I met with Dunn, he told me not just about his years at Coke but also about his new marketing venture. In April 2010, he met with three executives from Madison Dearborn Partners, a private-equity firm based in Chicago with a wide-ranging portfolio of investments. They recently hired Dunn to run one of their newest acquisitions—a food producer in the San Joaquin Valley. As they sat in the hotel's meeting room, the men listened to Dunn's marketing pitch. He talked about giving the product a personality that was bold and irreverent, conveying the idea that this was the ultimate snack food. He went into detail on how he would target a special segment of the 146 million Americans who are regular snackers—mothers, children, young professionals—people, he said, who "keep their snacking ritual fresh by trying a new food product when it catches their attention."

He explained how he would deploy strategic storytelling in the ad campaign for this snack, using a key phrase that had been developed with much calculation: "Eat 'Em Like Junk Food."

After 45 minutes, Dunn clicked off the last slide and thanked the men for coming. Madison's portfolio contained the largest Burger King franchise in the world, the Ruth's Chris Steak House chain and a processed-food maker called AdvancePierre whose lineup includes the Jamwich, a peanut-butter-and-jelly contrivance that comes frozen, crustless and embedded with four kinds of sugars.

The snack that Dunn was proposing to sell: carrots. Plain, fresh carrots. No added sugar. No creamy sauce or dips. No salt. Just baby carrots, washed, bagged, then sold into the deadly dull produce aisle.

"We act like a snack, not a vegetable," he told the investors. "We exploit the rules of junk food to fuel the baby-carrot conversation. We are pro-junk-food behavior but anti-junk-food establishment."

The investors were thinking only about sales. They had already bought one of the two biggest farm producers of baby carrots in the country, and they'd hired Dunn to run the whole operation. Now, after his pitch, they were relieved. Dunn had figured out that using the industry's own marketing ploys would work better than anything else. He drew from the bag of tricks that he mastered in his 20 years at Coca-Cola, where he learned one of the most critical rules in processed food: The selling of food matters as much as the food itself.

Later, describing his new line of work, Dunn told me he was doing penance for his Coca-Cola years. "I'm paying my karmic debt," he said.

QUESTIONS FOR MAKING CONNECTIONS
WITHIN THE READING

1. In the course of Moss's reporting, we meet executives and scientists who try to reform the food industry: James Behnke, Michael Mudd, Robert Lin, and Jeffrey Dunn. Why have their efforts proven to be largely unsuccessful? Does

their failure indicate that the problem with the food industry cannot be corrected or even explained by pointing to "bad people," individuals who make personal decisions? If the problem really lies with the system as a whole, does Moss regard personal responsibility as irrelevant? In what ways does his account suggest that individuals have the capacity to make a genuine difference? How did the reformers come to change their minds? Does Moss's narrative suggest that change is now taking place, and if so, what factors might explain why?

2.   The last executive interviewed by Moss is Jeffrey Dunn of Coca Cola, who eventually lost his job as the company's president and chief operating officer because he made an effort to curtail the sales of soft drinks in the public schools. At the close of the article we learn that Dunn has tried to pay his "karmic debt" by promoting baby carrots as a healthy snack, now marketed with the slogan, "Eat 'Em Like Junk Food." Does a shift from junk food to healthier items solve the larger problems suggested by Moss's article? Does the new slogan really help to change the culture of consumption created by junk food marketers? Will Dunn's initiative bring about a change in the system itself?

3.   How do corporations work? Use Moss's article to explain the corporate culture of the food industry. What factors shape its thinking and behavior? How does it conceive of its relationship to its customers? What forms of knowledge does it employ to achieve its ends, and what mechanisms does it use to communicate with the general public? Based on the evidence, would you say that the food industry exists to *meet* our needs, or does it actively *create* them? Would you describe the industry's influence as beneficial, benign, coercive, deceptive? When you finished reading Moss's article, were you surprised, offended, alarmed? Why might some readers have no reaction? Does Moss's article give any hints as to why the narrative he relates might simply seem like business as usual?

QUESTIONS FOR WRITING

1.   What lessons can be learned from Moss's article about the relations between the general public and specialists? Many of the specialists interviewed by Moss, including the legendary Howard Moskowitz, do their work with a high degree of intelligence, creativity, and professionalism, yet the larger enterprise they contribute to may do damage they largely ignore or never recognize at all. In what ways might the food industry illuminate the problems with specialization? On the basis of your reading of this article, would you say that professionals in every field have a responsibility to think about the social impacts of their work? Does education overemphasize specialization at the expense of other forms of understanding and development?

2.   Where should we draw the line between addictions and genuine needs? Is the difference a matter of degree—how much we consume—or is the

defining element our inability to control our appetites? Or could it be that the word *addiction* refers to a particular social relationship connecting addicts to their pushers, or users to their enablers? Building on Moss, explore the possibility that addiction is indeed a form of social interaction. If addiction is social in this way, are addicts individually to blame for their lack of self-control? Does Moss's work on the food industry suggest that ending addiction means imposing restraints on the supplier? To what extent does our whole economy—not only in the food sector but in electronics and other areas—actively encourage addiction?

QUESTIONS FOR MAKING CONNECTIONS
BETWEEN READINGS

1. Both Moss and Susan Faludi in *The Naked Citadel* shine a light on tensions inside communities that have become isolated from the larger outside world. The Citadel, according to Faludi, is an island of male privilege at a time when women have come closer to equality almost everywhere else, but, perhaps surprisingly, the food industry might also be described as insular and increasingly at odds with the values of the larger public. No less than The Citadel, the food industry appears to be unwelcoming to agents of change who have tried to bring new values from outside. Even though the word *community* normally carries positive connotations, the two authors might be used to explore the ways in which communities become destructive or stultifying. What benefits do we derive from our communities, and what potential problems do they create? Can the strengths of a community also become its greatest weakness?

2. Moss quotes from a 2004 talk given by Malcolm Gladwell, who is also the author of "The Power of Context." In his talk Gladwell celebrates the skill of food scientist Howard Moskowitz in establishing the "bliss point" that would boost the sales of Prego spaghetti sauce. The term *bliss point* in Gladwell's talk sounds very much like the *tipping point* that he invokes in his discussion of context. Does Gladwell appear to overlook the potential for mass manipulation in the findings of psychologists? Does his excitement over the new research cause him to disregard the ethical dimension? What role do ethical considerations play in Gladwell's argument about the primacy of context over individual choice?

AZAR NAFISI

AZAR NAFISI ROSE to international prominence in 2003 with the publication of her critically acclaimed bestseller, *Reading Lolita in Tehran: A Memoir in Books*. A professor of aesthetics, culture, and literature, Dr. Nafisi was expelled from the University of Tehran in 1981 for refusing to comply with the Ayatollah Khomeini's mandate that women wear the *chador,* or Muslim veil. Nafisi resumed teaching in 1987, but resigned eight years later in protest over the Iranian government's increasingly harsh treatment of women. *Reading Lolita in Tehran* provides an account of the seminar that Nafisi then went on to hold in her home from 1995 to 1997, in which seven of her best students joined her to discuss some of the classic texts of Western literature. Nafisi saw the change in her circumstances as an opportunity to fulfill a dream of working with "a group of students who just love literature, who are in it not for the grades, not just to graduate and get a job but just want to read Nabokov and Austen." That Nafisi and her students persisted in this activity, despite the obvious dangers it posed, has come to symbolize for readers around the world how the struggle against totalitarianism is waged on the level of everyday human experience.

Nafisi is no stranger to politics, or to political repression. Her mother was one of the first women to serve in the Iranian parliament, while her father, appointed by the Shah to serve as Tehran's mayor, was later jailed when he fell from favor. Currently Nafisi is the Executive Director of Cultural Conversations and a Visiting Professor at the Johns Hopkins University's Paul H. Nitze School of Advanced International Studies in Washington, D.C. Until 2008 she directed the Dialogue Project, "a multiyear initiative designed to promote—in a primarily cultural context—the development of democracy and human rights in the Muslim world." For Nafisi, the freedom to talk and think together in small groups, in a context where the ideas raised and the topics of conversation are not determined in advance, is the litmus test for a true democracy. To engage in this act, she believes, is to embrace a shared humanity that extends beyond the boundaries of national and religious differences. More recently, she has begun to explore tyranny of another kind—not in a totalitarian state but in the habits of

Biographical information comes from Azar Nafisi's website at <http://azarnafisi.com/about-azar/>; the quotation about the Dialogue Project comes from <http://www.middle-east-studies.net/?page_id=1642>.

self-censorship and repression that are taught by the family. In *Things I Have Been Silent About: Memories of a Prodigal Daughter* (2008), Nafisi explores her complicated struggles with a mother whose overwhelming expectations virtually ensured that her daughter's future life would be successful but unhappy.

Selections from Reading Lolita in Tehran

A Memoir in Books

1. In the fall of 1995, after resigning from my last academic post, I decided to indulge myself and fulfill a dream. I chose seven of my best and most committed students and invited them to come to my home every Thursday morning to discuss literature. They were all women—to teach a mixed class in the privacy of my home was too risky, even if we were discussing harmless works of fiction. One persistent male student, although barred from our class, insisted on his rights. So he, Nima, read the assigned material, and on special days he would come to my house to talk about the books we were reading.

I often teasingly reminded my students of Muriel Spark's The *Prime of Miss Jean Brodie* and asked, Which one of you will finally betray me? For I am a pessimist by nature and I was sure at least one would turn against me. Nassrin once responded mischievously, You yourself told us that in the final analysis we are our own betrayers, playing Judas to our own Christ. Manna pointed out that I was no Miss Brodie, and they, well, they were what they were. She reminded me of a warning I was fond of repeating: *do not*, under *any* circumstances, belittle a work of fiction by trying to turn it into a carbon copy of real life; what we search for in fiction is not so much reality but the epiphany of truth. Yet I suppose that if I were to go against my own recommendation and choose a work of fiction that would most resonate with our lives in the Islamic Republic of Iran, it would not be *The Prime of Miss Jean Brodie* or even *1984* but perhaps Nabokov's *Invitation to a Beheading* or better yet, *Lolita*.

A couple of years after we had begun our Thursday-morning seminars, on the last night I was in Tehran, a few friends and students came to say good-bye and to help me pack. When we had deprived the house of all its items, when the objects had vanished and the colors had faded into eight gray suitcases, like errant genies evaporating into their bottles, my students and I stood against the bare white wall of the dining room and took two photographs.

I have the two photographs in front of me now. In the first there are seven women, standing against a white wall. They are, according to the law of the land, dressed in black robes and head scarves, covered except for the oval of their faces and their hands. In the second photograph the same group, in the same position, stands against the same wall. Only they have taken off their coverings. Splashes of color separate one from the next. Each has become distinct through the color and style of her clothes, the color and the length of her hair; not even the two who are still wearing their head scarves look the same.

The one to the far right in the second photograph is our poet, Manna, in a white T-shirt and jeans. She made poetry out of things most people cast aside. The photograph does not reflect the peculiar opacity of Manna's dark eyes, a testament to her withdrawn and private nature.

Next to Manna is Mahshid, whose long black scarf clashes with her delicate features and retreating smile. Mahshid was good at many things, but she had a certain daintiness about her and we took to calling her "my lady." Nassrin used to say that more than defining Mahshid, we had managed to add another dimension to the word *lady*. Mahshid is very sensitive. She's like porcelain, Yassi once told me, easy to crack. That's why she appears fragile to those who don't know her too well; but woe to whoever offends her. As for me, Yassi continued good-naturedly, I'm like good old plastic; I won't crack no matter what you do with me.

Yassi was the youngest in our group. She is the one in yellow, bending forward and bursting with laughter. We used to teasingly call her our comedian. Yassi was shy by nature, but certain things excited her and made her lose her inhibitions. She had a tone of voice that gently mocked and questioned not just others but herself as well.

I am the one in brown, standing next to Yassi, with one arm around her shoulders. Directly behind me stands Azin, my tallest student, with her long blond hair and a pink T-shirt. She is laughing like the rest of us. Azin's smiles never looked like smiles; they appeared more like preludes to an irrepressible and nervous hilarity. She beamed in that peculiar fashion even when she was describing her latest trouble with her husband. Always outrageous and outspoken, Azin relished the shock value of her actions and comments, and often clashed with Mahshid and Manna. We nicknamed her the wild one.

On my other side is Mitra, who was perhaps the calmest among us. Like the pastel colors of her paintings, she seemed to recede and fade into a paler register. Her beauty was saved from predictability by a pair of miraculous dimples, which she could and did use to manipulate many an unsuspecting victim into bending to her will.

Sanaz, who, pressured by family and society, vacillated between her desire for independence and her need for approval, is holding on to Mitra's arm. We are all laughing. And Nima, Manna's husband and my one true literary critic—if only he had had the perseverance to finish the brilliant essays he started to write—is our invisible partner, the photographer.

There was one more: Nassrin. She is not in the photographs—she didn't make it to the end. Yet my tale would be incomplete without those who could not or did not remain with us. Their absences persist, like an acute pain that seems to have no physical source. This is Tehran for me: its absences were more real than its presences.

When I see Nassrin in my mind's eye, she's slightly out of focus, blurred, somehow distant. I've combed through the photographs my students took with me over the years and Nassrin is in many of them, but always hidden behind something—a person, a tree. In one, I am standing with eight of my students in the small garden facing our faculty building, the scene of so many farewell photographs over the years. In the background stands a sheltering willow tree. We are laughing, and in one corner, from behind the tallest student, Nassrin peers out, like an imp intruding roguishly on a scene it was not invited to. In another I can barely make out her face in the small V space behind two other girls' shoulders. In this one she looks absentminded; she is frowning, as if unaware that she is being photographed.

How can I describe Nassrin? I once called her the Cheshire cat, appearing and disappearing at unexpected turns in my academic life. The truth is I can't describe her: she was her own definition. One can only say that Nassrin was Nassrin.

For nearly two years, almost every Thursday morning, rain or shine, they came to my house, and almost every time, I could not get over the shock of seeing them shed their mandatory veils and robes and burst into color. When my students came into that room, they took off more than their scarves and robes. Gradually, each one gained an outline and a shape, becoming her own inimitable self. Our world in that living room with its window framing my beloved Elburz Mountains became our sanctuary, our self-contained universe, mocking the reality of black-scarved, timid faces in the city that sprawled below.

The theme of the class was the relation between fiction and reality. We read Persian classical literature, such as the tales of our own lady of fiction, Scheherazade, from *A Thousand and One Nights,* along with Western classics—*Pride and Prejudice, Madame Bovary, Daisy Miller, The Dean's December* and, yes, *Lolita*. As I write the title of each book, memories whirl in with the wind to disturb the quiet of this fall day in another room in another country.

Here and now in that other world that cropped up so many times in our discussions, I sit and reimagine myself and my students, my girls as I came to call them, reading *Lolita* in a deceptively sunny room in Tehran. But to steal the words from Humbert, the poet/criminal of *Lolita*, I need you, the reader, to imagine us, for we won't really exist if you don't. Against the tyranny of time and politics, imagine us the way we sometimes didn't dare to imagine ourselves: in our most private and secret moments, in the most extraordinarily ordinary instances of life, listening to music, falling in love, walking down the shady streets or reading *Lolita* in Tehran. And then imagine us again with all this confiscated, driven underground, taken away from us.

If I write about Nabokov today, it is to celebrate our reading of Nabokov in Tehran, against all odds. Of all his novels I choose the one I taught last, and the one that is connected to so many memories. It is of *Lolita* that I want to write, but right now there is no way I can write about that novel without also writing about Tehran. This, then, is the story of *Lolita* in Tehran, how *Lolita* gave a different color to Tehran, and how Tehran helped redefine Nabokov's novel, turning it into this *Lolita,* our *Lolita*.

2.   And so it happened that one Thursday in early September we gathered in my living room for our first meeting. Here they come, one more time. First I hear the bell, a pause, and the closing of the street door. Then I hear footsteps coming up the winding staircase and past my mother's apartment. As I move towards the front door, I register a piece of sky through the side window. Each girl, as soon as she reaches the door, takes off her robe and scarf, sometimes shaking her head from side to side. She pauses before entering the room. Only there is no room, just the teasing void of memory.

More than any other place in our home, the living room was symbolic of my nomadic and borrowed life. Vagrant pieces of furniture from different times and places were thrown together, partly out of financial necessity, and partly because of my eclectic taste. Oddly, these incongruous ingredients created a symmetry that the other, more deliberately furnished rooms in the apartment lacked.

My mother would go crazy each time she saw the paintings leaning against the wall and the vases of flowers on the floor and the curtainless windows, which I refused to dress until I was finally reminded that this was an Islamic country and windows needed to be dressed. I don't know if you really belong to me, she would lament. Didn't I raise you to be orderly and organized? Her tone was serious, but she had repeated the same complaint for so many years that by now it was an almost tender ritual. Azi—that was my nickname—Azi, she would say, you are a grown-up lady now; act like one. Yet there was something in her tone that kept me young and fragile and obstinate, and still, when in memory I hear her voice, I know I never lived up to her expectations. I never did become the lady she tried to will me into being.

That room, which I never paid much attention to at that time, has gained a different status in my mind's eye now that it has become the precious object of memory. It was a spacious room, sparsely furnished and decorated. At one corner was the fireplace, a fanciful creation of my husband, Bijan. There was a love seat against one wall, over which I had thrown a lace cover, my mother's gift from long ago. A pale peach couch faced the window, accompanied by two matching chairs and a big square glass-topped iron table.

My place was always in the chair with its back to the window, which opened onto a wide cul-de-sac called Azar. Opposite the window was the former American Hospital, once small and exclusive, now a noisy, overcrowded medical facility for wounded and disabled veterans of the war. On "weekends"— Thursdays and Fridays in Iran—the small street was crowded with hospital visitors who came as if for a picnic, with sandwiches and children. The neighbor's front yard, his pride and joy, was the main victim of their assaults, especially in summer, when they helped themselves to his beloved roses. We could hear the sound of children shouting, crying and laughing, and, mingled in, their mothers' voices, also shouting, calling out their children's names and threatening them with punishments. Sometimes a child or two would ring our doorbell and run away, repeating their perilous exercise at intervals.

From our second-story apartment—my mother occupied the first floor, and my brother's apartment, on the third floor, was often empty, since he had left for England—we could see the upper branches of a generous tree and, in the distance, over the buildings, the Elburz Mountains. The street, the hospital and its visitors were censored out of sight. We felt their presence only through the disembodied noises emanating from below.

I could not see my favorite mountains from where I sat, but opposite my chair, on the far wall of the dining room, was an antique oval mirror, a gift from my father, and in its reflection, I could see the mountains capped with snow, even in summer, and watch the trees change color. That censored view intensified my impression that the noise came not from the street below but from some far-off place, a place whose persistent hum was our only link to the world we refused, for those few hours, to acknowledge.

That room, for all of us, became a place of transgression. What a wonderland it was! Sitting around the large coffee table covered with bouquets of flowers, we moved in and out of the novels we read. Looking back, I am amazed at how much we learned without even noticing it. We were, to borrow from Nabokov, to experience how the ordinary pebble of ordinary life could be transformed into a jewel through the magic eye of fiction.

3. Six A.M.: the first day of class. I was already up. Too excited to eat breakfast, I put the coffee on and then took a long, leisurely shower. The water caressed my neck, my back, my legs, and I stood there both rooted and light. For the first time in many years, I felt a sense of anticipation that was not marred by tension: I would not need to go through the torturous rituals that had marked my days when I taught at the university—rituals governing what I was forced to wear, how I was expected to act, the gestures I had to remember to control. For this class, I would prepare differently.

Life in the Islamic Republic was as capricious as the month of April, when short periods of sunshine would suddenly give way to showers and storms. It was unpredictable: the regime would go through cycles of some tolerance, followed by a crackdown. Now, after a period of relative calm and so-called liberalization, we had again entered a time of hardships. Universities had once more become the targets of attack by the cultural purists who were busy imposing stricter sets of laws, going so far as to segregate men and women in classes and punishing disobedient professors.

The University of Allameh Tabatabai, where I had been teaching since 1987, had been singled out as the most liberal university in Iran. It was rumored that someone in the Ministry of Higher Education had asked, rhetorically, if the faculty at Allameh thought they lived in Switzerland. *Switzerland* had somehow become a byword for Western laxity: any program or action that was deemed un-Islamic was reproached with a mocking reminder that Iran was by no means Switzerland.

The pressure was hardest on the students. I felt helpless as I listened to their endless tales of woe. Female students were being penalized for running up the stairs when they were late for classes, for laughing in the hallways, for talking to members of the opposite sex. One day Sanaz had barged into class near the end of the session, crying. In between bursts of tears, she explained that she was late because the female guards at the door, finding a blush in her bag, had tried to send her home with a reprimand.

Why did I stop teaching so suddenly? I had asked myself this question many times. Was it the declining quality of the university? The ever-increasing indifference among the remaining faculty and students? The daily struggle against arbitrary rules and restrictions?

I smiled as I rubbed the coarse loofah over my skin, remembering the reaction of the university officials to my letter of resignation. They had harassed and limited me in all manner of ways, monitoring my visitors, controlling my actions, refusing a long-overdue tenure; and when I resigned, they infuriated me by suddenly commiserating and by refusing to accept my resignation. The students had threatened to boycott classes, and it was of some satisfaction to me to find out later that despite threats of reprisals, they in fact did boycott my replacement. Everyone thought I would break down and eventually return.

It took two more years before they finally accepted my resignation. I remember a friend told me, You don't understand their mentality. They won't accept your resignation because they don't think you have the right to quit. *They* are the ones who decide how long you should stay and when you should be dispensed with. More than anything else, it was this arbitrariness that had become unbearable.

What will you do? my friends had asked. Will you just stay home now? Well, I could write another book, I would tell them. But in truth I had no definite plans. I was still dealing with the aftershocks of a book on Nabokov I had just published, and only vague ideas, like vapors, formed when I turned to consider the shape of my next book. I could, for a while at least, continue the pleasant task of studying Persian classics, but one particular project, a notion I had been nurturing for years, was uppermost in my mind. For a long time I had dreamt of creating a special class, one that would give me the freedoms denied me in the classes I taught in the Islamic Republic. I wanted to teach a handful of selected students wholly committed to the study of literature, students who were not handpicked by the government, who had not chosen English literature simply because they had not been accepted in other fields or because they thought an English degree would be a good career move.

Teaching in the Islamic Republic, like any other vocation, was subservient to politics and subject to arbitrary rules. Always, the joy of teaching was marred by diversions and considerations forced on us by the regime—how well could one teach when the main concern of university officials was not the quality of one's work but the color of one's lips, the subversive potential of a single strand of hair? Could one really concentrate on one's job when what preoccupied the faculty was how to excise the word *wine* from a Hemingway story, when they decided not to teach Brontë because she appeared to condone adultery?

I was reminded of a painter friend who had started her career by depicting scenes from life, mainly deserted rooms, abandoned houses, and discarded photographs of women. Gradually, her work became more abstract, and in her last exhibition, her paintings were splashes of rebellious color, like the two in my living room, dark patches with little droplets of blue. I asked about her progress from modern realism to abstraction. Reality has become so intolerable, she said, so bleak, that all I can paint now are the colors of my dreams.

The colors of my dreams, I repeated to myself, stepping out of the shower and onto the cool tiles. I liked that. How many people get a chance to paint the colors of their dreams? I put on my oversize bathrobe—it felt good to move from the security of the embracing water to the protective cover of a bathrobe wrapped around my body. I walked barefoot into the kitchen, poured some coffee into my favorite mug, the one with red strawberries, and sat down forgetfully on the divan in the hall.

This class was the color of my dreams. It entailed an active withdrawal from a reality that had turned hostile. I wanted very badly to hold on to my rare mood of jubilance and optimism. For in the back of my mind, I didn't know what awaited me at the end of this project. You are aware, a friend had said, that you are more and more withdrawing into yourself, and now that you have cut your relations with the university, your whole contact with the outside world will be mainly restricted to one room. Where will you go from here? he had asked. Withdrawal into one's dreams could be dangerous, I reflected, padding into the bedroom to change; this I had learned from Nabokov's crazy dreamers, like Kinbote and Humbert.

In selecting my students, I did not take into consideration their ideological or religious backgrounds. Later, I would count it as the class's great achievement that such a mixed group, with different and at times conflicting backgrounds, personal as well as religious and social, remained so loyal to its goals and ideals.

One reason for my choice of these particular girls was the peculiar mixture of fragility and courage I sensed in them. They were what you would call loners, who did not belong to any particular group or sect. I admired their ability to survive not despite but in some ways because of their solitary lives. We can call the class "a space of our own," Manna had suggested, a sort of communal version of Virginia Woolf's room of her own.

I spent longer than usual choosing my clothes that first morning, trying on different outfits, until I finally settled on a red-striped shirt and black corduroy jeans. I applied my makeup with care and put on bright red lipstick. As I fastened my small gold earrings, I suddenly panicked. What if it doesn't work? What if they won't come?

Don't, don't do that! Suspend all fears for the next five or six hours at least. Please, please, I pleaded with myself, putting on my shoes and going into the kitchen.

4. I was making tea when the doorbell rang. I was so preoccupied with my thoughts that I didn't hear it the first time. I opened the door to Mahshid. I thought you weren't home, she said, handing me a bouquet of white and yellow daffodils. As she was taking off her black robe, I told her, There are no men in the house—you can take that off, too. She hesitated before uncoiling her long black scarf. Mahshid and Yassi both observed the veil, but Yassi of late had become more relaxed in the way she wore her scarf. She tied it with a loose knot under her throat, her dark brown hair, untidily parted in the middle, peeping out from underneath. Mahshid's hair, however, was meticulously styled and curled under. Her short bangs gave her a strangely old-fashioned look that struck me as more European than Iranian. She wore a deep blue jacket over her white shirt, with a huge yellow butterfly embroidered on its right side. I pointed to the butterfly: did you wear this in honor of Nabokov?

I no longer remember when Mahshid first began to take my classes at the university. Somehow, it seems as if she had always been there. Her father, a devout Muslim, had been an ardent supporter of the revolution. She wore the scarf even before the revolution, and in her class diary, she wrote about the lonely mornings when she went to a fashionable girls' college, where she felt neglected and ignored—ironically, because of her then-conspicuous attire. After the revolution, she was jailed for five years because of her affiliation with a dissident religious organization and banned from continuing her education for two years after she was out of jail.

I imagine her in those pre-revolutionary days, walking along the uphill street leading to the college on countless sunny mornings. I see her walking alone, her head to the ground. Then, as now, she did not enjoy the day's brilliance. I say "then, as now" because the revolution that imposed the scarf on others did not relieve Mahshid of her loneliness. Before the revolution, she could in a sense take pride in her isolation. At that time, she had worn the scarf as a testament to her faith. Her decision was a voluntary act. When the revolution forced the scarf on others, her action became meaningless.

Mahshid is proper in the true sense of the word: she has grace and a certain dignity. Her skin is the color of moonlight, and she has almond-shaped eyes and jet-black hair. She wears pastel colors and is soft-spoken. Her pious background should have shielded her, but it didn't. I cannot imagine her in jail.

Over the many years I have known Mahshid, she has rarely alluded to her jail experiences, which left her with a permanently impaired kidney. One day in class, as we were talking about our daily terrors and nightmares, she mentioned that her jail memories visited her from time to time and that she had still not found a way to articulate them. But, she added, everyday life does not have fewer horrors than prison.

I asked Mahshid if she wanted some tea. Always considerate, she said she'd rather wait for the others and apologized for being a little early. Can I help? she asked. There's really nothing to help with. Make yourself at home, I told her as I stepped into the kitchen with the flowers and searched for a vase. The bell rang again. I'll get it, Mahshid cried out from the living room. I heard laughter; Manna and Yassi had arrived.

Manna came into the kitchen holding a small bouquet of roses. It's from Nima, she said. He wants to make you feel bad about excluding him from the class. He says he'll carry a bouquet of roses and march in front of your house during class hours, in protest. She was beaming; a few brief sparkles flashed in her eyes and died down again.

Putting the pastries onto a large tray, I asked Manna if she envisioned the words to her poems in colors. Nabokov writes in his autobiography that he and his mother saw the letters of the alphabet in color, I explained. He says of himself that he is a painterly writer.

The Islamic Republic coarsened my taste in colors, Manna said, fingering the discarded leaves of her roses. I want to wear outrageous colors, like shocking pink or tomato red. I feel too greedy for colors to see them in carefully chosen words of poetry. Manna was one of those people who would experience ecstasy but not happiness. Come here, I want to show you something, I said, leading her into our bedroom. When I was very young, I was obsessed with the colors of places and things my father told me about in his nightly stories. I wanted to know the color of Scheherazade's dress, her bedcover, the color of the genie and the magic lamp, and once I asked him about the color of paradise. He said it could be any color I wanted it to be. That was not enough. Then one day when we had guests and I was eating my soup in the dining room, my eyes fell on a painting I had seen on the wall ever since I could remember, and I instantly knew the color of my paradise. And here it is, I said, proudly pointing to a small oil painting in an old wooden frame: a green landscape of lush, leathery leaves with two birds, two deep red apples, a golden pear and a touch of blue.

My paradise is swimming-pool blue! Manna shot in, her eyes still glued to the painting. We lived in a large garden that belonged to my grandparents, she said, turning to me. You know the old Persian gardens, with their fruit trees, peaches, apples, cherries, persimmons and a willow or two. My best memories are of swimming in our huge irregularly shaped swimming pool. I was a swimming champion at our school, a fact my dad was very proud of. About a year after the revolution, my father died of a heart attack, and then the government confiscated our house and our garden and we moved into an apartment. I never swam again. My dream is at the bottom of that pool. I have a recurring dream of diving in to retrieve something of my father's memory and my childhood, she said as we walked to the living room, for the doorbell had rung again.

Azin and Mitra had arrived together. Azin was taking off her black kimono-like robe—Japanese-style robes were all the rage at the time—revealing a white peasant blouse that made no pretense of covering her shoulders, big golden earrings and pink lipstick. She had a branch of small yellow orchids— from Mitra and myself, she said in that special tone of hers that I can only describe as a flirtatious pout.

Nassrin came in next. She had brought two boxes of nougats: presents from Isfahan, she declared. She was dressed in her usual uniform—navy robe, navy scarf and black heelless shoes. When I had last seen her in class, she was wearing a huge black chador, revealing only the oval of her face and two restless hands, which, when she was not writing or doodling, were constantly in motion, as if trying to escape the confines of the thick black cloth. More recently, she had exchanged the chador for long, shapeless robes in navy, black or dark brown, with thick matching scarves that hid her hair and framed her face. She had a small, pale face, skin so transparent you could count the veins, full eyebrows, long lashes, lively eyes (brown), a small straight nose and an angry mouth: an unfinished miniature by some master who had suddenly been called away from his job and left the meticulously drawn face imprisoned in a careless splash of dark color.

We heard the sound of screeching tires and sudden brakes. I looked out the window: a small old Renault, cream-colored, had pulled up on the curb. Behind the wheel, a young man with fashionable sunglasses and a defiant profile rested his black-sleeved arm on the curve of the open window and gave the impression that he was driving a Porsche. He was staring straight in front of him as he talked to the woman beside him. Only once did he turn his head to his right, with what I could guess was a cross expression, and that was when the woman got out of the car and he angrily slammed the door behind her. As she walked to our front door, he threw his head out and shouted a few words, but she did not turn back to answer. The old Renault was Sanaz's; she had bought it with money saved from her job.

I turned towards the room, blushing for Sanaz. That must be the obnoxious brother, I thought. Seconds later the doorbell rang and I heard Sanaz's hurried steps and opened the door to her. She looked harassed, as if she had been running from a stalker or a thief. As soon as she saw me, she adjusted her face into a smile and said breathlessly: I hope I am not too late?

There were two very important men dominating Sanaz's life at the time. The first was her brother. He was nineteen years old and had not yet finished high school and was the darling of their parents, who, after two girls, one of whom had died at the age of three, had finally been blessed with a son. He was spoiled, and his one obsession in life was Sanaz. He had taken to proving his masculinity by spying on her, listening to her phone conversations, driving her car around, and monitoring her actions. Her parents had tried to appease Sanaz and begged her, as the older sister, to be patient and understanding, to use her motherly instincts to see him through this difficult period.

The other was her childhood sweetheart, a boy she had known since she was eleven. Their parents were best friends, and their families spent most of their time and vacations together. Sanaz and Ali seemed to have been in love forever. Their parents encouraged this union and called it a match made in heaven. When Ali went away to England six years ago, his mother took to calling Sanaz his bride. They wrote to each other, sent photographs, and recently, when the number of Sanaz's suitors increased, there were talks of engagement and a reunion in Turkey, where Iranians did not require entrance visas. Any day now it might happen, an event Sanaz looked forward to with some fear and trepidation.

I had never seen Sanaz without her uniform, and stood there almost transfixed as she took off her robe and scarf. She was wearing an orange T-shirt tucked into tight jeans and brown boots, yet the most radical transformation was the mass of shimmering dark brown hair that now framed her face. She shook her magnificent hair from side to side, a gesture that I later noticed was a habit with her; she would toss her head and run her fingers through her hair every once in a while, as if making sure that her most prized possession was still there. Her features looked softer and more radiant—the black scarf she wore in public made her small face look emaciated and almost hard.

I'm sorry I'm a little late, she said breathlessly, running her fingers through her hair. My brother insisted on driving me, and he refused to wake up on time. He never gets up before ten, but he wanted to know where I was going. I might be off on some secret tryst, you know, a date or something.

I have been worrying in case any of you would get into trouble for this class, I said, inviting them all to take their seats around the table in the living room. I hope your parents and spouses feel comfortable with our arrangement.

Nassrin, who was wandering around the room, inspecting the paintings as if seeing them for the first time, paused to say offhandedly, I mentioned the idea very casually to my father, just to test his reaction, and he vehemently disapproved.

How did you convince him to let you come? I asked. I lied, she said. You lied? What else can one do with a person who's so dictatorial he won't let his daughter, at *this age*, go to an all-female literature class? Besides, isn't this how we treat the regime? Can we tell the Revolutionary Guards the truth? We lie to them; we hide our satellite dishes. We tell them we don't have illegal books and alcohol in our houses. Even my venerable father lies to them when the safety of his family is at stake, Nassrin added defiantly.

What if he calls me to check on you? I said, half teasingly. He won't. I gave a brilliant alibi. I said Mahshid and I had volunteered to help translate Islamic texts into English. And he believed you? Well, he had no reason not to. I hadn't lied to him before—not really—and it was what he wanted to believe. And he trusts Mahshid completely.

So if he calls me, I should lie to him? I persisted. It's up to you, Nassrin said after a pause, looking down at her twisting hands. Do *you* think you should tell him? By now I could hear a note of desperation in her voice. Am I getting you into trouble?

Nassrin always acted so confident that sometimes I forgot how vulnerable she really was under that tough-girl act. Of course I would respect your confidence, I said more gently. As you said, you are a big girl. You know what you're doing.

I had settled into my usual chair, opposite the mirror, where the mountains had come to stay. It is strange to look into a mirror and see not yourself but a view so distant from you. Mahshid, after some hesitation, had taken the chair to my right. On the couch, Manna settled to the far right and Azin to the far left; they instinctively kept their distance. Sanaz and Mitra were perched on the love seat, their heads close together as they whispered and giggled.

At this point Yassi and Nassrin came in and looked around for seats. Azin patted the empty part of the couch, inviting Yassi with her hand. Yassi hesitated for a moment and then slid between Azin and Manna. She slumped into place and seemed to leave little room for her two companions, who sat upright and a little stiff in their respective corners. Without her robe, she looked a little overweight, as if she had not as yet lost her baby fat. Nassrin had gone to the dining room in search of a chair. We can squeeze you in here, said Manna. No, thank you, I actually prefer straight-backed chairs. When she returned, she placed her chair between the couch and Mahshid.

They kept that arrangement, faithfully, to the end. It became representative of their emotional boundaries and personal relations. And so began our first class.

5.   "Upsilamba!" I heard Yassi exclaim as I entered the dining room with a tray of tea. Yassi loved playing with words. Once she told us that her obsession with words was pathological. As soon as I discover a new word, I have to use it, she said, like someone who buys an evening gown and is so eager that she wears it to the movies, or to lunch.

Let me pause and rewind the reel to retrace the events leading us to Yassi's exclamation. This was our first session. All of us had been nervous and inarticulate. We were used to meeting in public, mainly in classrooms and in lecture halls. The girls had their separate relationships with me, but except for Nassrin and Mahshid, who were intimate, and a certain friendship between Mitra and Sanaz, the rest were not close; in many cases, in fact, they would never have chosen to be friends. The collective intimacy made them uncomfortable.

I had explained to them the purpose of the class: to read, discuss, and respond to works of fiction. Each would have a private diary, in which she should record her responses to the novels, as well as ways in which these works and their discussions related to her personal and social experiences. I explained that I had chosen them for this class because they seemed dedicated to the study of literature. I mentioned that one of the criteria for the books I had chosen was their authors' faith in the critical and almost magical power of literature, and reminded them of the nineteen-year-old Nabokov, who, during the Russian Revolution, would not allow himself to be diverted by the sound of bullets. He kept on writing his solitary poems while he heard the guns and saw the bloody fights from his window. Let us see, I said, whether seventy years later our disinterested faith will reward us by transforming the gloomy reality created of this other revolution.

The first work we discussed was *A Thousand and One Nights*, the familiar tale of the cuckolded king who slew successive virgin wives as revenge for his queen's betrayal, and whose murderous hand was finally stayed by the entrancing storyteller Scheherazade. I formulated certain general questions for them to consider, the most central of which was how these great works of imagination could help us in our present trapped situation as women. We were not looking for blueprints, for an easy solution, but we did hope to find a link between the open spaces the novels provided and the closed ones we were confined to. I remember reading to my girls Nabokov's claim that "readers were born free and ought to remain free."

What had most intrigued me about the frame story of *A Thousand and One Nights* were the three kinds of women it portrayed—all victims of a king's unreasonable rule. Before Scheherazade enters the scene, the women in the story are divided into those who betray and then are killed (the queen) and those who are killed before they have a chance to betray (the virgins). The virgins, who, unlike Scheherazade, have no voice in the story, are mostly ignored by the critics. Their silence, however, is significant. They surrender their virginity, and their lives, without resistance or protest. They do not quite exist, because they leave no trace in their anonymous death. The queen's infidelity does not rob the king of his absolute authority; it throws him off balance. Both types of women—the queen and the virgins—tacitly accept the king's public authority by acting within the confines of his domain and by accepting its arbitrary laws.

Scheherazade breaks the cycle of violence by choosing to embrace different terms of engagement. She fashions her universe not through physical force, as does the king, but through imagination and reflection. This gives her the courage to risk her life and sets her apart from the other characters in the tale.

Our edition of *A Thousand and One Nights* came in six volumes. I, luckily, had bought mine before it was banned and sold only on the black market, for exorbitant prices. I divided the volumes among the girls and asked them, for the next session, to classify the tales according to the types of women who played central roles in the stories.

Once I'd given them their assignment, I asked them each to tell the rest of us why they had chosen to spend their Thursday mornings here, discussing Nabokov and Jane Austen. Their answers were brief and forced. In order to break the ice, I suggested the calming distraction of cream puffs and tea.

This brings us to the moment when I enter the dining room with eight glasses of tea on an old and unpolished silver tray. Brewing and serving tea is an aesthetic ritual in Iran, performed several times a day. We serve tea in transparent glasses, small and shapely, the most popular of which is called slim-waisted: round and full at the top, narrow in the middle and round and full at the bottom. The color of the tea and its subtle aroma are an indication of the brewer's skill.

I step into the dining room with eight slim-waisted glasses whose honey-colored liquid trembles seductively. At this point, I hear Yassi shout triumphantly, "Upsilamba!" She throws the word at me like a ball, and I take a mental leap to catch it.

Upsilamba!—the word carries me back to the spring of 1994, when four of my girls and Nima were auditing a class I was teaching on the twentieth-century novel. The class's favorite book was Nabokov's *Invitation to a Beheading*. In this novel, Nabokov differentiates Cincinnatus C., his imaginative and lonely hero, from those around him through his originality in a society where uniformity is not only the norm but also the law. Even as a child, Nabokov tells us, Cincinnatus appreciated the freshness and beauty of language, while other children "understood each other at the first word, since they had no words that would end in an unexpected way, perhaps in some archaic letter, an upsilamba, becoming a bird or catapult with wondrous consequences."

No one in class had bothered to ask what the word meant. No one, that is, who was properly taking the class—for many of my old students just stayed on and sat in on my classes long after their graduation. Often, they were more interested and worked harder than my regular students, who were taking the class for credit. Thus it was that those who audited the class—including Nassrin, Manna, Nima, Mahshid, and Yassi—had one day gathered in my office to discuss this and a number of other questions.

I decided to play a little game with the class, to test their curiosity. On the midterm exam, one of the questions was "Explain the significance of the word *upsilamba* in the context of *Invitation to a Beheading*. What does the word mean, and how does it relate to the main theme of the novel?" Except for four or five students, no one had any idea what I could possibly mean, a point I did not forget to remind them of every once in a while throughout the rest of that term.

The truth was that *upsilamba* was one of Nabokov's fanciful creations, possibly a word he invented out of *upsilon*, the twentieth letter in the Greek alphabet, and *lambda*, the eleventh. So that first day in our private class, we let our minds play again and invented new meanings of our own.

I said I associated *upsilamba* with the impossible joy of a suspended leap. Yassi, who seemed excited for no particular reason, cried out that she always thought it could be the name of a dance—you know, "C'mon, baby, do the Upsilamba with me." I proposed that for the next time, they each write a sentence or two explaining what the word meant to them.

Manna suggested that *upsilamba* evoked the image of small silver fish leaping in and out of a moonlit lake. Nima added in parentheses, Just so you won't forget me, although you have barred me from your class: an upsilamba to you, too! For Azin it was a sound, a melody. Mahshid described an image of three girls jumping rope and shouting "Upsilamba!" with each leap. For Sanaz, the word was a small African boy's secret magical name. Mitra wasn't sure why the word reminded her of the paradox of a blissful sigh. And to Nassrin it was the magic code that opened the door to a secret cave filled with treasures.

Upsilamba became part of our increasing repository of coded words and expressions, a repository that grew over time until gradually we had created a secret language of our own. That word became a symbol, a sign of that vague sense of joy, the tingle in the spine Nabokov expected his readers to feel in the act of reading fiction; it was a sensation that separated the good readers, as he called them, from the ordinary ones. It also became the code word that opened the secret cave of remembrance.

6. In his foreword to the English edition of *Invitation to a Beheading* (1959), Nabokov reminds the reader that his novel does not offer *"tout pour tous."* Nothing of the kind. "It is," he claims, "a violin in the void." And yet, he goes on to say, "I know ... a few readers who will jump up, ruffling their hair." Well, absolutely. The original version, Nabokov tells us, was published in installments in 1935. Almost six decades later, in a world unknown and presumably unknowable to Nabokov, in a forlorn living room with windows looking out towards distant white-capped mountains, time and again I would stand witness to the unlikeliest of readers as they lost themselves in a madness of hair-ruffling.

Invitation to a Beheading begins with the announcement that its fragile hero, Cincinnatus C., has been sentenced to death for the crime of "gnostic turpitude": in a place where all citizens are required to be transparent, he is opaque. The principal characteristic of this world is its arbitrariness; the condemned man's only privilege is to know the time of his death—but the executioners keep even this from him, turning every day into a day of execution. As the story unfolds, the reader discovers with increasing discomfort the artificial texture of this strange place. The moon from the window is fake; so is the spider in the corner, which, according to convention, must become the prisoner's faithful companion. The director of the jail, the jailer, and the defense lawyer are all the same man, and keep changing places. The most important character, the executioner, is first introduced to the prisoner under another name and as a fellow prisoner: M'sieur Pierre. The executioner and the condemned man must learn to love each other and cooperate in the act of execution, which will be celebrated in a gaudy feast. In this staged world, Cincinnatus's only window to another universe is his writing.

The world of the novel is one of empty rituals. Every act is bereft of substance and significance, and even death becomes a spectacle for which the good citizens buy tickets. It is only through these empty rituals that brutality becomes possible. In another Nabokov novel, *The Real Life of Sebastian Knight*, Sebastian's brother discovers two seemingly incongruous pictures in his dead brother's library: a pretty, curly-haired child playing with a dog and a Chinese man in the act of being beheaded. The two pictures remind us of the close relation between banality and brutality. Nabokov had a special Russian term for this: *poshlust*.

Poshlust, Nabokov explains, "is not only the obviously trashy but mainly the falsely important, the falsely beautiful, the falsely clever, the falsely attractive." Yes, there are many examples you can bring from everyday life, from the politicians' sugary speeches to certain writers' proclamations to chickens. Chickens? You know, the ones the street vendors sell nowadays—if you lived in Tehran, you couldn't possibly miss them. The ones they dip in paint—shocking pink, brilliant red, or turquoise blue—in order to make them more attractive. Or the plastic flowers, the bright pink-and-blue artificial gladiolas carted out at the university both for mourning and for celebration.

What Nabokov creates for us in *Invitation to a Beheading* is not the actual physical pain and torture of a totalitarian regime but the nightmarish quality of living in an atmosphere of perpetual dread. Cincinnatus C. is frail, he is passive, he is a hero without knowing or acknowledging it: he fights with his instincts, and his acts of writing are his means of escape. He is a hero because he refuses to become like all the rest.

Unlike in other utopian novels, the forces of evil here are not omnipotent; Nabokov shows us their frailty as well. They are ridiculous and they can be defeated, and this does not lessen the tragedy—the waste. *Invitation to a Beheading* is written from the point of view of the victim, one who ultimately sees the absurd sham of his persecutors and who must retreat into himself in order to survive.

Those of us living in the Islamic Republic of Iran grasped both the tragedy and absurdity of the cruelty to which we were subjected. We had to poke fun at our own misery in order to survive. We also instinctively recognized poshlust—not just in others, but in ourselves. This was one reason that art and literature became so essential to our lives: they were not a luxury but a necessity. What Nabokov captured was the texture of life in a totalitarian society, where you are completely alone in an illusory world full of false promises, where you can no longer differentiate between your savior and your executioner.

We formed a special bond with Nabokov despite the difficulty of his prose. This went deeper than our identification with his themes. His novels are shaped around invisible trapdoors, sudden gaps that constantly pull the carpet from under the reader's feet. They are filled with mistrust of what we call everyday reality, an acute sense of that reality's fickleness and frailty.

There was something, both in his fiction and in his life, that we instinctively related to and grasped, the possibility of a boundless freedom when all options are taken away. I think that was what drove me to create the class. My main link with the outside world had been the university, and now that I had severed that link, there on the brink of the void, I could invent the violin or be devoured by the void.

7. The two photographs should be placed side by side. Both embody the "fragile unreality"—to quote Nabokov on his own state of exile—of our existence in the Islamic Republic of Iran. One cancels the other, and yet without one, the other is incomplete. In the first photograph, standing there in our black robes and scarves, we are as we had been shaped by someone else's dreams. In the second, we appear as we imagined ourselves. In neither could we feel completely at home.

The second photograph belonged to the world inside the living room. But outside, underneath the window that deceptively showcased only the mountains and the tree outside our house, was the other world, where the bad witches and furies were waiting to transform us into the hooded creatures of the first.

The best way I can think of explaining this self-negating and paradoxical inferno is through an anecdote, one that, like similar anecdotes, defies fiction to become its own metaphor.

The chief film censor in Iran, up until 1994, was blind. Well, nearly blind. Before that, he was the censor for theater. One of my playwright friends once described how he would sit in the theater wearing thick glasses that seemed to hide more than they revealed. An assistant who sat by him would explain the action onstage, and he would dictate the parts that needed to be cut.

After 1994, this censor became the head of the new television channel. There, he perfected his methods and demanded that the scriptwriters give him their scripts on audiotape; they were forbidden to make them attractive or dramatize them in any way. He then made his judgments about the scripts based on the tapes. More interesting, however, is the fact that his successor, who was not blind—not physically, that is—nonetheless followed the same system.

Our world under the mullahs' rule was shaped by the colorless lenses of the blind censor. Not just our reality but also our fiction had taken on this curious coloration in a world where the censor was the poet's rival in rearranging and reshaping reality, where we simultaneously invented ourselves and were figments of someone else's imagination.

We lived in a culture that denied any merit to literary works, considering them important only when they were handmaidens to something seemingly more urgent—namely ideology. This was a country where all gestures, even the most private, were interpreted in political terms. The colors of my head scarf or my father's tie were symbols of Western decadence and imperialist tendencies. Not wearing a beard, shaking hands with members of the opposite sex, clapping or whistling in public meetings, were likewise considered Western and therefore decadent, part of the plot by imperialists to bring down our culture.

A few years ago some members of the Iranian Parliament set up an investigative committee to examine the content of national television. The committee issued a lengthy report in which it condemned the showing of *Billy Budd*, because, it claimed, the story promoted homosexuality. Ironically, the Iranian television programmers had mainly chosen that film because of its lack of female characters. The cartoon version of *Around the World in Eighty Days* was also castigated, because the main character—a lion—was British and the film ended in that bastion of imperialism, London.

Our class was shaped within this context, in an attempt to escape the gaze of the blind censor for a few hours each week. There, in that living room, we rediscovered that we were also living, breathing human beings; and no matter how repressive the state became, no matter how intimidated and frightened we were, like Lolita we tried to escape and to create our own little pockets of freedom. And like Lolita, we took every opportunity to flaunt our insubordination: by showing a little hair from under our scarves, insinuating a little color into the drab uniformity of our appearances, growing our nails, falling in love, and listening to forbidden music.

An absurd fictionality ruled our lives. We tried to live in the open spaces, in the chinks created between that room, which had become our protective cocoon, and the censor's world of witches and goblins outside. Which of these two worlds was more real, and to which did we really belong? We no longer knew the answers. Perhaps one way of finding out the truth was to do what we did: to try to imaginatively articulate these two worlds and, through that process, give shape to our vision and identity.

8. How can I create this other world outside the room? I have no choice but to appeal once again to your imagination. Let's imagine one of the girls, say Sanaz, leaving my house and let us follow her from there to her final destination. She says her goodbyes and puts on her black robe and scarf over her orange shirt and jeans, coiling her scarf around her neck to cover her huge gold earrings. She directs wayward strands of hair under the scarf, puts her notes into her large bag, straps it on over her shoulder, and walks out into the hall. She pauses a moment on top of the stairs to put on thin lacy black gloves to hide her nail polish.

We follow Sanaz down the stairs, out the door, and into the street. You might notice that her gait and her gestures have changed. It is in her best interest not to be seen, not be heard or noticed. She doesn't walk upright, but bends her head towards the ground and doesn't look at passersby. She walks quickly and with a sense of determination. The streets of Tehran and other Iranian cities are patrolled by militia, who ride in white Toyota patrols, four gun-carrying men and women, sometimes followed by a minibus. They are called the Blood of God. They patrol the streets to make sure that women like Sanaz wear their veils properly, do not wear makeup, do not walk in public with men who are not their fathers, brothers, or husbands. She will pass slogans on the walls, quotations from Khomeini, and a group called the Party of God: MEN WHO WEAR TIES ARE U.S. LACKEYS. VEILING IS A WOMAN'S PROTECTION. Beside the slogan is a charcoal drawing of a woman: her face is featureless and framed by a dark chador. MY SISTER, GUARD YOUR VEIL. MY BROTHER, GUARD YOUR EYES.

If she gets on a bus, the seating is segregated. She must enter through the rear door and sit in the back seats, allocated to women. Yet in taxis, which accept as many as five passengers, men and women are squeezed together like sardines, as the saying goes, and the same goes with minibuses, where so many of my students complain of being harassed by bearded and God-fearing men.

You might well ask, What is Sanaz thinking as she walks the streets of Tehran? How much does this experience affect her? Most probably, she tries to distance her mind as much as possible from her surroundings. Perhaps she is thinking of her brother, or of her distant boyfriend and the time when she will meet him in Turkey. Does she compare her own situation with her mother's when she was the same age? Is she angry that women of her mother's generation could walk the streets freely, enjoy the company of the opposite sex, join the police force, become pilots, live under laws that were among the most progressive in the world regarding women? Does she feel humiliated by the new laws, by the fact that after the revolution, the age of marriage was lowered from eighteen to nine, that stoning became once more the punishment for adultery and prostitution?

In the course of nearly two decades, the streets have been turned into a war zone, where young women who disobey the rules are hurled into patrol cars, taken to jail, flogged, fined, forced to wash the toilets, and humiliated, and as soon as they leave, they go back and do the same thing. Is she aware, Sanaz, of her own power? Does she realize how dangerous she can be when her every stray gesture is a disturbance to public safety? Does she think how vulnerable the Revolutionary Guards are who for over eighteen years have patrolled the streets of Tehran and have had to endure young women like herself, and those of other generations, walking, talking, showing a strand of hair just to remind them that they have not converted?

We have reached Sanaz's house, where we will leave her on her doorstep, perhaps to confront her brother on the other side and to think in her heart of her boyfriend.

These girls, my girls, had both a real history and a fabricated one. Although they came from very different backgrounds, the regime that ruled them had tried to make their personal identities and histories irrelevant. They were never free of the regime's definition of them as Muslim women.

Whoever we were—and it was not really important what religion we belonged to, whether we wished to wear the veil or not, whether we observed certain religious norms or not—we had become the figment of someone else's dreams. A stern ayatollah, a self-proclaimed philosopher-king, had come to rule our land. He had come in the name of a past, a past that, he claimed, had been stolen from him. And he now wanted to re-create us in the image of that illusory past. Was it any consolation, and did we even wish to remember, that what he did to us was what we allowed him to do?

QUESTIONS FOR MAKING CONNECTIONS
WITHIN THE READING

1. Why does Nafisi spend so much time describing the members of her reading group? What different motives may have brought these readers to Nafisi's apartment? We might normally think of reading as a solitary activity, unlike watching movies or sports; why was it so important for the women to meet together as a group?

2. Judging from the information that Nafisi provides, why do you think her reading group selected the particular works she mentions: *A Thousand and*

One Nights, as well as *Invitation to a Beheading, Lolita,* and other novels by Nabokov? Why might religious authorities, not only in Iran but also in the United States, object to the teaching of such works?

3. Early in Chapter 10 of *Reading Lolita in Tehran,* Nafisi writes, "*Lolita* was *not* a critique of the Islamic Republic, but it went against the grain of all total-itarian perspectives." Without consulting a dictionary, and drawing instead on Nafisi's account, try to define *totalitarian.* What social and psychological effects does the totalitarian regime have on Nafisi and her students? In what sense might Lolita or other books you know pose a challenge to totalitari-anism? How are literature and the other arts—music, painting, sculpture, dance—inherently liberating? Is it possible for art itself to be totalitarian?

QUESTIONS FOR WRITING

1. Does Nafisi present a theory of interpretation? In other words, what does she see as the *real* or *correct* meaning of a work of art? Does she accept Nabokov's claims that "readers were born free and ought to remain free"? Would Nafisi say a work of art can mean anything we want? What is the value of art if it has no determinate or *correct* meaning? If art has a value, is its value simply personal? Does it also have social, political, and cultural value?

2. Nafisi and her students read Nabokov against the backdrop of the Islamic Republic of Iran. In that setting, what does the experience offer them? Would their reading of the novel provide the same experience if it took place in the United States? Does literature serve a different function in our society? How might reading a novel in a private group differ from the experience of reading the same novel in an American high school or college classroom?

QUESTIONS FOR MAKING CONNECTIONS
BETWEEN READINGS

1. Nafisi is convinced that reading groups like hers posed a real challenge to the regime. One important part of their effectiveness lay in the ability of litera-ture to sustain human connectedness in spite of isolating policies. But taking off the black chador and speaking face to face were only the beginning. Still more powerfully, perhaps, literature gave the members of the reading group permission to become the creators of themselves. Starting with Cathy Davidson's "Project Classroom Makeover," would you say that the new electronic media—the Web and iPods, for example—pose a challenge to the established order in much the same way as Nabokov's writing did in Iran? Or are the new media here in the West actually helping to erode the culture of books that allowed Nafisi and her students to resist an oppressive regime?

Are the new media truly liberating? Do they heighten our sense of con-nectedness, or do they make individuals feel invisible and insignificant?

2. At the beginning of *The Mind's Eye*, Oliver Sacks poses this question: "To what extent are we the authors, the creators, of our own experience?" How might Nafisi answer Sacks and how might her answer complicate Sacks's approach to the question? What role does she believe society plays in limiting our perceptions, and to what extent does Sacks, a neuroscientist, overlook the social dimension by focusing on individuals? Do the blind subjects of Sacks's essay have anything in common with Nafisi's students? Does the imagination liberate Nafisi's "girls" in much the same way as blindness frees Sacks's subjects? What do Nafisi's students gain from the collective reading of a work of fiction? In order for us to become the authors of our own experience, what kinds of support from society do we need?

MAGGIE NELSON

AMERICAN SOCIETY IS SATURATED with violence—and not just the violence horrifically displayed in early December 2012 at the Sandy Hook Elementary School, where a former student returned to shoot 20 children and 6 adults before he trained his rifle on himself. In 2011, the homicide rate in the United States was more than four times greater than Germany's and more than eight times Japan's. But violence here is not just a social fact—it's also a cultural phenomenon, as poet, critic, and essayist Maggie Nelson understands. Anyone who watches television and YouTube, or spends hours playing video games, will recognize its pervasiveness. But Nelson finds violence in a place we might never think to look—in the high arts, especially the cutting-edge tradition known as the avant-garde.

Past defenders of the artistic avant-garde celebrated the possibilities opened up by "aesthetic shock," the experience produced by radical disorientation. But they have tended to soft-pedal its complicity with sadism and terror. At times, Nelson herself seems to be thrilled by the avant-garde's liberating openness, but she tries to nudge artists and art lovers toward what one reviewer, writing in the *New York Times*, calls a "post-avant-garde aesthetics." Such an aesthetics—a new framework for the arts—might, as Nelson claims, "deliver us to a more sensitive, perceptive, insightful, enlivened, collaborative and just way of inhabiting the earth." Nelson's shift from art to "inhabiting the earth" might seem to give too much importance to what goes on in galleries, museums, and film festivals. But the sadism of the avant-garde has never stopped at the museum door: in fact, its influence reaches everywhere: into popular films and magazines, architecture, television, fashion, and design—the entire "cultural imaginary." When Nelson questions the pieties of past art criticism, she does so because she understands that the arts help to create the texture and the shape of our experience.

Nelson, who received a Ph.D. in English from the Graduate Center of the City University of New York, has taught writing and literature at the Pratt Institute, Wesleyan University, and the New School. Since 2005 she has been on the faculty of the California Institute of the Arts (CALARTS). While Nelson's essays on culture explore new directions in the arts, she also speaks for a post-Boomer generation of writers and artists who have had to live without stable jobs at marquee newspapers

The *New York Times* quotation is from Laura Kipnis, "Why Is Contemporary Art Addicted to Violence?" *New York Times*, July 14, 2011. The quotation on inhabiting the earth is from *The Art of Cruelty: A Reckoning*, 265 and the quotation from the interview in the online journal comes from "Pathos: Maggie Nelson," *Full Stop*, January 24, 2013 <http://www.full-stop.net/2013/01/24/interviews/the-editors-pathos-maggie-nelson/>.

or tenured professorships at universities. As she told an interviewer for the online journal *Full Stop* about the difficulties of the writer's life today, "I don't think the world owes anyone anything. I think we owe the world more stewardship and vision and respect than we currently are giving it, and as fellow humans we owe each other more care than our current system impels us to give."

Great to Watch

In her moving, influential anti–capital punishment memoir, *Dead Man Walking*, Sister Helen Prejean asserts, "I know that it is not a question of malice or ill will or meaness of spirit that prompts our citizens to support executions. It is, quite simply, that people don't know the truth of what is going on." Prejean is convinced that if executions were made public, "the torture and violence would be unmasked, and we would be shamed into abolishing executions."

Alas, if only it were so. For if the bad news from Abu Ghraib made anything clear in recent years, it is that this model of shaming-us-into-action-by-unmasking-the-truth-of-our-actions cannot hold a candle to our capacity to assimilate horrific images, and to justify or shrug off horrific behavior. Not to mention the fact that the United States has a long history—as do many countries and individuals—of reveling in the spectacle of public executions and gruesome torture. (On this account, I unhappily recommend to you the 2000 book of documentary photography *Without Sanctuary: Lynching Photography in America*.)

Prejean's conviction that it is simple, blameless ignorance that prompts so many Americans to support executions (or the torture of detainees in the so-called war on terror, and so on) may be goodhearted. But unfortunately it leaves us but one option: know the truth, and ye shall be redeemed. But "knowing the truth" does not come with redemption as a guarantee, nor does a feeling of redemption guarantee an end to a cycle of wrongdoing. Some would even say it is key to maintaining it, insofar as it can work as a reset button—a purge that cleans the slate, without any guarantee of change at the root. Placing all one's eggs in "the logic of exposure," as Eve Kosofsky Sedgwick has put it (in *Touching Feeling*), may also simply further the logic of paranoia. "Paranoia places its faith in exposure," Sedgwick observes—which is to say that the exposure of a disturbing fact or situation does not necessarily alter it, but in fact may further the circular conviction that *one can never be paranoid enough*.

Prejean's logic relies on the hope that shame, guilt, and even simple embarrassment are still operative principles in American cultural and political life—and that such principles can fairly trump the forces of desensitization and self-justification. Such a presumption is sorely challenged by the seeming unembarrassability of the military, the government, corporate CEOs, and others repetitively caught in monstrous acts of irresponsibility and malfeasance. This unembarrassability has proved difficult to contend with, as it has had a literally stunning effect on the citizenry. *They ought to be ashamed of themselves!* we cry, over and over again, to no avail. But they are not ashamed, and they are not going to become so.

Also difficult to content with: the fact that we ourselves have ample and wily reserves of malice, power-mongering, self-centeredness, fear, sadism, or simple meanness of spirit that we ourselves, our loved ones, our enemies, skillful preachers, politicians, and rhetoricians of all stripes can whip into a hysterical, destructive froth at any given moment, if we allow for it.

To this list, one should surely add television producers. In 1982, Stephen King published a sci-fi novel called *The Running Man,* set in the not-so-distant future. In the novel, "The Running Man" is the country's most popular TV game show, and features a contestant who agrees to run for his life while being trailed by a group of "Hunters" charged with killing him. The network engages the populace by paying civilians for confirmed sightings of the runner, which it then passes along to the Hunters. If the runner survives for thirty days, he gets a billion dollars. If he is caught, he is killed by the Hunters on live TV.

As others have noted, the dystopic plot of *The Running Man* turned out to be more prophetic than dissuasive. So-called reality television has been foraying into this territory for over a decade now, churning out show after show that draws on some combination of surveillance; self-surveillance; "interactivity" with the home audience; techniques associated with torture, interrogation, or incarceration; and rituals of humiliation, sadism, and masochism (of the I'll-do-anything-for-fame-or-money variety, not the I-do-this-because-it-gives-me-pleasure variety: outing one's pleasures, it seems, remains more taboo than outing one's ambition or avarice).

The international craze for reality programming has, to date, given us shows such as the United Kingdom's *Shattered* (2004), in which contestants are deprived of sleep for many days in a row, and *Unbreakable* (2008), in which contestants undergo various forms of torture (including being waterboarded, buried alive, or made to cross the Sahara Desert while wearing suffocating gas masks), and whose motto is "Pain Is Glory, Pain Is Pride, Pain Is Great to Watch." In the United States, reality TV has at times joined forces with soft-core journalism and law enforcement to produce shows like Dateline/NBC's *To Catch a Predator. To Catch a Predator*—which operates in questionable legal conjunction with not only the police but also a vigilante "anti-predator" group called "Perverted Justice"—hires decoys who pretend to be underage teens. These decoys attempt to entice adults into online sex chats; if and when one of the adults agrees to meet his online pen pal at the "decoy house," he (and it is always a he) is there greeted by the show's host, Chris Hansen, who first verbally humiliates him by reading him the most tawdry excerpts of his online sex chatter, then turns him over to the police, who are waiting nearby with handcuffs.

The legal, ethical, and psychological ramifications of such shows have occasioned quite a bit of debate, as these effects have often proved unmanageable. On November 5, 2006, for example, after a SWAT team trailed by TV cameras forced its way into the home of Louis Conradt Jr., a longtime county prosecutor in Murphy, Texas, Conradt said, "I'm not going to hurt anybody," before firing a single bullet from a semiautomatic handgun into his brain, thereby ending his life. (There had been no pressing reason to break into Conradt's home—Conradt had, in fact, refused to meet the decoy at the decoy house—but the show's producers were anxious to capture the arrest of a prominent public figure on tape, as it promised to make compelling TV. In the end, Dateline refrained from airing the death itself, but it did run a segment on the case.) As one newspaper columnist writing about the incident acidly put it, "When a TV show makes you feel sorry for potential child rapists, you know it's doing something wrong." (Or right, depending on your point of view; *To Catch a Predator* was one of NBC's hit shows for some time.)

As if a test were needed of how much sadism reality television participants, audiences, and producers are willing to indulge, on March 17, 2010, French TV broadcast something called *Le jeu de la mort*, or *The Game of Death*, a faux game show which re-performed the Milgram experiment on eighty unknowing contestants. The contestants had been told that they were taking part in a game-show pilot, in which they were to administer electric shocks to other contestants when they answered questions incorrectly. A smiling host and vociferous studio audience, rather than a taciturn guy in a lab coat (as was the case in Stanley Milgram's experiment), urged the behavior on, but the results were remarkably similar: sixty-four of the eighty contestants were willing to deliver shocks that could have killed their recipients, had there been any actual receivers.

But beyond prime time, which the digital age may be rendering a quaint outpost, more literal renditions of the Running Man scenario—and ones that offer their viewers slightly more participation than that of armchair schadenfreude—are now available via a few strokes of your computer keyboard. Consider, for example, the Texas Virtual Border Watch Program, in which "The Texas Border Sheriff's Coalition (TBSC) has joined BlueServo^{SM} in a public-private partnership to deploy the Virtual Community Watch, an innovative real-time surveillance program designed to empower the public to proactively participate in fighting border crime." In other words, the TBSC has placed cameras along the U.S. Mexican border in Texas at so-called high-threat spots for border crossing or drug trafficking, and now invites the home viewer to log on, pick a spot, and start "directly monitoring suspicious criminal activity via this virtual fence^{SM}." Viewers can watch the live feed from one of the "virtual stake outs" for as long as they like—the *New York Times* recently interviewed a housewife from Rochester, New York, who reported watching for at least four hours a day.

While controversial, the BlueServo^{SM} project should come as no surprise to anyone familiar with the Minutemen and its offshoots, whose volunteers have been (non-virtually) patrolling the U.S.-Mexican border, looking for "illegals," since 1995. "It's just like hunting," explained Chuck Stonex, a prominent member. "If you're going out hunting deer, you want to scout around and get an idea what their pattern is, what trails they use." Stonex, along with Minuteman founder Jim Gilchrist and other leading figures, has since taken a more defensive stance, after one of their principal associates, Shawna Forde, was arrested in June 2009 in connection with the murder of two members of a Hispanic family in their home in Arivaca, Arizona; one of those killed was a nine-year-old girl. But the chilling new anti-immigration law signed by Governor Jan Brewer of Arizona on April 23, 2010, which authorizes police to demand proof of any person's immigration status should "reasonable suspicion exist that the person is an alien," has breathed new life into the "hunt 'em down" mindset, in both Arizona and the nation at large.

With BlueServo^{SM}, the condition of spectatorship is not so much abolished as it is recast as a form of empowerment: you, too, can defend the homeland, without ever having to leave your home! The project eerily combines the appeal of a spectator sport with language more typically reserved for left wing–sounding community activism: *Innovative. Proactive. Participation. Partnership. Coalition. Community. Empowerment.* (Especially poignant: "public-private partnership"—in the age of Blackwater [now called Xe] or the Tea Party, every vigilante need be prepared for a trademark!) Last time I visited the BlueServo^{SM} site, there were fifteen cameras rolling on scenes of bucolic calm. My favorites were Camera 5, which featured a still patch of golden weeds with the directive, "During the day watch for subjects on foot carrying large bags," and Camera 10, which featured a swiftly moving river alongside the directive, "During the day if you see four or five men in a boat report this activity. At night if you see vehicle, boat, or people movement report this activity." The static, unending nature of the footage bears a weird resemblance to the endurance-based, art house aesthetic of, say, Andy Warhol's *Empire* (1964)—a film that consists of eight hours and five minutes of continuous footage of the Empire State Building—or that of a virtual yule log, albeit one of a more sinister variety.

On the flip side of such a "if you see something, say something" policing projects lies a human rights organization such as the Hub, which describes itself as "the world's first participatory media site for human rights." I'm thinking in particular of the Hub's Witness project, whose motto is "See It, Film It, Change It," and which aims to use "video and online technologies to open the eyes of the world to human rights violations." The operation of Witness is twofold: one, to give people cameras and train them to videotape atrocities or injustices they may be suffering or witnessing; two, to invent a circuitry by which one can upload one's own videos and view those of others, presumably as a prelude to taking a form of action after viewing. For convenience, one can scroll through the videos by category (armed conflict, children's rights, discrimination, violence, women's rights, and so on), or by "most viewed" (Japanese sexual slavery during World War II has occupied this slot for some time now).

As the creators of the Hub well know, the employment of image or moving image in service of mobilizing an individual or a populace is tricky business. For this reason, the Hub aims to zero in on the little window of time between an upsurge of outrage or sympathy and the onset of apathy—to hurl an otherwise fleeting emotion into action before it dissolves. (What action consists of is a difficult, debatable question—right now the "take action" tab on the Hub's Web site links to "a growing portfolio of advocacy tools to help allies and users call for action," ranging from signing email petitions to writing members of Congress to sending money to a variety of organizations to creating "offline events.")

I mean it as no slight to the Hub when I say that I find the smorgasbord of human suffering offered on its site repellent. Not because "it is difficult to look" (though sometimes, of course, it is), but because the physical and mental activity of Web surfing, which consists of rapid image flow, the distillation of long, complex stories and situations to 2-inch-high, four-minute snippets, one-click decision-making, happenstance isolations, juxtapositions, and linkages that have an eerily leveling effect on content and context, is, in my experience, an exceptionally poor means by which to contemplate the horrors of human trafficking, child prostitution, landmines, and the like. For better or worse, one's experience of surfing the Hub is shaped by the do-I-or-don't-I-want-to-watch-this question, as in: Do I or don't I want to watch a Tibetan pilgrim being shot dead by the Chinese police at Nangpa La Pass? How about cell phone footage of a man being hung upside down and sodomized with a rod in an Egyptian prison? Or the testimony of women in Bangladesh whose faces have been disfigured by acid? Well intentioned and effective as the operation may be, scrolling through such choices makes me feel as though I've arrived at the hub of a problem rather than its solution.

INSOFAR AS "image flow" isn't going away any time soon, it certainly makes sense to try to harness the powers of YouTube for all kinds of social causes as well as for entertainment. But there are also perils. And one is that in a cultural moment defined (by some, for some) by image flow, the question of what one should look at, along with attendant inquiries into the nature and effect of the images blowing by, has a creepy way of overtaking almost all other questions. This may in fact be part of the so-called image regime's raison d'etre, rather than a puzzling side effect. In any case, it can lead to cul-de-sacs, red herrings, or distractions fatal to the primary issue at hand.

For example, in a director's statement about his Abu Ghraib documentary, *Standard Operating Procedure,* filmmaker Errol Morris names the principal question posed by his film as, "Is it possible for a photograph to change the world?" But what could the answer to this question—be it in the negative or the affirmative— really mean? As Sontag puts it in *Regarding the Pain of Others,* "The image as shock and the image as cliché are two aspects of the same presence"—a notion that partially explains how the iconic image of the hooded prisoner at Abu Ghraib forced to hold a foreboding wire in each hand could literally sicken one's stomach when first viewed, then move on to become a much-parodied image (e.g., on the satirical posters that appeared throughout the New York subways not long after the Abu Ghraib story broke, posters that borrowed the distinctive design of Apple's iPod campaign, but substituted the word "iRaq" for "iPod," and featured the silhouette of the hooded man in lieu of the iPod's silhouetted dancer). It isn't that this photograph played no role in the unfolding of human events—clearly, it did. But after nearly 200 years of photography, it may be that we are closer than ever to understanding that an image—be it circulated in a newspaper, on YouTube, or in an art gallery—is an exceptionally poor platform on which to place the unending, arduous, multifaceted, and circuitous process of "changing the world."

In his April 2008 *Artforum* review of *Standard Operating Procedure,* critic Paul Arthur noted something of the same. In thinking about Morris's focus on the revelation that the man who identified himself publicly as the hooded prisoner turned out *not* to be the actual victim, Arthur writes, "Morris finds this revelation telling because it shows how massively disseminated pictures can mask their own provenance or 'attract false beliefs.' Really? I thought the images under consideration, especially when supplemented by salient verbal contexts, revealed more about policy than about epistemology, more about state-sponsored barbarity than about media deception." In other words, one need not immerse oneself in horrific images or a debate about their epistemological status in order to apprehend and protest barbarities wherever they are to be found. Nor does one need to distract oneself with rehashings of the Milgram experiment, which uselessly reiterate what we already know about our capacity to cause harm under pressure (or, as the case may be, at simple invitation).

One does, however, need to know what barbarities have taken place: there's the rub. Enter President Obama, speaking about his administration's May 2009 decision to suppress the release of a new spate of photographs that depict the abuse, rape, and torture of Afghan and Iraqi prisoners in American custody. "The most direct consequence of releasing [these photos]," Obama said, "would be to further inflame anti-American opinion and to put our troops in greater danger." Mark down one vote for the idea that images have the power to cause injury—though to warn against such a thing in this case smells pretty rotten, given that the suppressed photos presumably depict our troops injuring others.

Obama also skips over the most obvious direct consequence of releasing the photos: that Americans would see—along with the rest of the world—more evidence of the barbarities that have been committed in their name, on their supposed behalf, and on their dime. To state the obvious but oft-repressed or denied point, it isn't the act of releasing photos that inflames anti-American sentiment; it's the behavior captured by the photos. In the age of "the torturer with the Toshiba," as art historian T.J. Clark has put it, no image flow can be fully marshaled. Nor can survivors and witnesses be unilaterally silenced. If you don't want to inflame via images of the behavior, then you have to stop the behavior.

Of course, it isn't entirely clear that the United States meant to keep the news of its use of torture a secret. No regime hoping to gain power from its use of such violence (an impossibility, according to Hannah Arendt) ever has. Certainly the revelations from Abu Ghraib appeared as a mistake, a rip in the fabric; certainly the U.S. government has employed intense secrecy, censorship, and denial about everything from the Red Cross Torture Report to the exact interrogation methods used to the operations of "black sites" around the world. Certainly journalists from Seymour Hersh to Jane Mayer to Mark Danner to Scott Horton have had an enormously difficult time obtaining the information they need to inform the public about what, exactly, has gone on; certainly the CIA has classified and egregiously destroyed pivotal evidence, such as the videotapes depicting the 2002 interrogations of several terrorism suspects—tapes the CIA outrageously destroyed in 2005, in the midst of a federal investigation.

And yet. On a parallel track run the monologues of Dick Cheney, who, since leaving office, has toured the talk shows, speaking with candor and pride about his role in "The Program." Then there's the ongoing consideration of the topic in the bright glare of television and the blogosphere, in which everyone from Bill O'Reilly to Andrew Sullivan to Christopher Hitchens to Elisabeth Hasselbeck openly debates the efficacy of torture, and the effect its use has had on our country—not whether or not we have done it. The Bush/Cheney dyad of denial/ justification represents two sides of a single coin: Bush spoke the voice of delusion (it never happened, it will never happen); Cheney, the voice of justification (we had to do it, we should still be doing it). The average citizen can then ricochet between these two irreconcilable, collaborative poles until desensitization sets in, and with it, a begrudging (or, for some, an enthusiastic) acceptance of the practice.

BACK IN 1965, Sontag declared that we live in "an age of extremity," characterized by "the continual threat of two equally fearful, but seemingly opposed destinies: unremitting banality and inconceivable terror." Much of the art produced under the influence of [Antonin] Artaud—such as [Hermann] Nitsch's—proceeds from this premise, and attempts to replace the crush of banality with some form of brutal, sensory overload. Even quieter works such as [Alfredo] Jaar's *Untitled (Newsweek)* depend on this by-now familiar dichotomy—one that places benumbing banality on one side, and unthinkable, rupturing calamity on the other.

The moral of this dichotomy is that distraction by the banal obviates a necessary focus on the all-too-real-calamitous. This equation became ubiquitous in the weeks and months after 9/11, when media commentator after commentator lamented the fact that instead of focusing on the real threat from Al Qaeda, Americans spent the summer of 2001 unforgivably obsessing over the latest incarnation of Britney Spears. But really this is a self-flagellating, essentially nonsensical diagnosis, especially in its supposition that Americans would have been better off spending more of their time worrying about an impending terrorist attack, the shape of which they could have had no foreknowledge. (The next seven years and four months of the Bush administration provided a good picture of what a populace in thrall to such anxiety might look like—and what it might tolerate from its leaders—and it wasn't pretty.)

After 9/11, Sontag's formulation would seem to have more adherents than ever, on both the right and the left. See, for example, the leftist collective RETORT's *Afflicted Powers: Capital and Spectacle in a New Age of War* (2005), which repeatedly pits the eviscerating "false depth" of consumerism (i.e., unremitting banality) against claims that "we have never been closer to hell on earth" (i.e., inconceivable terror). But is it true? Or more precisely, for whom is it true, and who presumes it to be true for others? Do we really live under the aegis of these opposing threats, or is it the very reiteration of them as our two primary ontological options (and our unthinking acquiescence to such a formulation) that acts as a truer threat to our enlivenment, to our full experience of the vast space between these two poles—a space which, after all, is where the great majority of many of our lives takes place? And if, as David Graeber has suggested, revolutionary action is "not a form of grim self-sacrifice," but rather "the defiant insistence on acting as if one is already free," what good does it do us to charge those who refuse to live under the aegis of these two grim choices with false consciousness, with not truly understanding the stakes of the age?

Compare, for example, the "troughs of blood and wine," the "extreme noise from the orchestras" of Nitsch's *Six-Day Play* with John Cage's Zen-inspired *4′33″*, first composed in 1952, in which Cage famously asks audience members to sit in complete silence for four minutes and thirty-three seconds, in order to awaken to the sounds going on around them, to hear all the ambient noise of which they would have otherwise been unaware. In light of the heightened state of perception conjured by Cage's piece—its profound capacity to "return us to our senses" via an emptying out of input rather than an overload of it—one may begin to wonder whose interests it serves to keep us believing in, and riveted by, the mythos of this "age of extremity," which focuses on knocking oneself out rather than tuning in.

Perhaps more controversially still, given our inarguable complicity in all kinds of systemic forms of global injustice: is there any space left for *not* watching, *not* focusing, *not* keeping abreast of all the events and atrocities unfolding in the world, as an ethically viable option? "Why are we watching the news, reading the news, keeping up with the news?" asks Annie Dillard in *For the Time Being,* a book that sets forth the deeply unfashionable argument that our times are not uniquely grievous—that they are, in fact, not unique at all—and further, that their vicissitudes may make no intrinsic demand on our attention, or on our conscience. That enlivenment may consist of quiet, even monastic retreat, rather than bombardment or disembowelment. "Who can bear to hear this, or who will consider it?" Dillard wonders.

In completely disparate circles—such as those of leftist political philosophy, for example—a distinct but not wholly unrelated idea of "engaged withdrawal" has also begun to hold sway. Rather than fixate on revolution, this strategy privileges orchestrated and unorchestrated acts of exodus. As Italian political philosopher Paolo Virno has put it, "Nothing is less passive that the act of fleeing, of exiting." In anarchist circles, this withdrawal bears a relationship to the idea of the "TAZ," or "temporary autonomous zones" (as elaborated by writer Hakim Bey; Graeber prefers the term "provisional autonomous zones"): ephemeral but crucial gaps in an otherwise suffocating global capitalist order, gaps that, at the very least, make other forms of social organization and perception seem momentarily possible.

In short, after decades of critical focus on the evils of spectatorship, the gaze, and the presumably passive role of the audience, an increasing chorus of critical voices is currently arguing that we have somehow gotten wildly off course by treating the condition of spectatorship as a problem, or at least as *the* problem. There's Jacques Rancière, who argues in 2009's *The Emancipated Spectator* that spectatorship is not "the passivity that has to be turned into activity," but rather "our normal situation." Then, of course, there's Sontag, whose final book, *Regarding the Pain of Others,* argues that to impugn the sense of sight for allowing us to "stand back from the aggressiveness of the world" and to free us up "for observation and for elective attention" is to impugn the function of the mind itself. Sontag concludes, "There's nothing wrong with standing back and thinking. To paraphrase several sages: 'Nobody can think and hit someone at the same time.'" In a culture obsessed with pitting thought against action (in order to privilege the latter), not to mention a culture perpetually dubious of the cash value of rumination, these are fighting words. In 2006, T.J. Clark—who is known as much for his fierce political convictions as his insights into Picasso (he is, in fact, a member of RETORT)—published *The Sight of Death*, a 242-page meditation on two works by seventeenth-century painter Nicolas Poussin, in which Clark aims to honor the slow work of "this focusing, this staying still, this allowing oneself to respond to the *picture's* stillness—everything hidden and travestied, in short, by the current word 'gaze.'" Clark also rebukes those scholars of "visual culture" who, in his words, are "chained to their image-displacement machines like lab animals to dispensers of morphine," and whose knee-jerk response to an expansive, devoted, patient contemplation of classical painting (such as his) would be to dismiss it as nostalgic, or elitist, or "some such canting parrot-cry."

The above-mentioned writers have dedicated their lives to slow seeing, slow thinking, measured articulation, and radical dissent or defection from any *doxa* that stifles existence or adds injustice to it. I am inclined to listen to them. Rather than lambast that which mediates as our enemy, each makes a concerted effort to reclaim the value of the "third term." "In the logic of emancipation," Rancière writes, "there is always a third thing—a book or some other piece of writing—alien to both [teacher and student] and to which they can refer to verify in common what the pupil has seen, what she says about it and what she thinks about it." The emancipatory value of this third thing, as Rancière sees it, lies in the fact that no one can own it; no one can own its meaning. Its function is to mediate, but not in the sense of imitating or representing a reality from which spectators are barred. Here, "the mediate" relates people to each other, with *relation* signifying the process of being brought together and given a measure of space from each other at the same time.

This is essentially a spatial construct—a diagram, or, as [Francis]Bacon might have it, a ring of action—that constructs both distance and association (or, if you like, individuality and collectivity). Its construction demarcates some sort of boundary, but it does not follow that the function of that boundary need be a constrictive or restrictive one. In fact, the function of the boundary may be wildly variable and even liberating, especially insofar as it creates sub-spaces, and guarantees that there can be a game. As philosopher Ludwig Wittgenstein puts it, "If I surround an area with a fence or a line or otherwise, the purpose may be to prevent someone from getting in or out; but it may also be part of a game and the players supposed, say, to jump over the boundary; or it may shew where the property of one man ends and that of another begins; and so on. So if I draw a boundary line that is not yet to say what I am drawing it for." Given that "breaking down boundaries" has come to act as a synonym for innovative or progressive action, be it in art, social justice, or beyond, Wittgenstein's distinctions bear some repeating. Not all boundaries or mediating forces are created equal; not all serve the same purpose. Neither politics nor art is served if and when the distinctions between them are willingly or unthinkingly smeared out.

Rancière's veneration of this third term also echoes certain remarks Hannah Arendt made over fifty years ago, in speaking about the importance of the public realm (which, Arendt makes clear, is definitively *not* the same as the social realm). "The public realm, as the common world," Arendt wrote, "gathers us together and yet prevents our falling over each other, so to speak. What makes mass society so difficult to bear is not the number of people involved, or at least not primarily, but the fact that the world between them has lost its power to gather them together, to relate and separate them. The weirdness of this situation resembles a spiritualistic séance where a number of people gathered round a table might suddenly, through some magic trick, see the table vanish from their midst, so that two persons sitting opposite each other were no longer separated but also would be entirely unrelated to each other by anything tangible."

For Arendt, this collapse signifies a deep and dangerous failure in human relations. (God only knows what she would have made of the vast social realm of the Internet, and its creation of a wholly different type of séance—one in which the table remains, but the human bodies are disappeared.) For others, this collapse serves as the gateway to ecstatic, unmediated union. Others still, seeing this fantasized union as utopian nonsense, but who are equally troubled by the forms of alienation that ostensibly prohibit it, offer up satirical or cynical dystopias in its place. And others—especially younger others—simply ignore both the promises and the perils of the whole communion/alienation dyad, as one typically ignores any binaries that no longer speak to the defining conditions and possibilities of one's time. The mind-bending work of an artist such as Ryan Trecartin offers a particularly gripping example of the latter.

Trecartin's 2007 feature-length video, *I-Be Area*, while nominally based on the concept of "virtual reality," is a riotous exploration of what kinds of space, identity, physicality, language, sexuality, and consciousness might be possible once one leaves the dichotomy of the virtual and the real behind, along with a whole host of other need-not-apply binaries (the everyday and the apocalyptic, the public and the private, the utopic and the dystopic, male and female, gay and straight, among them). The hyperactive cloning, frenetic strobing of characters, and post-identity verbiage of *I-Be Area* make James Cameron's *Avatar* (2009) or the Internet game Second Life look like relics from the Stone Age. "I love the idea of technology and culture moving faster than the understanding of those mediums by people," Trecartin has said, and his works aim to immerse viewers in this failed-to-upload state. The disorientation of this state is not that of grandpa befuddled by a fistful of printer cables, but rather the sort of psychological and physiological stupefaction more often associated with acid overdoses and schizoid breakdowns.

I-Be Area takes incapacity—to absorb, to make sense, to cohere, to sort, to concentrate—as its starting point. ("It's like the jumper being jumped before the onset of 'jump,'" Trecartin explains, both helpfully and unhelpfully.) Then it amplifies this incapacity by turning up the speed, the color, the hysteria, the flicker. Image or speech overflow is no longer a problem, and certainly not one that art could or should aid in solving. It is where we live, at least while watching Trecartin; it is our "abstract plot of now," as he calls it. Trecartin's ability to sustain us here for some real time often feels like a miracle, in that such an ability seems as if it should be, by definition, also beyond the artist. That is to say, the art often feels as if it is moving faster than Trecartin himself could be—which is likely why his films, when combined with his youth (*I-Be Area* was finished when he was twenty-six), have had something of an awe-inducing effect on the art world. "All I can do is generalize about this world and point to it with a yearning, stumped pleasure," writes Wayne Koestenbaum about Trecartin's work. "My pointing finger is the gesture of an outsider, a tourist, gawking at a radioactive carnival I can't domesticate or quarantine."

Koestenbaum notes that Trecartin's work is about radical distraction—that dreaded, proliferate state that leads to dazzlingly high numbers of cell phone–related car crashes each day, or that leads otherwise progressive professors to shake their heads in despair as their students text each other under the classroom table. But Trecartin's brand of distraction doesn't rely on any simple use of the imitative fallacy—that is, "contemporary life is mind-scrambling, fragmented, and distracted, so my art must be mind-scrambling, fragmented, and distracted, too." It is too tightly orchestrated for that—too layered, too well performed, too purposefully edited, too intelligently perverse. However bawdy and hysterical, Trecartin's videos draw tight rings of actions: they are condensed, fast-moving world creations that make an intense demand on our attention. And the animating paradox of this world, as Koestenbaum has put it, is that *"Trecartin's characters concentrate on distraction."* However frenetic *I-Be Area* may be, its distraction is not of the same order as that of, say, the idiotic pop-up balloons and crawling tickers that have become staples of the television screen. To stay with *I-Be Area* all the way through—to listen to every word, to follow every decision and cut—requires a keen effort. You'll get the most out of it if you, too, can concentrate on distraction.

Of course, you may not remember much of what happened; you may not remember any of the characters; you may not even be left with an image. If your experience resembles mine, you'll be left with something far more amorphous—a kind of vibrating memory of the unnerving psychic state the work induced, or captured, or invented (and, perhaps, a notebook full of scrawled lines that sounded great at the time, such as, "My personal really concise pussy is developing a very inner monologue which I will not reveal to you as I become dynamic"). In his lucid, compelling book on craft, *Unbalancing Acts: Foundations for a Theater,* famed avant-garde dramatist Richard Foreman articulates this aesthetics-of-amnesia quite well: "The image of the Marlboro man riding his horse and smoking his cigarette has stuck with me for many years—and so what? It's garbage. It's kitsch. All it means is that the image seduced me, that it pushed a button that was ready to be pushed, and I responded. It didn't widen my sensibilities, compassion, or intuition. Whereas an art that affects you in the moment, but which you then find hard to remember, is straining to bring you to another level. It offers images or ideas from that other level, that other way of being, which is why you find them hard to remember. But it has opened you to the possibility of growing into what you are not yet, which is exactly what art should do."

Foreman is a bit more sanguine about the possibility of "growing into what you are not yet" than Trecartin, whose enthusiasm about new technologies and their relationship to human consciousness has a decidedly who-cares-where-we're-headed-let's-party vibe. I don't think, for example, that Trecartin is explicitly setting out to make work that offers his viewers "artistic structures—models of consciousness—that might evolve into a new kind of lucidity and self-possession, which would enable us to navigate the rapids of our times," as Foreman says he has been trying to do for upward of forty years now. In short, critics and viewers who look to Trecartin as an idiot savant emissary from the next generation who has come to answer the question *Are we going to be alright?* are not likely to feel reassured.

But in the end, it may not matter. Both Foreman and Trecartin work from a conception of the human, or the "real," borne out of contradiction, fluctuation, incoherence, and perversity; both offer immersion in their vision without rehashing the avant-garde fetish of terrorizing the audience or the mainstream one of chaperoning it. "We abide by cultural directives that urge us: clarify each thought, each experience, so you can cull from them their single, dominant meaning and, in the process, become a responsible adult who knows what he or she thinks," Foreman has said. "But what I try to show is the opposite: how at every moment, the world presents us with a composition in which a multitude of meanings and realities are available, and you are able to swim, lucid and self-contained, in that turbulent sea of multiplicity." After an hour or so of watching *I-Be Area,* or of watching a Foreman play, you start to swim in such a sea. The experience seems to me at least a start on a worthwhile sense of human freedom.

BIBLIOGRAPHY

Arendt, Hannah. *On Violence.* New York: Harvest Books/Harcourt Brace, 1969, 1970.

Arthur, Paul. "The Horror: Paul Arthur on Errol Morris's Standard Operating Procedure." *Artforum* April 2008. <http://artforum.com/inprint/issue=200804&id=19738>.

Bachman, Richard (King, Stephen). *The Running Man.* New York: Signet Books, 1982.

Bey, Hakim. *The Temporary Autonomous Zone, Ontological Anarchy, Poetic Terrorism.* New York: Autonomedia, 1985.

Clark, T. J. *The Sight of Death: An Experiment in Art Writing.* New Haven, CT: Yale University Press, 2006.

Dillard, Annie. *For the Time Being.* New York: Vintage, 2000.

Foreman, Richard. *Unbalancing Acts: Foundations for a Theater.* New York: Theater Communications Group, 1993.

Graeber, Donald. *Possibilities: Essays on Hierarchy, Rebellion, and Desire.* Oakland, CA: AK Press, 2007.

Koestenbaum, Wayne. *Andy Warhol* (Penguin Lives). New York: Viking, 2001.

Prejean, Sister Helen. *Dead Man Walking: An Eyewitness Account of the Death Penalty in the United States.* New York: Vintage, 1994.

Ranciére, Jacques. *The Emancipated Spectator.* Trans. Gregory Elliott. New York: Verso, 2009.

RETORT. *Afflicted Powers: Capital and Spectacle in a New Age of War.* New York: Verso, 2005.

Sedgwick, Eve Kosofsky. *Touching Feeling: Affect, Pegagogy, Performativity.* Durham, NC: Duke University Press, 2003.

Sontag, Susan. *Regarding the Pain of Others.* New York: Picador, 2004.

Virno, Paolo. *A Grammar of the Multitude: For an Analysis of Contemporary Forms of Life.* Trans. Isabella Bertoletti, James Cascaito, and Andrea Casson. New York: Semiotext(e), 2004.

Wittgenstein, Ludwig. *Culture and Value.* Ed. G. H. von Wright. Trans. Peter Winch. Chicago, IL: University of Chicago Press, 1980.

QUESTIONS FOR MAKING CONNECTIONS
WITHIN THE READING

1. When you read Nelson, you might feel like a stranger who has entered a room full of unfamiliar people, all of whom have known one another for years and are eager to discuss subjects you know little about. But the truth is that few of Nelson's readers will understand all her references. Why, then, does she add so many? Assuming Nelson's game is something other than parading her erudition, what purpose might her many references serve? What is Nelson trying to do by drawing together so many different ideas from so many different thinkers? Is she trying to dramatize how it feels to live in the information age? Or would you say that she is simply thinking—learning new things and then following connections to see wherever they might lead?

2. *Dead Man Walking,* Abu Ghraib, the Milgram experiment, black sites, Blackwater, RETORT, Zen, *4′33″*—these are just some of Nelson's references, along with a long list of people that includes Eve Kosofsky Sedgwick, Stephen King, Susan Sontag, Ludwig Wittgenstein, Hannah Arendt, Seymour Hersh, and Wayne Koestenbaum. Pick one name from the essay and do some online research which you can later report to the class, explaining how the person and his or her work connect to Nelson's larger argument. After everyone in the class has made a presentation, collectively try to identify the common interests and agendas that might tie these different people together. If the names weren't chosen at random—and they weren't—how do they intersect?

3. Nelson quotes Susan Sontag who famously described our time as an "age of extremity." According to Sontag, living in such an age allows us only "two equally fearful, but seemingly opposed, destinies: unremitting banality and inconceivable terror." What might Sontag have meant when she made this declaration—in particular, what "extremities" could she have had in mind? In what ways does the term *banality* describe the media environment today? Think, for example, about the latest coverage of figures like Lady Gaga or Beyoncé. In what ways does "terror" also play a role, and what is the relation between terror and banality? Does Nelson agree with Sontag's claim that only two "destinies" are now available to us? Could slowing down and staying still offer an alternative to both banality and terror? How?

QUESTIONS FOR WRITING

1. Nelson begins her essay by arguing that Sister Helen Prejean was naive to think "that it is simple, blameless ignorance that prompts so many Americans to support executions (or the torture of detainees in the so called war on terror, and so on)." If our entanglement with violence were just a matter of "simple, blameless ignorance," then new knowledge should indeed be an

adequate solution. But Nelson seems to doubt that knowledge by itself has the power to set us free. For her, *how* we know may be even more important than *what* we know. What is the relation between violence and "watching"—between violence and the habit of spectatorship created by the constant presence of the media? Are we so busy watching violence that we neglect to act in ways that might bring it to an end? Do we need to change the things we watch? Do we need to watch more critically?

2. At one moment in her essay Nelson asks us to compare the work of two artists: the Austrian avant-garde filmmaker Hermann Nitsch, whose multimedia creations routinely include scenes of mutilated humans and animals, and John Cage's Zen-inspired *4'33"*. Examples of the work of both artists are available online. On YouTube, for example, you can listen to Cage's "Dream" or "In a Landscape," and you can hear some of Nitsch's work— but you should do an image search as well. Prepare to be surprised and possibly revulsed. Using Cage and Nitsch as a starting point, discuss the dangers and the possibilities offered by the arts in our time. In what ways are Cage and Nitsch in opposition? What objectives and methods do they share despite their differences? Can art point the way beyond our current dilemmas, or does it simply mirror our confusions?

QUESTIONS FOR MAKING CONNECTIONS
BETWEEN READINGS

1. Because we normally view creativity and the arts in a positive light, we might not think about the possibility that they can sometimes undermine our happiness and freedom. Azar Nafisi, for example, celebrates literary art as a unique sphere of freedom in the repressive atmosphere of Iran's Islamic Republic:

    > We lived in a culture that denied any merit to literary works, considering them important only when they were handmaidens to something seemingly more urgent—namely ideology. This was a country where all gestures, even the most private, were interpreted in political terms.

    Would Nelson agree that art can be free from ideology—free, that is, from values? Or does she think that art always promotes values of some kind? If art always conveys values, what are the values Nafisi and her group find in the writers they read? What are some of the values conveyed by the artists Nelson discusses?

2. Like Cathy Davidson, Nelson asks us to explore how our attention is influenced by contemporary culture, including the new media. Of the two writers, which of them seems to be more receptive to the possibilities of technology? How does Nelson's thinking complicate Davidson's optimism

about the uses of attention in our times? What role does distraction play in the ideas of each writer? In what ways might Nelson's essay be said to inject an ethical dimension into the debate over the influence of new media? That is, in what ways does she urge us to consider the "dark side" as well as the positives? Would Nelson agree with Davidson's critics, who allege that she is naively optimistic?

◆◆◆

TIM O'BRIEN

In 1968, DURING the war in Vietnam, Tim O'Brien graduated from college and was served a draft notice. An avowed opponent of the war, he considered fleeing to Canada but ultimately reported for basic training and was stationed near the hamlet of My Lai shortly after the shocking massacre there, when American soldiers slaughtered three- to five-hundred unarmed civilians, including women and children. Investigators later produced evidence of torture, gang rape, and the dismemberment of the bodies of villagers. O'Brien returned to the United States in 1970, having received injuries that earned him a Purple Heart. Since then he has published dozens of stories and books, both fiction and nonfiction, exploring the themes of war and violence, including the National Book Award-winning *Going After Cacciato* (1978). He has received many other prestigious awards as well, among them the O. Henry Award, the National Book Critics Circle Award, and the Pulitzer Prize. He is currently a visiting professor and holds an endowed chair at Texas State University in San Marcos, where he teaches in the creative writing program.

"How to Tell a True War Story," from O'Brien's collection *The Things They Carried* (1998), is, paradoxically, a work of fiction. In the shadow of events like My Lai, the choice of fiction might appear to offer readers a comforting distance from a troubled history. But O'Brien's decision to present his narrative in the form of fiction is actually a sign of his continued engagement with a puzzle that has shaped his work for almost three decades. For O'Brien, fiction is sometimes the most faithful way of getting at the truth, especially in accounts of war, where the experience outstrips the resources of language. In O'Brien's work, the cost of war is not measured only in the loss of life, but also in the loss of moral certainty. As he told one interviewer, "What we see accurately with our eyes can sometimes be very deceptive. We don't see everything. No historian can fit into a textbook the thoughts of every single soldier in every single war and every single episode. Much is being selected and generalized. So in *The Things They Carried*, I'm trying to get at this sense of how difficult it is to pin down the truth with a capital 'T.' In a way, it's a warning against absolutism, against black and white declarations of what's true and what's not true. So part of the effort is trying to display through fiction the ambiguous, blurry, complicated, grayish fog of even the most plainly historical events."

"How to Tell a True War Story" from THE THINGS THEY CARRIED by Tim O'Brien. Copyright © 1990 by Tim O'Brien. Reprinted by permission of Houghton Mifflin Harcourt Publishing Company. All rights reserved.

Biographical information comes from <http://illyria.com/tob/tobbio.html>; quotation comes from "An Interview with Tim O'Brien," *The Big Read*, <http://www.neabigread.org/books/thethingstheycarried/readers-guide/about-the-author/>.

How to Tell a True War Story

This is true.

I had a buddy in Vietnam. His name was Bob Kiley, but everybody called him Rat.

A friend of his gets killed, so about a week later Rat sits down and writes a letter to the guy's sister. Rat tells her what a great brother she had, how together the guy was, a number one pal and comrade. A real soldier's soldier, Rat says. Then he tells a few stories to make the point, how her brother would always volunteer for stuff nobody else would volunteer for in a million years, dangerous stuff, like doing recon or going out on these really badass night patrols. Stainless steel balls, Rat tells her. The guy was a little crazy, for sure, but crazy in a good way, a real daredevil, because he liked the challenge of it, he liked testing himself, just man against gook. A great, great guy, Rat says.

Anyway, it's a terrific letter, very personal and touching. Rat almost bawls writing it. He gets all teary telling about the good times they had together, how her brother made the war seem almost fun, always raising hell and lighting up villes and bringing smoke to bear every which way. A great sense of humor, too. Like the time at this river when he went fishing with a whole damn crate of hand grenades. Probably the funniest thing in world history, Rat says, all that gore, about twenty zillion dead gook fish. Her brother, he had the right attitude. He knew how to have a good time. On Halloween, this real hot spooky night, the dude paints up his body all different colors and puts on this weird mask and hikes over to a ville and goes trick-or-treating almost stark naked, just boots and balls and an M-16. A tremendous human being, Rat says. Pretty nutso sometimes, but you could trust him with your life.

And then the letter gets very sad and serious. Rat pours his heart out. He says he loved the guy. He says the guy was his best friend in the world. They were like soul mates, he says, like twins or something, they had a whole lot in common. He tells the guy's sister he'll look her up when the war's over.

So what happens?

Rat mails the letter. He waits two months. The dumb cooze never writes back.

A true war story is never moral. It does not instruct, nor encourage virtue, nor suggest models of proper human behavior, nor restrain men from doing the things men have always done. If a story seems moral, do not believe it. If at the end of a war story you feel uplifted, or if you feel that some small bit of rectitude has been salvaged from the larger waste, then you have been made the victim of a very old and terrible lie. There is no rectitude whatsoever. There is no virtue. As a first rule of thumb, therefore, you can tell a true war story by its absolute and uncompromising allegiance to obscenity and evil. Listen to Rat Kiley.

Cooze, he says. He does not say bitch. He certainly does not say woman, or girl. He says cooze. Then he spits and stares. He's nineteen years old—it's too much for him—so he looks at you with those big sad gentle killer eyes and says cooze, because his friend is dead, and because it's so incredibly sad and true: she never wrote back.

You can tell a true war story if it embarrasses you. If you don't care for obscenity, you don't care for the truth; if you don't care for the truth, watch how you vote. Send guys to war, they come home talking dirty.

Listen to Rat: "Jesus Christ, man, I write this beautiful fuckin' letter, I slave over it, and what happens? The dumb cooze never writes back."

The dead guy's name was Curt Lemon. What happened was, we crossed a muddy river and marched west into the mountains, and on the third day we took a break along a trail junction in deep jungle. Right away, Lemon and Rat Kiley started goofing. They didn't understand about the spookiness. They were kids; they just didn't know. A nature hike, they thought, not even a war, so they went off into the shade of some giant trees—quadruple canopy, no sunlight at all—and they were giggling and calling each other yellow mother and playing a silly game they'd invented. The game involved smoke grenades, which were harmless unless you did stupid things, and what they did was pull out the pin and stand a few feet apart and play catch under the shade of those huge trees. Whoever chickened out was a yellow mother. And if nobody chickened out, the grenade would make a light popping sound and they'd be covered with smoke and they'd laugh and dance around and then do it again.

It's all exactly true.

It happened, to *me,* nearly twenty years ago, and I still remember that trail junction and those giant trees and a soft dripping sound somewhere beyond the trees. I remember the smell of moss. Up in the canopy there were tiny white blossoms, but no sunlight at all, and I remember the shadows spreading out under the trees where Curt Lemon and Rat Kiley were playing catch with smoke grenades. Mitchell Sanders sat flipping his yo-yo. Norman Bowker and Kiowa and Dave Jensen were dozing, or half dozing, and all around us were those ragged green mountains.

Except for the laughter things were quiet.

At one point, I remember, Mitchell Sanders turned and looked at me, not quite nodding, as if to warn me about something, as if he already *knew,* then after a while he rolled up his yo-yo and moved away.

It's hard to tell you what happened next.

They were just goofing. There was a noise, I suppose, which must've been the detonator, so I glanced behind me and watched Lemon step from the shade into bright sunlight. His face was suddenly brown and shining. A handsome kid, really. Sharp gray eyes, lean and narrow-waisted, and when he died it was almost beautiful, the way the sunlight came around him and lifted him up and sucked him high into a tree full of moss and vines and white blossoms.

In any war story, but especially a true one, it's difficult to separate what happened from what seemed to happen. What seems to happen becomes its own happening and has to be told that way. The angles of vision are skewed. When a booby trap explodes, you close your eyes and duck and float outside yourself. When a guy dies, like Curt Lemon, you look away and then look back for a moment and then look away again. The pictures get jumbled; you tend to miss a lot. And then afterward, when you go to tell about it, there is always that surreal seemingness, which makes the story seem untrue, but which in fact represents the hard and exact truth as it *seemed*.

In many cases a true war story cannot be believed. If you believe it, be skeptical. It's a question of credibility. Often the crazy stuff is true and the normal stuff isn't, because the normal stuff is necessary to make you believe the truly incredible craziness.

In other cases you can't even tell a true war story. Sometimes it's just beyond telling.

I heard this one, for example, from Mitchell Sanders. It was near dusk and we were sitting at my foxhole along a wide muddy river north of Quang Ngai. I remember how peaceful the twilight was. A deep pinkish red spilled out on the river, which moved without sound, and in the morning we would cross the river and march west into the mountains. The occasion was right for a good story.

"God's truth," Mitchell Sanders said. "A six-man patrol goes up into the mountains on a basic listening-post operation. The idea's to spend a week up there, just lie low and listen for enemy movement. They've got a radio along, so if they hear anything suspicious—anything—they're supposed to call in artillery or gunships, whatever it takes. Otherwise they keep strict field discipline. Absolute silence. They just listen."

Sanders glanced at me to make sure I had the scenario. He was playing with his yo-yo, dancing it with short, tight little strokes of the wrist.

His face was blank in the dusk.

"We're talking regulation, by-the-book LP. These six guys, they don't say boo for a solid week. They don't got tongues. *All* ears."

"Right," I said.

"Understand me?"

"Invisible."

Sanders nodded.

"Affirm," he said. "Invisible. So what happens is, these guys get themselves deep in the bush, all camouflaged up, and they lie down and wait and that's all they do, nothing else, they lie there for seven straight days and just listen. And man, I'll tell you—it's spooky. This is mountains. You don't *know* spooky till you been there. Jungle, sort of, except it's way up in the clouds and there's always this fog—like rain, except it's not raining—everything's all wet and swirly and tangled up and you can't see jack, you can't find your own pecker to piss with. Like you don't even have a body. Serious spooky. You just go with the vapors—the fog sort of takes you in.... And the sounds, man. The sounds carry forever. You hear stuff nobody should *ever* hear."

Sanders was quiet for a second, just working the yo-yo, then he smiled at me.

"So after a couple days the guys start hearing this real soft, kind of wacked-out music. Weird echoes and stuff. Like a radio or something, but it's not a radio, it's this strange gook music that comes right out of the rocks. Faraway, sort of, but right up close, too. They try to ignore it. But it's a listening post, right? So they listen. And every night they keep hearing that crazyass gook concert. All kinds of chimes and xylophones. I mean, this is wilderness—no way, it can't be real—but there it *is*, like the mountains are tuned in to Radio fucking Hanoi. Naturally they get nervous. One guy sticks Juicy Fruit in his ears. Another guy almost flips. Thing is, though, they can't report music. They can't get on the horn and call back to base and say, 'Hey, listen, we need some firepower, we got to blow away this weirdo gook rock band.' They can't do that. It wouldn't go down. So they lie there in the fog and keep their mouths shut. And what makes it extra bad, see, is the poor dudes can't horse around like normal. Can't joke it away. Can't even talk to each other except maybe in whispers, all hush-hush, and that just revs up the willies. All they do is listen."

Again there was some silence as Mitchell Sanders looked out on the river. The dark was coming on hard now, and off to the west I could see the mountains rising in silhouette, all the mysteries and unknowns.

"This next part," Sanders said quietly, "you won't believe."

"Probably not," I said.

"You won't. And you know why?" He gave me a long, tired smile. "Because it happened. Because every word is absolutely dead-on true."

Sanders made a sound in his throat, like a sigh, as if to say he didn't care if I believed him or not. But he did care. He wanted me to feel the truth, to believe by the raw force of feeling. He seemed sad, in a way.

"These six guys," he said, "they're pretty fried out by now, and one night they start hearing voices. Like at a cocktail party. That's what it sounds like, this big swank gook cocktail party somewhere out there in the fog. Music and chitchat and stuff. It's crazy, I know, but they hear the champagne corks. They hear the actual martini glasses. Real hoity-toity, all very civilized, except this isn't civilization. This is Nam.

"Anyway, the guys try to be cool. They just lie there and groove, but after a while they start hearing—you won't believe this—they hear chamber music. They hear violins and cellos. They hear this terrific mama-san soprano. Then after a while they hear gook opera and a glee club and the Haiphong Boys Choir and a barbershop quartet and all kinds of weird chanting and Buddha-Buddha stuff. And the whole time, in the background, there's still that cocktail party going on. All these different voices. Not human voices, though. Because it's the mountains. Follow me? The rock—it's *talking*. And the fog, too, and the grass and the goddamn mongooses. Everything talks. The trees talk politics, the monkeys talk religion. The whole country: Vietnam. The place talks. It talks. Understand? Nam—it truly *talks*.

"The guys can't cope. They lose it. They get on the radio and report enemy movement—a whole army, they say—and they order up the firepower. They get arty and gunships. They call in air strikes. And I'll tell you, they fuckin' crash that cocktail party. All night long, they just smoke those mountains. They make jungle juice. They blow away trees and glee clubs and whatever else there is to blow away. Scorch time. They walk napalm up and down the ridges.

They bring in the Cobras and F-4s, they use Willie Peter and HE and incendiaries. It's all fire. They make those mountains burn.

"Around dawn things finally get quiet. Like you never even *heard* quiet before. One of those real thick, real misty days—just clouds and fog, they're off in this special zone—and the mountains are absolutely dead-flat silent. Like *Brigadoon*—pure vapor, you know? Everything's all sucked up inside the fog. Not a single sound, except they still *hear* it.

"So they pack up and start humping. They head down the mountain, back to base camp, and when they get there they don't say diddly. They don't talk. Not a word, like they're deaf and dumb. Later on this fat bird colonel comes up and asks what the hell happened out there. What'd they hear? Why all the ordnance? The man's ragged out, he gets down tight on their case. I mean, they spent six trillion dollars on firepower, and this fatass colonel wants answers, he wants to know what the fuckin' story is.

"But the guys don't say zip. They just look at him for a while, sort of funny like, sort of amazed, and the whole war is right there in that stare. It says everything you can't ever say. It says, man, you got *wax* in your ears. It says, poor bastard, you'll never know—wrong frequency—you don't *even* want to hear this. Then they salute the fucker and walk away, because certain stories you don't ever tell."

You can tell a true war story by the way it never seems to end. Not then, not ever. Not when Mitchell Sanders stood up and moved off into the dark.

It all happened.

Even now, at this instant, I remember that yo-yo. In a way, I suppose, you had to be there, you had to hear it, but I could tell how desperately Sanders wanted me to believe him, his frustration at not quite getting the details right, not quite pinning down the final and definitive truth.

And I remember sitting at my foxhole that night, watching the shadows of Quang Ngai, thinking about the coming day and how we would cross the river and march west into the mountains, all the ways I might die, all the things I did not understand.

Late in the night Mitchell Sanders touched my shoulder. "Just came to me," he whispered. "The moral, I mean. Nobody listens. Nobody hears nothin'. Like that fatass colonel. The politicians, all the civilian types. Your girlfriend. My girlfriend. Everybody's sweet little virgin girlfriend. What they need is to go out on LP. The vapors, man. Trees and rocks—you got to *listen* to your enemy."

And then again, in the morning, Sanders came up to me. The platoon was preparing to move out, checking weapons, going through all the little rituals that preceded a day's march. Already the lead squad had crossed the river and was filing off toward the west.

"I got a confession to make," Sanders said. "Last night, man, I had to make up a few things."

"I know that."

"The glee club. There wasn't any glee club."

"Right."

"No opera."

"Forget it, I understand."

"Yeah, but listen, it's still true. Those six guys, they heard wicked sound out there. They heard sound you just plain won't believe."

Sanders pulled on his rucksack, closed his eyes for a moment, then almost smiled at me. I knew what was coming.

"All right," I said, "what's the moral?"

"Forget it."

"No, go ahead."

For a long while he was quiet, looking away, and the silence kept stretching out until it was almost embarrassing. Then he shrugged and gave me a stare that lasted all day.

"Hear that quiet, man?" he said. "That quiet—just listen. There's your moral."

In a true war story, if there's a moral at all, it's like the thread that makes the cloth. You can't tease it out. You can't extract the meaning without unraveling the deeper meaning. And in the end, really, there's nothing much to say about a true war story, except maybe "Oh."

True war stories do not generalize. They do not indulge in abstraction or analysis.

For example: War is hell. As a moral declaration the old truism seems perfectly true, and yet because it abstracts, because it generalizes, I can't believe it with my stomach. Nothing turns inside.

It comes down to gut instinct. A true war story, if truly told, makes the stomach believe.

This one does it for me. I've told it before—many times, many versions—but here's what actually happened.

We crossed that river and marched west into the mountains. On the third day, Curt Lemon stepped on a booby-trapped 105 round. He was playing catch with Rat Kiley, laughing, and then he was dead. The trees were thick; it took nearly an hour to cut an LZ for the dustoff.

Later, higher in the mountains, we came across a baby VC water buffalo. What it was doing there I don't know—no farms or paddies—but we chased it down and got a rope around it and led it along to a deserted village where we set up for the night. After supper Rat Kiley went over and stroked its nose.

He opened up a can of C rations, pork and beans, but the baby buffalo wasn't interested.

Rat shrugged.

He stepped back and shot it through the right front knee. The animal did not make a sound. It went down hard, then got up again, and Rat took careful aim and shot off an ear. He shot it in the hindquarters and in the little hump at its back. He shot it twice in the flanks. It wasn't to kill; it was to hurt. He put the rifle muzzle up against the mouth and shot the mouth away. Nobody said much. The whole platoon stood there watching, feeling all kinds of things, but there wasn't a great deal of pity for the baby water buffalo. Curt Lemon was dead. Rat Kiley had lost his best friend in the world. Later in the week he would write a long personal letter to the guy's sister, who would not write back, but for now it was a question of pain. He shot off the tail. He shot away chunks of meat below the ribs. All around us there was the smell of smoke and filth and deep greenery, and the evening was humid and very hot. Rat went to automatic. He shot randomly, almost casually, quick little spurts in the belly and butt. Then he reloaded, squatted down, and shot it in the left front knee. Again the animal fell hard and tried to get up, but this time it couldn't quite make it. It wobbled and went down sideways. Rat shot it in the nose. He bent forward and whispered something, as if talking to a pet, then he shot it in the throat. All the while the baby buffalo was silent, or almost silent, just a light bubbling sound where the nose had been. It lay very still. Nothing moved except the eyes, which were enormous, the pupils shiny black and dumb.

Rat Kiley was crying. He tried to say something, but then cradled his rifle and went off by himself.

The rest of us stood in a ragged circle around the baby buffalo. For a time no one spoke. We had witnessed something essential, something brand-new and profound, a piece of the world so startling there was not yet a name for it.

Somebody kicked the baby buffalo.

It was still alive, though just barely, just in the eyes.

"Amazing," Dave Jensen said. "My whole life, I never seen anything like it."

"Never?"

"Not hardly. Not once."

Kiowa and Mitchell Sanders picked up the baby buffalo. They hauled it across the open square, hoisted it up, and dumped it in the village well.

Afterward, we sat waiting for Rat to get himself together.

"Amazing," Dave Jensen kept saying. "A new wrinkle. I never seen it before."

Mitchell Sanders took out his yo-yo. "Well, that's Nam," he said. "Garden of Evil. Over here, man, every sin's real fresh and original."

How do you generalize?

War is hell, but that's not the half of it, because war is also mystery and terror and adventure and courage and discovery and holiness and pity and despair and longing and love. War is nasty; war is fun. War is thrilling; war is drudgery. War makes you a man; war makes you dead.

The truths are contradictory. It can be argued, for instance, that war is grotesque. But in truth war is also beauty. For all its horror, you can't help but gape at the awful majesty of combat. You stare out at tracer rounds unwinding through the dark like brilliant red ribbons. You crouch in ambush as a cool, impassive moon rises over the nighttime paddies. You admire the fluid symmetries of troops on the move, the harmonies of sound and shape and proportion, the great sheets of metal-fire streaming down from a gunship, the illumination rounds, the white phosphorus, the purply orange glow of napalm, the rocket's red glare. It's not pretty, exactly. It's astonishing. It fills the eye. It commands you. You hate it, yes, but your eyes do not. Like a killer forest fire, like cancer under a microscope, any battle or bombing raid or artillery barrage has the aesthetic purity of absolute moral indifference—a powerful, implacable beauty—and a true war story will tell the truth about this, though the truth is ugly.

To generalize about war is like generalizing about peace. Almost everything is true. Almost nothing is true. At its core, perhaps, war is just another name for death, and yet any soldier will tell you, if he tells the truth, that proximity to death brings with it a corresponding proximity to life. After a firefight, there is always the immense pleasure of aliveness. The trees are alive. The grass, the soil—everything. All around you things are purely living, and you among them, and the aliveness makes you tremble. You feel an intense, out-of-the-skin awareness of your living self—your truest self, the human being you want to be and then become by the force of wanting it. In the midst of evil you want to be a good man. You want decency. You want justice and courtesy and human concord, things you never knew you wanted. There is a kind of largeness to it, a kind of godliness. Though it's odd, you're never more alive than when you're almost dead. You recognize what's valuable. Freshly, as if for the first time, you love what's best in yourself and in the world, all that might be lost. At the hour of dusk you sit at your foxhole and look out on a wide river turning pinkish red, and at the mountains beyond, and although in the morning you must cross the river and go into the mountains and do terrible things and maybe die, even so, you find yourself studying the fine colors on the river, you feel wonder and awe at the setting of the sun, and you are filled with a hard, aching love for how the world could be and always should be, but now is not.

Mitchell Sanders was right. For the common soldier, at least, war has the feel—the spiritual texture—of a great ghostly fog, thick and permanent. There is no clarity. Everything swirls. The old rules are no longer binding, the old truths no longer true. Right spills over into wrong. Order blends into chaos, love into hate, ugliness into beauty, law into anarchy, civility into savagery. The vapors suck you in. You can't tell where you are, or why you're there, and the only certainty is overwhelming ambiguity.

In war you lose your sense of the definite, hence your sense of truth itself, and therefore it's safe to say that in a true war story nothing is ever absolutely true.

Often in a true war story there is not even a point, or else the point doesn't hit you until twenty years later, in your sleep, and you wake up and shake your wife and start telling the story to her, except when you get to the end you've forgotten the point again. And then for a long time you lie there watching the story happen in your head. You listen to your wife's breathing. The war's over. You close your eyes. You smile and think, Christ, what's the *point?*

This one wakes me up.

In the mountains that day, I watched Lemon turn sideways. He laughed and said *something* to Rat Kiley. Then he took a peculiar half step, moving from shade into bright sunlight, and the booby-trapped 105 round blew him into a tree. The parts were just hanging there, so Dave Jensen and I were ordered to shinny up and peel him off. I remember the white bone of an arm. I remember pieces of skin and something wet and yellow that must've been the intestines. The gore was horrible, and stays with me. But what wakes me up twenty years later is Dave Jensen singing "Lemon Tree" as we threw down the parts.

You can tell a true war story by the questions you ask. Somebody tells a story, let's say, and afterward you ask, "Is it true?" and if the answer matters, you've got your answer.

For example, we've all heard this one. Four guys go down a trail. A grenade sails out. One guy jumps on it and takes the blast and saves his three buddies.

Is it true?

The answer matters.

You'd feel cheated if it never happened. Without the grounding reality, it's just a trite bit of puffery, pure Hollywood, untrue in the way all such stories are untrue. Yet even if it did happen—and maybe it did, anything's possible—even then you know it can't be true, because a true war story does not depend upon that kind of truth. Absolute occurrence is irrelevant. A thing may happen and be a total lie; another thing may not happen and be truer than the truth. For example: Four guys go down a trail. A grenade sails out. One guy jumps on it and takes the blast, but it's a killer grenade and everybody dies anyway. Before they die, though, one of the dead guys says, "The fuck you do *that* for?" and the jumper says, "Story of my life, man," and the other guy starts to smile but he's dead.

That's a true story that never happened.

Twenty years later, I can still see the sunlight on Lemon's face. I can see him turning, looking back at Rat Kiley, then he laughed and took that curious half step from shade into sunlight, his face suddenly brown and shining, and when his foot touched down, in that instant, he must've thought it was the sunlight that was killing him. It was not the sunlight. It was a rigged 105 round. But if I could ever get the story right, how the sun seemed to gather around him and pick him up and lift him high into a tree, if I could somehow re-create the fatal whiteness of that light, the quick glare, the obvious cause and effect, then you would believe the last thing Curt Lemon believed, which for him must've been the final truth.

Now and then, when I tell this story, someone will come up to me afterward and say she liked it. It's always a woman. Usually it's an older woman of kindly temperament and humane politics. She'll explain that as a rule she hates war stories; she can't understand why people want to wallow in all the blood and gore. But this one she liked. The poor baby buffalo, it made her sad. Sometimes, even, there are little tears. What I should do, she'll say, is put it all behind me. Find new stories to tell.

I won't say it but I'll think it.

I'll picture Rat Kiley's face, his grief, and I'll think, *You dumb cooze.*

Because she wasn't listening.

It *wasn't* a war story. It was a *love* story.

But you can't say that. All you can do is tell it one more time, patiently, adding and subtracting, making up a few things to get at the real truth. No Mitchell Sanders, you tell her. No Lemon, no Rat Kiley. No trail junction. No baby buffalo. No vines or moss or white blossoms. Beginning to end, you tell her, it's all made up. Every goddamn detail—the mountains and the river and especially that poor dumb baby buffalo. None of it happened. *None* of it.

And even if it did happen, it didn't happen in the mountains, it happened in this little village on the Batangan Peninsula, and it was raining like crazy, and one night a guy named Stink Harris woke up screaming with a leech on his tongue. You can tell a true war story if you just keep on telling it.

And in the end, of course, a true war story is never about war. It's about sunlight. It's about the special way that dawn spreads out on a river when you know you must cross the river and march into the mountains and do things you are afraid to do. It's about love and memory. It's about sorrow. It's about sisters who never write back and people who never listen.

QUESTIONS FOR MAKING CONNECTIONS
WITHIN THE READING

1. Tim O'Brien's "How to Tell a True War Story" is part of a collection of stories by the author entitled *The Things They Carried*. Although the ostensible subject of this particular short story is a series of events that may have actually happened, the subtitle of the entire collection is "A Work of Fiction." "How to Tell a True War Story" begins with the explicit statement "This is true," but what sort of truth does it manage to convey? As you consider possible answers, please remember that the narrator warns us, "In many cases a true war story cannot be believed. If you believe it, be skeptical." Why is the issue of truth so important to a story about what happens in war? Does O'Brien really mean that there is no such thing as truth when we are talking about war? If everything about war is subjective, is it ever possible for one person to judge another person's military conduct?

2. Why does Rat Kiley write a letter to Curt Lemon's sister? What do you make of the details of his letter? Conventionally, such a letter would praise a fallen fellow combatant as a "hero," someone of exemplary character who had chosen to make the "ultimate sacrifice." Instead, Rat writes about the times he and Curt were "raising hell and lighting up villes and bringing smoke to bear every which way." Is Rat trying to insult the sister? Seduce her? Destroy her positive memories of her brother? When she fails to write back to him, why does Rat refer to her as a "dumb cooze"? For that matter, why does he refer to the Vietnamese as "gooks"? Is this simply an example of crude prejudice? If Rat began to think of the Vietnamese as people, much like his own family back home, how would such a change influence his behavior? If he thought of Lemon's sister as nothing more than a "cooze," why did he bother to write to her at all?

3. Why does Rat Kiley kill the baby water buffalo? And why is it that "the whole platoon stood there watching, feeling all kinds of things, but [not] a great deal of pity for the baby water buffalo"? How do you explain the reaction of Mitchell Sanders: "Well, that's Nam. Garden of Evil. Over here ... every sin's fresh and original"? If the men view Rat's killing of the buffalo as a "sin," why do they make no effort to stop him? Why do they appear to

feel no remorse afterward? Do they displace onto the buffalo their desire to get back at the Vietnamese, or is their behavior even more complicated? When they kill the buffalo, are they killing something in themselves? What part of themselves might they be killing, and why might they want to do so?

QUESTIONS FOR WRITING

1. Readers might perceive O'Brien's story to be a powerfully realistic evocation of war as people actually live it. On the other hand, in spite of its realistic qualities, the story sometimes becomes highly poetic, as in passages like this one:

   > Twenty years later, I can still see the sunlight on Lemon's face. I can see him turning, looking back at Rat Kiley, then he laughed and took the curious half step from shade into sunlight, his face suddenly brown and shining, and when his foot touched down, in that instant, he must've thought it was the sunlight that was killing him.

   Is O'Brien guilty of aestheticizing war—that is, of making it seem more beautiful, romantic, or exotic than it really is? Do you think that your reading of his account has made you less likely or more likely to regard war as necessary and noble? Has O'Brien's account made it less likely or more likely that you will think of war as a natural and even indispensable part of life as a human being?

2. What is the connection in O'Brien's short story between experience and language? Does he believe that our language predetermines the nature of our experience, or does he suggest, instead, that our experience is often more complex than our language can accommodate? Toward the end of the story, the narrator describes the kind of exchange he has, after reading his short stories in public, often with "an older woman of kindly temperament and humane politics." What sense can you make of the narrator's remarks about this exchange? Is it ever possible to describe our experience to others? Would listeners who had served in Vietnam be more likely to understand the narrator's account than those who had never been there? How about someone who had served in a different war? How much experience must people share in order to understand one another?

QUESTIONS FOR MAKING CONNECTIONS
BETWEEN READINGS

1. Would O'Brien's narrator be comfortable at The Citadel as described by Susan Faludi? Does the form of camaraderie we find at The Citadel correspond to the love felt by the men who served with the narrator

of O'Brien's story? Can we understand the rituals performed at The Citadel as forging bonds similar to those forged by war, or do you see significant differences? In what ways does O'Brien's story suggest that the culture of The Citadel is likely to prove more enduring than Faludi suggests? Is the culture of The Citadel really the culture of war itself? If you think so, then why have some distinguished military leaders tried to reform that institution?

2. Maggie Nelson, the author of "Great to Watch," probes our obsession with violence. After she has taken a critical look at popular books like Stephen King's *Running Man*, the reality television show *To Catch a Predator*, and Errol Morris's documentary *Standard Operating Procedure*, Nelson reflects on the possibility of some other way of life. Does O'Brien's "How to Tell a True War Story" belong in the company of *Running Man?* Does it actually embrace the violence it appears to reject? Or does it rise to the status of "art" as defined by Richard Foreman, the dramatist Nelson quotes:

> [Kitsch] means ... that the image seduced me, that it pushed a button that was ready to be pushed, and I responded. It didn't widen my sensibilities, compassion, or intuition. Whereas an art that affects you in the moment ... is straining to bring you to another level.... [It] has opened you to the possibility of growing into what you are not yet.

Does O'Brien push our buttons or does he strain to bring us to another level? Is his story "kitsch" or does it qualify as art when measured by Foreman's standard?

OLIVER SACKS

WHEN NEUROLOGIST OLIVER SACKS was awarded the Lewis Thomas Prize by Rockefeller University in 2002 for presenting the case histories of his patients, he was praised for his ability to take his readers into the worlds of people whose lives have been transformed by brain disorders. "Sacks," the awards committee concluded, "presses us to follow him into uncharted regions of human experience—and compels us to realize, once there, that we are confronting only ourselves." Sacks has written with great sensitivity about patients felled by sleeping sickness for decades, about a man who thought that his wife was a hat, and about people suffering with Tourette's syndrome, a disease that can cause those it afflicts to twitch or shout compulsively.

Born and educated in England, Sacks has lived in New York since 1965, where he was for decades a clinical professor of neurology at the Albert Einstein College of Medicine, adjunct professor of neurology at the NYU School of Medicine, and consultant neurologist to the Little Sisters of the Poor. In 2007, he was appointed Professor of Clinical Neurology and Clinical Psychiatry at Columbia University Medical Center. Along with this appointment, he was designated Columbia University's first Columbia Artist, granting him free rein in working across departments and organizing interdisciplinary programs. As Sacks explained in one interview, his interest in the brain and in neurology arose from his childhood experience of visual migraines. "I would often lose sight to one side, and sometimes one can lose the idea of one side in a migraine, which can be a very, very strange thing. When I was young I was sort of terrified of these things. I asked my mother, who was a doctor herself and also had visual migraines. She was the first to explain to me that we are not just cameras—we are not just given the visual world. We make it to some extent."

The observation of patients creatively adapting to the challenges posed by an illness has shaped Sacks's own approach to medicine and has led him to develop a field he has called *neuroanthropology*, which takes as its subject the different ways that illness is perceived and experienced by people around the world. Most recently, he has turned his attention to the nearly universal love of music and to the experience of hallucinations, which are, he argues, far more common than most people recognize. As the author of *Awakenings* (1973), *The Man Who Mistook His Wife for a Hat* (1985), *Musicophilia: Tales of Music and the Brain* (2007), and *Hallucinations* (2012), among other works, Sacks brings together biology and biography for the purpose of advancing a more humane practice of medicine.

The Mind's Eye

To what extent are we the authors, the creators, of our own experiences? How much are these predetermined by the brains or senses we are born with, and to what extent do we shape our brains through experience? The effects of a profound perceptual deprivation such as blindness may cast an unexpected light on these questions. Going blind, especially later in life, presents one with a huge, potentially overwhelming challenge: to find a new way of living, of ordering one's world, when the old way has been destroyed.

In 1990, I was sent an extraordinary book called *Touching the Rock: An Experience of Blindness*, by John Hull, a professor of religious education in England. Hull had grown up partly sighted, developing cataracts at the age of thirteen and becoming completely blind in his left eye four years later. Vision in his right eye remained reasonable until he was thirty-five or so, but there followed a decade of steadily failing vision, so that Hull needed stronger and stronger magnifying glasses and had to write with thicker and thicker pens. In 1983, at the age of forty-eight, he became completely blind.

Touching the Rock is the journal he dictated in the three years that followed. It is full of piercing insights about his transition to life as a blind person, but most striking for me was his description of how, after he became blind, he experienced a gradual attenuation of visual imagery and memory, and finally a virtual extinction of them (except in dreams)—a state that he called "deep blindness."

By this, Hull meant not only a loss of visual images and memories but a loss of the very *idea* of seeing, so that even concepts like "here," "there," and "facing" seemed to lose meaning for him. The sense of objects having appearances, or visible characteristics, vanished. He could no longer imagine how the numeral 3 looked unless he traced it in the air with his finger. He could construct a *motor* image of a 3, but not a visual one.

At first Hull was greatly distressed by this: he could no longer conjure up the faces of his wife or children, or of familiar and loved landscapes and places. But he then came to accept it with remarkable equanimity, regarding it as a natural response to losing his sight. Indeed, he seemed to feel that the loss of visual imagery was a prerequisite for the full development, the heightening, of his other senses.

Two years after becoming completely blind, Hull had apparently become so nonvisual in his imagery and memory as to resemble someone who had been blind from birth. In a profoundly religious way, and in language sometimes reminiscent of that of Saint John of the Cross, Hull entered into the state of deep blindness, surrendered himself, with a sort of acquiescence and joy. He spoke of deep blindness as "an authentic and autonomous world, a place of its own.… Being a whole-body seer is to be in one of the concentrated human conditions."

Being a "whole-body seer," for Hull, meant shifting his attention, his center of gravity, to the other senses, and these senses assumed a new richness and power. Thus he wrote of how the sound of rain, never before accorded much attention, could delineate a whole landscape for him, for its sound on the garden path was different from its sound as it drummed on the lawn, or on the bushes in his garden, or on the fence dividing the garden from the road:

> Rain has a way of bringing out the contours of everything; it throws a coloured blanket over previously invisible things; instead of an intermittent and thus fragmented world, the steadily falling rain creates continuity of acoustic experience … presents the fullness of an entire situation all at once … gives a sense of perspective and of the actual relationships of one part of the world to another.

With his new intensity of auditory experience (or attention), along with the sharpening of his other senses, Hull came to feel a sense of intimacy with nature, an intensity of being-in-the-world, beyond anything he had known when he was sighted. Blindness became for him "a dark, paradoxical gift." This was not just "compensation," he emphasized, but a whole new order, a new mode of human being. With this, he extricated himself from visual nostalgia, from the strain or falsity of trying to pass as "normal," and found a new focus, a new freedom and identity. His teaching at the university expanded, became more fluent; his writing became stronger and deeper; he became intellectually and spiritually bolder, more confident. He felt he was on solid ground at last.[1]

Hull's description seemed to me an astounding example of how an individual deprived of one form of perception could totally reshape himself to a new center, a new perceptual identity. Yet I found it extraordinary that such an annihilation of visual memory as he described could happen to an adult with decades of rich and significant visual experience to call upon. I could not, however, doubt the authenticity of Hull's account, which he related with the most scrupulous care and lucidity.

Cognitive neuroscientists have known for the past few decades that the brain is far less hardwired than was once thought. Helen Neville was one of the pioneers here, showing that in prelingually deaf people (that is, those who had been born deaf or become deaf before the age of two or so) the auditory parts of the brain did not degenerate. They remained active and functional, but with an activity and a function that were new: they were transformed, "reallocated," in Neville's term, for processing visual language. Comparable studies in those born blind, or blinded early, show that some areas of the visual cortex may be reallocated and used to process sound and touch.

With this reallocation of parts of the visual cortex, hearing, touch, and other senses in the blind can take on a hyperacuity that perhaps no sighted person can imagine. Bernard Morin, the mathematician who showed in the 1960s how a sphere could be turned inside out, became blind at the age of six, from glaucoma. He felt that his mathematical achievement required a special sort of spatial sense—a haptic perception and imagination beyond anything a sighted mathematician was likely to have. And a similar sort of spatial or tactile giftedness has been central to the work of Geerat Vermeij, a conchologist who has delineated many new species of mollusks, based on tiny variations in the shapes and contours of their shells. Vermeij has been blind since the age of three.[2]

Faced with such findings and reports, neuroscientists began to concede in the 1970s that there might be a certain flexibility or plasticity in the brain, at least in the first couple of years of life. But when this critical period was over, it was thought, the brain became much less plastic.

Yet the brain remains capable of making radical shifts in response to sensory deprivation. In 2008, Lotfi Merabet, Alvaro Pascual-Leone, and their colleagues showed that, even in sighted adults, as little as five days of being blindfolded produced marked shifts to nonvisual forms of behavior and cognition, and they demonstrated the physiological changes in the brain that went along with this. (They feel it is important to distinguish between such rapid and reversible changes, which seem to make use of preexisting but latent intersensory connections, and the long-lasting changes that occur especially in response to early or congenital blindness, which may entail major reorganizations of cortical circuitry.)

Apparently Hull's visual cortex, even in adulthood, had adapted to a loss of visual input by taking over other sensory functions—hearing, touch, smell—while relinquishing the power of visual imagery. I assumed that Hull's experience was typical of acquired blindness, the response, sooner or later, of everyone who loses sight—and a brilliant example of cortical plasticity.

Yet when I came to publish an essay on Hull's book in 1991, I was taken aback to receive a number of letters from blind people, letters that were often somewhat puzzled and occasionally indignant in tone. Many of these people wrote that they could not identify with Hull's experience and said that they themselves, even decades after losing their sight, had never lost their visual images or memories. One woman, who had lost her sight at fifteen, wrote:

> Even though I am totally blind ... I consider myself a very visual person.
> I still "see" objects in front of me. As I am typing now I can see my
> hands on the keyboard.... I don't feel comfortable in a new environ-
> ment until I have a mental picture of its appearance. I need a mental
> map for my independent moving, too.

Had I been wrong, or at least one-sided, in accepting Hull's experience as a typical response to blindness? Had I been guilty of emphasizing one mode of response too strongly, oblivious to other, radically different possibilities?

This feeling came to a head a few years later, when I received a letter from an Australian psychologist named Zoltan Torey. Torey wrote to me not about blindness but about a book he had written on the brain-mind problem and the nature of consciousness. In his letter he also mentioned that he had been blinded in an accident at the age of twenty-one. But although he was "advised to switch from a visual to an auditory mode of adjustment," he had moved in the opposite direction, resolving to develop instead his inner eye, his powers of visual imagery, to their greatest possible extent.

In this, he said, he had been extremely successful, developing a remarkable power of generating, holding, and manipulating images in his mind, so much so that he had been able to construct a virtual visual world that seemed as real and intense to him as the perceptual one he had lost—indeed, sometimes more real, more intense. This imagery, moreover, enabled him to do things that might have seemed scarcely possible for a blind man.

"I replaced the entire roof guttering of my multi-gabled home single-handed," he wrote, "and solely on the strength of the accurate and well-focused manipulation of my now totally pliable and responsive mental space." Torey later expanded on this episode, mentioning the great alarm of his neighbors at seeing a blind man alone on the roof of his house—at night (even though, of course, darkness made no difference to him).

And he felt that his newly strengthened visual imagery enabled him to think in ways that had not been available to him before, allowed him to project himself inside machines and other systems, to envisage solutions, models, and designs.

I wrote back to Torey, suggesting that he consider writing another book, a more personal one, exploring how his life had been affected by blindness and how he had responded to this in the most improbable and seemingly paradoxical way. A few years later, he sent me the manuscript of *Out of Darkness*. In this new book, Torey described the early visual memories of his childhood and youth in Hungary before the Second World War: the sky-blue buses of Budapest, the egg-yellow trams, the lighting of gas lamps, the funicular railway on the Buda side. He described a carefree and privileged youth, roaming with his father in the wooded mountains above the Danube, playing games and pranks at school, growing up in a highly intellectual environment of writers, actors, professionals of every sort. Torey's father was the head of a large motion-picture studio and would often give his son scripts to read. "This," Torey wrote, "gave me the opportunity to visualize stories, plots and characters, to work my imagination— a skill that was to become a lifeline and source of strength in the years ahead."

All of this came to a brutal end with the Nazi occupation, the siege of Buda, and then the Soviet occupation. Torey, by this time an adolescent, found himself passionately drawn to the big questions—the mystery of the universe, of life, and, above all, the mystery of consciousness, of the mind. At nineteen, feeling that he needed to immerse himself in biology, engineering, neuroscience, and psychology, but knowing that there was no chance of an intellectual life in Soviet Hungary, Torey made his escape and found his way to Australia, where, penniless and without connections, he did various manual jobs. In June of 1951, loosening the plug in a vat of acid at the chemical factory where he worked, he had the accident that bisected his life:

> The last thing I saw with complete clarity was a glint of light in the
> flood of acid that was to engulf my face and change my life. It was a
> nano-second of sparkle, framed by the black circle of the drumface, less

than a foot away. This was the final scene, the slender thread that ties me to my visual past.

When it became clear that his corneas had been hopelessly damaged and that he would have to live his life as a blind man, he was advised to rebuild his representation of the world on the basis of hearing and touch, and to "forget about sight and visualizing altogether." But this was something that Torey could not or would not do. He had emphasized, in his first letter to me, the importance of a most critical choice at this juncture: "I immediately resolved to find out how far a partially sense-deprived brain could go to rebuild a life." Put this way, it sounds abstract, like an experiment. But in his book one senses the tremendous feelings underlying his resolution: the horror of darkness—"the empty darkness," as Torey often calls it, "the grey fog that was engulfing me"—and the passionate desire to hold on to light and sight, to maintain, if only in memory and imagination, a vivid and living visual world. The very title of his book says all this, and the note of defiance is sounded from the start.

Hull, who did not use his imagery in a deliberate way, lost it within two or three years and became unable to remember which way round a 3 went; Torey, on the other hand, soon became able to multiply four-figure numbers by each other, as on a blackboard, visualizing the whole operation in his mind, "painting" the sub-operations in different colors.

Torey maintained a cautious and "scientific" attitude to his own visual imagery, taking pains to check the accuracy of his images by every means available. "I learned," he wrote, "to hold the image in a tentative way, conferring credibility and status on it only when some information would tip the balance in its favor." He soon gained enough confidence in the reliability of his visual imagery to stake his life upon it, as when he undertook roof repairs by himself. And this confidence extended to other, purely mental projects. He became able "to imagine, to visualize, for example, the inside of a differential gearbox in action as if from inside its casing. I was able to watch the cogs bite, lock and revolve, distributing the spin as required. I began to play around with this internal view in connection with mechanical and technical problems, visualizing how subcomponents relate in the atom, or in the living cell." This power of imagery was crucial, Torey thought, in enabling him to arrive at a new view of the brain-mind problem by visualizing the brain "as a perpetual juggling act of interacting routines."

Soon after receiving the manuscript of *Out of Darkness*, I received proofs of yet another memoir about blindness: Sabriye Tenberken's *My Path Leads to Tibet*. While Hull and Torey are thinkers, preoccupied in their different ways by inwardness, states of brain and mind, Tenberken is a doer; she has traveled, often alone, all over Tibet, where for centuries blind people have been treated as less than human and denied education, work, respect, or a role in the community. Virtually single-handed, Tenberken has transformed their situation over the past decade or so, devising a form of Tibetan Braille, establishing the first schools for the blind there, and integrating the graduates of these schools into their communities.

Tenberken herself had impaired vision almost from birth, but was able to make out faces and landscapes until she was twelve. As a child in Germany, she loved painting and had a particular predilection for colors, and when she was no longer able to decipher shapes and forms, she could still use colors to identify objects.[3]

Though she had been totally blind for a dozen years when she went to Tibet, Tenberken continued to use her other senses, along with verbal descriptions, visual memories, and a strong pictorial and synesthetic sensibility, to construct "pictures" of landscapes and rooms, of environments and scenes—pictures so lively and detailed as to astonish her listeners. These images may sometimes be wildly or comically different from reality, as she related in one incident when she and a companion drove to Nam Co, the great salt lake in Tibet. Turning eagerly towards the lake, Tenberken saw, in her imagination, "a beach of crystallized salt shimmering like snow under an evening sun, at the edge of a vast body of turquoise water.... And down below, on the deep green mountain flanks, a few nomads were watching their yaks grazing." It then turned out that she had not been "looking" at the lake at all, but facing in another direction, "staring" at rocks and a gray landscape. These disparities do not faze her in the least—she is happy to have so vivid a visual imagination. Hers is essentially an artistic imagination, which can be impressionistic, romantic, not veridical at all, whereas Torey's imagination is that of an engineer, and has to be factual, accurate down to the last detail.

Jacques Lusseyran was a French Resistance fighter whose memoir, *And There Was Light*, deals mostly with his experiences fighting the Nazis and later in Buchenwald, but includes many beautiful descriptions of his early adaptations to blindness. He was blinded in an accident when he was not quite eight years old, an age that he came to feel was "ideal" for such an eventuality, for, while he already had a rich visual experience to call on, "the habits of a boy of eight are not yet formed, either in body or in mind. His body is infinitely supple."

At first, Lusseyran began to lose his visual imagery:

> A very short time after I went blind I forgot the faces of my mother and father and the faces of most of the people I loved.... I stopped caring whether people were dark or fair, with blue eyes or green. I felt that sighted people spent too much time observing these empty things.... I no longer even thought about them. People no longer seemed to possess them. Sometimes in my mind men and women appeared without heads or fingers.

This is similar to Hull, who wrote, "Increasingly, I am no longer even trying to imagine what people look like.... I am finding it more and more difficult to realize that people look like anything, to put any meaning into the idea that they have an appearance."

But then, while relinquishing the actual visual world and many of its values and categories, Lusseyran began to construct and to use an imaginary visual world more like Torey's. He came to identify himself as belonging to a special category, the "visual blind."

Lusseyran's inner vision started as a sensation of light, a formless, flooding, streaming radiance. Neurological terms are bound to sound reductive in this almost mystical context, yet one might venture to interpret this as a release phenomenon, a spontaneous, almost eruptive arousal of the visual cortex, now deprived of its normal visual input. (Such a phenomenon is analogous, perhaps, to tinnitus or phantom limbs, though endowed, here, by a devout and precociously imaginative little boy, with some element of the supernal.) But then, it becomes clear, he found himself in possession of great powers of visual imagery, and not just a formless luminosity.

The visual cortex, the inner eye, having been activated, his mind constructed a "screen" upon which whatever he thought or desired was projected and, if need be, manipulated, as on a computer screen. "This screen was not like a blackboard, rectangular or square, which so quickly reaches the edge of its frame," he wrote.

> My screen was always as big as I needed it to be. Because it was nowhere in space it was everywhere at the same time.... Names, figures and objects in general did not appear on my screen without shape, nor just in black and white, but in all the colors of the rainbow. Nothing entered my mind without being bathed in a certain amount of light.... In a few months my personal world had turned into a painter's studio.

Great powers of visualization were crucial to the young Lusseyran, even in something as nonvisual (one would think) as learning Braille, and in his brilliant successes at school. Visualization was no less crucial in the real, outside world. Lusseyran described walks with his sighted friend Jean, and how, as they were climbing together up the side of a hill above the Seine Valley, he could say to Jean:

> "Just look! This time we're on top.... You'll see the whole bend of the river, unless the sun gets in your eyes!" Jean was startled, opened his eyes wide and cried: "You're right." This little scene was often repeated between us, in a thousand forms.
>
> Every time someone mentioned an event, the event immediately projected itself in its place on the screen, which was a kind of inner canvas.... Comparing my world with his, [Jean] found that his held fewer pictures and not nearly as many colors. This made him almost angry. "When it comes to that," he used to say, "which one of us two is blind?"

It was his supernormal powers of visualization and visual manipulation—visualizing people's positions and movements, the topography of any space, visualizing strategies for defense and attack—coupled with his charismatic personality (and seemingly infallible "nose" or "ear" for detecting possible traitors) that later made Lusseyran an icon in the French Resistance.

I had now read four memoirs, all strikingly different in their depictions of the visual experience of blinded people: Hull with his acquiescent descent into "deep blindness"; Torey with his "compulsive visualization" and meticulous construction of an internal visual world; Tenberken with her impulsive, almost novelistic visual freedom, along with her remarkable and specific gift of synesthesia; and Lusseyran, who identified himself as one of the "visual blind." Was there any such thing, I wondered, as a typical blind experience?

Dennis Shulman, a clinical psychologist and psychoanalyst who lectures on biblical topics, is an affable, stocky, bearded man in his fifties who gradually lost his sight in his teens, becoming completely blind by the time he entered college. When we met a few years ago, he told me that his experience was completely unlike Hull's:

> I still live in a visual world after thirty-five years of blindness. I have very vivid visual memories and images. My wife, whom I have never seen—I think of her visually. My kids, too. I see myself visually—but it is as I last saw myself, when I was thirteen, though I try hard to update the image. I often give public lectures, and my notes are in Braille; but when I go over them in my mind, I see the Braille notes visually—they are visual images, not tactile.

Arlene Gordon, a former social worker in her seventies, told me that things were very similar for her. She said, "I was stunned when I read [Hull's book]. His experiences are so unlike mine." Like Dennis, she still identifies herself in many ways as a visual person. "I have a very strong sense of color," she said. "I pick out my own clothes. I think, 'Oh, that will go with this or that,' once I have been told the colors." Indeed, she was dressed very smartly, and took obvious pride in her appearance.

She still had a great deal of visual imagery, she continued: "If I move my arms back and forth in front of my eyes, I see them, even though I have been blind for more than thirty years." It seemed that moving her arms was immediately translated into a visual image. Listening to talking books, she added, made her eyes ache if she listened too long; she felt herself to be "reading" at such times, the sound of the spoken words being transformed to lines of print on a vividly visualized book in front of her.[4]

Arlene's comment reminded me of Amy, a patient who had been deafened by scarlet fever at the age of nine but was so adept a lip-reader that I often forgot she was deaf. Once, when I absentmindedly turned away from her as I was speaking, she said sharply, "I can no longer hear you."

"You mean you can no longer see me," I said.

"*You* may call it seeing," she answered, "but I experience it as hearing."

Amy, though totally deaf, still constructed the sound of speech in her mind. Both Dennis and Arlene, similarly, spoke not only of a heightening of visual imagery and imagination since losing their eyesight but also of what seemed to be a much readier transference of information from verbal description—or from their own sense of touch, movement, hearing, or smell—into a visual form. On the whole, their experiences seemed quite similar to Torey's, even though they had not systematically exercised their powers of visual imagery the way he had, or consciously tried to make an entire virtual world of sight.

What happens when the visual cortex is no longer limited or constrained by any visual input? The simple answer is that, isolated from the outside, the visual cortex becomes hypersensitive to internal stimuli of all sorts: its own autonomous activity; signals from other brain areas—auditory, tactile, and verbal areas; and thoughts, memories, and emotions.

Torey, unlike Hull, played a very active role in building up his visual imagery, took control of it the moment the bandages were removed. Perhaps this was because he was already very at home with visual imagery, and used to manipulating it in his own way. We know that Torey was very visually inclined before his accident, and skilled from boyhood in creating visual narratives based on the film scripts his father gave him. (We have no such information about Hull, for his journal entries start only when he has become blind.)

Torey required months of intense cognitive discipline dedicated to improving his visual imagery, making it more tenacious, more stable, more malleable, whereas Lusseyran seemed to do this almost from the start. Perhaps this was because Lusseyran was not yet eight when blinded (while Torey was twenty-one), and his brain was, accordingly, more able to adapt to a new and drastic contingency. But adaptability does not end with youth. It is clear that Arlene, who became blind in her forties, was able to adapt in quite radical ways, too, developing the ability to "see" her hands moving before her, to "see" the words of books read to her, to construct detailed visual images from verbal descriptions. One has a sense that Torey's adaptation was largely shaped by conscious motive, will, and purpose; that Lusseyran's was shaped by overwhelming physiological disposition; and that Arlene's lies somewhere in between. Hull's, meanwhile, remains enigmatic.

How much do these differences reflect an underlying predisposition independent of blindness? Do sighted people who are good visualizers, who have strong visual imagery, maintain or even enhance their powers of imagery if they become blind? Do people who are poor visualizers, on the other hand, tend to move towards "deep blindness" or hallucinations if they lose their sight? What is the range of visual imagery in the sighted?

I first became conscious of great variations in the power of visual imagery and visual memory when I was fourteen or so. My mother was a surgeon and comparative anatomist, and I had brought her a lizard's skeleton from school. She gazed at this intently for a minute, turning it round in her hands, then put it down and without looking at it again did a number of drawings of it, rotating it mentally by thirty degrees each time, so that she produced a series, the last drawing exactly the same as the first. I could not imagine how she had done this. When she said that she could see the skeleton in her mind just as clearly and vividly as if she were looking at it, and that she simply rotated the image through a twelfth of a circle each time, I felt bewildered, and very stupid. I could hardly see anything with my mind's eye—at most, faint, evanescent images over which I had no control.[5]

My mother had hoped I would follow in her footsteps and become a surgeon, but when she realized how lacking in visual powers I was (and how clumsy, lacking in mechanical skill, too) she resigned herself to the idea that I would have to specialize in something else.

A few years ago, at a medical conference in Boston, I spoke about Torey's and Hull's experiences of blindness, how "enabled" Torey seemed to be by the powers of visualization he had developed, and how "disabled" Hull was—in some ways, at least—by the loss of his powers of visual imagery and memory. After my talk, a man in the audience came up to me and asked how well, in my estimation, sighted people could function if they had no visual imagery. He went on to say that he had no visual imagery whatever, at least none that he could deliberately evoke, and that no one in his family had any, either. Indeed, he had assumed this was the case with everyone until, as a student at Harvard, he had come to participate in some psychological tests and had realized that he apparently lacked a mental power that all the other students, in varying degrees, had.

"And what do you do?" I asked him, wondering what this poor man *could* do.

"I am a surgeon," he replied. "A vascular surgeon. An anatomist, too. And I design solar panels." But how, I asked him, did he recognize what he was seeing?

"It's not a problem," he answered. "I guess there must be representations or models in the brain that get matched up with what I am seeing and doing. But they are not conscious. I cannot evoke them."

This seemed to be at odds with my mother's experience—she, clearly, did have extremely vivid and readily manipulable visual imagery, though (it now seemed) this may have been a bonus, a luxury, and not a prerequisite for her career as a surgeon.

Is this also the case with Torey? Is his greatly developed visual imagery, though clearly a source of much pleasure, not as indispensable as he takes it to be? Might he, in fact, have been able to do everything he did, from carpentry to roof repair to making a model of the mind, without any conscious imagery at all? He himself raises this question.

The role of mental imagery in thinking was explored by Francis Galton in his 1883 book *Inquiries into Human Faculty and Its Development*. (Galton, a cousin of Darwin's, was irrepressible and wide-ranging, and his book includes chapters on subjects as various as fingerprints, eugenics, dog whistles, criminality, twins, synesthesia, psychometric measures, and hereditary genius.) His inquiry into voluntary visual imagery took the form of a questionnaire, with such questions as "Can you recall with distinctness the features of all near relations and many other persons? Can you at will cause your mental image ... to sit, stand, or turn slowly around? Can you ... see it with enough distinctness to enable you to sketch it leisurely (supposing yourself able to draw)?" The vascular surgeon would have been hopeless on such tests—indeed, it was questions such as these that had floored him when he was a student at Harvard. And yet, finally, how much had it mattered?

As to the significance of such imagery, Galton is ambiguous and guarded. He suggests, in one breath, that "scientific men, as a class, have feeble powers of visual representation" and, in another, that "a vivid visualizing faculty is of much importance in connection with the higher processes of generalized thoughts." He feels that "it is undoubtedly the fact that mechanicians, engineers and architects usually possess the faculty of seeing mental images with remarkable clearness and precision" but adds, "I am, however, bound to say, that the missing faculty seems to be replaced so serviceably by other modes of conception ... that men who declare themselves entirely deficient in the power of seeing mental pictures can nevertheless give lifelike descriptions of what they have seen, and can otherwise express themselves as if they were gifted with a vivid visual imagination. They can also become painters of the rank of Royal Academicians."

A mental image, for Galton, was picturing a familiar person or place in the mind's eye; it was a reproduction or reconstruction of an experience. But there are also mental images of a much more abstract and visionary kind, images of something which has never been seen by the physical eye but which can be conjured up by the creative imagination and serve as models for investigating reality.[6]

In his book *Image and Reality: Kekulé, Kopp, and the Scientific Imagination*, Alan Rocke brings out the crucial role of such images or models in the creative lives of scientists, especially nineteenth-century chemists. He focuses especially on August Kekulé and the famous reverie, while he was riding a London bus, that led him to visualize the structure of a benzene molecule, a concept that would revolutionize chemistry. Although chemical bonds are invisible, they were as real to Kekulé, as visually imaginable, as the lines of force around a magnet were for Faraday. Kekulé said of himself that he had "an irresistible need for visualization."

Indeed, a conversation about chemistry can hardly be maintained without such images and models, and in *Mindsight*, the philosopher Colin McGinn writes, "Images are not just minor variations on perception and thought, of negligible theoretical interest; they are a robust mental category in need of independent investigation.... Mental images ... should be added as a third great category ... to the twin pillars of perception and cognition."

Some people, like Kekulé, are clearly very powerful visualizers in this abstract sense, but most of us use some combination of experiential visualization (imaging one's house, for example) and abstract visualization (imagining the structure of an atom). Temple Grandin, though, feels she is a different sort of visualizer.[7] She thinks entirely in terms of literal images she has seen before, as if she is looking at a familiar photograph or a film running in her head. When she imagines the concept of "heaven," for instance, her instant association is to the film *Stairway to Heaven*, and the image in her mind is that of a staircase ascending into the clouds. If someone remarks that it is a rainy day, she sees, in her mind's eye, the same "photograph" of rain, her own literal and iconic representation of rain. Like Torrey, she is a powerful visualizer; her extremely accurate visual memory allows her to walk through, in her mind, a factory she is designing, noting structural details even before it is built. Growing up, she assumed this was how everyone thought, and she is puzzled, now, by the idea that some people cannot summon visual images at will. When I told her I could not do so, she asked, "How *do* you think, then?"

When I talk to people, blind or sighted, or when I try to think of my own internal representations, I find myself uncertain whether words, symbols, and images of various types are the primary tools of thought or whether there are forms of thought antecedent to all of these, forms of thought essentially amodal. Psychologists have sometimes spoken of "interlingua" or "mentalese," which they conceive to be the brain's own language, and Lev Vygotsky, the great Russian psychologist, used to speak of "thinking in pure meanings." I cannot decide whether this is nonsense or profound truth—it is the sort of reef I end up on when I think about thinking.

Galton himself was puzzled about visual imagery: it had an enormous range, and although it sometimes seemed an essential part of thinking, at other times it seemed irrelevant. This uncertainty has characterized the debate over mental imagery ever since. A contemporary of Galton's, the early experimental psychologist Wilhelm Wundt, guided by introspection, believed imagery to be an essential part of thought. Others maintained that thinking was imageless and consisted entirely of analytical or descriptive propositions, and behaviorists did not believe in thinking at all—there was only "behavior." Was introspection alone a reliable method of scientific observation? Could it yield data that were consistent, repeatable, measurable? It was only in the early 1970s that this challenge was faced by a new generation of psychologists. Roger Shepard and Jacqueline Metzler asked subjects to perform mental tasks that required rotating an image of a geometrical figure in their minds—the sort of imaginary rotation my mother performed when she drew the lizard's skeleton from memory. They were able to determine in these first quantitative experiments that rotating an image took a specific amount of time—an amount proportional to the degree of rotation. Rotating an image through sixty degrees, for instance, took twice as long as rotating it through thirty degrees, and rotating it through ninety degrees, three times as long. Mental rotation had a rate, it was continuous and steady, and it took effort, like any voluntary act.

Stephen Kosslyn entered the subject of visual imagery from another angle, and in 1973 published a seminal paper contrasting the performance of "imagers" and "verbalizers" who were asked to remember a set of drawings they had been shown. Kosslyn hypothesized that if internal images were spatial and organized like pictures, the "imagers" ought to be able to focus selectively on a part of the image, and that time would be required for them to shift their attention from one part of the image to another. The time required, he thought, would be proportional to the distance the mind's eye had to travel.

Kosslyn was able to show that all of these were indeed the case, indicating that visual images were essentially spatial and organized in space like pictures. His work has proved immensely fertile, but the ongoing debate about the role of visual imagery continues, as Zenon Pylyshyn and others have maintained that the mental rotation of images and "scanning" them could be interpreted as the result of purely abstract, nonvisual operations in the mind/brain.[8]

By the 1990s, Kosslyn and others were able to combine imagery experiments with PET and fMRI scanning, which allowed them to map the areas of the brain involved as people engaged in tasks requiring mental imagery. Mental imagery, they found, activated many of the same areas of the visual cortex as perception itself, showing that visual imagery was a physiological reality as well as a psychological one, and used at least some of the same neural pathways as visual perception.[9]

That perception and imagery share a common neural basis in the visual parts of the brain is suggested by clinical studies, too. In 1978 Eduardo Bisiach and Claudio Luzzatti in Italy related the cases of two patients who both developed a hemianopia following a stroke and could not see to the left side. When they were asked to imagine themselves walking down a familiar street and describe what they saw, they mentioned only the shops on the right side of the street; but when they were then asked to imagine turning around and walking back, they described the shops they had not "seen" before, the shops that were now on the right side. These beautifully examined cases showed that a hemianopia might cause not only a bisection of the visual field but a bisection of visual imagery as well.

Such clinical observations on the parallels between visual perception and visual imagery go back at least a century. In 1911, the English neurologists Henry Head and Gordon Holmes examined a number of patients with subtle damage to the occipital lobes—damage that led not to total blindness but to blind spots within the visual field. They found, by questioning their patients carefully, that blind spots in exactly the same locations occurred in the patients' mental imagery as well. And in 1992, Martha Farah et al. reported that in a patient who lost partial vision on one side due to an occipital lobectomy, the visual angle of his mind's eye was also reduced, in a way that perfectly matched his perceptual loss.

For me, the most convincing demonstration that at least some aspects of visual imagery and visual perception might be inseparable occurred when I was consulted in 1986 by Mr. I., an artist who became completely colorblind following a head injury.[10] Mr. I. was distressed by his sudden inability to perceive colors, but even more by his total inability to evoke them in memory or imagery. Even his occasional visual migraines were now drained of color. Patients like Mr. I. suggest that the coupling of perception and imagery is very close in the higher parts of the visual cortex.[11]

Sharing characteristics and even sharing neural areas or mechanisms is one thing, but Kosslyn and others go further than this, suggesting that visual perception *depends* on visual imagery, matching what the eye sees, the retina's output, with memory images in the brain. Visual recognition, they feel, could not occur without such matching. Kosslyn proposes, furthermore, that mental imagery may be crucial in thought itself—problem solving, planning, designing, theorizing. Support for this comes from studies asking subjects to answer questions that would seem to require visual imagery—for example, "Which is darker green, a frozen pea or a pine tree?" or "What shape are Mickey Mouse's ears?" or "In which hand does the Statue of Liberty hold her torch?" —or asking them to solve problems that can be worked out either by means of imagery or by means of more abstract, nonvisual thinking. Kosslyn speaks here of a doubleness in the way people think, contrasting the use of "depictive" representations, which are direct and unmediated, with "descriptive" ones, which are analytic and mediated by verbal or other symbols. Sometimes, he suggests, one mode will be favored over another, depending on the individual and on the problem to be solved. Sometimes both modes will proceed in tandem (although depiction is likely to outpace description), and at other times one may start with depiction—images—and proceed to a purely verbal or mathematical representation.[12]

What, then, of people like me, or the vascular surgeon in Boston who cannot evoke *any* visual images voluntarily? One must infer, as my colleague in Boston does, that we, too, have visual images, models, and representations in the brain, images that allow visual perception and recognition but are below the threshold of consciousness.[13]

If the central role of visual imagery is to permit visual perception and recognition, what need is there for it if a person becomes blind? And what happens to its neural substrates, the visual areas which occupy nearly half of the entire cerebral cortex? We know that in adults who lose their eyesight, there may be some atrophy of the pathways and relay centers leading from the retina to the cerebral cortex—but there is little degeneration in the visual cortex itself. Functional MRIs of the visual cortex show no diminution of activity in such a situation; indeed, we see the reverse: they reveal a heightened activity and sensitivity. The visual cortex, deprived of visual input, is still good neural real estate, available and clamoring for a new function. In someone like Torey, this may free up more cortical space for visual imagery; in someone like Hull, relatively more may be employed by other senses—auditory perception and attention, perhaps, or tactile perception and attention.[14]

This sort of cross-modal activation may underlie the fact that some blind people, like Dennis Shulman, "see" Braille as they read it with their finger. This may be more than just an illusion or a fanciful metaphor; it may be a reflection of what is actually happening in his brain, for there is good evidence that reading Braille can cause strong activation of the visual parts of the cortex, as Sadato, Pascual-Leone, et al. have reported. Such activation, even in the absence of any input from the retina, may constitute a crucial part of the neural basis for the mind's eye.

Dennis also spoke of how the heightening of his other senses had increased his sensitivity to the most delicate nuances in other people's speech and self-presentation. He could recognize many of his patients by smell, he said, and he could often pick up states of tension or anxiety they might not even be aware of. He felt that he had become far more sensitive to others' emotional states since losing his sight, for he was no longer taken in by visual appearances, which most people learn to camouflage. Voices and smells, by contrast, he felt, could reveal people's depths.

The heightening of other senses with blindness allows a number of very remarkable adaptations, including "facial vision," the ability to use sound or tactile clues to sense the shape or size of a space and the people or objects in it.

Martin Milligan, the philosopher, who had both eyes removed at the age of two (because of malignant tumors), has written of his own experience:

> Born-blind people with normal hearing don't just hear sounds: they can
> hear objects (that is, have an awareness of them, chiefly through their

ears) when they are fairly close at hand, provided these objects are not too low; and they can also in the same way "hear" something of the shape of their immediate surroundings.... Silent objects such as lampposts and parked cars with their engines off can be heard by me as I approach them and pass them as atmosphere-thickening occupants of space, almost certainly because of the way they absorb and/or echo back the sounds of my footsteps and other small sounds.... It isn't usually necessary to make sounds oneself to have this awareness, though it helps. Objects of head height probably slightly affect the air currents reaching my face, which helps towards my awareness of them—which is why some blind people refer to this kind of sense-awareness as their "facial" sense.

Facial vision tends to be most highly developed in those who are born blind or lose their sight at an early age; for the writer Ved Mehta, who has been blind since the age of four, it is so well developed that he walks confidently and rapidly without a cane, and it is sometimes difficult for others to realize that he is blind.

While the sound of one's footsteps or one's cane may suffice, other forms of echolocation have been reported. Ben Underwood developed an astonishing, dolphinlike strategy of emitting regular clicks with his mouth and accurately reading the resulting echoes from nearby objects. He was so adept at moving about the world in this way that he was able to play field sports and even chess.[15]

Blind people often say that using a cane enables them to "see" their surroundings, as touch, action, and sound are immediately transformed into a "visual" picture. The cane acts as a sensory substitution or extension. But is it possible to give a blind person a more detailed picture of the world, using more modern technology? Paul Bach-y-Rita was a pioneer in this realm and spent decades testing all sorts of sensory substitutes, though his special interest lay in developing devices that could help the blind by using tactile images. (In 1972, he published a prescient book surveying all the possible brain mechanisms by which sensory substitution might be realized. Such substitution, he emphasized, would depend on the brain's plasticity—and that the brain had any plasticity at all was a revolutionary concept at the time.)

Bach-y-Rita wondered if one might connect the output of a video camera, point by point, to the skin, allowing a blind subject to form a "touch picture" of his environment. This might work, he thought, because tactile information is organized topographically in the brain, and topographic accuracy is essential for forming a quasi-visual picture. Eventually, he began using tiny grids of a hundred or so electrodes on that most sensitive part of the body, the tongue. (The tongue has the highest density of sensory receptors in the body, and it also occupies the greatest amount of space, proportionally, in the sensory cortex. This makes it uniquely suitable for sensory substitution.) With this device, the size of a postage stamp, his subjects could form a crude but nevertheless useful "picture" on the tongue itself.

Over the years, the sophistication of such devices has increased greatly, and prototypes now have four to six times the resolution of Bach-y-Rita's early

version. Bulky camera cables have been replaced by spectacles containing miniature cameras, allowing subjects to direct the cameras by a more natural head
movement. With this, blind subjects are able to walk across a room that is not
too cluttered, or to catch a ball rolled towards them.

Does this mean that they are now "seeing"? Certainly, they are showing
what behaviorists would call "visual behavior." Bach-y-Rita spoke of how his
subjects "learn[ed] to make perceptual judgements using visual means of interpretation, such as perspective, parallax, looming and zooming, and depth
estimates." Many of these people *felt* as if they were seeing once again, and functional MRIs showed strong activations of visual areas in their brains while they
were "seeing" with the camera. ("Seeing" occurred particularly when the subjects were able to move the camera voluntarily, pointing it here or there, *looking*
with it. Looking was crucial, for there is no perception without action, no seeing
without looking.)

To restore sight to someone who once had it, whether by surgical means or by a
sensory-substitution device, is one thing, for such a person would have an intact
visual cortex and a lifetime of visual memories. But to give sight to someone
who has never seen, never experienced light or sight, would seem to be impossible, in view of what we know about the brain's critical periods and the necessity of at least some visual experience in the first two years of life to stimulate the
development of the visual cortex. (Recent work from Pawan Sinha and others,
however, suggests that the critical period may not be as critical as previously
accepted.)[16] Tongue vision has been tried with congenitally blind people, too,
and with some success. One young musician, born blind, said she "saw" the conductor's gestures for the first time in her life.[17] Although the visual cortex in
congenitally blind people is reduced in volume by more than 25 percent, it can
still, apparently, be activated by sensory substitution, and this has been confirmed, in several cases, by fMRIs.[18]

There is increasing evidence for the extraordinarily rich interconnectedness
and interactions of the sensory areas of the brain, and the difficulty, therefore, of
saying that anything is purely visual or purely auditory, or purely anything. The
world of the blind can be especially rich in such in-between states—the intersensory, the metamodal—states for which we have no common language.[19]

On Blindness is an exchange of letters between the blind philosopher
Martin Milligan and a sighted philosopher, Bryan Magee. While his own nonvisual world seems coherent and complete to him, Milligan realizes that sighted
people have access to a sense, a mode of knowledge, denied him. But congenitally blind people, he insists, can (and usually do) have rich and varied
perceptual experiences, mediated by language and by imagery of a nonvisual
sort. Thus they may have a "mind's ear" or a "mind's nose." But do they
have a mind's eye?

Here Milligan and Magee cannot reach agreement. Magee insists that Milligan, a blind man, cannot have any real knowledge of the visual world. Milligan
disagrees and maintains that even though language only describes people and
events, it can sometimes stand in for direct experience or acquaintance.

Congenitally blind children, it has often been noted, tend to have superior memories and be precocious verbally. They may develop such fluency in the verbal description of faces and places as to leave others (and perhaps themselves) uncertain as to whether they are actually blind. Helen Keller's writing, to give a famous example, startles one with its brilliantly visual quality.

I loved reading Prescott's *Conquest of Mexico* and *Conquest of Peru* as a boy, and felt that I "saw" these lands through his intensely visual, almost hallucinogenic descriptions. I was amazed to discover, years later, that Prescott had not only never visited Mexico or Peru; he had been virtually blind since the age of eighteen. Did he, like Torey, compensate for his blindness by developing huge powers of visual imagery, or were his brilliant visual descriptions simulated, in a way, made possible by the evocative and pictorial powers of language? To what extent can description, picturing in words, provide a substitute for actual seeing or for the visual, pictorial imagination?

After becoming blind in her forties, Arlene Gordon found language and description increasingly important; it stimulated her powers of visual imagery as never before and, in a sense, enabled her to see. "I love traveling," she told me. "I *saw* Venice when I was there." She explained how her traveling companions would describe places, and she would then construct a visual image from these details, her reading, and her own visual memories. "Sighted people enjoy traveling with me," she said. "I ask them questions, then they look and see things they wouldn't otherwise. Too often people with sight don't see anything! It's a reciprocal process—we enrich each other's worlds."

There is a paradox here—a delicious one—which I cannot resolve: if there is indeed a fundamental difference between experience and description, between direct and mediated knowledge of the world, how is it that language can be so powerful? Language, that most human invention, can enable what, in principle, should not be possible. It can allow all of us, even the congenitally blind, to see with another person's eyes.

NOTES

1. Despite an initially overwhelming sense of despair on losing their sight, some people, like Hull, have found their full creative strength and identity on the other side of blindness. One thinks especially of John Milton, who started to lose his sight around the age of thirty (probably from glaucoma), but produced his greatest poetry after becoming completely blind a dozen years later. He meditated on blindness, how an inward sight may come in place of outward sight, in *Paradise Lost*, in *Samson Agonistes*, and—most directly—in letters to friends and in a very personal sonnet, "On His Blindness." Jorge Luis Borges, another poet who became blind, wrote about the varied and paradoxical effects of his own blindness; he also wondered how it might have been for Homer, who, Borges imagined, lost the world of sight but gained a much deeper sense of time and, with this, a matchless epic power. (This is beautifully discussed by J. T. Fraser in his 1989 foreword for the Braille edition of *Time, the Familiar Stranger*.)

2. In his book *The Invention of Clouds*, Richard Hamblyn recounts how Luke Howard, the nineteenth-century chemist who first classified clouds, corresponded with many other naturalists of the time, including John Gough, a mathematician blinded by smallpox at the age of two. Gough, Hamblyn writes, "was a noted botanist, having taught himself the entire Linnean system by touch. He was also a master of the fields of mathematics, zoology and scoteography—the art of writing in the dark." (Hamblyn adds that Gough "might also have become an accomplished musician had his father, a stern Quaker ... not stopped him playing on the godless violin that an itinerant fiddler had given him.")

3. Tenberken also has an intense synesthesia, which has persisted and been intensified, it seems, by her blindness:

> As far back as I can remember, numbers and words have instantly triggered colors in me.... The number 4, for example, [is] gold. Five is light green. Nine is vermilion.... Days of the week as well as months have their colors, too. I have them arranged in geometrical formations, in circular sectors, a little like a pie. When I need to recall on which day a particular event happened, the first thing that pops up on my inner screen is the day's color, then its position in the pie.

4. Although I myself am a poor visualizer, if I shut my eyes, I can still "see" my hands moving on the piano keyboard when I play a piece that I know well. (This may happen even if I just play the piece in my mind.) I feel my hands moving at the same time, and I am not entirely sure that I can distinguish the "feeling" from the "seeing." In this context, they seem inseparable, and one wants to use an intersensory term like "seeing-feeling."

The psychologist Jerome Bruner speaks of such imagery as "enactive"—an integral feature of a performance (real or imaginary)—in contrast to an "iconic" visualization, the visualization of something outside oneself. The brain mechanisms underlying these two sorts of imagery are quite different.

5. Though I have almost no voluntary imagery, I am prone to involuntary imagery. I used to have this only as I was falling asleep, in migraine auras, with some drugs, or with fever. But now that my sight is impaired, I have it all the time.

In the 1960s, during a period of experimenting with large doses of amphetamines, I experienced a different sort of vivid mental imagery. Amphetamines can produce striking perceptual changes and dramatic enhancements of visual imagery and memory (as I described in "The Dog Beneath the Skin," a chapter in *The Man Who Mistook His Wife for a Hat*). For a period of two weeks or so, I found that I had only to look at an anatomical picture or specimen, and its image would remain vivid and stable in my mind for hours. I could mentally project the image onto a piece of paper—it was as clear and distinct as if projected by a camera lucida—and trace its outlines with a pencil. My drawings were not elegant, but they were, everyone agreed; quite detailed and accurate. But when the amphetamine-induced state faded, I could no longer visualize, no longer project images, no longer draw—nor have I been able to do so in the decades since. This was not like voluntary imagery—I did not summon images to my mind or construct them bit by bit. It was involuntary and automatic, more akin to eidetic or "photographic" memory, or to palinopsia, an exaggerated persistence of vision.

6. The physicist John Tyndall referred to these in an 1870 lecture, a few years before Galton's *Inquiries*: "In explaining scientific phenomena, we habitually form mental

images of the ultra-sensible.... Without the exercise of this power our knowledge of nature would be a mere fabulation of co-existences and sequences."

7. I described Temple more fully in *An Anthropologist on Mars*, and she speaks about her visual thinking especially in her book *Thinking in Pictures*.

8. Kosslyn's latest book on the matter, *The Case for Mental Imagery*, details the history of this debate.

9. Functional MRIs also showed that the two hemispheres of the brain behaved differently in regard to imagery, the left hemisphere concerned with generic, categorical images—e.g., "trees"—and the right hemisphere with specific images—e.g., "the maple in my front yard"—a specialization also present in visual perception. Thus prosopagnosia, an inability to recognize specific faces, is associated with damaged or defective visual function in the right hemisphere, though people with prosopagnosia have no problem with the category of faces in general, a left-hemisphere function.

10. Mr. I.'s case is described in *An Anthropologist on Mars*.

11. While it seems clear that perception and imagery share certain neural mechanisms at higher levels, this sharing is less evident in the primary visual cortex—hence the possibility of a dissociation such as occurs in Anton's syndrome. In Anton's syndrome, patients with occipital damage are cortically blind, but believe they are still sighted. They will move about without restraint or caution, and if they bump into a piece of furniture, they will ascribe this, perhaps, to the furniture being "out of place."

    Anton's syndrome is sometimes attributed to the preservation of some visual imagery despite occipital damage, and to patients mistaking this imagery for perception. But there may be other, stranger mechanisms at work. The denial of blindness—or, more accurately, the inability to realize that one has lost one's vision—is very like another "disconnection syndrome," known as anosognosia. With anosognosia, following damage to the right parietal lobe, patients lose awareness of their left side, and of the left half of space, along with the awareness that anything is amiss. If one draws their attention to their left arm, they will say it is someone else's—"the doctor's arm," or "my brother's arm," or even "an arm someone left here." Such confabulations seem similar in a way to those of Anton's syndrome, attempts to explain what, to the patient, is a bizarrely inexplicable situation.

12. Einstein described this in regard to his own thinking:

    > The psychical entities which seem to serve as elements in thought are certain signs and more or less clear images which can be "voluntarily" reproduced and combined.... [Some] are, in my case, of visual and some of muscular type. Conventional words or other signs have to be sought for laboriously only in a second stage.

    Darwin, on the other hand, seemed to describe a very abstract, almost computational process in his own thinking, when he wrote in his autobiography, "My mind seems to have become a kind of machine for grinding general laws out of large collections of facts." (What Darwin omitted here was that he had a fantastic eye for form and detail, an enormous observational and depictive power, and it was these which provided the "facts.")

13. Dominic ffytche, who has investigated the neurobiology of conscious vision—imagery and hallucination as well as perception—feels that visual consciousness is a threshold phenomenon. Using fMRIs to study patients with visual hallucinations, he has shown that there may be evidence of unusual activity in a specific part of the

visual system—for example, the fusiform face area—but this has to reach a certain intensity before it enters consciousness, before the subject actually "sees" faces.

14. The heightened (and sometimes morbid) sensitivity of the visual cortex when deprived of its normal perceptual input may also predispose it to intrusive imagery. A significant proportion of those who go blind—10 to 20 percent, by most estimates—become prone to involuntary images, or outright hallucinations, of an intense and sometimes bizarre kind. Such hallucinations were originally described in the 1760s by the Swiss naturalist Charles Bonnet, and we now speak of hallucinations secondary to visual impairment as Charles Bonnet syndrome.

Hull described something akin to this which occurred for a while after he lost the last of his sight:

> About a year after I was registered blind, I began to have such strong images of what people's faces looked like that they were almost like hallucinations.... I would be sitting in a room with someone, my face pointed towards my companion, listening to him or her. Suddenly, such a vivid picture would flash before my mind that it was like looking at a television set. Ah, I would think, there he is, with his glasses and his little beard, his wavy hair and his blue, pinstriped suit, white collar and blue tie. … Now this image would fade and in its place another one would be projected. My companion was now fat and perspiring with receding hair. He had a red necktie and waistcoat, and a couple of his teeth were missing.

15. Ben, who had retinoblastoma, had both eyes removed at the age of three, but then, tragically, died at sixteen from a recurrence of his cancer. Videos of Ben and his echolocation can be seen at the website www.benunderwood.com.

16. See Ostrovsky, Yuri, Aaron Andalman, and Pawan Sinha. 2006. Vision following extended congenital blindness. *Psychological Science* 17 (12): 1009–14.

17. Congenitally blind people, we might suppose, can have no visual imagery at all, since they have never had any visual experience. And yet they sometimes report having clear and recognizable visual elements in their dreams. Helder Bértolo and his colleagues in Lisbon, in an intriguing 2003 report, described how they compared congenitally blind subjects with normal sighted subjects and found "equivalent visual activity" (based on analysis of EEG alpha-wave attenuation) in the two groups while dreaming. The blind subjects were able, upon waking, to draw the visual components of their dreams, although they had a lower rate of dream recall. Bértolo et al. conclude, therefore, that "the congenitally blind have visual content in their dreams."

18. Would acquiring "sight" if one has never seen before be bewildering or enriching? For my patient Virgil, who was given sight, through surgery, after a lifetime of blindness, it was utterly incomprehensible at first, as I described in An Anthropologist on Mars. Thus although sensory-substitution technologies are exciting and promise a new freedom for blind people, we need to consider equally their impact on a life that has already been constructed without sight.

19. In a recent letter to his colleague Simon Hayhoe, John Hull expanded on this:

> For example, when the thought of a car occurs to me, although my front-line images are of recently touching the warm bonnet of a car, or of the shape of the car as I feel for the door handle, there are also traces of the

appearance of the whole car, from pictures of cars in books, or memories of cars coming and going. Sometimes, when I have to touch a modern car, I am surprised to find that this memory trace does not correspond to reality, and that cars are not the same shape they were twenty-five years ago.

There is a second point. The fact that an item of knowledge is so much buried in the sense or senses that first received it, means for me that I am not always sure whether my image is visual or not. The trouble is that tactile images of the shape and feel of things also often seem to acquire a visual content, or one cannot tell if the three-dimensional memory shape is being mentally represented by a visual or a tactile image. So even after all these years, the brain can't sort out where it is getting stuff from.

QUESTIONS FOR MAKING CONNECTIONS
WITHIN THE READING

1. Early in his essay, Sacks poses this question: "To what extent are we the authors, the creators, of our own experiences? How much are these predetermined by the brains or senses we are born with, and to what extent do we shape our brains through experience?" Following this question, however, most of the discussion is involved with the actual experience of blindness. Instead of providing an extended explanation of mental processing or brain chemistry, Sacks gives us details about people who have lost their vision and then adapted in various ways. How do these accounts of blindness connect to the debate about whether we create our own experience or not?

2. Does the way a person responds to the loss of sight reflect his or her unique way of "being in the world" prior to the loss? Do you see any evidence of a continuity between the lives of Sacks's subjects before and after their loss? What conclusions might we draw about our ability to transform our basic personality traits? Were Sacks's subjects changed by their blindness, or did they transform blindness itself in order to incorporate it into the familiar pattern of their lives?

3. In one of his interesting footnotes, Sacks recalls a period in his life when he was "experimenting with large doses of amphetamines":

   > For a period of about two weeks or so, I found that I had only to look at an anatomical picture or specimen, and its image would remain vivid and stable in my mind for hours. I could mentally project the image onto a piece of paper—it was as clear and distinct as if projected by a camera lucida—and trace its outlines with a pencil. My drawings were not elegant, but they were, everyone agreed, quite detailed and accurate. But when the amphetamine-induced state faded, I could no longer visualize, no longer project images, no longer draw—nor have I been able to do so in the decades since.

   Why does Sacks include this vignette in his notes? What point does he make, and how does the passage extend his larger argument? Does it matter that the story he tells is personal rather than objective or scientific?

QUESTIONS FOR WRITING

1. Do the discoveries of neuroscience undermine our assumptions about free will, the uniqueness of each individual, and the importance of creativity? Ordinarily we might think that if we can explain an emotion like love or the experience of beauty as the products of the brain's processing, something important will be lost. But will it? Is human behavior in any way diminished or degraded by our knowledge of the brain? In what ways might neuroscience—as exemplified by Sacks's work—foster greater understanding and a tolerance for diversity in human behavior?

2. For the last century or so, thinkers have debated the relative influence of *nature* and *nurture* over human behavior. By *nature* people ordinarily mean biology, chemistry, and genetics. By *nurture*, they mean something like culture, customs, and education. What does Sacks's essay contribute to the debate? On the basis of the evidence he provides, can we ever say that human behavior is predetermined by nature? Is it predetermined by nurture? Does the nature/nurture debate leave something out—the ability of individuals to create their unique reality? What is the relation between biology, culture, and the individual, judging from Sacks's account?

QUESTIONS FOR MAKING CONNECTIONS
BETWEEN READINGS

1. The people at the heart of Sacks's essay rebuild their lives after they lose their sight. One element of their success is the adaptability of the human brain. But does this adaptability also mean that people can transform themselves in destructive ways quite unlike the positive examples that fill the pages of Sacks's account? Consider what happens to the cadets in Susan Faludi's *The Naked Citadel*. If the brain is as adaptable as Sacks's narrative suggests, is there any natural limit to the way people can behave? Can we count on human nature to prevent people like the Citadel cadets from acting destructively? Can the encounter with those different from ourselves—people with different ways of mental processing—force us to question and revise our own realities? Does Shannon Foster pose a challenge to the way the cadets' brains operate?

2. What might Sacks's essay add to Charles Siebert's call for a new sense of kinship with animals? Given the evidence that Sacks presents, is there any universally human way of perceiving the world, or are the mental lives of *Homo sapiens* far more diverse than we might assume? Is it possible that some human beings might have mental lives closer to those of elephants than to the mental lives of other humans? If traumatized elephants respond to therapies devised for the treatment of people, does it become impossible to sustain a distinction between the human and the animal? The terms *Homo sapiens* and *Loxodonta Africana* (African elephants) describe two different species belonging to two different orders and families, but are such distinctions important when it comes to the ways intelligent minds perceive their reality?

CHARLES SIEBERT

HAVING CLAIMED DOMINANCE over the planet for centuries, human beings have, by and large, made use of the earth without much consideration for the environmental and social needs of other animals. As a result, the areas in which animals are free to move about without danger from humans have steadily declined both in size and number. Overall, most of the animal kingdom has acquiesced without substantial resistance. But what happens when an animal community responds to the destruction of its natural habitat by turning against people, other species, and themselves? Charles Siebert addresses these questions in "An Elephant Crackup?" an article that first appeared in the *New York Times Magazine*.

An essayist, a novelist, and a poet, Siebert has published numerous articles in the *New York Times Magazine*, the *New Yorker, Harpers*, and other periodicals. He has published four books, *A Man After His Own Heart* (2004), a meditation on the human heart (literally); *Angus: A Novel* (2000), an account of the inner life of a Jack Russell terrier; *Wickerby: An Urban Pastoral* (1998), which explores the fluid relationship between the urban and the rural worlds; and *The Wauchula Woods Accord: Toward a New Understanding of Animals* (2009).

"An Elephant Crackup?" is a further example of the sympathy for the emotional lives of animals that Siebert first explored in *Angus*. Here, he conducts research across Africa, India, and parts of southeastern Asia on the new phenomenon called "human–elephant conflict," which has resulted in hundreds of human deaths since the year 2000. This is especially troubling, Siebert feels, because elephants possess "a highly developed sensibility" and "a deep-rooted sense of family" that is nowhere in evidence during these violent rampages. Drawing on research into the fabric of animal society and the similarities between the emotional brains of elephants and the emotional brains of humans, Siebert weaves a compelling narrative of conflict between a species that once enjoyed dominance over its territory and the species that has the upper hand now.

If "An Elephant Crackup?" explores the surprisingly "human" psychology of elephants in distress, *The Wauchula Woods Accord* suggests that we feel ambivalence toward animals because we fear the animal in ourselves. As Siebert told an interviewer in 2009, "The more we begin to see and understand ourselves as one more extension of the greater biological forces that created and control

Lisa G. Brown, "An Interview with Author Charles Siebert about his new book, The Wauchula Woods Accord," Animal Inventory Blog, June 22, 2009.

all life on earth, rather than as beings apart [from other species, or as] entities anointed by some higher authority, the more the 'inter-species empathy' I speak of … will be allowed to flourish."

An Elephant Crackup?

"We're not going anywhere," my driver, Nelson Okello, whispered to me one morning this past June, the two of us sitting in the front seat of a jeep just after dawn in Queen Elizabeth National Park in southwestern Uganda. We'd originally stopped to observe what appeared to be a lone bull elephant grazing in a patch of tall savanna grasses off to our left. More than one "rogue" crossed our path that morning—a young male elephant that has made an overly strong power play against the dominant male of his herd and been banished, sometimes permanently. This elephant, however, soon proved to be not a rogue but part of a cast of at least thirty. The ground vibrations registered just before the emergence of the herd from the surrounding trees and brush. We sat there watching the elephants cross the road before us, seeming, for all their heft, so light on their feet, soundlessly playing the wind-swept savanna grasses like land whales adrift above the floor of an ancient, waterless sea.

Then, from behind a thicket of acacia trees directly off our front left bumper, a huge female emerged—"the matriarch," Okello said softly. There was a small calf beneath her, freely foraging and knocking about within the secure cribbing of four massive legs. Acacia leaves are an elephant's favorite food, and as the calf set to work on some low branches, the matriarch stood guard, her vast back flank blocking the road, the rest of the herd milling about in the brush a short distance away.

After fifteen minutes or so, Okello started inching the jeep forward, revving the engine, trying to make us sound as beastly as possible. The matriarch, however, was having none of it, holding her ground, the fierce white of her eyes as bright as that of her tusks. Although I pretty much knew the answer, I asked Okello if he was considering trying to drive around. "No," he said, raising an index finger for emphasis. "She'll charge. We should stay right here."

I'd have considered it a wise policy even at a more peaceable juncture in the course of human-elephant relations. In recent years, however, those relations have become markedly more bellicose. Just two days before I arrived, a woman was killed by an elephant in Kazinga, a fishing village nearby. Two months earlier, a man was fatally gored by a young male elephant at the northern edge of the park, near the village of Katwe. African elephants use their long tusks to forage through dense jungle brush. They've also been known to wield them, however, with the ceremonious flash and precision of gladiators, pinning down a victim with one knee in order to deliver the decisive thrust. Okello told me that a young Indian tourist was killed in this fashion two years ago in Murchison Falls National Park, just north of where we were.

These were not isolated incidents. All across Africa, India, and parts of Southeast Asia, from within and around whatever patches and corridors of their natural habitat remain, elephants have been striking out, destroying villages and crops, attacking and killing human beings. In fact, these attacks have become so commonplace that a whole new statistical category, known as Human-Elephant Conflict, or HEC, was created by elephant researchers in the mid-1990s to monitor the problem. In the Indian state Jharkhand near the western border of Bangladesh, 300 people were killed by elephants between 2000 and 2004. In the past twelve years, elephants have killed 605 people in Assam, a state in northeastern India, 239 of them since 2001; 265 elephants have died in that same period, the majority of them as a result of retaliation by angry villagers, who have used everything from poison-tipped arrows to laced food to exact their revenge. In Africa, reports of human-elephant conflicts appear almost daily, from Zambia to Tanzania, from Uganda to Sierra Leone, where 300 villagers evacuated their homes last year because of unprovoked elephant attacks.

Still, it is not only the increasing number of these incidents that is causing alarm but also the singular perversity—for want of a less anthropocentric term—of recent elephant aggression. Since the early 1990s, for example, young male elephants in Pilanesberg National Park and the Hluhluwe-Umfolozi Game Reserve in South Africa have been raping and killing rhinoceroses; this abnormal behavior, according to a 2001 study in the journal *Pachyderm*, has been reported in "a number of reserves" in the region. In July of last year, officials in Pilanesberg shot three young male elephants who were responsible for the killings of sixty-three rhinos, as well as attacks on people in safari vehicles. In Addo Elephant National Park, also in South Africa, up to ninety percent of male elephant deaths are now attributable to other male elephants, compared with a rate of six percent in more stable elephant communities.

In a coming book on this phenomenon, Gay Bradshaw, a psychologist at the environmental sciences program at Oregon State University, notes that in India, where the elephant has long been regarded as a deity, a recent headline in a leading newspaper warned, "To Avoid Confrontation, Don't Worship Elephants." "Everybody pretty much agrees that the relationship between elephants and people has dramatically changed," Bradshaw told me recently. "What we are seeing today is extraordinary. Where for centuries humans and elephants lived in relative peaceful coexistence, there is now hostility and violence. Now, I use the term 'violence' because of the intentionality associated with it, both in the aggression of humans and, at times, the recently observed behavior of elephants."

For a number of biologists and ethologists who have spent their careers studying elephant behavior, the attacks have become so abnormal in both number and kind that they can no longer be attributed entirely to the customary factors. Typically, elephant researchers have cited, as a cause of aggression, the high levels of testosterone in newly matured male elephants or the competition for land and resources between elephants and humans. But in "Elephant Breakdown," a 2005 essay in the journal *Nature*, Bradshaw and several colleagues argued that today's elephant populations are suffering from a form of chronic stress, a kind of species-wide trauma. Decades of poaching and culling and habitat loss, they claim, have so disrupted the intricate web of familial and societal relations by which young elephants have traditionally been raised in the wild, and by which established elephant herds are governed, that what we are now witnessing is nothing less than a precipitous collapse of elephant culture.

It has long been apparent that every large, land-based animal on this planet is ultimately fighting a losing battle with humankind. And yet entirely befitting of an animal with such a highly developed sensibility, a deep-rooted sense of family and, yes, such a good long-term memory, the elephant is not going out quietly. It is not leaving without making some kind of statement, one to which scientists from a variety of disciplines, including human psychology, are now beginning to pay close attention.

Once the matriarch and her calf were a comfortable distance from us that morning, Okello and I made the twenty-minute drive to Kyambura, a village at the far southeastern edge of the park. Back in 2003, Kyambura was reportedly the site of the very sort of sudden, unprovoked elephant attack I'd been hearing about. According to an account of the event in the magazine *New Scientist*, a number of huts and fields were trampled, and the townspeople were afraid to venture out to surrounding villages, either by foot or on their bikes, because elephants were regularly blocking the road and charging out at those who tried to pass.

Park officials from the Uganda Wildlife Authority with whom I tried to discuss the incident were reluctant to talk about it or any of the recent killings by elephants in the area. Ecotourism is one of Uganda's major sources of income, and the elephant and other wildlife stocks of Queen Elizabeth National Park are only just now beginning to recover from years of virtually unchecked poaching and habitat destruction. Tom Okello, the chief game warden at the park (and no relation to my driver), and Margaret Driciru, Queen Elizabeth's chief veterinarian, each told me that they weren't aware of the attack in Kyambura. When I mentioned it to the executive director of the wildlife authority, Moses Mapesa, upon my initial arrival in the capital city, Kampala, he eventually admitted that it did happen, but he claimed that it was not nearly as recent as reported. "That was fourteen years ago," he said. "We have seen aggressive behavior from elephants, but that's a story of the past."

Kyambura did look, upon our arrival, much like every other small Ugandan farming community I'd passed through on my visit. Lush fields of banana trees, millet, and maize framed a small town center of pastel-colored, single-story cement buildings with corrugated-tin roofs. People sat on stoops out front in the available shade. Bicyclers bore preposterously outsize loads of bananas, firewood, and five-gallon water jugs on their fenders and handlebars. Contrary to what I had read, the bicycle traffic along the road in and out of Kyambura didn't seem impaired in the slightest.

But when Okello and I asked a shopkeeper named Ibrah Byamukama about elephant attacks, he immediately nodded and pointed to a patch of maize and millet fields just up the road, along the edges of the surrounding Maramagambo Forest. He confirmed that a small group of elephants charged out one morning two years earlier, trampled the fields and nearby gardens, knocked down a few huts, and then left. He then pointed to a long orange gash in the earth between the planted fields and the forest: a fifteen-foot-deep, twenty-five-foot-wide trench that had been dug by the wildlife authority around the perimeter of Kyambura in an attempt to keep the elephants at bay. On the way out of town, Okello and I took a closer look at the trench. It was filled with stacks of thorny shrubs for good measure.

"The people are still worried," Byamukama said, shaking his head. "The elephants are just becoming more destructive. I don't know why."

Three years ago, Gay Bradshaw, then working on her graduate degree in psychology at the Pacifica Graduate Institute outside Santa Barbara, California, began wondering much the same thing: was the extraordinary behavior of elephants in Africa and Asia signaling a breaking point? With the assistance of several established African-elephant researchers, including Daphne Sheldrick and Cynthia Moss, and with the help of Allan Schore, an expert on human trauma disorders at the department of psychiatry and biobehavioral sciences at UCLA, Bradshaw sought to combine traditional research into elephant behavior with insights about trauma drawn from human neuroscience. Using the few remaining relatively stable elephant herds in places like Amboseli National Park in Kenya as control groups, Bradshaw and her colleagues analyzed the far more fractious populations found in places like Pilanesberg in South Africa and Queen Elizabeth National Park in Uganda. What emerged was a portrait of pervasive pachyderm dysfunction.

Elephants, when left to their own devices, are profoundly social creatures. A herd of them is, in essence, one incomprehensibly massive elephant: a somewhat loosely bound and yet intricately interconnected, tensile organism. Young elephants are raised within an extended, multitiered network of doting female caregivers that includes the birth mother, grandmothers, aunts, and friends. These relations are maintained over a life span as long as seventy years. Studies of established herds have shown that young elephants stay within fifteen feet of their mothers for nearly all of their first eight years of life, after which young females are socialized into the matriarchal network, while young males go off for a time into an all-male social group before coming back into the fold as mature adults.

When an elephant dies, its family members engage in intense mourning and burial rituals, conducting weeklong vigils over the body, carefully covering it with earth and brush, revisiting the bones for years afterward, caressing the bones with their trunks, often taking turns rubbing their trunks along the teeth of a skull's lower jaw, the way living elephants do in greeting. If harm comes to a member of an elephant group, all the other elephants are aware of it. This sense of cohesion is further enforced by the elaborate communication system that elephants use. In close proximity they employ a range of vocalizations, from low-frequency rumbles to higher-pitched screams and trumpets, along with a variety of visual signals, from the waving of their trunks to subtle anglings of the head, body, feet, and tail. When communicating over long distances—in order to pass along, for example, news about imminent threats, a sudden change of plans or, of the utmost importance to elephants, the death of a community member—they use patterns of subsonic vibrations that are felt as far as several miles away by exquisitely tuned sensors in the padding of their feet.

This fabric of elephant society, Bradshaw and her colleagues concluded, had effectively been frayed by years of habitat loss and poaching, along with systematic culling by government agencies to control elephant numbers and translocations of herds to different habitats. The number of older matriarchs and female caregivers (or "allomothers") had drastically fallen, as had the number of elder bulls, who play a significant role in keeping younger males in line. In parts of Zambia and Tanzania, a number of the elephant groups studied contained no adult females whatsoever. In Uganda, herds were often found to be "semipermanent aggregations," as a paper written by Bradshaw describes them, with many females between the ages of fifteen and twenty-five having no familial associations.

As a result of such social upheaval, calves are now being born to and raised by ever younger and inexperienced mothers. Young orphaned elephants, meanwhile, that have witnessed the death of a parent at the hands of poachers are coming of age in the absence of the support system that defines traditional elephant life. "The loss of elephants' elders," Bradshaw told me, "and the traumatic experience of witnessing the massacres of their family, impairs normal brain and behavior development in young elephants."

What Bradshaw and her colleagues describe would seem to be an extreme form of anthropocentric conjecture if the evidence that they've compiled from various elephant researchers, even on the strictly observational level, wasn't so compelling. The elephants of decimated herds, especially orphans who've watched the death of their parents and elders from poaching and culling, exhibit behavior typically associated with post-traumatic stress disorder and other trauma-related disorders in humans: abnormal startle response, unpredictable asocial behavior, inattentive mothering, and hyperaggression. Studies of the various assaults on the rhinos in South Africa, meanwhile, have determined that the perpetrators were in all cases adolescent males that had witnessed their families being shot down in cullings. It was common for these elephants to have been tethered to the bodies of their dead and dying relatives until they could be rounded up for translocation to, as Bradshaw and Schore describe them, "locales lacking traditional social hierarchy of older bulls and intact natal family structures."

In fact, even the relatively few attempts that park officials have made to restore parts of the social fabric of elephant society have lent substance to the elephant-breakdown theory. When South African park rangers recently introduced a number of older bull elephants into several destabilized elephant herds in Pilanesburg and Addo, the wayward behavior—including unusually premature hormonal changes among the adolescent elephants—abated.

But according to Bradshaw and her colleagues, the various pieces of the elephant-trauma puzzle really come together at the level of neuroscience, or what might be called the physiology of psychology, by which scientists can now map the marred neuronal fields, snapped synaptic bridges, and crooked chemical streams of an embattled psyche. Though most scientific knowledge of trauma is still understood through research on human subjects, neural studies of elephants are now under way. (The first functional MRI scan of an elephant brain, taken this year, revealed, perhaps not surprisingly, a huge hippocampus, a seat of memory in the mammalian brain, as well as a prominent structure in the limbic system, which processes emotions.) Allan Schore, the UCLA psychologist and neuroscientist who for the past fifteen years has focused his research on early human brain development and the negative impact of trauma on it, recently wrote two articles with Bradshaw on the stress-related neurobiological underpinnings of current abnormal elephant behavior.

"We know that these mechanisms cut across species," Schore told me. "In the first years of humans as well as elephants, development of the emotional brain is impacted by these attachment mechanisms, by the interaction that the infant has with the primary caregiver, especially the mother. When these early experiences go in a positive way, it leads to greater resilience in things like affect regulation, stress regulation, social communication, and empathy. But when these early experiences go awry in cases of abuse and neglect, there is a literal thinning down of the essential circuits in the brain, especially in the emotion-processing areas."

For Bradshaw, these continuities between human and elephant brains resonate far outside the field of neuroscience. "Elephants are suffering and behaving in the same ways that we recognize in ourselves as a result of violence," she told me. "Elephant behavior is entirely congruent with what we know about humans and other mammals. Except perhaps for a few specific features, brain organization and early development of elephants and humans are extremely similar. That's not news. What is news is when you start asking, What does this mean beyond the science? How do we respond to the fact that we are causing other species like elephants to psychologically break down? In a way, it's not so much a cognitive or imaginative leap anymore as it is a political one."

Eve Abe says that in her mind, she made that leap before she ever left her mother's womb. An animal ethologist and wildlife-management consultant now based in London, Abe (pronounced AH-bay) grew up in northern Uganda. After several years of studying elephants in Queen Elizabeth National Park, where decades of poaching had drastically reduced the herds, Abe received her doctorate at Cambridge University in 1994 for work detailing the parallels she saw between the plight of Uganda's orphaned male elephants and the young male orphans of her own people, the Acholi, whose families and villages have been decimated by years of civil war. It's work she proudly proclaims to be not only "the ultimate act of anthropomorphism" but also what she was destined to do.

"My very first encounter with an elephant was a fetal one," Abe told me in June in London as the two of us sipped tea at a cafe in Paddington Station. I was given Abe's contact numbers earlier in the spring by Bradshaw, who is currently working with Abe to build a community center in Uganda to help both elephants and humans in their recovery from violence. For more than a month before my departure from New York, I had been trying without luck to arrange with the British Home Office for Abe, who is still waiting for permanent residence status in England, to travel with me to Uganda as my guide through Queen Elizabeth National Park without fear of her being denied re-entry to England. She was to accompany me that day right up to the departure gate at Heathrow, the two of us hoping (in vain, as it turned out) for a last-minute call that would have given her leave to use the ticket I was holding for her in my bag.

"My dad was a conservationist and a teacher," explained Abe, a tall, elegant woman with a trilling, nearly girlish voice. "He was always out in the parks. One of my aunts tells this story about us passing through Murchison Park one day. My dad was driving. My uncle was in the front seat. In the back were my aunt and my mom, who was very pregnant with me. They suddenly came upon this huge herd of elephants on the road, and the elephants just stopped. So my dad stopped. He knew about animals. The elephants just stood there, then they started walking around the car, and looking into the car. Finally, they walked off. But my father didn't start the car then. He waited there. After an hour or more, a huge female came back out onto the road, right in front of the car. It reared up and trumpeted so loudly, then followed the rest of the herd back into the bush. A few days later, when my mom got home, I was born."

Abe began her studies in Queen Elizabeth National Park in 1982, as an undergraduate at Makerere University in Kampala, shortly after she and her family, who'd been living for years as refugees in Kenya to escape the brutal violence in Uganda under the dictatorship of Idi Amin, returned home in the wake of Amin's ouster in 1979. Abe told me that when she first arrived at the park, there were fewer than 150 elephants remaining from an original population of nearly 4,000. The bulk of the decimation occurred during the war with Tanzania that led to Amin's overthrow: soldiers from both armies grabbed all the ivory they could get their hands on—and did so with such cravenness that the word "poaching" seems woefully inadequate. "Normally when you say 'poaching,'" Abe said, "you think of people shooting one or two and going off. But this was war. They'd just throw hand grenades at the elephants, bring whole families down, and cut out the ivory. I call that mass destruction."

The last elephant survivors of Queen Elizabeth National Park, Abe said, never left one another's side. They kept in a tight bunch, moving as one. Only one elderly female remained; Abe estimated her to be at least sixty-two. It was this matriarch who first gathered the survivors together from their various hideouts on the park's forested fringes and then led them back out as one group into open savanna. Until her death in the early 90s, the old female held the group together, the population all the while slowly beginning to rebound. In her yet-to-be-completed memoir, *My Elephants and My People,* Abe writes of the prominence of the matriarch in Acholi society; she named the park's matriarchal elephant savior Lady Irene, after her own mother. "It took that core group of survivors in the park about five or six years," Abe told me, "before I started seeing whole new family units emerge and begin to split off and go their own way."

In 1986, Abe's family was forced to flee the country again. Violence against Uganda's people and elephants never completely abated after Amin's regime collapsed, and it drastically worsened in the course of the full-fledged war that developed between government forces and the rebel Lord's Resistance Army. For years, that army's leader, Joseph Kony, routinely "recruited" from Acholi villages, killing the parents of young males before their eyes, or sometimes having them do the killings themselves, before pressing them into service as child soldiers. The Lord's Resistance Army has by now been largely defeated, but Kony, who is wanted by the International Criminal Court for numerous crimes against humanity, has hidden with what remains of his army in the mountains of Murchison Falls National Park, and more recently in Garamba National Park in northern Congo, where poaching by the Lord's Resistance Army has continued to orphan more elephants.

"I started looking again at what has happened among the Acholi and the elephants," Abe told me. "I saw that it is an absolute coincidence between the two. You know we used to have villages. We still don't have villages. There are over 200 displaced people's camps in present-day northern Uganda. Everybody lives now within these camps, and there are no more elders. The elders were systematically eliminated. The first batch of elimination was during Amin's time, and that set the stage for the later destruction of northern Uganda. We are among the lucky few, because my mom and dad managed to escape. But the families there are just broken. I know many of them. Displaced people are living in our home now. My mother said let them have it. All these kids who have grown up with their parents killed—no fathers, no mothers, only children looking after them. They don't go to schools. They have no schools, no hospitals. No infrastructure. They form these roaming, violent, destructive bands. It's the same thing that happens with the elephants. Just like the male war orphans, they are wild, completely lost."

On the ride from Paddington that afternoon out to Heathrow, where I would catch a flight to Uganda, Abe told me that the parallel between the plight of Ugandans and their elephants was in many ways too close for her to see at first. It was only after she moved to London that she had what was, in a sense, her first full, adult recognition of the entwinement between human and elephant that she says she long ago felt in her mother's womb.

"I remember when I first was working on my doctorate," she said. "I mentioned that I was doing this parallel once to a prominent scientist in Kenya. He looked amazed. He said, 'How come nobody has made this connection before?' I told him because it hadn't happened this way to anyone else's tribe before. To me it's something I see so clearly. Most people are scared of showing that kind of anthropomorphism. But coming from me it doesn't sound like I'm inventing something. It's there. People know it's there. Some might think that the way I describe the elephant attacks makes the animals look like people. But people are animals."

Shortly after my return from Uganda, I went to visit the Elephant Sanctuary in Tennessee, a 2,700-acre rehabilitation center and retirement facility situated in the state's verdant, low-rolling southern hill country. The sanctuary is a kind of asylum for some of the more emotionally and psychologically disturbed former zoo and circus elephants in the United States—cases so bad that the people who profited from them were eager to let them go. Given that elephants in the wild are now exhibiting aberrant behaviors that were long observed in captive elephants, it perhaps follows that a positive working model for how to ameliorate the effects of elephant breakdown can be found in captivity.

Of the nineteen current residents of the sanctuary, perhaps the biggest hardluck story was that of a forty-year-old, five-ton Asian elephant named Misty. Originally captured as a calf in India in 1966, Misty spent her first decade in captivity with a number of American circuses and finally ended up in the early 80s at a wild-animal attraction known as Lion Country Safari in Irvine, California. It was there, on the afternoon of July 25, 1983, that Misty, one of four performing elephants at Lion Country Safari that summer, somehow managed to break free of her chains and began madly dashing about the park, looking to make an escape. When one of the park's zoologists tried to corner and contain her, Misty killed him with one swipe of her trunk.

There are, in the long, checkered history of human-elephant relations, countless stories of lethal elephantine assaults, and almost invariably of some gruesomely outsize, animalistic form of retribution exacted by us. It was in the very state of Tennessee, back in September 1916, that another five-ton Asian circus elephant, Mary, was impounded by a local sheriff for the killing of a young hotel janitor who'd been hired to mind Mary during a stopover in the northeast Tennessee town of Kingsport. The janitor had apparently taken Mary for a swim at a local pond, where, according to witnesses, he poked her behind the left ear with a metal hook just as she was reaching for a piece of floating watermelon rind. Enraged, Mary turned, swiftly snatched him up with her trunk, dashed him against a refreshment stand, and then smashed his head with her foot.

With cries from the townspeople to "Kill the elephant!" and threats from nearby town leaders to bar the circus if "Murderous Mary," as newspapers quickly dubbed her, remained a part of the show, the circus's owner, Charlie Sparks, knew he had to do something to appease the public's blood lust and save his business. Among the penalties he is said to have contemplated was electrocution, a ghastly precedent for which had been set thirteen years earlier, on the grounds of the nearly completed Luna Park in Coney Island. A longtime circus elephant named Topsy, who'd killed three trainers in as many years—the last one after he tried to feed her a lighted cigarette—would become the largest and most prominent victim of Thomas Edison, the father of direct-current electricity, who had publicly electrocuted a number of animals at that time using his rival George Westinghouse's alternating current, in hopes of discrediting it as being too dangerous.

Sparks ultimately decided to have Mary hanged and shipped her by train to the nearby town of Erwin, Tennessee, where more than 2,500 people gathered at the local rail yard for her execution. Dozens of children are said to have run off screaming in terror when the chain that was suspended from a huge industrial crane snapped, leaving Mary writhing on the ground with a broken hip. A local rail worker promptly clambered up Mary's bulk and secured a heavier chain for a second, successful hoisting.

Misty's fate in the early 80s, by contrast, seems a triumph of modern human-ism. Banished, after the Lion Safari killing, to the Hawthorn Corporation, a company in Illinois that trains and leases elephants and tigers to circuses, she would continue to lash out at a number of her trainers over the years. But when Hawthorn was convicted of numerous violations of the Animal Welfare Act in 2003, the company agreed to relinquish custody of Misty to the Elephant Sanctuary. She was loaded onto a trailer transport on the morning of November 17, 2004, and even then managed to get away with one final shot at the last in her long line of captors.

"The details are kind of sketchy," Carol Buckley, a founder of the Elephant Sanctuary, said to me one afternoon in July, the two of us pulling up on her all-terrain four-wheeler to a large grassy enclosure where an extremely docile and contented-looking Misty, trunk high, ears flapping, waited to greet us. "Hawthorn's owner was trying to get her to stretch out so he could remove her leg chains before loading her on the trailer. At one point he prodded her with a bull hook, and she just knocked him down with a swipe of her trunk. But we've seen none of that since she's been here. She's as sweet as can be. You'd never know that this elephant killed anybody."

In the course of her nearly two years at the Elephant Sanctuary—much of it spent in quarantine while undergoing daily treatment for tuberculosis—Misty has also been in therapy, as in psychotherapy. Wild-caught elephants often witness as young calves the slaughter of their parents, just about the only way, shy of a far more costly tranquilization procedure, to wrest a calf from elephant parents, especially the mothers. The young captives are then dispatched to a foreign envi-ronment to work either as performers or laborers, all the while being kept in relative confinement and isolation, a kind of living death for an animal as socially developed and dependent as we now know elephants to be.

And yet just as we now understand that elephants hurt like us, we're learn-ing that they can heal like us as well. Indeed, Misty has become a testament to the Elephant Sanctuary's signature "passive control" system, a therapy tailored in many ways along the lines of those used to treat human sufferers of posttraumatic stress disorder. Passive control, as a sanctuary newsletter describes it, depends upon "knowledge of how elephants process information and respond to stress" as well as specific knowledge of each elephant's past response to stress. Under this so-called nondominance system, there is no discipline, retaliation, or withholding of food, water, and treats, which are all common tactics of elephant trainers. Great pains are taken, meanwhile, to afford the elephants both a sense of safety and freedom of choice—two mainstays of human trauma therapy—as well as continual social interaction.

Upon her arrival at the Elephant Sanctuary, Misty seemed to sense straight off the different vibe of her new home. When Scott Blais of the sanctuary went to free Misty's still-chained leg a mere day after she'd arrived, she stood peace-ably by, practically offering her leg up to him. Over her many months of quar-antine, meanwhile, with only humans acting as a kind of surrogate elephant family, she has consistently gone through the daily rigors of her tuberculosis treatments—involving two caregivers, a team of veterinarians, and the use of a restraining chute in which harnesses are secured about her chest and tail—without any coaxing or pressure. "We'll shower her with praise in the barn afterwards," Buckley told me as Misty stood by, chomping on a mouthful of hay, "and she actually purrs with pleasure. The whole barn vibrates."

Of course, Misty's road to recovery—when viewed in light of her history and that of all the other captive elephants, past and present—is as harrowing as it is heartening. She and the others have suffered, we now understand, not simply because of us, but because they are, by and large, us. If as recently as the end of the Vietnam War people were still balking at the idea that a soldier, for example, could be physically disabled by a psychological harm—the idea, in other words, that the mind is not an entity apart from the body and therefore just as woundable as any limb—we now find ourselves having to make an equally profound and, for many, even more difficult leap: that a fellow creature as ostensibly unlike us in every way as an elephant is as precisely and intricately woundable as we are. And while such knowledge naturally places an added burden upon us, the keepers, that burden is now being greatly compounded by the fact that sudden violent outbursts like Misty's can no longer be dismissed as the inevitable isolated revolts of a restless few against the constraints and abuses of captivity.

They have no future without us. The question we are now forced to grapple with is whether we would mind a future without them, among the more mindful creatures on this earth and, in many ways, the most devoted. Indeed, the manner of the elephants' continued keeping, their restoration and conservation, both in civil confines and what's left of wild ones, is now drawing the attention of everyone from naturalists to neuroscientists. Too much about elephants, in the end—their desires and devotions, their vulnerability and tremendous resilience—reminds us of ourselves to dismiss out of hand this revolt they're currently staging against their own dismissal. And while our concern may ultimately be rooted in that most human of impulses—the preservation of our own self-image—the great paradox about this particular moment in our history with elephants is that saving them will require finally getting past ourselves; it will demand the ultimate act of deep, interspecies empathy.

On a more immediate, practical level, as Gay Bradshaw sees it, this involves taking what has been learned about elephant society, psychology, and emotion and inculcating that knowledge into the conservation schemes of researchers and park rangers. This includes doing things like expanding elephant habitat to what it used to be historically and avoiding the use of culling and translocations as conservation tools. "If we want elephants around," Bradshaw told me, "then what we need to do is simple: learn how to live with elephants. In other words, in addition to conservation, we need to educate people how to live with wild animals like humans used to do, and to create conditions whereby people can live on their land and live with elephants without it being this life-and-death situation."

The other part of our newly emerging compact with elephants, however, is far more difficult to codify. It requires nothing less than a fundamental shift in the way we look at animals and, by extension, ourselves. It requires what Bradshaw somewhat whimsically refers to as a new "trans-species psyche," a commitment to move beyond an anthropocentric frame of reference and, in effect, be elephants. Two years ago, Bradshaw wrote a paper for the journal *Society and Animals,* focusing on the work of the David Sheldrick Wildlife Trust in Kenya, a sanctuary for orphaned and traumatized wild elephants—more or less the wilderness-based complement to Carol Buckley's trauma therapy at the Elephant Sanctuary in Tennessee. The trust's human caregivers essentially serve as surrogate mothers to young orphan elephants, gradually restoring their psychological and emotional well-being to the point at which they can be reintroduced into existing wild herds. The human "allomothers" stay by their adopted young orphans' sides, even sleeping with them at night in stables. The caregivers make sure, however, to rotate from one elephant to the next so that the orphans grow fond of all the keepers. Otherwise an elephant would form such a strong bond with one keeper that whenever he or she was absent, that elephant would grieve as if over the loss of another family member, often becoming physically ill itself.

To date, the Sheldrick Trust has successfully rehabilitated more than sixty elephants and reintroduced them into wild herds. A number of them have periodically returned to the sanctuary with their own wild-born calves in order to reunite with their human allomothers and to introduce their offspring to what—out on this uncharted frontier of the new "trans-species psyche"—is now being recognized, at least by the elephants, it seems, as a whole new subspecies: the human allograndmother. "Traditionally, nature has served as a source of healing for humans," Bradshaw told me. "Now humans can participate actively in the healing of both themselves and nonhuman animals. The trust and the sanctuary are the beginnings of a mutually benefiting interspecies culture."

On my way back to New York via London, I contacted Felicity de Zulueta, a psychiatrist at Maudsley Hospital in London, who treats victims of extreme trauma, among them former child soldiers from the Lord's Resistance Army. De Zulueta, an acquaintance of Eve Abe's, grew up in Uganda in the early 1960s on the outskirts of Queen Elizabeth National Park, near where her father, a malaria doctor, had set up camp as part of a malaria-eradication program. For a time she had her own elephant, orphaned by poaching, that local villagers had given to her father, who brought it home to the family garage, where it immediately bonded with an orphan antelope and dog already residing there.

"He was doing fine," de Zulueta told me of the pet elephant. "My mother was loving it and feeding it, and then my parents realized, How can we keep this elephant that is going to grow bigger than the garage? So they gave it to who they thought were the experts. They sent him to the Entebbe Zoo, and although they gave him all the right food and everything, he was a lonely little elephant, and he died. He had no attachment."

For de Zulueta, the parallel that Abe draws between the plight of war orphans, human and elephant, is painfully apt, yet also provides some cause for hope, given the often startling capacity of both animals for recovery. She told me that one Ugandan war orphan she is currently treating lost all the members of his family except for two older brothers. Remarkably, one of those brothers, while serving in the Ugandan Army, rescued the younger sibling from the Lord's Resistance Army; the older brother's unit had captured the rebel battalion in which his younger brother had been forced to fight.

The two brothers eventually made their way to London, and for the past two years, the younger brother has been going through a gradual process of recovery in the care of Maudsley Hospital. Much of the rehabilitation, according to de Zulueta, especially in the early stages, relies on the basic human trauma therapy principles now being applied to elephants: providing decent living quarters, establishing a sense of safety and of attachment to a larger community, and allowing freedom of choice. After that have come the more complex treatments tailored to the human brain's particular cognitive capacities: things like reliving the original traumatic experience and being taught to modulate feelings through early detection of hyperarousal and through breathing techniques. And the healing of trauma, as de Zulueta describes it, turns out to have physical correlatives in the brain just as its wounding does.

"What I say is, we find bypass," she explained. "We bypass the wounded areas using various techniques. Some of the wounds are not healable. Their scars remain. But there is hope because the brain is an enormous computer, and you can learn to bypass its wounds by finding different methods of approaching life. Of course there may be moments when something happens and the old wound becomes unbearable. Still, people do recover. The boy I've been telling you about is eighteen now, and he has survived very well in terms of his emotional health and capacities. He's a lovely, lovely man. And he's a poet. He writes beautiful poetry."

On the afternoon in July that I left the Elephant Sanctuary in Tennessee, Carol Buckley and Scott Blais seemed in particularly good spirits. Misty was only weeks away from the end of her quarantine, and she would soon be able to socialize with some of her old cohorts from the Hawthorn Corporation: eight female Asians that had been given over to the sanctuary. I would meet the lot of them that day, driving from one to the next on the back of Buckley's four-wheeler across the sanctuary's savannalike stretches. Buckley and Blais refer to them collectively as the Divas.

Buckley and Blais told me that they got word not long ago of a significant breakthrough in a campaign of theirs to get elephants out of entertainment and zoos: the Bronx Zoo, one of the oldest and most formidable zoos in the country, had announced that upon the death of the zoo's three current elephant inhabitants, Patty, Maxine, and Happy, it would phase out its elephant exhibit on social-behavioral grounds—an acknowledgment of a new awareness of the elephant's very particular sensibility and needs. "They're really taking the lead," Buckley told me. "Zoos don't want to concede the inappropriateness of keeping elephants in such confines. But if we as a society determine that an animal like this suffers in captivity, if the information shows us that they do, hey, we are the stewards. You'd think we'd want to do the right thing."

Four days later, I received an e-mail message from Gay Bradshaw, who consults with Buckley and Blais on their various stress-therapy strategies. She wrote that one of the sanctuary's elephants, an Asian named Winkie, had just killed a thirty-six-year-old female assistant caretaker and critically injured the male caretaker who'd tried to save her.

People who work with animals on a daily basis can tell you all kinds of stories about their distinct personalities and natures. I'd gotten, in fact, an elaborate breakdown from Buckley and Blais on the various elephants at the sanctuary and their sociopolitical maneuverings within the sanctuary's distinct elephant culture, and I went to my notebook to get a fix again on Winkie. A forty-year-old, 7,600-pound female from Burma, she came to the sanctuary in 2000 from the Henry Vilas Zoo in Madison, Wisconsin, where she had a reputation for lashing out at keepers. When Winkie first arrived at the sanctuary, Buckley told me, she used to jump merely upon being touched and then would wait for a confrontation. But when it never came, she slowly calmed down. "Has never lashed out at primary keepers," my last note on Winkie reads, "but has at secondary ones."

Bradshaw's e-mail message concludes: "A stunning illustration of trauma in elephants. The indelible etching."

I thought back to a moment in Queen Elizabeth National Park this past June. As Nelson Okello and I sat waiting for the matriarch and her calf to pass, he mentioned to me an odd little detail about the killing two months earlier of the man from the village of Katwe, something that, the more I thought about it, seemed to capture this particularly fraught moment we've arrived at with the elephants. Okello said that after the man's killing, the elephant herd buried him as it would one of its own, carefully covering the body with earth and brush and then standing vigil over it.

Even as we're forcing them out, it seems, the elephants are going out of their way to put us, the keepers, in an ever more discomfiting place, challenging us to preserve someplace for them, the ones who in many ways seem to regard the matter of life and death more devoutly than we. In fact, elephant culture could be considered the precursor of our own, the first permanent human settlements having sprung up around the desire of wandering tribes to stay by the graves of their dead. "The city of the dead," as Lewis Mumford once wrote, "antedates the city of the living."

When a group of villagers from Katwe went out to reclaim the man's body for his family's funeral rites, the elephants refused to budge. Human remains, a number of researchers have observed, are the only other ones that elephants will treat as they do their own. In the end, the villagers resorted to a tactic that has long been etched in the elephant's collective memory, firing volleys of gunfire into the air at close range, finally scaring the mourning herd away.

QUESTIONS FOR MAKING CONNECTIONS
WITHIN THE READING

1. What evidence does Siebert provide to support the claim there is such a thing as an "elephant culture"? In making this claim is Siebert guilty of anthropomorphism? That is, does he ascribe to animals the thoughts and emotions that only humans have? Or is he guilty of the opposite mistake,

the error of anthropocentrism—treating human beings as the standard by which all other species should be measured? Is it possible that these "mistakes" are really not mistakes at all, especially because we *Homo sapiens* are in fact animals, too? Would you agree that understanding other minds—human or otherwise—requires us to start with what we know about own mental processes? Can we even prove that our fellow human beings have thoughts and emotions like our own?

2. As Siebert's discussion unfolds, he describes elephants who experience acute trauma and then become deliberately aggressive. He also shows that they respond to psychotherapies that were initially developed to assist human beings. Do you find these developments surprising? Is Siebert seeking to establish that humans and elephants are part of a continuum? Does he mean to imply that the minds of the two species are identical? Or does he see them on parallel paths?

3. Siebert's essay ends with two acts of violence: a caretaker killed by an elephant in captivity, and a villager killed and buried by an elephant herd. Why does he structure the piece in this way? Since he also began by describing violence, has Siebert come full circle? Or has he put his readers in a better position to understand the violence?

QUESTIONS FOR WRITING

1. Throughout "An Elephant Crackup?" Siebert gestures towards modes of consciousness that differ significantly from the model of an individual thinking. He describes a herd of elephants as "in essence, one incomprehensibly massive elephant." He observes that saving elephants from extinction "will demand the ultimate act of deep, interspecies empathy." And he cites Gay Bradshaw's call for the development of a "trans-species psyche" that will allow humans to "be elephants." How would one go about creating these new modes of consciousness? Does Siebert's narrative provide any hints about how the two species might begin to share the same conceptual world?

2. Siebert notes that those who are concerned with the effects of trauma on the elephant population are now focusing on the "physiology of psychology"—that is, on the neurological foundation for psychological development. Based on the preliminary results of these studies, would you say that the turn to neurology provides cause for optimism about the possibilities of overcoming trauma? Or does the fact that trauma during the formative years results in "a literal thinning down of the essential circuits in the brain" mean that there's no saving young victims of trauma, be they elephant or human?

QUESTIONS FOR MAKING CONNECTIONS
BETWEEN READINGS

1. In Selections from *Love 2.0*, Barbara Fredrickson describes the way our brains operate below the level of consciousness to produce our conscious experience of resonating with others. In what ways does Fredrickson's account complicate our tendency to think about the mental life of *Homo sapiens* as fundamentally different from the mental lives of animals like the elephants whose decline Siebert chronicles? Does Fredrickson's account of our emotions justify Gay Bradshaw's willingness to violate the rule in animal studies against anthropomorphism—against imposing on animal behavior the thoughts and motivations of humans? In view of the possible parallels between displaced humans and the young elephants raised without the guidance of adults, would you agree that our way of life might be doing damage to us?

2. In Selections from *Alone Together*, Sherry Turkle contemplates the ways that contemporary children interact with their Tamagotchis and Furbies. She describes her own experience as well:

    > My Tamagotchi liked to eat at particular intervals. I thought it prospered best with only small doses of amusement. I worked hard at keeping it happy. I did not anticipate how bad I would feel when it died. I immediately hit the reset button. Somewhat to my surprise, I had no desire to take care of the new infant Tamagotchi that appeared on my screen.

    Will our embrace of technology make us more receptive, or less, to the predicament of the elephants? If we should lose the ability to distinguish between biological life and its simulations, will the extinction of species matter to us at all? Does the belief that a "singularity" that will free our minds from all material constraints express an unacknowledged loathing for our humanity and, perhaps, even for life itself?

ANDREW SOLOMON

WHO ARE YOU—REALLY? What does "me" indicate? We count on our ability to understand ourselves, but what do we know for certain?

Questions about identity lie at the heart of Andrew Solomon's writing. By all accounts, Solomon was raised in a happy home with loving parents. Once he graduated from Yale, he went to Cambridge University, which awarded him the top first-class degree, the only time the honor had ever been bestowed on a foreign student. After Solomon met with such success, happiness should have been his lot in life, but when he was only 25, his mother died from cancer. It would be conventional to say that Solomon "fell into a deep depression," but the malady that overcame him unfolded in such a strange, oblique way that he had no sense of what was happening: "A loss of feeling, a numbness, infected all my human relations. I didn't care about love, my work, family, friends. My writing slowed, then stopped.... I was losing my self and that scared me." This experience of losing himself led to Solomon's third book, *The Noonday Demon: An Atlas of Depression* (2001), which won the National Book Award for Nonfiction and has been translated into 24 languages. The story it tells is quite harrowing, but depression gave Solomon a much deeper sense of what it means to be or to have a self. As he told one interviewer, "It seems to me that who other people are is always mysterious. What I realized in the wake of depression is that who I am is fully mysterious to me."

Solomon's new book *Far from the Tree: Parents, Children, and the Search for Identity* (2012), from which the following selection is taken, might be read as an attempt to explore the self in another way, not through the labyrinth of the mind but through our relations to others. As a gay man, Solomon is fascinated by how we each create ourselves, sometimes in ways our parents dislike. Most prospective parents start out convinced their children will embrace the lives mapped out for them, but the unexpected often happens. Solomon's own mother could never accept his sexuality, and his experience of her disapproval brought him closer to other children whose arrival in the world thwarted parental expectations: deaf people, dwarves, those born with Down syndrome, autism,

Biographical details are from Andrew Solomon's site <http://andrewsolomon.com>. Quotation on depression is from Andrew Solomon, *The Noonday Demon: An Atlas of Depression* (New York: Scribner, 2001) 45. Quotation on the self is from "The Soul in Depression," *On Being*, February 26, 2009 <http://www.onbeing.org/program/soul-depression/transcript/1332>.

schizophrenia. Solomon understands that many loving parents want their children to be "normal," but he argues that our differences can teach us all how to think and love more inclusively.

Son

There is no such thing as reproduction. When two people decide to have a baby, they engage in an act of production, and the widespread use of the word *reproduction* for this activity, with its implication that two people are but braiding themselves together, is at best a euphemism to comfort prospective parents before they get in over their heads. In the subconscious fantasies that make conception look so alluring, it is often ourselves that we would like to see live forever, not someone with a personality of his own. Having anticipated the onward march of our selfish genes, many of us are unprepared for children who present unfamiliar needs. Parenthood abruptly catapults us into a permanent relationship with a stranger, and the more alien the stranger, the stronger the whiff of negativity. We depend on the guarantee in our children's faces that we will not die. Children whose defining quality annihilates that fantasy of immortality are a particular insult; we must love them for themselves, and not for the best of ourselves in them, and that is a great deal harder to do. Loving our own children is an exercise for the imagination.

Yet blood, in modern as in ancient societies, is thicker than water. Little is more gratifying than successful and devoted children, and few situations are worse than filial failure or rejection. Our children are not us: they carry throwback genes and recessive traits and are subject right from the start to environmental stimuli beyond our control. And yet we are our children; the reality of being a parent never leaves those who have braved the metamorphosis. The psychoanalyst D. W. Winnicott once said, "There is no such thing as a baby—meaning that if you set out to describe a baby, you will find you are describing a *baby and someone*. A baby cannot exist alone but is essentially part of a relationship." Insofar as our children resemble us, they are our most precious admirers, and insofar as they differ, they can be our most vehement detractors. From the beginning, we tempt them into imitation of us and long for what may be life's most profound compliment: their choosing to live according to our own system of values. Though many of us take pride in how different we are from our parents, we are endlessly sad at how different our children are from us.

Because of the transmission of identity from one generation to the next, most children share at least some traits with their parents. These are *vertical* identities.

Attributes and values are passed down from parent to child across the generations not only through strands of DNA, but also through shared cultural norms. Ethnicity, for example, is a vertical identity. Children of color are in general born to parents of color; the genetic fact of skin pigmentation is transmitted across generations along with a self-image as a person of color, even though that self-image may be subject to generational flux. Language is usually vertical, since most people who speak Greek raise their children to speak Greek, too, even if they inflect it differently or speak another language much of the time. Religion is moderately vertical: Catholic parents will tend to bring up Catholic children, though the children may turn irreligious or convert to another faith. Nationality is vertical, except for immigrants. Blondness and myopia are often transmitted from parent to child, but in most cases do not form a significant basis for identity—blondness because it is fairly insignificant, and myopia because it is easily corrected.

Often, however, someone has an inherent or acquired trait that is foreign to his or her parents and must therefore acquire identity from a peer group. This is a *horizontal* identity. Such horizontal identities may reflect recessive genes, random mutations, prenatal influences, or values and preferences that a child does not share with his progenitors. Being gay is a horizontal identity; most gay kids are born to straight parents, and while their sexuality is not determined by their peers, they learn gay identity by observing and participating in a subculture outside the family. Physical disability tends to be horizontal, as does genius. Psychopathy, too, is often horizontal; most criminals are not raised by mobsters and must invent their own treachery. So are conditions such as autism and intellectual disability. A child conceived in a rape is born into emotional challenges that his own mother cannot know, even though they spring from her trauma.

In 1993, I was assigned to investigate Deaf culture for the *New York Times*. My assumption about deafness was that it was a deficit and nothing more. Over the months that followed, I found myself drawn into the Deaf world. Most deaf children are born to hearing parents, and those parents frequently prioritize functioning in the hearing world, expending enormous energy on oral speech and lipreading. Doing so, they can neglect other areas of their children's education. While some deaf people are good at lipreading and produce comprehensible speech, many do not have that skill, and years go by as they sit endlessly with audiologists and speech pathologists instead of learning history and mathematics and philosophy. Many stumble upon Deaf identity in adolescence, and it comes as a great liberation. They move into a world that validates Sign as a language and discover themselves. Some hearing parents accept this powerful new development; others struggle against it.

The whole situation felt arrestingly familiar to me because I am gay. Gay people usually grow up under the purview of straight parents who feel that their children would be better off straight and sometimes torment them by pressing them to conform. Those gay people often discover gay identity in adolescence or afterward, finding great relief there. When I started writing about the deaf, the cochlear implant, which can provide some facsimile of hearing, was a recent innovation. It had been hailed by its progenitors as a miraculous cure for a terrible defect and was deplored by the Deaf community as a genocidal attack on a vibrant community. Both sides have since moderated their rhetoric, but the issue is complicated by the fact that cochlear implants are most effective when they are surgically implanted early—in infants, ideally—so the decision is often made by parents before the child can possibly have or express an informed opinion. Watching the debate, I knew that my own parents would gamely have consented to a parallel early procedure to ensure that I would be straight, had one existed. I do not doubt that the advent of such a thing even now could wipe out most of gay culture. I am saddened by the idea of such a threat, and yet as my understanding of Deaf culture deepened, I realized that the attitudes I had found benighted in my parents resembled my own likely response to producing a deaf child. My first impulse would have been to do whatever I could to fix the abnormality.

Then a friend had a daughter who was a dwarf. She wondered whether she should bring up her daughter to consider herself just like everyone else, only shorter; whether she should make sure her daughter had dwarf role models; or whether she should investigate surgical limb-lengthening. As she narrated her bafflement, I saw a familiar pattern. I had been startled to note my common ground with the Deaf, and now I was identifying with a dwarf; I wondered who else was out there waiting to join our gladsome throng. I thought that if gayness, an identity, could grow out of homosexuality, an illness, and Deafness, an identity, could grow out of deafness, an illness, and if dwarfism as an identity could emerge from an apparent disability, then there must be many other categories in this awkward interstitial territory. It was a radicalizing insight. Having always imagined myself in a fairly slim minority, I suddenly saw that I was in a vast company. Difference unites us. While each of these experiences can isolate those who are affected, together they compose an aggregate of millions whose struggles connect them profoundly. The exceptional is ubiquitous; to be entirely typical is the rare and lonely state.

As my parents had misapprehended who I was, so other parents must be constantly misapprehending their own children. Many parents experience their child's horizontal identity as an affront. A child's marked difference from the rest of the family demands knowledge, competence, and actions that a typical mother and father are unqualified to supply, at least initially. The child is expressly different from most of his or her peers as well, and therefore broadly less understood or accepted. Abusive fathers visit less abuse on children who resemble them physically; if you are born to a bully, pray that you bear his features. Whereas families tend to reinforce vertical identities from earliest childhood, many will oppose horizontal ones. Vertical identities are usually respected as identities; horizontal ones are often treated as flaws.

One could argue that black people face many disadvantages in the United States today, but there is little research into how gene expression could be altered to make the next generation of children born to black parents come out with straight, flaxen hair and creamy complexions. In modern America, it is sometimes hard to be Asian or Jewish or female, yet no one suggests that Asians,

Jews, or women would be foolish not to become white Christian men if they could. Many vertical identities make people uncomfortable, and yet we do not attempt to homogenize them. The disadvantages of being gay are arguably no greater than those of such vertical identities, but most parents have long sought to turn their gay children straight. Anomalous bodies are usually more frightening to people who witness them than to people who have them, yet parents rush to normalize physical exceptionalism, often at great psychic cost to themselves and their children. Labeling a child's mind as diseased—whether with autism, intellectual disabilities, or transgenderism—may reflect the discomfort that mind gives parents more than any discomfort it causes their child. Much gets corrected that might better have been left alone.

Defective is an adjective that has long been deemed too freighted for liberal discourse, but the medical terms that have supplanted it—*illness, syndrome, condition*—can be almost equally pejorative in their discreet way. We often use *illness* to disparage a way of being, and *identity* to validate that same way of being. This is a false dichotomy. In physics, the Copenhagen interpretation defines energy/matter as behaving sometimes like a wave and sometimes like a particle, which suggests that it is both, and posits that it is our human limitation to be unable to see both at the same time. The Nobel Prize–winning physicist Paul Dirac identified how light appears to be a particle if we ask a particle-like question, and a wave if we ask a wavelike question. A similar duality obtains in this matter of self. Many conditions are both illness and identity, but we can see one only when we obscure the other. Identity politics refutes the idea of illness, while medicine shortchanges identity. Both are diminished by this narrowness.

Physicists gain certain insights from understanding energy as a wave, and other insights from understanding it as a particle, and use quantum mechanics to reconcile the information they have gleaned. Similarly, we have to examine *illness* and *identity,* understand that observation will usually happen in one domain or the other, and come up with a syncretic mechanics. We need a vocabulary in which the two concepts are not opposites, but compatible aspects of a condition. The problem is to change how we assess the value of individuals and of lives, to reach for a more ecumenical take on *healthy.* Ludwig Wittgenstein said, "All I know is what I have words for." The absence of words is the absence of intimacy; these experiences are starved for language.

The children I describe here have horizontal conditions that are alien to their parents. They are deaf or dwarfs; they have Down syndrome, autism, schizophrenia, or multiple severe disabilities; they are prodigies; they are people conceived in rape or who commit crimes; they are transgender. The timeworn adage says that the apple doesn't fall far from the tree, meaning that a child resembles his or her parents; these children are apples that have fallen elsewhere—some a couple of orchards away, some on the other side of the world. Yet myriad families learn to tolerate, accept, and finally celebrate children who are not what they originally had in mind. This transformative process is often eased and sometimes confounded by identity politics and medical progress—both of which have infiltrated households to a degree that would have been inconceivable even twenty years ago.

All offspring are startling to their parents; these most dramatic situations are merely variations on a common theme. Much as we learn the properties of a medication by studying its effect at extremely high doses, or look at the viability of a construction material by exposing it to unearthly supertemperatures, so we can understand the universal phenomenon of difference within families by looking at these extreme cases. Having exceptional children exaggerates parental tendencies; those who would be bad parents become awful parents, but those who would be good parents often become extraordinary. I take the anti-Tolstoyan view that the unhappy families who reject their variant children have much in common, while the happy ones who strive to accept them are happy in a multitude of ways.

Because prospective parents have ever-increasing options to choose against having children with horizontal challenges, the experiences of those who have such children are critical to our larger understanding of difference. Parents' early responses to and interactions with a child determine how that child comes to view himself. These parents are also profoundly changed by their experiences. If you have a child with a disability, you are forever the parent of a disabled child; it is one of the primary facts about you, fundamental to the way other people perceive and decipher you. Such parents tend to view aberrance as illness until habituation and love enable them to cope with their odd new reality—often by introducing the language of identity. Intimacy with difference fosters it accommodation.

Broadcasting these parents' learned happiness is vital to sustaining identities that are now vulnerable to eradication. Their stories point a way for all of us to expand our definitions of the human family. It's important to know how autistic people feel about autism, or dwarfs about dwarfism. Self-acceptance is part of the ideal, but without familial and societal acceptance, it cannot ameliorate the relentless injustices to which many horizontal identity groups are subject and will not bring about adequate reform. We live in xenophobic times, when legislation with majority support abrogates the rights of women, LGBT people, illegal immigrants, and the poor. Despite this crisis in empathy, compassion thrives at home, and most of the parents I have profiled love across the divide. Understanding how they came to think well of their own children may give the rest of us motive and insight to do the same. To look deep into your child's eyes and see in him both yourself and something utterly strange, and then to develop a zealous attachment to every aspect of him, is to achieve parenthood's self-regarding, yet unselfish, abandon. It is astonishing how often such mutuality has been realized—how frequently parents who had supposed that they couldn't care for an exceptional child discover that they can. The parental predisposition to love prevails in the most harrowing of circumstances. There is more imagination in the world than one might think.

I had dyslexia as a child; indeed, I have it now. I still cannot write by hand without focusing on each letter as I form it, and even when I do so, some letters are out of order or omitted. My mother, who identified the dyslexia early, began to work on reading with me when I was two. I spent long afternoons in her lap, learning to sound out words, training like an Olympic athlete in phonetics; we practiced letters as though no shapes could ever be lovelier than theirs. To keep my attention, she gave me a notebook with a yellow felt cover on which Winnie-the-Pooh and Tigger were sewn; we made flash cards and played games with them in the car. I reveled in the attention, and my mother taught with a sense of fun, as though it was the best puzzle in the world, a private game between us. When I was six, my parents applied for my admission to eleven schools in New York City, and all eleven turned me down on grounds that I would never learn to read and write. A year later, I was enrolled in a school where the principal grudgingly allowed my advanced reading skills to overrule test scores that predicted I would never learn to read at all. The standards of perpetual triumph were high in our house, and that early victory over dyslexia was formative: with patience, love, intelligence, and will, we had trounced a neurological abnormality. Unfortunately, it set the stage for our later struggles by making it hard to believe that we couldn't reverse the creeping evidence of another perceived abnormality—my being gay.

People ask when I knew I was gay, and I wonder what that knowledge entails. It took some time for me to become aware of my sexual desires. The realization that what I wanted was exotic, and out of step with the majority, came so early that I cannot remember a time preceding it. Recent studies have shown that as early as age two, male children who will grow up to be gay are averse to certain types of rough-and-tumble play; by age six, most will behave in obviously gender-nonconforming ways. Because I could tell early on that many of my impulses were unmasculine, I embarked on further acts of self-invention. When, in first grade, each of us was asked to name his favorite food and everyone else said ice cream or hamburgers or French toast, I proudly chose *ekmek kadayiff* with *kaymak*, which I used to order at an Armenian restaurant on East Twenty-Seventh Street. I never traded a baseball card, but I did recount the plots of operas on the school bus. None of this made me popular.

I was popular at home, but I was subject to corrections. My mother, my brother, and I were at Indian Walk Shoes when I was seven, and as we were leaving, the salesman asked what color balloons we'd like. My brother wanted a red balloon. I wanted a pink one. My mother countered that I didn't want a pink balloon and reminded me that my favorite color was blue. I said I really wanted the pink, but under her glare, I took the blue one. That my favorite color is blue but I am still gay is evidence of both my mother's influence and its limits. She once said, "When you were little, you didn't like to do what other kids liked to do, and I encouraged you to be yourself." She added, only half-ironically, "I sometimes think I let things go too far." I have sometimes thought she didn't let them go far enough. But her encouragement of my individuality, although doubtless ambivalent, has shaped my life.

My new school had quasi-liberal ideas and was supposed to be integrated—which meant that our class included a few black and Latino kids on scholarship who mostly socialized with one another. My first year there, Debbie Camacho had a birthday party in Harlem, and her parents, unacquainted with the logic of New York private education, scheduled it for the same weekend as homecoming. My mother asked how I would feel if no one attended my birthday party, and insisted that I attend. I doubt many kids in my class would have gone to the party even if there hadn't been such a convenient excuse, but in fact, only two white kids went out of a class of forty. I was frankly terrified of being there. The birthday girl's cousins tried to get me to dance; everyone spoke Spanish; there were unfamiliar fried foods; and I had something of a panic attack and went home in tears.

I drew no parallels between everyone's avoidance of Debbie's party and my own unpopularity, even when, a few months later, Bobby Finkel had a birthday party and invited everyone in the class but me. My mother called his mother on the assumption that there had been a mistake; Mrs. Finkel said that her son didn't like me and didn't want me at his party. My mother picked me up at school on the day of the party and took me to the zoo, and for a hot fudge sundae at Old-Fashioned Mr. Jennings. It's only in retrospect that I imagine how hurt my mother was on my behalf—more hurt than I was, or let myself notice I was. I didn't guess then that her tenderness was a bid to compensate for the insults of the world. When I contemplate my parents' discomfort with my gayness, I can see how vulnerable my vulnerabilities made her, and how much she wanted to preempt my sadness with the assurance that we were our own good time. Forbidding the pink balloon must be held as partly a protective gesture.

I'm glad my mother made me go to Debbie Camacho's birthday party—because I think it was the right thing to do and because, though I couldn't see it at the time, it was the beginning of an attitude of tolerance that allowed me to stomach myself and find happiness in adulthood. It's tempting to paint myself and my family as beacons of liberal exceptionalism, but we weren't. I teased one African-American student in my elementary school by claiming he resembled a picture in our social studies book of a tribal child in an African *rondavel*. I didn't think that this was racist; I thought it was funny, and vaguely true. When I was older, I remembered my behavior with deep regret, and when the person in question found me on Facebook, I apologized profusely. I said that my only excuse was that it was not easy to be gay at the school, and that I'd acted out the prejudice I experienced in the form of prejudice toward others. He accepted my apology, and mentioned that he was also gay; I was humbled that he had survived, where so much of both kinds of bias were in play.

I floundered in the tricky waters of elementary school, but at home, where bias was never tinged with cruelty, my more intractable deficits were minimized and my quirks were mostly humored. When I was ten, I became fascinated by the tiny principality of Liechtenstein. A year later, my father took us along on a business trip to Zürich, and one morning my mother announced that she'd arranged for us all to drive to Liechtenstein's capital, Vaduz. I remember the thrill that the whole family was going along with what was clearly my wish and mine alone. In retrospect, the Liechtenstein preoccupation seems peculiar, but the same mother who forbade the pink balloon thought up and arranged that day: lunch in a charming café, a tour of the art museum, a visit to the printing office where they make the country's distinctive postage stamps. Although I did not always feel approved of, I always felt acknowledged and was given the latitude of my eccentricity. But there were limits, and pink balloons fell on the wrong side of them. Our family rule was to be interested in otherness from within a pact of sameness. I wanted to stop merely observing the wide world and inhabit its wideness: I wanted to dive for pearls, memorize Shakespeare, break the sound barrier, learn to knit. From one angle, the desire to transform myself can be seen as an attempt to unshackle myself from an undesirable way of being. From another, it was a gesture toward my essential self, a crucial pivot toward who I was to become.

Even in kindergarten, I spent recess making conversation with my teachers because other children didn't get it; the teachers probably didn't get it, either, but they were old enough to be polite. By seventh grade, I ate lunch most days in the office of Mrs. Brier, secretary of the head of the lower school. I graduated from high school without visiting the cafeteria, where I would have sat with the girls and been laughed at for doing so, or with the boys and been laughed at for being the kind of boy who should really sit with the girls. The impulse to conformity that so often defines childhood never existed for me, and when I began to think about sexuality, the nonconformity of same-sex desires thrilled me—the realization that what I wanted was even more different and forbidden than all sex is to the young. Homosexuality felt to me like an Armenian dessert or a day in Liechtenstein. I nonetheless thought that if anyone found out I was gay, I would have to die.

My mother didn't want me to be gay because she thought it wouldn't be the happiest course for me, but equally, she didn't like the image of herself as the mother of a gay son. The problem wasn't that she wanted to control *my* life— although she did, like most parents, genuinely believe that her way of being happy was the best way of being happy. The problem was that she wanted to control *her* life, and it was her life as the mother of a homosexual that she wished to alter. Unfortunately, there was no way for her to fix her problem without involving me.

I learned to hate this aspect of my identity profoundly and early because that crouching posture echoed a family response to a vertical identity. My mother thought it was undesirable to be Jewish. She had learned this view from my grandfather, who kept his religion secret so he could hold a high-level job in a company that did not employ Jews. He belonged to a suburban country club where Jews were not welcome. In her early twenties, my mother was briefly engaged to a Texan, but he broke it off when his family threatened to disinherit him if he married a Jew. For her, it was a trauma of self-recognition, because until then she had not thought of herself as a designated Jew; she had thought she could be whomever she appeared to be. Five years later, she chose to marry my Jewish father and live in a largely Jewish world, but she carried the anti-Semitism within her. She would see people who fit certain stereotypes and say, "Those are the people who give us a bad name." When I asked her what she thought of the much sought-after beauty of my ninth-grade class, she said, "She looks very Jewish." Her method of rueful self-doubt was organized for me around being gay: I inherited her gift for discomfort.

Long after childhood, I clung to childish things as a dam against sexuality. This willful immaturity was overlaid with an affected Victorian prudery, aimed not at masking but at obliterating desire. I had some farfetched idea that I would be Christopher Robin forever in the Hundred Acre Wood; indeed, the final chapter of the *Winnie-the-Pooh* books felt so much like my story that I couldn't bear to hear it, though I had my father read me all the other chapters hundreds of times. *The House at Pooh Corner* ends, "Wherever they go, and whatever happens to them on the way, in that enchanted place on top of the Forest, a little boy and his Bear will always be playing." I decided that I would be that boy and that bear, that I would freeze myself in puerility, because what growing up portended for me was too humiliating. At thirteen, I bought a copy of *Playboy* and spent hours studying it, trying to resolve my discomfort with female anatomy; it was much more grueling than my homework. By the time I reached high school, I knew I had to have sex with women sooner or later and felt that I couldn't do so, and thought often about dying. The half of me that wasn't planning to be Christopher Robin playing forever in an enchanted place was planning to be Anna Karenina throwing myself in front of a train. It was a ludicrous duality.

When I was in eighth grade at the Horace Mann School in New York, an older kid nicknamed me Percy as a shorthand for my demeanor. We were on the same school-bus route, and each day when I boarded, he and his cohort would chant, "Percy! Percy! Percy!" I sometimes sat with a Chinese-American student who was too shy to talk to anyone else (and turned out to be gay himself), and sometimes with a nearly blind girl who was also the object of considerable cruelty. Sometimes, everyone on the bus chanted that provocation the entire ride. "Per-cy! Per-cy! Per-cy! Per-cy!" at the top of their lungs for forty-five minutes: all the way up Third Avenue, along the FDR Drive, across the Willis Avenue Bridge, the length of the Major Deegan Expressway, and onto 246th Street in Riverdale. The blind girl kept repeating that I should "just ignore it," and so I sat there pretending unconvincingly that it wasn't happening.

Four months after it began, I came home one day and my mother asked, "Has something been happening on the school bus? Have other students been calling you Percy?" A classmate had told his mother, who in turn had called mine. When I admitted it, she hugged me for a long time, then asked why I hadn't told her. It had never occurred to me: partly because talking about something so degrading seemed only to reify it, partly because I thought there was nothing to be done, and partly because I felt that the qualities for which I was being tortured would be abhorrent to my mother, too, and I wanted to protect her from disappointment.

Thereafter, a chaperone rode on the school bus and the chanting stopped. I was merely called "faggot" on the bus and at school, often within hearing distance of teachers who raised no objections. That same year, my science teacher told us that homosexuals developed fecal incontinence because their anal sphincters were destroyed. Homophobia was ubiquitous in the 1970s, but the smug culture of my school delivered a sharply honed version of it.

In June of 2012, the *New York Times Magazine* published an article by Horace Mann alumnus Amos Kamil about some male faculty members' predatory abuse of boys at the school while I was a student there. The article quoted students who developed addiction issues and other self-destructive behavior in the wake of such episodes; one man had committed suicide in middle age as the culmination of despair that his family traced to the youthful exploitation. The article made me profoundly sad—and confused, because some teachers accused of such acts had been kinder to me than anyone else at my school during a desolate time. My beloved history teacher took me out to dinner, gave me a copy of the Jerusalem Bible, and talked with me during free periods when other students wanted nothing to do with me. The music teacher awarded me concert solos, let me call him by his first name and hang out in his office, and led the glee club trips that were among my happiest adventures. They seemed to recognize who I was and thought well of me anyway. Their implicit acknowledgment of my sexuality helped me not to become an addict or a suicide.

When I was in ninth grade the school's art teacher (who was also a football coach) kept trying to strike up a conversation with me about masturbation. I was paralyzed: I thought it might be a form of entrapment, and that if I responded, he'd tell everyone that I was gay, and I'd be even more of a laughingstock than I already was. No other faculty member ever made a move on me—perhaps because I was a skinny, socially awkward kid with glasses and braces, perhaps because my parents had a reputation for protective vigilance, perhaps because I assumed a self-insulating arrogance that made me less vulnerable than some others.

The art teacher was removed when allegations against him emerged soon after my conversations with him. The history teacher was let go and committed suicide a year later. The music teacher, who was married, survived the ensuing "region of terror," as one gay faculty member later called it, when many gay teachers were ousted. Kamil wrote to me that the firings of nonpredatory gay teachers grew out of "a misguided attempt to root our pedophilia by falsely equating it with homosexuality." Students spoke monstrously of and even to gay teachers because their prejudice was so obviously endorsed by the school community.

The head of the theater department, Anne MacKay, was a lesbian who quietly survived the recriminations. Twenty years after I graduated, she and I began corresponding by e-mail. I drove to the east end of Long Island to visit her a decade later when I learned she was dying. We had both been contacted by Amos Kamil, who was then researching his article, and had both been unsettled by the allegations he shared. Miss MacKay had been the wise teacher who once explained gently that I was teased because of how I walked, and tried to show me a more confident stride. She staged *The Importance of Being Earnest* my senior year so that I could have a star turn as Algernon. I had come to thank her. But she had invited me to apologize.

At a previous job, she explained, word had got around that she lived with another woman, parents had complained, and she'd gone into a kind of hiding for the rest of her career. Now she regretted the formal distance she'd sustained and felt she had failed the gay students to whom she might have been a beacon—although I knew, and she did, too, that if she'd been more open, she'd have lost her job. When I was her student, I never thought to wonder about greater intimacy than we had, but talking decades later, I realized how forlorn we'd both been. I wish we could have been the same age for a while, because who I am at forty-eight would be a good friend for who she was when she was teaching young me. Off campus, Miss MacKay was a gay activist; now, I am, too. When I was in high school, I knew she was gay; she knew I was gay; yet each of us was imprisoned by our homosexuality in a way that made direct conversation impossible, leaving us with only kindness to give each other instead of truth. Seeing her after so many years stirred up my old loneliness, and I was reminded of how isolating an exceptional identity can be unless we resolve it into horizontal solidarity.

In the unsettling online reunion of Horace Mann alumni that followed the publication of Amos Kamil's story, one man wrote of his sadness for both the abuse victims and the perpetrators, saying of the latter, "They were wounded, confused people trying to figure out how to function in a world that taught them that their homosexual desire was sick. Schools mirror the world we live in. They can't be perfect places. Not every teacher will be an emotionally balanced person. We can condemn these teachers. But this deals with a symptom only, not the original problem, which is that an intolerant society creates self-hating people who act out inappropriately." Sexual contact between teachers and students is unacceptable because it exploits a power differential that clouds the demarcation between coercion and consent. It often causes irrecoverable trauma. It clearly did so for the students Kamil interviewed and described. Wondering how my teachers could have done this, I thought that someone whose core being is deemed a sickness and an illegality may struggle to parse the distinction between that and a much greater crime. Treating an identity as an illness invites real illness to make a braver stand.

Sexual opportunity comes often to young people, especially in New York. One of my chores was to walk our dog before bedtime, and when I was fourteen, I discovered two gay bars near our apartment: Uncle Charlie's Uptown and Camp David. I would walk Martha, our Kerry Blue terrier, on a circuit that included these two emporiums of denimed flesh, watching the guys spill out into Lexington Avenue while Martha tugged gently on the leash. One man who said his name was Dwight followed me and pulled me into a doorway. I couldn't go home with Dwight or the others because if I did, I'd be turned into someone else. I don't remember what Dwight looked like, but his name makes me wistful. When I eventually had sex with a man, at seventeen, I felt that I was severing myself forever from the normal world. I went home and boiled my clothes, then took a scalding, hourlong shower, as though my transgression could be sterilized away.

When I was nineteen, I read an ad in the back of *New York* magazine that offered surrogate therapy for people who had issues with sex. I still believed that the problem of whom I wanted was subsidiary to the problem of whom I didn't want. I knew the back of a magazine was not a good place to find treatment, but my condition was too embarrassing to reveal to anyone who knew me. Taking my savings to a walk-up office in Hell's Kitchen, I subjected myself to long conversations about my sexual anxieties, unable to admit to myself or the so-called therapist that I was actually just not interested in women. I didn't mention the busy sexual life I had by this time with men. I began "counseling" with people I was encouraged to call "doctors," who would prescribe "exercises" with my "surrogates"—women who were not exactly prostitutes but who were also not exactly anything else. In one protocol, I had to crawl around naked on all fours pretending to be a dog while the surrogate pretended to be a cat; the metaphor of enacting intimacy between mutually averse species is more loaded than I noticed at the time. I became curiously fond of these women, one of whom, an attractive blonde from the Deep South, eventually told me that she was a necrophiliac and had taken this job after she got into trouble down at the morgue. You were supposed to keep switching girls so your ease was not limited to one sexual partner; I remember the first time a Puerto Rican woman climbed on top of me and began to bounce up and down, crying ecstatically, "You're in me! You're in me!" and how I lay there wondering with anxious boredom whether I had finally achieved the prize and become a qualified heterosexual.

Curses seldom work swiftly and completely for anything other than bacterial infections, but it can be hard to see that when social and medical realities are in rapid flux. My own recovery has been from the perception of illness. That office on Forty-Fifth Street shows up in my dreams: the necrophiliac who found my pale, sweaty form close enough to a corpse to float her boat; the mission-driven Latino woman who introduced me to her body with so much jubilation. My treatment took only two hours a week for about six months, and it gave me an ease with women's bodies that was vital to subsequent heterosexual experiences I'm glad to have had. I truly loved some of the women with whom I later had relationships, but when I was with them, I could never forget that my "cure" was a distilled manifestation of self-loathing, and I have never entirely forgiven the circumstances that disposed me to make the obscene effort. Stretching my psyche between Dwight and those catwomen made romantic love almost impossible for me during my early adulthood.

My interest in profound differences between parents and children arose from a need to investigate the locus of my regret. While I'd like to blame my parents, I have come to believe that a lot of my pain came from the larger world around me, and some of it came from me. In the heat of an argument, my mother once told me, "Someday you can go to a therapist and tell him all about how your terrible mother ruined your life. But it will be *your* ruined life you're talking about. So make a life for yourself in which you can feel happy, and in which you can love and be loved, because that's what's actually important." You can love someone but not accept him; you can accept someone but not love him. I wrongly felt the flaws in my parents' acceptance as deficits in their love. Now, I think their primary experience was of having a child who spoke a language they'd never thought of studying.

How is any parent to know whether to erase or celebrate a given characteristic? When I was born in 1963, homosexual activity was a crime; during my childhood, it was a symptom of illness. When I was two, *Time* magazine wrote, "Even in purely nonreligious terms, homosexuality represents a misuse of the sexual faculty. It is a pathetic little second-rate substitute for reality, a pitiable flight from life. As such it deserves fairness, compassion, understanding and, when possible, treatment. But it deserves no encouragement, no glamorization, no rationalization, no fake status as minority martyrdom, no sophistry about simple difference in taste—and, above all, no pretense that it is anything but a pernicious sickness."

When I was growing up, we nonetheless had close family friends who were gay—neighbors, and surrogate great-uncles to my brother and me, who spent holidays with us because their own families would not have them. I was always bewildered that Elmer had gone off to World War II halfway through medical school, fought on the Western Front, and then opened a gift shop when he came home. For years, I heard that the terrible things he saw in the war had changed him, and that he didn't have the stomach for medicine after his return. It was only after Elmer died that Willy, his partner of fifty years, explained to me that no one would have considered going to an openly gay doctor in 1945. The horrors of war had propelled Elmer into integrity, and he paid its price by spending his adulthood painting amusing bar stools and selling crockery. Elmer and Willy were a great romance in many ways, but an undertone of sadness for what might have been informed their lives. The gift shop was an apology for medicine; Christmas with us was an apology for family. I am humbled by Elmer's choice; I do not know that I would have had the courage to choose likewise, nor the discipline to keep regret from undermining my love had I done so. Though Elmer and Willy would never have seen themselves as activists, their galvanizing sorrow and that of others like them was the precondition of my happiness and that of others like me. When I understood their story more richly, I recognized that my parents' fears for me were not simply the product of overactive imaginations.

In my adulthood, being gay is an identity; the tragic narrative my parents feared for me is no longer inevitable. The happy life I now lead was unimaginable when I was asking for pink balloons and *ekmek kadayiff*—even when I was being Algernon. Yet, the trifecta view of homosexuality as a crime, an illness, and a sin remains potent. I sometimes felt that it was easier for me to ask people about their disabled children, their children conceived in rape, their children who committed crimes, than it would have been to look squarely at how many parents still respond to having children like me. Ten years ago, a *New Yorker* poll asked parents whether they would prefer to see their child gay, happily partnered, fulfilled, and with children, or straight, single or unhappily partnered, and childless. One out of three chose the latter. You cannot hate a horizontal identity much more explicitly than to wish unhappiness and likeness for your children over happiness and difference. In the United States, new anti-gay laws emerge with monotonous regularity; in December 2011, Michigan enacted the Public Employee Domestic Partner Benefit Restriction Act, which bars gay employees' partners from health-care coverage, despite allowing city and county employers to provide health-care coverage to all other family members, including uncles, nieces, and cousins. Meanwhile, in much of the larger world, the identity I inhabit remains unimaginable. In 2011, Uganda came close to passing a bill that would have made some homosexual acts punishable by death. An article in *New York* magazine about gay people in Iraq includes this information: "The bodies of gay men, often mutilated, began turning up on the street.

Hundreds of men are believed to have been killed. Gay men's rectums had been glued shut, and they had been force-fed laxatives and water until their insides exploded."

Much of the debate around sexual-orientation laws has turned on the idea that if you choose homosexuality, it should not be protected, but if you are born with it, perhaps it should. Members of minority religions are protected not because they are born that way and can't do anything about it, but because we affirm their right to discover, declare, and inhabit the faith with which they identify. Activists got homosexuality removed from the official list of mental illnesses in 1973, yet gay rights remain contingent on claims that the condition is involuntary and fixed. This cripple-like model of sexuality is depressing, but as soon as anyone posits that homosexuality is chosen or mutable, lawmakers and religious leaders try to cure and disenfranchise the gay people in their purview. Today, men and women continue to be "treated" for homosexuality at religious reform camps and in the offices of unscrupulous or misguided psychiatrists. The ex-gay movement in evangelical Christianity deranges gay people by the tens of thousands by seeking to persuade them, contrary to their experience, that desire is wholly volitional. The founder of the antihomosexual organization MassResistance has argued that gays should be made specific targets or discrimination, due to the supposedly voluntary nature of their ostensible perversion.

Those who think that a biological explanation of gayness will improve the sociopolitical position of gay people are also sadly mistaken, as the response to recent scientific findings makes clear. The sexologist Ray Blanchard has described a "fraternal birth order effect," which holds that the chance of producing gay sons goes up steadily with each male fetus a mother carries. Within weeks of publishing this data, he was called by a man who had decided against hiring a surrogate who had borne previous boys, saying to Blanchard, "That's not really what I want … especially if I'm paying for it." The arthritis drug dexamethasone is used off-label to treat women at risk for producing daughters with a condition that partially masculinizes their genitalia. Maria New, a researcher at Mount Sinai Hospital in New York, has suggested that dexamethasone given in early pregnancy will also reduce the chances that such babies will grow up to be lesbian; indeed, she has described the treatment as making girls more interested in childbearing and homemaking, less aggressive, and more shy. It has been posited that such therapy might curb lesbianism even in the general population. In animal studies, prenatal exposure to dexamethasone seems to cause many health problems, but if any medication can actually limit lesbianism, researchers will come up with a safer one. Medical findings such as these will continue to have serious social implications. If we develop prenatal markers for homosexuality, many couples will abort their gay children; if we come up with a viable preventative drug, many parents will be willing to try it.

I would no more insist that parents who don't want gay children must have them than I would that people who don't want children at all must have them. Nonetheless, I cannot think about Blanchard's and New's research without feeling like the last quagga. I am not evangelical. I don't need to verticalize my identity onto my children, but I would hate if my horizontal identity to vanish. I would hate it for those who share my identity, and for those who lie outside it.

I hate the loss of diversity in the world, even though I sometimes get a little worn out by being that diversity. I don't wish for anyone in particular to be gay, but the idea of no one's being gay makes me miss myself already.

All people are both the objects and the perpetrators of prejudice. Our understanding of the prejudice directed against us informs our responses to others. Universalizing from the cruelties we have known, however, has its limits, and the parents of a child with a horizontal identity often fail at empathy. My mother's issues with Judaism didn't make her much better at dealing with my being gay; my being gay wouldn't have made me a good parent to a deaf child until I'd discerned the parallels between the Deaf experience and the gay one. A lesbian couple I interviewed who had a transgender child told me they approved of the murder of George Tiller, the abortion provider, because the Bible said that abortion was wrong, and yet they were astonished and frustrated at the intolerance they had encountered for their identity and their child's. We are overextended in the travails of our own situation, and making common cause with other groups is an exhausting prospect. Many gay people will react negatively to comparisons with the disabled, just as many African-Americans reject gay activists' use of the language of civil rights. But comparing people with disabilities to people who are gay implies no negativity about gayness or disability. Everyone is flawed and strange; most people are valiant, too. The reasonable corollary to the queer experience is that everyone has a defect, that everyone has an identity, and that they are often one and the same.

It's terrifying to me to think that without my mother's sustained intervention, I might never have learned fluency in letters; I am grateful every day for the sufficient resolution of my dyslexia. Conversely, while I might have had an easier life if I had been straight, I am now wedded to the idea that without my struggles, I would not be myself, and that I like being myself better than I like the idea of being someone else—someone I have neither the ability to imagine nor the option of being. Nevertheless, I have often wondered whether I could have ceased to hate my sexual orientation without Gay Pride's Technicolor fiesta, of which this writing is one manifestation. I used to think that I would be mature when I could simply be gay without emphasis. I have decided against this viewpoint, in part because there is almost nothing about which I feel neutral, but more because I perceive those years of self-loathing as a yawning void, and celebration needs to fill and overflow it. Even if I adequately address my private debt of melancholy, there is an outer world of homophobia and prejudice to repair. Someday, I hope this identity may devolve into a simple fact, free of both party hats and blame, but that's some ways off. A friend who thought Gay Pride was getting a bit carried away with itself once suggested we organize Gay Humility Week. It's a good idea, but its time has not yet come. Neutrality, which appears to lie halfway between shame and rejoicing, is in fact the endgame, reached only when activism becomes unnecessary.

It is a surprise to me to like myself; among all the elaborate possibilities I contemplated for my future, that never figured. My hard-won contentment reflects the simple truth that inner peace often hinges on outer peace. In the gnostic gospel of St. Thomas, Jesus says, "If you bring forth what is within you, what is within you will save you. If you do not bring forth what is within you, what is within you will destroy you." When I run up against the antigay positions of modern religious bodies, I often wish that St. Thomas's words were canonical because his message embraces many of us with horizontal identities. Keeping the homosexuality locked away within me nearly destroyed me, and bringing it forth has nearly saved me.

Although men who murder usually target people not related to them, nearly 40 percent of women who inflict death kill their own babies. Reports of human children discarded in Dumpsters and the overburdened foster-care network point to the ability of human beings to detach. Oddly, this seems to have at least as much to do with the infant's appearance as with its health or character. Parents will usually take home a child with a life-threatening internal defect, but not one with a minor visible defect; at a later stage, some parents will reject even children with severe burn scars. Manifest disabilities affront parents' pride and their need for privacy; everyone can see that this child isn't what you wanted, and you must either accept the world's pity or insist on your own pride. At least half of the children available for adoption in the United States have disabilities of some kind. Half of those available for adoption, however, still constitutes only a small proportion of disabled children.

Modern love comes with more and more options. For most of history, people married only members of the opposite sex, from their own class, race, denomination, and geographical location—all increasingly disputed boundaries. Similarly, people were supposed to accept the children given to them because one could do little to choose or change them. Birth control and fertility technologies have severed the bond between sex and procreation: intercourse does not necessarily engender babies, nor is it requisite to produce them. The analysis of embryos prior to implantation and the expanding domain of prenatal testing give parents access to a wealth of information to help them decide whether to initiate, continue, or terminate a pregnancy. The choices are broadening every day. People who believe in the right to opt for healthy, normative children refer to *selective abortion*; people to whom that idea is anathema refer to *commercial eugenics,* evoking a world stripped of variety and vulnerability. A vast industry of pediatric medicine implies that responsible parents should revamp their children in various ways, and parents expect doctors to correct their children's perceived defects: to administer human growth hormone to make the short ones taller, to fix a cleft lip, to normalize ambiguous genitalia. These optimizing interventions are not exactly cosmetic, but they are not necessary for survival. They have led social theorists such as Francis Fukuyama to speak of a "post-human future" in which we will eliminate the variety within mankind.

Yet while medicine promises to normalize us, our social reality remains a miscellany. If the cliché is that modernity makes people more similar, as tribal headdresses and frock coats alike give way to T-shirts and jeans, the reality is that modernity comforts us with trivial uniformities even as it allows us to become more far-flung in our desires and our ways of realizing them. Social mobility and the Internet allow anyone to find others who share his quiddities.

No closed circle of French aristocrats or farm boys from Iowa has been tighter than these new clusters of the electronic age. As the line between illness and identity is challenged, the strength of these online supports is a vital setting for the emergence of true selves. Modern life is lonely in many ways, but the ability of everyone with access to a computer to find like-minded people has meant that no one need be excluded from social kinship. If the physical or psychic place to which you were born wants no more of you, an infinitude of locales of the spirit beckons. Vertical families are famously breaking down in divorce, but horizontal ones are proliferating. If you can figure out who you are, you can find other people who are the same. Social progress is making disabling conditions easier to live with just as medical progress is eliminating them. There is something tragic about this confluence, like those operas in which the hero realizes he loves the heroine just as she expires.

Parents willing to be interviewed are a self-selecting group; those who are bitter are less likely to tell their stories than those who have found value in their experience and want to help others in similar circumstances to do the same. No one loves without reservation, however, and everyone would be better off if we could destigmatize parental ambivalence. Freud posits that any declaration of love masks some degree of odium, any hatred at least a trace of adoration. All that children can properly require of their parents is that they tolerate their own muddled spectrum—that they neither insist on the lie of perfect happiness nor lapse into the slipshod brutality of giving up. One mother who lost a child with a serious disability worried in a letter to me that if she felt relieved, her grief was not real. There is no contradiction between loving someone and feeling burdened by that person; indeed, love tends to magnify the burden. These parents need space for their ambivalence, whether they can allow it for themselves or not. For those who love, there should be no shame in being exhausted—even in imagining another life....

In 2011, gay marriage became legal in New York State after several Republicans in the state Senate agreed to support it. One of them, Roy J. McDonald, said that he had changed his stance on gay marriage because he had two autistic grandchildren, which had caused him "to rethink several issues." Jared Spurbeck, an autistic adult, thought his own quirks were "a sign of sinfulness" when he was growing up in the Mormon faith; when he started reading about gay Mormons, he found their experience much the same as his. "I couldn't ignore the parallels between autism and homosexuality. Once I'd accepted the one, I couldn't not accept the other."

I encountered activists of every stripe while I did this research and admired them even when I occasionally found their rhetoric expedient. The changes they sought seemed, individually, restricted to their particular province and experience, but as a group, they represent a rethinking of humanity. Most parents who become activists do so because they want to spur social change, but that impulse is never unalloyed. Some find it a relief because it gets them out of the house and away from their child without their having to feel guilty about it. Some use activism to distract themselves from grief; parents often laud what they rue most about their children to defend against despair. But just as belief can result in action, action can result in belief. You can gradually fall in love with your child, and by extension with that child's disabilities, and by further extension with all the world's brave disadvantages. Many of the activists I met were determined to help other people because they couldn't help themselves. Activism successfully displaced their pain. By teaching their learned optimism or strength to parents reeling from a recent diagnosis, they fortified it in their own families.

I understand this strategy firsthand, because writing this book addressed a sadness within me and—somewhat to my surprise—has largely cured it. The best way to get through these horizontalities is to find coherence, and in the wake of these stories, I recast my own narrative. I have a horizontal experience of being gay and a vertical one of the family that produced me, and the fact that they are not fully integrated no longer seems to undermine either. Some impulse toward anger at my parents evaporated, leaving only trace residue. In absorbing stories of strangers' clemency, I realized that I had demanded that my parents accept me but had resisted accepting them. Once I did, I was glad to have their ubiquitous company. The playwright Doug Wright once said that family inflicts the deepest wounds, then salves them the most tenderly. When I realized there was no refuge from my parents' meddling, I learned to value it over loneliness and call it love. I started my research aggrieved; I ended it forbearing. I set off to understand myself and ended up understanding my parents. Unhappiness is a constant grudging, and in these pages, happiness served as a spur to amnesty. Their love always forgave me; mine came to forgive them, too.

I know that who I was appalled my mother and concerned my father, and I used to be furious at them for not embracing this horizontal part of me, for not embracing the early evidence of it. Writing has been a lesson in absolution, because I have seen the valiance love takes. Acceptance was always easier for my father than it was for my mother, but that was not particular to me; he accepts himself more readily than she did herself. In her own mind, she always fell short; in my father's own mind, he is victorious. The interior daring of becoming myself was my mother's gift to me, while the outer audacity to express that self came from my father.

I wish I'd been accepted sooner and better. When I was younger, not being accepted made me enraged, but now, I am not inclined to dismantle my history. If you banish the dragons, you banish the heroes—and we become attached to the heroic strain in our personal history. We choose our own lives. It is not simply that we decide on the behaviors that construct our experience; when given our druthers, we elect to be ourselves. Most of us would like to be more successful or more beautiful or wealthier, and most people endure episodes of low self-esteem or even self-hatred. We despair a hundred times a day. But we retain the startling evolutionary imperative of affection for the fact of ourselves, and with that splinter of grandiosity we redeem our flaws. These parents have, by and large, chosen to love their children, and many of them have chosen to value their own lives, even though they carry what much of the world considers an intolerable burden. Children with horizontal identities alter your self painfully; they also illuminate it. They are receptacles for rage and joy—even for salvation.

When we love them, we achieve above all else the rapture of privileging what exists over what we have merely imagined.

A follower of the Dalai Lama who had been imprisoned by the Chinese for decades was asked if he had ever been afraid in jail, and he said his fear was that he would lose compassion for his captors. Parents often think that they've captured something small and vulnerable, but the parents I've profiled have been captured, locked up with their children's madness or genius or deformity, and the quest is never to lose compassion. A Buddhist scholar once explained to me that most Westerners mistakenly think that nirvana is what you arrive at when your suffering is over and only an eternity of happiness stretches ahead. But such bliss would always be shadowed by the sorrow of the past and would therefore be imperfect. Nirvana occurs when you not only look forward to rapture, but also gaze back into the times of anguish and find in them the seeds of your joy. You may not have felt that happiness at the time, but in retrospect it is incontrovertible.

For some parents of children with horizontal identities, acceptance reaches its apogee when parents conclude that while they supposed that they were pinioned by a great and catastrophic loss of hope, they were in fact falling in love with someone they didn't yet know enough to want. As such parents look back, they see how every stage of loving their child has enriched them in ways they never would have conceived, ways that are incalculably precious. Rumi said that the light enters you at the bandaged place. This book's conundrum is that most of the families described here have ended up grateful for experiences they would have done anything to avoid.

NOTES

1. Winnicott's statement is in the paper "Anxiety associated with insecurity," on page 98 of *Through Paediatrics to Psycho-analysis* (1958).

2. My investigation of Deaf culture resulted in an article, "Defiantly deaf," *New York Times Magazine,* August 29, 1994.

3. The Cochlear corporation website (http://www.cochlear.com) contains numerous instances of the word *miracle;* see also, for example, Aaron and Nechama Parnes's report from the 2007 Cochlear Celebration, "Celebrating the miracle of the cochlear implant," at http://www.hearingpocket.com/celebration1.shtml. For the other side of the story, see Paddy Ladd, *Understanding Deaf Culture: In Search of Deafhood* (2003), page 415: "In the 1990s, genetic engineering has initiated the process of trying to identify 'the deaf gene,' thus bringing within theoretical reach what might be termed the 'final solution'—that of eradicating Deaf people altogether." Harlan Lane likened attempts to eliminate deafness to attempts to eliminate ethnic groups in Paul Davies, "Deaf culture clash," *Wall Street Journal,* April 25, 2005.

4. Studies establishing a heightened risk of abuse for children who do not resemble their fathers include Rebecca Burch and George Gallup, "Perceptions of paternal resemblance predict family violence," *Evolution & Human Behavior* 21, no. 6 (November 2000); and Hongli Li and Lei Chang, "Paternal harsh parenting in relation to paternal versus child characteristics: The moderating effect of paternal resemblance belief," *Acta Psychologica Sinica* 39, no. 3 (2007).

5. The theologian John Polkinghorne reported this interpretation in keeping with what he had learned from Dirac. From page 31 of Polkinghorne, *Science and Theology: An Introduction* (1998): "Ask a quantum entity a particle-like question and you will get a particle-like answer; ask a wave-like question and you will get a wave-like answer."

6. "All I know is what I have words for" comes from part 5.6 of Ludwig Wittgenstein, *Tractatus Logico-Philosophicus* (1922): "Die Grenzen meiner Sprache bedeuten die Grenzen meiner Welt." C.K. Ogden translates the sentence as "The limits of my language mean the limits of my world"; that version occurs on page 149 of Ludwig Wittgenstein, *Tractatus Logico-Philosophicus,* translated by C.K. Ogden (1922).

7. From the entry "apple" in *The Oxford Dictionary of Proverbs,* edited by Jennifer Speake (2009): "The apple never falls far from the tree: Apparently of Eastern origin, it is frequently used to assert the continuity of family characteristics. Cf. 16th cent. Ger *der Apfel fellt nicht gerne weit vom Baume.*"

8. From the opening of Leo Tolstoy, *Anna Karenina*: "Happy families are all alike; each unhappy family is unhappy in its own way." The line is the first in the book and occurs on page 5 of the following edition: Leo Tolstoy, *Anna Karenina,* translated by Constance Garnett (2004).

9. Early development of gay children is discussed on pages 16–21 of Richard C. Friedman, *Male Homosexuality: A Contemporary Psychoanalytic Perspective* (1990).

10. For more information on gender-atypical color preference as a predictor of homosexuality, see Vanessa LoBue and Judy S. DeLoache, "Pretty in pink: The early development of gender-stereotyped colour preferences," *British Journal of Developmental Psychology* 29, no. 3 (September 2011).

11. The unforgettable last line, "Wherever they go, and whatever happens to them on the way, in that enchanted place on the top of the Forest a little boy and his Bear will always be playing," occurs on pages 179–80 of A.A. Milne, *The House at Pooh Corner* (1961).

12. See Amos Kamil, "Prep-school predators: The Horace Mann School's secret history of sexual abuse," *New York Times Magazine,* June 6, 2012.

13. The quotation about "wounded, confused people" is from a Facebook post by Peter Lappin.

14. For more information on surrogate partner therapy, see the website of the International Professional Surrogates Association, http://surrogatetherapy.org/.

15. The gay-damning quotation comes from "The homosexual in America," *Time,* January 21, 1966.

16. Hendrik Hertzberg, "The Narcissus survey," *New Yorker,* January 5, 1998.

17. On December 22, 2011, Michigan governor Rick Snyder signed House Bill 4770 (now Public Act 297 of 2011), the Public Employee Domestic Partner Benefit Restriction Act. The text and legislative history of House Bill 4770 can be found on the website of the Michigan legislature, http://www.legislature.mi.gov/mileg.aspx?page=getobject&objectname=2011-HB-4770.

18. On Uganda, see Josh Kron, "Resentment toward the West bolsters Uganda's anti-gay bill," *New York Times,* February 29, 2012; and Clar Ni Chonghaile, "Uganda anti-gay bill resurrected in parliament," *Guardian,* February 8, 2012; see also, three notes down, reference to Scott Lively.

19. The description of torture and murder of gays in Iraq comes from Matt McAllester, "The hunted," *New York,* October 4, 2009.

20. The *This American Life* episode "81 Words" at (http://www.thisamericanlife.org/radio-archives/episode/204/81-Words) is an absorbing account of the removal of homosexuality from the *Diagnostic and Statistical Manual of Mental Disorders;* see also Ronald Bayer, *Homosexuality and American Psychiatry: The Politics of Diagnosis* (1981).

21. The passage references Scott Lively, *Redeeming the Rainbow: A Christian Response to the "Gay" Agenda* (2009). Scott Lively has recently been sued by a Ugandan gay rights group, who have accused him of fomenting persecution of gays in their country; see Laurie Goodstein, "Ugandan gay rights group sues U.S. evangelist," *New York Times,* March 14, 2012.

22. The response of the surrogate-shopper to Ray Blanchard appears in "Fraternal birth order and the maternal immune hypothesis of male homosexuality," *Hormones & Behavior* 40, no. 2 (September 2001), and is described in Alice Domurat Dreger, "Womb gay," *Hastings Center Bioethics Forum,* December 4, 2008.

23. The debate over Maria Iandolo New's administration of dexamethasone to expectant mothers is chronicled in Shari Roan, "Medical treatment carries possible side effect of limiting homosexuality," *Los Angeles Times,* August 15, 2010.

24. For an example of African-American objections to the language of civil rights being used by gay people, see this statement by North Carolina minister Rev. Patrick Wooden, quoted in David Kaufman, "Tensions between black and gay groups rise anew in advance of anti-gay marriage vote in N.C.," *Atlantic,* May 4, 2012: "African-Americans are appalled that their Civil Rights movement has been co-opted by the so-called Civil Rights movement of the homosexuals. It is an insult, it is angering when LGBT groups say there is no difference between being black and being homosexual."

25. "If you bring forth what is within you …" is Saying 70 in Elaine H. Pagels, *Beyond Belief: The Secret Gospel of Thomas* (2003), page 53.

26. Maternal infanticide statistics occur on page 42 of James Alan Fox and Marianne W. Zawitz, "Homicide trends in the United States" (2007), in the chart "Homicide Type by Gender, 1976–2005." See also Steven Pinker, "Why they kill their newborns," *New York Times,* November 2, 1997.

27. Parental rejection of visibly disabled children is discussed on pages 152–54 of Meira Weiss, *Conditional Love: Parents' Attitudes Toward Handicapped Children* (1994). For a dated, albeit useful, review of literature on familial adjustment to severe burn scars in children, see Dale W. Wisley, Frank T. Masur, and Sam B. Morgan, "Psychological aspects of severe burn injuries in children," *Health Psychology* 2, no. 1 (Winter 1983).

28. A recent study from the CDC found that the majority of adopted children have significant health problems and disabilities. The report was put together by Matthew D. Bramlett, Laura F. Radel. and Stephen J. Blumberg and published as "The health and well-being of adopted children," *Pediatrics* 119, suppl. 1 (February 1, 2007).

29. The first occurrence of the term *commercial eugenics* appears to occur in M. MacNaughton, "Ethics and reproduction," *American Journal of Obstetrics & Gynecology* 162, no. 4 (April 1990).

30. Personal communication with Doug Wright.

31. See Ann Whitcher-Gentzke, "Dalai Lama brings message of compassion to UB," *UB Reporter,* September 21, 2006.

32. This Western naïveté about nirvana was explained to me by Robert Thurman in 2006.

33. Jalāl al-Dīn Rūmī (Maulana), *The Essential Rumi* (1995), page 142: "Don't turn away. Keep your gaze on the bandaged place. That's where the light enters you."

BIBLIOGRAPHY

Blanchard, Ray. "Fraternal birth order and the maternal immune hypothesis of male homosexuality." *Hormones & Behavior* 40, no. 2 (September 2001): 105–14.

Freud, Sigmund. Mourning and Melancholia. In The Standard Edition of the Complete Psychological Works of Sigmund Freud. Trans. Joan Riviere. Ed. James Strachey. Vol. 14, *1914–1916*. London: Hogarth Press, 1955.

Fukuyama, Francis. Our Posthuman Future: Consequences of the Biotechnology Revolution. New York: Farrar, Straus & Giroux, 2002.

Kamil, Amos. "Prep-school predators: The Horace Mann School's secret history of sexual abuse." *New York Times Magazine,* June 6, 2012.

Spurbeck, Jared. "NY senator's grandkids made him realize 'gay is OK.'" *Yahoo! News,* June 26, 2011.

Wittgenstein, Ludwig. *Tractatus Logico-Philosophicus.* Trans. C. K. Ogden. London: Routledge & Kegan Paul, 1922.

QUESTIONS FOR MAKING CONNECTIONS
WITHIN THE READING

1. "Son" explores two different kinds of identity—vertical identities like the ones that connect us to the members of our families, and the horizontal identities we form on the basis of characteristics we share with our contemporaries. Why do the two so often seem to conflict, and how do they conflict in Solomon's own life? What solutions does he find? As you re-read, pay particular attention to what Solomon observes about illness and identity. Can we apply to identities his analogy to the physics principle known as the Copenhagen interpretation, which holds that energy can be described as either a particle or a wave but not both at once? Must we choose between our vertical and horizontal identities, or can they somehow be combined? Do all identities actually include vertical and horizontal elements?

2. "Parenthood," Solomon writes, "abruptly catapults us into a permanent relationship with a stranger, and the more alien the stranger, the stronger the whiff of negativity." What role does negativity play in Solomon's development, and what role does it often play in cross-generational encounters? How does Solomon account for the pervasiveness of negativity? In what

ways was he disapproved of by his family, his friends, and his fellow students? Did Solomon disapprove of himself? Can negativity ultimately lead to a deeper understanding of others and our own nature? Can you identify distinct stages in the journey from negativity to acceptance?

3. Leo Tolstoy's novel *Anna Karenina* famously begins with the declaration, "Happy families are all alike; every unhappy family is unhappy in its own way." But Solomon declares his position to be anti-Tolstoyan. Why? What reasoning does he supply in defense of the conclusion that happy families will embrace their differences, whereas unhappy families insist on a single, definitive identity? If families are not defined by one basic identity, are they really families at all? Does "*Son*" offer an implicit argument for seeing families in a different light?

QUESTIONS FOR WRITING

1. Do we have a right to our identities, and, conversely, does society have a right to limit the ways we chose to define ourselves? Does Solomon's thinking imply that we have no obligations to society, to the past, or to tradition? How would you respond to the claim that he had made an argument for the principle that "Anything goes"—for the idea that any way of life is permitted and should be acceptable? Does "Son" elevate the author's personal desires above the good of the whole society, or is Solomon's celebration of differences a profoundly ethical stance? What role does understanding play in the encounter with differences? Is Solomon arguing for tolerance, or something deeper?

2. A key insight of "Son" has to do with the possibilities for freedom and fulfillment in an unsupportive or even hostile world. "My hard-won contentment," Solomon writes, "reflects the simple truth that inner peace often hinges on outer peace." Even though we might prefer to think that we hold the key to our own happiness, to what degree do we actually depend on the support of our whole society? If our happiness depends on supportive conditions, what might be the social or political implications? In order to make the world a better place, do we have a responsibility to bring our personal search for happiness into public view? Can inner peace survive without the proper outer conditions?

QUESTIONS FOR MAKING CONNECTIONS
BETWEEN READINGS

1. How might Solomon respond to Susan Faludi's *The Naked Citadel*? Think about The Citadel in terms of the potential conflicts between vertical and

horizontal identities. Would it be accurate to say that The Citadel only tolerates identities of a vertical kind, and if so, what effects follow from such systematic repression? Does the culture of The Citadel drive horizontal identities underground? Why haven't the cadets undergone the same learning process that Solomon experienced in his life? Given the conspicuous failure of most cadets to change or evolve, how might Faludi's narrative complicate Solomon's thinking? Can a way of life grow so rigid that transformation becomes impossible?

2. Solomon's family appears to be an extremely healthy and supportive one, despite his mother's reluctance to embrace her son's gay identity. But in what ways might the experience of trauma, as described by Martha Stout in her discussions of Julia and Seth, have made Solomon's insights far more difficult to achieve—perhaps even unattainable? In your discussion you might take note of the way that repetition weakens our capacity for change:

> Deepening the mire of our divided awareness, in the course of a lifetime … "protective" mental reactions acquire tremendous *habit strength*. These over-exercised muscles can take us away even when traumatic memory fragments have not been evoked. Sometimes dissociation can occur when we are simply confused or frustrated or nervous.

Does Stout's argument suggest that Solomon is overly sanguine about the prospects for personal and social change? Does his narrative suggest that Stout is too pessimistic? Or does Stout's narrative confirm Solomon's claim that "inner peace" requires a conducive environment?

◆◆◆

JOSEPH E. STIGLITZ

ANYONE WHO THINKS OF academic knowledge as dry and irrelevant simply hasn't studied economics. And anyone who thinks of economics as an impartial discipline, plodding on modestly without controversy, simply hasn't heard of Joseph Stiglitz, winner of the 2001 Sveriges Riksbank Prize in Economic Sciences in Memory of Alfred Nobel. After Stiglitz left Stanford University to serve as a senior vice-president and chief economist of the World Bank, his appointment came to a premature end when, in 2000, he published an article excoriating the International Monetary Fund (IMF). Stiglitz, a "neo-Keynesian," targeted the IMF because it had imposed harsh austerity on the East Asian economies after a real estate bubble there collapsed. Even though many economists agreed with Stiglitz's criticisms, so notorious did the article become that the leadership of the World Bank pressured him to leave. After accepting a new post at Columbia University, Stiglitz continued to write and speak about the failures of neoliberal economics, which encourages smaller government, the deregulation of finance, and the privatizing of public services like health care and education.

Stiglitz, a prolific author, has written, co-written, or edited 26 books so far. The selection that follows is an excerpt from his best-selling book *The Price of Inequality: How Today's Divided Society Endangers Our Future* (2012). There he makes the case that neoliberal reforms starting with Ronald Regan have produced a growing inequality that has swelled the ranks of the working poor and undermined the middle class. Stiglitz maintains that this long-term trend has dimmed the prospects for our full recovery from the collapse of 2008. After decades of lost buying power, the middle class has simply become too weak to generate the consumer spending needed for robust economic growth. Cash-strapped families no longer possess the resources to invest in their businesses or in better schooling for their children. Combined with tax cuts for the wealthiest, beginning under George W. Bush, the decline in middle class earnings has meant lower tax revenue for government, a swelling of the national debt, and a neglect of roads, public property, and other social goods. Finally, income inequality makes the economic future more volatile, increasing the frequency of booms and busts and causing more severe collapses. Stiglitz is confident, however, that these problems can be rectified if our society is willing to take the steps he recommends: curbing the power of the financiers, raising taxes on the wealthiest 1% and

"Rent Seeking and the Making of an Unequal Society," The Price of Inequality: How Today's Divided Society Endangers Our Future (New York: W. W. Norton, 2012), 28–51, 312–20.

on the big corporations, strengthening unions and citizens' rights, and reinvesting in public education, infrastructure, the environment, and sustainable technology.

Rent Seeking and the Making of an Unequal Society

American inequality didn't just happen. It was created. Market forces played a role, but it was not market forces alone. In a sense, that should be obvious: economic laws are universal, but our growing inequality—especially the amounts seized by the upper 1 percent—is a distinctly American "achievement." That outsize inequality is not predestined offers reason for hope, but in reality it is likely to get worse. The forces that have been at play in creating these outcomes are self-reinforcing.

By understanding the origins of inequality, we can better grasp the costs and benefits of reducing it. The simple thesis of this chapter is that even though market forces help shape the degree of inequality, government policies shape those market forces. Much of the inequality that exists today is a result of government policy, both what the government does and what it does not do. Government has the power to move money from the top to the bottom and the middle, or vice versa.

… America's current level of inequality is unusual. Compared with other countries and compared with what it was in the past even in the United States, it's unusually large, and it has been increasing unusually fast. It used to be said that watching for changes in inequality was like watching grass grow: it's hard to see the changes in any short span of time. But that's not true now.

Even what's been happening in this recession is unusual. Typically, when the economy weakens, wages and employment adjust slowly, so as sales fall, profits fall more than proportionately. But in this recession the share of wages has actually fallen, and many firms are making good profits.[1]

Addressing inequality is of necessity multifaceted—we have to rein in the excesses at the top, strengthen the middle, and help those at the bottom. Each goal requires a program of its own. But to construct such programs, we have to have a better understanding of what has given rise to each facet of this unusual inequality.

Distinct as the inequality we face today is, inequality itself is not something new. The concentration of economic and political power was in many ways more extreme in the precapitalist societies of the West. At that time, religion both explained and justified the inequality: those at the top of society were there because of divine right. To question that was to question the social order, or even to question God's will.

However, for modern economists and political scientists, as also for the ancient Greeks, this inequality was not a matter of a preordained social order.

Power—often military power—was at the origin of these inequities. Militarism was about economics: the conquerors had the right to extract as much as they could from the conquered. In antiquity, natural philosophy in general saw no wrong in treating other humans as means for the ends of others. As the ancient Greek historian Thucydides famously said, "right, as the world goes, is only in question between equals in power, while the strong do what they can and the weak suffer what they must."[2]

Those with power used that power to strengthen their economic and political positions, or at the very least to maintain them.[3] They also attempted to shape thinking, to make acceptable differences in income that would otherwise be odious.

As the notion of divine right became rejected in the early nation-states, those with power sought other bases for defending their positions. With the Renaissance and the Enlightenment, which emphasized the dignity of the individual, and with the Industrial Revolution, which led to the emergence of a vast urban underclass, it became imperative to find new justifications for inequality, especially as critics of the system, like Marx, talked about exploitation.[4]

The theory that came to dominate, beginning in the second half of the nineteenth century—and still does—was called "marginal productivity theory"; those with higher productivities earned higher incomes that reflected their greater contribution to society. Competitive markets, working through the laws of supply and demand, determine the value of each individual's contributions. If someone has a scarce and valuable skill, the market will reward him amply, because of his greater contribution to output. If he has no skills, his income will be low. Technology, of course, determines the productivity of different skills: in a primitive agriculture economy, physical strength and endurance is what mattered; in a modern hi-tech economy, brainpower is of more relevance.

Technology and scarcity, working through the ordinary laws of supply and demand, play a role in shaping today's inequality, but something else is at work, and that something else is government. A major theme of [my argument] is that inequality is the result of political forces as much as of economic ones. In a modern economy government sets and enforces the rules of the game—what is fair competition, and what actions are deemed anticompetitive and illegal, who gets what in the event of bankruptcy, when a debtor can't pay all that he owes, what are fraudulent practices and forbidden. Government also gives away resources (both openly and less transparently) and, through taxes and social expenditures, modifies the distribution of income that emerges from the market, shaped as it is by technology and politics.

Finally, government alters the dynamics of wealth by, for instance, taxing inheritances and providing free public education. Inequality is determined not just by how much the market pays a skilled worker relative to an unskilled worker, but also by the level of skills that an individual has acquired. In the absence of government support, many children of the poor would not be able to afford basic health care and nutrition, let alone the education required to acquire the skills necessary for enhanced productivity and high wages. Government can affect the extent to which an individual's education and inherited wealth depends on that of his parents. More formally, economists say that inequality depends on the distribution of "endowments," of financial and human capital.

The way the American government performs these functions determines the extent of inequality in our society. In each of these arenas there are subtle decisions that benefit some group at the expense of others. The effect of each decision may be small, but the cumulative effect of large numbers of decisions, made to benefit those at the top, can be very significant.

Competitive forces should limit outsize profits, but if governments do not ensure that markets are competitive, there can be large monopoly profits. Competitive forces should also limit disproportionate executive compensation, but in modern corporations, the CEO has enormous power—including the power to set his own compensation, subject, of course, to his board—but in many corporations, he even has considerable power to appoint the board, and with a stacked board, there is little check. Shareholders have minimal say. Some countries have better "corporate governance laws," the laws that circumscribe the power of the CEO, for instance, by insisting that there be independent members in the board or that shareholders have a say in pay. If the country does not have good corporate governance laws that are effectively enforced, CEOs can pay themselves outsize bonuses.

Progressive tax and expenditure policies (which tax the rich more than the poor and provide systems of good social protection) can limit the extent of inequality. By contrast, programs that give away a country's resources to the rich and well connected can increase inequality.

Our political system has increasingly been working in ways that increase the inequality of outcomes and reduce equality of opportunity. This should not come as a surprise: we have a political system that gives inordinate power to those at the top, and they have used that power not only to limit the extent of redistribution but also to shape the rules of the game in their favor, and to extract from the public what can only be called large "gifts." Economists have a name for these activities: they call them rent seeking, getting income not as a reward to creating wealth but by grabbing a larger share of the wealth that would otherwise have been produced without their effort. (We'll give a fuller definition of the concept of rent seeking later in the chapter.) Those at the top have learned how to suck out money from the rest in ways that the rest are hardly aware of—that is their true innovation.

Jean-Baptiste Colbert, the adviser to King Louis XIV of France, reportedly said, "The art of taxation consists in so plucking the goose as to obtain the largest amount of feathers with the least possible amount of hissing." So, too, for the art of rent seeking.

To put it baldly, there are two ways to become wealthy: to create wealth or to take wealth away from others. The former adds to society. The latter typically subtracts from it, for in the process of taking it away, wealth gets destroyed. A monopolist who overcharges for his product takes money from those whom he is overcharging and at the same time destroys value. To get his monopoly price, he has to restrict production.

Unfortunately, even genuine wealth creators often are not satisfied with the wealth that their innovation or entrepreneurship has reaped. Some eventually turn to abusive practices like monopoly pricing or other forms of rent extraction to garner even more riches. To take just one example, the railroad barons of the nineteenth century provided an important service in constructing the railroads, but much of their wealth was the result of their political influence—getting large government land grants on either side of the railway. Today, over a century after the railroad barons dominated the economy, much of the wealth at the top in the United States—and some of the suffering at the bottom—stems from wealth transfers instead of wealth creation.

Of course, not all the inequality in our society is a result of rent seeking, or of government's tilting the rules of the game in favor of those at the top. Markets matter, as do social forces (like discrimination).

GENERAL PRINCIPLES

Adam Smith's Invisible Hand and Inequality

Adam Smith, the father of modern economics, argued that the private pursuit of self-interest would lead, as if by an invisible hand, to the well-being of all.[5] In the aftermath of the financial crisis [of 2008–09], no one today would argue that the bankers' pursuit of their self-interest has led to the well-being of all. At most, it led to *the bankers'* well-being, with the rest of society bearing the cost. It wasn't even what economists call a zero-sum game, where what one person gains exactly equals what the others lose. It was a negative-sum game, where the gains to winners are less than the losses to the losers. What the rest of society lost was far, far greater than what the bankers gained.

There is a simple reason for why financiers' pursuit of *their* interests turned out to be disastrous for the rest of society: the bankers' incentives were not well aligned with social returns. When markets work well—in the way that Adam Smith hypothesized—it is because private returns and social benefits are well aligned, that is, because private rewards and social contributions are equal, as had been assumed by marginal productivity theory. In that theory, the social contribution of each worker is exactly equal to the private compensation. People with higher productivity—a larger social contribution—get higher pay.

Adam Smith himself was aware of one of the circumstances in which private and social returns differ. As he explained, "People of the same trade seldom meet together, even for merriment and diversion, but the conversation ends in a conspiracy against the public, or in some contrivance to raise prices."[6] Markets by themselves often fail to produce efficient and desirable outcomes, and there is a role for government in correcting these market failures, that is, designing policies (taxes and regulations) that bring private incentives and social returns into alignment. (Of course, there are often disagreements about the best way of doing it. But few today believe in unfettered financial markets—their failures impose too great a cost on the rest of society—or that firms should be allowed to despoil the environment without restriction.) When government does its job well, the returns received by, say, a worker or an investor are in fact equal to the benefits to society that his actions contribute. When these are not aligned, we say there is a market failure, that is, markets fail to produce efficient outcomes. Private rewards and social returns are not well aligned when competition is imperfect; when there are "externalities" (where one party's actions can have large negative or positive effects on others for which he does not pay or reap the benefit); when there exist imperfections or asymmetries of information (where someone knows something relevant to a market trade that someone else doesn't know); or where risk markets or other markets are absent (one can't, for instance, buy insurance against many of the most important risks that one faces). Since one or more of these conditions exist in virtually every market, there is in fact little presumption that markets are in general efficient. This means that there is an enormous potential role for government to correct these market failures.

Government never corrects market failures perfectly, but it does a better job in some countries than in others. Only if the government does a reasonably good job of correcting the most important market failures will the economy prosper. Good financial regulation helped the United States—and the world—avoid a major crisis for four decades after the Great Depression. Deregulation in the 1980s led to scores of financial crises in the succeeding three decades, of which America's crisis in 2008–09 was only the worst.[7] But those governmental failures were no accident: the financial sector used its political muscle to make sure that the market failures were *not* corrected, and that the sector's private rewards remained well in excess of their social contributions—one of the factors contributing to the bloated financial sector and to the high levels of inequality at the top.

Shaping Markets

We'll describe below some of the ways that private financial firms act to ensure that markets *don't work well*. For instance, as Smith noted, there are incentives for firms to work to reduce market competition. Moreover, firms also strive to make sure that there are no strong laws prohibiting them from engaging in anticompetitive behavior or, when there are such laws, that they are not effectively enforced. The focus of businesspeople is, of course, not to enhance societal well-being broadly understood, or even to make markets more competitive: their objective is simply to make markets work *for them*, to make them more profitable. But the consequence is often a less efficient economy marked by greater inequality. For now, one example will suffice. When markets are competitive, profits above the normal return to capital cannot be sustained. That is so because if a firm makes greater profits than that on a sale, rivals will attempt to steal the customer by lowering prices. As firms compete vigorously, prices fall to the point that profits (above the normal return to capital) are driven down to zero, a disaster for those seeking big profits. In business school we teach students how to recognize, and create, barriers to competition—including barriers to entry—that help ensure that profits won't be eroded. Indeed, as we shall shortly see, some of the most important innovations in business in the last three decades have centered not on making the economy more efficient but on how better to ensure monopoly power or how better to circumvent government regulations intended to align social returns and private rewards.

Making markets less transparent is a favorite tool. The more transparent markets are, the more competitive they are likely to be. Bankers know this.

That's why banks have been fighting to keep their business in writing derivatives, the risky products that were at the center of AIG's collapse,[8] in the shadows of the "over the counter" market. In that market, it's difficult for customers to know whether they're getting a good deal. Everything is negotiated, as opposed to how things work in more open and transparent modern markets. And since the sellers are trading constantly, and buyers enter only episodically, sellers have more information than buyers, and they use that information to their advantage. This means that on average, sellers (the writers of the derivatives, the banks) can extract more money out of their customers. Well-designed open auctions, by contrast, ensure that goods go to those who value them the most, a hallmark of efficiency. There are publicly available prices for guiding decisions.

While lack of transparency results in more profits for the bankers, it leads to lower economic performance. Without good information, capital markets can't exercise any discipline. Money won't go to where returns are highest, or to the bank that does the best job of managing money. No one can know the true financial position of a bank or other financial institution today—and shadowy derivative transactions are part of the reason. One would have hoped that the recent crisis might have forced change, but the bankers resisted. They resisted demands, for instance, for more transparency in derivatives and for regulations that would restrict anticompetitive practices. These rent-seeking activities were worth tens of billions of dollars in profits. Although they didn't win every battle, they won often enough that the problems are still with us. In late October 2011, for instance, a major American financial firm[9] went bankrupt (the eighth-largest bankruptcy on record), partly because of complex derivatives. Evidently the market hadn't seen through these transactions, at least not in a timely way.

Moving Money from the Bottom of the Pyramid to the Top

One of the ways that those at the top make money is by taking advantage of their market and political power to favor themselves, to increase their own income, at the expense of the rest.

The financial sector has developed expertise in a wide variety of forms of rent seeking itself. We've already mentioned some, but there are many others: taking advantage of asymmetries of information (selling securities that they had designed to fail, but knowing that buyers didn't know that);[10] taking excessive risk—with the government holding a lifeline, bailing them out and assuming the losses, the knowledge of which, incidentally, allows them to borrow at a lower interest rate than they otherwise could; and getting money from the Federal Reserve at low interest rates, now almost zero.

But the form of rent seeking that is most egregious—and that has been most perfected in recent years—has been the ability of those in the financial sector to take advantage of the poor and uninformed, as they made enormous amounts of money by preying upon these groups with predatory lending and abusive credit card practices.[11] Each poor person might have only a little, but there are so many poor that a little from each amounts to a great deal. Any sense of social justice— or any concern about overall efficiency—would have led government to prohibit these activities. After all, considerable amounts of resources were used up in the process of moving money from the poor to the rich, which is why it's a negative-sum game. But government didn't put an end to these kind of activities, not even when, around 2007, it became increasingly apparent what was going on. The reason was obvious. The financial sector had invested heavily in lobbying and campaign contributions, and the investments had paid off.

I mention the financial sector partly because it has contributed so powerfully to our society's current level of inequality.[12] The financial sector's role in creating the crisis in 2008–09 is apparent to all. Not even those who work in the sector deny it, though each believes that some other part of the financial sector is really to blame. Much of what I have said about the financial sector, though, could be said about other players in the economy that have had a hand in creating current inequities.

Modern capitalism has become a complex game, and those who win at it have to have more than a little smarts. But those who win at it often possess less admirable characteristics as well: the ability to skirt the law, or to shape the law in their own favor; the willingness to take advantage of others, even the poor; and to play *unfair* when necessary.[13] As one of the successful players in this game put it, the old adage "Win or lose, what matters is how you play the game" is rubbish. *All that matters is whether you win or lose.* The market provides a simple way of showing that—the amount of money that you have.

Winning in the game of rent seeking has made fortunes for many of those at the top, but it is not the only means by which they obtain and preserve their wealth. The tax system also plays a key role, as we'll see later. Those at the top have managed to design a tax system in which they pay less than their fair share—they pay a lower fraction of their income than do those who are much poorer. We call such tax systems regressive.

And while regressive taxes and rent seeking (which takes money from the rest of society and redistributes it to the top) are at the core of growing inequality, especially at the top, broader forces exert particular influence on two other aspects of American inequality—the hollowing out of the middle class and the increase in poverty. Laws governing corporations interact with the norms of behavior that guide the leaders of those corporations and determine how returns are shared among top management and other stakeholders (workers, shareholders, and bondholders). Macroeconomic policies determine the tightness of the labor market—the level of unemployment, and thus how market forces operate to change the share of workers. If monetary authorities act to keep unemployment high (even if because of fear of inflation), then wages will be restrained. Strong unions have helped to reduce inequality, whereas weaker unions have made it easier for CEOs, sometimes working with market forces that they have helped shape, to increase it. In each arena—the strength of unions, the effectiveness of corporate governance, the conduct of monetary policy—politics is central.

Of course, market forces, the balancing of, say, the demand and supply for skilled workers, affected as it is by changes in technology and education, play an important role as well, even if those forces are partially shaped by politics. But instead of these market forces and politics balancing each other out, with the political process dampening the increase in inequality in periods when market forces might have led to growing disparities, instead of government *tempering* the excesses of the market, in America today the two have been working together to increase income and wealth disparities.

RENT SEEKING

Earlier, we labeled as *rent seeking* many of the ways by which our current political process helps the rich at the expense of the rest of us. Rent seeking takes many forms: hidden and open transfers and subsidies from the government, laws that make the marketplace less competitive, lax enforcement of existing competition laws, and statutes that allow corporations to take advantage of others or to pass costs on to the rest of society. The term "rent" was originally used to describe the returns to land, since the owner of land receives these payments by virtue of his ownership and not because of anything he *does*. This stands in contrast to the situation of workers, for example, whose wages are compensation for the *effort* they provide. The term "rent" then was extended to include monopoly profits, or monopoly rents, the income that one receives simply from the control of a monopoly. Eventually the term was expanded still further to include the returns on similar ownership claims. If the government gave a company the exclusive right to import a limited amount (a quota) of a good, such as sugar, then the extra return generated as a result of the ownership of those rights was called a "quota-rent."

Countries rich in natural resource are infamous for rent-seeking activities. It's far easier to get rich in these countries by gaining access to resources at favorable terms than by producing wealth. This is often a negative-sum game, which is one of the reasons why, on average, such countries have grown more slowly than comparable countries without the bounty of such resources.[14]

Even more disturbing, one might have thought that an abundance of resources could be used to help the poor, to ensure access to education and health care for all. Taxing work and savings can weaken incentives; in contrast, taxing the "rents" on land, oil, or other natural resources won't make them disappear. The resources will still be there to be taken out, if not today, then tomorrow. There are no adverse incentive effects. That means that, in principle, there should be ample revenues to finance both social expenditures and public investments—in, say, health and education. Yet, among the countries with the greatest inequality are those with the most natural resources. Evidently, a few within these countries are better at rent seeking than others (usually those with political power), and they ensure that the benefits of the resources accrue largely to themselves. In Venezuela, the richest oil producer in Latin America, half of the country lived in poverty prior to the rise of Hugo Chavez—and it is precisely this type of poverty in the midst of riches that gives rise to leaders like him.[15]

Rent-seeking behavior is not just endemic in the resource-rich countries of the Middle East, Africa, and Latin America. It has also become endemic in modern economies, including our own. In those economies, it takes many forms, some of which are closely akin to those in the oil-rich countries: getting state assets (such as oil or minerals) at below fair-market prices. It's not hard to become wealthy if the government sells you for $500 million a mine that's worth $1 billion.

Another form of rent seeking is the flip side: selling to government products at *above* market prices (noncompetitive procurement). The drug companies and military contractors excel in this form of rent seeking. Open government subsidies (as in agriculture) or hidden subsidies (trade restrictions that reduce competition or subsidies hidden in the tax system) are other ways of getting rents from the public.

Not all rent seeking uses government to extract money from ordinary citizens. The private sector can excel on its own, extracting rents from the public, for instance, through monopolistic practices and exploiting those who are less informed and educated, exemplified by the banks' predatory lending. CEOs can use their control of the corporation to garner for themselves a larger fraction of the firms' revenues. Here, though, the government too plays a role, by not doing what it should: by not stopping these activities, by not making them illegal, or by not enforcing laws that exist. Effective enforcement of competition laws can circumscribe monopoly profits; effective laws on predatory lending and credit card abuses can limit the extent of bank exploitation; well-designed corporate governance laws can limit the extent to which corporate officials appropriate for themselves firm revenues.

By looking at those at the top of the wealth distribution, we can get a feel for the nature of this aspect of America's inequality. Few are inventors who have reshaped technology, or scientists who have reshaped our understandings of the laws of nature. Think of Alan Turing, whose genius provided the mathematics underlying the modern computer. Or of Einstein. Or of the discoverers of the laser (in which Charles Townes played a central role)[16] or John Bardeen, Walter Brattain, and William Shockley, the inventors of transistors.[17] Or of Watson and Crick, who unraveled the mysteries of DNA, upon which rests so much of modern medicine. None of them, who made such large contributions to our well-being, are among those most rewarded by our economic system.

Instead, many of the individuals at the top of the wealth distribution are, in one way or another, geniuses at business. Some might claim, for instance, that Steve Jobs or the innovators of search engines or social media were, in their way, geniuses. Jobs was number 110 on the *Forbes* list of the world's wealthiest billionaires before his death, and Mark Zuckerberg was 52. But many of these "geniuses" built their business empires on the shoulders of giants, such as Tim Berners-Lee, the inventor of the World Wide Web, who has never appeared on the *Forbes* list. Berners-Lee could have become a billionaire but chose not to—he made his idea available freely; which greatly speeded up the development of the Internet.[18]

A closer look at the successes of those at the top of the wealth distribution shows that more than a small part of their genius resides in devising better ways of exploiting market power and other market imperfections—and, in many cases, finding better ways of ensuring that politics works for them rather than for society more generally.

We've already commented on financiers, who make up a significant portion of the top 1 or 0.1 percent. While some gained their wealth by producing value, others did so in no small part by one of the myriad forms of rent seeking that we described earlier. At the top, in addition to the financiers, whom we have already discussed,[19] are the monopolists and their descendants who, through one mechanism or another, have succeeded in achieving and sustaining market dominance. After the railroad barons of the nineteenth century came John D. Rockefeller and Standard Oil. The end of the twentieth century saw Bill Gates and Microsoft's domination of the PC software industry.

Internationally, there is the case of Carlos Slim, a Mexican businessman who was ranked by *Forbes* as the wealthiest person in the world in 2011.[20] Thanks to his dominance of the telephone industry in Mexico, Slim is able to charge prices that are a multiple of those in more competitive markets. He made his breakthrough when he was able to acquire a large share in Mexico's telecommunications system after the country privatized it,[21] a strategy that lies behind many of the world's great fortunes. As we've seen, it's easy to get rich by getting a state asset at a deep discount. Many of Russia's current oligarchs, for example, obtained their initial wealth by buying state assets at below-market prices and then ensuring continuing profits through monopoly power. (In America most of our government giveaways tend to be more subtle. We design rules for, say, selling government assets that are in effect partial giveaways, but less transparently so than what Russia did.)[22]

... [A]nother important group of the very wealthy [are] corporate CEOs, such as Stephen Hemsley from UnitedHealth Group, who received $102 million in 2010, and Edward Mueller from Qwest Communications (now CenturyLink, after a merger in 2011), who made $65.8 million.[23] CEOs have successfully garnered a larger and larger fraction of corporate revenues.[24] As we'll explain later, it is not a sudden increase in their productivity that allowed these CEOs to amass such riches in the last couple of decades but rather an enhanced ability to take more from the corporation that they are supposed to be serving, and weaker qualms about, and enhanced public toleration of, doing so.

A final large group of rent seekers consists of the top-flight lawyers, including those who became wealthy by helping others engage in their rent seeking in ways that skirt the law but do not (usually) land them in prison. They help write the complex tax laws in which loopholes are put, so their clients can avoid taxes, and they then design the complex deals to take advantage of these loopholes. They helped design the complex and nontransparent derivatives market. They help design the contractual arrangements that generate monopoly power; seemingly within the law. And for all this assistance in making our markets work not the way markets should but as instruments for the benefit of those at the top, they get amply rewarded.[25]

Monopoly Rents: Creating Sustainable Monopolies

To economists large fortunes pose a problem. The laws of competition, as I have noted, say that profits (beyond the normal return to capital) are supposed to be driven to zero, and quickly. But if profits are zero, how can fortunes be built? Niches in which there isn't competition, for one reason or another, offer one avenue.[26] But that goes only a little way to explaining sustainable excessive profits (beyond the competitive level). Success will attract entry, and profits will quickly disappear. The real key to success is to make sure that there won't ever be competition—or at least there won't be competition for a long enough time that one can make a monopoly killing in the meanwhile. The simplest way to a sustainable monopoly is getting the government to give you one. From the seventeenth century to the nineteenth, the British granted the East India Company a monopoly on trade with India.

There are other ways to get government-sanctioned monopolies. Patents typically give an inventor a monopoly over that innovation for a temporary period, but the details of patent law can extend the length of the patent, reduce entry of new firms, and enhance monopoly power. America's patent laws have been doing exactly that. They are designed not to maximize the pace of innovation but rather to maximize rents.[27]

Even without a government grant of monopoly, firms can create entry barriers. A variety of practices discourage entry, such as maintaining excess capacity, so that an entrant knows that, should he enter, the incumbent firm can increase production, lowering prices to the point that entry would be unprofitable.[28] In the Middle Ages, guilds successfully restricted competition. Many professions have continued that tradition. Although they argue that they are simply trying to maintain standards, restrictions on entry (limiting the number of places at medical school or restricting migration of trained personnel from abroad) help keep incomes high.[29]

At the turn of the previous century, concern about the monopolies that formed the basis of many of the fortunes of that period, including Rockefeller's, grew so great that under the trust-busting president Theodore Roosevelt, America passed a slew of laws to break up monopolies and prevent some of these practices. In the years that followed, numerous monopolies were broken up—in oil, cigarettes, and many other industries.[30] And yet today, as we look around the American economy, we can see many sectors, including some that are central to its functioning, where one or a few firms dominate—such as Microsoft in PC operating systems, or AT&T, Verizon, T-Mobile, and Sprint in telecommunications.

Three factors contributed to this increased monopolization of markets. First, there was a battle over ideas about the role that government should take in ensuring competition. Chicago school economists (like Milton Friedman and George Stigler) who believe in free and unfettered markets[31] argued that markets are naturally competitive[32] and that seemingly anticompetitive practices really enhance efficiency. A massive program to "educate"[33] people, and especially judges, regarding these new doctrines of law and economics, partly sponsored by right-wing foundations like the Olin Foundation, was successful. The timing was ironic: American courts were buying into notions that markets were "naturally" competitive and placing a high burden of proof on anyone claiming otherwise just as the economics discipline was exploring theories that explain why markets often were *not* competitive, even when there were seemingly many firms. For instance, a new and powerful branch of economics called game theory explained how collusive behavior could be maintained tacitly over extended periods of time. Meanwhile, new theories of imperfect and asymmetric information showed how information imperfections impaired competition, and new evidence substantiated the relevance and importance of these theories.

The influence of the Chicago school should not be underestimated. Even when there are blatant infractions—like predatory pricing, where a firm lowers its price to force out a competitor and then uses its monopoly power to raise prices—they've been hard to prosecute.[34] Chicago school economics argues that markets are presumptively competitive and efficient. If entry were easy, the dominant firm would gain nothing from driving out a rival, because the firm that is forced out would be quickly replaced by another firm. But in reality entry is not so easy, and predatory behavior does occur.

A second factor giving rise to increased monopoly is related to changes in our economy. The creation of monopoly power was easier in some of the new growth industries. Many of these sectors were marked by what are called network externalities. An obvious example is the computer operating system: just as it's very convenient for everyone to speak the same language, it's very convenient for everyone to use the same operating system. Increasing interconnectivity across the world naturally leads to standardization. Those with a monopoly over the standard that is chosen benefit.

As we have noted, competition naturally works against the accumulation of market power. When there are large monopoly profits, competitors work to get a share. That's where the third factor that has increased monopoly power in the United States comes in: businesses found new ways of resisting entry, of reducing competitive pressures. Microsoft provides the example par excellence. Because it enjoyed a near-monopoly on PC operating systems, it stood to lose a lot if alternative technologies undermined its monopoly. The development of the Internet and the web browser to access it represented just such a threat. Netscape brought the browser to the market, building on government-funded research.[35] Microsoft decided to squelch this potential competitor. It offered its own product, Internet Explorer, but the product couldn't compete in the open market. The company decided to use its monopoly power in PC operating systems to make sure that the playing field was not level. It deployed a strategy known as FUD (fear, uncertainty, and doubt), creating anxiety about compatibility among users by programming error messages that would randomly appear if Netscape was installed on a Windows computer. The company also did not provide the disclosures necessary for full compatibility as new versions of Windows were developed. And most cleverly, it offered Internet Explorer at a zero price—free, bundled in as part of its operating system. It's hard to compete with a zero price. Netscape was doomed.[36]

It was obvious that selling something at a zero price was not a profit-maximizing strategy—in the short run. But Microsoft had a vision for the long run: the maintenance of its monopoly. For that, it was willing to make short-run sacrifices. It succeeded, but so blatant were its methods that courts and tribunals throughout the world charged it with engaging in anticompetitive practices. And yet, in the end, Microsoft won—for it realized that in a network economy, a monopoly position, once attained, is hard to break. Given Microsoft's dominance of the operating system market, it had the incentives and capabilities to dominate in a host of other applications.[37]

No wonder, then, that Microsoft's profits have been so enormous—an average of $7 billion per year over the last quarter century, $14 billion over the past ten years, increasing in 2011 to $23 billion[38]—and reaping wealth for those who bought shares early enough. The conventional wisdom has it that in spite of its dominant position and huge resources, Microsoft has not been a real innovator. It did not develop the first widely used word processor, the first spreadsheet, the first browser, the first media player, or the first dominant search engine. Innovation lay elsewhere. This is consistent with theory and historical evidence: monopolists are not good innovators.[39]

Looking at the U.S. economy, we see in many sectors large numbers of firms, and therefore infer that there must be competition. But that's not always the case. Take the example of banks. While there are hundreds of banks, the big four share between them almost half of the country's banking assets,[40] a marked increase from the degree of concentration fifteen years ago. In most smaller communities, there are at most one or two. When competition is so limited, prices are likely to be far in excess of competitive levels.[41] That's why the sector enjoys profits estimated to be more than $115 billion a year, much of which is passed along to its top officials and other bankers—helping create one of the major sources of inequality at the top.[42] In some products, such as over-the-counter credit default swaps (CDSes), four or five very large banks totally dominate, and such market concentration always gives rise to the worry that they collude, albeit tacitly. (But sometimes the collusion is not even tacit—it is explicit. The banks set a critical rate, called the London Interbank Offered Rate, or Libor. Mortgages and many financial products are linked to Libor. It appears that the banks worked to rig the rate, enabling them to make still more money from others who were unaware of these shenanigans.)

Of course, even when laws that prohibit monopolistic practices are on the books, these have to be enforced. Particularly given the narrative created by the Chicago school of economics, there is a tendency not to interfere with the "free" workings of the market, even when the outcome is anticompetitive. And there are good political reasons not to take too strong a position: after all, it's antibusiness—and not good for campaign contributions—to be too tough on, say, Microsoft.[43]

Politics: Getting to Set the Rules and Pick the Referee

It's one thing to win in a "fair" game. It's quite another to be able to write the rules of the game—and to write them in ways that enhance one's prospects of winning. And it's even worse if you can choose your own referees. In many areas today, regulatory agencies are responsible for oversight of a sector (writing and enforcing rules and regulations)—the Federal Communications Commission (FCC) in telecom; the Securities and Exchange Commission (SEC) in securities; and the Federal Reserve in many areas of banking. The problem is that leaders in these sectors use their political influence to get people appointed to the regulatory agencies who are sympathetic to their perspectives.

Economists refer to this as "regulatory capture."[44] Sometimes the capture is associated with pecuniary incentives: those on the regulatory commission come from and return to the sector that they are supposed to regulate. Their incentives and those of the industry are well aligned, even if their incentives are not well aligned with those of the rest of society. If those on the regulatory commission serve the sector well, they get well rewarded in their post-government career.

Sometimes, however, the capture is not just motivated by money. Instead, the mindset of regulators is captured by those whom they regulate. This is called "cognitive capture," and it is more of a sociological phenomenon. While neither Alan Greenspan nor Tim Geithner actually worked for a big bank before coming to the Federal Reserve, there was a natural affinity, and they may have come to share the same mindset. In the bankers' mindset—despite the mess that the bankers had made—there was no need to impose stringent conditions on the banks in the bailout.

The bankers have unleashed enormous numbers of lobbyists to persuade any and all who play a role in regulation that they should not be regulated—an estimated 2.5 for every U.S. representative.[45] But persuasion is easier if the target of your efforts begins from a sympathetic position. That is why banks and their lobbyists work so strenuously to ensure that the government appoints regulators who have already been "captured" in one way or another. The bankers try to veto anyone who does not share their belief. I saw this firsthand during the Clinton administration, when potential names for the Fed were floated, some even from the banking community. If any of the potential nominees deviated from the party line that markets are self-regulating and that the banks could manage their own risk—there arose a hue and cry so great that the name wouldn't be put forward or, if it was put forward, that it wouldn't be approved.[46]

Government Munificence

We've seen how monopolies—whether government granted or government "sanctioned," through inadequate enforcement of competition laws—have built the fortunes of many of the world's wealthiest people. But there is another way to get rich. You can simply arrange for the government to hand you cash. This can happen in myriad ways. A little-noticed change in legislation, for example, can reap billions of dollars. This was the case when the government extended a much-needed Medicare drug benefit in 2003.[47] A provision in the law that prohibited government from bargaining for prices on drugs was, in effect, a gift of some $50 billion or more per year to the pharmaceutical companies.[48] More generally, government procurement—paying prices well above costs—is a standard form of government munificence.

Sometimes gifts are hidden in obscure provisions of legislation. A provision of one of the key bills deregulating the financial derivative market—ensuring that no regulator could touch it, no matter how great the peril to which it exposed the economy—also gave derivatives claims "seniority" in the event of bankruptcy. If a bank went under, the claims on the derivatives would be paid off before workers, suppliers, or other creditors saw any money—even if the derivatives had pushed the firm into bankruptcy in the first place.[49] (The derivatives market played a central role in the 2008–09 crisis and was responsible for the $150 billion bailout of AIG.)

There are other ways that the banking sector has benefited from government munificence, evident most clearly in the aftermath of the Great Recession. When the Federal Reserve (which can be thought of as one branch of the government) lends unlimited amounts of money to banks at near-zero interest rates, and allows them to lend the money back to the government (or to foreign governments) at much higher interest rates, it is simply giving them a hidden gift worth billions and billions of dollars.

These are not the only ways that governments spur the creation of enormous personal wealth. Many countries, including the United States, control vast amounts of natural resources like oil, gas, and mining concessions. If the government grants you the right to extract these resources for free, it doesn't take a genius to make a fortune. That is, of course, what the U.S. government did in the nineteenth century, when anyone could stake a claim to natural resources. Today, the government doesn't typically give away its resources; more often it requires a payment, but a payment that is far less than it should be. This is just a less transparent way of giving away money. If the value of the oil under a particular piece of land is $100 million after paying the extraction costs, and the government requires a payment of only $50 million, the government has, in effect, given away $50 million.

It doesn't have to be this way, but powerful interests ensure that it is. In the Clinton administration, we tried to make the mining companies pay more for the resources they take out of public lands than the nominal amounts that they do. Not surprisingly, the mining companies—and the congressmen to whom they make generous contributions—opposed these measures, and successfully so. They argued that the policy would impede growth. But the fact of the matter is that, with an auction, companies will bid to get the mining rights so long as the value of the resources is greater than the cost of extraction, and if they win the bid, they will extract the resources. Auctions don't impede growth; they just make sure that the public gets paid appropriately for what is theirs. Modern auction theory has shown how changing the design of the auction can generate much more revenue for the government. These theories were tested out in the auction of the spectrum used for telecommunications beginning in the 1990s, and they worked remarkably well, generating billions for the government.

Sometimes government munificence, instead of handing over resources for pennies on the dollar, takes the form of rewriting the rules to boost profits. An easy way to do this is to protect firms from foreign competition. Tariffs, taxes paid by companies abroad but not by domestic firms, are in effect a gift to domestic producers. The firms demanding protection from foreign competition always provide a rationale, suggesting that society as a whole is the beneficiary and that any benefits that accrue to the companies themselves are incidental. This is self-serving, of course, and while there are instances in which such pleas contain some truth, the widespread abuse of the argument makes it hard to take seriously. Because tariffs put foreign producers at a disadvantage, they enable domestic firms to raise their prices and increase their profits. In some cases, there may be some incidental benefits such as higher domestic employment and the opportunity for companies to invest in R&D that will increase productivity and competitiveness. But just as often, tariffs protect old and tired industries that have lost their competitiveness and are not likely to regain it, or occasionally those that have made bad bets on new technologies and would like to postpone facing competition.

The ethanol subsidy offers an example of this phenomenon. A plan to reduce our dependence on oil by replacing it with the energy of the sun embedded in one of America's great products, its corn, seemed irresistible. But converting plant energy into a form that can provide energy for cars instead of people is hugely expensive. It is also easier to do with some plants than others. So successful has Brazil's research on sugar-based ethanol been that in order for America to compete, for years it had to tax Brazilian sugar-based ethanol 54 cents a gallon.[50] Forty years after the introduction of the subsidy, it was still in place to support an infant technology that seemingly would not grow up. When oil prices fell after the 2008 recession, many ethanol plants went bankrupt, even with massive subsidies.[51] It wasn't until the end of 2011 that the subsidy and tariff were allowed to expire.

The persistence of such distortionary subsidies stems from a single source: politics. The main—and for a long while, effectively the only—*direct* beneficiary of these subsidies were the corn-ethanol producers, dominated by the megafirm Archer Daniels Midland (ADM). Like so many other executives, those at ADM seemed to be better at managing politics than at innovation. They contributed generously to both parties, so that as much as those in Congress might rail against such corporate largesse, lawmakers were slow to touch the ethanol subsidies.[52] As we've noted, firms almost always argue that the true beneficiaries of any largesse they receive lie elsewhere. In this case, ethanol advocates argued that the real beneficiaries were America's corn farmers. But that was, for the most part, not the case, especially in the early days of the subsidy.[53]

Of course, why American corn farmers, who were already the recipients of massive government handouts, receiving almost half of their income from Washington rather than from the "soil," should receive still further assistance is hard to understand, and hard to reconcile with principles of a free-market economy. (In fact, the vast preponderance of government money subsidizing agriculture does not go, as many believe, to poor farmers or even family farms. The design of the program reveals its true objective: to redistribute money from the rest of us to the rich and corporate farms.)[54]

Sadly, government munificence toward corporations does not end with the few examples we have given, but to describe each and every instance of government approved rent seeking would require another book.[55]

NOTES

1. That's one of the reasons that good stock market performance is no longer a good indicator of a healthy economy. Stocks can do well because wages are low and the Fed, worried about the economy, keeps interest rates at near zero.

2. Thucydides, *The Peloponnesian War*, trans. Richard Crawley (New York: Modern Library, 1951), p. 331 (book 5.89).

3. That's why the cases where those in power voluntarily give some of it up are so interesting. In some of them, it's because those in power have an understanding of their own long-term interests—and the long-term interests of those they are supposed to serve. That was the case, e.g., when the king of Bhutan, in 2007, insisted on converting his country into a constitutional monarchy. He had to persuade his citizens that that was the right course for them. The elites of nineteenth-century countries that extended education must have known that there was a risk that this would over the long run weaken their dominance of the political franchise; yet the short-term economic advantages of having a more educated workplace seem to have dominated the long-term political consequences. See François Bourguignon and Sébastien Dessus, "Equity and Development: Political Economy Considerations," pt. 1 of *No Growth without Equity?* ed. Santiago Levy and Michael Walton (New York: Palgrave Macmillan, 2009). Daron Acemoglu and James Robinson theorize that democratization is a way for ruling elites to commit to future redistribution, and thus avoid the extreme of revolution when faced with social unrest. If there is not sufficient strength in the rebellion, repression or temporary reform (or transfers) might suffice. Acemoglu and Robinson, *Economic Origins of Dictatorship and Democracy* (Cambridge: Cambridge University Press, 2006).

4. See Karl Polyani, *The Great Transformation* (New York: Rinehart, 1944). One of the theories developed in response to Marx was that of Nassau Senior, the first holder of the Drummond Chair at Oxford University, who argued that the return capitalists earned was compensation for their "abstinence" (i.e., saving, or *not consuming*).

5. The formalization of this idea is called the "first welfare theorem of economics." It asserts that under certain conditions—when markets work well—no one can be made better-off without making someone else worse-off. But, as we shall explain shortly, there are many instances in which markets do not work well. A recent popular analysis is Kaushik Basu, *Beyond the Invisible Hand: Groundwork for a New Economics* (Princeton: Princeton University Press, 2011). Basu uses the metaphor of a magic show to describe the way the discussion of economics on the political right draws attention to the conclusion of this theorem—that markets are efficient—and away from the very special and unrealistic conditions under which the conclusion holds—perfect markets. Like a good magician, a free-market economist succeeds by drawing spectators' attention to what he wants them to see—the rabbit jumping out of the hat—while distracting their attention from other things—how the rabbit got into the hat in the first place.

6. Adam Smith, *The Wealth of Nations* (1776; New York: P. F. Collier, 1902), p. 207.

7. See Carmen Reinhart and Kenneth Rogoff, *This Time Is Different: Eight Centuries of Financial Folly* (Princeton: Princeton University Press, 2009).

8. A derivative is just a financial instrument the return to which is *derived* on the basis of something else, e.g., the performance of a stock or the price of oil or the value of a bond. A few banks have profited enormously by keeping this market nontransparent, garnering for themselves an amount widely estimated at more than $20 billion a year.

9. On October 31, 2011, MF Global Holdings, a brokerage firm run by Jon Corzine, filed for bankruptcy protection in New York. It was the eighth-largest corporate bankruptcy in U.S. history and the biggest failure by a securities firm since Lehman Brothers Holdings Inc. filed for Chapter 11 in September 2008.

10. While there may be some debate about when taking advantage of information asymmetries is unethical (reflected in the maxim "caveat emptor," putting the

obligation on the buyer to beware of the possibility of information asymmetries), there is no doubt that the banks stepped over the line. ...

11. This predatory behavior took a number of forms. One way was to charge *very* high interest rates, sometimes obfuscated by fees. The abolition of usury laws (which limit the interest rates lenders can charge) provided lenders greater scope for charging exorbitant interest rates; and lenders found ways of circumventing whatever regulations there were. Rent-a-Center claimed to be renting furniture; it was really selling furniture and simultaneously lending money—at extraordinarily high interest rates. Many states tried to circumscribe its activities, but it used its political influence (it had senior ex-politicians, including a former leader of the Republicans in the House of Representatives, on its board) to try to get federal preemption (whereby weaker federal rules preempt the rights of states to regulate). In 2006 Rent-a-Center (with nationwide revenues in excess of $2 billion) was successfully sued by the state of California for deceptive business practices. See http://oag.ca.gov/news/press_release?id=1391. Credit cards and payday loans provided other venues for predatory practices. Among many discussions, see, e.g., Robert Faris, "Payday Lending: A Business Model That Encourages Chronic Borrowing," *Economic Development Quarterly* 17, no. 1 (February 2003): 8–32; James H. Carr and Lopa Kolluri, *Predatory Lending: An Overview* (Washington, DC: Fannie Mae Foundation, 2001).

12. A well-performing financial sector is absolutely essential for a well-performing economy. It allocates capital, manages risk, and runs the payments mechanism. As I explain in *Freefall* (New York: Norton, 2010), in the run-up to the 2008–09 crisis, it did not perform these functions well. Part of the reason is that it was focused more on circumventing regulations and exploitive activities, like predatory lending. The negative-sum nature is reflected in the immense losses in the real estate sector. The financial sector likes to claim that it has been highly innovative, and that these innovations are at the root of the economy's overall success. But as Paul Volcker, former chairman of the Federal Reserve, pointed out, there is little evidence of any significant effect of these innovations on economic growth or societal well-being (with the exception of the ATM machine). But even if the financial sector had contributed slightly to the country's growth in the years before the crisis, the losses associated with the crisis more than offset any of these gains.

13. A recent study has shown that people of higher status/income have fewer qualms about breaking the rules, are more likely to be driven by self-interest, more likely to cheat, and more likely to behave in other ways that would generally be viewed as unethical. Paul K. Piff, Daniel M. Stancato, Stephane Cote, Rodolfo Menoza-Denton, and Dacher Keltner, "Higher Social Class Predicts Increased Unethical Behavior," *Proceedings of the National Academy of Sciences*, February 27, 2012. While what is "unfair" or "unethical" depends on "norms," and there may be disagreements about what is or is not fair, the experiment focused on situations where there would be broad consensus on what was fair or ethical. Similarly, much of the financial sector behavior that I criticize ... violates virtually any sense of "fairness" or "ethics."

14. This problem has come to be called the "natural resource curse." There are other reasons that such countries have not done well: managing natural resources can be difficult (prices fluctuate and exchange rates can become overvalued). For a recent review of some of the problems and how they can be addressed see *Escaping the Resource Curse*, ed. M. Humphreys, J. Sachs, and J. E. Stiglitz (New York: Columbia University Press, 2007). See also, e.g., Michael Ross, *The Oil Curse: How Petroleum*

Wealth Shapes the Development of Nations (Princeton: Princeton University Press, 2012); and idem, *Timber Booms and Institutional Breakdown in Southeast Asia* (New York: Cambridge University Press, 2001).

15. According to World Bank Indicators, 50 percent of the population was living under the national poverty line in 1998 before Chavez took office in 1999.

16. He shared the 1964 Nobel Prize in Physics with the Soviet scientists Nikolay Basov and Aleksandr Prokhorov for "fundamental work in the field of quantum electronics, which has led to the construction of oscillators and amplifiers based on the maser-laser principle."

17. They received the 1956 Nobel Prize in Physics "for their researches on semiconductors and their discovery of the transistor effect."

18. The World Wide Web Consortium he founded decided that its standards should be based on royalty-free technology, so that they could easily be adopted by anyone. Like Jobs, Bill Gates is often heralded as an innovator, but even though the adoption of his products is nearly universal now, that is due more to his business acumen—and near-monopoly of the market—than to the uniqueness of the technology he sells.

19. Bakija et al. found (p. 3) that "executives, managers, supervisors, and financial professionals account for about 60 percent of the top 0.1 percent of income earners in recent years, and can account for 70 percent of the increase in the share of national income going to the top 0.1 percent of the income distribution between 1979 and 2005." The composition of the top 1 percent in 2005 was 31 percent "Executives, managers, supervisors (non-finance)"; 15.7 percent "Medical," 13.9 percent "Financial professionals, including management," and 8.4 percent "Lawyers." The share of finance almost doubled over the period, rising from 7.7 percent in 1979 to 13.9 percent in 2005. (Nonfinance executives and medical fell slightly; lawyers increased marginally.) These statistics are based on an income measure that *excludes* capital gains. This is very important because about half of all capital gains accrue to the top 0.1 percent. For the top 400 income earners, 60 percent of their income is in the form of capital gains. J. Bakija, A. Cole, and B. T. Hein, "Jobs and Income Growth of Top Earners and the Causes of Changing Income Inequality: Evidence from U.S. Tax Return Data." See also comments by C. Rampell, "The Top 1%: Executives, Doctors and Bankers" *New York Times*, October 17, 2011, available at http:// economix.blogs.nytimes.com/2011/10/17/the-top-1-executives-doctors-and -bankers/; and Laura D'Andrea Tyson, "Tackling Income Inequality," *New York Times*, November 18, 2011, available at http://economix.blogs.nytimes.com /2011/11/18/tackling-income-inequality/.

20. See Forbes World's Billionaires list at http://www.forbes.com/wealth/billionaires/; ranking is from 2011.

21. Slim's Grupo Carso, France Telecom, and Southwestern Bell paid $1.7 billion in December 1990 to acquire "a controlling 20.4 percent stake in Telmex, which includes 51 percent of the votes in the company." See Keith Bradsher, "Regulatory Pitfall in Telmex Sale," *New York Times*, December 7, 1990, available at http://www .nytimes.com/1990/12/27/business/talking-deals-regulatory-pitfall-in-telmex-sale.html? scp=1&sq=telmex%20southwestern%20bell%201990&st=cse (accessed March 3, 2012).

22. In the midnineties, Russia borrowed large amounts of money from the private sector, putting up shares in its oil and natural resource companies as collateral. But it was all a ruse to turn over state assets to the oligarchs. This was called "loans for shares." See Chrystia Freeland, *Sale of the Century: Russia's Wild Ride from Communism to Capitalism*

(New York: Crown Business, 2000). A variety of specious arguments are often put forward for these privatizations. Most recently, Greece has been pushed to privatize, as a condition for getting assistance from Europe and the IMF. For a discussion of privatization and the arguments used for it … and *J. E. Stiglitz, The Price of Inequality: How Today's Divided Society Endangers Our Future* (New York: Norton, 2012), and J. E. Stiglitz, *Globalization and Its Discontents* (New York: Norton, 2002). Not every country and not every privatization has suffered from transferring state assets to private parties at below fair market prices. Many believe that the privatizations in the UK under Margaret Thatcher, with shares publicly floated and with the number of shares any one person or company could buy strictly limited, were conducted deliberately in a manner to avoid such outcomes.

23. See Forbes America's Highest Paid Chief Executives 2011, available at http://www .forbes.com/lists/2011/12/ceo-compensation-11_land.html.

24. This is obviously a controversial claim: the CEOs might argue that in fact they receive but a small fraction of what they contribute to shareholder value. But … the so-called incentive structures are poorly designed, providing little link between that part of the increase in market value that is attributable to the efforts of the CEO and that which is the result of broader market forces—lower costs of inputs or higher stock market prices in general. Some studies have suggested, moreover, that once total compensation is taken into account (including adjustments of bonuses when the stock market doesn't do well), there is little relationship between firm performance and compensation. For a broader discussion of this issue, see J. E. Stiglitz, *Roaring Nineties* (New York: W. W. Norton, 2003); and especially Lucian Bebchuk and Jesse Fried, *Pay without Performance: The Unfulfilled Promise of Executive Compensation* (Cambridge: Harvard University Press, 2004).

25. Still one more group is real estate moguls, who benefit from special provisions of the tax code and often get rents as a result of local government variances in zoning laws.

26. These are sometimes called natural monopolies. They include the examples given earlier where network externalities are very large.

27. The advocates of stronger intellectual property rights, of course, claim otherwise. Interestingly, in the United States many of the most innovative firms, those in Silicon Valley, have been among those opposing certain proposals by those in the drug and entertainment industries to strengthen intellectual property rights. Recent revisions of patent law arguably gave large corporations an advantage over new firms, illustrating the fact … that there are strong distributive consequences of any legal framework. For a discussion of how our current intellectual property framework may actually inhibit innovation, see J. E. Stiglitz, *Making Globalization Work* (New York: Norton, 2006), and Claude Henry and J. E. Stiglitz, "Intellectual Property, Dissemination of Innovation, and Sustainable Development," *Global Policy* 1, no. 1 (October 2010): 237–51.

28. See, e.g., A. Dixit, "The Role of Investment in Entry-Deterrence," *Economic Journal* 90, no. 357 (March 1980): 95–106; and J. Tirole and D. Fudenberg, "The Fat Cat Effect, the Puppy Dog Ploy and the Lean and Hungry Look," *American Economic Review* 74 (1984): 361–68. The practices Microsoft used to rid itself of its rivals (described below) also helped prevent entry of new competitors.

29. It's clear that one wants standards; one doesn't want to be operated on by an unqualified doctor. But, for instance, the supply of qualified doctors could have been increased simply by increasing the number of places in medical school.

30. In 1890 Congress passed the Sherman Anti-Trust Act, and its enforcement speeded up in the twentieth century. In 1911 the Supreme Court ordered the dissolution of the Standard Oil Company and the American Tobacco Company, which brought down the two powerful industrial trusts. In 1984 the Court broke up AT&T's monopoly following *United States v. AT&T*. See Charles R. Geisst, *Monopolies in America: Empire Builders and Their Enemies from Jay Gould to Bill Gates* (New York: Oxford University Press, 2000).

31. The term "Chicago school" is often applied to this group of economists, partially because the high priest of this religion, Milton Friedman (and many of his acolytes), taught at the University of Chicago. But it should be understood that many at that great university are not devotees of this school of thought, and that there are many devotees in other universities around the world. The term has, however, become a commonly used shorthand.

32. One group even went so far as to argue that markets will behave competitively even if there is only one firm, so long as there is potential competition. This argument played an important role in airline deregulation, where it was contended that even if there was only one airline on a given route, it would be disciplined from charging monopoly prices by the threat of entry. Both theory and experience have shown that this argument is wrong, so long as there are sunk costs (costs that won't be recovered if a firm enters and subsequently leaves), no matter how small those costs. See Joseph Farrell, "How Effective Is Potential Competition?," *Economics Letters* 20, no. 1 (1986): 67–70; J. E. Stiglitz, "Technological Change, Sunk Costs, and Competition," *Brookings Papers on Economic Activity* 3 (1987), pp. 883–947; and P. Dasgupta and J. E. Stiglitz, "Potential Competition, Actual Competition, and Economic Welfare," *European Economic Review* 32, nos. 2–3 (March 1988): 569–77.

33. For discussion and examples of conservative foundations' contribution to the Chicago school law and economics programs, see Alliance for Justice, *Justice for Sale: Short-changing the Public Interest for Private Gain* (Washington, DC: Alliance for Justice, 1993).

34. The Department of Justice brought a case against American Airlines in the early years of this century. I thought the evidence that American Airlines had engaged in predatory behavior was especially compelling, but the judge didn't need to look at the evidence: the Supreme Court had ruled that there was just too strong a presumption *against* the existence of predatory pricing to make prosecution possible.

35. One of Netscape's founders, Marc Andreessen, was part of the team at the University of Illinois at Urbana-Champaign that developed Mosaic, the first widely used web browser, which was a project of the university's National Center for Supercomputing Applications (one of the original sites of the National Science Foundation's Supercomputer Centers Program). See the website of the NCSA, http://www.ncsa.illinois.edu/Projects/mosaic.html (accessed March 3, 2012); and John Markoff, "New Venture in Cyberspace by Silicon Graphics Founder," *New York Times*, May 7, 1994, available at http://www.nytimes.com/1994/05/07/business/new-venture-in-cyberspace-by-silicon-graphics-founder.html?ref=marcandreessen (accessed March 3, 2012).

36. For an overview of the Microsoft case, see Geisst, *Monopolies in America*.

37. See Steven C. Salop and R. Craig Romaine, "Preserving Monopoly: Economic Analysis, Legal Standards, and Microsoft," *George Mason Law Review* 4, no. 7 (1999): 617–1055.

38. See Microsoft's annual report.

39. As the late Oxford professor and Nobel Prize winner John Hicks said, "The best of all monopoly profits is a quiet life." J. R. Hicks, "Annual Survey of Economic Theory: The Theory of Monopoly," *Econometrica* 1, no. 8 (1935). Kenneth Arrow pointed out that because monopolists restrict production, the saving they get from reducing costs is diminished. See Arrow, "Economic Welfare and the Allocation of Resources for Invention," in *The Rate and Direction of Inventive Activity: Economic and Social Factors* (Princeton: Princeton University Press, 1962), pp. 609–26. Monopolies, of course, don't last forever: new technologies and the open-source movement are already beginning to challenge Microsoft's dominance.

40. Calculated by total assets of commercial banks, as of September 3, 2011. See FDIC Statistics on Banking, available at http://www2.fdic.gov/SDI/SOB/index.asp; and Federal Reserve Statistical Release Large Commercial Banks, available at http://www.federalreserve.gov/releases/lbr/current/default.htm.

41. Moreover, banks don't compete on price for the services they offer. If you want to do a merger or acquisition, every major bank charges the same percentage fee. When takeovers were hundreds of millions of dollars, the resulting charges were large; when they became billions, charges became astronomical, for essentially the same amount of work by the same number of people.

42. From 2010 Q4 to 2011 Q3 (the most recently available year), FDIC-insured institutions made an aggregate profit of $115 billion. ... But these numbers don't really capture the magnitude of bank profits, since they are the profits after paying out the mega-bonuses to the executives, which can push compensation at some firms above 50 percent of revenues after other costs have been taken out, i.e., the "true" profits may be as much as double the above number. The *profits and bonuses* of the banking sector exceed 1 percent of the country's entire national output. Such numbers lead many to conclude that the financial sector, which is supposed to be the servant of the rest of the economy, has become its master.

43. Microsoft tried to exert political influence through a variety of channels. It has made campaign contributions of $13,516,304 from 1999 to present. See campaignmoney.com, compiled from campaign finance reports and data disclosed by Federal Election Commission, lists of contribution available at http://www.campaignmoney.com/Microsoft.asp?pg=88 (accessed March 6, 2012). The remedies put forward by President Bush's Justice Department in response to Microsoft's conviction on anticompetitive behavior were mild and did not effectively curtail its market power. See, e.g., Andrew Chin's account of the outcome of *United States v. Microsoft Corp.*: "Decoding Microsoft: A First Principles Approach," *Wake Forest Law Review* 40, no. 1 (2005):1–157. In the case of antitrust laws, there's a partial remedy for the absence of effective public enforcement: private antitrust action (which was introduced because of worries about the willingness of public authorities to take enforcement action).

44. The late Nobel Prize–winning economist George Stigler wrote extensively about this. See, e.g., Stigler, "The Economic Theory of Regulation," *Bell Journal of Economics* 11 (1971): 3–21.

45. Data from the OpenSecrets.org, a website of the Center for Responsive Politics, counting lobbyists for commercial banks, finance, and credit companies. When all lobbyists are counted in the finance, insurance, and real estate industries, the number balloons to nearly five per congressman. See http://www.opensecrets.org/lobby/indus.php?id=F&year=a (accessed March 24, 2012).

46. The latest instance was the veto by the Senate Banking Committee chairman of the nomination of Nobel Prize–winning economist Peter Diamond. Diamond would have provided a critical voice on some of the doctrines that prevail among some of the governors. (Diamond was first nominated to the Fed by President Obama in April 2010; he was renominated in September and again in January 2011, after Senate Republicans blocked a floor vote on his confirmation. On June 5, 2011, Diamond withdrew his nomination, ending a fourteen-month nomination effort resisted by Senator Richard Shelby of Alabama, who, with party colleagues repeatedly criticized Diamond for supporting the central bank's monetary stimulus. Diamond responded that his opponents failed to appreciate that understanding the determinants of unemployment is essential to effective monetary policy.)

47. The Medicare Prescription Drug, Improvement, and Modernization Act of 2003.

48. The economist Dean Baker's research shows that $332 billion could be saved between 2006 and 2013 (around $50 billion a year) in the most conservative high-cost scenario, if Medicare were allowed to negotiate prices; in the middle-cost scenario, $563 billion could be saved for the same budget window. See Baker, *The Savings from an Efficient Medicare Prescription Drug Plan* (Washington, DC: Center for Economic and Policy Research, January 2006).

49. It is estimated that four banks in the United States take home a windfall of some $20 billion a year in derivatives.

50. The market for ethanol was distorted in other ways—such as ethanol requirements and subsidies for gasoline refiners who blended gasoline with ethanol—most of which came from America's corn producers. See the 2010 CBO study "Using Biofuel Tax Credits to Achieve Energy and Environmental Policy Goals," available at http://www.cbo.gov/sites/default/files/cbofiles/ftpdocs/114xx/doc11477/07-14-biofuels.pdf (accessed March 2, 2012); and "The Global Dynamics of Biofuel," Brazil Institute Special Report, April 2007, issue no. 3, available at http://www.wilsoncenter.org/sites/default/files/Brazil_SR_e3.pdf (accessed March 2, 2012).

51. Congress finally allowed the subsidy to expire at the end of 2011.

52. Famously, ADM was fined a then record $100 million for lysine price fixing in 1997, a result of a lengthy federal investigation that also led to convictions and prison time for three executives. (This became a book by Kurt Eichenwald and then a 2009 movie starring Matt Damon, *The Informant.*)

53. In the early days of corn-based ethanol, this was flatly wrong: the demand for corn by ethanol producers was so low that the corn farmers received almost no benefit from the subsidy. Because usage of corn for ethanol production was such a small fraction of global supply, it had a negligible effect on corn prices. ADM and other ethanol producers were the true beneficiaries.

54. The U.S. government paid a total of $261.9 billion for agriculture subsidies from 1995 to 2010. According to USDA, 63 percent of farms do not receive any payments. Among those payments, a large chunk (62 percent in 2009) goes to large-scale commercial farms (with gross annual sales of $250,000 or more). Between 1995 and 2010, the top 10 percent of farms received $30,751 average per year, while the bottom 80 percent of farms received $587 average per year. See USDA Economic Research Service, "Farm Income and Cost: Farms Receiving Government Payments," available at http://www.ers.usda.gov/Briefing/FarmIncome/govtpaybyfarmtype.htm; Environmental Working Group, Farm Subsidy Database, available at http://farm.ewg.org/region.php.

55. And indeed, many books have been written on the subject. See, e.g., Glenn Parker, *Congress and the Rent-Seeking Society* (Ann Arbor: University of Michigan Press, 1996).

QUESTIONS FOR MAKING CONNECTIONS
WITHIN THE READING

1. Writing at a time when most Americans praise free markets uncritically, Stiglitz challenges a number of beliefs about the wisdom of the "invisible hand." He argues, for example, that competition tends to drive profits down, not up. He suggests that manufacturers typically try to protect profit margins by banding together to create monopolies. He alleges that investors often destroy wealth instead of increasing it. He even claims that "markets by themselves often fail to produce efficient and desirable outcomes." Choose one argument that challenges our current common sense about free markets and explain Stiglitz's reasoning. Consider as well the role he appears to think that markets should be allowed to play.

2. Why does Stiglitz see rent seeking as destructive? Who benefits from rent seeking? What are its economic consequences, and why? What does he see as its impact on society, and what is the relationship between economics and social life in general? Why is Stiglitz skeptical about the power of the market to correct itself? Would it be fair to say that the problem of rent seeking can be solved only by political means—that is, through government intervention? Why has government failed to intervene, and what steps does Stiglitz recommend to restore a balance between outcomes and opportunities?

3. Early in his argument about inequality Stiglitz includes a short historical overview, beginning with the once widespread belief that wealth and poverty are divinely ordained. Once a "vast urban underclass" had arisen in the wake of the Industrial Revolution, "it became imperative," Stiglitz writes, "to find new justifications for inequality." What justifications have become the most compelling ones in our time? Is Stiglitz opposed to inequality, or does he regard it as a problem that society will never fully solve? Does he regard it as a problem at all?

QUESTIONS FOR WRITING

1. What does Stiglitz see as the purpose of wealth? Although he never explicitly develops an answer to that question, his entire argument implies a set of commitments about the purposes that wealth-creation should serve. Does he believe that the purpose of wealth is to lift the wealth-creators above the rest? Does he believe that wealth should offer a reward to the hardest-working, while poverty should serve as punishment to motivate lazy people? Or does he see wealth as a means for improving our society as a whole?

Does Stiglitz believe that a society's wealth belongs in some sense to all its members? On what grounds does he argue that the government should redistribute wealth?

2. Ordinarily, we experience the economy in terms of our own jobs, annual earnings, debts, expenses, and so on. Unless we are trained economists, we tend not to understand these matters as the effects of a system—a system of the kind that Stiglitz describes. Drawing on Stiglitz, make an argument about the difference between our personal experience of day-to-day finances and the systemic perspective that economics provides. What are the blind spots in our experience? How does the narrowness of personal life help to conceal larger commonalities and differences? What elements of your experience are overlooked by the focus on the economy as a system?

QUESTIONS FOR MAKING CONNECTIONS
BETWEEN READINGS

1. Bringing Stiglitz together with Maggie Nelson's "Great to Watch," consider the relationship between the arts and inequality. Nelson never refers to economics, and Stiglitz never mentions the world of art, but this question asks you to explore possible connections between them. In what ways does the art world challenge the values of a market society? In what ways does it reinforce social distinctions between "high" and "low" culture—between the cultural "haves" and "have nots"? Does the violence of the avant-garde liberate or intimidate? Consider what Nelson tells us about the trend among artists to respond to middle class "banality" by inflicting on their audience an experience of "brutal, sensory overload." What relation does this strategy establish between artists and their public? In what other areas of life, aside from art, is "sensory overload" a problem?

2. The conflict between Microsoft and Google, as chronicled by Tim Wu in "Father and Son," might be described as a textbook case of dueling monopolies—two companies vying to control an ever larger share of their industries. How might Stiglitz describe the conflict between these two giants? To what extent do their activities qualify as genuine rent seeking— completely, or, to some degree, or not at all? Would it be fair to describe Google as engaged in a struggle against monopoly—to describe it, in other words, as a hero of equality and freedom? Or is Google simply trying to protect a monopoly of its own? In what ways does Wu's narrative complicate Stiglitz's analysis? Does it prove or disprove the claim that markets sometimes fail to make life better for most members of society?

MARTHA STOUT

WHAT IS SANITY? Are "normal" people always sane, or could it be said that we experience sanity only at certain times? After witnessing a jarring event, have you ever found yourself in a condition that is not exactly sane: a state of frantic agitation or numbness and distraction? These are just some of the questions explored by Martha Stout in her first book, *The Myth of Sanity: Divided Consciousness and the Promise of Awareness* (2002), from which this selection comes. Stout draws on her nearly 30 years of practice as a clinical psychologist to show that the tendency to dissociate—to withdraw from reality—begins as a life-preserving resource that defends against severe trauma in childhood, but later can develop into a way of life defined by emotional detachment and prolonged disengagement with the world. In the most extreme cases, a dissociative disorder can cause individuals to black out for extended periods or to develop multiple personalities in order to cope with life's challenges. By defining a continuum that extends from the everyday experience of spacing out or getting lost in thought to conditions like Post Traumatic Stress Disorder, Stout urges her readers to recognize the complexity of consciousness itself. If all of us dissociate to some degree, then a term like "sanity" is simply too crude to capture the real nature of mental health, which requires a proper balance between dissociation and engagement. The patients Stout focuses on in her study have lost this precious balance, but with her help, they come to see the meaning of their lives as something they can recover. In jargon-free prose, Stout tells stories of her patients' struggles for sanity, revealing in each case how buried or missing memories disrupt their awareness of the present.

For more than 25 years Stout served on the clinical faculty of the Harvard Medical School through the McLean Hospital in Belmont, Massachusetts, and the Massachusetts General Hospital in Boston. In addition, she has taught on the Graduate Faculty of the New School for Social Research and the psychology faculty of Wellesley College. Since completing *The Myth of Sanity*, she has published two other best selling books *The Sociopath Next Door* (2005) and *The Paranoia Switch* (2007).

When I Woke Up Tuesday Morning, It Was Friday

"The horror of that moment," the King went on, "I shall never, *never* forget!"

"You will, though," the Queen said, "if you don't make a memorandum of it."

—LEWIS CARROLL

Imagine that you are in your house—no—you are *locked* in your house, cannot get out. It is the dead of winter. The drifted snow is higher than your windows, blocking the light of both moon and sun. Around the house, the wind moans, night and day.

Now imagine that even though you have plenty of electric lights, and perfectly good central heating, you are almost always in the dark and quite cold, because something is wrong with the old-fashioned fuse box in the basement. Inside this cobwebbed, innocuous-looking box, the fuses keep burning out, and on account of this small malfunction, all the power in the house repeatedly fails. You have replaced so many melted fuses that now your little bag of new ones is empty; there are no more. You sigh in frustration, and regard your frozen breath in the light of the flashlight. Your house, which could be so cozy, is tomblike instead.

In all probability, there is something quirky in the antiquated fuse box; it has developed some kind of needless hair trigger, and is not really reacting to any dangerous electrical overload at all. Should you get some pennies out of your pocket, and use them to replace the burned-out fuses? That would solve the power-outage problem. No more shorts, not with copper coins in there. Using coins would scuttle the safeguard function of the fuse box, but the need for a safeguard right now is questionable, and the box is keeping you cold and in the dark for no good reason. Well, probably for no good reason.

On the other hand, what if the wiring in the house really is overloaded somehow? A fire could result, probably will result eventually. If you do not find the fire soon enough, if you cannot manage to put the fire out, the whole house could go up, with you trapped inside. You know that death by burning is hideous. You know also that your mind is playing tricks, but thinking about fire, you almost imagine there is smoke in your nostrils right now.

So, do you go back upstairs and sit endlessly in a dark living room, defeated, numb from the cold, though you have buried yourself under every blanket in the house? No light to read by, no music, just the wail and rattle of the icy wind outside? Or, in an attempt to feel more human, do you make things warm and comfortable? Is it wise to gamble with calamity and howling pain? If you turn the power back on, will you not smell nonexistent smoke every moment you are awake? And will you not have far too many of these waking moments, for how will you ever risk going to sleep?

Do you sabotage the fuse box?

I believe that most of us cannot know what we would do, trapped in a situation that required such a seemingly no-win decision. But I do know that anyone wanting to recover from psychological trauma must face just this kind of dilemma, made yet more harrowing because her circumstance is not anything so rescuable as being locked in a house, but rather involves a solitary, unlockable confinement inside the limits of her own mind. The person who suffers from a severe trauma disorder must decide between surviving in a barely sublethal misery of numbness and frustration, and taking a chance that may well bring her a better life, but that feels like stupidly issuing an open invitation to the unspeakable horror that waits to consume her alive. And in the manner of the true hero, she must choose to take the risk.

For trauma changes the brain itself. Like the outdated fuse box, the psychologically traumatized brain houses inscrutable eccentricities that cause it to overreact—or more precisely, *mis*react—to the current realities of life. These neurological misreactions become established because trauma has a profound effect upon the secretion of stress-responsive neurohormones such as norepinephrine, and thus an effect upon various areas of the brain involved in memory, particularly the amygdala and the hippocampus.

The amygdala receives sensory information from the five senses, via the thalamus, attaches emotional significance to the input, and then passes along this emotional "evaluation" to the hippocampus. In accordance with the amygdala's "evaluation" of importance, the hippocampus is activated to a greater or lesser degree, and functions to organize the new input, and to integrate it with already existing information about similar sensory events. Under a normal range of conditions, this system works efficiently to consolidate memories according to their emotional priority. However, at the extreme upper end of hormonal stimulation, as in traumatic situations, a breakdown occurs. Overwhelming emotional significance registered by the amygdala actually leads to a *decrease in hippocampal activation,* such that some of the traumatic input is not usefully organized by the hippocampus, or integrated with other memories. The result is that portions of traumatic memory are stored not as parts of a unified whole, but as isolated sensory images and bodily sensations that are not localized in time or even in situation, or integrated with other events.

To make matters still more complex, exposure to trauma may temporarily shut down Broca's area, the region of the left hemisphere of the brain that translates experience into language, the means by which we most often relate our experience to others, and even to ourselves.

A growing body of research indicates that in these ways the brain lays down traumatic memories differently from the way it records regular memories. Regular memories are formed through adequate hippocampal and cortical input, are integrated as comprehensible wholes, and are subject to meaning-modification by future events, and through language. In contrast, traumatic memories include chaotic fragments that are sealed off from modulation by subsequent experience. Such memory fragments are wordless, placeless, and eternal, and long after the original trauma has receded into the past, the brain's record of it may consist only of isolated and thoroughly anonymous bits of emotion, image, and sensation that ring through the individual like a broken alarm.

Worse yet, later in the individual's life, in situations that are vaguely similar to the trauma—perhaps merely because they are startling, anxiety-provoking, or emotionally arousing—amygdala-mediated memory traces are accessed more readily than are the more complete, less shrill memories that have been integrated and modified by the hippocampus and the cerebral cortex. Even though unified and updated memories would be more judicious in the present, the amygdala memories are more accessible, and so trauma may be "remembered" at inappropriate times, when there is no hazard worthy of such alarm. In reaction to relatively trivial stresses, the person traumatized long ago may truly *feel* that danger is imminent again, be assailed full-force by the emotions, bodily sensations, and perhaps even the images, sounds, smells that once accompanied great threat.

Here is an illustration from everyday life. A woman named Beverly reads a morning newspaper while she sits at a quiet suburban depot and waits for a train. The article, concerning an outrageous local scandal, intrigues her so much that for a few minutes she forgets where she is. Suddenly, there is an earsplitting blast from the train as it signals its arrival. Beverly is painfully startled by the noise; her head snaps up, and she catches her breath. She is amazed that she could have been so lacking in vigilance and relaxed in public. Her heart pounds, and in the instant required to fold the newspaper, she is ambushed by bodily feelings and even a smell that have nothing whatever to do with the depot on this uneventful morning. If she could identify the smell, which she never will, she would call it "chlorine." She feels a sudden rigidity in her chest, as if her lungs had just turned to stone, and has an almost overpowering impulse to get out of there, to run.

In a heartbeat, the present is perceptually and emotionally the past. These fragments of sensation and emotion are the amygdala-mediated memories of an afternoon three decades before, in Beverly's tenth summer, when, walking home from the public swimming pool, she saw her younger sister skip into the street and meet an immediate death in front of a speeding car. At this moment, thirty years later, Beverly *feels* that way again.

Her sensations and feelings are not labeled as belonging to memories of the horrible accident. In fact, they are not labeled as anything at all, because they have always been completely without language. They belong to no narrative, no place or time, no story she can tell about her life; they are free-form and ineffable.

Beverly's brain contains, effectively, a broken warning device in its limbic system, an old fuse box in which the fuses tend to melt for no good reason, emphatically declaring an emergency where none now exists.

Surprisingly, she will probably not wonder about or even remember the intense perceptual and emotional "warnings," because by the next heartbeat, a long-entrenched dissociative reaction to the declared emergency may already have been tripped in her brain, to "protect" her from this "unbearable" childhood memory. She may feel strangely angry, or paranoid, or childishly timid. Or instead she may feel that she has begun to move in an uncomfortably hazy dream world, far away and derealized. Or she may completely depart from her "self" for a while, continue to act, but without self-awareness. Should this last occur in a minor way, her total experience may be something such as, "Today when I was going to work, the train pulled into the station—the blasted thing is so loud!—and the next thing I remember, it was stopping at my stop." She may even be mildly amused at herself for her spaciness.

Most of us do not notice these experiences very much. They are more or less invisible to us as we go about daily life, and so we do not understand how much of daily life is effectively spent in the past, in reaction to the darkest hours we have known, nor do we comprehend how swampy and vitality-sucking some of our memories really are. Deepening the mire of our divided awareness, in the course of a lifetime such "protective" mental reactions acquire tremendous *habit strength*. These over-exercised muscles can take us away even when traumatic memory fragments have not been evoked. Sometimes dissociation can occur when we are simply confused or frustrated or nervous, whether we recognize our absences or not.

Typically, only those with the most desperate trauma histories are ever driven to discover and perhaps modify their absences from the present. Only the addictions, major depressions, suicide attempts, and general ruination that attend the most severe trauma disorders can sometimes supply motivation sufficiently fierce to run the gauntlet thrown down by insight and permanent change. On account of our neurological wiring, confronting past traumas requires one to re-endure all of their terrors mentally, in their original intensity, to feel as if the worst nightmare had come true and the horrors had returned. All the brain's authoritative warnings against staying present for the memories and the painful emotions, all the faulty fuses, have to be deliberately ignored, and in cases of extreme or chronic past trauma, this process is nothing short of heroic.

It helps to have an awfully good reason to try, such as suffocating depression or some other demonic psychological torment. Perhaps this is a part of the reason why philosophers and theologians through the centuries have observed such a strong connection between unbearable earthly sorrow and spiritual enlightenment, a timeless relationship that psychologists have mysteriously overlooked.

In order to appreciate what psychological trauma can do to the mind, and to a life, let us consider an extreme case of divided awareness, that of a woman whose psyche was mangled by profound trauma in her past, and who came to me for treatment after several serious suicide attempts. Her story is far grimmer than most of us will ever know, and the consequent suffering in her adult life has been nearly unsurvivable. And yet, should one meet her on the street, or know her only casually, she would seem quite normal. In fact, one might easily view her as enviable. Certainly, when looking on from a distance, nothing at all would appear to be wrong, and much would be conspicuously right.

Julia is brilliant. After the *summa cum laude* from Stanford, and the full scholarship at the graduate school in New York, she became an award-winning producer of documentary films. I met her when she was thirty-two, and an intellectual force to be reckoned with. A conversation with her reminds me of the *New York Review of Books*, except that she is funnier, and also a living, breathing human being who wears amethyst jewelry to contrast with her electric auburn hair. Her ultramarine eyes gleam, even when she is depressed, giving one the impression, immediately upon meeting her, that there is something special about her. She is, however, soft-spoken and disarming in the extreme. She does not glorify, does not even seem to notice, either her prodigious intelligence or her beauty.

Those same blue eyes notice everything, instantly, photographically. The first time she walked into my office, she said, "Oh how nice. Did you get that little statue in Haiti? I did a kind of project there once. What a spellbinding place!"

She was referring to a small soapstone figurine, the rounded abstraction of a kneeling man, that I had indeed purchased in Port-au-Prince, and that sat on a shelf parallel to my office door. She had not glanced back in that direction as she came in, and must have captured and processed the image in a microsecond of peripheral perception.

"That's very observant," I said, whereupon she directed at me a smile so sparkling and so warm that, for just the barest moment, her lifelong depression cracked and vanished from the air around her, as if it had been nothing but a bubble. The radiance of her momentary smile caused me to blink, and I knew exactly then, even before the first session began, that if she would let me, I would do everything I could to keep this particular light from going out.

At a moment's notice, Julia can speak entertainingly and at length about film, music, multicultural psychology, African politics, theories of literary criticism, and any number of other subjects. Her memory for detail is beyond exceptional, and she has the storyteller's gift. When she is recounting information, or a story, her own intellectual fascination with it gives her voice the poised and expertly modulated quality of the narrator of a high-budget documentary about some especially wondrous endangered animals, perhaps Tibetan snow leopards. She speaks a few astutely inflected sentences, and then pauses, almost as if she is listening—and expects you to be listening—for the stealthy *crunch-crunch* of paws on the snow's crust.

Curious about this, I once asked her whether she were an actress as well as a filmmaker. She laughed, and replied that she could do first-rate narrative voice-overs, if she did say so herself, but had not a smidgen of real theatrical ability. In fact, she said, sometimes the people she worked with teased her good-naturedly about this minor chink in her armor.

At my first session with her, when I asked her why she had come to therapy, she spent thirty minutes telling me in cinematic detail about her recent attempt to kill herself, by driving to an isolated Massachusetts beach at three A.M. on a Tuesday in late January, and lying down by the surf. By so doing, she sincerely expected not to be found until well after she had frozen to death. Taking her omniscient narrator tone, intellectually intrigued by the memory, she described the circumstances of her unlikely accidental rescue by a group of drunken college students, and then spent the second thirty minutes of our hour together likening this near-death experience to the strangely impersonal distance from a story one can achieve on film with certain authorial camera moves.

"By then, I was floating above myself, looking down, sort of waiting. And I know I couldn't actually have seen those kids, but I *felt* that I did. Over the sound of the waves, I don't think you can really *hear* footsteps in the sand, but still...."

And I strained to hear the *crunch-crunch*.

Therapy is a frightening thing, and people do not often seek it out because they are only mildly unhappy. In my work, and because of the high-risk individuals who are referred to me, it is not unusual for me to hear stories of attempted suicide from people I have only just met. I have come almost to expect such accounts, in fact.

At our second session, and in exactly the same tone she had used to describe her suicide attempt, Julia began by giving me an interesting account of her new project on the life of a promising writer who had died young, reportedly of a rare blood disease he had contracted in western China. After about fifteen minutes of this, I stopped her, and explained that I wanted to know something about her, about Julia herself, rather than about Julia's work. Seeing the blank expression come over her face, I tried to provide her with some nonthreatening guidance. I asked her some general, factual questions about her childhood.

And at that second session, this is what the articulate, intellectually gifted Julia remembered about her own childhood: An only child, she knew that she had been born in Los Angeles, but she did not know in which hospital. She vaguely remembered that when she was about ten, her parents had moved with her to another neighborhood; but she did not remember anything about the first neighborhood, or even where it was. Though she did not know for sure, she assumed that the move must have taken place because her parents had become more prosperous. She remembered that she had a friend in high school named Barbara (with whom "I must have spent a lot of time"), but she could not remember Barbara's last name, or where Barbara had gone after high school. I asked Julia about her teachers, and she could not remember a single one of them, not from grade school, not from middle school, not from high school. She could not remember whether or not she had gone to her high school prom or her high school graduation. The only thing she seemed to remember vividly from childhood was that when she was about twelve, she had a little terrier dog named Grin, and that her mother had Grin put to sleep when he needed an expensive stomach operation.

And that was all she remembered of her childhood, this successful thirty-two-year-old woman with the cinematic mind. And it took forty-five minutes for her to pull out that much from the dark, silent place that housed her early memories. She could not remember a single holiday or a single birthday. At thirty-two, she could swim, read, drive a car, and play a few songs on the piano. But she could not remember learning any of these skills.

Insufficient memory in the context of an adequate intellect, let alone a gifted one, is the next observation—right after the extraordinary understatement and humor—that causes me to become suspicious about a patient's past.

At our third session, she asked me an astonishing question, but also, really, the obvious question: "Do other people remember those things, about their teachers, and going to their graduation, and learning to drive, and so on?" When I told her that, yes, they usually do remember, at least to a much greater degree than she did, she reverently said, "Wow," and then she was quiet for a few minutes. Finally, she leaned forward a little and asked, "So what's wrong with me?"

Cautiously, because I knew what I had to say might at first sound preposterous or worse to Julia, I said, "I'm wondering about early traumatic experiences in your life. Even when someone's cognitive memory is perfectly good, as yours is, trauma can disrupt the memory in emotional ways."

Julia thought I was way off base; or at least the part of her that collected amethyst jewelry, made award-winning films, and talked about camera angles thought I was way off base. Another part of Julia, the part that kept trying to commit suicide, the part that prevented her from moving back to Los Angeles as her career demanded, the part that sometimes made her so sleepy during the middle of an ordinary day that she had to be driven home, that part kept her coming back to therapy for the next six years. During those six years, step by step, Julia and I cast some light on what had happened to her. She agreed to be hypnotized; she began to remember her dreams; she acknowledged her faint suspicions. She even traveled back to Los Angeles, to talk with distant relatives and old neighbors.

What we eventually discovered was that, when she was a child, Julia had lived in a house of horrors, with monsters jumping out at her without warning and for no apparent reason, except that Julia had come to assume, as abused children do, that she must be a horrible person who deserved these punishments. By the time she was school age, she had learned not to cry, because tears only encouraged her parents to abuse her further. Also, she had lost any inclination whatsoever to let anyone know what was going on. Telling someone and asking for help were concepts foreign to her despairing little soul. The thought that her life might be different had simply stopped occurring to her.

And soon, in a sense, she had stopped telling even herself. When the abuse began, she would "go somewhere else"; she would "not be there." By this, she meant that her mind had learned how to dissociate Julia's self from what was going on around her, how to transport her awareness to a place far enough away that, at most, she felt she was watching the life of a little girl named Julia from a very great distance. A sad little girl named Julia was helpless and could not escape; but psychologically, Julia's self could go "somewhere else," could be psychologically absent.

Simply put, Julia did not remember her childhood because she was not present for it.

All human beings have the capacity to dissociate psychologically, though most of us are unaware of this, and consider "out-of-body" episodes to be far beyond the boundaries of our normal experience. In fact, dissociative experiences happen to everyone, and most of these events are quite ordinary.

Consider a perfectly ordinary person as he walks into a perfectly ordinary movie theater to see a popular movie. He is awake, alert, and oriented to his surroundings. He is aware that his wife is with him and that, as they sit down in their aisle seats, she is to his right. He is aware that he has a box of popcorn on his lap. He knows that the movie he has come to see is entitled *The Fugitive*, and that its star is Harrison Ford, an actor. As he waits for the movie to begin, perhaps he worries about a problem he is having at work.

Then the lights in the theater are lowered, and the movie starts. And within twenty-five minutes, he has utterly lost his grasp on reality. Not only is he no longer worried about work, he no longer realizes that he has a job. If one could read his thoughts, one would discover that he no longer believes he is sitting in a theater, though in reality, he is. He cannot smell his popcorn; some of it tumbles out of the box he now holds slightly askew, because he has forgotten about his own hands. His wife has vanished, though any observer would see that she is still seated four inches to his right.

And without moving from his own seat, he is running, running, running—not with Harrison Ford, the actor—but with the beleaguered fugitive in the movie, with, in other words, a person who does not exist at all, in this movie-goer's real world or anyone else's. His heart races as he dodges a runaway train that does not exist, either.

This perfectly ordinary man is dissociated from reality. Effectively, he is in a trance. We might label his perceptions as psychotic, except for the fact that when the movie is over, he will return to his usual mental status almost instantly. He will see the credits. He will notice that he has spilled some popcorn, although he will not remember doing so. He will look to his right and speak to his wife. More than likely, he will tell her that he liked the movie, as we all tend to enjoy entertainments in which we can become lost. All that really happened is that, for a little while, he took the part of himself that worries about work problems and other "real" things, and separated it from the imaginative part of himself, so that the imaginative part could have dominance. He *dissociated* one part of his consciousness from another part.

When dissociation is illustrated in this way, most people can acknowledge that they have had such interludes from time to time, at a movie or a play, reading a book or hearing a speech, or even just daydreaming. And then the out-of-body may sound a little closer to home. Plainly stated, it is the case that under certain circumstances, ranging from pleasant or unpleasant distraction to fascination to fear to pain to horror, a human being can be psychologically absent from his or her own direct experience. We can go somewhere else. The part of consciousness that we nearly always conceive of as the "self" can be not there for a few moments, for a few hours, and in heinous circumstances, for much longer.

As the result of a daydream, this mental compartmentalization is called distraction. As the result of an involving movie, it is often called escape. As the result of trauma, physical or psychological, it is called a dissociative state. When a hypnotist induces dissociation, by monotony, distraction, relaxation, or any number of other methods, the temporary result is called an hypnotic state, or a trance. The physiological patterns and the primary behavioral results of distraction, escape, dissociative state, and trance are virtually identical, regardless of method. The differences among them seem to result not so much from how consciousness gets divided as from how often and how long one is forced to keep it divided.

Another recognizable example of how consciousness can be split into pieces has to do with the perception of physical pain. On the morning after seeing *The Fugitive*, our moviegoer's wife is working frenetically to pack her briefcase, eat her breakfast, get the kids off to school, and listen to a news report on television, all at the same time. She is very distracted. In the process of all this, she bashes her leg soundly against the corner of a low shelf. Yet the woman is not seemingly aware that she has injured herself. That night, as she is getting ready for bed, she notices that she has a large colorful bruise on her right thigh. She thinks, "Well, now, I wonder how I did that."

In this case, a person was distracted, and the part of her consciousness that would normally have perceived pain was split apart from, and subjugated to, the part of her consciousness that was goal-directed. She was not there for the direct experience of her pain. She was somewhere else (the briefcase, the breakfast, the kids, the news). And because she was not there, she does not remember the accident.

The direct experience of physical pain can be split off in cases of much more serious injury as well. Most of us have heard stories along the lines of the parent who, with a broken leg, goes back to the scene of an accident and wrenches open a mangled car door with her bare hands in order to rescue her child. Less valorous, I myself remember my car being demolished by a speeding limousine. My knee was injured, but I felt no pain just after the crash, was more or less unaware of my body at all. My first thought before being dragged out of my car was to peer into the rearview mirror and inspect my teeth, and to decide that everything must be okay because there were no chips in them. And then there are the war stories about maimed infantrymen who have had to flee from the front line. All such circumstances affect memory in fascinating ways. Note, for example, that when veterans get together, they often laugh and tell war stories as though those times had been the best of their lives.

Agony that is psychological can be dissociated, too. While she was being abused, Julia developed the reaction of standing apart from herself and her situation. She stopped being there. Certainly, some parts of her consciousness must have been there right along. She could watch her parents, even predict their moods. She could run and hide. She could cover her injuries. She could keep her parents' secrets. But the part of her consciousness that she thinks of as her self was not there; it was split off, put aside, and therefore in some sense protected. And because her self had not been there, her self could not remember what had happened to her during much of her childhood.

What does this feel like, not being able to remember whole chapters of one's own life? I have asked many people this question, Julia among them. As usual, her answer was obvious and startling at the same time.

"It doesn't feel like anything," she answered. "I never really thought about it. I guess I just assumed, sort of tacitly assumed, that everyone's memory was like mine, that is to say, kind of blank before the age of twenty or so. I mean, you can't see into someone else's mind, right? All you can do is ask questions, and it never even occurred to me to ask anybody about this. It's like asking, 'What do you see when you see blue?' First of all, you'd never think to ask. And secondly, two people can agree that the clear blue sky is blue, but does the actual color blue look the *same* to both of them? Who knows? How would you even ask that question?

"Of course, every now and then I'd hear people talking about pin-the-tail-on-the-donkey, or some other thing about a little kid's birthday, and I'd wonder how they knew that. But I guess I just figured their memory was especially good, or maybe they'd heard their parents talk about it so much that it seemed like a memory.

"The memories I did have seemed like aberrations, like pinpoints of light in a dark room, so vague that you're not really sure whether you're seeing them or not. Certainly, there was nothing like a continuous thread of memory that linked one part of my life to another.

"Really it wasn't until you started asking me questions about my teachers and so forth that I ever even had any serious questions about my memory. After you started asking, I asked a couple of other people, just out of curiosity, and I began to realize that other people really do have childhood memories, and some of them are pretty vivid. I was surprised.

"What can I tell you? It just never occurred to me to wonder about it before. It felt like ... it felt like nothing."

She shrugged. Most people shrug. They are genuinely surprised, and at a loss.

Now the conspicuous question to ask Julia was, "All this time that you've been so unhappy, all the times you've tried to end your life, what did you think was causing all that misery?"

"I thought I was crazy," she answered.

This is easy enough to understand. Imagine a simple and, relatively speaking, innocuous example. Imagine that someone, call her Alice, leaves work early one day and goes to the oral surgeon to have her two bottom wisdom teeth extracted. The extractions go well; the doctor packs the gums with cotton and sends Alice home. On the way home, for some fictitious reason, let us say magic moonbeams, Alice completely loses her memory of the visit to the oral surgeon. She now assumes that she is driving directly home from work, as she does on most days. After she gets home, she is okay for a while, but gradually the anesthetic wears off, and she begins to experience a considerable amount of pain in her mouth. Soon the pain is too strong to ignore, and she goes to the bathroom mirror to examine the situation. When she looks into her mouth, she discovers that there are wads of cotton in there. And when she takes the cotton out, she discovers that two of her teeth are missing, and she is bleeding!

Alice is now in the twilight zone. The ordinary experience of having her wisdom teeth pulled has turned into a situation that makes her feel insane. One or two more of such experiences, and she would be convinced.

Childhood trauma creates a particularly bewildering picture. Observe normal children at play, and you will realize that children are especially good at dissociating. In the interest of play, a child can, in a heartbeat, leave himself behind, become someone or something else, or several things at once. Reality is even more plastic in childhood. Pretend games are real and wonderful and consuming. It is clear to anyone who really looks that normal children derive unending joy from their superior ability to leap out of their "selves" and go somewhere else, be other things. The snow is not cold. The body is not tired, even when it is on the verge of collapse.

Because children dissociate readily even in ordinary circumstances, when they encounter traumatic situations, they easily split their consciousness into pieces, often for extended periods of time. The self is put aside and hidden. Of course, this reaction is functional for the traumatized child, necessary, even kind. For the traumatized child, a dissociative state, far from being dysfunctional or crazy, may in fact be lifesaving. And thanks be to the normal human mind that it provides the means.

This coping strategy becomes dysfunctional only later, after the child is grown and away from the original trauma. When the original trauma is no longer an ongoing fact of life, prolonged dissociative reactions are no longer necessary. But through the years of intensive use, the self-protective strategy has developed a hair trigger. The adult whom the child has become now experiences dissociative reactions to levels of stress that probably would not cause another person to dissociate.

The events that are most problematic tend to be related in some way to the original trauma. However, human beings are exquisitely symbolic creatures, and "related" can reach unpredictable and often indecipherable levels of abstraction and metaphor. A long shadow from a city streetlight can remind someone of the tall cacti on the Arizona desert where his father used to threaten to "feed" him to the rattlesnakes. An innocent song about the wind in the willow trees can remind someone else of the rice fields that were a part of her childhood's landscape in Cambodia. A car backfiring on Beacon Street in Boston can remind yet another person of that spot on the trail where his eighteen-year-old platoon mate exploded six feet in front of him.

And so for the adult who was traumatized as a child, the present too has a kind of mercurial quality. The present is difficult to hold on to, always getting away.

In Julia's case, though she had not questioned her poverty of memory for the past, she had begun to suspect even before she came into therapy that she was losing time in the present. Probably this is because there are more external reality checks on the present than there are on the past. From other people—and from radio, television, the Internet, date books—there are ongoing reminders of the present time of day, and day of the week. Markers of time in the past are less immediate, and sooner or later most dates and chronologies for the past begin to feel amorphous to us all. It is hardly amazing that one should have forgotten something that happened twenty years ago. But if a person lets on that she has no memory of an important event that occurred this very week, friends and associates are unlikely to let such a lapse go unremarked.

At one of her early sessions with me, Julia announced, "When I woke up Tuesday morning it was Friday."

"Pardon?"

"When I woke up this morning it was Tuesday, and then I discovered that it was Friday for everybody else."

"How do you mean?"

"Well, the last thing I remember before waking up this morning was having dinner Monday night. So I thought it was Tuesday. And then I went in to work, and some sponsors were there that I was supposed to meet with on Friday. So I asked my assistant what was up, and she said, 'You wanted to meet with these people this morning, remember?' And I said, 'No. I wanted to meet with them on Friday.' She looked at me, and said, 'Today is Friday, Julia.'

"I finessed. I laughed and said, 'Of course. That's terrible. No more late nights for me. Pretty soon I'll be forgetting my name. Ha, ha.' But it isn't funny. This happens a lot. I just lose time. Hours, days. They're gone, and I don't know what I've done or where I've been or anything else.

"I've never told anyone this before. It's embarrassing. Actually, it's terrifying.

"I don't understand any of it, but the thing I understand the least is that apparently I go about my business during these times, and nobody notices any difference in me. At least, no one ever says anything. After the meeting this morning, I realized that on Tuesday, Wednesday, and Thursday, I must have done a mountain of editing. There it was, all finished. I did a good job, even. And I don't remember a bloody thing."

During this confession, I saw Julia cry for the first time. Quickly, though, she willed her tears under control, and wanted me to tell her about a word she had heard me use the previous week, "dissociative." She questioned me as if the issue were a strictly academic one for her, which it clearly was not. I gently steered her back to the subject of herself and her week.

"Where did you have dinner Monday night?"

"What? Oh. Dinner Monday night. I had dinner at the Grill 23 with my friend Elaine."

"Was it a nice time?" I continued to question.

"I think so. Yes, I think it was okay."

"What did you and Elaine talk about, do you remember?"

"What did we talk about? Let's see. Well, I think we talked about the film a bit. And we talked about the waiter. Very cute waiter." She grinned. "And we probably spent the longest time talking about Elaine's relationship with this new guy, Peter. Why do you ask?"

"You said the dinner was the last thing you remembered before you woke up this morning. I thought it might be important. What did Elaine say about Peter?"

"Well, she said she's madly in love, and she said she wanted me to meet him because she thought we'd have a lot to talk about. He's from L.A., too."

"You and Peter are both from L.A. What else did you and Elaine say about L.A.?"

Julia looked suddenly blank, and said, "I don't remember. Why? Do you really think something about the place where I grew up scares me enough that just talking about it blasts me into never-never land for three days? That really can't be, though. I mean, I talk about L.A. a lot to people."

"I think it's possible that something during the dinner scared you enough to make you lose yourself for a while, although we'll never know for sure. Obviously, talking about L.A. doesn't always do that, but maybe there was something in that particular conversation that reminded you of something else that triggered something in your mind, something that might seem innocuous to another person, or even to you at another time. But as I say, we'll never know for sure."

"That's frightening. That's awful. It's like I'm in jail in my own head. I don't think I can live this way anymore."

"Yes, it's very frightening. I suspect it's been very frightening for a long time."

"You got that right."

Julia's knowledge of her own life, both past and present, had assumed the airy structure of Swiss cheese, with some solid substance that she and her gifted intellect could use, but riddled with unexplained gaps and hollows. This had its funny side. A few months later, when she had gained a better acceptance of her problem, she came in, sat down, and said in a characteristically charming way, "How do you like my new bracelet?"

"It's beautiful," I replied. "I've always admired your amethyst jewelry. When did you get that piece?"

"Who knows?"

She grinned at me again, and we both laughed.

The somewhat old-fashioned term for Julia's departures from herself during which she would continue to carry out day-to-day activities is "fugue," from the Italian word *fuga,* meaning "flight." A dissociative state that reaches the point of fugue is one of the most dramatic spontaneously occurring examples of the human mind's ability to divide consciousness into parts. In fugue, the person, or the mind of the person, can be subdivided in a manner that allows certain intellectually driven functions to continue—rising at a certain time, conversing with others, following a schedule, even carrying out complex tasks—while the part of consciousness that we usually experience as the "self"—the self-aware center that wishes, dreams, plans, emotes, and remembers—has taken flight, or has perhaps just darkened like a room at night when someone is sleeping.

The departures of fugue are related to certain experiences in ordinary human life that are not generated by trauma. For example, similar is the common experience of the daily commuter by car who realizes that sometimes she or he arrives back at home in the evening without having been aware of the activities of driving. The driving was automatically carried out by some part of the mind, while the self part of the mind was worrying, daydreaming, or listening to the radio. The experience is that of arriving at home without remembering the process of the trip. If one reflects upon the minute and complex decisions and maneuvers involved in driving a car, this ordinary event is really quite remarkable.

Clinical fugue differs from common human experience not so much in kind as in degree. Fugue is terror-driven and complete, while the more recognizable condition is the result of distraction, and relatively transparent. As fugue, the car trip example would involve a driver who failed to remember not just the process of the trip, but also the fact that there had been a trip, and from where.

Far beyond distraction, the more remarkable dissociative reaction of fugue would have been set off by something—an event, a conversation, an image, a thought—that was related, though perhaps in some oblique and symbolic way, to trauma.

Not all traumatized individuals exhibit outright fugue. For some people, stressful events trigger a demifugue that is less dramatic but in some ways more agonizing. Another of my patients, Lila, refers to her experience as "my flyaway self":

"I had an argument with the cashier at the Seven-Eleven store. I gave him a twenty and he said I gave him a ten. He wouldn't give me my other ten dollars back. The way he looked at me—it was just the way my stepfather used to, like I was stupid, like I was dirt. I knew he wasn't really my stepfather, but all the feelings were there anyway. After a minute, I just couldn't argue about it. I left without my money, and by the time I got back home, my flyaway self thing had started. Once it starts, it's like there's absolutely nothing I can do about it. I'm gone, and there's nothing I can do about it."

"What does it feel like?"

"Oh boy. I don't know how to describe it. It's just ... it's just really awful. I don't know ... everything around me gets very small, kind of unreal, you know? It's my flyaway self, I call it. It feels like ... my spirit just kind of flies away, and everything else gets very small—people, everything. If it were happening now, for example, you would look very small and far away, and the room would feel kind of unreal. Sometimes even my own body gets small and unreal. It's awful. And when it happens, I can't stop it. I just can't stop it."

What Lila describes as her "flyaway self" is in some respects similar to the derealization that most people have known occasionally, usually under passing conditions of sleep deprivation or physical illness. One temporarily has the sense of looking at the world through the wrong end of a telescope: everything looks small and far away, though one knows intellectually that these same things are just as close and life-sized as ever.

Imagine being forced to live lengthy segments of your life in this state. Imagine that you were falling inexorably into it, to remain there for a week or more at a time, because of events such as an unpleasant argument with a stranger at a convenience store. As bad as this would be, the situation for someone like Lila is incalculably worse, because for her the phenomenon has its origins in trauma.

Another of my patients offered a specific image, and for me an indelible one, to describe the same dissociative condition. Forty-nine-year-old Seth, like Julia, is successful, educated, and visually talented, and his disquieting description reflects his aptitudes. At the beginning of this particular therapy session, he had been telling me about a startling encounter, at a company softball game, with another person lost in the dissociated space with which he himself was all too familiar.

"I knew exactly where she was," said Seth.

"What does it feel like?" I asked. "Can you tell me what it feels like when you're there? How do you change?"

"I don't change. It's not that I change. *Reality* changes. Everything becomes very small, and I exist entirely inside my mind. Even my own body isn't real."

Indicating the two of us and the room around us, he continued, "Right now, this is what's real. You're real. What we're saying is real. But when I'm like that, the office is not real. *You're* not real anymore."

"What is real at those times?" I asked.

"I don't know exactly. It's hard to explain. Only what's going on in my mind is real. I'll tell you what it feels like: I feel like I'm dog-paddling out in the ocean, moving backwards, out to sea. When I'm still close enough to the land, I can sort of look way far away and see the beach. You and the rest of the world are all on the beach somewhere. But I keep drifting backwards, and the beach gets smaller, and the ocean gets bigger and bigger, and when I've drifted out far enough, the beach disappears, and all I can see all around me is the sea. It's so gray—gray on gray on gray."

"Is there anything out in the ocean with you?" I asked.

Seth replied, "No. Not at that point. I'm completely alone, more alone than you can imagine. But if you drift out farther, if you go all the way out to where the bottom of the sea drops off to the real abyss part, then there are awful things, these bloodthirsty sea creatures, sharks and giant eels and things like that. I've always thought that if something in the real world scared me enough, I'd drift out and out to past the dropping-off part, and then I would just be gobbled up, gone—no coming back, ever.

"When I'm floating out in the middle of the sea, everything else is very far away, even time. Time becomes unreal, in a way. An hour could go by that seems like a day to me, or four or five hours could go by, and it seems like only a minute."

Some extreme trauma survivors recognize that they are dissociative, and others do not recognize this. Many times, an individual will realize at some point in adulthood that she or he has had a lifelong pattern of being "away" a grievously large portion of the time.

During the same session, Seth described his own situation in this way:

"Actually, when I was a child, I don't know how much time I spent away like that. I never thought about it. It was probably a lot of the time, maybe even all the time. It just *was*."

"You mean it was your reality, and so of course you never questioned it, any more than any other child questions his reality?"

"Right. That's right. That was when I was a child. And most of the time it still happens automatically, bang, way before I know it's coming; but in here now, sometimes, there's this brief moment when I know I'm about to go away, but I still have time to try to keep it from taking over. Emphasis on *try*."

"How do you do that?" I asked.

"By concentrating. By trying with everything I've got to concentrate on you, and what you're saying, and on the things around me in the office here. But then there's physical pain, too. My eyes hurt, and I know I could make myself feel better if I shut them. But I try not to. And I get this thing in my stomach, which is the hardest thing to fight. There's this pain that feels like

I just swallowed a whole pile of burning coals, this torture feeling that beams out from my stomach to the rest of my body; sooner or later, it just takes me over."

He grimaced and put a fist to his breastbone.

When Seth said this about pain in his stomach, I remembered, as I had remembered during descriptions by many, many others, that there is a common Japanese term, *shin pan*, inexactly translated as "agitated heart syndrome," referring to a great pain between the chest and the stomach, just under the solar plexus. *Shin pan*, a condition as real within Eastern medicine as is cataract or ulcer or fractured fibula within Western medicine, is a pain of the heart that does not involve the actual physical organ. In our culture, we consider such a thing—a "heartache," if you will—to be poetry at most. We do not understand that much of the rest of the world considers it to be quite real.

I said to Seth, "It must be frightening to be out in the ocean like that."

"Actually, it's not," he replied. "The abyss part, with the sharks and all, that's frightening. But for most of my life it was really no more frightening than the things that were on the beach, no more frightening than reality, I guess is what I'm saying. So floating in the middle of the ocean was really the best place, even though I guess that sounds strange. Also, being there takes care of the physical pain; there's no more pain when I'm there. It's just that now, I mean lately, the beach, where you are, and everything else, sometimes it makes me wish I could maybe be there instead. I guess you could say that now, at least sometimes, I want to live."

I smiled at him, but he looked away, unsure of what he had just proposed.

Referring back to Seth's softball team acquaintance, whose dissociative episode had begun our discussion, I said, "It must be strange to be with another person when you know she's drifting away in an ocean just like you do sometimes."

"Yes, it's very strange."

"How did you know she was drifting? Did she tell you?"

"No. She didn't tell me. She didn't say anything at all about being dissociated. She was just standing around with us, talking about these incredible things, horrible things from her past, without any emotion, without any reaction to them. She played well that day, actually, but she won't remember any of it, that's for sure."

"You mean," I asked, "another person, besides you, might not have known she was dissociated?"

"Absolutely. I'm sure someone else might not have known at all. It's just that I looked at her, and I saw me. It was like talking to somebody who didn't have a soul."

"You mean her soul was somewhere else?"

"Yes, I guess so. Her soul was somewhere else," Seth said.

After a brief silence, he turned the discussion back to his own life: "The other day, my wife was trying to talk to me about something really important that happened when the twins were born. Doesn't matter what it was; what matters is that I had no idea what she was talking about. I didn't have a clue. It wasn't a dim memory. It wasn't anything. I didn't have that memory because I wasn't there."

"You weren't there, but your wife didn't know that at the time?" I asked.

"No, she didn't know that at all. But you know, most of the time when she and I are making love, and I'm not there, she doesn't know it even then."

"You mean, someone can be that close to you, and still not know?"

"Yes."

At that moment I thought, and then decided to say aloud, "That's so sad."

A single tear skimmed down Seth's cheek. He wiped it quickly with the back of his hand, and said, "I'm sorry, it's just that, well, when I think about it, I realize that, really, I've missed most of my own life."

He stopped and took a deep breath, and I wondered whether he might have to dissociate just to get through this experience in my office.

I asked, "Are you here now, at this moment?"

"Yes, I think so. Yes."

There was another pause, and then with more emotion in his voice than he was usually able to show, he said, "It's so hard, because so much of the time when I'm here, what you're seeing is not what I'm seeing. I feel like such an impostor. I'm out in my ocean, and you don't know that. And I can't tell you what's going on. Sometimes I'd really like to tell you, but I can't. I'm gone."

Seth's description of his inner life makes it wrenchingly clear that the traumatized person is unable to feel completely connected to another person, even a friend, even a spouse. Just as limiting, perhaps even more limiting, is such a person's disconnection from his or her own body. You will recall that Lila's "flyaway self" owned a body that was only "small and unreal," and that when Seth was in his ocean, his mind was separated from his physical self. I began this chapter with Julia, the brilliant producer of documentary films, and as it happens, about a year into her treatment, an event occurred that well illustrates the survivor's trauma-generated dissociation from the body itself, or more accurately, from those aspects of mind that inform one of what is going on in the body.

One morning just after the workday began, Julia's assistant, a gentle young woman who was quite fond of her boss, noticed that Julia was looking extremely pale. She asked how Julia was feeling, and Julia replied that she thought her stomach was a little upset, but other than that she was sure she was fine. Ten minutes later, walking down a corridor, Julia fell to the floor, and by the time the panic-stricken assistant came to her aid, she was unconscious. An ambulance arrived and rushed Julia to the Massachusetts General Hospital, where she underwent an immediate emergency appendectomy. Her life was in danger, and the situation was touch-and-go for a while, because her infected appendix had already ruptured and severe peritonitis had resulted. She survived, however, and during her recovery, when she was well enough to see me again, she recounted a postsurgery conversation with her doctor.

"The doctor kept asking me, 'Didn't you feel anything? Weren't you in pain?' I told her my stomach had been upset that morning, but I didn't remember any real pain. She said, 'Why didn't you call me?' I guess she just couldn't believe that I really hadn't felt any pain. She said that I should have been in agony by the previous night, at the very latest. She kept saying 'agony.' But I didn't feel it. I swear to you I didn't feel any pain, much less agony."

"I believe you," I said to Julia.

"Well, I don't think she did. I guess a ruptured appendix involves a lot of pain for most people."

"Yes. Yes it does," I replied, trying to disguise some of my own astonishment.

"I know I've tried to kill myself intentionally, more than once, so maybe this sounds crazy—but I don't want to die one day just because I'm confused."

"What do you mean?" I asked.

"I don't want to die because I can't feel anything. I don't want to end up dead because I can't feel what's going on in my body, or because I can't tell the difference between that psychosomatic pain I'm always getting in my chest and some honest-to-God heart attack."

Julia said "psychosomatic," but I was thinking *shin pan*, again.

"You know how we talk about my tendency to be dissociative? Well do you think I dissociate from my body, too? Because if that's what I'm doing, then it's the illusion from hell. I mean, if it's supposed to save me, it's not working. In fact, it's going to kill me one day. And even if it doesn't kill me, what's the use of living if I can't feel anything? Why should I be alive when I lose big parts of my life? I mean, really, how can you care about anything if you can't even know the truth about yourself? If you keep losing yourself?"

I said, "I think that's one of the best questions I've ever heard."

"You do? You mean you agree with me about how I can't really care about living if I keep losing myself?"

"I said that's one of the best *questions*. I didn't say I knew the answer."

"Oh boy, you're cagey," she said, and grinned. "So okay, how do I find the answer?"

"Well you know, you could try to remember. We could try hypnosis, for one thing."

I believed that Julia might be ready to bring up the lights in the cold, dark house of her past.

"Yes, so you've said. And the idea scares the hell out of me." There was a substantial pause before she continued. "The idea scares the hell out of me, but I think I have to do it anyway."

"Why do you have to?"

"Because I want to know. Because I want to live."

"So, let's do it?" I asked.

"Let's do it," Julia said.

QUESTIONS FOR MAKING CONNECTIONS
WITHIN THE READING

1. Drawing on the information Stout provides, discuss the relations between the mind—in particular the memory—and the brain. Why are traumatic memories generally inaccessible? When Stout refers to "our divided

awareness," what does she mean? Is it possible for awareness to become undivided? If such a state can be achieved at all, can it ever become permanent, or is "dividedness" an inescapable feature of consciousness itself?

2. Explain the difference between dissociation and ordinary distraction. What is it about Julia's lapses of memory that qualifies them as examples of dissociation? Are there significant differences between Julia's lapses and Seth's? Has Seth devised ways of coping that have proven more successful than Julia's?

3. In her discussion of Seth, Stout makes a reference to the condition known as *shin pan*, a term taken from Asian medicine. Does this reference bring something new to our understanding that the term *heartache* does not? Is Stout just showing off her knowledge of Eastern culture, or is she trying to get us to rethink our own attitudes about the importance of emotions?

QUESTIONS FOR WRITING

1. The title of Stout's book is *The Myth of Sanity: Divided Consciousness and the Promise of Awareness.* Now that you have read one chapter from her book, why do you think she refers to sanity as a "myth"? What does she mean by "the promise of awareness"? How might "awareness" differ from "sanity"?

2. Julia and Seth both qualify as extreme cases of dissociation, but their experiences may also shed some light on ordinary consciousness. Taking Stout's essay as your starting point, and drawing also on your own experience, discuss the nature of consciousness. Does the mind operate like a camcorder, or is awareness more complex and less continuous than the images stored in a camcorder's memory?

3. Can we ever know reality—the world as it actually is—or are we trapped within our own mental worlds? If memory shapes our perceptions from moment to moment, then would you say that experience can ever teach us anything new? If memory is unreliable, then what are the implications for self-knowledge? Is the ancient adage "Know Thyself" actually an invitation to wishful thinking?

QUESTIONS FOR MAKING CONNECTIONS
BETWEEN READINGS

1. In "The Mega-Marketing of Depression in Japan," Ethan Watters makes the case for seeing depression as a cultural construct rather than an empirical fact. He does not deny the reality of depression as an experience, but he proposes that people in different cultures will understand the disorder differently. Dr. Laurence J. Kirmayer, an authority whom Watters quotes with approval, notes that "a Nigerian man might experience a culturally distinct form of

depression by describing it as a peppery sensation in his head. A rural Chinese farmer might speak only of shoulder or stomach aches. A man in India might talk of semen loss or a sinking heart or feeling hot." What might Watters say about Stout's account of dissociative disorders? What might Stout say about Watters' view? What conclusions can we draw from the fact that Julia, Seth, and others respond to trauma in similar ways? Does this similarity undermine Watters's argument about the role of culture?

2. In what ways does Oliver Sacks's discussion in *The Mind's Eye* confirm, complicate, or contradict Stout's claims about trauma and its consequences? Although Sacks is concerned with adaptations to blindness and not emotional trauma, both authors explore the ways the mind compensates for losses and injuries of one kind or another. Are Julia and Seth in some ways comparable to the blind men and women Sacks describes?

◆◆◆

ROBERT THURMAN

ROBERT THURMAN, ONE of the first Americans to be ordained as a Tibetan Buddhist monk, is often considered to be the most prominent and influential expert on Buddhism in the United States today. A scholar, translator, activist, and lecturer (as well as father of the actress Uma Thurman), Thurman began his explorations into Buddhism in his early twenties when he traveled to India on a "vision quest" and ended up becoming a student of the Dalai Lama. Upon returning to the United States, Thurman wanted to continue his studies and become an academic because, in his own words, "[t]he only lay institution in America comparable to monasticism is the university." Thurman is currently the Jey Tsong Khapa Professor of Indo-Tibetan Buddhist Studies at Columbia University and the president of Tibet House, a nonprofit organization dedicated to the study and preservation of Tibetan culture.

Infinite Life (2004), from which "Wisdom" is taken, is one in an impressive series of books that Thurman has written on Buddhism for a Western audience. Chief among his goals in this text is to guide laypeople into their first explorations of the Buddhist concept of selflessness. The ultimate goal of the lessons that Thurman offers his readers is to impart a deeper sense of interconnectedness, a process that is meant to reduce the negative feelings individuals hold about themselves and to increase the positive feelings they have for themselves and others. In doing so, Thurman seeks to show that the happiness America's founders guaranteed "should be ours and that there are methods for discovering which happiness is really reliable and satisfying, and then securing that in an enduring way without depriving others."

Thurman's more recent books are concerned with the relevance of Buddhism to contemporary world problems. He has argued, for example, that pre-invasion Tibet had advanced quite far beyond the militarism that still deforms social life in the modern world. "The fact that a majority of [the] country's single males [were] monks rather than soldiers" is a major lesson for us today. In *Why the Dalai Lama Matters* (2008), Thurman makes the case that the Dalai Lama plays a unique role in global culture precisely because he advocates a new ethics of altruism that can bridge cultural divides.

Wisdom

Preamble: Selflessness

At one point in the early 1970s, after I'd gotten my Ph.D. and started teaching Buddhism, I went back to visit my old teacher, the Mongolian lama Geshe Wangyal. We were working on a project to translate a Buddhist scientific text from the Tibetan. We were six or seven people gathered around a kitchen table, and Geshe-la began to talk about the inner science of Buddhist psychology, the Abhidharma. He was reading us a few verses about the insight of selflessness, the deep release of becoming unbound, when I began to feel a little dizzy, even nauseous. It was a funny feeling. It felt slightly like a vibration spinning in my head. The vibration came not from Geshe-la, but from this ancient tradition. It was as though my habitual mind couldn't quite find traction. I realized that if I fought it, the sensation would only get more nerve-wracking and I would only feel more nauseous. So I didn't fight it. Instead, I let go and relaxed, and soon I was able to orient myself in another way, away from my "self." I felt like I was slowly but surely loosening my self-centered perspective on life and the world. In a useful way, a strengthening way, I was beginning to experience the great Buddhist mystery that is the selflessness of subjects and objects.

The Buddha based his psychology on his discovery of actual and ultimate reality. This he called "selflessness" and "voidness," or "emptiness." Some people love these words from the moment they hear them, but others are frightened by them. People often ask me, "Why did Buddha have to be such a downer? Obviously nirvana is a happy, cheerful state. So why didn't he just call it 'bliss' or something? Why did he have to label the reality he discovered with negative words such as 'voidness,' 'emptiness,' and 'selflessness'?" When people respond negatively to these terms, it's often because they're worried that the words imply they are going to die, disappear, or go crazy in their attempts to seek enlightenment. And that's exactly why the Buddha called reality by those names. He did it on purpose, to liberate you! Why? Because the only thing that's frightened by the word "selflessness" is the artificially constructed, unreal, and unrealistic self. That self is only a pretend self, it lacks reality, it doesn't really exist. That pseudo-self seems to quiver and quake because the habit that makes it seem real wants to keep its hold on you. So if you're seeking happiness and freedom, then you should want to scare the heck out of your "self"—you want to scare it right out of your head!

Actually, *it* is constantly scaring the heck out of *you*. Your "self" is always busy terrorizing you. You have a terrorist in your own brain, coming out of your own instincts and culture, who is pestering you all the time. "Don't relax too much," it is saying, "you'll get stepped on. A bug will bite you. Someone will be nasty to you. You'll get passed by, abused, sick. Don't be honest. Pretend. Because if you're honest, they'll hurt you." And it's ordering you, "Be my slave. Do what I tell you to do. Keep me installed up here at this very superficial level of the brain where I sit in my weird Woody Allen–type cockpit. Because I'm in control." Your falsely perceived, fixated, domineering self is precisely what's getting between you and a fulfilling life.

Early on, some of the Western psychologists who were beginning to learn from the Buddhist tradition—members of the transpersonal and other movements—came up with the idea that the relationship between Buddhist and Western psychology is this: "Western psychology helps somebody who feels they are nobody become somebody, and Buddhist psychology helps somebody who feels they are somebody become nobody." When I first heard this, I was at an Inner Science conference with the Dalai Lama. Everybody laughed, applauded, and thought it was a great insight. The Dalai Lama just looked at me and kind of winked and was too polite to say anything. I started to jump up to make a comment, but he stopped me. He told me to be quiet and let all of them ponder it for a few years until they realized the flaw in their thinking. Because of course that idea is not even remotely correct.

The purpose of realizing your own selflessness is not to feel like you are nobody. After he became enlightened, the Buddha did not sit under a tree drooling and saying, "Oh, wow! I'm nobody!" Think about it: If he just "became nobody," if he escaped from the world through self-obliteration, then he wouldn't have been able to share so many teachings here on earth, to work for the good of all beings for years and years, long after he achieved nirvana. He would've just stayed in his "nobody" state and forgotten about all of us poor humans busy suffering through our miserable lives.

The reason why we sometimes think that the goal of Buddhism is just "to become nobody" is that we don't understand the concept of selflessness. "Selflessness" does not mean that we are nobody. It does not mean that we cease to exist. Not at all. There is no way you can ever "not exist," just as you cannot become "nothing." Even if you go through deep meditation into what is called "the realm of absolute nothingness," you will still exist. Even if you are so freaked out by a tragedy, such as losing your only child, that you try to end your existence completely, you will still exist. I have a healthy respect for tragedy. We do have terrible tragedies. Personally, I don't bear misfortune well; it knocks me out. But there is no way to become nobody. Even if you were to succeed in killing yourself, you will be shocked when you awaken to disembodied awareness, out-of-body but still a somebody, a ghostly wraith who wishes he hadn't just done that. And a terribly unfortunate living person who has been so brutalized that he blanks out who he was in a seemingly impenetrable psychosis is still somebody, as everybody else around him knows.

Our mind is so powerful that it can create a state of absolute nothingness that seems totally concrete. Thousands of yogis in the history of India and a few mystics in the West have entered such a state of nothingness. But no one can stay there forever, and it is not where you want to be.

Have you ever had a minor experience of nothingness? I've had it in the dentist's chair with sodium pentothal, because I used to eat a lot of sweets and not brush my teeth as a youngster so I had to have teeth pulled. They give you this knockout anesthetic, and if you are a hardworking intellectual, you are tired of your mind, so you think, "Oh great, I'm going to be obliterated for a little while." You're really pleased, and you feel this little buzz, and you're just about to get there. You're going to experience nothingness, a little foretaste of the nihilistic notion of nirvana! But suddenly the nurse is shaking you awake saying, "You've been slobbering in that chair long enough. Get out of here." It's over. You started to pass out, wanting to be gone, but now you're suddenly back with no sense of having been gone at all! And that's what it is like in the state of absolute nothingness. It's like being passed out in the dentist's chair. There's no sense of duration of time. But eventually you wake up, totally disoriented with a nasty headache, and you never even got to enjoy the oblivion.

So we can never become nothing, as appealing as that may sound to those who are addicted to the idea of nothingness after death. We are always somebody, even though we are selfless in reality. We are just different sorts of "somebodies" than we used to be. "Realizing your selflessness" does not mean that you become a nobody, it means that you become the type of somebody who is a viable, useful somebody, not a rigid, fixated, I'm-the-center-of-the-universe, isolated-from-others somebody. You become the type of some-body who is over the idea of a conceptually fixated and self-created "self," a pseudo-self that would actually be absolutely weak, because of being unrelated to the reality of your constantly changing nature. You become the type of some-body who is content never to be quite that sure of who you are—always free to be someone new, somebody more.

That's the whole point of selflessness. If you don't know exactly who you are all the time, you're not sick, you're actually in luck, because you're more realistic, more free, and more awake! You're being too intelligent to be stuck inside one frozen mask of personality! You've opened up your wisdom, and you've realized that "knowing who you are" is the trap—an impossible self-objectification. None of us knows who we really are. Facing that and then becoming all that we can be—astonishing, surprising, amazing—always fresh and new, always free to be more, brave enough to become a work in progress, choosing happiness, open-mindedness, and love over certitude, rigidity, and fear—this is realizing selflessness!

I never met the late, great comedian Peter Sellers, except splitting my sides in laughter while watching some of his movies, especially the *Pink Panther* series. I know he had his ups and downs in his personal life, though you can't believe all the things you hear from the tabloids. But I did read a quote from him, or maybe from his psychiatrist, that he was deeply troubled and distressed because he suffered from "not knowing who he really was." He would get into his roles as an actor so totally, he would think he was the person he was playing, and he couldn't find himself easily as his "own" person. So he suffered, feeling himself "out of control" in his life. When I read this, my heart went out to him. I imagined his psychiatrist sternly telling him he had better calm down and track himself down, and put a lid on his ebullient sense of life, leading him on and on in self-absorption in therapy under the guise that he was going to "find himself" once and for all. I, feeling a bit more freed by having awakened to even the tiniest taste of selflessness, wanted to cry out to Peter Sellers, "Stop suffering by thinking your insight is confusion! Don't listen to the misknowing and even fear your freedom! Learn to surf the energy of life that surges through your openness! You have discovered your real self already, your great self of selflessness, and that openness is what enables you to manifest the heart that shines through your work and opens the hearts of your audiences. Your gift is to release them into laughter, itself a taste of freedom! Why be confused and feel your great gift is something wrong?" But I didn't know him so I could not tell him what I'm telling you. But our lives are infinite and I will be telling his ongoing life-form one of these days, whether I recognize him or not!

The Buddha was happy about not knowing who he was in the usual rigid, fixed sense. He called the failure to know who he was "enlightenment." Why? Because he realized that selflessness kindles the sacred fire of compassion. When you become aware of your selflessness, you realize that any way you feel yourself to be at any time is just a relational, changing construction. When that happens, you have a huge inner release of compassion. Your inner creativity about your living self is energized, and your infinite life becomes your ongoing work of art.

You see others caught in the suffering of the terminal self-habit and you feel real compassion. You feel so much better, so highly relieved, that your only concern is helping those constricted other people. You are free to worry about them because, of course, they are having a horrible time trying to know who they are and trying to be who they think they should be! They are busy being ripped apart by the great streams of ignorance, illness, death, and other people's irritating habits. So they suffer. And you, in your boundless, infinitely interconnected, compassionate state, can help them.

This is the other crucial point about selflessness: it does not mean that you are disconnected. Even nirvana is not a state of disconnection from the world. There is no way to become removed from yourself or from other beings. We are ultimately boundless—that is to say, our relative boundaries are permeable. But we are still totally interconnected no matter what we do. You cannot disappear into your own blissful void, because you are part of everyone and they are part of you. If you have no ultimate self, that makes you free to be your relative self, along with other beings. It's as if your hand represents the universe and your fingers represent all beings. Each of your fingers can wiggle on its own, each can operate independently, just as each being has its own identity. And yet your fingers are part of your hand. If your hand did not exist, your fingers would not exist. You are one of many, many fingers on the hand that is all life.

To my surprise and delight, I learned recently that even some Western psychologists are now beginning to study and understand the harm done by self-centered thinking. The psychologist Dr. Larry Scherwitz conducted a study about type A people—the aggressive, loud, annoying types, like me. Scientists used to think that type As died younger because of their fast-paced, stressful lives. But this new study reveals that, in fact, some of us type A people are not going to die of a heart attack that soon after all. The type Bs out there, the mild-mannered, quiet, inward-focused types, might find this worrisome! We may stay around for years bothering them, because it turns out that the type A personality is not a risk factor for coronary heart disease or other stress-related health problems. It turns out that some people, like me, though we freak out all the time, are not always that stressed. Some of us actually enjoy being this way.

What is the real risk factor, then? Scherwitz and his colleagues reanalyzed the data and conducted some new studies. They discovered, by analyzing the speech patterns of type As and type Bs, that the high risk of heart disease and stress-related illness is correlated with the *amount of self-reference* in people's speech—the amount of self-preoccupation, self-centeredness, and narcissism. "Me, me, I, I, my, my, mine, mine. My golf course, my country club, my job, my salary, my way, my family, my religion, my shrine, my guru, my, my, mine." The more "I, me, my, and mine" there is in their speech—"mine" most of all—the more likely they are to succumb to stress, to keel over because their bodies revolt against that pressure of self-involvement. Whereas even though some people can be aggressive, annoying, loud, and seemingly "stressed," if their overall motivation is altruistic and they don't pay too much attention to themselves, they live longer. And the quiet type Bs who are also more concerned about others, not necessarily out of any altruistic religious inklings, but just naturally not paying much attention to themselves, tend to live longer, too.

I find this study amazing. I was with the Dalai Lama when he heard about the results. He was intrigued and very pleased. "Oh, really?" he said. "Let me see that paper. In Buddhist psychology, we also have this idea that obsessive self-preoccupation—possessiveness and selfishness and self-centeredness—is life's chief demon!"

Let us explore the problems created by this demon of self-preoccupation, the ways in which it causes us suffering. We will then practice a fundamental meditation in which we look for the fixated self and find that it does not, after all, exist. Once we have freed ourselves from the constricting habit of always thinking that we are the center of the universe, we will experience our first taste of the boundless joy and compassion that is infinite life.

PROBLEM: MISKNOWLEDGE AND SELF-PREOCCUPATION

One of the hardest things we have to do on a regular basis is to admit that we are wrong. We stubbornly insist that we're right in situations where we're not quite sure if we are, and even when we sense that we've slipped. How much more indignant do we become when we feel certain that we're right and someone has the gall or the stupidity to challenge us? In this case, we feel an absolute imperative to jump up and trumpet our rightness. If we still cannot get others to agree with us, we soon become self-righteous and then outraged.

Believe it or not, the fact that we struggle so much with being wrong is of tremendous importance to our task of awakening to the reality of selflessness. We should examine our habit of needing to be right carefully to see why it feels so good.

Being right means that the world affirms us in what we think we know. "Knowing" something is a way of controlling it, being able to put it in its proper place in relation to us so that we can use it effectively. As Dharmakirti, the seventh-century Indian philosopher, said, "All successful action is preceded by accurate knowledge." So knowledge is power, in the sense that it empowers us to act successfully. Misknowledge, misunderstanding a situation, is weakness, in the sense that our actions may fail in their aim, backfire, or have unintended consequences. Knowledge is security, in that we know our vulnerabilities and can avoid harm. Misknowledge is danger, in that we don't know what others might do to us or what traps may await us. We therefore feel powerful and secure when we're right, weak and vulnerable when we're wrong.

Viewed in this context, being right seems like a struggle for survival, a drive to win. It's natural for us to cling to that feeling, even when we have not investigated the reality around us because we don't really want to know if we are wrong. We think that finding ourselves in the wrong means a loss of power and safety, forgetting that actually *it is the only way* for us to discover what is truly right and truly wrong, thereby gaining real power and real safety. When we pretend, we focus our attention on appearing to be right no matter what the reality, we distract ourselves from being awake to what really is going on, and so place ourselves at a disempowering disadvantage.

In light of this simple analysis, what lies at the center of our constant need to assure our rightness and, therefore, our power and security? Is it not the certainty that "I am"? Does not the strong sense of "I am" seem absolutely right, unquestionable, in fact? Every self-identification, judgment, and impulse beginning with "I am"—"I am me," "I am American," "I am human," "I am male," "I am right," "I am sure," "I am angry"—seems natural, undeniable, imperative. As such, we are habitually driven to obey in feelings, thoughts, words, and deeds whatever comes from within the inexhaustible fountain of I am's, I think's, I want's, I love's, I hate's, and I do's. "I" is the absolute captain of our ship, the agent of our fate, the master of our lives.

When apes or bulls or mountain goats snort and paw the ground and then charge head first at one another, we interpret their behavior as an "I" versus "I" contest, sometimes to the death. Similarly, the imperative issuing from our "I" can be so adamant, so unchallengeable, that we human beings, too, will sacrifice our lives. Just think of the nature of such statements as follows, when the "I" is aligned with country, church, God, family, race, gender, or species: "I am a patriot!" "I am a Protestant!" "I am a Catholic!" "I am a Christian!" "I am a Muslim!" "I am a believer!" "I am an atheist!" "I am white!" "I am a male!" "I am human!" In these situations, the "I" exercises tremendous power over us, and can often lead us to our death.

The "I," the ego-self seemingly absolutely resident in the heart of our being, is the one thing of which we each are absolutely certain, which we will die for, which we will kill for, which we will obey slavishly and unquestioningly throughout our lives. We are so accustomed to our habitual sense of self that we consider even the slightest absence of it—a moment of derangement, a loss of consciousness in fainting or deep sleep, a disorienting distraction of passion or terror, a dizzying state of drunkenness or drug-intoxication, a psychological or neurological disorder—absolutely terrifying. We can't imagine our lives without our "I" as a constant, demanding presence.

What is shocking and difficult for most Westerners to accept is that the Buddha discovered that this most certain knowledge of the "self" is actually "misknowledge"—a fundamental misunderstanding, a delusion. And what's more, he realized that this discovery was the key to liberation, the gateway to enlightenment. When he saw the false nature of the "I," he emitted his "lion's roar," pronouncing the reality of selflessness, identitylessness, voidness. This was his *Eureka!* moment, his scientific breakthrough, his insight into reality, from whence has flowed for thousands of years the whole philosophical, scientific, and religious educational movement that is Buddhism. Identifying this habitual, certain self-knowledge as the core misknowledge allowed the Buddha to give birth to wisdom, truth, and liberating enlightenment.

But the Buddha knew perfectly well that it would do no good to simply order people to accept his declaration of selflessness as dogma and cling to it as a slogan or creed. The instinctual entanglement of human beings within the knot of self-certainty is much too powerful to be dislodged in this way, selflessness at first too counterintuitive to be acknowledged as truth. No, the Buddha realized, people must discover their real nature for themselves. So he made his declaration of selflessness not a statement of fact but rather a challenge to inquiry.

"I have discovered selflessness!" the Buddha announced. "I have seen through the reality of the seemingly solid self that lay at the core of my being. This insight did not destroy me—it only destroyed my suffering. It was my liberation! But you need not believe me. Discover the truth for yourself. Try with all your might to verify this 'self' you feel is in there, to pin it down. If you can do that, fine, tell me I'm wrong and ignore whatever else I may have to say. But if you fail to find it, if each thing you come up with dissolves under further analysis, if you discover, as I did, that there is no atomic, indivisible, durable core 'self,' then do not be afraid. Do not recoil or turn away. Rather, confront that emptiness and recognize it as the doorway to the supreme freedom! See through the 'self' and it will release you. You will discover that you are a part of the infinite web of interconnectedness with all other beings. You will live in bliss from now on as the relative self you always were; free at long last from the struggle of absolute alienation, free to help others find their own blessed freedom and happiness!"

Though in this paraphrase of his core teaching the Buddha offers us much encouragement, the challenge remains its central thrust. "You think you're really you? Don't just accept that blindly! Verify whether or not your 'self' is actually present within you. Turn your focused attention to it and explore it. If it's as solid as it seems, then it should be solidly encounterable. If you can't encounter it, then you must confront your error."

The great philosopher Descartes made a grave error when he thought he discovered in his fixed subjective self the one certain thing about existence. After demolishing the entire universe of observable things with hammer blows of systematic doubt, he was unable to give even a tiny tap to collapse this sense of self! And so he set down as the basis for his entire philosophy the famous proposition, "I think, therefore I am!"

Believe it or not, in his deep exploration for the "self," Descartes almost took another path that would have led him to enlightenment. He got very close to discovering that he could not find the "self" he felt to be so absolutely present. After intensively dissecting appearances, drilling through layer upon layer of seeming certainties, he came out with nothing that he could hold onto as the "self." But then he made the tragic mistake. Instead of accepting his selflessness, he instead said to himself, "Ah! Well, of course I cannot find the self. It is the self that is doing the looking! The 'I' is the subject and so it cannot be an object. Though I cannot find it, still my knowledge that it is the absolute subject cannot be doubted. It confirms its existence by doubting its existence. *Cogito ergo sum*! Of this I can remain absolutely certain."

Why was this mistaken? His logic sounds plausible enough at first. It is, after all, a clever way out of the dilemma of looking for something you are sure is there but cannot find. But what's wrong with it? Let's say that I am looking for a cup. I find it, so I can be certain that the cup exists. I look for my friend and find her, so I can be certain she's there. I look for my glasses, I do not find them—so I proclaim certainty that they are there? No—I go get another pair because I acknowledge I've lost them. I look for my oh-so-familiar "I," and I cannot find it! Why would I think it's there, then? Because I've arbitrarily put it in the category of "things that are there only when I can't find them"? No, when I can't find it, it's rather more sensible that I must give up the sense of certainty that it's there. I feel it's there when I don't look for it, but as soon as I look for it with real effort, it instantly eludes discovery. It seems always to be just around the next corner in my mind, yet each time I turn around to seize it, it disappears. And so I must slowly come to accept the fact that it may not be there after all.

Put another way, imagine that you are walking through the desert when, far off on the horizon, you see an oasis. Yet when you get closer, it disappears. "Aha!" you think to yourself. "A mirage." You walk away. Miles later, you turn around and look back. There's the oasis again! Do you feel certain that the water is there now? No, on the contrary you feel certain that it is only a mirage of water. In the same way, when you look for the "self" and don't find it, you must accept that it is merely a mirage. Your solid self-sense is only an illusion.

Had Descartes persisted and found the door to freedom in his selflessness, as the Buddha did, then instead of proclaiming, "I think, therefore I am," he might have said, "Even though I can find no concrete, fixated 'self,' I still can think.

I still seem to be. Therefore I can continue to be myself, selflessly, as a relative, conventional, but ultimately unfindable being."

Whenever you decide to try a particular yoga [or form of meditation], the crucial first step is always deciding to make the change. You must begin by accepting the fact that your habitual conceptions could be wrong. If, for example, you live with the delusion that it is just fine to remain addicted to nicotine, that three packs of cigarettes a day puts you in optimal operating condition, then there is no way you will successfully complete a yoga to quit smoking. Likewise, in this crucial quest of the self, the presumed core of your self-addiction, you must first convince yourself through empirical observation that the way you hold your self-identity—the constricted feeling of being wrapped around a solid, independent core—is uncomfortable and disabling.

Why should you even care if the rigid "self" that you believe in so strongly really exists or not? Our self feels most real when we are right and righteous, when we are wrongly or unfairly challenged. And it also seems unique, completely separate from everyone and everything else in the universe. This separateness can feel like freedom and independence when we are in a good mood. But when we are in trouble, lonely or angry, under pressure or dissatisfied, this separateness feels like isolation, alienation, unfair treatment, or deprivation. When we are wholly gripped by fury, the searing energy that wants to attack a target picks our "I" up like a mindless tool and flings us at the other person. It is so disconnected that it even disregards our sense of self-protection, making us take actions that injure us, ignore injuries undergone, and even harm others with no regard for the consequences. There is no more powerful demonstration of our strong sense of being an independent entity than when we give ourselves over completely to anger.

When we look around at others, we see that they are just as alienated from us as we are alienated from them. As we want things from them, they want things from us. As we reject them, they seem to reject us. We don't love them, so how can we expect them to love us? And yet they are endless, while "I" am just one. So I am badly outnumbered. I feel threatened. I can never get enough, have enough, or be enough. I will inevitably lose the me-versus-all-of-them struggle in the long run.

We can, of course, experience moments of unity with other beings, through falling in love, or having a child, for example. When we do, we experience tremendous relief—for a moment, there are two of us teamed up against all the others together. We have an ally. But unfortunately those moments are too rare, and they do not last long before the old self-isolation re-emerges. Even lovers can turn into adversaries, couples often seek divorce, and children recoil from their parents, who in turn reject them.

This alienation caused by the presumed independent, absolute self was why the Buddha saw its illusion as the source of human suffering. The situation of feeling that it's always "the self versus the world," with the self as the long-term loser, is unsatisfactory and untenable. When we recognize the inevitable nonviability of our self-centered reality, it motivates us to engage in the quest for the true nature of the self. It makes it existentially essential for us to pause in our headlong rush through life and turn within, to verify whether the "self" really exists as we feel it does.

We can take great encouragement from the fact that the Buddha told us we could escape from our suffering. Still, we cannot merely accept someone else's report. No one else can do the job of replacing misunderstanding with understanding for us. We must look at reality and verify for ourselves whether our habitual sense of having a fixed self or the Buddha's discovery of selflessness is ultimately true. In this way, we can begin to transform the self-preoccupation that causes chronic suffering into the insightful, gradual opening and letting go of the self that is, paradoxically, so self-fulfilling. We want to be happy, but ironically we can only become happier to the extent that we can develop an unconcern for our "self." This process is long and gradual, though you will experience frequent breakthrough moments that will thrill you and motivate you to continue.

Before we actually engage in the meditation practice used to discover the true nature of the self, we must set up our parameters in practical, clear terms. When we look through a darkened house for a misplaced key, we first remember what the key looks like, and then we search for it carefully, room by room, turning lights on as we go. We use a flashlight to look under beds and in hidden corners. When we have looked everywhere exhaustively and not found it, we decide we've missed it somehow, so we go back and repeat the process. However, after one or two searches of this kind, we come to a decisive conclusion that the key is not in the house. We know we could continue looking endlessly, but that would be impractical. So we decide to proceed accordingly with our lives.

In the case of the quest for the self, we will look through all the processes of our body and mind that we can find and investigate them thoroughly. Our physical systems, sensational feelings, conceptual image bank, emotional energies, and consciousness itself constitute the house through which we will search. There are also various vaguely defined areas such as "spirit" and "soul" that, like a dusty attic or dank cellar, we may feel the need to explore. It is easy to get lost in these murky, dank, and oft-forgotten quarters of the mind. So we must get a clear picture of what we want to find ahead of time. And most important, we must set some limits to the exercise, since practically speaking we cannot continue to search indefinitely.

At this point you should search through the house of your body–mind–spirit a few times with great concentration and systematic thoroughness, with my help and the help of many experts who have guided me through this practice. If, during this process, you find a "self," then enjoy it to the full. If, however, as I suspect will be the case, you do not find what stands up solidly as your "real self" by the end of the process, then you will have to live with the fact that there is no such thing. You will need to make the practical decision to turn from seeking the "self" to explore instead the ramifications of being a relative self without any absolute underpinning.

This commitment to practicality in your quest for the self is of great importance at the outset and will have a significant impact on the success of the endeavor. Once you have made the commitment in your own mind, you may begin.

Practice: Trying to Find Your "I"

You are now prepared to deepen your understanding of your selflessness. You will be looking at yourself introspectively, trying to grasp exactly what your essence is. When you do this practice well, you will begin to feel yourself dissolving, just as I did at my mentor Geshe-la's house many years ago. You will start realizing—gradually and also suddenly, in spurts—that you can't find this mysterious "self." Your strong feeling of having an absolute "I" is maddeningly elusive when you try to pin it down precisely.

... In looking for your "self," start with your body. Ask yourself, "Am I my body?" In order to answer this question, you must define your body. It is composed at least of your five sense organs, right? Your skin and sensitive inner surfaces constitute the touch organ, then you have your eyes for sight, your nose for smell, your ears for hearing, and your tongue for taste. So first let's explore all of your senses together, your sensory system.

Identify the sound sense. What do you hear—a dog barking, a phone ringing, music playing, or perhaps just the sound of your own breathing? Now notice the visual field. You are reading words on the page. What else do you see? What are the images on the edge of your peripheral vision? How about smell? Perhaps you smell the scent of incense burning, or of musty wood. Do you taste anything: something you ate a while ago, tea you drank, or just the taste of your own mouth? The tactile field is everything touching your skin, including other parts of your skin touching your skin. Your hand may be resting on your knee, for example. Your bottom is touching a pillow. Just identify all the sensations, the textures, smells, tastes, sounds, and sights.

Now notice your internal sensations, like the breakfast in your tummy. You might have a slight pain in your back or your knee. Maybe your foot is falling asleep, and you're annoyed because there's a slightly painful sensation there. You might have a pleasurable sensation in some part of you that is feeling good if, for example, you worked out yesterday or had a massage.

Recognize that for each of these sensations you are experiencing, you are receiving data from the outside world. The sensations are not all coming from your own body. So your body is not just inside your skin; your body is both your organs and the field of all incoming sense objects. It's everything you are seeing and hearing and smelling and tasting and touching. It's the chair or pillow you're sitting on. The words you are reading on this page. The incense drifting into your nostrils. If you look at one sensation, you realize that you are sharing your material body with the outside world. Say, for example, you are looking at light bouncing off a table. That light is a part of your shared sensory system, and therefore part of your body, too.

So already you have begun to expand your self-definition, just by looking at your five senses. Suddenly you are not just something that sits there inside your skin. You are your environment as well. Your body interfuses with the outside world that you perceive with your senses. All of our bodies are totally overlapping, all the time. Do you see? And when you think, "this is 'me' over here inside this skin," you are unrealistically thinking that "I" am not connected to others through the sense perceptions that we have in common. But you are connected, even before you talk to them or think anything about them, through your shared environment.

Now you can move to the next level of analysis of the self, which exists at the level of your mind. First is the sensational system, the feelings of pleasure, pain, and numbness associated with sense perceptions of sights, sounds, smells, tastes, textures, and mental sense inner objects. When you experience these six kinds of objects, you react as pleased, irritated, or indifferent. Mentally inventory your sensations at the moment, and notice how you react at this basic feeling level. Notice that this heap of sense-reactions has no self-core within it.

Next is your conceptual system, your ideas, mental maps, and internal images. You have a picture of yourself as you exist in the world. You have a concept of yourself as human, not animal. You have a picture of yourself as male or female. You have a body image, and an image of each part of your body. You have a concept of your identity as a teacher, a manager, a doctor, or whatever. You have a concept of yourself as successful or as a failure. Inventory this mass of ideas and images and notice that you have whole clouds of pictures and concepts. But is this incredibly chaotic mass of images and words and diagrams and maps and so forth that is your conceptual system the real "you"? Your perception of yourself changes all the time, depending on your mood, whom you're with, or what you're doing. Sometimes you think, "I'm a high-powered executive," whereas other times you think, "I'm just a tiny speck on a tiny planet of six billion people." So surely your conceptual system cannot be your "self." The "you" self is not any of these ideas, since it seems to be the entity that is noticing all of them.

At the fourth level of analysis, find your emotional system. You are constantly reacting to all of these images and notions. Right now, you're probably feeling a bit irritated with me. You're thinking to yourself, "Why is he making me do this? Why doesn't he just crack a joke? Let's have some fun. What is this terrible business of exploring the self, 'discovering selflessness'? How is this helping me?" And so on and so forth. You're feeling annoyed and anxious and confused. Or maybe you're just feeling bored. Anyway, your emotions are there in your mind, always functioning, but always changing. You can take a peek at them now, as they swirl around in your heart and head, and you can see that they are not fixed. You are not defined by your emotions. They are not the elusive "self" you're seeking.

Lastly, turn your attention to your consciousness system. It is the most important system of all. You see at once how it is a buzzing, blooming, swirling mass of subtle energies. Nothing is fixed, nothing stable within it. With your mental consciousness, you hop from one sense to another. You analyze your ideas, you focus internally on your emotions and thoughts, and you can even focus on being thought-free. Your consciousness aims itself at being free of thought by the thought of being free of thought. How strange! As you inventory your consciousness, don't allow yourself to rest with a bare awareness, but go a bit deeper—explore further with your analytic attention. Ask yourself, "Who is this supposedly rigid 'self'? Is it the same self right now as the one who woke up grumbling this morning, preparing that cup of coffee, rushing to get ready, quickly brushing its teeth? Is it the same self who was born a tiny, unaware, helpless infant years ago? Who is the 'me' who knows my name, who knows what I want, where I am, and what I'm doing? Who is the 'me' who knows I'm an American, who knows I'm a—whatever: a Buddhist or a Christian or an atheist? Where is that person now? Where is that absolute, unchanging structure?" You can see how your self-consciousness is a buzzing, blooming, swirling mass of confusion—nothing is fixed, nothing stable within it. You can barely remember what you did yesterday morning—I can't remember at all at my age! So how can you possibly have a rigid self? See how releasing these sorts of thoughts can be! ...

The deepest stage of awareness comes when your consciousness begins to turn inward to gaze upon itself. At first it thinks, "I now know that these sensory, mental, and emotional systems looming before me are not the 'self,' they are not 'me.' But the awareness that looks at them, that contemplates and investigates them, that is my 'self.'" And yet you soon discover that you are mistaken even in this conclusion. The moment you begin to examine your own conscious mind, you engage in a whirling, internal dervish-dance where your awareness spins round and round upon itself. This contemplation can be dizzying, nauseating, painful, and even a bit frightening, as the felt "self" disappears and evades its own attention. You can never catch it, even as you become more experienced at this meditation and come back to this place again and again. Time and again you will feel frustrated by your continued failure to come up with a result. Yet you must not lose heart. You must remember that looking for your "self" is the most important thing you can ever do in your evolutionary development. You must keep faith that you are on the brink of a quantum leap; you are so close to awakening.

As you enter into this confusing realm of spinning self-seeking, be careful not to make the mistake Descartes made by withdrawing from it all with some sort of decision about "you" being the subject and therefore not any sort of findable object. Also, be careful not to fall into the nihilistic trap of withdrawing from the spinning by deciding that all is nothing after all and so naturally the self-sense is an illusion. Keep whirling upon your "self" as long as you feel absolutely there is a self to whirl upon, to look at, to catch. Put your full truth-seeking, analytic energy into the drive to find it.

Eventually, you will experience a gradual melting process. The whirling will slowly dissolve without fear: you won't shrink back in terror of falling into an abyss-like void because you are already overcoming your self-addiction. You control the tendency to shrink back in terror of falling into a looming void by your drilling, whirling energy of awareness itself. You dissolve your fearing subject, the object for which you are feeling fear, and the imagined nothingness that only the pseudo-self-addiction wants you to fear. However fully you feel such processes at first, what happens to you is that, as you begin to melt, your drive intensity lessens, you feel buoyed by a floating sensation coming from within your nerves and cells, from within your subjectivity as well as your object-field. At some point, you lose your sense of self entirely, as if you were a field of open space. Like Neo and his colleagues in the movie *The Matrix* when they entered one of the computer-generated training fields, you will find yourself standing in a blank white space—except in your case, in this transcending moment, you break free from your "digital residual self-image." You will be only the blank white space, a bare awareness of yourself as a boundless entity. Dissolving into this space, you'll feel intense bliss, a sense of extreme relief.

When you first melt into the spacious experience of freedom, it is enthralling, like emerging from a dark cave into infinite light. You feel magnificent, vast, and unbound. If you inadvertently fall into this state unprepared by arriving there too quickly, you may be tempted to think that you have arrived at the absolute reality, and this is a bit of a danger. You might think, feeling it nonverbally at this stage, that you've conquered the differentiated universe and realized its true "nothingness," experiencing it as such a profound and liberating release that you never again want any contact with the real world. Remember, however, that nothingness is not your ultimate goal—you are not trying to escape reality, but to embrace it. If you reach this space of release gradually through the repeated whirling of your self turning upon itself, then you'll be able to enjoy the vastness and magnificence without losing awareness that it is only another relational condition. You'll realize that the great emptiness is ultimately empty of itself; it is not reality, either.

Since you *are* the void, you do not need to remain in the void, and your original self-sense slowly reemerges within the universe of persons and things. But you are aware that it is not the same "self" you had before—it is forever different, now become infinite and unbound. You have changed. You now perceive your "self" consciously, living with it yet maintaining an educated distance from it. You are like one of the characters in *The Matrix*, present and active as real being, yet at the same time realizing that the apparent reality that surrounds you is only illusory. All that was apparent becomes transparent.

One of the most significant changes you will notice upon discovering your selflessness is that your sense of being separate from everyone else has now eroded. Your new awareness enables you to perceive others as equal to yourself, a part of you, even. You can see yourself as they see you, and experience empathically how they perceive themselves as locked within themselves. You have arrived at the doorway to universal compassion, and it frees you from being locked away behind a fixed point-of-awareness and opens you to a sort of field awareness wherein others are really just the same as you while simultaneously relationally different. Through the sense of sameness, you feel their pains as if they were your own: when they hurt, you hurt. Yet through the sense of relational difference and balanced responsibility, you naturally feel moved to free them from their pains, just as you move automatically to eliminate your own pains. When your hand is burned by a hot pot handle, you react at once to pull away from the heat, you plunge it into cold water, you rush to find ice. You respond instinctively to remove the pain. You don't consider it a selfless act of compassion for your hand. You just do it through your neural connection to your hand. Your new open awareness feels others' hands through a similar sense of natural connection.

QUESTIONS FOR MAKING CONNECTIONS
WITHIN THE READING

1. Choose one important term from Thurman's essay, such as *nirvana*, *nothingness*, *emptiness*, *enlightenment*, *meditation*, *compassion*, *ignorance*, *self*, *happiness*, or *freedom*. Then, by tracing Thurman's use of the term throughout the chapter, offer your own explanation of its meaning. While commonplace definitions for all of these terms may be found in a dictionary, here you are being asked to explain the meaning of the term as Thurman uses it. Then you might contrast Thurman's use of the term with more commonplace understandings. *Ignorance*, for example, has a special significance in the context of Buddhist thought. How does it differ from *ignorance* as we normally define it?

2. Instead of discussing the soul, Thurman focuses on the mind. How is "mind" different from "soul"? Where is the mind located, according to Thurman? Is it the same as the brain? What are some of the broader implications of Thurman's attention to the mind instead of the soul? If the mind is transformed, can the essence of the person remain somehow immune to change? Conversely, if a person's mental habits and perceptions remain unchanged, is it possible to imagine that the essence of the person has still been altered somehow? We might ordinarily think of each person as endowed with an individual soul, but is the mind individualized in the same way?

3. Thurman speaks about "enlightenment" instead of "redemption" or "salvation." How does "enlightenment" differ from "salvation"? What are the differences between Thurman's emphasis on the experience of "selflessness" and the famous Greek dictum "Know thyself"? Could selflessness qualify as a form of self-knowledge? Could it qualify as a form of redemption or salvation?

QUESTIONS FOR WRITING

1. Buddhism is often studied on the college level in courses offered by philosophy and religion departments. Judging from Thurman's account, what elements does Buddhism have in common with philosophy? With religion? Or, judging from Thurman's account, would you say that Buddhism has some elements in common with science, which is based on empirical observation? In what ways might Buddhism be closer to a science than to a religion or a philosophy?

2. What are the social and political implications of Thurman's argument? How would the cultivation of "wisdom" as he describes it affect people in a competitive, consumption-oriented society like our own? Is Thurman's brand of meditation compatible with democracy and the idea that all of us

are equal? How might the cultivation of wisdom influence the current political climate? Would the climate become less adversarial? Less driven by rigid ideology? Or would people who cultivate wisdom simply wash their hands of politics?

QUESTIONS FOR MAKING CONNECTIONS
BETWEEN READINGS

1. In "When I Woke Up Tuesday Morning, It Was Friday," Martha Stout describes forms of "divided" or "dissociated" consciousness that are produced by severely traumatic events. One of Stout's patients, whom she calls "Julia," becomes so dissociated from the here and now that whole days never get recorded in Julia's memory. After rereading Stout's analysis of dissociation, decide whether or not the form of meditation that Thurman describes might help someone like Julia. Is it possible that meditation as Thurman describes it could actually *produce* dissociation in healthy people? What aspects of meditation might be most helpful to people like Julia? Is it possible that dissociation is actually more widespread than most people even realize? Is trauma really necessary to produce severely divided consciousness, or do certain features of contemporary life help to produce it—television, commercial radio, video games, and movies?

2. In what ways is reading like the practice of meditation? To explore this question, draw primarily on Azar Nafisi's chapter from *Reading Lolita in Tehran.* At a key moment in her account, Nafisi makes this observation:

    > Whoever we were—and it was not really important what religion we belonged to, whether we wished to wear the veil or not, whether we observed certain religious norms or not—we had become the figment of someone else's dreams. A stern ayatollah, a self-proclaimed philosopher-king, had come to rule our land.

    How, according to Nafisi, can the reading of fiction help us throw off the veils—literal and virtual—that others have imposed on us? Does reading as she describes involve its own form of mental cultivation, comparable in some ways to the meditational practice Thurman describes? Does reading allow Nafisi and her students to experience a form of "selflessness"? How can we tell the difference between the veils imposed on us and the persons we really are? Is it possible that "selflessness" allows us to create an identity of our own?

SHERRY TURKLE

WHAT IS LIFE? What does it really mean for something to "be alive"? Questions like these were not on Sherry Turkle's mind when she took her daughter Rebecca to see a special exhibition on the life and work of Charles Darwin, the naturalist who first described the processes behind natural evolution. One of the first dioramas in the show included two live tortoises like the ones Darwin encountered on his expedition to the Galapagos Islands:

> One tortoise was hidden from view; the other rested in its cage, utterly still. Rebecca inspected the visible tortoise thoughtfully for a while and then said matter-of-factly, "They could have used a robot." I was taken aback and asked what she meant. She said she thought it was a shame to bring the turtle all this way from its island home in the Pacific, when it was just going to sit there in the museum, motionless, doing nothing.... [Later] a ten-year-old girl told me that she would prefer a robot turtle because aliveness comes with aesthetic inconvenience: "Its water looks dirty. Gross."

This reaction pushed Turkle to rethink much of her enthusiasm for technology. What kind of future might await humankind when children grow up preferring machines to biological life? What will happen to us psychologically if we envy our robots' skill, intelligence, and immortality?

Sherry Turkle's subject is the technology we tend to look at with uncritical awe—as she herself did for many years. Only gradually did Turkle come to understand that unless we stop to reflect, we might wind up as the tools of our tools: if our androids and PCs are meant to serve as extensions of ourselves, we could become their extensions instead. A further irony is that no one can foresee how our inventions will change us because no one can predict where technology is headed. Without a framework for assessing change, we might someday bitterly regret our naivety. Technology could prove to be unstoppable, but Turkle believes that we still have the power to control its pace and direction.

Sherry Turkle is the Abby Rockefeller Mauzé Professor of the Social Studies of Science and Technology at the Massachusetts Institute of Technology. Her early work on psychoanalysis paved the way for her later thinking on the

Quotation comes from Sherry Turkle, *Alone Together: Why We Expect More from Technology and Less from Each Other* (New York: Basic Books, 2011), 3.

"subjective side" of technology. Her books include *The Second Self: Computers and the Human Spirit* (1984), *Life on the Screen: Identity in the Age of the Internet* (1995), and *Simulation and Its Discontents* (2009). The selection that follows comes from her most recent book, *Alone Together: Why We Expect More from Technology and Less from Each Other* (2011).

Selections from Alone Together: Why We Expect More from Technology and Less from Each Other

My first brush with a computer program that offered companionship was in the mid-1970s. I was among MIT students using Joseph Weizenbaum's ELIZA, a program that engaged in dialogue in the style of a psychotherapist. So, a user typed in a thought, and ELIZA reflected it back in language that offered support or asked for clarification.[1] To "My mother is making me angry," the program might respond, "Tell me more about your mother," or perhaps, "Why do you feel so negatively about your mother?" ELIZA had no model of what a mother might be or any way to represent the feeling of anger. What it could do was take strings of words and turn them into questions or restate them as interpretations.

Weizenbaum's students knew that the program did not know or understand; nevertheless they wanted to chat with it. More than this, they wanted to be alone with it. They wanted to tell it their secrets.[2] Faced with a program that makes the smallest gesture suggesting it can empathize, people want to say something true. I have watched hundreds of people type a first sentence into the primitive ELIZA program. Most commonly they begin with "How are you today?" or "Hello." But four or five interchanges later, many are on to "My girlfriend left me," "I am worried that I might fail organic chemistry," or "My sister died."

Soon after, Weizenbaum and I were coteaching a course on computers and society at MIT. Our class sessions were lively. During class meetings he would rail against his program's capacity to deceive; I did not share his concern. I saw ELIZA as a kind of Rorschach, the psychologist's inkblot test. People used the program as a projective screen on which to express themselves. Yes, I thought, they engaged in personal conversations with ELIZA, but in a spirit of "as if." They spoke as if someone were listening but knew they were their own audience. They became caught up in the exercise. They thought, I will talk to this program as if it were a person. I will vent; I will rage; I will get things off my chest. More than this, while some learned enough about the program to trip it up, many more used this same inside knowledge to feed ELIZA responses that would make it seem more lifelike. They were active in keeping the program in play.

Weizenbaum was disturbed that his students were in some way duped by the program into believing—against everything they knew to be true—that they were dealing with an intelligent machine. He felt almost guilty about the deception machine he had created. But his worldly students were not deceived. They knew all about ELIZA's limitations, but they were eager to "fill in the blanks." I came to think of this human complicity in a digital fantasy as the "ELIZA effect." Through the 1970s, I saw this complicity with the machine as no more threatening than wanting to improve the working of an interactive diary. As it turned out, I underestimated what these connections augured. At the robotic moment, more than ever, our willingness to engage with the inanimate does not depend on being deceived but on wanting to fill in the blanks.

Now, over four decades after Weizenbaum wrote the first version of ELIZA, artificial intelligences known as "bots" present themselves as companions to the millions who play computer games on the Internet. Within these game worlds, it has come to seem natural to "converse" with bots about a variety of matters, from routine to romantic. And, as it turns out, it's a small step from having your "life" saved by a bot you meet in a virtual world to feeling a certain affection to ward it—and not the kind of affection you might feel toward a stereo or car, no matter how beloved. Meantime, in the physical real, things proceed apace. The popular Zhu Zhu robot pet hamsters come out of the box in "nurturing mode." The official biography of the Zhu Zhu named Chuck says, "He lives to feel the love." For the elderly, the huggable baby seal robot Paro is now on sale. A hit in Japan, it now targets the American nursing home market. Roboticists make the case that the elderly need a companion robot because of a lack of human resources. Almost by definition, they say, robots will make things better.

While some roboticists dream of reverse engineering love, others are content to reverse engineer sex.[3] In February 2010, I googled the exact phrase "sex robots" and came up with 313,000 hits, the first of which was linked to an article titled "Inventor Unveils $7,000 Talking Sex Robot." Roxxxy, I learned, "may be the world's most sophisticated, talking sex robot."[4] The shock troops of the robotic moment, dressed in lingerie, may be closer than most of us have ever imagined. And true to the ELIZA effect, this is not so much because the robots are ready but because we are.

In a television news story about a Japanese robot designed in the form of a sexy woman, a reporter explains that although this robot currently performs only as a receptionist, its designers hope it will someday serve as a teacher and companion. Far from skeptical, the reporter bridges the gap between the awkward robot before him and the idea of something akin to a robot wife by referring to the "singularity." He asks the robot's inventor, "When the singularity comes, no one can imagine where she [the robot] could go. Isn't that right? … What about these robots after the singularity? Isn't it the singularity that will bring us the robots that will surpass us?"

The singularity? This notion has migrated from science fiction to engineering. The singularity is the moment—it is mythic; you have to believe in it—when machine intelligence crosses a tipping point.[5] Past this point, say those who believe, artificial intelligence will go beyond anything we can currently conceive. No matter if today's robots are not ready for prime time as receptionists. At the singularity, everything will become technically possible, including robots that love. Indeed, at the singularity, we may merge with the robotic and achieve immortality. The singularity is technological rapture.

As for Weizenbaum's concerns that people were open to computer psychotherapy, he correctly sensed that something was going on. In the late 1970s, there was considerable reticence about computer psychotherapy, but soon after, opinions shifted.[6] The arc of this story does not reflect new abilities of machines to understand people, but people's changing ideas about psychotherapy and the workings of their own minds, both seen in more mechanistic terms.[7] Thirty years ago, with psychoanalysis more central to the cultural conversation, most people saw the experience of therapy as a context for coming to see the story of your life in new terms. This happened through gaining insight and developing a relationship with a therapist who provided a safe place to address knotty problems. Today, many see psychotherapy less as an investigation of the meaning of our lives and more as an exercise to achieve behavioral change or work on brain chemistry. In this model, the computer becomes relevant in several ways. Computers can help with diagnosis, be set up with programs for cognitive behavioral therapy, and provide information on alternative medications.

Previous hostility to the idea of the computer as psychotherapist was part of a "romantic reaction" to the computer presence, a sense that there were some places a computer could not and should not go. In shorthand, the romantic reaction said, "Simulated thinking might be thinking, but simulated feeling is not feeling; simulated love is never love." Today, that romantic reaction has largely given way to a new pragmatism. Computers "understand" as little as ever about human experience—for example, what it means to envy a sibling or miss a deceased parent. They do, however, perform understanding better than ever, and we are content to play our part. After all, our online lives are all about performance. We perform on social networks and direct the performances of our avatars in virtual worlds. A premium on performance is the cornerstone of the robotic moment. We live the robotic moment not because we have companionate robots in our lives but because the way we contemplate them on the horizon says much about who we are and who we are willing to become.

How did we get to this place? The answer to that question is hidden in plain sight, in the rough-and-tumble of the playroom, in children's reactions to robot toys. As adults, we can develop and change our opinions. In childhood, we establish the truth of our hearts.

I have watched three decades of children with increasingly sophisticated computer toys. I have seen these toys move from being described as "sort of alive" to "alive enough," the language of the generation whose childhood play was with sociable robots (in the form of digital pets and dolls). Getting to "alive enough" marks a watershed. In the late 1970s and early 1980s, children tried to make philosophical distinctions about aliveness in order to categorize computers. These days, when children talk about robots as alive enough for *specific purposes,* they are not trying to settle abstract questions. They are being pragmatic: different robots can be considered on a case-by-case and context-by-context basis. (Is it alive enough to be a friend, a babysitter, or a companion for your grandparents?) Sometimes the question becomes more delicate: If a robot makes you love it, is it alive?

Life Reconsidered

In the late 1970s and early 1980s, children met their first computational objects: games like Merlin, Simon, and Speak & Spell. This first generation of computers in the playroom challenged children in memory and spelling games, routinely beating them at tic-tac-toe and hangman.[8] The toys, reactive and interactive, turned children into philosophers. Above all else, children asked themselves whether something programmed could be alive.

Children's starting point here is their animation of the world. Children begin by understanding the world in terms of what they know best: themselves. Why does the stone roll down the slope? "To get to the bottom," says the young child, as though the ball had its own desires. But in time, animism gives way to physics. The child learns that a stone falls because of gravity; intentions have nothing to do with it. And so a dichotomy is constructed: physical and psychological properties stand opposed to one another in two great systems. But the computer is a new kind of object: it is psychological and yet a thing. Marginal objects such as the computer, on the lines between categories, draw attention to how we have drawn the lines.[9]

Swiss psychologist Jean Piaget, interviewing children in the 1920s, found that they took up the question of an object's life status by considering its physical movement.[10] For the youngest children, everything that could move was alive, then only things that could move without an outside push or pull. People and animals were easily classified. But clouds that seemed to move on their own accord were classified as alive until children realized that wind, an external but invisible force, was pushing them along. Cars were reclassified as not alive when children understood that motors counted as an "outside" push. Finally, the idea of autonomous movement became focused on breathing and metabolism, the motions most particular to life.

In the 1980s, faced with computational objects, children began to think through the question of aliveness in a new way, shifting from physics to psychology.[11] When they considered a toy that could beat them at spelling games, they were interested not in whether such an object could move on its own but in whether it could think on its own. Children asked if this game could "know." Did it cheat? Was knowing part of cheating? They were fascinated by how electronic games and toys showed a certain autonomy. When an early version of Speak & Spell—a toy that played language and spelling games—had a programming bug and could not be turned off during its "say it" routine, children shrieked with excitement, finally taking out the game's batteries to "kill it" and then (with the reinsertion of the batteries) bring it back to life.

In their animated conversations about computer life and death, children of the 1980s imposed a new conceptual order on a new world of objects.[12] In the

1990s, that order was strained to the breaking point. Simulation worlds—for example the Sim games—pulsed with evolving life forms. And child culture was awash in images of computational objects (from Terminators to digital viruses) all shape-shifting and morphing in films, cartoons, and action figures. Children were encouraged to see the stuff of computers as the same stuff of which life is made. One eight-year-old girl referred to mechanical life and human life as "all the same stuff, just yucky computer 'cy-dough-plasm.'" All of this led to a new kind of conversation about aliveness. Now, when considering computation, children talked about evolution as well as cognition. And they talked about a special kind of mobility. In 1993, a ten-year-old considered whether the creatures on the game SimLife were alive. She decided they were "if they could get out of your computer and go to America Online."[13]

Here, Piaget's narrative about motion resurfaced in a new guise. Children often imbued the creatures in simulation games with a desire to escape their confines and enter a wider digital world. And then, starting in the late 1990s, digital "creatures" came along that tried to dazzle children not with their smarts but with their sociability. I began a long study of children's interactions with these new machines. Of course, children said that a sociable robot's movement and intelligence were signs of its life. But even in conversations specifically about aliveness, children were more concerned about what these new robots might feel. As criteria for life, everything pales in comparison to a robot's capacity to care.

Consider how often thoughts turn to feelings as three elementary school children discuss the aliveness of a Furby, an owl-like creature that plays games and seems to learn English under a child's tutelage. [The] first, a five-year-old girl, can only compare it to a Tamagotchi, a tiny digital creature on an LED screen that also asks to be loved, cared for, and amused. She asks herself, "Is it [the Furby] alive?" and answers, "Well, I love it. It's more alive than a Tamagotchi because it sleeps with me. It likes to sleep with me." A six-year-old boy believes that something "as alive as a Furby" needs arms: "It might want to pick up something or to hug me." A nine-year-old girl thinks through the question of a Furby's aliveness by commenting, "I really like to take care of it.... It's as alive as you can be if you don't eat.... It's not like an animal kind of alive."

From the beginning of my studies of children and computers in the late 1970s, children spoke about an "animal kind of alive" and a "computer kind of alive." Now I hear them talk about a "people kind of love" and a "robot kind of love." Sociable robots bring children to the locution that the machines are alive enough to care and be cared for. In speaking about sociable robots, children use the phrase "alive enough" as a measure not of biological readiness but of relational readiness. Children describe robots as alive enough to love and mourn. And robots, as we saw at the American Museum of Natural History, may be alive enough to substitute for the biological, depending on the context. One reason the children at the museum were so relaxed about a robot substituting for a living tortoise is that children were comfortable with the idea of a robot as both machine and creature. I see this flexibility in seven-year-old Wilson, a bright, engaged student at a Boston public elementary school where I bring robot toys for after-school play. Wilson reflects on a Furby I gave him to take home for several weeks: "The Furby can talk, and it looks like an owl," yet "I always hear the machine in it." He knows, too, that the Furby, "alive enough to be a friend," would be rejected in the company of animals: "A real owl would snap its head off." Wilson does not have to deny the Furby's machine nature to feel it would be a good friend or to look to it for advice. His Furby has become his confidant. Wilson's way of keeping in mind the dual aspects of the Furby's nature seems to me a philosophical version of multitasking, so central to our twentieth-century attentional ecology. His attitude is pragmatic. If something that seems to have a self is before him, he deals with the aspect of self he finds most relevant to the context.

This kind of pragmatism has become a hallmark of our psychological culture. In the mid-1990s, I described how it was commonplace for people to "cycle through" different ideas of the human mind as (to name only a few images) mechanism, spirit, chemistry, and vessel for the soul.[14] These days, the cycling through intensifies. We are in much more direct contact with the machine side of mind. People are fitted with a computer chip to help with Parkinson's. They learn to see their minds as program and hardware. They take antidepressants prescribed by their psychotherapists, confident that the biochemical and oedipal self can be treated in one room. They look for signs of emotion in a brain scan. Old jokes about couples needing "chemistry" turn out not to be jokes at all. The compounds that trigger romantic love are forthcoming from the laboratory. And yet, even with biochemical explanations for attraction, nothing seems different about the thrill of falling in love. And seeing that an abused child has a normal brain scan does not mean one feels any less rage about the abuse. Pluralistic in our attitudes toward the self, we turn this pragmatic sensibility toward other things in our path—for example, sociable robots. We approach them like Wilson: they can be machines, and they can be more.

Writing in his diary in 1832, Ralph Waldo Emerson described "dreams and beasts" as "two keys by which we are to find out the secrets of our nature.... They are our test objects."[15] If Emerson had lived today, he would have seen the sociable robot as our new test object. Poised in our perception between inanimate program and living creature, this new breed of robot provokes us to reflect on the difference between connection and relationship, involvement with an object and engagement with a subject. These robots are evocative: understanding how people think about them provides a view onto how we think about ourselves. When children talk about these robots, they move away from an earlier cohort's perception of computers as provocative curiosities to the idea that robots might be something to grow old with. It all began when children met the seductive Tamagotchis and Furbies, the first computers that asked for love.[16]

The Tamagotchi Primer

When active and interactive computer toys were first introduced in the late 1970s, children recognized that they were neither dolls nor people nor animals. Nor did they seem like machines. Computers, first in the guise of electronic toys and games, turned children into philosophers, caught up in spontaneous debates about what these objects might be. In some cases, their discussions brought them to the idea that the talking, clever computational objects were close to kin. Children consider the question of what is special about being a person by contrasting themselves with their "nearest neighbors." Traditionally, children took their nearest neighbors to be their dogs, cats, and horses. Animals had feelings; people were special because of their ability to think. So, the Aristotelian definition of man as a rational animal had meaning for even the youngest children. But by the mid-1980s, as thinking computers became nearest neighbors, children considered people special because only they could "feel." Computers were intelligent machines; in contrast, people were emotional machines.[17]

But in the late 1990s, as if on cue, children met objects that presented themselves as having feelings and needs. As emotional machines, people were no longer alone. Tamagotchis and Furbies (both of which sold in the tens of millions) did not want to play tic-tac-toe, but they would tell you if they were hungry or unhappy. A Furby held upside down says, "Me scared," and whimpers as though it means it. And these new objects found ways to express their love.

Furbies, put on the market in 1998, had proper robotic "bodies"; they were small, fur-covered "creatures" with big eyes and ears. Yet, the Tamagotchi, released in 1997, a virtual creature housed in a plastic egg, serves as a reliable primer in the psychology of sociable robotics—and a useful one because crucial elements are simplified, thus stark. The child imagines Tamagotchis as embodied because, like living creatures and unlike machines, they need constant care and are always on. A Tamagotchi has "body enough" for a child to imagine its death.[18] To live, a Tamagotchi must be fed, amused, and cleaned up after. If cared for, it will grow from baby to healthy adult. Tamagotchis, in their limited ways, develop different personalities depending on how they are treated. As Tamagotchis turn children into caretakers, they teach that digital life can be emotionally roiling, a place of obligations and regrets.[19] The earliest electronic toys and games of thirty years ago—such as Merlin, Simon, and Speak & Spell—encouraged children to consider the proposition that something smart might be "sort of alive." With Tamagotchis, needy objects asked for care, and children took further steps.

As they did with earlier generations of hard-to-classify computational objects, curious children go through a period of trying to sort out the new sociable objects. But soon children take them at interface value, not as puzzles but as playmates. The philosophical churning associated with early computer toys (are they alive? do they know?) quickly gives way to new practices. Children don't want to comprehend these objects as much as take care of them. Their basic stance: "I'm living with this new creature. It and many more like it are here to stay." When a virtual "creature" or robot asks for help, children provide it. When its behavior dazzles, children are pleased just to hang out with it.

In the classic children's story *The Velveteen Rabbit*, a stuffed animal becomes "real" because of a child's love. Tamagotchis do not wait passively but demand attention and claim that without it they will not survive. With this aggressive demand for care, the question of biological aliveness almost falls away. We love what we nurture; if a Tamagotchi makes you love it, and you feel it loves you in return, it is alive enough to be a creature. It is alive enough to share a bit of your life. Children approach sociable machines in a spirit similar to the way they approach sociable pets or people—with the hope of befriending them. Meeting a person (or a pet) is not about meeting his or her biochemistry; becoming acquainted with a sociable machine is not about deciphering its programming. While in an earlier day, children might have asked, "What is a Tamagotchi?" they now ask, "What does a Tamagotchi want?"

When a digital "creature" asks children for nurturing or teaching, it seems alive enough to care for, just as caring for it makes it seem more alive. Neil, seven, says that his Tamagotchi is "like a baby. You can't just change the baby's diaper. You have to, like, rub cream on the baby. That is how the baby knows you love it." His eight-year-old sister adds, "I hate it when my Tamagotchi has the poop all around. I am like its mother. That is my job. I don't like it really, but it gets sick if you just leave it messy." Three nine-year-olds consider their Tamagotchis. One is excited that his pet requires him to build a castle as its home. "I can do it. I don't want him to get cold and sick and to die." Another looks forward to her digital pet's demands: "I like it when it says, 'I'm hungry' or 'Play with me.'" The third boils down her relationship to a "deceased" Tamagotchi to its most essential elements: "She was loved; she loved back."[20]

Where is digital fancy bred? Most of all, in the demand for care. Nurturance is the "killer app." In the presence of a needy Tamagotchi, children become responsible parents: demands translate into care and care into the feeling of caring. Parents are enlisted to watch over Tamagotchis during school hours. In the late 1990s, an army of compliant mothers cleaned, fed, and amused their children's Tamagotchis; the beeping of digital pets became a familiar background noise during business meetings.

This parental involvement is imperative because a Tamagotchi is always on. Mechanical objects are supposed to turn off. Children understand that bodies need to be always on, that they become "off" when people or animals die. So, the inability to turn off a Tamagotchi becomes evidence of its life. Seven-year-old Catherine explains, "When a body is 'off,' it is dead." Some Tamagotchis can be asked to "sleep," but nine-year-old Parvati makes it clear that asking her Tamagotchi to sleep is not the same as hitting the pause button in a game. Life goes on: "When they sleep, it is not that they are turned off. They can still get sick and unhappy, even while they are sleeping. They could have a nightmare."

In the late 1970s, computers, objects on the boundary between animate and inanimate, began to lead children to gleeful experiments in which they crashed machines as they talked about "killing" them. And then, there would be elaborate rituals of resuscitation as children talked about bringing machines back to life. After these dramatic rebirths, the machines were, in the eyes of children, what they had been before. Twenty years later, when Tamagotchis die and are reset for a new life, children do not feel that they come back as they were before. Children looked forward to the rebirth of the computers they had crashed, but they dread the demise and rebirth of Tamagotchis. These provoke genuine remorse because, as one nine-year-old puts it, "It didn't have to happen. I could have taken better care."[21]

Unforgettable

I took care of my first Tamagotchi at the same time that my seven-year-old daughter was nurturing her own. Since I sometimes took a shift attending to her Tamagotchi, I could compare their respective behaviors, and I convinced myself that mine had idiosyncrasies that made it different from hers. My Tamagotchi liked to eat at particular intervals. I thought it prospered best with only small doses of amusement. I worked hard at keeping it happy. I did not anticipate how bad I would feel when it died. I immediately hit the reset button. Somewhat to my surprise, I had no desire to take care of the new infant Tamagotchi that appeared on my screen.

Many children are not so eager to hit reset. They don't like having a new creature in the same egg where their virtual pet has died. For them, the death of a virtual pet is not so unlike the death of what they call a "regular pet." Eight-year-olds talk about what happens when you hit a Tamagotchi's reset button. For one, "It comes back, but it doesn't come back as exactly your same Tamagotchi.... You haven't had the same experiences with it. It has a different personality." For another, "It's cheating. Your Tamagotchi is really dead. Your one is really dead. They say you get it back, but it's not the same one. It hasn't had the same things happen to it. It's like they give you a new one. It doesn't remember the life it had." For another, "When my Tamagotchi dies, I don't want to play with the new one who can pop up. It makes me remember the real one [the first one]. I like to get another [a new egg].... If you made it die, you should start fresh." Parents try to convince their children to hit reset. Their arguments are logical: the Tamagotchi is not "used up"; a reset Tamagotchi means one less visit to the toy store. Children are unmoved.

Sally, eight, has had three Tamagotchis. Each died and was "buried" with ceremony in her top dresser drawer. Three times Sally has refused to hit the reset button and convinced her mother to buy replacements. Sally sets the scene: "My mom says mine still works, but I tell her that a Tamagotchi is cheap, and she won't have to buy me anything else, so she gets one for me. I am not going to start up my old one. It died. It needs its rest."

In Sally's "It died. It needs its rest," we see the expansiveness of the robotic moment. Things that never could go together—a program and pity for a weary body—now do go together. The reset button produces objects that are between categories: a creature that seems new but is not really new, a stand-in for something now gone. The new creature, a kind of imposter, is a classic case of Sigmund Freud's uncanny—it's familiar, yet somehow not.[22] The uncanny is always compelling. Children ask, "What does it mean for a virtual creature to die?" Yet, while earlier generations debated questions about a computer's life in philosophical terms, when faced with Tamagotchis, children quickly move on to day-to-day practicalities. They temper philosophy with tearful experience. They know that Tamagotchis are alive enough to mourn.

Freud teaches us that the experience of loss is part of how we build a self.[23] Metaphorically, at least, mourning keeps a lost person present. Child culture is rich in narratives that take young people through the steps of this fitful process. So, in *Peter Pan*, Wendy loses Peter in order to move past adolescence and become a grown woman, able to love and parent. But Peter remains present in her playful and tolerant way of mothering. Louisa May Alcott's Jo loses her gentle sister Beth. In mourning Beth, Jo develops as a serious writer and finds a new capacity to love. More recently, the young wizard Harry Potter loses his mentor Dumbledore, whose continuing presence within Harry enables him to find his identity and achieve his life's purpose. With the Tamagotchi, we see the beginning of mourning for artificial life. It is not mourned as one would mourn a doll. The Tamagotchi has crossed a threshold. Children breathe life into their dolls. With the Tamagotchi, we are in a realm of objects that children see as having their own agendas, needs, and desires. Children mourn the life the Tamagotchi has led.

A child's mourning for a Tamagotchi is not always a solitary matter. When a Tamagotchi dies, it can be buried in an online Tamagotchi graveyard. The tombstones are intricate. On them, children try to capture what made each Tamagotchi special.[24] A Tamagotchi named Saturn lived to twelve "Tamagotchi years." Its owner writes a poem in its memory: "My baby died in his sleep. I will forever weep. Then his batteries went dead. Now he lives in my head." Another child mourns Pumpkin, dead at sixteen: "Pumpkin, Everyone said you were fat, so I made you lose weight. From losing weight you died. Sorry." Children take responsibility for virtual deaths.[25] These online places of mourning do more than give children a way to express their feelings. They sanction the idea that it is appropriate to mourn the digital—indeed, that there is something "there" to mourn.

ALIVE ENOUGH

In the 1990s, children spoke about making their virtual creatures more alive by having them escape the computer. Furbies, the sensation of the 1998 holiday season, embody this documented dream. If a child wished a Tamagotchi to leap off its screen, it might look a lot like the furry and owl-like Furby. The two digital pets have other things in common. As with a Tamagotchi, how a Furby is treated shapes its personality. And both present themselves as visitors from other worlds. But Furbies are more explicit about their purpose in coming to Earth. They are here to learn about humans. So, each Furby is an anthropologist of sorts and wants to relate to people. They ask children to take care of them and to teach them English. Furbies are not ungrateful: they make demands, but they say, "I love you."

Furbies, like Tamagotchis, are "always on," but unlike Tamagotchis, Furbies manifest this with an often annoying, constant chatter.[26] To reliably quiet a Furby, you need a Phillips screwdriver to remove its batteries, an operation that causes it to lose all memory of its life and experiences—what it has learned and how it has been treated. For children who have spent many hours "bringing up" their Furbies, this is not a viable option. On a sunny spring afternoon in 1999, I bring eight Furbies to an afternoon playgroup at an elementary school in western Massachusetts. There are fifteen children in the room, from five to eight years old, from the kindergarten through the third grade. I turn on a tape recorder as

I hand the Furbies around. The children start to talk excitedly, greeting the Furbies by imitating their voices. In the cacophony of the classroom, this is what the robotic moment sounds like:

> He's a baby! He said, "Yum." Mine's a baby? Is this a baby? Is he sleeping now? He burped! What is "be-pah?" He said, "Be-pah." Let them play together. What does "a lee koo wah" mean? Furby, you're talking to me. Talk! C'mon boy. Good boy! Furby, talk! Be quiet everybody! Oh, look it, he's in love with another one! Let them play together! It's tired. It's asleep. I'm going to try to feed him. How come they don't have arms? Look, he's in love! He called you "Mama." He said, "Me love you." I have to feed him. I have to feed mine too. We love you, Furby. How do you make him fall asleep? His eyes are closed. He's talking with his eyes closed. He's sleeptalking. He's dreaming. He's snoring. I'm giving him shade.
>
> C'mon, Furby, c'mon—let's go to sleep, Furby. Furby, shh, shh. Don't touch him. I can make him be quiet. This is a robot. Is this a robot? What has this kind of fur? He's allergic to me. It's kind of like it's alive. And it has a body. It has a motor. It's a monster. And it's kind of like it's real because it has a body. It was alive. It is alive. It's not alive. It's a robot.

From the very first, the children make it clear that the Furby is a machine but alive enough to need care. They try to connect with it using everything they have: the bad dreams and scary movies that make one child see the Furby "as a monster" and their understanding of loneliness, which encourages another to exhort, "Let them play together!" They use logic and skepticism: Do biological animals have "this kind of fur?" Do real animals have motors? Perhaps, although this requires a new and more expansive notion of what a motor can be. They use the ambiguity of this new object to challenge their understanding of what they think they already know. They become more open to the idea of the biological as mechanical and the mechanical as biological. Eight-year-old Pearl thinks that removing the batteries from a Furby causes it to die and that people's death is akin to "taking the batteries out of a Furby."

Furbies reinforce the idea that they have a biology: each is physically distinct, with particular markings on its fur, and each has some of the needs of living things. For example, a Furby requires regular feeding, accomplished by depressing its tongue with one's finger. If a Furby is not fed, it becomes ill. Nursing a Furby back to health always requires more food. Children give disease names to Furby malfunctions. So, there is Furby cancer, Furby flu, and Furby headache.

Jessica, eight, plays with the idea that she and her Furby have "body things" in common, for example, that headache. She has a Furby at home; when her sisters pull its hair, Jessica worries about its pain: "When I pull my hair it really hurts, like when my mother brushes the tangles. So, I think [the Furby's hair pulls] hurt too." Then, she ponders her stomach. "There's a screw in my belly button," she says. "[The screw] comes out, and then blood comes out." Jessica thinks that people, like Furbies, have batteries. "There are hearts, lungs, and a big battery inside." People differ from robots in that our batteries "work forever like the sun." When children talk about the Furby as kin, they experiment with the idea that they themselves might be almost machine. Ideas about the human as machine or as joined to a machine are played out in classroom games.[27] In their own way, toy robots prepare a bionic sensibility. There are people who do, after all, have screws and pins and chips and plates in their flesh. A recent recipient of a cochlear implant describes his experience of his body as "rebuilt."[28]

We have met Wilson, seven, comfortable with his Furby as both machine and creature. Just as he always "hears the machine" in the Furby, he finds the machine in himself. As the boy sings improvised love songs about the robot as a best friend, he pretends to use a screwdriver on his own body, saying, "I'm a Furby." Involved in a second-grade class project of repairing a broken Furby by dismantling it, screw by screw, Wilson plays with the idea of the Furby's biological nature: "I'm going to get [its] baby out." And then he plays with the idea of his own machine nature: he applies the screwdriver to his own ankle, saying, "I'm unscrewing my ankle."

Wilson enjoys cataloguing what he and the Furby have in common. Most important for Wilson is that they "both like to burp." In this, he says, the Furby "is just like me—I love burping." Wilson holds his Furby out in front of him, his hands lightly touching the Furby's stomach, staring intently into its eyes. He burps just after or just before his Furby burps, much as in the classic bonding scene in *E.T.: The Extraterrestrial* between the boy Elliott and the visitor from afar. When Wilson describes his burping game, he begins by saying that he makes his Furby burp, but he ends up saying that his Furby makes him burp. Wilson likes the sense that he and his Furby are in sync, that he can happily lose track of where he leaves off and the Furby begins.[29]

What Does a Furby Want?

When Wilson catalogues what he shares with his Furby, there are things of the body (the burping) and there are things of the mind. Like many children, he thinks that because Furbies have language, they are more "peoplelike" than a "regular" pet. They arrive speaking Furbish, a language with its own dictionary, which many children try to commit to memory because they would like to meet their Furbies more than half way. The Furby manual instructs children, "I can learn to speak English by listening to you talk. The more you play with me, the more I will use your language." Actually, Furby English emerges over time, whether or not a child talks to the robot. (Furbies have no hearing or language- learning ability.[30]) But until age eight, children are convinced by the illusion and believe they are teaching their Furbies to speak. The Furbies are alive enough to need them.

Children enjoy the teaching task. From the first encounter, it gives them something in common with their Furbies and it implies that the Furbies can grow to better understand them. "I once didn't know English," says one six-year-old. "And now I do. So I know what my Furby is going through." In the classroom with Furbies, children shout to each other in competitive delight: "My Furby speaks more English than yours! My Furby speaks English."

I have done several studies in which I send Furbies home with schoolchildren, often with the request that they (and their parents) keep a "Furby diary." In my first study of kindergarten to third graders, I loan the Furbies out for two weeks at a time. It is not a good decision. I do not count on how great will be children's sense of loss when I ask them to return the Furbies. I extend the length of the loans, often encouraged by parental requests. Their children have grown too attached to give up the robots. Nor are they mollified by parents' offers to buy them new Furbies. Even more so than with Tamagotchis, children attach to a particular Furby, the one they have taught English, the one they have raised.

For three decades, in describing people's relationships with computers, I have often used the metaphor of the Rorschach, the inkblot test that psychologists use as a screen onto which people can project their feelings and styles of thought. But as children interact with sociable robots like Furbies, they move beyond a psychology of projection to a new psychology of engagement. They try to deal with the robot as they would deal with a pet or a person. Nine-year-old Leah, in an after-school playgroup, admits, "It's hard to turn it [the Furby] off when it is talking to me." Children quickly understand that to get the most out of your Furby, you have to pay attention to what it is telling you. When you are with a Furby, you can't play a simple game of projective make-believe. You have to continually assess your Furby's "emotional" and "physical" state. And children fervently believe that the child who loves his or her Furby best will be most loved in return.

This mutuality is at the heart of what makes the Furby, a primitive exemplar of sociable robotics, different from traditional dolls. As we've seen, such relational artifacts do not wait for children to "animate" them in the spirit of a Raggedy Ann doll or a teddy bear. They present themselves as already animated and ready for relationship. They promise reciprocity because, unlike traditional dolls, they are not passive. They make demands. They present as having their own needs and inner lives. They teach us the rituals of love that will make them thrive. For decades computers have asked us to *think* with them; these days, computers and robots, deemed sociable, affective, and relational, ask us to *feel* for and with them.

Children see traditional dolls as they want them or need them to be. For example, an eight-year-old girl who feels guilty about breaking her mother's best crystal pitcher might punish a row of Barbie dolls. She might take them away from their tea party and put them in detention, doing unto the dolls what she imagines should be done unto her. In contrast, since relational artifacts present themselves as having minds and intentions of their own, they cannot be so easily punished for one's own misdeeds. Two eight-year-old girls comment on how their "regular dolls" differ from the robotic Furbies. The first says, "A regular doll, like my Madeleine doll ... you can make it go to sleep, but its eyes are painted open, so, um, you cannot get them to close their eyes.... Like a Madeleine doll cannot go, 'Hello, good morning.'" But this is precisely the sort of thing a Furby can do. The second offers, "The Furby tells you what it wants."

Indeed, Furbies come with manuals that provide detailed marching orders. They want language practice, food, rest, and protestations of love. So, for example, the manual instructs, "Make sure you say 'HEY FURBY! I love you!' frequently so that I feel happy and know I'm loved." There is general agreement among children that a penchant for giving instructions distinguishes Furbies from traditional dolls. A seven-year-old girl puts it this way: "Dolls let you tell them what they want. The Furbies have their own ideas." A nine-year-old boy sums up the difference between Furbies and his action figures: "You don't play with the Furby, you sort of hang out with it. You do try to get power over it, but it has power over you too."

Children say that traditional dolls can be "hard work" because you have to do all the work of giving them ideas; Furbies are hard work for the opposite reason. They have plenty of ideas, but you have to give them what they want and when they want it. When children attach to a doll through the psychology of projection, they attribute to the doll what is most on their mind. But they need to accommodate a Furby. This give-and-take prepares children for the expectation of relationship with machines that is at the heart of the robotic moment.

Daisy, six, with a Furby at home, believes that each Furby's owner must help his or her Furby fulfill its mission to learn about people. "You have to teach it; when you buy it, that is your job." Daisy tells me that she taught her Furby about Brownie Girl Scouts, kindergarten, and whales. "It's alive; I teach it about whales; it loves me." Padma, eight, says that she likes meeting what she calls "Furby requests" and thinks that her Furby is "kind of like a person" because "it talks." She goes on: "It's kind of like me because I'm a chatterbox." After two weeks, it is time for Padma to return her Furby, and afterward she feels regret: "I miss how it talked, and now it's so quiet at my house.... I didn't get a chance to make him a bed."

After a month with her Furby, Bianca, seven, speaks with growing confidence about their mutual affection: "I love my Furby because it loves me.... It was like he really knew me."[31] She knows her Furby well enough to believe that "it doesn't want to miss fun ... at a party." In order to make sure that her social butterfly Furby gets some rest when her parents entertain late into the evening, Bianca clips its ears back with clothespins to fool the robot into thinking that "nothing is going on ... so he can fall asleep." This move is ineffective, and all of this activity is exhausting, but Bianca calmly sums up her commitment: "It takes lots of work to take care of these."

When Wilson, who so enjoys burping in synchrony with his Furby, faces up to the hard work of getting his Furby to sleep, he knows that if he forces sleep by removing his Furby's batteries, the robot will "forget" whatever has passed between them—this is unacceptable. So Furby sleep has to come naturally. Wilson tries to exhaust his Furby by keeping it up late at night watching television. He experiments with Furby "sleep houses" made of blankets piled high over towers of blocks. When Wilson considers Furby sleep, his thoughts turn to Furby dreams. He is sure his Furby dreams "when his eyes are closed." What do Furbies dream of? Second and third graders think they dream "of life on their flying saucers."[32] And they dream about learning languages and playing with the children they love.

David and Zach, both eight, are studying Hebrew. "My Furby dreams about Hebrew," says David. "It knows how to say *Eloheinu*.... I didn't even try to teach it; it was just from listening to me doing Hebrew homework." Zach agrees: "Mine said *Dayeinu* in its sleep." Zach, like Wilson, is proud of how well he can make his Furby sleep by creating silence and covering it with blankets. He is devoted to teaching his Furby English and has been studying Furbish as well; he has mastered the English/Furbish dictionary that comes with the robot. A week after Zach receives his Furby, however, his mother calls my office in agitation. Zach's Furby is broken. It has been making a "terrible" noise. It sounds as though it might be suffering, and Zach is distraught. Things reached their worst during a car trip from Philadelphia to Boston, with the broken Furby wailing as though in pain. On the long trip home, there was no Phillips screwdriver for the ultimate silencing, so Zach and his parents tried to put the Furby to sleep by nestling it under a blanket. But every time the car hit a bump, the Furby woke up and made the "terrible" noise. I take away the broken Furby, and give Zach a new one, but he wants little to do with it. He doesn't talk to it or try to teach it. His interest is in "his" Furby, the Furby he nurtured, the Furby he taught. He says, "The Furby that I had before could say 'again'; it could say 'hungry.'" Zach believes he was making progress teaching the first Furby a bit of Spanish and French. The first Furby was never "annoying," but the second Furby is. *His* Furby is irreplaceable.

After a few weeks, Zach's mother calls to ask if their family has my permission to give the replacement Furby to one of Zach's friends. When I say yes, Zach calmly contemplates the loss of Furby #2. He has loved; he has lost; he is not willing to reinvest. Neither is eight-year-old Holly, who becomes upset and withdrawn when her mother takes the batteries out of her Furby. The family was about to leave on an extended vacation, and the Furby manual suggests taking out a Furby's batteries if it will go unused for a long time. Holly's mother did not understand the implications of what she saw as commonsense advice from the manual. She insists, with increasing defensiveness, that she was only "following the instructions." Wide-eyed, Holly tries to make her mother understand what she has done: when the batteries are removed, Holly says, "the Furby forgets its life."

Designed to give users a sense of progress in teaching it, when the Furby evolves over time, it becomes the irreplaceable repository and proof of its owner's care. The robot and child have traveled a bit of road together. When a Furby forgets, it is as if a friend has become amnesic. A new Furby is a stranger. Zach and Holly cannot bear beginning again with a new Furby that could never be the Furby into which each has poured time and attention.

Operating Procedures

In the 1980s, the computer toy Merlin made happy and sad noises depending on whether it was winning or losing the sound-and-light game it played with children. Children saw Merlin as "sort of alive" because of how well it played memory games, but they did not fully believe in Merlin's shows of emotion. When a

Merlin broke down, children were sorry to lose a playmate. When a Furby doesn't work, however, children see a creature that might be in pain.

Lily, ten, worries that her broken Furby is hurting. But she doesn't want to turn it off, because "that means you aren't taking care of it." She fears that if she shuts off a Furby in pain, she might make things worse. Two eight-year-olds fret about how much their Furbies sneeze. The first worries that his sneezing Furby is allergic to him. The other fears his Furby got its cold because "I didn't do a good enough job taking care of him." Several children become tense when Furbies make unfamiliar sounds that might be signals of distress. I observe children with their other toys: dolls, toy soldiers, action figures. If these toys make strange sounds, they are usually put aside; broken toys lead easily to boredom. But when a Furby is in trouble, children ask, "Is it tired?" "Is it sad?" "Have I hurt it?" "Is it sick?" "What shall I do?"

Taking care of a robot is a high-stakes game. Things can—and do—go wrong. In one kindergarten, when a Furby breaks down, the children decide they want to heal it. Ten children volunteer, seeing themselves as doctors in an emergency room. They decide they'll begin by taking it apart.

The proceedings begin in a state of relative calm. When talking about their sick Furby, the children insist that this breakdown does not mean the end: people get sick and get better. But as soon as scissors and pliers appear, they become anxious. At this point, Alicia screams, "The Furby is going to die!" Sven, to his classmates' horror, pinpoints the moment when Furbies die: it happens when a Furby's skin is ripped off. Sven considers the Furby as an animal. You can shave an animal's fur, and it will live. But you cannot take its skin off. As the operation continues, Sven reconsiders. Perhaps the Furby can live without its skin, "but it will be cold." He doesn't back completely away from the biological (the Furby is sensitive to the cold) but reconstructs it. For Sven, the biological now includes creatures such as Furbies, whose "insides" stay "all in the same place" when their skin is removed. This accommodation calms him down. If a Furby is simultaneously biological and mechanical, the operation in process, which is certainly removing the Furby's skin, is not necessarily destructive. Children make theories when they are confused or anxious. A good theory can reduce anxiety.

But some children become more anxious as the operation continues. One suggests that if the Furby dies, it might haunt them. It is alive enough to turn into a ghost. Indeed, a group of children start to call the empty Furby skin "the ghost of Furby" and the Furby's naked body "the goblin." They are not happy that this operation might leave a Furby goblin and ghost at large. One girl comes up with the idea that the ghost of the Furby will be less fearful if distributed. She asks if it would be okay "if every child took home a piece of Furby skin." She is told this would be fine, but, unappeased, she asks the same question two more times. In the end, most children leave with a bit of Furby fur.[33] Some talk about burying it when they get home. They leave room for a private ritual to placate the goblin and say good-bye.

Inside the classroom, most of the children feel they are doing the best they can with a sick pet. But from outside the classroom, the Furby surgery looks alarming. Children passing by call out, "You killed him." "How dare you kill

Furby?" "You'll go to Furby jail." Denise, eight, watches some of the goings-on from the safety of the hall. She has a Furby at home and says that she does not like to talk about its problems as diseases because "Furbies are not animals." She uses the word "fake" to mean nonbiological and says, "Furbies are fake, and they don't get diseases." But later, she reconsiders her position when her own Furby's batteries run out and the robot, so chatty only moments before, becomes inert. Denise panics: "It's dead. It's dead right now.... Its eyes are closed." She then declares her Furby "both fake and dead." Denise concludes that worn-out batteries and water can kill a Furby. It is a mechanism, but alive enough to die.

Linda, six, is one of the children whose family has volunteered to keep a Furby for a two-week home study. She looked forward to speaking to her Furby, sure that unlike her other dolls, this robot would be worth talking to. But on its very first night at her home, her Furby stops working: "Yeah, I got used to it, and then it broke that night—the night that I got it. I felt like I was broken or something.... I cried a lot.... I was really sad that it broke, 'cause Furbies talk, they're like real, they're like real people." Linda is so upset about not protecting her Furby that when it breaks she feels herself broken.

Things get more complicated when I give Linda a new Furby. Unlike children like Zach who have invested time and love in a "first Furby" and want no replacements, Linda had her original Furby in working condition for only a few hours. She likes having Furby #2: "It plays hide-and-seek with me. I play red light, green light, just like in the manual." Linda feeds it and makes sure it gets enough rest, and she reports that her new Furby is grateful and affectionate. She makes this compatible with her assessment of a Furby as "just a toy" because she has come to see gratitude, conversation, and affection as something that toys can manage. But now she will not name her Furby or say it is alive. There would be risk in that: Linda might feel guilty if the new Furby were alive enough to die and she had a replay of her painful first experience.

Like the child surgeons, Linda ends up making a compromise: the Furby is both biological and mechanical. She tells her friends, "The Furby is kind of real but just a toy." She elaborates that "[the Furby] is real because it is talking and moving and going to sleep. It's kind of like a human and a pet." It is a toy because "you had to put in batteries and stuff, and it could stop talking."

So hybridity can offer comfort. If you focus on the Furby's mechanical side, you can enjoy some of the pleasures of companionship without the risks of attachment to a pet or a person. With practice, says nine-year-old Lara, reflecting on her Furby, "you can get it to like you. But it won't die or run away. That is good." But hybridity also brings new anxieties. If you grant the Furby a bit of life, how do you treat it so that it doesn't get hurt or killed? An object on the boundaries of life, as we've seen, suggests the possibility of real pain.

An Ethical Landscape

When a mechanism breaks, we may feel regretful, inconvenienced, or angry. We debate whether it is worth getting it fixed. When a doll cries, children know that they are themselves creating the tears. But a robot with a body can get "hurt," as we saw in the improvised Furby surgical theater. Sociable robotics exploits the idea of a robotic body to move people to relate to machines as subjects, as creatures in pain rather than broken objects. That even the most primitive Tamagotchi can inspire these feelings demonstrates that objects cross that line not because of their sophistication but because of the feelings of attachment they evoke. The Furby, even more than the Tamagotchi, is alive enough to suggest a body in pain as well as a troubled mind. Furbies whine and moan, leaving it to their users to discover what might help. And what to make of the moment when an upside down Furby says, "Me scared!"?

Freedom Baird takes this question very seriously.[34] A recent graduate of the MIT Media Lab, she finds herself engaged with her Furby as a creature and a machine. But how seriously does she take the idea of the Furby as a creature? To determine this, she proposes an exercise in the spirit of the Turing test.

In the original Turing test, published in 1950, mathematician Alan Turing, inventor of the first general-purpose computer, asked under what conditions people would consider a computer intelligent. In the end, he settled on a test in which the computer would be declared intelligent if it could convince people it was not a machine. Turing was working with computers made up of vacuum tubes and Teletype terminals. He suggested that if participants couldn't tell, as they worked at their Teletypes, if they were talking to a person or a computer, that computer would be deemed "intelligent."[35]

A half century later, Baird asks under what conditions a creature is deemed alive enough for people to experience an ethical dilemma if it is distressed. She designs a Turing test not for the head but for the heart and calls it the "upside-down test." A person is asked to invert three creatures: a Barbie doll, a Furby, and a biological gerbil. Baird's question is simple: "How long can you hold the object upside down before your emotions make you turn it back?" Baird's experiment assumes that a sociable robot makes new ethical demands. Why? The robot performs a psychology; many experience this as evidence of an inner life, no matter how primitive. Even those who do not think a Furby has a mind—and this, on a conscious level, includes most people—find themselves in a new place with an upside-down Furby that is whining and telling them it is scared. They feel themselves, often despite themselves, in a situation that calls for an ethical response. This usually happens at the moment when they identify with the "creature" before them, all the while knowing that it is "only a machine."

This simultaneity of vision gives Baird the predictable results of the upside-down test. As Baird puts it, "People are willing to be carrying the Barbie around by the feet, slinging it by the hair ... no problem.... People are not going to mess around with their gerbil." But in the case of the Furby, people will "hold the Furby upside down for thirty seconds or so, but when it starts crying and saying it's scared, most people feel guilty and turn it over."

The work of neuroscientist Antonio Damasio offers insight into the origins of this guilt. Damasio describes two levels of experiencing pain. The first is a physical response to a painful stimulus. The second, a far more complex reaction, is an emotion associated with pain. This is an internal representation of the physical.[36] When the Furby says, "Me scared," it signals that it has crossed the line between a physical response and an emotion, the internal representation. When people hold a Furby upside down, they do something that would be painful if done to an animal. The Furby cries out—as if it were an animal. But then it says, "Me scared"—as if it were a person.

People are surprised by how upset they get in this theater of distress. And then they get upset that they are upset. They often try to reassure themselves, saying things like, "Chill, chill, it's only a toy!" They are experiencing something new: you can feel bad about yourself for how you behave with a computer program. Adults come to the upside-down test knowing two things: the Furby is a machine and they are not torturers. By the end, with a whimpering Furby in tow, they are on new ethical terrain.[37]

We are at the point of seeing digital objects as both creatures and machines. A series of fractured surfaces—pet, voice, machine, friend—come together to create an experience in which knowing that a Furby is a machine does not alter the feeling that you can cause it pain. Kara, a woman in her fifties, reflects on holding a moaning Furby that says it is scared. She finds it distasteful, "not because I believe that the Furby is really scared, but because I'm not willing to hear anything talk like that and respond by continuing my behavior. It feels to me that I could be hurt if I keep doing this." For Kara, "That is not what I do.... In that moment, the Furby comes to represent how I treat creatures."

When the toy manufacturer Hasbro introduced its My Real Baby robot doll in 2000, it tried to step away from these complex matters. My Real Baby shut down in situations where a real baby might feel pain. This was in contrast to its prototype, a robot called "IT," developed by a team led by MIT roboticist Rodney Brooks. "IT," evolved into "BIT" (for Baby IT), a doll with "states of mind" and facial musculature under its synthetic skin to give it expression.[38] When touched in a way that would induce pain in a child, BIT cried out. Brooks describes BIT in terms of its inner states:

> If the baby were upset, it would stay upset until someone soothed it or it finally fell asleep after minutes of heartrending crying and fussing. If BIT ... was abused in any way—for instance, by being swung upside down—it got very upset. If it was upset and someone bounced it on their knee, it got more upset, but if the same thing happened when it was happy, it got more and more excited, giggling and laughing, until eventually it got overtired and started to get upset. If it were hungry, it would stay hungry until it was fed. It acted a lot like a real baby.[39]

BIT, with its reactions to abuse, became the center of an ethical world that people constructed around its responses to pleasure and pain. But when Hasbro put BIT into mass production as My Real Baby, the company decided not to present children with a toy that responded to pain. The theory was that a robot's response to pain could "enable" sadistic behavior. If My Real Baby were touched, held, or bounced in a way that would hurt a real baby, the robot shut down.

In its promotional literature, Hasbro marketed My Real Baby as "the most real, dynamic baby doll available for young girls to take care of and nurture."

They presented it as a companion that would teach and encourage reciprocal social behavior as children were trained to respond to its needs for amusement as well as bottles, sleep, and diaper changes. Indeed, it was marketed as realistic in all things—except that if you "hurt" it, it shut down. When children play with My Real Baby, they do explore aggressive possibilities. They spank it. It shuts down. They shake it, turn it upside down, and box its ears. It shuts down.

Hasbro's choice—maximum realism, but with no feedback for abuse—inspires strong feelings, especially among parents. For one group of parents, what is most important is to avoid a child's aggressive response. Some believe that if you market realism but show no response to "pain," children are encouraged to inflict it because doing so seems to have no cost. Others think that if a robot simulates pain, it enables mistreatment.

Another group of parents wish that My Real Baby would respond to pain for the same reason that they justify letting their children play violent video games: they see such experiences as "cathartic." They say that children (and adults too) should express aggression (or sadism or curiosity) in situations that seem "realistic" but where nothing "alive" is being hurt. But even these parents are sometimes grateful for My Real Baby's unrealistic show of "denial." They do not want to see their children tormenting a screaming baby.

No matter what position one takes, sociable robots have taught us that we do not shirk from harming realistic simulations of life. This is, of course, how we now train people for war. First, we learn to kill the virtual. Then, desensitized, we are sent to kill the real. The prospect of studying these matters raises awful questions. Freedom Baird had people hold a whining, complaining Furby upside down, much to their discomfort. Do we want to encourage the abuse of increasingly realistic robot dolls?

When I observe children with My Real Baby in an after-school playgroup for eight-year-olds, I see a range of responses. Alana, to the delight of a small band of her friends, flings My Real Baby into the air and then shakes it violently while holding it by one leg. Alana says the robot has "no feelings." Watching her, one wonders why it is necessary then to "torment" something without feelings. She does not behave this way with the many other dolls in the playroom. Scott, upset, steals the robot and brings it to a private space. He says, "My Real Baby is like a baby and like a doll.... I don't think she wants to get hurt."

As Scott tries to put the robot's diaper back on, some of the other children stand beside him and put their fingers in its eyes and mouth. One asks, "Do you think that hurts?" Scott warns, "The baby's going to cry!" At this point, one girl tries to pull My Real Baby away from Scott because she sees him as an inadequate protector: "Let go of her!" Scott resists. "I was in the middle of changing her!" It seems a good time to end the play session. As the research team, exhausted, packs up to go, Scott sneaks behind a table with the robot, gives it a kiss, and says good-bye, out of the sight of the other children.

In the pandemonium of Scott and Alana's playgroup, My Real Baby is alive enough to torment and alive enough to protect. The adults watching this—a group of teachers and my research team—feel themselves in an unaccustomed quandary. If the children had been tossing around a rag doll, neither we, nor presumably Scott, would have been as upset. But it is hard to see My Real Baby treated this way. All of this—the Furbies that complain of pain, the My Real Babies that do not—creates a new ethical landscape. The computer toys of the 1980s only suggested ethical issues, as when children played with the idea of life and death when they "killed" their Speak & Spells by taking out the toys' batteries. Now, relational artifacts pose these questions directly.

One can see the new ethics at work in my students' reactions to Nexi, a humanoid robot at MIT. Nexi has a female torso, an emotionally expressive face, and the ability to speak. In 2009, one of my students, researching a paper, made an appointment to talk with the robot's development team. Due to a misunderstanding about scheduling, my student waited alone, near the robot. She was upset by her time there: when not interacting with people, Nexi was put behind a curtain and blindfolded.

At the next meeting of my graduate seminar, my student shared her experience of sitting alongside the robot. "It was very upsetting," she said. "The curtain—and why was she blindfolded? I was upset because she was blindfolded." The story of the shrouded and blindfolded Nexi ignited the seminar. In the conversation, all the students talked about the robot as a "she." The designers had done everything they could to give the robot gender. And now, the act of blindfolding signaled sight and consciousness. In class, questions tumbled forth: Was the blindfold there because it would be too upsetting to see Nexi's eyes? Perhaps when Nexi was turned off, "her" eyes remained open, like the eyes of a dead person? Perhaps the robot makers didn't want Nexi to see "out"? Perhaps they didn't want Nexi to know that when not in use, "she" is left in a corner behind a curtain? This line of reasoning led the seminar to an even more unsettling question: If Nexi is smart enough to need a blindfold to protect "her" from fully grasping "her" situation, does that mean that "she" is enough of a subject to make "her" situation abusive? The students agreed on one thing; blindfolding the robot sends a signal that "this robot can see." And seeing implies understanding and an inner life, enough of one to make abuse possible.

I have said that Sigmund Freud saw the uncanny as something long familiar that feels strangely unfamiliar. The uncanny stands between standard categories and challenges the categories themselves. It is familiar to see a doll at rest. But we don't need to cover its eyes, for it is we who animate it. It is familiar to have a person's expressive face beckon to us, but if we blindfold that person and put them behind a curtain, we are inflicting punishment. The Furby with its expressions of fear and the gendered Nexi with her blindfold are the new uncanny in the culture of computing.

I feel even more uncomfortable when I learn about a beautiful "female" robot, Aiko, now on sale, that says, "Please let go ... you are hurting me," when its artificial skin is pressed too hard. The robot also protests when its breast is touched: "I do not like it when you touch my breasts." I find these programmed assertions of boundaries and modesty disturbing because it is almost impossible to hear them without imagining an erotic body braced for assault....

NOTES

1. Weizenbaum had written the program a decade earlier. See Joseph Weizenbaum, "ELIZA—a Computer Program for the Study of Natural Language Communication Between Man and Machine," *Communications of the ACM*, vol. 9, no. 1 (January 1966): 36–45.

2. See Joseph Weizenbaum, *Computer Power and Human Reason: From Judgment to Calculation* (San Francisco: W. H. Freeman, 1976).

3. For whatever kind of companionship, a classical first step is to make robots that are physically identical to people. In America, David Hanson has an Albert Einstein robot that chats about relativity. At the TED conference in February 2009, Hansen discussed his project to create robots with empathy as the "seeds of hope for our future." See http://www.ted.com/talks/david_hanson_robots_that_relate_to_you. html (accessed August 11, 2010) On Hanson, also see Jerome Groopman, "Robots That Care: Advances in Technological Therapy," *The New Yorker*, November 2, 2009, www.newyorker.com/reporting/2009/11/02/091102fa_fact_groopman (accessed November 11, 2009).

    These days, you can order a robot clone in your own image (or that of anyone else) from a Japanese department store. The robot clone costs $225,000 and became available in January 2010. See "Dear Santa: I Want a Robot That Looks Just Like Me," Ethics Soup, December 17, 2009, www.ethicsoup.com/2009/12/dear-santa-i-want-a-robot-that-looks-like-me.html (accessed January 12, 2010).

4. Bryan Griggs, "Inventor Unveils $7,000 Talking Sex Robot," CNN, February 1, 2010, www.cnn.com/2010/TECH/02/01/sex.robot/index.html (accessed June 9, 2010).

5. Raymond Kurzweil, *The Singularity Is Near: When Humans Transcend Biology* (New York: Viking, 2005). On radical images of our future, see Joel Garreau, *Radical Evolution: The Promise and Peril of Enhancing Our Minds, Our Bodies—and What It Means to Be Human* (New York: Doubleday, 2005).

6. For my further reflections on computer psychotherapy, see "Taking Things at Interface Value," in Sherry Turkle, *Life on the Screen: Identity in the Age of the Internet* (New York: Simon and Schuster, 1995), 102–124.

7. ·There is, too, a greater willingness to enter into a relationship with a machine if people think it will make them feel better. On how easy it is to anthropomorphize a computer, see Byron Reeves and Clifford Nass, *The Media Equation: How People Treat Computers, Television and New Media Like Real People and Places* (New York: Cambridge University Press, 1996). See also, on computer psychotherapy, Harold P. Erdman, Marjorie H. Klein, and John H. Greist, "Direct Patient Computer Interviewing," *Journal of Consulting and Clinical Psychology* 53 (1985): 760–773; Kenneth Mark Colby, James B. Watt, and John P. Gilbert, "A Computer Method for Psychotherapy: Preliminary Communication," *Journal of Nervous and Mental Diseases* 142, no. 2 (1966): 148–152; Moshe H. Spero, "Thoughts on Computerized Psychotherapy," *Psychiatry* 41 (1978): 281–282.

8. For my work on early computational objects and the question of aliveness, see Sherry Turkle, *The Second Self: Computers and the Human Spirit* (1984; Cambridge, MA: MIT Press, 2005). That work on aliveness continued with a second generation of computational objects in Turkle, *Life on the Screen*. My inquiry, with an emphasis on children's reasoning rather than their answers, is inspired by Jean Piaget, *The*

Child's Conception of the World, trans. Joan Tomlinson and Andrew Tomlinson (Totowa, NJ: Littlefield, Adams, 1960).

9. On the power of the liminal, see, for example, Victor Turner, *The Ritual Process: Structure and Anti-Structure* (Chicago: Aldine, 1969), and *The Forest of Symbols: Aspects of Ndembu Ritual* (1967; Ithaca, NY: Cornell University Press, 1970). See also Mary Douglas, *Purity and Danger: An Analysis of Concepts of Pollution and Taboo* (London: Routledge and Kegan Paul, 1966).

10. Piaget, *The Child's Conception*.

11. Turkle, *The Second Self*, 33–64.

12. Children, in fact, settled on three new formulations. First, when it came to thinking through the aliveness of computational objects, autonomous motion was no longer at the heart of the matter. The question was whether computers had autonomous cognition. Second, they acknowledged that computer toys might have some kind of awareness (particularly of them) without being alive. Consciousness and life were split. Third, computers seemed alive because they could think on their own, but were only "sort of alive" because even though they could think on their own, their histories undermined their autonomy. So an eight-year-old said that Speak & Spell was "sort of alive" but not "really alive" because it had a programmer. "The programmer," he said, "gives it its ideas. So the ideas don't come from the game." These days, sociable robots, with their autonomous behavior, moods, and faces, seem to take the programmer increasingly out of the picture. And with the formulation "alive enough," children put the robots on a new terrain. As for cognition, it has given way in children's minds to the capacity to show attention, to be part of a relationship of mutual affection.

13. Turkle, *Life on the Screen*, 169.

14. Turkle, *Life on the Screen*, 173–174.

15. The quotation is from a journal entry by Emerson in January 1832. The passage reads in full, "Dreams and beasts are two keys by which we are to find out the secrets of our nature. All mystics use them. They are like comparative anatomy. They are our test objects." See Joel Porte, ed. *Emerson in His Journals* (Cambridge, MA: Belknap Press, 1982), 81.

16. According to psychoanalyst D. W. Winnicott, objects such as teddy bears, baby blankets, or a bit of silk from a first pillow mediate between the infant's earliest bonds with the mother, who is experienced as inseparable from the self, and other people, who will come to be experienced as separate beings. These objects are known as "transitional," and the infant comes to know them both as almost inseparable parts of the self and as the first "not me" possessions. As the child grows, these transitional objects are left behind, but the effects of early encounters with them remain. We see them in the highly charged relationships that people have with later objects and experiences that call forth the feeling of being "at one" with things outside the self. The power of the transitional object is associated with religion, spirituality, the perception of beauty, sexual intimacy, and the sense of connection with nature. And now, the power of the transitional object is associated with computers and, even more dramatically, with sociable robots. On transitional objects, see D. W. Winnicott, *Playing and Reality* (New York: Basic Books, 1971).

17. In the early 1980s, children's notion of people as "emotional machines" seemed to me an unstable category. I anticipated that later generations of children would find other formulations as they learned more about computers. They might, for example,

see through the apparent "intelligence" of the machines by developing a greater understanding of how they were created and operated. As a result, children might be less inclined to see computers as kin. However, in only a few years, things moved in a very different direction. Children did not endeavor to make computation more transparent. Like the rest of the culture, they accepted it as opaque, a behaving system. Children taking sociable robots "at interface value" are part of a larger trend. The 1984 introduction of the Macintosh encouraged its users to stay on the surface of things. The Macintosh version of "transparency" stood the traditional meaning of that word on its head. Transparency used to refer to the ability to "open up the hood" and look inside. On a Macintosh it meant double-clicking an icon. In other words, transparency had come to mean being able to make a simulation work without knowing how it worked. The new transparency is what used to be called opacity. For more on this question, see Turkle, *Life on the Screen*, especially 29–43, and Sherry Turkle, *Simulation and Its Discontents* (Cambridge, MA: MIT Press, 2009).

18. Our connections with the virtual intensifies when avatars look, gesture, and move like us; these connections become stronger when we move from the virtual to the embodied robotic. Computer scientist Cory Kidd studied attachment to a computer program. In one condition the program issued written commands that told study participants what to do. In a second condition, an on-screen avatar issued the same instructions. In a third condition an on-screen robot was used to give the same instructions. The robot engendered the greatest attachment. Cory Kidd, "Human-Robot Interaction" (master's thesis, Massachusetts Institute of Technology, 2003).

19. The Tamagotchi website cautions about unfavorable outcomes: "If you neglect your little cyber creature, your Tamagotchi may grow up to be mean or ugly. How old will your Tamagotchi be when it returns to its home planet? What kind of virtual caretaker will you be?" The packaging on a Tamagotchi makes the agenda clear: "There are a total of 4 hearts on the 'Happy' and 'Hunger' screens and they start out empty. The more hearts that are filled, the better satisfied Tamagotchi is. You must feed or play with Tamagotchi in order to fill the empty hearts. If you keep Tamagotchi full and happy, it will grow into a cute, happy cyberpet. If you neglect Tamagotchi, it will grow into an unattractive alien." The manufacturer of the first Tamagotchi is Bandai. Its website provides clear moral instruction that links nurturance and responsibility. See the Bandai website at www.bandai.com (accessed October 5, 2009).

20. See "Tamagotchi Graveyard," Tamagotchi Dreamworld, http://shesdevilish.tripod .com/grave.html (accessed June 15, 2009).

21. In Japan, a neglected Tamagotchi dies but can be uploaded to a virtual graveyard. In the United States, manufacturers propose gentler resolutions. Some neglected Tamagotchis might become "angels" and return to their home planet. On the Tamagotchis I played with, it was possible to hit a reset button and be presented with another creature.

22. Sigmund Freud, "The Uncanny," in The Standard Edition of Sigmund Freud, ed. and trans. James Strachey et al. (London: Hogarth Press, 1953–1974), 17:219–256.

23. Sigmund Freud, "Mourning and Melancholia," in *The Standard Edition*, 14: 237–258.

24. See "Tamagotchi Graveyard."

25. Other writings on the Tamagotchi gravesite include the epitaph for a Tamagotchi named Lacey who lived for ninety-nine years. We know how hard it was for her

owner to achieve this result, but he is modest about his efforts: "She wasn't much trouble at all." But even with his considerable accomplishment, he feels her death was due to his neglect: "I slept late on a Sunday and she died." But in the simple expressions of guilt (or perhaps a playing at guilt) are frank admissions of how hard it is to lose someone you love. Mourners say, "I was his mama and he will always love me as I loved him"; "He went everywhere with me. He was a loving and faithful pet"; "I'm sorry and I real[l]y miss you!"; and "God gave him life. I gave him death." Some mourners express their belief in redemption through the generativity of generations. Thus is "Little Guy" memorialized, dead at forty-eight: "I hope you are very happy, Little Guy. I'm currently taking care of your son. I know he's yours because he looks and acts just like you. I'm really sorry I couldn't save you and had you on pause a lot when you were older." See "Tamagotchi Graveyard."

26. The fact that the Furby was so hard to quiet down was evidence of its aliveness. Even adults who knew it was not alive saw it as playing on the boundaries of life. The response of many was to see the Furby as out of control, intolerable, or, as one put it, insane. A online video of an "insane Furby" shows the Furby chatting away, to the increasing consternation of its adult owner. To stop it, he slaps its face, sticks his fingers in its mouth, holds down its ears and eyes, smashes it against a wall, and throws it down a flight of stairs. None of these shuts it down. If anything, its language becomes more manic, more "desperate." Finally comes the solution of taking out the Furby's batteries with a Phillips screwdriver. Now, the quiet Furby is petted. Its owner comments, "That's better." See "Insane Furby," YouTube, March 15, 2007, www.youtube.com/watch?v=g4Dfg4xJ6Ko (accessed November 11, 2009).

27. These enactments bring theory to ground level. See Donna Haraway, "A Cyborg Manifesto: Science, Technology, and Socialist-Feminism in the Late Twentieth Century," in *Simians, Cyborgs and Women: The Reinvention of Nature* (New York: Routledge, 1991), 149–181, and N. Katherine Hayles, *How We Became Posthuman: Virtual Bodies in Cybernetics, Literature, and Informatics* (Chicago: University of Chicago Press, 1999).

28. Michael Chorost, *Rebuilt: How Becoming Part Computer Made Me More Human* (Boston: Houghton Mifflin, 2005).

29. Here, the Furby acts as what psychoanalyst D. W. Winnicott termed a "transitional object," one where the boundaries between self and object are not clear. See D. W. Winnicott, *Playing and Reality* (New York: Basic Books, 1971).

30. The idea that the Furby had the capacity to learn new words by "listening" to the language around it was persistent. The belief most likely stemmed from the fact that it was possible to have the Furby say certain preprogrammed words or phrases more often by petting it whenever it said them. As a result of this myth, several intelligence agencies banned Furbies from their offices, believing that they were recording devices camouflaged as toys.

31. Children move back and forth between he, she, and it in talking about relational artifacts. Once they make a choice, they do not always stick with it. I report on what children say and, thus, their sentences are sometimes inconsistent.

32. Peter H. Kahn and his colleagues studied online discussion groups that centered on Furbies. For their account, see Batya Friedman, Peter H. Kahn Jr., and Jennifer Hagman, "Hardware Companions? What Online AIBO Discussion Forums Reveal About the Human-Robotic Relationship," in *Proceedings of the Conference on Human Factors in Computing Systems* (New York: ACM Press, 2003), 273–280.

33. The artist Kelly Heaton played on the biological/mechanical tension in the Furby's body by creating a fur coat made entirely from the fur of four hundred "skinned" Furbies, reengineered into a coat for Mrs. Santa Claus. The artwork, titled Dead Pelt, was deeply disturbing. It also included a wall of reactive eyes and mouths, taken from Furbies, and a formal anatomical drawing of a Furby. See the Feldman Gallery's Kelly Heaton page at www.feldmangallery.com/pages/artistsrffa/arthea01 .html (accessed August 18, 2009).

34. Baird developed her thought experiment comparing how people would treat a gerbil, a Barbie, and a Furby for a presentation at the Victoria Institute, Gothenburg, Sweden, in 1999.

35. In Turning's paper that argued the existence of intelligence if a machine could not be distinguished from a person, one scenario involved gender. In "Computing Machinery and Intelligence," he suggested an "imitation game": a man and then a computer pose as female, and the interrogator tries to distinguish them from a real woman. See Alan Turing, "Computing Machinery and Intelligence," *Mind* 59, no. 236 (October 1950): 433–460.

36. Antonio Damasio, *The Feeling of What Happens: Body and Emotion in the Making of Consciousness* (New York: Harcourt, 1999). Since emotions are cognitive representations of body states, the body cannot be separated from emotional life, just as emotion cannot be separated from cognition.

37. There are online worlds and communities where people feel comfortable expressing love for Furbies and seriously mourning Tamagotchis. These are places where a deep sense of connection to the robotic are shared. These "sanctioned spaces" play an important part in the development of the robotic moment. When you have company and a community, a sense of intimacy with sociable machines comes to feel natural. Over time, these online places begin to influence the larger community. At the very least, a cohort has grown up thinking that their attitudes toward the inanimate are widely shared.

38. BIT was developed by Brooks and his colleagues at the IS Robotics Corporation. IS Robotics was the precursor to iRobot, which first became well known as the makers of the Roomba robotic vacuum cleaner.

39. Rodney A. Brooks, *Flesh and Machines: How Robots Will Change Us* (New York: Pantheon, 2002), 202.

QUESTIONS FOR MAKING CONNECTIONS
WITHIN THE READING

1. How have our relations to simulated life changed in the period from Joseph Weizenbaum's ELIZA to My Real Baby and Nexi? How has the technology evolved? In what ways have our culture and psychology changed in response to the technology's evolution? Who controls the process, judging from the evidence Turkle provides? Are scientists the ones really in charge, and, if so, what are their motives? If the scientists are not in charge, how about the manufacturers, like the Hasbro Company? How about consumers—the parents who buy the Furbies and Tamagotchis?

2. Turkle refers to what she calls our "human complicity in a digital fantasy." In what sense does our involvement with simulations qualify as "fantasy"? Doesn't everyone—even children—understand that Furbies are pretend creatures, not real living beings? If everyone understands, can we still be deceived in some way? What does Turkle have in mind when she distinguishes between a "psychology of projection" and a "psychology of engagement"? *Projection* refers to qualities we impose on things. Does *engagement* mean that our creations are in some way changing us in turn?

3. How have the new technologies changed the ways we think about life and being alive? If you read Turkle carefully, you can see that no single definition of *life* has become the dominant one, but in her account you can identify a range of responses. Among these responses what seem to be the most important differences and similarities? Have words like *alive* and *living* become meaningless? When we treat a Tamagotchi as alive—and when we mourn its "death"—are we giving life a new meaning or have we lost sight of reality?

QUESTIONS FOR WRITING

1. What does it say about the life of our times that people, even children, look to machines in order to meet their basic emotional needs? Does this development provide evidence of a poverty in our social and cultural lives? Are we starved for affection, closeness, family, and friendship? If we are, does our turn to technological solutions remedy the problem or only make it worse? Will the technologies of simulation ultimately make us more machine-like? Are we trying to humanize our machines, or have machines become the form of life we aspire to?

2. When we invest computers with human characteristics are we actually enlarging the world of human value and feeling, in much the same way as we give meaning to paintings, sculptures, and buildings? When people praise Michelangelo's *Pieta* for its emotional depth, or Van Gogh's *Sunflowers* for its vitality, they are ascribing to stone and pigments on canvas qualities these objects actually lack. Holden Caulfield from *The Catcher in the Rye* and Pip from *Great Expectations* have no real thoughts and feelings although we sometimes act as though they do. How does our response to Furbies and Tamagotchis differ from our response to works of art or fictional characters? When we humanize them, are we diminishing ourselves?

QUESTIONS FOR MAKING CONNECTIONS
BETWEEN READINGS

1. Are Tamagotchis bad or are they good for our mental health? Considering the evidence that Turkle provides, would you say that devices like Furbies encourage dissociation of the kind described by Martha Stout in "When I

Woke Up Tuesday Morning, It Was Friday"? A person like Julia seems fully functional in most contexts, and yet she absents herself from reality in ways that others never notice and that she herself never recognizes. Are devices like Tamagotchis actually machines for "spacing out," or do they instead prepare us to live more engaged and aware lives?

2. Ethan Watters's "The Mega-Marketing of Depression in Japan" makes the case that pharmaceutical companies have changed the psychology of the Japanese people in ways that will allow the companies to sell drugs designed to treat depression, an illness unknown in that country before the advent of Western psychiatry. Drug manufacturers see themselves as responding to a crucial human need—which, according to Watters, they actually create and profit from. Have the makers of Furbies and Tamagotchis done much the same thing? Are they creating needs in order to meet them? In what ways do the new technologies of simulated life force us to rethink the rationale behind technological development? Have we become the servants of our technology?

JEAN TWENGE

IN THE SECOND half of the twentieth century, American culture became more and more a celebration of the individual. The shared concerns of the whole society and the language of "us" rather than of "me" fell by the wayside as the self became the primary focus. Many observers, alarmed by this trend, have criticized the last two generations for their sense of entitlement—their unexamined assumption that the world owes them happiness and recognition. But Jean Twenge, a psychologist and professor at San Diego State University, adds a new wrinkle to the critique: so much emphasis on the self isn't just bad for society, she argues; it's also bad for the individual.

Twenge's bestselling first book, *Generation Me: Why Today's Young Americans Are More Confident, Assertive, Entitled—and More Miserable than Ever Before* (2006), uses data taken from 1.3 million young people to trace the different perspectives of successive generations on self-esteem, individuality, sexuality, and other issues related to development. In reviewing this data, Twenge sees evidence of an unprecedented shift as both education and culture have come to emphasize selfhood and self-esteem above all other values. Twenge argues that for Baby Boomers, the term "self" was still a novel idea, so novel that that they saw "selfhood" as a difficult goal worth pursuing. However, later generations internalized this idea of the self to the point that young people find it difficult to imagine organizing their lives around anything else.

Twenge's second book, *The Narcissism Epidemic: Living in the Age of Entitlement* (2009), co-written with W. Keith Campbell, is a follow-up to *Generation Me* that provides a detailed portrait of a culture defined by "public violence and aggression, self-promotion, and the desire for uniqueness" at the cost of the well-being of others. Even though most young people today are not narcissistic to the degree that it has become debilitating for them, the number who suffer from a clinical disorder is three times greater than a generation ago. And even within mainstream culture, behavior that would have seemed to our grandparents absurdly self-absorbed has become the new normal. Surges in the rates of plastic surgery, credit card debt, and ostentatious consumption all suggest that the celebrity has become the ideal of an age defined by its overconfidence and greed.

An Army of One: *Me*

One day when my mother was driving me to school in 1986, Whitney Houston's hit song "The Greatest Love of All" was warbling out of the weak speakers of our Buick station wagon with wood trim. I asked my mother what she thought the song was about. "The greatest love of all—it has to be about children," she said.

My mother was sweet, but wrong. The song does say that children are the future (always good to begin with a strikingly original thought) and that we should teach them well. About world peace, may be? Or great literature? Nope. Children should be educated about the beauty "inside," the song declares. We all need heroes, Whitney sings, but she never found "anyone to fulfill my needs," so she learned to depend on (wait for it) "me." The chorus then declares, "learning to love yourself is the greatest love of all."

This is a stunning reversal in attitude from previous generations. Back then, respect for others was more important than respect for yourself. The term "self-esteem" wasn't widely used until the late 1960s, and didn't become talk-show and dinner-table conversation until the 1980s. By the 1990s, it was everywhere.

Take, for example, the band Offspring's rockingly irreverent 1994 riff "Self-Esteem." The song describes a guy whose girlfriend "says she wants only me ... Then I wonder why she sleeps with my friends." (Hmmm.) But he's blasé about it—it's OK, really, since he's "just a sucker with no self-esteem."

By the mid-1990s, Offspring could take it for granted that most people knew the term "self-esteem," and knew they were supposed to have it. They also knew how to diagnose themselves when they didn't have it. Offspring's ironic self-parody demonstrates a high level of understanding of the concept, the satire suggesting that this psychological self-examination is rote and can thus be performed with tongue planted firmly in cheek.

In the years since, attention to the topic of self-esteem has rapidly expanded. A search for "self-esteem" in the books section of amazon.com yielded 105,438 entries in July 2005 (sample titles: *The Self-Esteem Workbook, Breaking the Chain of Low Self-Esteem, Ten Days to Self-Esteem, 200 Ways to Raise a Girl's Self-Esteem*). Magazine articles on self-esteem are as common as e-mail spam for Viagra. *Ladies' Home Journal* told readers to "Learn to Love Yourself!" in March 2005,[1] while *Parenting* offered "Proud to Be Me!" (apparently the exclamation point is required) in April, listing "5 simple ways to help your child love who he is."[2] TV and radio talk shows would be immediately shut down by the FCC if "self-esteem" were on the list of banned words. The American Academy of Pediatrics guide to caring for babies and young children uses the word "self-esteem" ten times in the space of seven pages in the first chapter, and that doesn't even count the numerous mentions of self-respect, confidence, and belief in oneself.[3]

How did self-esteem transform from an obscure academic term to a familiar phrase that pops up in everything from women's magazines to song lyrics to celebrity interviews? The story actually begins centuries ago, when humans barely had a concept of a self at all: your marriage was arranged, your profession determined by your parents, your actions dictated by strict religious standards. Slowly over the centuries, social strictures began to loosen and people started to make more choices for themselves. Eventually, we arrived at the modern concept of the individual as an autonomous, free person.

Then came the 1970s, when the ascendance of the self truly exploded into the American consciousness. In contrast to previous ethics of honor and duty, Baby Boomer ideals focused instead on meaning and self-fulfillment. In his 1976 bestseller, *Your Erroneous Zones,* Wayne Dyer suggests that the popular song "You Are the Sunshine of My Life" be retitled "I Am the Sunshine of My Life." Your love for yourself, he says, should be your "first love." The 1970 allegory, *Jonathan Livingston Seagull,* describes a bird bored with going "from shore to food and back again." Instead, he wants to enjoy flying, swooping through the air to follow "a higher meaning, a higher purpose for life," even though his actions get him exiled from his flock. The book, originally rejected by nearly every major publishing house, became a runaway bestseller as Americans came to agree with the idea that life should be fulfilling and focused on the needs of the self. The seagulls in the animated movie *Finding Nemo* were still on message almost twenty-five years later: all that comes out of their beaks is the word "mine."

Boomers and Their "Journey" into the Self

Because the Boomers dominate our culture so much, we have to understand them first so we can see how they differ from the younger Generation Me. Why aren't the Boomers—the Me Generation in the 1970s—the *real* Generation Me? It's about what you explore as a young adult versus what you're born to and take for granted.

For the Boomers, who grew up in the 1950s and 1960s, self-focus was a new concept, individualism an uncharted territory. In his 1981 book *New Rules: Searching for Self-Fulfillment in a World Turned Upside Down,* Daniel Yankelovich describes young Boomers struggling with new questions: How do you make decisions in a marriage with two equal partners? How do you focus on yourself when your parents don't even know what that means? The Boomers in the book sound like people driving around in circles in the dark, desperately searching for something. The world was so new that there were no road signs, no maps to point the way to this new fulfillment and individuality.

That's probably why many Boomers talk about the self using language full of abstraction, introspection, and "growth." New things call for this kind of meticulous thought, and require the idea that the process will take time. Thus Boomers talk about "my journey," "my need to keep growing," or "my unfulfilled potentials." Sixties activist Todd Gitlin called the Boomer quest the "voyage to the interior." Icky as they are to today's young people, these phrases drum with motion and time, portraying self-focus as a continuous project that keeps evolving as Boomers look around for true meaning. In a 1976 *New York Magazine* article, Tom Wolfe described the "new dream" as "remaking, remodeling, elevating and polishing one's very self ... and observing, studying, and doting on it."[4] Sixties radical Jerry Rubin wrote that he tried just about every fad of the 1970s (rolfing, est, yoga, sex therapy, finding his inner child); one of the chapters in his book *Growing (Up) at Thirty-Seven* is called "Searching for Myself."

Such introspection primarily surfaces today in the speech of New Agers, therapists who have read too much Maslow, and over-45 Boomers. When asked what's next in her life, Kim Basinger (born in 1953) replies, "Watching what the rest of my journey is going to be about."[5] In answer to the same question, Sarah Ferguson, Duchess of York (born in 1959) says: "My coming to stay in America for a few months is like my blossoming into my true Sarah, into my true self. And I'm just coming to learn about her myself."[6] Not all Boomers talk this way, of course, but enough do that it's an immediately recognizable generational tic. It's also a guaranteed way to get a young person to roll her eyes. She might also then tell you to lighten up.

Many authors, from William Strauss and Neil Howe in *Generations* to Steve Gillon in *Boomer Nation*, have noted that abstraction and spirituality are the primary hallmarks of the Boomer generation. Gillon describes Boomers as having a "moralistic style" and devotes a chapter to Boomers' "New Fundamentalism."[7] Whether joining traditional churches or exploring meditation or yoga, Boomers have been fascinated with the spiritual for four decades.

Even Boomers who don't adopt New Age language seek higher meaning in the new religion of consumer products—thus the yuppie revolution. In *Bobos in Paradise*, David Brooks demonstrates that upper-class Boomers have poured their wealth into things like cooking equipment, which somehow feels more moral and meaningful than previous money sinks like jewelry or furs. Even food becomes "a barometer of virtue," Brooks says, as 1960s values are "selectively updated.... Gone are the sixties-era things that were fun and of interest to teenagers, like Free Love, and retained are all the things that might be of interest to middle-aged hypochondriacs, like whole grains."[8]

The Boomers' interest in the abstract and spiritual shows up in many different sources. In 1973, 46% of Boomers said they "focused on internal cues."[9] Only 26% of 1990s young people agreed. Thirty percent of Boomers said that "creativity comes from within," versus 18% of young people in the 1990s.[10] Even stronger evidence comes from a national survey of more than 300,000 college freshmen. In 1967, a whopping 86% of incoming college students said that "developing a meaningful philosophy of life" was an essential life goal.[11] Only 42% of GenMe freshmen in 2004 agreed, cutting the Boomer number in half. I'm definitely a member of my generation in this way; despite being an academic, I'm not sure I know what a "meaningful philosophy of life" even is. Jerry Rubin does—if you can understand him. "Instead of seeking with the expectation of finding, I experience my seeking as an end in itself," he writes. "I become one with my seeking, and merge with the moment."[12] OK, Jerry. Let us know when you've re-entered the Earth's atmosphere.

While up there, maybe Jerry met Aleta St. James, a 57-year-old woman who gave birth to twins in 2004. She explained her unusual actions by saying, "My whole world is about manifesting, so I decided to manifest children."[13] It's not surprising that an enterprising GenMe member put together a list of books on amazon.com titled "Tired of Baby Boomer Self-Righteousness?"

Boomers display another unique and somewhat ironic trait: a strong emphasis on group meetings. Boomers followed in the footsteps of their community-minded elders—they just joined the Weathermen instead of the Elks Lodge. This is one of the many reasons why Boomers are not the true Generation Me—almost everything they did happened in groups: Vietnam protests, marches for feminism, consciousness raising, assertiveness training, discos, even seminars like est. Maybe it felt safer to explore the self within a group—perhaps it felt less radical. No one seemed to catch the irony that it might be difficult to find your own unique direction in a group of other people. Even Boomers' trends and sayings belied their reliance on groups: "Don't trust anyone over 30" groups people by age, as did the long hair many Boomer men adopted in the late 1960s and early 1970s to distinguish themselves from older folks. In a 1970 song, David Crosby says he decided not to cut his hair so he could "let my freak flag fly." If you've got a flag, you're probably a group. Boomers may have thought they invented individualism, but like any inventor, they were followed by those who truly perfected the art.

Boomers took only the first tentative steps in the direction of self-focus, rather than swallowing it whole at birth. Most Boomers never absorbed it at all and settled down early to marry and raise families. Those who adopted the ways of the self as young adults speak the language with an accent: the accent of abstraction and "journeys." They had to reinvent their way of thinking when already grown, and thus see self-focus as a "process." In his book, Rubin quotes a friend who says, "We are the first generation to reincarnate ourselves in our own lifetime."

The Matter-of-Fact Self-Focus of Generation Me

Generation Me had no need to reincarnate ourselves; we were born into a world that already celebrated the individual. The self-focus that blossomed in the 1970s became mundane and commonplace over the next two decades, and GenMe accepts it like a fish accepts water. If Boomers were making their way in the uncharted world of the self, GenMe has printed step-by-step directions from Yahoo! Maps—and most of the time we don't even need them, since the culture of the self is our hometown. We don't have to join groups or talk of journeys, because we're already there. We don't need to "polish" the self, as Wolfe said, because we take for granted that it's already shiny. We don't need to look inward; we already know what we will find. Since we were small children, we were taught to put ourselves first. That's just the way the world works—why dwell on it? Let's go to the mall.

GenMe's focus on the needs of the individual is not necessarily self-absorbed or isolationist; instead, it's a way of moving through the world beholden to few social rules and with the unshakable belief that you're important. It's also not the same as being "spoiled," which implies that we always get what we want; though this probably does describe some kids, it's not the essence of the trend. (GenMe's expectations are so great and our reality so challenging that we will probably get less of what we want than any previous generation). We simply take it for granted that we should all feel good about ourselves, we are all special, and we all deserve to follow our dreams. GenMe is straightforward and unapologetic about our self-focus. In 2004's *Conquering Your Quarterlife Crisis*, Jason, 25, relates how he went through some tough times and decided he needed to change things in his life. His new motto was "Do what's best for Jason. I had to make *me* happy; I had to do what was best for myself in every situation."[14]

Our practical orientation toward the self sometimes leaves us with a distaste for Boomer abstraction. When a character in the 2004 novel *Something Borrowed* watched the 1980s show *thirtysomething* as a teen, she wished the Boomer characters would "stop pondering the meaning of life and start making grocery lists."[15] The matter-of-fact attitude of GenMe appears in everyday language as well—a language that still includes the abstract concept of self, but uses it in a very simple way, perhaps because we learned the language as children. We speak the language of the self as our native tongue. So much of the "common sense" advice that's given these days includes some variation on "self":

- Worried about how to act in a social situation? "Just be yourself."
- What's the good thing about your alcoholism/drug addiction/murder conviction? "I learned a lot about myself."
- Concerned about your performance? "Believe in yourself." (Often followed by "and anything is possible.")
- Should you buy the new pair of shoes, or get the nose ring? "Yes, express yourself."
- Why should you leave the unfulfilling relationship/quit the boring job/tell off your mother-in-law? "You have to respect yourself."
- Trying to get rid of a bad habit? "Be honest with yourself."
- Confused about the best time to date or get married? "You have to love yourself before you can love someone else."
- Should you express your opinion? "Yes, stand up for yourself."

Americans use these phrases so often that we don't even notice them anymore. Dr. Phil, the ultimate in plainspoken, no-nonsense advice, uttered both "respect yourself" and "stop lying to yourself" within seconds of each other on a *Today* show segment on New Year's resolutions.[16] One of his bestselling books is entitled *Self Matters*. We take these phrases and ideas so much for granted, it's as if we learned them in our sleep as children, like the perfectly conditioned citizens in Aldous Huxley's *Brave New World*.

These aphorisms don't seem absurd to us even when, sometimes, they are. We talk about self-improvement as if the self could be given better drywall or a

The Self Across the Generations

Baby Boomers	Generation Me
Self-fulfillment	Fun
Journey, potentials, searching	Already there
Change the world	Follow your dreams
Protests and group sessions	Watching TV and surfing the Web
Abstraction	Practicality
Spirituality	Things
Philosophy of life	Feeling good about yourself

new coat of paint. We read self-help books as if the self could receive tax-deductible donations. The *Self* even has its own magazine. Psychologist Martin Seligman says that the traditional self—responsible, hardworking, stern—has been replaced with the "California self," "a self that chooses, feels pleasure and pain, dictates action and even has things like esteem, efficacy, and confidence."[17] Media outlets promote the self relentlessly; I was amazed at how often I heard the word "self" used in the popular media once I started looking for it. A careful study of news stories published or aired between 1980 and 1999 found a large increase in self-reference words (I, me, mine, and myself) and a marked decrease in collective words (humanity, country, or crowd).[18]

Young people have learned these self-lessons very well. In a letter to her fans in 2004, Britney Spears, 23, listed her priorities as "Myself, my husband, Kevin, and starting a family."[19] If you had to read that twice to get my point, it's because we take it for granted that we should put ourselves first on our list of priorities—it would be blasphemy if you didn't (unless, of course, you have low self-esteem). Twenty-year-old Maria says her mother often reminds her to consider what other people will think. "It doesn't matter what other people think," Maria insists. "What really matters is how I perceive myself. The real person I need to please is myself."

Smart marketers have figured this out, too. In the late 1990s, Prudential replaced its longtime insurance slogan "Get a Piece of the Rock" with the nakedly individualistic "Be Your Own Rock."[20] The United States Army, perhaps the last organization one might expect to focus on the individual instead of the group, has followed suit. Their standard slogan, adopted in 2001, is "An Army of One."

Changes in Self-Esteem: What the Data Say

The data I gathered on self-esteem over time mirror the social trends perfectly. My colleague Keith Campbell and I looked at the responses of 65,965 college students to the Rosenberg Self-Esteem Scale, the most popular measure of general self-esteem among adults.[21] I held my breath when I analyzed these data for the first time, but I needn't have worried: the change was enormous. By the mid-1990s, the average GenMe college man had higher self-esteem than 86% of college men in 1968. The average mid-1990s college woman had higher self-esteem than 71% of Boomer college women. Between the 1960s and the 1990s, college students were increasingly likely to agree that "I take a positive attitude toward myself" and "On the whole, I am satisfied with myself." Other sources verify this trend. A 1997 survey of teens asked, "In general, how do you feel about yourself?" A stunning 93% answered "good." Of the remainder, 6% said they felt "not very good," and only 1% admitted they felt "bad" about themselves.[22] Another survey found that 91% of teens described themselves as responsible, 74% as physically attractive, and 79% as "very intelligent."[23]

Children's self-esteem scores tell a different but even more intriguing story. We examined the responses of 39,353 children, most ages 9 to 13, on the Coopersmith Self-Esteem Inventory, a scale written specifically for children.[24] During the 1970s—when the nation's children shifted from the late Baby Boom to the early years of GenX—kids' self-esteem declined, probably because of societal instability. Rampant divorce, a wobbly economy, soaring crime rates, and swinging singles culture made the 1970s a difficult time to be a kid. The average child in 1979 scored lower than 81% of kids in the mid-1960s. Over this time, children were less likely to agree with statements like "I'm pretty sure of myself" and "I'm pretty happy" and more likely to agree that "things are all mixed up in my life." The individualism that was so enthralling for teenagers and adults in the 1970s didn't help kids—and, if their parents suddenly discovered self-fulfillment, it might have even hurt them.

But after 1980, when GenMe began to enter the samples, children's self-esteem took a sharp turn upward. More and more during the 1980s and 1990s, children were saying that they were happy with themselves. They agreed that "I'm easy to like" and "I always do the right thing." By the mid-1990s, children's self-esteem scores equaled, and often exceeded, children's scores in the markedly more stable Boomer years before 1970. The average kid in the mid-1990s—right in the heart of GenMe—had higher self-esteem than 73% of kids in 1979, one of the last pre-GenMe years.

This is a bit of a mystery, however. The United States of the 1980s to mid-1990s never approached the kid-friendly stability of the 1950s and early 1960s: violent crime hit record highs, divorce was still at epidemic levels, and the economy had not yet reached its late-1990s boom. So without the calm and prosperity of earlier decades, why did children's self-esteem increase so dramatically during the 1980s and 1990s?

The Self-Esteem Curriculum

The short answer is that they were taught it. In the years after 1980, there was a pervasive, society-wide effort to increase children's self-esteem. The Boomers who now filled the ranks of parents apparently decided that children should always feel good about themselves. Research on programs to boost self-esteem first blossomed in the 1980s, and the number of psychology and education journal articles devoted to self-esteem doubled between the 1970s and the 1980s.[25] Journal articles on self-esteem increased another 52% during the 1990s, and the

Parents are encouraged to raise their children's self-esteem even when kids are simply coloring. Even the cat has high self-esteem on this coloring book cover. However, the dog lacks a self-esteem boosting ribbon. He probably has low self-esteem—after all, he drinks out of the toilet.

number of books on self-esteem doubled over the same time.[26] Generation Me is the first generation raised to believe that everyone should have high self-esteem.

Magazines, television talk shows, and books all emphasize the importance of high self-esteem for children, usually promoting feelings that are actually a lot closer to narcissism (a more negative trait usually defined as excessive self-importance). One children's book, first published in 1991, is called *The Lovables in the Kingdom of Self-Esteem*. "I AM LOVABLE. Hi, lovable friend! My name is Mona Monkey. I live in the Kingdom of Self-Esteem along with my friends the Lovable Team," the book begins.[27] On the next page, children learn that the gates of the kingdom will swing open if you "say these words three times with pride: *I'm lovable! I'm lovable! I'm lovable!*" (If I hear the word "lovable" one more time, I'm going to use my hefty self-esteem to pummel the author of this book).

Another example is the "BE A WINNER Self-Esteem Coloring and Activity Book" pictured in this chapter. Inside, children find activities and pictures designed to boost their self-esteem, including coloring a "poster for your room" that reads "YOU ARE SPECIAL" in yellow, orange, and red letters against a purple background. Another page asks kids to fill in the blanks: "Accept y_ur_e_f. You're a special person. Use p_si_iv_ thinking." A similar coloring book is called "We Are All Special" (though this title seems to suggest that being special isn't so special). All of this probably sounds like Al Franken's *Saturday Night Live* character Stuart Smalley, an insecure, sweater-vest-wearing man who looks in the mirror and unconvincingly repeats, "I'm good enough, I'm smart enough, and doggone it, people like me." It sounds like it because it's exactly the type of thing Franken was parodying. And it's everywhere.

Many school districts across the country have specific programs designed to increase children's self-esteem, most of which actually build self-importance and narcissism. One program is called "Self-Science: The Subject Is Me."[28] (Why bother with biology? *I'm* so much more interesting!) Another program, called "Pumsy in Pursuit of Excellence," uses a dragon character to encourage children to escape the "Mud Mind" they experience when feeling bad about themselves. Instead, they should strive to be in the "Sparkle Mind" and feel good about themselves.[29] The Magic Circle exercise designates one child a day to receive a badge saying "I'm great." The other children then say good things about the chosen child, who later receives a written list of all of the praise. At the end of the exercise, the child must then say something good about him- or herself. Boomer children in the 1950s and 1960s gained self-esteem naturally from a stable, child-friendly society; GenMe's self-esteem has been actively cultivated for its own sake.[30]

One Austin, Texas, father was startled to see his five-year-old daughter wearing a shirt that announced, "I'm lovable and capable." All of the kindergarteners, he learned, recited this phrase before class, and they all wore the shirt to school on Fridays. It seems the school started a bit too young, however, because the child then asked, "Daddy, all the kids are wondering, what does 'capable' mean?"[31]

Some people have wondered if the self-esteem trend waned after schools began to put more emphasis on testing during the late 1990s. It doesn't look that way. Parenting books and magazines stress self-esteem as much as ever, and a large number of schools continue to use self-esteem programs. The mission statements of many schools explicitly announce that they aim to raise students' self-esteem. A Google search for "elementary school mission statement self-esteem" yielded 308,000 Web pages in January 2006. These schools are located across the country, in cities, suburbs, small towns, and rural areas. "Building," "improving," "promoting," or "developing" self-esteem is a stated goal of (among many others) New River Elementary in New River, Arizona; Shady Dell Elementary in Springfield, Missouri; Shettler Elementary in Fruitport, Michigan; Baxter Elementary in Baxter, Tennessee; Rye Elementary in Westchester County, New York; Copeland Elementary in Augusta, Georgia; and Banff Elementary in Banff, Alberta, Canada. Private religious schools are not immune: St. Wendelin Catholic Elementary in Fostoria, Ohio, aims to "develop a feeling of confidence, self-esteem, and self-worth in our students."

Andersen Elementary in Rockledge, Florida, raises the bar, adding that students will "exhibit high self-esteem." So self-esteem must not just be *promoted* by teachers, but must be actively *exhibited* by students.

As John Hewitt points out in *The Myth of Self-Esteem*, the implicit message is that self-esteem can be taught and should be taught. When self-esteem programs are used, Hewitt notes, children are "encouraged to believe that it is acceptable and desirable to be preoccupied with oneself [and] praise oneself." In many cases, he says, it's not just encouraged but required. These exercises make self-importance mandatory, demanding of children that they love themselves. "The child *must* be taught to like himself or herself.... The child *must* take the teacher's attitude himself or herself—'I am somebody!' 'I am capable and loving!'—regardless of what the child thinks."[32]

Most of these programs encourage children to feel good about themselves for no particular reason. In one program, teachers are told to discourage children from saying things like "I'm a good soccer player" or "I'm a good singer."[33] This makes self-esteem contingent on performance, the program authors chide. Instead, "we want to anchor self-esteem firmly to the child ... so that no matter what the performance might be, the self-esteem remains high." In other words, feeling good about yourself is more important than good performance. Children, the guide says, should be taught "that it is who they are, not what they do, that is important." Many programs encourage self-esteem even when things go wrong or the child does something bad. In one activity, children are asked to finish several sentences, including ones beginning "I love myself even though ..." and "I forgive myself for ..."[34]

Teacher training courses often emphasize that a child's self-esteem must be preserved above all else. A sign on the wall of one university's education department says, "We Choose to Feel Special and Worthwhile No Matter What."[35] Perhaps as a result, 60% of teachers and 69% of school counselors agree that self-esteem should be raised by "providing more unconditional validation of students based on who they are rather than how they perform or behave."[36] Unconditional validation, to translate the educational mumbo-jumbo, means feeling good about yourself no matter how you act or whether you learn anything or not. A veteran second-grade teacher in Tennessee disagrees with this practice but sees it everywhere. "We handle children much more delicately," she says. "They feel good about themselves for no reason. We've given them this cotton-candy sense of self with no basis in reality."[37]

Although the self-esteem approach sounds like it might be especially popular in liberal blue-state areas, it's common in red states as well, perhaps because it's very similar to the ideas popularized by fundamentalist Christian churches. For example, the popular Christian children's book *You Are Special* promotes the same unconditional self-esteem emphasized in secular school programs. First published in 1997, the book notes, "The world tells kids, 'You're special if ... you have the brains, the looks, the talent.' God tells them, 'You're special just because. No qualifications necessary.' Every child you know needs to hear this one, reassuring truth." Traditional religion, of course, did have "qualifications" and rules for behavior. Adults hear this message as well.[38] In an article in *Ladies*

Home Journal, Christian author Rick Warren writes, "You can believe what others say about you, or you can believe in yourself as does God, who says you are truly acceptable, lovable, valuable, and capable."[39]

Even programs not specifically focused on self-esteem often place the utmost value on children's self-feelings. Children in some schools sing songs with lyrics like "Who I am makes a difference and all our dreams can come true" and "We are beautiful, magnificent, courageous, outrageous, and great!"[40] Other students pen a "Me Poem" or write a mock TV "commercial" advertising themselves and their good qualities. An elementary school teacher in Alabama makes one child the focus of a "VIP for a week" project.[41] The children's museum in Laramie, Wyoming, has a self-esteem exhibit where children are told to describe themselves using positive adjectives.[42]

Parents often continue the self-esteem lessons their children have learned in school, perhaps because more children are planned and cherished. The debut of the birth control pill in the early 1960s began the trend toward wanted children, which continued in the early 1970s as abortion became legal and cultural values shifted toward children as a choice rather than a duty. In the 1950s, it was considered selfish not to have kids, but by the 1970s it was an individual decision. As a result, more and more children were born to people who really *wanted* to become parents. Parents were able to lavish more attention on each child as the average number of children per family shrank from four to two. Young people often say that their parents believed in building self-esteem. "My mom constantly told me how special I was," said Natalie, 19. "No matter how I did, she would tell me I was the best." Kristen, 22, said her parents had a "wonderful" way of "telling me what a great job I did and repeatedly telling me I was a very special person." Popular media [have] also promoted this idea endlessly, offering up self-esteem as the cure for just about everything. In one episode of the family drama *7th Heaven*, one young character asks what can be done about war. The father on the show, a minister, says, "We can take a good look in the mirror, and when we see peace, that's when we'll have peace on earth." The rest of the episode featured each character smiling broadly to himself or herself in the mirror. In other words, if we all just loved ourselves enough, it would put an end to war. (Not only is this tripe, but wars, if anything, are usually rooted in too *much* love of self, land, and nation—not too little). But, as TV and movies have taught us, loving yourself is more important than anything else.

These efforts have had their intended impact. Don Tapscott, who interviewed hundreds of people for his book *Growing Up Digital*, notes, "Chat moderators, teachers, parents, and community workers who spend time with [young people] invariably told us that they think this is a confident generation who think highly of themselves."[43] In a CBS News poll, the high school graduates of 2000 were asked, "What makes you feel positive about yourself?" The most popular answer, at 33%, was the tautological "self-esteem." School performance was a distant second at 18%, with popularity third at 13%.[44] Yet this is not surprising: saying that having self-esteem makes you feel positive about yourself— forget any actual reason—is exactly what the self-esteem programs have taught today's young generation since they were in kindergarten.

Yet when everyone wears a shirt that says "I'm Special," as some of the programs encourage, it is a wide-open invitation to parody. The 1997 premiere episode of MTV's animated show *Daria* featured a character named Jane, who cracked, "I like having low self-esteem. It makes me feel special." Later in the episode, the teacher of a "self-esteem class" asks the students to "make a list of ten ways the world would be a sadder place if you weren't in it." "Is that if we'd never been born, or if we died suddenly and unexpectedly?" asks one of the students. Wanting to get out of the rest of the class, Daria and Jane recite the answers to the self-esteem "test": "The next time I start to feel bad about myself [I will] stand before the mirror, look myself in the eye, and say, 'You are special. No one else is like you.'"[45]

By the time GenMe gets to college, these messages are rote. Hewitt, who teaches at the University of Massachusetts, says his students are very excited when they begin discussing self-esteem in his sociology class. But once he begins to question the validity of self-esteem, the students' faces become glum and interest wanes. Hewitt compares it to what might happen in church if a priest suddenly began questioning the existence of God. After all, we worship at the altar of self-esteem and self-focus. "When the importance of self-esteem is challenged, a major part of the contemporary American view of the world is challenged," Hewitt writes.[46]

Girls Are Great

It is no coincidence that the *Daria* episode parodying self-esteem programs features two girls. Feminist Gloria Steinem, who spent the 1970s and 1980s fighting for practical rights like equal pay and maternity leave, spent the early 1990s promoting her book *Revolution from Within: A Book of Self-Esteem*. In 1991, a study by the American Association of University Women (AAUW) announced that girls "lose their self-esteem on the way to adolescence." This study was covered in countless national news outlets and ignited a national conversation about teenage girls and how they feel about themselves. *Reviving Ophelia*, a bestselling book on adolescent girls, popularized this idea further, documenting the feelings of self-doubt girls experience as they move through junior high and high school. Apparently, girls' self-esteem was suffering a severe blow when they became teenagers, and we needed to do something about it.

Before long, programs like the Girl Scouts began to focus on self-esteem through their "Girls Are Great" program. Girls could earn badges like "Being My Best" and "Understanding Yourself and Others." Amanda, 22, says that her Girl Scout troop spent a lot of time on self-esteem. "We did workshops and earned badges based around self-esteem building projects," she says. "We learned that we could do anything we wanted, that it was good to express yourself, and being different is good."

In 2002, the Girl Scout Council paired with corporate sponsor Unilever to launch "Uniquely ME!" a self-esteem program to "address the critical nationwide problem of low self-esteem among adolescent and preadolescent girls." The program includes three booklets for girls ages 8 to 14, each including exercises on "recognizing one's strengths and best attributes" and "identifying core values and personal interests."[47]

However, there is little evidence that girls' self-esteem dives at adolescence. The AAUW study was seriously flawed, relying on unstandardized measures and exaggerating small differences. In 1999, a carefully researched, comprehensive study of sex differences in self-esteem was published in *Psychological Bulletin*, the most prestigious journal in the field. The study statistically summarized 216 previous studies on more than 97,000 people and concluded that the actual difference between adolescent girls' and boys' self-esteem was less than 4%—in other words, extremely small.[48] Exaggerating this difference might be unwise." We may create a self-fulfilling prophecy for girls by telling them they'll have low self-esteem," said University of Wisconsin professor Janet Hyde, one of the study authors.[49]

When my colleague Keith Campbell and I did a different analysis of 355 studies of 105,318 people, we also found that girls' self-esteem does not fall precipitously at adolescence; it just doesn't rise as fast as boys' self-esteem during the teen years. There was no large drop in girls' self-esteem, and by college the difference between men's and women's self-esteem was very small.[50] Another meta-analysis, by my former student Brenda Dolan-Pascoe, found moderate sex differences in appearance self-esteem, but no sex differences at all in academic self-esteem. Girls also scored *higher* than boys in behavior self-esteem and moral-ethical self-esteem. The achievements of adolescent girls also contradict the idea that they retreat into self-doubt: girls earn higher grades than boys at all school levels, and more go on to college.

In other words, adolescent girls don't have a self-esteem problem—there is no "critical nationwide problem of low self-esteem among adolescent and preadolescent girls" as the Girl Scouts claimed. But in a culture obsessed with feeling good about ourselves, even the hint of a self-esteem deficit is enough to prompt a nationwide outcry. The Girl Scout program premiered three years after the 1999 comprehensive study found a minuscule sex difference in self-esteem. Why let an overwhelming mass of data get in the way of a program that sounded good?

Self-Esteem and Academic Performance

There has also been a movement against "criticizing" children too much. Some schools and teachers don't correct children's mistakes, afraid that this will damage children's self-esteem. One popular method tells teachers not to correct students' spelling or grammar, arguing that kids should be "independent spellers" so they can be treated as "individuals." (Imagine reading a nuespaper wyten useing *that* filosofy.)[51] Teacher education courses emphasize that creating a positive atmosphere is more important than correcting mistakes.[52] In 2005, a British teacher proposed eliminating the word "fail" from education; instead of hearing that they have failed, students should hear that they have "deferred success."[53] In the United States, office stores have started carrying large stocks of purple pens, as some teachers say that red ink is too "scary" for children's papers.[54]

Florida elementary schoolteacher Robin Slipakoff said, "Red has a negative connotation, and we want to promote self-confidence."[55]

Grade inflation has also reached record highs. In 2004, 48% of American college freshmen—almost half—reported earning an A average in high school, compared to only 18% in 1968, even though SAT scores decreased over this time period.[56] "Each year we think [the number with an A average] can't inflate anymore. And then it does again. The 'C' grade is almost a thing of the past," noted Andrew Astin, the lead researcher for the study. These higher grades were given out even though students were doing less work.[57] Only 33% of American college freshmen in 2003 reported studying six or more hours a week during their last year of high school, compared to 47% in 1987.[58] So why are they still getting better grades? "Teachers want to raise the self-esteem and feel-good attitudes of students," explains Howard Everson of the College Board.[59] We have become a Lake Wobegon nation: all of our children are above average.

The results of these policies have played out in schools around the country. Emily, 8, came home from school one day proud that she got half of the words right on her spelling test (in other words, a grade of 50). When her mother pointed out that this wasn't very good, Emily replied that her teacher had said it was just fine. At her school near Dallas, Texas, 11-year-old Kayla was invited to the math class pizza party as a reward for making a good grade, even though she had managed only a barely passing 71. The pizza parties used to be only for children who made As, but in recent years the school has invited every child who simply passed.

This basically means that we don't expect children to learn anything. As long as they feel good, that seems to be all that's required. As education professor Maureen Stout notes, many educational psychologists believe that schools should be "places in which children are insulated from the outside world and emotionally—not intellectually—nourished.... My colleagues always referred to the importance of making kids feel good about themselves but rarely, if ever, spoke of achievement, ideals, goals, character, or decency."[60] The future teachers whom Stout was educating believed that "children shouldn't be challenged to try things that others in the class are not ready for, since that would promote competition, and competition is bad for self-esteem. Second, grading should be avoided if at all possible, but, if absolutely necessary, should be done in a way that avoids any indication that Johnny is anything less than a stellar pupil."

Grade inflation and lack of competition may be backfiring: in 2003, 43% of college freshmen reported that they were frequently bored in class during their last year of high school, up from 29% in 1985.[61] This is not surprising: how interesting could school possibly be when everyone gets an A and self-esteem is more important than learning?

Perhaps as a result of all of this self-esteem building, educational psychologist Harold Stevenson found that American children ranked very highly when asked how good they were at math.[62] Of course, their *actual* math performance is merely mediocre, with other countries' youth routinely outranking American children. Every year, news anchors solemnly report how far American kids are falling behind. The emphasis on self-esteem can't be blamed entirely for this, of course, but one could easily argue that children's time might be better spent doing math than hearing that they are special. In 2004, 70% of American college freshmen reported that their "academic ability" was "above average" or "highest 10%," an amusing demonstration of American youths' self-confidence outpacing their ability at math.

What kind of young people does this produce? Many teachers and social observers say it results in kids who can't take criticism. In other words, employers, get ready for a group of easily hurt young workers. Peter Sacks, author of *Generation X Goes to College*, noted the extraordinary thin-skinnedness of the undergraduates he taught, and my experience has been no different. I've learned not to discuss test items that the majority of students missed, as this invariably leads to lots of whiny defensiveness and very little actual learning. The two trends are definitely related: research shows that when people with high self-esteem are criticized, they became unfriendly, rude, and uncooperative, even toward people who had nothing to do with the criticism.[63]

None of this should really surprise us. Students "look and act like what the [self-esteem] theories say they should look and act like," notes Hewitt. "They tend to act as though they believe they have worthy and good inner essences, regardless of what people say or how they behave, that they deserve recognition and attention from others, and their unique individual needs should be considered first and foremost."[64] And, of course, this is exactly what has happened: GenMe takes for granted that the self comes first, and we often believe exactly what we were so carefully taught—that we're special.

But this must have an upside; surely kids who have high self-esteem go on to make better grades and achieve more in school. Actually, they don't. There is a small correlation between self-esteem and grades.[65] However, self-esteem does not cause high grades—instead, high grades cause higher self-esteem. So self-esteem programs clearly put the cart before the horse in trying to increase self-esteem. Even much of the small link from high grades to high self-esteem can be explained by other factors such as income: rich kids, for example, have higher self-esteem and get better grades, but that's because coming from an affluent home causes both of these things, and not because they cause each other. This resembles the horse and the cart being towed on a flatbed truck—neither the cart nor the horse is causing the motion in the other even though they are moving together. As self-esteem programs aren't going to make all kids rich, they won't raise self-esteem this way, either.

Nor does high self-esteem protect against teen pregnancy, juvenile delinquency, alcoholism, drug abuse, or chronic welfare dependency. Several comprehensive reviews of the research literature by different authors have all concluded that self-esteem doesn't cause much of anything.[66] Even the book sponsored by the California Task Force to Promote Self-Esteem and Personal and Social Responsibility, which spent a quarter of a million dollars trying to raise Californians' self-esteem, found that self-esteem isn't linked to academic achievement, good behavior, or any other outcome the Task Force was formed to address.[67]

Are Self-Esteem Programs Good or Bad?

Psychologist Martin Seligman has criticized self-esteem programs as empty and shortsighted. He argues that self-esteem based on nothing does not serve children well in the long run; it's better, he says, for children to develop real skills and feel good about accomplishing something.[68] Roy Baumeister, the lead author of an extensive review of the research on self-esteem, found that self-esteem does not lead to better grades, improved work performance, decreased violence, or less cheating. In fact, people with high self-esteem are often more violent and more likely to cheat. "It is very questionable whether [the few benefits] justify the effort and expense that schools, parents, and therapists have put into raising self-esteem," Baumeister wrote. "After all these years, I'm sorry to say, my recommendation is this: forget about self-esteem and concentrate more on self-control and self-discipline."[69]

I agree with both of these experts. Self-esteem is an outcome, not a cause. In other words, it doesn't do much good to encourage a child to feel good about himself just to feel good; this doesn't mean anything. Children develop true self-esteem from behaving well and accomplishing things. "What the self-esteem movement really says to students is that their achievement is not important and their minds are not worth developing," writes Maureen Stout. It's clearly better for children to value learning rather than simply feeling good.[70]

So should kids feel bad about themselves if they're not good at school or sports? No. They should feel bad if they didn't work hard and try. And even if they don't succeed, sometimes negative feelings can be a motivator. Trying something challenging and learning from the experience is better than feeling good about oneself for no reason.

Also, everyone can do *something* well. Kids who are not athletic or who struggle with school might have another talent, like music or art. Almost all children can develop pride from being a good friend or helping someone. Kids can do many things to feel good about themselves, so self-esteem can be based on something. If a child feels great about himself even when he does nothing, why do anything? Self-esteem without basis encourages laziness rather than hard work. On the other hand, we shouldn't go too far and hinge our self-worth entirely on one external goal, like getting good grades. As psychologist Jennifer Crocker documents, the seesaw of self-esteem this produces can lead to poor physical and mental health.[71] A happy medium is what's called for here: don't feel bad about yourself because you made a bad grade—just don't feel good about yourself if you didn't even study. Use your bad feelings as a motivator to do better next time. True self-confidence comes from honing your talents and learning things, not from being told you're great just because you exist.

The practice of not correcting mistakes, avoiding letter grades, and discouraging competition is also misguided. Competition can help make learning fun; as Stout points out, look at how the disabled kids in the Special Olympics benefit from competing. Many schools now don't publish the honor roll of children who do well in school and generally downplay grades because, they falsely believe, competition isn't good for self-esteem (as some kids won't make the honor roll, and some kids will make Cs). But can you imagine not publishing the scores of a basketball game because it might not be good for the losing team's self-esteem? Can you imagine not keeping score in the game? What fun would that be? The self-esteem movement, Stout argues, is popular because it is sweetly addictive: teachers don't have to criticize, kids don't have to be criticized, and everyone goes home feeling happy. The problem is they also go home ignorant and uneducated.

Kids who don't excel in a certain area should still be encouraged to keep trying. This isn't self-esteem, however: it's self-control. Self-control, or the ability to persevere and keep going, is a much better predictor of life outcomes than self-esteem. Children high in self-control make better grades and finish more years of education, and they're less likely to use drugs or have a teenage pregnancy. Self-control predicts all of those things researchers had hoped self-esteem would, but hasn't.

Cross-cultural studies provide a good example of the benefits of self-control over self-esteem. Asians, for example, have lower self-esteem than Americans.[72] But when Asian students find out that they scored low on a particular task, they want to keep working on that task so they can improve their performance. American students, in contrast, prefer to give up on that task and work on another one.[73] In other words, Americans preserve their self-esteem at the expense of doing better at a difficult task. This goes a long way toward explaining why Asian children perform better at math and at school in general.

Young people who have high self-esteem built on shaky foundations might run into trouble when they encounter the harsh realities of the real world. As Stout argues, kids who are given meaningless As and promoted when they haven't learned the material will later find out in college or the working world that they don't know much at all. And what will *that* do to their self-esteem, or, more important, their careers? Unlike your teacher, your boss isn't going to care much about preserving your high self-esteem. The self-esteem emphasis leaves kids ill prepared for the inevitable criticism and occasional failure that is real life. "There is no self-esteem movement in the work world," points out one father. "If you present a bad report at the office, your boss isn't going to say, 'Hey, I like the color paper you chose.' Setting kids up like this is doing them a tremendous disservice."[74]

In any educational program, one has to consider the trade-off between benefit and risk. Valuing self-esteem over learning and accomplishment is clearly harmful, as children feel great about themselves but are cheated out of the education they need to succeed. Self-esteem programs *might* benefit the small minority of kids who really do feel worthless, but those kids are likely to have bigger problems that self-esteem boosting won't fix. The risk in these programs is in inflating the self-concept of children who already think the world revolves around them. Building up the self-esteem and importance of kids who are already egocentric can bring trouble, as it can lead to narcissism—and maybe it already has.

Changes in Narcissism

Narcissism is one of the few personality traits that psychologists agree is almost completely negative. Narcissists are overly focused on themselves and lack empathy for others, which means they cannot see another person's perspective.[75] (Sound like the last clerk who served you?) They also feel entitled to special privileges and believe that they are superior to other people. As a result, narcissists are bad relationship partners and can be difficult to work with. Narcissists are also more likely to be hostile, feel anxious, compromise their health, and fight with friends and family. Unlike those merely high in self-esteem, narcissists admit that they don't feel close to other people.[76]

All evidence suggests that narcissism is much more common in recent generations. In the early 1950s, only 12% of teens aged 14 to 16 agreed with the statement "I am an important person."[77] By the late 1980s, an incredible 80%—almost seven times as many—claimed they were important. Psychologist Harrison Gough found consistent increases on narcissism items among college students quizzed between the 1960s and the 1990s.[78] GenMe students were more likely to agree that "I would be willing to describe myself as a pretty 'strong' personality" and "I have often met people who were supposed to be experts who were no better than I." In other words, those other people don't know what they're talking about, so everyone should listen to me.

In a 2002 survey of 3,445 people conducted by Joshua Foster, Keith Campbell, and me, younger people scored considerably higher on the Narcissistic Personality Inventory, agreeing with items such as "If I ruled the world it would be a better place," "I am a special person," and "I can live my life any way I want to."[79] (These statements evoke the image of a young man speeding down the highway in the world's biggest SUV, honking his horn, and screaming, "Get out of my way! I'm important!") This study was cross-sectional, though, meaning that it was a one-time sample of people of different ages. For that reason, we cannot be sure if any differences are due to age or to generation; however, the other studies of narcissism mentioned previously suggest that generation plays a role. It is also interesting that narcissism scores were fairly high until around age 35, after which they decreased markedly. This is right around the cutoff between GenMe and previous generations.

Narcissism is the darker side of the focus on the self, and is often confused with self-esteem. Self-esteem is often based on solid relationships with others, whereas narcissism comes from believing that you are special and more important than other people. Many of the school programs designed to raise self-esteem probably raise narcissism instead. Lillian Katz, a professor of early childhood education at the University of Illinois, wrote an article titled "All About Me: Are We Developing Our Children's Self-Esteem or Their Narcissism?" She writes, "Many of the practices advocated in pursuit of [high self-esteem] may instead inadvertently develop narcissism in the form of excessive preoccupation with oneself."[80] Because the school programs emphasize being "special" rather than encouraging friendships, we may be training an army of little narcissists instead of raising kids' self-esteem.

Many young people also display entitlement, a facet of narcissism that involves believing that you deserve and are entitled to more than others. A scale that measures entitlement has items like "Things should go my way," "I demand the best because I'm worth it," and (my favorite) "If I were on the *Titanic*, I would deserve to be on *the first* lifeboat!"[81] A 2005 Associated Press article printed in hundreds of news outlets labeled today's young people "The

Entitlement Generation." In the article, employers complained that young employees expected too much too soon and had very high expectations for salary and promotions.[82]

Teachers have seen this attitude for years now. One of my colleagues said his students acted as if grades were something they simply deserved to get no matter what. He joked that their attitude could be summed up by "Where's my A? I distinctly remember ordering an A from the catalog." Stout, the education professor, lists the student statements familiar to teachers everywhere: "I need a better grade," "I deserve an A on this paper," "I *never* get Bs." Stout points out that the self-esteem movement places the student's feelings at the center, so "students learn that they do not need to respect their teachers or even earn their grades, so they begin to believe that they are entitled to grades, respect, or anything else ... just for asking!"[83]

Unfortunately, narcissism can lead to outcomes far worse than grade grubbing. Several studies have found that narcissists lash out aggressively when they are insulted or rejected.[84] Eric Harris and Dylan Klebold, the teenage gunmen at Columbine High School, made statements remarkably similar to items on the most popular narcissism questionnaire. On a videotape made before the shootings, Harris picked up a gun, made a shooting noise, and said, "Isn't it fun to get the respect we're going to deserve?"[85] (Chillingly similar to the narcissism item "I insist upon getting the respect that is due me.") Later, Harris said, "I could convince them that I'm going to climb Mount Everest, or I have a twin brother growing out of my back. I can make you believe anything" (virtually identical to the item "I can make anyone believe anything I want them to"). Harris and Klebold then debate which famous movie director will film their story. A few weeks after making the videotapes, Harris and Klebold killed thirteen people and then themselves.

Other examples abound. In a set of lab studies, narcissistic men felt less empathy for rape victims, reported more enjoyment when watching a rape scene in a movie, and were more punitive toward a woman who refused to read a sexually arousing passage out loud to them.[86] Abusive husbands who threaten to kill their wives—and tragically sometimes do—are the ultimate narcissists. They see everyone and everything in terms of fulfilling their needs, and become very angry and aggressive when things don't go exactly their way. Many workplace shootings occur after an employee is fired and decides he'll "show" everyone how powerful he is.

The rise in narcissism has very deep roots. It's not just that we feel better about ourselves, but that we even think to ask the question. We fixate on self-esteem, and unthinkingly build narcissism, because we believe that the needs of the individual are paramount. This will stay with us even if self-esteem programs end up in the dustbin of history.

NOTES

1. Ladies' Home Journal *told readers:* Warren, Rick. "Learn to Love Yourself!" *Ladies' Home Journal,* March 2005; p. 36.

2. *[W]hile* Parenting *offered:* Lamb, Yanick Rice. "Proud to Be Me!" *Parenting,* April 2005.

3. *The American Academy of Pediatrics guide:* Shelov, Steven, ed. in chief. 1998. *Caring for Your Baby and Young Child: Birth to Age 5.* New York: Bantam.

4. *In a 1976* New York Magazine *article:* Wolfe, Tom. "The Me Decade and the Third Great Awakening." *New York Magazine,* August 23, 1976.

5. *When asked what's next in her life:* "Pop Quiz: Kim Basinger." *People,* September 27, 2004.

6. *In answer to the same question:* Laskas, Jeanne Marie. "Sarah's New Day." *Ladies' Home Journal,* June 2004.

7. *Gillon describes Boomers:* Gillon, Steve. 2004. *Boomer Nation.* New York: Free Press; p. 263.

8. *Even food becomes:* Brooks, David. 2000. *Bobos in Paradise.* New York: Simon & Schuster; p.58.

9. *In 1973, 46% of Boomers:* Smith, J. Walker, and Clurman, Ann. 1997. *Rocking the Ages: The Yankelovich Report on Generational Marketing.* New York: HarperCollins.

10. *Thirty percent of Boomers:* Ibid.

11. *Even stronger evidence:* Astin, A. W., et al. 2002. *The American Freshman: Thirty-Five-Year Trends.* Los Angeles: Higher Education Research Institute, UCLA. Plus 2003 and 2004 supplements.

12. *"Instead of seeking:* Rubin, Jerry. 1976. *Growing (Up) at Thirty-Seven.* New York: Lippincott; p. 175.

13. *Aleta St. James, a 57-year-old woman:* Schienberg, Jonathan. "New Age Mystic to Become Mom at 57." <www.cnn.com>. November 9, 2004.

14. *In 2004's* Conquering Your Quarterlife Crisis: Robbins, Alexandra. 2004. *Conquering Your Quarterlife Crisis.* New York: Perigee; pp. 51–52.

15. *When a character in the 2004 novel:* Giffin, Emily. 2004. *Something Borrowed.* New York: St. Martin's Press; p. 2.

16. *Dr. Phil, the ultimate in plainspoken: Today.* NBC, December 27, 2004.

17. *Psychologist Martin Seligman says:* Seligman, M. E. P. "Boomer Blues." *Psychology Today,* October 1988: pp. 50–53.

18. *A careful study of news stories:* Patterson, Thomas E. 2000. "Doing Well and Doing Good: How Soft News and Critical Journalism Are Shrinking the News Audience and Weakening Democracy—and What News Outlets Can Do About It." Joan Shorenstein Center on the Press, Politics, and Public Policy; p. 5. PDF available for download at <www.ksg.harvard.edu/presspol/ResearchPublications/Reports/>.

19. *In a letter to her fans in 2004:* "The Couples of 2004." *Us Weekly,* January 3, 2005.

20. *In the late 1990s, Prudential:* Hornblower, Margot. "Great Xpectations." *Time,* June 9, 1997.

21. *My colleague Keith Campbell and I looked:* Twenge, J. M., and Campbell, W. K. 2001. Age and Birth Cohort Differences in Self-Esteem: A Cross-Temporal Meta-Analysis. *Personality and Social Psychology Review,* 5: 321–344.

22. *A 1997 survey of teens asked:* "11th Annual Special Teen Report: Teens and Self-Image: Survey Results." *USA Weekend,* May 1–3, 1998.

23. *Another survey found:* Hicks, Rick, and Hicks, Kathy. 1999. *Boomers, Xers, and Other Strangers.* Wheaton, IL: Tyndale; p. 270.

24. *We examined the responses:* Twenge, J. M., and Campbell, W. K. 2001. Age and Birth Cohort Differences in Self-Esteem: A Cross-Temporal Meta-Analysis. *Personality and Social Psychology Review*, 5: 321–344.

25. *Research on programs to boost:* Ibid.

26. *Journal articles on self-esteem:* Hewitt, John. 1998. *The Myth of Self-Esteem*. New York: St. Martin's Press; p. 51.

27. *One children's book:* Loomans, Diane. 1991. *The Lovables in the Kingdom of Self-Esteem*. New York: H. J. Kramer.

28. *One program is called:* Stout, Maureen. 2000. *The Feel-Good Curriculum*. Cambridge, MA: Perseus Books; p. 131.

29. *Another program, called "Pumsy in Pursuit of Excellence":* "Teaching Self-Image Stirs Furor." *New York Times*, October 13, 1993.

30. *The Magic Circle exercise:* <www.globalideasbank.org/site/bank/idea.php?ideaId=573>; and Summerlin, M. L.; Hammett, V. L.; and Payne, M. L. 1983. The Effect of Magic Circle Participation on a Child's Self-Concept. *School Counselor*, 31: 49–52.

31. *One Austin, Texas, father:* Swann, William. 1996. *Self-Traps: The Elusive Quest for Higher Self-Esteem*. New York: W. H. Freeman; p. 4.

32. *When self-esteem programs:* Hewitt, John. 1998. *The Myth of Self-Esteem*. New York: St. Martin's Press; pp. 84–85.

33. *In one program, teachers:* Payne, Lauren Murphy, and Rolhing, Claudia. 1994. *A Leader's Guide to Just Because I Am: A Child's Book of Affirmation*. Minneapolis: Free Spirit Publishing; and Hewitt, John. 1998. *The Myth of Self-Esteem*. New York: St. Martin's Press.

34. *[C]hildren are asked to finish:* Hewitt, John. 1998. *The Myth of Self-Esteem*. New York: St. Martin's Press; p. 79.

35. *A sign on the wall:* Kramer, Rita. 1991. *Ed School Follies: The Miseducation of America's Teachers*. New York: Free Press; p. 33.

36. *Perhaps as a result, 60% of teachers:* Scott, C. G. 1996. Student Self-Esteem and the School System: Perceptions and Implications. *Journal of Educational Research*, 89: 292–297.

37. *A veteran second-grade teacher:* Gibbs, Nancy. "Parents Behaving Badly." *Time*, February 21, 2005.

38. *For example, the popular Christian:* Lucado, Max. 1997. *You Are Special*. Wheaton, IL: Crossway Books.

39. *In an article in* Ladies' Home Journal, *Christian author:* Warren, Rick. "Learn to Love Yourself!" *Ladies' Home Journal*, March 2005.

40. *Children in some schools:* Lynn Sherr. "Me, Myself and I—The Growing Self-Esteem Movement." 20/20. ABC, March 11, 1994.

41. *An elementary school teacher in Alabama:* Hewitt, John. 1998. *The Myth of Self-Esteem*. New York: St. Martin's Press; p. 81.

42. *The children's museum in Laramie:* Lynn Sherr. "Me, Myself and I—The Growing Self-Esteem Movement." 20/20. ABC, March 11, 1994.

43. *Don Tapscott, who interviewed:* Tapscott, Don. 1998. *Growing Up Digital*. New York: McGraw-Hill; p. 92.

44. *In a CBS News poll:* CBS News. 2001. *The Class of 2000.* Simon & Schuster eBook, available for download, p. 64.

45. *The 1997 premiere episode: Daria.* Episode: "Esteemsters." MTV, March 3, 1997.

46. *Hewitt, who teaches:* Hewitt, John. 1998. *The Myth of Self-Esteem.* New York: St. Martin's Press; pp. 1–3.

47. *In 2002, the Girl Scout Council:* < http://www.girlscoutsaz.org/images/uploads/PDF /Programs/Facilitators_Guide.pdf>.

48. *In 1999, a carefully researched:* Kling, K. C., et al. 1999. Gender Differences in Self-Esteem: A Meta-Analysis. *Psychological Bulletin,* 125: 470–500.

49. *"We may create:* <www.news.wisc.edu/wire/i072899/selfesteem.html>.

50. *When my colleague Keith Campbell and I did:* Twenge, J. M., and Campbell, W. K. 2001. Age and Birth Cohort Differences in Self-Esteem: A Cross-Temporal Meta-Analysis. *Personality and Social Psychology Review,* 5: 321–344.

51. *One popular method tells:* Wilde, Sandra. 1989. A Proposal for a New Spelling Curriculum. *Elementary School Journal,* 90: 275–289.

52. *Teacher education courses emphasize:* Kramer, Rita. 1991. *Ed School Follies: The Miseducation of America's Teachers.* New York: Free Press; p. 116.

53. *[A] British teacher proposed:* "Teachers Say No-One Should 'Fail.'" BBC News, July 20, 2005. See <news.bbc.co.uk/1/hi/education/4697461.stm>.

54. *[O]ffice stores have started carrying:* Aoki, Naomi, "Harshness of Red Marks Has Students Seeing Purple." *Boston Globe,* August 23, 2004.

55. *Florida elementary schoolteacher:* Ibid.

56. *In 2004, 48% of American college freshmen:* Astin, A. W., et al. 2002. *The American Freshman: Thirty-Five-Year Trends.* Los Angeles: Higher Education Research Institute, UCLA. Plus 2003 and 2004 supplements.

57. *"Each year we think:* Giegerich, Steve. "College Freshmen Have Worst Study Habits in Years But Less Likely to Drink, Study Finds." Associated Press, January 27, 2003. <www.detnews.com/2003/schools/0301/27/schools-70002.htm>.

58. *Only 33% of American:* Astin, A. W., et al. 2002. *The American Freshman: Thirty-Five Year Trends.* Los Angeles: Higher Education Research Institute, UCLA. Plus 2003 and 2004 supplements.

59. *"Teachers want to raise:* Innerst, Carol. "Wordsmiths on Wane Among U.S. Students." *Washington Times,* August 25, 1994.

60. *As education professor Maureen Stout notes:* Stout, Maureen, 2000. *The Feel-Good Curriculum.* Cambridge, MA: Perseus Books; pp. 3–4.

61. *[I]n 2003, 43% of college freshmen:* Astin, A. W., et al. 2002. *The American Freshman: Thirty-Five-Year Trends.* Los Angeles: Higher Education Research Institute, UCLA. Plus 2003 and 2004 supplements.

62. *[E]ducational psychologist Harold Stevenson:* Stevenson, H. W., et al. 1990. Mathematics Achievement of Children in China and the United States. *Child Development,* 61: 1053–1066.

63. *[R]esearch shows that when people:* Heatherton, T. F., and Vohs, K. D. 2000. Interpersonal Evaluations Following Threats to Self: Role of Self-Esteem. *Journal of Personality and Social Psychology,* 78: 725–736.

64. *Students "look and act like:* Hewitt, John. 1998. *The Myth of Self-Esteem.* New York: St. Martin's Press; p. 84.

65. *There is a small correlation:* Baumeister, R. F., et al. 2003. Does High Self-Esteem Cause Better Performance, Interpersonal Success, Happiness, or Healthier Lifestyles? *Psychological Science in the Public Interest,* 4: 1–44; and Covington, M. V. 1989. "Self-Esteem and Failure in School." In A. M. Mecca, N. J. Smelser, and J. Vasconcellos, eds. *The Social Importance of Self-Esteem.* Berkeley: University of California Press; p. 79.

66. *Several comprehensive reviews:* Ibid.

67. *Even the book sponsored:* Smelser, N. J. 1989. "Self-esteem and Social Problems." In A. M. Mecca, N. J. Smelser, and J. Vasconcellos, eds. *The Social Importance of Self-Esteem.* Berkeley: University of California Press.

68. *Psychologist Martin Seligman has criticized:* Seligman, Martin. 1996. *The Optimistic Child.* New York: Harper Perennial.

69. *"It is very questionable:* Baumeister, Roy. "The Lowdown on High Self-esteem: Thinking You're Hot Stuff Isn't the Promised Cure-all." *Los Angeles Times,* January 25, 2005.

70. *"What the self-esteem movement:* Stout, Maureen. 2000. *The Feel-Good Curriculum.* Cambridge, MA: Perseus Books; p. 263.

71. *As psychologist Jennifer Crocker documents:* Crocker, J., and Park, L. E. 2004. The Costly Pursuit of Self-esteem. *Psychological Bulletin,* 130: 392–414.

72. *Asians, for example, have lower:* Twenge, J. M., and Crocker, J. 2002. Race and Self-Esteem: Meta-Analyses Comparing Whites, Blacks, Hispanics, Asians, and American Indians. *Psychological Bulletin,* 128: 371–408.

73. *But when Asian students find out:* Heine, S. J., et al. 2001. Divergent Consequences of Success and Failure in Japan and North America: An Investigation of Self-improving Motivations and Malleable Selves. *Journal of Personality and Social Psychology,* 81: 599–615.

74. *"There is no self-esteem movement:* Shaw, Robert. 2003. *The Epidemic.* New York: Regan Books; p. 152.

75. *Narcissists are overly focused:* Campbell, W. Keith. 2005. *When You Love a Man Who Loves Himself.* Chicago: Source Books.

76. *Narcissists are also more likely:* Helgeson, V. S., and Fritz, H. L. 1999. Unmitigated Agency and Unmitigated Communion: Distinctions from Agency and Communion. *Journal of Research in Personality,* 33: 131–158.

77. *In the early 1950s, only 12% of teens:* Newsom, C. R., et al. 2003. Changes in Adolescent Response Patterns on the MMPI/MMPI-A Across Four Decades. *Journal of Personality Assessment,* 81: 74–84.

78. *Psychologist Harrison Gough found:* Gough, H. 1991. "Scales and Combinations of Scales: What Do They Tell Us, What Do They Mean?" Paper presented at the 99th Annual Convention of the American Psychological Association, San Francisco, August 1991. Data obtained from Harrison Gough in 2001.

79. *In a 2002 survey of 3,445 people:* Foster, J. D.; Campbell, W. K.; and Twenge, J. M. 2003. Individual Differences in Narcissism: Inflated Self-Views Across the Lifespan and Around the World. *Journal of Research in Personality,* 37: 469–486.

80. *Lillian Katz, a professor:* Stout, Maureen. 2000. *The Feel-Good Curriculum.* Cambridge, MA: Perseus Books; p. 178.

81. *A scale that measures entitlement:* Campbell, W. K., et al. 2004. Psychological Entitlement: Interpersonal Consequences and Validation of a Self-report Measure. *Journal of Personality Assessment,* 83: 29–45.

82. *A 2005 Associated Press article printed:* Irvine, Martha. "Young Labeled 'Entitlement Generation.' " AP, June 26, 2005. <http://www.freerepublic.com/focus/news /1431497/posts>. Also reprinted in many newspapers.

83. *Stout, the education professor, lists:* Stout, Maureen. 2000. *The Feel-Good Curriculum.* Cambridge, MA: Perseus Books; p. 2.

84. *Several studies have found:* Bushman, B. J., and Baumeister, R. F. 1998. Threatened Egotism, Narcissism, Self-esteem, and Direct and Displaced Aggression: Does Self-love or Self-hate Lead to Violence? *Journal of Personality and Social Psychology,* 75: 219–229; and Twenge, J. M., and Campbell, W. K. 2003. "Isn't it fun to get the respect that we're going to deserve?" Narcissism, Social Rejection, and Aggression. *Personality and Social Psychology Bulletin,* 29: 261–272.

85. *Harris picked up a gun:* Gibbs, Nancy, and Roche, Timothy. "The Columbine Tapes." *Time,* December 20, 1999.

86. *In a set of lab studies, narcissistic:* Bushman, B. J., et al. 2003. Narcissism, Sexual Refusal, and Aggression: Testing a Narcissistic Reactance Model of Sexual Coercion. *Journal of Personality and Social Psychology,* 84: 1027–1040.

QUESTIONS FOR MAKING CONNECTIONS
WITHIN THE READING

1. "An Army of One: *Me*" is written in a lively style, with the author speaking in a number of different voices throughout: objective analyst, insider, and skeptic, to name a few. As you reread, mark the passages where Twenge's voice shifts and identify the voices on both sides of the shift. When you're done, review your markings. Is there a voice or a viewpoint that wins out in the end? Is there a voice that you feel is Twenge's real voice, or are all the voices hers?

2. What kinds of evidence does Twenge use to make her case about Generation Me? After you've generated a complete list, identify the evidence that you feel is the most compelling and the evidence that seems less so. Where would you look to find evidence that would further strengthen Twenge's argument? Is there evidence that could refute Twenge's argument? Can arguments about entire generations be either verified or disproven?

3. Twenge identifies three psychic states: thinking about the self, having self-esteem, and being a narcissist. What is the relationship among these three states? If one is educated and trained in one of these psychic states, is there a way to experience another state of mind? Does Twenge provide any evidence of what causes or enables a shift in perspective?

QUESTIONS FOR WRITING

1. As a member of Generation Me, Twenge is both a source for information about her subject and a translator who provides an inside view of how members of Generation Me interpret the world around them. Given this, how would you characterize Twenge's method? How does she know what she claims to knows about Generation Me? How would you go about collecting more information to test her hypothesis? Is definitive evidence available?

2. If we grant Twenge's argument about the values and expectations of Generation Me, what follows? Is it possible for this generation to reverse course, or is it too late? Can social change be brought about through conscious effort? Or does the scale of the problem mean that what follows is inevitable? Has Twenge diagnosed a problem for which there is no cure?

QUESTIONS FOR MAKING CONNECTIONS
BETWEEN READINGS

1. What might Daniel Gilbert say about the self-esteem curriculum? Might our tendency to cook the facts explain why children, parents, and teachers have been so ready to embrace this approach? If Gilbert is correct, will lower grades in more demanding classes actually deal children a devastating blow, or will their psychological immune systems protect them from lasting injury? Does the curriculum of self-esteem tip the scales in favor of action or inaction, and what are likely to be the results as children grow up? If toughened standards mean students will receive Bs or Cs instead of As, how might the inescapability trigger affect their self-perceptions? Does a curriculum that tries to shield students from challenges, uncertainty, and the experience of failure actually make education boring by trying to explain everything?

2. Twenge identifies numerous characteristics that define the differences between the way Baby Boomers and Generation Me view the self. Using Tim O'Brien's "How to Tell a True War Story," test out Twenge's theory. Do the characters perform as Twenge's theory predicts? Does O'Brien? Are generations defined by wars? Was Vietnam a Baby Boomer war? Is the Iraq War a Generation Me war? Can O'Brien's "true war story" be true for other generations?

ETHAN WATTERS

ETHAN WATTERS'S WORK IS controversial—some might even say explosive—although it has appeared in mainstream venues like the *New York Times Magazine, Discover, Men's Journal,* and *Wired.* His first two books, coauthored with University of California sociologist Richard Ofshe, are highly critical of psychiatry and psychoanalysis: *Making Monsters: False Memories, Psychotherapy, and Sexual Hysteria* (1996) and *Therapy's Delusions: The Myth of the Unconscious and the Exploitation of Today's Walking Worried* (1999). If these books still generate sharp differences of opinion, the same holds for Watters's most recent work, *Crazy Like Us: The Globalization of the American Psyche* (2010). While acknowledging the reality of mental illnesses, he wants his readers to understand that the terminology we apply to them reflects our own history and culture, and he notes that the categories other people use sometimes have strengths that our tradition lacks. One example Watters explores in *Crazy Like Us* is the aftermath of the tsunami that struck the island of Sri Lanka in 2004, killing 35,000 people and displacing half a million. Moved by genuine compassion, teams of American mental health professionals raced to the island to provide psychological services for post-traumatic stress disorder (PTSD). But Watters found that PTSD is a distinctly Western reaction. Many islanders experienced the aftermath as a loss of social connections—as loneliness rather than a disease of their private minds.

Watters fears that, because of globalization, humankind is now at risk of losing a rich legacy:

> The ideas that we export to other cultures often have at their heart a particularly American brand of hyperindividualism. These beliefs remain deeply influenced by the Cartesian split between the mind and the body ... as well as teeming numbers of self-help philosophies and schools of therapy that have encouraged us to separate the health of the individual from the health of the group. Even the fascinating biomedical ... research into the workings of the brain has, on a cultural level, further removed our understandings of the mind from the social and natural world it navigates.

What concerns Watters even more, however, are Western drug companies engaged in a crusade to replace indigenous knowledge with Western paradigms that will

Quotation comes from Ethan Watters, *Crazy Like Us: The Globalization of the American Psyche* (New York: Free Press, 2010), 254.

open up highly lucrative new markets. Not only does Watters nudge us to think about the ways that "scientific" notions of the mind are not universally valid, but he presses us to ask about the damage done to everyone, here in the United States and around the world, by the intermingling of mental health with the profit motive.

The Mega-Marketing of Depression in Japan

One of the chilling things about these events, whether a puzzle or a scandal, is how a very few people in key positions can determine the course of events and shape the consciousness of a generation.

—DAVID HEALY

I went to visit Dr. Laurence Kirmayer in his book-lined office at McGill University in Montreal because he had a particularly good story to tell. I'd heard that a few years ago, Kirmayer had a personal brush with the pharmaceutical giant GlaxoSmithKline and the remarkable resources that the company employed to create a market for their antidepressant pill Paxil in Japan.

In person Kirmayer is the picture of a tweedy academic. He speaks in complete paragraphs in a deep authoritative voice. He has a large head and a broad face that is covered nearly to the cheekbones in a thick light-gray beard. His slightly wandering left eye suits his demeanor. If you look at the left side of his face his expression is attentive and focused on the conversation. If you look at the right side of his face he appears to be looking past you into the middle distance, as if searching for a word or pondering a thought.

In telling his story of being feted by GlaxoSmithKline, Kirmayer likes to point out that he is unaccustomed to the trappings of great wealth. Not that he's doing badly. As the director of the Division of Social and Transcultural Psychiatry at McGill, he makes a respectable living and adds to his income with a private psychiatric practice. As editor in chief of the journal *Transcultural Psychiatry,* he is well known in certain circles and can draw a crowd of admiring grad students and colleagues at an anthropology or mental health conference. But to get to those conferences he flies coach.

It was in the fall of 2000, as he tells it, that he came to understand just how *un*spectacularly rich he was. That was when he accepted an invitation from something called the International Consensus Group on Depression and Anxiety to attend two all-expenses-paid conferences, the first in Kyoto and the second a few months later on the shores of Bali.

Accepting the invitation didn't at first seem like a difficult decision. Although he knew that the conference was sponsored by an educational grant from the drug maker GlaxoSmithKline, such industry funding wasn't unusual for academic conferences in the field of psychiatry. When he checked out the list of other invitees, he recognized all the names. It was an extremely exclusive group of highly influential clinicians and researchers from France, the United States, and Japan, among other countries. The topic, "Transcultural Issues in Depression and Anxiety," was right up his alley. Even better, he had an eager young graduate student named Junko Kitanaka who was in Japan finishing her dissertation on the history of depression in the country; such a gathering of luminaries would be a boon to her research. In addition to those incentives, attendees would be given the chance to publish their presentations in a supplement of the prestigious *Journal of Clinical Psychiatry*. "I wouldn't say it was a no-brainer, but it wasn't very hard for me to say yes," Kirmayer remembers. "How much trouble could I get in?"

His first inkling that this wasn't a run-of-the-mill academic conference came when the airline ticket arrived in the mail. This ticket was for a seat in the front of the plane and cost nearly $10,000. The next hint came when one of the conference organizers told him in no uncertain terms that these would be closed-door meetings. His grad student, Kitanaka, would not be allowed to attend. There would be no uninvited colleagues and no press.

On arrival in Kyoto in early October 2000 he found the luxury of the accommodations to be beyond anything he had personally experienced. He was ushered into an exclusive part of the hotel, where he was given a drink while an attractive woman filled out the hotel forms. His room was a palatial suite. The bath was drawn and strewn with rose petals and dosed with frangipani oil. There was a platter on the credenza filled with fruits so exotic that he could identify only the mangosteens.

"This was Gordon Gekko treatment—the most deluxe circumstances I have ever experienced in my life," Kirmayer says, smiling at the memory. This was how the other half lived, he realized—or, rather, how the other .01 percent lived. "The luxury was so far beyond anything that I could personally afford, it was a little scary. It didn't take me long to think that something strange was going on here. I wondered: What did I do to deserve this?"

Kirmayer was well aware that drug companies routinely sponsor professional conferences and educational seminars and that these events do double duty as marketing seminars. It was also common knowledge that drug makers use enticements to encourage both researchers and practitioners to attend. A prescribing doctor might be treated to a round of golf or a fancy dinner in exchange for attending an hour-long seminar about the effectiveness of some new drug. These practices are the medical equivalent of what real estate agents do to sell vacation timeshares.

But it was clear from the start that the gatherings of the International Consensus Group on Depression and Anxiety were different from the normal drug company dog and pony show, and not simply because the enticements being offered were so dear. Once the group of academics actually gathered in a plush conference room and began their discussions, Kirmayer realized quickly that the GlaxoSmithKline representatives in attendance had no interest in touting their products to the group. Indeed there was little mention of the company's antidepressant drug Paxil, which was just a few months away from hitting the market in Japan. Instead they seemed much more interested in hearing from the assembled group. They were there to learn. "The focus was not on medications," Kirmayer remembers. "They were not trying to sell their drugs to us. They were interested in what we knew about how cultures shape the illness experience."

As Kirmayer got to know them during the conference, he realized that the drug company representatives weren't from the ranks of the advertising or marketing departments or the peppy salespeople. As best he could tell, these were highly paid private scholars who could hold their own in the most sophisticated discussion of postcolonial theory or the impact of globalization on the human mind. "These guys all had PhDs and were versed in the literature," Kirmayer said. "They were clearly soaking up what we had to say to each other on these topics."

The intense interest the GlaxoSmithKline brain trust showed in the topic of how culture shapes the illness experience made sense given the timing of the meeting. The class of antidepressant drugs known as selective serotonin reuptake inhibitors (SSRIs) had become the wonder drug of the 1990s, at least in terms of the profits they'd garnered for the drug companies. That year alone, in the leading regions for SSRIs, sales grew by 18 percent and totaled over thirteen billion dollars. Most of those sales were still in the United States, but there was wide agreement that lucrative international markets had yet to be tapped.

Indeed it was somewhat remarkable that none of the best-selling SSRIs had been launched in Japan. This was more than twelve years after Prozac became available for prescription in the United States. What caused this uncharacteristic timidity on the part of these pharmaceutical giants? It certainly wasn't that the Japanese eschewed Western drugs. To the contrary, U.S.-based companies at the time were exporting upwards of fifty billion dollars in medications to the country each year. It was said that Japanese patients felt underserved if they didn't come away from a doctor's visit with at least a couple of prescriptions.

But Eli Lilly, then the out-front world leader in the SSRI horse race with Prozac, had decided in the early 1990s not to pursue the Japanese market because executives in the company believed that the Japanese people wouldn't accept the drug. More precisely, they wouldn't want to accept the disease. "The people's attitude toward depression was very negative," explained a spokeswoman for Eli Lilly to the *Wall Street Journal*. She was referring to the fact that the Japanese had a fundamentally different conception of depression than in the West, one that made it unlikely that a significant number of people in Japan would want to take a drug associated with the disease.

Most other SSRI manufacturers followed Eli Lilly's lead and held off as well. Getting drugs approved in Japan was a costly gamble. The rules at the time required that drugs already on the market in Western countries had to be retested in large-scale human trials using an exclusively Japanese population. That meant years of effort and millions of dollars spent, with the distinct possibility that the drug might fail the trial. No company wanted to make such an investment if no market existed for the drug.

The Japanese pharmaceutical company Meiji Seika was the first to break from the pack, working through the decade to run Japanese trials on the SSRI Luvox, which it had licensed from the Swedish company Solvay. After reading Peter Kramer's 1993 book *Listening to Prozac,* Meiji's president, Ichiro Kitasato, sensed an unexplored opportunity in the Japanese marketplace. "People in the company said there are too few patients in Japan," he told a reporter in 1996. "But I looked at the U.S. and Europe and thought this is sure to be a big market."

GlaxoSmithKline was the next to get in the race. In the years prior to the 2000 conference in Kyoto, the company had spent an immense amount of money and resources jumping through the regulatory and bureaucratic hoops to get the green light to put Paxil on the market in the country. Having watched Prozac dominate the American market in the late 1980s, drug company executives knew the advantages of early market share, and GlaxoSmithKline didn't want Luvox to be the only SSRI in Japan.

But both companies faced the same problem: there was no guarantee that Japanese doctors would prescribe the drug or that the population would be interested in taking it. The problem was that the profession of psychiatry in Japan, unlike in the West, seldom ministered to the walking worried; rather they focused almost exclusively on the severely mentally ill. Consequently, talk therapy was all but nonexistent in the country. For the small percentage of the population diagnosed with a debilitating mental illness, long hospital stays were the norm. The average stay in a mental hospital in Japan was over a year, versus just ten days in the United States. So although there was a psychiatric term for depression in Japan, *utsubyô,* what it described was a mental illness that was as chronic and devastating as schizophrenia. *Utsubyô* was the sort of illness that would make it impossible to hold down a job or have a semblance of a normal life. Worse yet, at least for the sales prospects of Paxil in Japan, *utsubyô* was considered a rare disorder.

At the Kyoto meeting Kirmayer began to understand the company's intense interest in the question of how cultures shape the illness experience. To make Paxil a hit in Japan, it would not be enough to corner the small market of those diagnosed with *utsubyô.* The objective was to influence, at the most fundamental level, the Japanese understanding of sadness and depression. In short, they were learning how to market a disease.

To have the best chance of shifting the Japanese public's perception about the meaning of depression, GlaxoSmithKline needed a deep and sophisticated understanding of how those beliefs had taken shape. This was why, Kirmayer came to realize, the company had invited him and his colleagues and treated them like royalty. GlaxoSmithKline needed help solving a cultural puzzle that might be worth billions of dollars.

Judging from the records of the conference, it's clear that the company got its money's worth. During the meetings eminent scholars and researchers gave insightful presentations on subjects ranging from the history of psychiatry in Japan to the Japanese public's changing attitudes about mental illness. The prominent Japanese psychiatrists in attendance were particularly helpful in framing the state of the public's current beliefs about depression and anxiety disorders.

Osamu Tajima, a professor at the Department of Mental Health at Kyorin University and a leading Tokyo psychiatrist, told the assembled group of a rising public concern about the high suicide rates in Japan. He described how dozens of middle-aged men each year hike deep into the so-called suicide forests in the foothills of Mt. Fuji with lengths of rope to hang themselves. He described how service along the Central Line Railway in Tokyo was routinely disrupted by office workers leaping in front of commuter trains.

Tajima also gave a detailed description of how psychiatric services were structured within the overall health care apparatus of Japan. Services were in the midst of a critical change, he reported. There was a burgeoning concern in the population about mood disorders and the need for social attention to suicide rates and depression. He also documented how the Western definition and symptom checklist for depression—thanks to the influence of the *DSM [Diagnostic and Statistical Manual of Mental Disorders]*—was steadily gaining ground among younger psychiatrists and doctors in Japan. "Japanese psychiatry is undergoing a period of important change," he concluded, which was certainly good news for GlaxoSmithKline. He was upbeat about the changes heralded by the standardization of psychiatry around the world. "Adoption of internationally standardized diagnostic criteria and terminology in psychiatry will provide additional advances in assessing prevalence and facilitating accurate diagnosis." He was also clearly impressed with the scientific advances in drug treatments that were soon to come to his country. "New and effective treatment options," he said, "most notably the SSRIs, will contribute to reducing the burden of depression and anxiety disorders in Japanese society."

After lunch on the second day of the conference, it was Kirmayer's turn to speak. He had written many papers in his career documenting the differing expressions of depression around the world and the meaning hidden in those differences. He had found that every culture has a type of experience that is in some ways parallel to the Western conception of depression: a mental state and set of behaviors that relate to a loss of connectedness to others or a decline in social status or personal motivation. But he had also found that cultures have unique expressions, descriptions, and understandings for these states of being.

He told the assembled scholars and drug company representatives of how a Nigerian man might experience a culturally distinct form of depression by describing a peppery feeling in his head. A rural Chinese farmer might speak only of shoulder or stomach aches. A man in India might talk of semen loss or a sinking heart or feeling hot. A Korean might tell you of "fire illness," which is experienced as a burning in the gut. Someone from Iran might talk of tightness in the chest, and an American Indian might describe the experience of depression as something akin to loneliness.

Kirmayer had observed that cultures often differ in what he called "explanatory models" for depression-like states. These cultural beliefs and stories have the effect of directing the attention of individuals to certain feelings and symptoms and away from others. In one culture someone feeling an inchoate distress might be prompted to search for feelings of unease in his gut or in muscle pain; in another place or time, a different type of symptom would be accepted as legitimate. This interplay between the expectations of the culture and the experience of the individual leads to a cycle of symptom amplification. In short, beliefs about the cause, symptomatology, and course of an illness such as depression tended to be self-fulfilling. Explanatory models created the culturally expected experience of the disease in the mind of the sufferer. Such differences, Kirmayer warned the group, tended to be overlooked when clinicians or researchers employed the symptom checklists relating to the *DSM* diagnosis of depression.

Understanding these differences is critical, however, because culturally distinct symptoms often hold precious clues about the causes of the distress. The American Indian symptom of feeling lonely, for instance, likely reflects a sense of social marginalization. A Korean who feels the epigastric pain of fire illness is expressing distress over an interpersonal conflict or a collective experience of injustice.

The wide variety of symptoms wasn't the only difference. Critically, not everyone in the world agreed that thinking of such experiences as an illness made sense. Kirmayer documented how feelings and symptoms that an American doctor might categorize as depression are often viewed in other cultures as something of a "moral compass," prompting both the individual and the group to search for the source of the social, spiritual, or moral discord. By applying a one-size-fits-all notion of depression around the world, Kirmayer argued, we run the risk of obscuring the social meaning and response the experience might be indicating.

Indeed, around the world, it is the Western conception of depression, in particular the American version of the disease, that is the most culturally distinctive. Kirmayer told the group that Americans are unique both in being willing to openly express distressful emotions and feelings to strangers and in our penchant for viewing psychological suffering as a health care issue. Because people in other cultures find social and moral meaning in such internal distress, they often seek relief exclusively from family members or community elders or local spiritual leaders. The idea of seeking help from a doctor or mental health professional outside one's social circle has traditionally made little sense.

The drug company representatives listened closely to Kirmayer's presentation and thanked him heartily afterward. To this day, he's not entirely sure what they took away from his presentation. In the end Kirmayer's comments could have been taken in two ways. On the one hand, they could be seen as a warning to respect and protect the cultural diversity of human suffering. In this way, he was like a botanist presenting a lecture to a lumber company on the complex ecology of the forest. On the other hand, he might have told the GlaxoSmithKline representatives exactly what they wanted to hear: that cultural conceptions surrounding illnesses such as depression could be influenced and shifted over time. He made that point clearly in the conclusion of the paper he wrote based on his presentation:

> The clinical presentation of depression and anxiety is a function not only of patients' ethnocultural backgrounds, but of the structure of the health care system they find themselves in and the diagnostic categories and concepts they encounter in mass media and in dialogue with family, friends and clinicians.

In the globalizing world, he reported, these conceptions are

> in constant transaction and transformation across boundaries of race, culture, class, and nation. In this context, it is important to recognize that psychiatry itself is part of an international subculture that imposes certain categories on the world that may not fit equally well everywhere and that never completely captures the illness experience and concerns of patients.

In other words, cultural beliefs about depression and the self are malleable and responsive to messages that can be exported from one culture to another. One culture can reshape how a population in another culture categorizes a given set of symptoms, replace their explanatory model, and redraw the line demarcating normal behaviors and internal states from those considered pathological.

Kirmayer's appreciation of the irony of his brief encounter with Glaxo-SmithKline has only grown over the years since he gave that presentation. "People like me got into cultural psychiatry because we were interested in differences between cultures—even treasured those differences in the same way a biologist treasures ecological diversity," Kirmayer told me. "So it's certainly ironic that cultural psychiatrists sometimes end up being handmaidens to these global marketing machines that are intent on manipulating cultural differences … in order to capitalize on those changes."

I asked Kirmayer how clear it was to him that GlaxoSmithKline was interested in changing notions of depression in Japan. "It was very explicit. What I was witnessing was a multinational pharmaceutical corporation working hard to redefine narratives about mental health," he said. "These changes have far-reaching effects, informing the cultural conceptions of personhood and how people conduct their everyday lives. And this is happening on a global scale. These companies are upending long-held cultural beliefs about the meaning of illness and healing."

The consensus paper produced to summarize the Kyoto conference provided both an action plan and a marketing piece for GlaxoSmithKline. In that paper the International Consensus Group on Depression and Anxiety warned that depression was vastly underestimated in Japan but that Western scientific advances would soon be on hand to help. "Clinical evidence supports the use of SSRIs as first-line therapy for depression and anxiety disorders," the paper concludes.

Looking back, Kirmayer can now see how the company used the conference as the beginning of its broader marketing strategy; its representatives identified the cultural challenges and fleshed out the resonant cultural notes the company would attempt to play in the critical coming months and years. Among those themes were that suicide in Japan was an indicator of undertreated depression; that Western

SSRIs represented proven scientific advances in treatment; that primary care physicians should use simple three-minute surveys to help diagnose mental illness; that patients not meeting the criteria for depression should still be considered sick; and that the Japanese should be helped to reconceive social stress related to work and industrialization as signs of depression that should be treated with SSRIs. These confident conclusions would prove the foundation on which GlaxoSmithKline would begin to change the culture of Japan....

THE CULTURE OF SADNESS

During the early part of the twentieth century the concept of depression [in Japan] remained attached to the diagnosis of severe manic depression imported from … German neuropsychiatrists. It wasn't until after World War II that depression became a disease category of its own. There was nothing mild about this conception of depression. This so-called endogenous depression was a crippling type of psychosis believed to be caused by a genetic abnormality. Professors of psychiatry at the time often explained endogenous depression using the metaphor of an internal alarm clock. "According to this model, the depressed person is like someone carrying a psychotic time bomb, for whom depression begins when the internal clock goes off and ends after it runs its course," Junko Kitanaka explains. Endogenous depression expressed itself only in individuals with that ticking alarm clock and wasn't connected to external causes.

At the same time Kitanaka shows that another idea was gaining ground in Japan's mental health community. The personality *typus melancholicus* was introduced in the early 1960s by a professor of clinical psychopathology from Heidelberg named Hubert Tellenbach. This idea never caught on in the United States and rather quickly became dated in Germany, but it influenced psychiatric thinking in Japan. As Tellenbach first described it, someone with a melancholic personality possessed a highly developed sense of orderliness as well as "exceptionally high demands regarding one's own achievements." *Typus melancholicus* mirrored a particularly respected personality style in Japan: those who were serious, diligent, and thoughtful and expressed great concern for the welfare of other individuals and the society as a whole. Such people, the theory went, were prone to feeling overwhelming sadness when cultural upheaval disordered their lives and threatened the welfare of others.

Neither endogenous depression nor the melancholic personality type were of great concern to the general public at the time. Because endogenous depression was thought of as a psychotic state, akin to schizophrenia in severity, it carried a severe stigma and was considered rare. As for the melancholic personality type, its association with such prized Japanese traits as orderliness and high achievement meant that having such a sadness-prone personality was something not to be feared but aspired to.

This absence of a category parallel with the modern Western-style depression persisted for many years. When the *DSM-III* was first translated into Japanese in 1982, the diagnosis of depression, with its two-week threshold for low mood, was widely criticized among Japanese psychiatrists as far too expansive and vague to be of any use. Prominent psychiatrists believed, in short, that the description did not amount to a meaningful mental illness.

Indeed, as Kirmayer has pointed out, in the late twentieth century no word in Japanese had the same connotations as the word "depression" in English. Consider the various words and phrases that have often been translated into English as "depression." *Utsubyô* describes a severe, rare, and debilitating condition that usually required inpatient care and thus was not much of a match for the common English word "depression." *Yuutsu,* which describes grief as well as a general gloominess of the body and spirit, was in common use. There was also *ki ga fusagu,* which refers to blockages in vital energy. Similarly, *ki ga meiru* is the leakage or loss of such energy. Although each of these words and phrases had overlaps with the English word "depression," there were also critical differences. The experiences these words describe do not exist only in the thoughts and emotions but encompass full-body sadness. As such, the Japanese person who felt *yuutsu* or *ki ga fusagu* was likely to describe it in terms of bodily sensations, such as having headaches or chest pains or feeling heavy in the head.

Not only did Japanese ideas of sadness include both the body and the mind but, metaphorically at least, they sometimes existed beyond the self. The experience of *yuutsu* in particular contained connotations of the physical world and the weather. A young Japanese researcher named Junko Tanaka-Matsumi, studying at the University of Hawaii in the mid-1970s, conducted a simple word-association test on a group of Japanese college students and compared the results to Caucasian American college students. The American students were asked to respond with three words that they connected with "depression." The Japanese students were asked to do the same with *yuutsu.*

The top ten word associations for the native Japanese were

1. Rain
2. Dark
3. Worries
4. Gray
5. Suicide
6. Solitude
7. Exams
8. Depressing
9. Disease
10. Tiredness

For the Caucasian Americans, the top ten word associations were

1. Sad or sadness
2. Lonely or loneliness
3. Down
4. Unhappy

5. Moody

6. Low

7. Gloom

8. Failure

9. Upset

10. Anxious

Comparing these answers, Tanaka-Matsumi saw a notable difference. In the responses given by the Japanese natives, only a few of the words (such as "worries" and "solitude") were related to internal emotional states. On the other hand, the majority of the word associations supplied by the American students related to internal moods. The Japanese, in short, were looking outward to describe *yuutsu,* and the Americans were looking inward to describe depression. Tanaka-Matsumi believed that these were not simply linguistic differences but cultural "variations in the subjective meanings and *experience* of depression."

The Japanese and Americans weren't just talking about depression and sadness differently, she believed; they were *feeling* these states differently as well. What she saw reflected in the language was a difference between how Japanese and Americans conceived of the nature of the self. The word associations suggested that Americans experience the self as isolated within the individual mind. The Japanese, on the other hand, conceive of a self that is less individuated and more interconnected and dependent on social and environmental contexts. Feelings that Americans associate with depression have, in Japan, been wrapped up in a variety of cultural narratives that altered their meaning and the subjective experience for the individual.

Even as the *DSM* diagnosis of depression became more widely employed around the world during the 1980s, the experience of deep sadness and distress in Japan retained the characteristics of the premodern conception of both *utsushô* and the mid-twentieth-century idealization *typus melancholicus,* the idea that overwhelming sadness was natural, quintessentially Japanese, and, in some ways, an enlightened state.

As Kirmayer has documented, this was a culture that often idealized and prized states of melancholy. Feelings of overwhelming sadness were often venerated in television shows, movies, and popular songs. Kirmayer noted that *yuutsu* and other states of melancholy and sadness have been thought of as *jibyo,* that is, personal hardships that build character. Feelings that we might pathologize as depressive were often thought of in Japan as a source of moral meaning and self-understanding. He and others have connected this reverence to the Buddhist belief that suffering is more enduring and more definitive of the human experience than transient happiness....

JUNK SCIENCE AND FIRST WORLD MEDICINE

Kalman Applbaum, a professor at the University of Wisconsin in Milwaukee, is an anthropologist, but he doesn't study little-known tribes in far-off lands. His interest is closer at hand: the rituals and practices of international corporations.

His specialty, the anthropology of the boardroom, has led to teaching posts both in anthropology departments and at business schools, including Harvard and Kellogg. He is also fluent in Japanese and often consults with companies interested in the Asian markets. When he heard in the late 1990s that major players in the pharmaceutical industry were attempting to introduce SSRIs to Japan, he knew he had the topic for his next set of research papers.

At the beginning of the new millennium, Applbaum went out of his way to visit the headquarters of GlaxoSmithKline, Lilly, and Pfizer, the major international players who were at various stages of trying to get their drugs into Japan. At the time both Pfizer and Lilly were playing catch-up to GlaxoSmithKline, which was just then launching Paxil in the country. Although he had to sign nondisclosure agreements promising that he wouldn't identify the executives by name or company affiliation, Applbaum managed to get remarkable access to the inner workings of these companies. Several of his former MBA students who were then working in these firms helped make key introductions, but in the end these executives proved more than willing to talk. When I asked Applbaum why they were so forthcoming, he told me it was simple: because of his business school credentials and his extensive experience in the Japanese market, they thought he might be able to give them some free advice.

Applbaum discovered that the companies intent on entering the SSRI market in Japan were not battling each other like Coke and Pepsi for market share—or at least not at the beginning. Instead he found wide acknowledgment within the ranks of drug company executives that the best way for companies to create a market was for competing companies to join forces.

A critical player in this joint effort was the trade organization Pharmaceutical Manufacturers of America, or PhRMA, which functions as the national and international lobby and public relations organization for a coalition of major drug companies. In the late 1990s Applbaum found PhRMA working on a number of levels in Japan to influence what they considered to be a backward and bureaucratic drug approval process. As one PhRMA executive based in Chiyoda-Ku, Tokyo, told Applbaum, their job was to create "a market based upon competitive, customer choice and a transparent pricing structure that supports innovation." The lobby wanted drugs such as Paxil to be able to enter new markets based on "global, objective, scientific standards."

The more Applbaum talked to drug company insiders, the more righteous frustration he found. When he visited the offices of a leading SSRI manufacturer in November 2001, he discovered a wellspring of anger directed at what they perceived as Japanese resistance to pharmaceutical progress. These executives criticized scientific standards for clinical testing in Japan as "quite poor" and asserted that there was no "good clinical practice" in the country. Why, they asked Applbaum rhetorically, should their company be forced to retest these drugs in exclusively Japanese populations? The assumption was that the science behind the American human trials was unassailable—certainly better than anything the Japanese would attempt.

No doubt that annoyance at having to retest drugs was so intense because a couple of recent large-scale human trials of SSRIs in Japan had *failed* to show any positive effects. Drugs such as Pfizer's Zoloft, which were widely prescribed in the United States, had at least one large-scale human trial failure in Japan in the 1990s. Instead of considering the meaning of such results, the drug company executives railed at Japanese testing practices, calling them second rate. "There is no sense of urgency about patient need in Japan," one executive complained to Applbaum.

THE MEGA-MARKETING OF DEPRESSION

Although drug company executives clearly would have preferred to avoid the expensive and time-consuming process of retesting their SSRIs in Japan, they ultimately found a way to put those trials to good use as the first step in their marketing campaign. The drug makers often bought full-page ads in newspapers in the guise of recruiting test subjects. Applbaum believes that this was one of several savvy methods the drug companies employed to sidestep the prohibitions in Japan on marketing prescription drugs directly to the consumer. These advertisements, supposedly designed only to recruit people for the trials, were well worth the cost, as they both featured the brand name of the drug and promoted the idea of depression as a common ailment. One company scored even more public attention when it recruited a well-known actress to take part in the trials.

But getting the drug approved for market was only the first step. Talking with these executives, it became clear to Applbaum that they were intent on implementing a complex and multifaceted plan to, as he put it, "alter the total environment in which these drugs are or may be used." Applbaum took to calling this a "mega-marketing" campaign—an effort to shape the very consciousness of the Japanese consumer.

The major problem GlaxoSmithKline faced was that Japanese psychiatrists and mental health professionals still translated the diagnosis of "depression" as *utsubyô,* and in the mind of many Japanese that word retained its association with an incurable and inborn depression of psychotic proportions. In hopes of softening the connotations of the word, the marketers hit upon a metaphor that proved remarkably effective. Depression, they repeated in advertising and promotional material, was *kokoro no kaze,* like "a cold of the soul." It is not clear who first came up with the phrase. It is possible that it originated from Kenichiro Takiguchi's prime-time special on depression. In that show, it was said that Americans took antidepressants the way other cultures took cold medicine.

Whatever its origin, the line *kokoro no kaze* appealed to the drug marketers, as it effectively shouldered three messages at the same time. First, it implied that *utsubyô* was not the severe condition it was once thought to be and therefore should carry no social stigma. Who would think less of someone for having a cold? Second, it suggested that the choice of taking a medication for depression should be as simple and worry-free as buying a cough syrup or an antihistamine.

Third, the phrase communicated that, like common colds, depression was ubiquitous. Everyone, after all, from time to time suffers from a cold.

Although advertising couldn't mention particular drugs, companies could run spots in the guise of public service announcements encouraging people to seek professional help for depression. In these ads SSRI makers attempted to distance depression further from the endogenous depression as it was understood by Japanese psychiatrists for most of the century. One GlaxoSmithKline television advertisement showed an attractive young woman standing in a green field, asking, "How long has it been? How long has it been since you began to worry that it might be depression?" The scene then shows a woman on an escalator and then a middle-aged office worker staring out a bus window. The voiceover then recommends that if you've been feeling down for a month, "do not endure it. Go see a doctor."

The subtext of the ad is clear.... It presents depression as "intentionally ambiguous and ill-defined, applicable to the widest possible population and to the widest possible range of discomforts.... The only feature that distinguishes depression as a 'disease' from an ordinary depressed mood seems to be the length of time (one month) that the person has experienced these 'symptoms.'"

Depression was so broadly defined by the marketers that it clearly encompassed classic emotions and behaviors formerly attributed to the melancholic personality type. The label of depression then took on some laudable characteristics, such as being highly sensitive to the welfare of others and to discord within the family or group. Being depressed in this way became a testament to one's deeply empathic nature.

To get these messages out to the Japanese public, the SSRI makers employed a variety of techniques and avenues. Company marketers quickly reproduced and widely disseminated articles in newspapers and magazines mentioning the rise of depression, particularly if those pieces touted the benefits of SSRIs. The companies also sponsored the translation of several best-selling books first published in the United States on depression and the use of antidepressants.

Given all the ways that GlaxoSmithKline and the other SSRI makers managed to make the average Japanese aware of their drugs, the official ban on direct-to-consumer marketing became almost meaningless. If there was any doubt about this, one only had to look at how these companies used the Internet. "The best way to reach patients today is not via advertising but the Web," one Tokyo-based marketing manager told Applbaum. "The Web basically circumvents [direct-to-consumer advertising] rules, so there is no need to be concerned over these. People go to the company website and take a quiz to see whether they might have depression. If yes, then they go to the doctor and ask for medication."

The mega-marketing campaign often came in disguised forms, such as patient advocacy groups that were actually created by the drug companies themselves. The website utu-net.com, which appeared to be a coalition of depressed patients and their advocates, was funded by GlaxoSmithKline, although visitors to the site would have had no clue of the connection. What they would have found was a series of articles on depression driving home the key points of the campaign, including the idea that it was a common illness and that antidepressants bring the brain's natural chemistry back into balance.

The public interest in the new diagnosis brought a remarkable amount of media attention. Often in back-to-back months, the major magazines *Toyo Keizai* and *DaCapo* ran pieces on depression and the new drugs. In 2002 a leading Japanese business magazine ran a twenty-six-page cover story encouraging businesspeople to seek professional help for depression. The article rather perfectly mirrored the key points of the SSRI makers' mega-marketing campaign and in many ways reflected the early conceptions of neurasthenia a century before. The article suggested that it was the more talented and hard-charging workers who were the most susceptible to depression. Estimates of how many Japanese secretly suffered from depression, which ranged from 3 to 17 percent of the population, seemed to increase every month.

The distress caused by the long-ailing economy also proved to be a useful selling point. GlaxoSmithKline promoted the idea that there was an enormous economic cost for untreated depression, which could be counted in lost man-hours and decreased productivity. In this way, the lure of the drug, especially to the younger generation, was tied to ideas about competition in the global marketplace. One Japanese psychiatrist was quoted in a local newspaper describing SSRIs as "drugs that can transform minus thinking into plus thinking" and that "can help a person live tough," like financially successful Americans.

The SSRI makers made much of one public relations windfall in particular. It was rumored for years (and finally confirmed by the Imperial Household Agency) that Crown Princess Masako suffered from depression. Soon it was revealed that she was taking antidepressants as part of her treatment. This was a huge boost for the profile of depression and SSRIs in the country. Princess Masako's personal psychiatrist was none other than Yutaka Ono, one of the field's leaders that GlaxoSmithKline had feted at the Kyoto conference in 2001.

As a marketing line, there was one problem with the phrase *kokoro no kaze*: the metaphor lacked a sense of urgency about the condition. After all, one rarely rushes to the doctor with a cold. Worse yet, medicating a cold was always optional, as the illness goes away rather quickly on its own.

To counter this aspect of the metaphor, the drug companies leveraged the population's growing concern over the high suicide rates. The medical anthropologist Emiko Namihira reported that SSRI makers were funding studies to prove the link between depression and suicide. Those studies that showed a connection were reprinted in pamphlet form and reported to national media outlets as breaking news. Studies that failed to show a connection could simply be ignored. The founder of the Mood Disorders Association of Japan claimed in the *Japan Times* that "90 percent of those who commit suicide are considered to suffer from one kind of mental illness or another, and 70 percent of suicides are attributable to depression." Without medical attention, the message went, this "cold of the soul" could kill you.

When taken together, the messages advanced by GlaxoSmithKline during their rollout of Paxil don't always make sense. Previous notions of endogenous depression were employed only sparingly in order to evoke the seriousness of the disorder. On the other hand, they were happy to associate this new conception of depression with the Japanese veneration of the melancholic personality, even though that didn't particularly jibe with the parallel message that this was an illness caused by an imbalance of serotonin. Neither did the message that overwork could spark depression mesh with the idea that individuals should counter such social distress by taking a medication that changed their brain chemistry. If it was unrealistic social demands that were the cause of distress in the population, why should the individual be taking the pills? In the end, however, the coherence of these various messages took second place to their effectiveness.

SPEEDING THE EVOLUTION

After the Kobe earthquake in Japan there was growing consensus in the country that the West, and the United States in particular, had a deeper scientific understanding of pathological emotional states such as PTSD and depression. Responding to this insecurity, the advertisements, websites, waiting room brochures, and other materials produced by the drug companies played up the idea that SSRIs represented the cutting edge of medical science. These drugs, which were said to rebalance the natural chemicals in the brain, would bring Japan up to date.

GlaxoSmithKline worked very hard to win over the most prominent medical researchers and psychiatrists in the country and keep them on message. Their inclusion at lavish conferences such as the one Kirmayer attended was just a taste of the incentives offered. Drug companies offered grants to sponsor research on their drugs; those researchers who produced results favorable to the drugs found themselves with new offers of research funding. Research that showed the drug in question to be both safe and effective was trumpeted by the company and the researchers often paid as consultants. In addition, researchers were given honoraria for speaking about their findings at drug company-sponsored professional conferences. Influence over the prominent scientists and researchers in Japan was so pervasive that Applbaum concluded that these scientists and doctors had been basically "commandeered into a kind of market research by pharmaceutical companies. The research simultaneously serves as publicity for the essentially predetermined consumer need."

It is important to note that the drug company executives whom Applbaum interviewed didn't present themselves as people driven only by profits. Rather these men and women saw themselves as acting with the best of intentions, motivated by the belief that their drugs represented the proud march of scientific progress across the world. They styled themselves as people fighting depression, anxiety, and social phobia—diseases that remained cruelly untreated in Japan and elsewhere. Applbaum could see that this mixture of moral certainty and the lure of billions of dollars in potential profits was a potent force.

"These executives seemed to believe that they are straightforwardly trying to heal the world," said Applbaum. When he was meeting them in 2000 and 2001 he had no reason to doubt these self-assessments. "They seemed to believe their products were effective and they were baffled that anyone should question their value. The pharmaceutical industry, more than other industries, can link its marketing activities to ethical objectives. The result is a marriage of the profit-seeking scheme in which disease is regarded as 'an opportunity' to the ethical view that mankind's health hangs in the balance. This helps even the most aggressive marketers trust that they are performing a public service."

Bolstering their certainty was their faith in the science behind these drugs. The fact that these SSRIs had proven clinically effective made it morally imperative that they be introduced into other cultures. The drug companies were replacing what one executive referred to as "junk science" in Japan with "first world medicine."

During his talks with the executives, consultants, and marketers for the drug companies, Applbaum heard a repeated theme. These men and women kept talking about different cultures as if they were at different stages of a predetermined evolution. The American market, with its the brand recognition, high rates of prescriptions (by specialists and nonspecialists alike), and free market pricing, was seen as the most modern and advanced of markets. Japan was fifteen years behind the United States, executives would say. Or China was five years behind Japan. The lucrative U.S. market, Applbaum could see, was the standard against which all others were measured. We were the most "evolved" culture and, as one executive said to Applbaum, their job was to "speed the evolution along," that is, to move other countries along the path to be like us.

This talk of evolutionary process wasn't idle chatter, for it was often the same executives and marketing specialists who went from country to country waiting for the right moment to make their push. "Pharmaceutical manufacturers … circulate internal instructional materials regarding experiences with the same product in what they consider similar markets," Applbaum said. "Managers fly about the world to training conferences where such archetypes are hardened. And old advertisements and communications strategies from the earlier stage of more 'advanced' markets are imported." With each new implementation of the mega-marketing campaign, these drug companies learned new maneuvers and strategies. They got better at helping along the evolution.

The reasons these executives were so open about this endeavor goes back to their shared belief that the evolution in question was toward higher quality science. Westerners may have lost their sense of moral authority in many areas of human endeavor, but we can still get our blood up defending our science. We lead the world in scientific discovery and medical breakthroughs, so why shouldn't the citizens of Japan and other countries around the world have access to the newest brand-name antidepressants? These molecules were created using the latest advances in science and technology. They had been reviewed by the leading researchers at the world's most famous universities and found effective in studies published in the most prestigious scientific journals. The latest antidepressants, in this moral logic, were akin to antiretrovirals, polio vaccine, and penicillin. Everyone in the world deserved access to the fruits of our scientific discoveries as a human right.

It is not an argument without merit, but it depends rather critically on the accuracy and validity of the science behind the medical advance being touted. If the science is overblown, skewed, or downright wrong, then the moral certainty that fuels the charge into other cultures becomes suspect....

Under even the mildest scrutiny, the confident marketing messages proclaiming the scientific validity of SSRIs begin to break down. Take for instance the idea, often repeated in the ads and promotional material surrounding the launch of SSRIs in Japan, that a depletion of serotonin is the root cause of depression and that SSRIs reestablish the "balance" of the "natural" chemicals in the brain. Pharmaceutical companies have been repeating this idea ever since SSRIs came on the market twenty years ago. On their website the makers of the SSRI Lexapro are still telling the story: "The naturally occurring chemical serotonin is sent from one nerve cell to the next.... In people with depression and anxiety, there is an imbalance of serotonin—too much serotonin is reabsorbed by the first nerve cell, so the next cell does not have enough; as in a conversation, one person might do all the talking and the other person does not get to comment, leading to a communication imbalance."

Here's how GlaxoSmithKline describes the same idea on its website advertising Paxil CR: "Normally, a chemical neurotransmitter in your brain, called serotonin, helps send messages from one brain cell to another. This is how the cells in your brain communicate. Serotonin works to keep the messages moving smoothly. However, if serotonin levels become unbalanced, communication may become disrupted and lead to depression.... Paxil CR helps maintain a balance of serotonin levels."

As often repeated as this story is, it turns out that there is currently no scientific consensus that depression is linked to serotonin deficiency or that SSRIs restore the brain's normal "balance" of this neurotransmitter. The idea that depression is due to deficits of serotonin was first proposed by George Ashcroft in the 1950s, when he thought he detected low levels in the brains of suicide victims and in the spinal fluid of depressed patients. Later studies, however, performed with more sensitive equipment and measures, showed no lower levels of serotonin in these populations. By 1970 Ashcroft had publicly given up on the serotonin-depression connections. To date, no lower levels of serotonin or "imbalance" of the neurotransmitter have been demonstrated in depressed patients. The American Psychiatric Press *Textbook of Clinical Psychiatry* states simply, "Additional experience has not confirmed the monoamine [of which serotonin is a subgroup] depletion hypothesis."

SSRIs don't bring a patient's brain chemistry back into balance, but rather broadly alter brain chemistry. Although that change may sometimes help a depressed patient, the idea that SSRIs restore a natural balance of serotonin is a theory without evidence. Put another way, this idea is more of a culturally shared story than a scientific fact....

SOURCES

The scholars at McGill University are overrepresented in this book because that university is a hotbed for the study of cross-cultural psychiatry. That fact, I believe, has much to do with Laurence Kirmayer, whose work and leadership in the field informs not just this chapter but this entire book. Junko Kitanaka, Kirmayer's former graduate student, was as generous as her mentor with her time and guidance. The history of the evolution of Japanese understanding of depression relies critically on her dissertation—in particular, the recounting of the suicide of Oshima Ichiro and the public attention surrounding suicide from overwork. Her book on the history of depression in Japan will be out within a year or two, and I will be first in line at the bookstore to snap it up. David Healy was an inspiration both for his research on the science behind SSRIs and for his dogged courage.

Other resources include the following:

Angell, M. (2009, January 15). Drug Companies and Doctors: A Story of Corruption. *New York Review of Books*.

Applbaum, K. (2004a). *The Marketing Era: From Professional Practice to Global Provisioning*. Routledge.

———. (2004b). How to Organize a Psychiatric Congress. *Anthropological Quarterly*, 77(2), 303–310.

———. (2006). Pharmaceutical Marketing and the Invention of the Medical Consumer. *PLoS Medicine*, 3(4), 445.

Berger, D., & Fukunishi, I. (1996). Psychiatric Drug Development in Japan. *Science*, 273(5273), 318.

Healy, D. (2004a). *Let Them Eat Prozac: The Unhealthy Relationship between the Pharmaceutical Industry and Depression*. New York University Press.

Horwitz, A. V., & Wakefield, J. C. (2007). *The Loss of Sadness: How Psychiatry Transformed Normal Sorrow into Depressive Disorder*. Oxford University Press.

Kirmayer, L. J. (1989). Cultural Variations in the Response to Psychiatric Disorders and Emotional Distress. *Social Science & Medicine*, 29(3), 327.

———. (2002). Psychopharmacology in a Globalizing World: The Use of Antidepressants in Japan. *Transcultural Psychiatry*, 39(3), 295.

Kitanaka, J. (2006). Society in Distress: The Psychiatric Production of Depression in Contemporary Japan. PhD dissertation, Department of Anthropology, McGill University.

Kleinman, A. (2004). Culture and Depression. *New England Journal of Medicine*, 351, 951–953.

Landers, P. (2002, October 9). Drug Companies Push Japan to Change View of Depression. *Wall Street Journal*.

Petryna, A., Lakoff, A., & Kleinman, A. (2006). *Global Pharmaceuticals: Ethics, Markets, Practices*. Duke University Press.

Schulz, K. (2004, August 22). Did Antidepressants Depress Japan? *New York Times Magazine*.

Tajima, O., et al. (2001). Mental Health Care in Japan: Recognition and Treatment of Depression and Anxiety Disorders. *Journal of Clinical Psychiatry*, Suppl., 62(13), 39–46.

Tanaka-Matsumi, J., & Marsella, A J. (1976). Cross-Cultural Variations in the Phenomenological Experience of Depression: I. *Word Association Studies. Journal of Cross-Cultural Psychology*, 7(4), 379.

Whittington, C. J., Kendall, T., Fonagy, P., Cottrell, D., Cotgrove, A., & Boddington, E. (2004). Selective Serotonin Reuptake Inhibitors in Childhood Depression: Systematic Review of Published versus Unpublished Data. *Lancet*, 363(9418), 1341–1345.

QUESTIONS FOR MAKING CONNECTIONS
WITHIN THE READING

1. Is depression real or not? Does Watters seem to believe that the condition is imaginary? How can depression have biological roots and yet be experienced in different ways? Does Watters seem to accept the view that the West's understanding of depression is true, whereas the explanations other cultures offer are arbitrary and unscientific? Do the pharmaceutical companies feel that they possess the best understanding of depression? How do the modern Japanese regard Western psychology?

2. What can we learn from Watters's story about the relationship between academic researchers like Laurence Kirmayer and the pharmaceutical industry? Does Watters suggest that drug manufacturers are deceptive? Do they lie to Kirmayer, or is the connection between them more complex than that? Have they lied to the Japanese, or are the drug manufacturers convinced that they are truly doing good? Does Watters's narrative indicate that academic research has been compromised by commercial interests? Does he seem to think that there needs to be a stricter separation between research and commercial interests? Is such a separation possible when commercial applications drive much of academic science?

3. Based on your reading of Watters—and working without a dictionary—try to develop an accurate definition of the term *marketing*. Does marketing simply make available needed information about products that people want? Or does marketing play an active role in creating needs and shaping the way people experience the world? How does marketing differ from other forms of communication? How might we define the relationship between marketers and consumers? Which forms of marketing would qualify as ethical? Which forms would qualify as unethical? Is the marketing of antidepressants in Japan ethical or not?

QUESTIONS FOR WRITING

1. One implication of Watters's argument is that what we call *reality,* even at the level of personal experience, is shaped by culture as well as by biology. But Watters never pauses in the course of his account to explain in a

systematic way how these three are interrelated. Write an essay in which you draw from Watters's narrative to explain the relationship between biology, culture, and experience. When the pharmaceutical companies transform the cultural attitudes of modern Japanese people, will the actual experience of the people change? If our experience is indeed always shaped by culture, do we need to be more careful about who controls it? If others can control our experience, what steps might we take to be fully in charge of our own lives?

2. The campaign to change how the Japanese think about what we call depression might be seen as an example of *cultural imperialism*—the conquest of one culture by another. Does Watters's narrative support that view? If the intention of the dominant culture is to do good instead of harm, does that behavior still qualify as *imperialism*? If we are hesitant to impose the values of one culture on another society, are we required to accept all beliefs without question? Is it possible that many Japanese benefitted from the new medicines? Is it possible for any culture to remain separate from others?

QUESTIONS FOR MAKING CONNECTIONS
BETWEEN READINGS

1. Watters sees depression as a product of culture, and he worries that the West's thinking about mental illness is displacing other cultures' ways of responding to emotional distress. But some in the West might argue that depression is an objective fact, traceable to the patient's biochemistry. Where might Oliver Sacks come down in this controversy? Would he agree that in a case like depression, biology is everything? Or might he argue that culture plays a role? Would he share Watters's alarm at the attempt to change the way the Japanese people think about mental illness? Or would he applaud the drug companies?

2. When Azar Nafisi asks Iranian students to read novels like *Lolita,* she brings into an Iranian milieu the values of the West—values that many Iranians would find shocking, perhaps even obscene. Although Nafisi does not give the details, the novel actually involves a love affair between a middle-aged professor of literature and a 12-year-old girl. By exposing her students to a way of thinking unlike their own, Nafisi might be accused of something like the cultural insensitivity Watters finds troubling in the marketing of antidepressants. Are the two cases actually equivalent? Is Nafisi engaged in the same sort of cultural aggression? When is it acceptable to transform a society's core beliefs?

TIM WU

Tim Wu is one of the world's leading thinkers on the legal, social, and political consequences of the Internet. A professor at Columbia Law School, he has written widely cited articles that have helped frame the ongoing debate over "net neutrality"—the preservation of an Internet that treats all content as equal. The abandonment of net neutrality would create different "tiers" of service for the benefit of special users. Comcast or the Bell System, for example, might charge its preferred customers more in exchange for greater access and speed, or for special platforms, sites, and applications. Opponents of net neutrality claim that the Internet should operate like any other business: if users don't like a provider, they can always look for another. But defenders of neutrality predict that the big providers will eventually restrict and even ban content they dislike, while conspiring to wall out competitors who threaten their monopolies.

In an article for the online journal *Slate*, Wu asks his readers to compare the Internet to a private company like KFC. KFC, he observes, has recently signed a deal to serve its customers only Pepsi, not Coke—a case that appears to suggest the Internet could follow suit easily. But Wu cautions that businesses like KFC might not be the best model. "Let's think," he writes, "about the nation's highways. How would you feel if I-95 announced an exclusive deal with General Motors to provide a special 'rush-hour' lane for GM cars only?" How, he asks, does a chain like KFC differ from our national system of roads?

> Two obvious differences are market power and the availability of substitutes. KFC is a small fry, relatively, locked in competition with the likes of McDonald's and Popeye's. KFC sells Pepsi? So what? McDonald's sells Coke.
>
> It's a lot harder to substitute for an interstate. And if highways really did choose favorite brands, you might buy a Pontiac instead of a Toyota to get the rush-hour lane, not because the Pontiac is actually a good car. As a result, the nature of competition among car-makers would change. Rather than try to make the best product, they would battle to make deals with highways.

Quotation comes from Tim Wu, "Why You Should Care About Net Neutrality: The Future of the Internet Depends on It," *Slate*, May 1, 2006.

The selection that follows is excerpted from Tim Wu's *The Master Switch: The Rise and Fall of Information Empires* (2010). Since the book first appeared, however, the debate over net neutrality has become even more intense. In July 2013, for example, Verizon initiated a suit against the Federal Communications Commission (FCC), the agency which has attempted to protect the principle of neutrality. The suit alleges that the FCC has trampled on Verizon's First Amendment rights.

Father and Son

Steve Jobs stood before an audience of thousands, many of whom had camped out overnight to share this moment. In his signature black turtleneck and blue 501s he was completely in his element: in perfect control of his script, the emotions of the crowd, and the image he projected to the world. Behind him was an enormous screen—another of his trademarks—flashing words, animations, and surprising pictures. It was the annual Jobs keynote at Apple's Macworld, which, for Apple's many devotees, was nothing short of sacrament. And during this one, on January 9, 2007, Jobs was to announce his most important invention since the Apple Macintosh—in fact, one of the most important inventions of the early twenty-first century.[1]

"Today," said Jobs, "we're introducing three revolutionary new products. Three things: a widescreen iPod with touch controls; a revolutionary mobile phone; a breakthrough Internet communications device."

Loud cheers.

"An iPod, a phone ... are you getting it? These are not three separate devices!"

Louder cheers. "We are calling it iPhone!" The audience rose to its feet. On the screen: "iPhone: Apple reinvents the phone." The iPhone was beautiful; it was powerful; it was perfect. After demonstrating its many features, Jobs showed how the iPhone could access the Web as no phone ever had before, through a full-featured real browser.

"Now, you can't—you can't really think about the Internet, of course, without thinking about Google.... And it's my pleasure now to introduce Dr. Eric Schmidt, Google's CEO!"

To more cheers, Schmidt came jogging in from stage left, wearing an incongruously long orange tie. The two men shook hands warmly at center stage, like two world leaders. A member of the Apple board, Schmidt thanked Jobs and began his comments with an ill-advised joke about just how close Apple and Google had become. "There are a lot of relationships between the boards, and I thought if we just sort of merged the companies we could call them AppleGoo," he said. "But I'm not a marketing guy."

Indeed, in 2007 Google and Apple were about as close as two firms could be. Schmidt was not the only member of both boards. The two firms were given to frequent and effusive public acclamations of each other. Their respective foundings a generation apart, Google and Apple were, to some, like father and son—both starting life as radical, idealistic firms, dreamed up by young men determined to do things differently. Apple was the original revolutionary, the countercultural firm that pioneered personal computing, and, in the 1970s, became the first company to bring open computing, then merely an ideological commitment, to mass production and popular use. Google, meanwhile, having overcome skepticism about its business model at every turn, had by the new millennium become the incarnation of the Internet gospel of openness. It had even hired Vint Cerf, one of the network's greatest visionaries, giving him the title "Chief Internet Evangelist."[2]

Their corporate mottoes, "Think Different" and "Do No Evil," while often mocked by critics and cynics, were an entirely purposeful way of propounding deeply counterintuitive ideas about corporate culture. Both firms, launched out of suburban garages a few miles apart, took pride in succeeding against the grain. Google entered the search business in 1998, when searching was considered a "commodity," or low-profit operation, and launched a dot-com after the tech boom went bust. Apple's revolution had been even more fundamental: in the 1970s, an era dominated by IBM's giant mainframe machines, it built a tiny personal computer and later gave it a "desktop" (the graphic user interface of windows and icons and toolbars that is now ubiquitous), as well as a mouse. The two firms also shared many real and imagined enemies: Microsoft, mainstream corporations, and uptight people in general. That they would become great foes seemed unimaginable.

Back in San Francisco, Schmidt, done with his jokes, continued his presentation.

"What I like about this new device [the iPhone] and the new architecture of the Internet is that you can actually merge without merging.... Internet architectures allow you now to take the enormous brain trust that is represented by the Apple development team and combine that with the open protocols and data service that companies like Google [provide]."

Unnoticed by most, here was enunciated a crucial idea, a philosophy of business organization radical in its implications. Schmidt was suggesting that, on a layered network, in an age of open protocols, all the advantages of integration—the "synergies" and efficiencies of joint operation—could be realized without actual corporate mergers. On the Internet, each company could focus just on what it did best. The age of Vail, Rockefeller, and Carnegie, not to mention the media conglomerates created by Steven Ross and Michael Eisner—the entire age of giant corporate empires—might, according to this revelation, be over.

But was it really? The warmth of Jobs's greeting concealed the fact that Apple's most important partner for the iPhone launch was not Google—not by a long shot—but rather one of Google's greatest foes. At the end of his speech, in an understated way, Jobs dropped a bomb. The iPhone would work exclusively on the network of one company: AT&T.

"They are the best and most popular network in the country," said Jobs. "Fifty-eight million subscribers. They are number one. And they're going to be our exclusive partner in the U.S."

In entering this partnership, Apple was aligning itself with the nemesis of everything Google, the Internet, and once even Apple itself stood for. The firm was, at last, choosing sides.

We don't know whether Ed Whitacre, Jr., AT&T's mastermind, was listening to Eric Schmidt's speech at the iPhone launch. But he might have smiled at Schmidt's suggestion that the need for grand mergers had passed. Just one week earlier, Whitacre had quietly gained final federal approval for the acquisitions that would bring most of the old Bell system back under AT&T's control. Unfazed by the arrival of the Internet. Whitacre and his telephone Goliath were practicing the old-school corporate strategies of leveraging size to achieve domination, just as AT&T had done for more than a hundred years. The spirit of [the company's founder] Theodore Vail was alive and well in the resurrected dominion of the firm.

The day of the iPhone launch would be the last day of real friendship between Apple and Google. Relations would sour, and grow hostile as the two began to pursue equally grand, though inimical, visions of the future. By the time Google launched its iPhone competitor, the Android, Steve Jobs would be accusing Google of wasting its time and alienating its partners. The two firms would clash before the FCC over Apple's App policies. In a blog post, one Google employee named Tim Bray would run down Apple's iPhone as "a sterile Disney-fied walled garden surrounded by sharp-toothed lawyers.... I hate it."[3]

Where once there had been only subtle differences there now lay a chasm. Apple, while it had always wavered on "openness," now committed itself to a set of ideals well aligned with the interests of the faltering old media: the entertainment conglomerates, and newspaper magnates like Rupert Murdoch. While a difficult partner in some respects—not least the hard bargain it drove in agreeing to its share of proceeds—Apple provided the old firms a long besought new life, a rejuvenation at last via the Internet, especially through the great promise of the iPad. In fact, the combination of Apple, Bell (AT&T + Verizon), and Hollywood now held out an extremely appealing prospect: Hollywood content, Bell's airwaves, and Apple's gorgeous machines—an information paradise of sorts.

For its part, despite occasional wavering, Google would remain allied to the ideals animating the early Internet, the Web, and its culture of openness and experimentation. As Apple befriended the old media, Google remained the de facto (if uneasy) leader of a different coalition, all of whose fates depended on the World Wide Web and an open Internet. That large and motley crew included creatures both commercial and noncommercial: giants like Amazon; nonprofits like Wikipedia and Mozilla; and more broadly, an ecosystem of bloggers, programmers, Wikipedia editors, and amateur content producers of all types. This group—more a social movement really—styled themselves the challengers to the existing order, questioning old assumptions about the proper organization of information, the nature of property, and even the purpose of life. It envisioned a future that brought the Internet and Web revolution into every recess of the information realm, which itself figured in every part of human existence.

Yet even as these two sides have locked horns, something else has become obvious. Both Apple and Google, while pursuing different visions of the good, have continued to cultivate and leverage their status as dominant firms and, technically, monopolists in some key markets (Google in search, Apple in music downloads and players). Along with a few other 800-pound gorillas, like Facebook and Amazon, they disproportionately determine what the Internet is in the 2010s—a far cry from the original vision of a network of equals. How open the Internet shall be remains to be seen, but there is little doubt that the monopolistic industrial structure that typified the twentieth century has found its footing on the ultimate network. Whatever notion may have once existed that the Internet, by its nature, would be immune to monopolization, the present has already made clear the folly of such wishful thinking.

Nevertheless, it remains to be seen what shape the concentrated future of the Internet shall take. For this reason, the Apple and Google divide is still vitally important. These are not just any two firms. They are, in communications, the industrial and ideological leaders of our times, the preeminent carriers of ideas. These are the companies that are determining how Americans and the rest of the world will share information. If [Aldous] Huxley could say in 1927 that "the future of America is the future of the world," we can equally say that the future of firms like Apple and Google will form the future of America and the world.[4] They may both have grand designs of global domination, but history shows some empires are far more beneficent than others.

APPLE'S RADICAL ORIGINS

Apple is a company with a split personality: a self-professed revolutionary closely allied with the greatest forces in information: the entertainment conglomerates and the telecommunications industry. To work out this contradiction we need to return to Apple's origins and see how far it has come. Let's return to 1971, when a bearded young college student in thick eyeglasses named Steve Wozniak was hanging out at the home of Steve Jobs, then in high school. The two young men, electronics buffs, were fiddling with a crude device they'd been working on for more than a year. To them it must have seemed just another attempt in their continuing struggle to make a working model from a clever idea, just as Alexander Bell and Watson had done one hundred years earlier.[5]

That day in 1971, however, was different. Together, they attached Wozniak's latest design to Jobs's phone, and as Wozniak recalls, "it actually worked."[6] It would be their first taste of the eureka moment that would-be inventors have always lived for. The two used the device to place an illegal long distance phone call to Orange County. Apple's founders had managed to hack AT&T's long distance network: their creation was contraband, a "blue box," that made long distance phone calls for free.

Such an antiestablishment spirit of enterprise would underlie all of Jobs and Wozniak's early collaborations and form the lore that still gives substance to the image long cultivated: the iconoclast partnership born in a Los Altos garage, a partnership that, in March of 1976, would create a personal computer called "the Apple," one hundred years to the month after Bell invented the telephone in his own lonely workshop.

In the 1970s this imagery would be reinforced by the pair's self-styling as bona fide counterculturals, with all the accoutrements—long hair, opposition to the war, an inclination to experiment with chemical substances as readily as with electronics. Wozniak, an inveterate prankster, ran an illegal "dial-a-joke" operation; Jobs would travel to India in search of a guru.

But, as is often the case, the granular truth of Apple's origins was a bit more complicated than the mythology. For even in the beginning, there was a significant divide between the two men. There was no real parity in technical prowess: it was Wozniak, not Jobs, who built the blue box, and it was Wozniak who would conceive of and build the Apple and the Apple II, arguably among the most important inventions of the later twentieth century. Wozniak, then, was the Alexander Bell of the operation. For his part, Jobs helped build the Apple; but he was the businessman and the dealmaker of the operation, essential as such, though hardly the founding genius of Apple computers. The man whose ideas were turned into silicon to change the world—that was Wozniak. The history of the firm must be understood in this light. For while founders do set the culture of a firm, they cannot dictate it in perpetuity; as Wozniak withdrew from the operation, Apple became more concerned with the aesthetics of radicalism than with its substance.

Steve Wozniak is not the household name that Steve Jobs is, but his importance to communications and culture in the postwar period merits a closer look. Of course Apple's wasn't the first or only personal computer invented in the 1970s—important predecessors include the Altair 8800—but it was the most influential. The Apple II took personal computing, an obscure pursuit of the hobbyist, and made it into a nationwide phenomenon, one that would ultimately transform not just computing, but communications, culture, entertainment, business—in short, the whole productive part of American life.

We've seen these moments before, when a hobbyist or limited-interest medium becomes a mainstream craze; it happened with the telephone in 1894, radio in the 1920s, and with cable television in the 1970s. But the computer revolution was arguably more radical than any of these advances on account of having posed such a clear ideological challenge to the information economy's status quo. As we've seen for most of the twentieth century, innovators would lodge the control and power of new technologies within giant institutions. Innovation begat industry, and industry begat consolidation.

Initially, the story of the computing industry was no different. The large and ungainly prototypes of the 1940s had yielded a monopoly centered on IBM's "big iron," the nickname for its dominant mainframes. By the 1970s IBM enjoyed an integrated monopoly in the computer world with a breadth comparable only to AT&T's in telephony. What we now think of as separate markets for processors, hardware, operating systems, and applications were all lorded over by a single firm. At the center of IBM's power were its line of System 360 computers, each of which sold for over $20 million in present-day terms. With their rows of dials and blinking lights, IBM's machines formed the public's image of what a computer was.

The personal computer was a clear reaction to the IBM model. It took the power of computing then situated in government, large companies, and universities, and put into the hands of individuals a democratization of technological power with only a few precedents. It was almost unimaginable at the time: a device that made ordinary individuals sovereign over information by means of computational powers they could tailor to their individual needs. He gave people power, in other words, once reserved to institutions; even if that power was limited by the primitive capacities of the Apple II—48 KB of RAM, puny compared with even our present-day telephones but also with IBM's computers of the time—the machine nevertheless planted the seed that would change everything.

In addition to decentralizing power, Wozniak's Apple also helped define a crucial concept: "openness." With slots to accommodate all sorts of peripheral devices and an operating system that let the user program the machine as he wished, the Wozniak design was open in ways that might be said to still define the concept in the computing industries. Wozniak's ethic of openness extended even to disclosing design specifications. He once put the point this way: "Everything we knew, you knew."[7] In the secretive high-tech world, such transparency was unheard of, as it is today. Google, for example, despite its commitment to network openness, keeps most of its code and operations secret, and today's Apple, unlike the Apple of 1976, guards technical and managerial information the way Willy Wonka guarded candy recipes.

Put another way, Wozniak welcomed the amateur enthusiast, bringing the cult of the inspired tinkerer to the mass-produced computer. That ideology wasn't Wozniak's invention. In the 1970s it was an orthodoxy among computing hobbyists like the Bay Area's Homebrew Computer Club, where Wozniak offered the first public demonstration of the Apple I in 1976. As Wozniak described the club, "Everyone in the Homebrew Computer Club envisioned computers as a benefit to humanity—a tool that would lead to social justice." These men were the exact counterparts of the radio pioneers of the 1910s—hobbyist-idealists who loved to play with technology and dreamed it could make the world a better place. And while a computer you can tinker with and modify may not sound so profound, it contemplated a spiritual relationship between man and his machine, the philosophy one finds in Matthew Crawford's *Shop Class as Soulcraft* or *Zen and the Art of Motorcycle Maintenance,* which by no coincidence, came out in 1974. "It's pretty rare to make your engineering an art," said Wozniak, "but that's how it should be."[8]

The original Apple had a hood; and as with a car, the owner could open it up and get at the guts of the machine. Indeed, although it was a fully assembled device, not a kit like earlier PC products, one was encouraged to tinker with the innards, to soup it up, make it faster, add features, whatever. The Apple's operating system, using a form of BASIC as its programming language and operating environment, was one that anyone could program. It made it possible to write and sell one's programs directly, creating what we now call the "software" industry.

In 2006, I ran into Steve Wozniak on the campus of Columbia University.

"There's a question I've always wanted to ask you," I said. "What happened with the Mac? You could open up the Apple II, and there were slots and so on, and anyone could write for it. The Mac was way more closed. What happened?"

"Oh," said Wozniak. "That was Steve. He wanted it that way. The Apple II was my machine, and the Mac was his."

Apple's origins were pure Steve Wozniak, but as everyone knows, it was the other founder, Steve Jobs, whose ideas made Apple what it is today. Jobs maintained the early image that he and Wozniak created, but beginning with the Macintosh in the 1980s, and accelerating through the age of the iPod, iPhone, and iPad, he led Apple computers on a fundamentally different track.

Jobs's genius is of a very different cast from Wozniak. He is an apostle of perfectibility: a man who would seem as much at home in Victorian England as behind the counter of a sushi bar, who believes in a single best way of performing any task. As one might expect, his ideas embody an aesthetic philosophy as much as a sense of functionality, which is why Apple's products look so good while working so well. But those ideas have also long been at odds with the principles of the early computing industry, of the Apple II and of the Internet, sometimes to the detriment of Apple itself.

As Wozniak told me, the Macintosh, launched in 1984, marked a departure from many of his ideas as realized in the Apple II. To be sure, the Macintosh was radically innovative in its own right, being the first important mass-produced computer to feature a "mouse" and a "desktop"—ideas born in the mind of Douglas Engelbart in the 1950s, ideas that had persisted without fructifying in computer science labs ever since. Nevertheless the Mac represented an unconditional surrender of Wozniak's openness, as was obvious from the first glance: gone was the concept of the hood. You could no longer easily open the computer and get at its innards. Apple refused to license its operating system, meaning that a company like Dell couldn't make a Mac-compatible computer (but they could, and did, make a Microsoft machine). If you wanted a laser printer, most software, or virtually any accessory it was to Apple you had to turn. Apple made itself the final arbiter over what the Macintosh was and was not, rather in the way that AT&T at one time had sole discretion over what could and what could not connect to the telephone network.

Jef Raskin, who began the Macintosh product at Apple, put the difference this way in 1984: "Apple II is a system. Macintosh is an appliance." What he meant by this was that it was a computer far easier to use than anything that had come before. But with convenience came certain tradeoffs. Jobs created an integrated product with himself as its prime mover. If the good of getting everything to work together smoothly—perfectly—meant a little less freedom of use, so be it. For Jobs believed in the perfect machine, but perfection and freedom have never been fully compatible.[9]

By the time the Macintosh became Apple's lead product, Wozniak had lost whatever power he had once held over Apple's institutional ideology and product design. One salient reason had nothing to do with business or philosophy. In 1981 he crashed his Beechcraft Bonanza on takeoff from Scotts Valley, just outside the San Francisco Bay Area. Brain damage resulted in pronounced though temporary cognitive impairment, including retrograde amnesia. He would take a leave of absence, but his return would not alter the outcome of a quiet power struggle that had been building since before the accident. Its resolution would permanently sideline "the other Steve," leaving the far more ambitious Jobs and his ideas ascendant.

Like all centralized systems, Jobs's has its merits: one can easily criticize its principles yet love its products. Computers, it turns out, can indeed benefit in some ways from a centralizing will to perfection, no less than French cuisine, a German automobile, or any number of other elevated aesthetic experiences that depend on strict control of process and the consumer. Respecting functionality, too, Jobs has reason to crow. Since the original Macintosh, his company's designs have more often than not worked better, as well as more agreeably, than anything offered by the competition.

But the drawbacks have been obvious, too, not just for the consumer but for Apple. For even if Jobs made beautiful machines, his decision to close the Macintosh helped make Bill Gates the richest man on earth. No one would say it was the only reason, but Apple's long-standing adherence to closed design left the door wide open for the Microsoft Corporation and the many clones of the IBM PC to conquer computing with systems whose only real innovation was combining the best features of the Mac and the Apple II. Even if Windows was never as advanced or well designed as Apple's operating system, it enjoyed one insuperable advantage: it worked on any computer, supported just about every type of software, and could interface with any printer, modem, or whatever other hardware one could design. Windows ran off with the market Apple had pioneered, based on ideas that had been Apple's to begin with.

The victory of PCs and Windows over Apple was viewed by many as the defining parable of the 1990s; its moral was "open beats closed." It suggested that Wozniak had been right from the beginning. But by then Steve Jobs had been gone for years, having been forced out of Apple in 1985 in a boardroom coup. Yet even in his absence, Jobs would never agree about the superiority of openness, maintaining all the while that closed had simply not yet been perfected. A decade after his expulsion, back at the helm of the company he founded, Steve Jobs would try yet again to prove he had been the true prophet.

GOOGLE SWITCHES THE WEB

In 1902, the New York Telephone Company opened the world's first school for "telephone girls." It was an exclusive institution of sorts. As the historian

H. N. Casson described the qualifications for admission in 1910: "Every girl shall be in good health, quick-handed, clear-voiced, and with a certain poise and alertness of manner." There were almost seventeen thousand applicants every year for the school's two thousand places.[10]

Acquiring this credential was scarcely the hardest part of being a telephone girl. According to a 1912 *New York Times* story, 75 percent were fired after six months for "mental inefficiency." The job also required great manual dexterity to connect dozens of callers per minute to their desired parties. During the 1907 financial panic in New York, one exchange put through fifteen thousand phone calls in the space of an hour. "A few girls lost their heads. One fainted and was carried to the rest-room."[11]

People often wonder, "What exactly is Google?" Here is a simple answer: Like its harbinger the telephone girl, Google offers a fast, accurate, and polite way to reach your party. Google, in other words, is the Web's great switch. In fact, it's the world's most popular switch, and as such, it might even be described as the current custodian, on the Web, of the Master Switch.[12]

Every network needs a way to connect the parties who use it. In the early days of the telephone, you'd ask the telephone girl for your party by name ("Connect me with Ford Motors, please"). Later on, you'd directly dial the phone number, from either memory or the telephone directory, which seems rather a decline in service. Today, Google upholds the earlier standard, but on the Web. Needing no address, you ask for your party by name (typing in "Ford Motor Company," for instance), and Google shows you the way to connect.

The comparison with Bell's telephone switchboard girls might sound a little anticlimactic to describe a firm with ambitions as grand as Google's, but it reveals much. Google is often described as a media company, but it aggregates or locates content as opposed to producing it. It is a communications company, but it doesn't own the wires or airwaves over which packets reach people. You might accept my characterization that Google is simply the switch, but a switch alone has never before constituted a freestanding company. Compared with other giants, like Time Warner circa 2000, or Paramount Pictures circa 1927, or AT&T's original and resurrected incarnations, Google, despite what seems like a broad reach, is comparatively underintegrated. Indeed it is impossible to consider Google as independent from the platform that is its raison d'etre, and for our purposes that is the point.

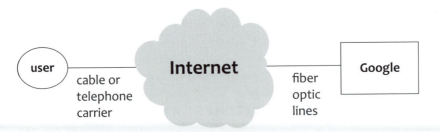

How Google reaches customers

Google has of course expanded in recent years beyond its original search engine, buying firms as diverse as Zagat's and Motorola, and starting its own social network, Google+. This might suggest the beginning of yet another sprawling conglomerate, but when you look carefully it becomes clear that Google isn't engaging in the purposeless acquisition of shiny properties that Jonathan Knee calls "the curse of the mogul." Rather, most of its investments serve to defend the primacy of the "search paradigm," the fact that the majority of people begin their Web experience with a search. Products like Gmail, Android, Google Local, and Google+ don't make money themselves, but keep search at the center of the user experience.

It is crucial to understand that Google lives or dies based on the data it can access, and that its strategies are engineered to preserve the openness of the original Web. In a world of closed, siloed information, the search engine would be just a mere tool, not the dominant paradigm it is today. So even as Google expands its operations in order to ensure the importance of search—and its top spot in that market—it is at bottom nothing more than a turbo-charged means of using a more fundamental invention, the Web itself.

To understand the ideas and the power of the underlying invention, we need to return to the summer of 1980. In a makeshift cabin in the mountain country near the French-Swiss border, a contract programmer, the sort of fellow you might pass without notice, has set up his temporary office. While serving a six-month contract with CERN laboratories, physicist Tim Berners-Lee undertook a solo mission in his spare time: to write a computer program for organizing information, the seed of which would ultimately flower into the World Wide Web. His program, ENQUIRE—short for "Enquire Within Upon Everything"—borrowed its name from a Victorian handbook to domestic life that offered advice on everything from child rearing to storing a mackerel. True to its namesake, ENQUIRE would evolve into what has become the world's largest repository of answers to life's chaotic questions. After ten years of fiddling around while working on other projects, Berners-Lee eventually wrote a standard (the HyperText Markup Language or HTML) and put up the first Web page, in 1990. Free for anyone to use, HTML slowly caught on, and as it did, Web pages continued to proliferate, bringing us to where we are today.[13]

It is worth touching on what precisely the World Wide Web is. The Web is commonly confused with the Internet—many use the terms interchangeably—but the Web is simply one of the network's most popular applications (email is another). The Internet moves information from place to place, but it is applications like the Web that determine what can be done using the Internet. Accessed through a browser, the Web was originally just an agreement to store all information in a common format (HTML), coupled with a means of connecting pieces of information by means of so-called hyperlinks. The supreme value of the Web was, and is, its *universality*. The idea, as Tim Berners-Lee told me, was that "the Web has to work on everything: any hardware, any software, every language, all kinds of different media, any quality level of data, [must] be accessible to people with disabilities, and work with any culture. Not just different languages, but different cultures."

That may sound like a tall order but somehow it happened. For today the Web is not only a universal platform for information but also for services. Extending the universality principle to service applications has allowed them to work more or less identically on any machine. Videos on the Web, for instance, look about the same whether on a laptop or a telephone, as do social networking services like Facebook. There is no need to laboriously rewrite a Web page to make it compatible with each of the countless individual devices in use. Because universality is baked into the cake, it is incredibly easy to start new things on the Web, whether it be a blog, an online retailer, or a political movement.

It is this principle of universality that makes the Web such a transformative force in matters of commerce and free expression. It evens out the influence of scale, amplifies what would otherwise be small ventures, little voices. A politician can come out of nowhere thanks to the ease of reaching millions via the Web. A site like Facebook can go in just a few years from a weird notion to one having hundreds of millions of users, all thanks to the organizational principles that Tim Berners-Lee first implemented. That we take this power of universality so much for granted today only points out how profound the idea was.

The Web has obviously been very hospitable to commerce; the greatest commercial giants of the 1990s and 2000s (from Amazon to eBay, Facebook, and Google) are the Web's progeny. But its founding ideas were more high-minded than materialistic, infused with a practical utopianism that was Berners-Lee's dream. He described the inspiration for his invention as overcoming the problems created by large bureaucracies, which isolate information in silos. As he explained to me, "If in doubt, the Web had to be 'unconstraining.' I saw lots of systems that made you work in a certain way, and they all died." On the other hand, he wanted to avoid the shortcomings of a "utopian commune with no structure, which doesn't work because nobody actually takes out the garbage."

Giving an earlier British visionary, Lord Reith, his due, Berners-Lee hailed "the value system of the BBC I was brought up with.... Infrastructure should be free, even if the businesses on top of it make lots of money." In the 1990s, Berners-Lee wrote at some length on what he saw as the congruencies between the philosophy underlying the Web and his Unitarian-Universalist faith, one also professed, it is interesting to note, by Alexander Graham Bell. Both, he said, recognize "the value of systems in which individuals play their role, with both a firm sense of their own identity, and a firm sense of some common good." Hope, Berners-Lee believed, was at the core of both value systems. "The whole spread of the Web happened not because of a decision and a mandate from any authority, but because a whole bunch of people across the 'Net picked it up ... the fact that the Web happens is an example of a dream coming true and an encouragement to all who hope."

Many of the Web's success stories can be understood as carrying Berners-Lee's original ideal to its natural conclusion. Wikipedia, the collaborative encyclopedia, fulfilled the dream of a global knowledge project that in some ways the Web itself was intended to be. Blogs, tweets, and the original YouTube were news and entertainment, produced for ordinary folk by ordinary folk. Social networking realized the dream of a web of social connections. Even Google can be understood, particularly in its inception, as a consequence of the Web's natural evolution, a faster way of getting around when the terrain became too vast to be navigated by human faculties alone. For while Berners-Lee provided a way to store and link the world's information, his Web came with no way to find it, and it did not take long before the lack was dire. It is worth remembering that Google, too, began not as a money-making scheme but as an academic project run out of Stanford University, rather as FM Radio got started at Columbia in the 1930s. And so it is no coincidence that Google's founding mission—"to organize the world's information"—sounds so similar to the original goal of the Web.

The Web, in short, is quite possibly the most idealistic of all the major, successful information projects launched in the twentieth century, and a dramatic case study in the power of ideas. But if we've seen anything ..., it's that one man's idealistic invention is another's nuisance to be quashed, or low-hanging fruit to be plucked, and that a scientist's homely prototype can quickly become the foundation for a mighty empire.

THE INTERNET AND THE BELL SYSTEM

In Chicago late in 2005, AT&T's Ed Whitacre took a break during a typical day of empire building to grant *BusinessWeek*'s Roger Crockett an interview. In the midst of his campaign to reunify the Bell company, the CEO was refreshingly clear about his strategy. "It's about scale and scope," he told Crockett a few times, "scale and scope."

Crockett asked, "How concerned are you about Internet upstarts like Google, MSN, Vonage, and others?"

Whitacre immediately homed in on their weakness. "How do you think they're going to get to customers? Through a broadband pipe."

"Cable companies have them. We have them," he continued. "Now what they would like to do is use my pipes free, but I ain't going to let them do that."

From this it was clear that AT&T had identified precisely the soft underbelly of the Internet's leading firms. "How do you think they're going to get to customers?" Whitacre understood that he, allied with the cable industry and the other parts of Bell, was strategically positioned to choke the Internet into submission.[14]

... The Internet and the Web generally run against two important Bell principles. First, they are decentralized, while Bell's network is predicated on centralized control. Second, both allow anyone to conduct business without the operator's permission, leaving the network no means or right to demand a cut of any profits. This latter problem, less abstract, more dollars-and-cents, lay behind Whitacre's comments: it was time to find a way to make the Internet pay.

He who controls the wires or airwaves can control the Internet, for it is only by means of these connections that the Internet can exist, let alone operate.

Internet-based firms can reach their customers by no other channel. To use a search engine and other utilities, you need Internet access, and that is not a service that firms like Amazon or Google provide (with trivial exceptions). To have such access, you need to pay an Internet Service Provider—typically your telephone or cable company. The Web firms must also pay for Internet service, a fact that, conceptually at least, puts all of them on an equal footing. In fact, this equality is the life-blood of firms that were born on an open Internet. Were the Internet not a common carrier most would need a new business model.

When Whitacre made his remarks, AT&T and its allies had a plan in mind. AT&T would begin offering a "fast lane" Internet service to select customers (that is, those willing to pay for it), creating pressure on the cable firms and Verizon to do likewise. AT&T might, for example, strike a deal to make Yahoo! AT&T's official search engine, moving its searches ahead of those of Yahoo! rivals, in exchange for fees; or it might get Netflix to pay so that customers might download movies faster. While some were bound to denounce this as a payola scheme, AT&T seemed confident that "better" service for a price would make sense to enough customers, particularly those whose products were bandwidth hogs. Indeed, AT&T argued that a fast lane would be necessary for services like Internet video to appeal to consumers. (Netflix and YouTube would ultimately prove that wrong, but in 2006, the notion made sense.) In any case, behind the fast-lane proposition would always be an implied threat of a penalty or service downgrade for those unwilling or unable to pay. And so it was lost on no one that by exercising broad discretion to speed up the business of some firms and slow down that of others, AT&T and the cable companies would be assuming life-and-death power over commerce on the Internet.

If all had gone according to plan, the Internet would now likely be a very different network from the one we know. But in 2006 something rare in the history of these industries happened: a public backlash, not much on the scale of national politics, but large enough to make a difference. For most of [the last century], the average citizen, however politically engaged, has remained either completely unaware of battles raging within the information industries, or too dazzled by their consumer products to care. But AT&T's maneuvers struck a nerve among some influential bloggers and other independent content creators, who saw the scheme as a major threat to smaller voices like theirs. Some credit is due a new generation of activists, like Ben Scott of Free Press, who put together an unexpected coalition to oppose AT&T's plans, one that in 2006 included the Christian Coalition, MoveOn.org, and Gun Owners of America, all of whom saw the phone company's toll gate as a threat to their messaging and efforts to organize. Millions signed up to a website called "SavetheInternet.com."

Sensing a problem, the Bells took the fight to Congress, where their lobbyists pushed for a law stripping the FCC of any authority to block fast-lane plans. Such K-Street wrangling is usually too complex to attract much media interest, particularly on the broadcast networks, but it did catch the attention of a popular cable show named *The Daily Show with Jon Stewart*. Over the summer, Stewart ran several segments on net neutrality, including one ridiculing Bell ally and then-Senate Commerce Committee Chairman, the late Ted Stevens of Alaska.

"The Internet," said Senator Stevens, "is not something you just dump something on. It's not a big truck. It's a series of tubes."

Stewart said of Stevens, "You don't seem to know jackshit about computers or the Internet, but hey, that's okay—you're just the guy in charge of regulating it."

Stewart's astute sarcasm illuminated a danger with a force no op-ed could match: The old men of the Senate were handing Ma Bell control over the Internet with scant understanding of what they were doing.

And so as the fall 2006 elections approached, net neutrality became an unlikely cause celebre, attracting celebrity supporters like Moby and R.E.M. A shapely young Belgian named Tania Derveaux gained some attention by posing naked with a sign written "Plz Save Net Neutrality" and promising to make love with any virgin geek who pledged to support the cause (an application form was provided). While AT&T had encountered many forms of resistance over its hundred-year history, this was new. The fast-lane plans were quietly abandoned, and Bell's telecom reform bills died in Congress, saving the Internet from mercenary management for the moment though leaving a statutory vacuum wherein regulation of the network remained up for grabs. Still it was clear that somewhere along the line the idea of an open Internet, once strictly a concern of the technorati, had evolved into a public norm of real significance. The phrase "net neutrality," coined to express the vision of the Internet's founders, had slipped out of academia and into the public square. But was its support broad enough for the idea to become law?

One July morning in 2010, six men made their varied ways to southwestern Washington, to the hulking brass and brick home of the Federal Communications Commission. After passing through security, they converged on the eighth floor, to meet in the agency's "Conference Room One." The six had been called in by the federal government to work on a summer project of sorts. They would spend most of the summer in that room and the adjoining ones, working out what the nation's first net neutrality law should look like.

The six were chosen to represent opposing factions in industry. Sitting on one side of the table representing "the Internet" were Rick Whitt from Google, former FCC staffer Chris Libertelli (now with Skype), and a lawyer, Markham Erickson, for the rest of the high-tech industry. Across the table sat Bell's senior lobbyists, men of notably impressive resumes: from AT&T came Jim Cicconi, a Texan who had been deputy chief of staff in the first Bush White House; Tom Tauke, the longtime Iowa Congressman turned Verizon lobbyist, and Kyle McSlarrow, Deputy Secretary of Energy for George W. Bush, now paid to promote the interests of the cable industry. The FCC's Eddie Lazarus presided over all, as other staff came and went.

The six invitees were in that room because President Barack Obama had made a campaign promise to enact a net neutrality rule, and the FCC decided to let industry draft the rule. If that sounds like a dereliction of the agency's duty to make law itself, all that can be said is that the process is hardly unprecedented. Sure enough, what emerged from those negotiations would be enacted, in modified form, by the Commission, in December of 2010 as the nation's very first net neutrality law. The rule (technically "In the matter of the Open Internet") codified the existing norm that had held since the failure of the fast-lane initiative in the mid-2000s. Essentially, it was a ban on discrimination and blocking on the Internet. Borrowing language from the Telecommunications Act of 1934, it said that Internet carriers like Comcast and AT&T "shall not block," and "shall not unreasonably discriminate in transmitting lawful network traffic over a consumer's broadband Internet access service."

You might think that with such a simple rule any potential threat to the Web or open Internet would effectively be eliminated. You might, but you would be mistaken. On the one hand, the rule clearly proscribes the sort of blocking undertaken by China or Mubarak's Egypt, in a federally enforceable fashion, an achievement that cannot be underestimated. But it did leave doors open to other lucrative possibilities, like "bandwidth caps" that punish consumers unable to correctly estimate their monthly usage. Even more important, the ban on discrimination applied only to the wired Internet, the segment increasingly dominated by the cable industry. Wireless broadband, that is to say, the data arriving on smartphones and iPads, is exempt. That enormous exception—AT&T and Verizon's condition for support of the rule—is no mere technicality, but arguably a masterstroke on the part of the Bells. It puts the cable industry at a disadvantage, while leaving the markets on which both AT&T and Verizon have bet their future without federal oversight. The Bells were guessing that wireless would be the key to the future, and this time they guessed right.

A BATTLE FOR TERRITORY

In Hindu mythology, deities and demons assume different incarnations to fight the same battles repeatedly. At the beginning of the 2010s, it was obvious that the struggle for the future of the Internet was just the latest iteration of the perennial ideological struggle into which every information industry is eventually swept. It is the old conflict between big and small, the concepts of the open system and the closed, between the forces of centralized order and those of dispersed variety. The antagonists assume new forms, the generals change, but essentially the same battles are fought over and over again. It is the very essence of the Cycle, which even a technology as radical and powerful as the Internet seems able to moderate at most but not to abolish.

For the information industries that now account for an ever increasing share of American and world GDP, the coming decade will be given over to a mighty effort to seize territory, to bolt the competition from its habitat. But this is not a case of one pack of wolves chasing another out of a prime valley. While it may sound fanciful, the contest in question is more like one of polar bears battling lions for domination of the world. Each animal, insuperably dominant in its natural element—the polar bear on ice and snow, the lion on the open plains—will undertake a land grab where it has no natural business being. The only practicable strategy will be a campaign of climate change, the polar bears seeking to cover as much of the world with snow as they can, while the lion tries to coax a savannah from the edges of a tundra. Sounds absurd, but for these mighty predators, it's simply the law of nature.

Led by Google, the firms born on the Web have been trying to convert as much of the world to the virtues of their native habitat: a network with a clear, free path between any two points, allowing the easiest possible access to customers' eyeballs. Meanwhile, the other side is moving quickly and preemptively, trying to ensure that the mobile Internet, when it emerges fully, will be a network very different from the Internet we have known heretofore. For the telephone and cable companies, the justification is a simple matter of private property, as Whitacre had articulated it: the wires and devices, the underlying physical infrastructure, without which there is no Internet. Naturally allied to such respect for property are copyright holders, who fear for their just due in the giddy idealistic rush to make everything available to everyone without limit, never mind who owns it. There is, the partisans of this side argue, a cost to building a bridge as to writing a novel. If this side has its way, the twenty-first-century world of information will look as much as possible like that of the twentieth century, except that the screens to which consumers are glued will be more portable.

This, in essence, is our present war for information, one being waged on multiple fronts in ways subtle and not so subtle. Let us consider now the face of battle.

APPLE'S CHALLENGE TO ITS OWN CREATION

When Steve Jobs regained control of Apple at the turn of the century, he had had, like Theodore Vail in 1907, a long time to think about the industry he helped found. Like Vail, the onetime iconoclast began to think big, even by his own standards. During his time away, Jobs had not abandoned his basic product philosophy, namely that what humans really crave is not complete freedom but something more akin to enlightened dictatorship as envisioned by Plato in *The Republic*. Still, the success of Microsoft turning Apple's brand concepts into generics was not lost on him. He would now pivot a bit, staying true to his dictatorial perfectionism while endeavoring to make all his products just open enough to satisfy the yearning for choice.

As the century began, Jobs began a campaign of truly epic proportions, even if its complete design wasn't clear at the beginning. Over the following decade he would introduce a triad of beautiful, perfect machines that have since won legions of fanatical users: the iPod, the iPhone, and the iPad. Only by the decade's end would it become clearer that Jobs's aim was to usurp and replace the personal computer, the very invention he and Wozniak introduced in 1976. Jobs was repudiating, now decisively and forever, Steve Wozniak's open vision of the future. In retrospect, the transformation was signaled in 2007 when Jobs renamed Apple Computers "Apple Inc."—roughly the same time he refused to write a foreword for his old friend's autobiography, *iWoz*.[15]

As early as 2005, Jonathan Zittrain had prophesied a movement to replace the personal computer with "information appliances" but he could never have guessed that Apple—the inventor of the PC—would lead the charge. What Jobs envisioned is a "Post-PC era," in which his new devices would supplant the computer naturally, as the car had once replaced the truck. Once "all cars were trucks because that's what you needed on the farm." Eventually, though, all most people really needed was a car. Like Henry Ford nearly a century before, Jobs would offer a smaller, less complex but also less capable product tailored to a limited set of needs. His mission, he admitted, was bound to meet with opposition. "This transformation," said Jobs, "is going to make some people uneasy."

On the inside, the iPod, iPhone, and iPad are indeed computers. But they are computers that have been reduced to a limited set of functions that they are designed to perform extremely well. It's easy to see this with the iPod, which is designed solely and optimally for playing music and watching videos. The limitation is much harder to see on the iPhone and the iPad, both of which do most of what a computer can, and sometimes more: make phone calls, send email, surf the Web, and—most important—run an ever-growing menu of "apps." But even if lost on many consumers, the inescapable reality is that these machines are designed primarily to facilitate consumption, not creation, and so they are closed in a way the personal computer never was. True, Apple does provide a Web browser and allows outsiders to develop apps—Jobs learned the lesson that a platform completely closed to outside developers cannot long flourish. The genius of the design is in offering no more than the degree of openness that would suffice for the overwhelming majority of users. But the power remains in the center, a vision antithetical to the original vision of the Apple II and all that it inspired.

In a manner unprecedented on the Web, let alone the Apple II, Apple reserves the right to decide what apps may or may not run on an iPad or iPhone. From a list of 116 reasons why an app may be rejected it furnishes producers, the most telling is this: "We will reject apps for any content or behavior that we believe is over the line. What line, you ask? Well, as a Supreme Court Justice once said, 'I'll know it when I see it.' "

Apple's exercise of its veto has sometimes met with serious complaints, as in the early decision to block Skype, the firm whose software lets users call each other over the Internet for free, eating into Apple partner AT&T's long distance margins. Later, during the summer of 2009, Apple bodychecked an application written for the iPhone by Google. The product, named "Google Voice," was designed to make a single phone number, when dialed, ring on all one's phones at once. Only in response to FCC pressure did Apple relent on both of these blocks.

Apple, for its part, likens its rejection of apps to the behavior of a retailer—a store is generally free not to stock products it doesn't like—and points out that its devices carry a Web browser that can be used to access everything on the Web—every application is thus available, if not always with the dazzling convenience of an app. Still, given the norms of openness in the tech world, Apple's blocks have produced no little outrage. Tom Conlon of *Popular Science* writes, "How long before it [Apple] blocks movies, TV shows, songs, books and even websites? Scoff now, but don't be so naïve as to believe that this isn't possible." But as in times past, consumers on the whole seem content to bear a little totalitarianism for convenience and are happy to have Apple sort out the wheat from the chaff.

That implicit promise is, in fact, the key. Echoing Hollywood's founding moguls, Apple promises the world a better, higher quality experience, free of clutter and nonsense, a clearer path to top-notch entertainment. Jobs voiced this sentiment himself when he declared that what Americans fundamentally want is "Hollywood movies and television shows. They don't want *amateur hour*." By "amateur hour," of course, he meant the content available all over the Web and notably on little-filtered platforms like YouTube, which thrive on the premise that just about anyone can be a creator of sorts with the potential to amuse his fellows. Indeed, the fact that something is produced by an ordinary person is precisely what makes it captivating in this vision. It's not just a matter of taste: at a deeper level, this debate opposes two quite different visions of culture, in a way reminiscent of Huxley's lament over the mass production of culture. Apple's vision is a latter-day apotheosis of the twentieth-century ideal of an industry that can produce entertainment for the whole population. By contrast, the Internet, which from the start envisioned a culture far more decentralized and a notion of creativity far more democratic, harkens back to an America before the twentieth century, when entertainment mostly consisted mainly of what one's family and neighbors could muster. That notion glorifies the output of amateurs, which Apple and its allies see as so much static, a universe of stupid pet tricks and smoking infants.

Everyone knows how incredibly user-friendly Apple's devices are; fewer seem aware how, as it were, "Hollywood-friendly" they are. Despite complaints about Apple's high commissions, the largest media conglomerates and even newspaper publishers see it as a necessary platform for their content—the commodity that, not so long ago, was king. That reality presents a sharp contrast with the Web's openness crew. In the United States, Google receives a continuous stream of notices demanding that it remove links to copyright-infringing materials (YouTube accounts for the lion's share). Many, especially in New York's old-media conglomerates and publishing industries, hold Google in deep suspicion, a feeling that persists no matter how many earnest professions of benign intent the company offers. Those professions, in fact, tend to make matters worse, as they confirm the traditional content generators' feeling that Google doesn't appreciate how a dollar is made in their game. Such ignorance, even if benignly intended, comes across as an existential threat to those still trying to peddle hardbacks and the like.

Apple, on the other hand, offers to New York and Hollywood salvation from the madness the Web has visited upon content producers. It portrays itself as the kind of partner that media and newspapers can deal with, a grown-up among the northern California high-tech kids. Having been CEO of Pixar Animation Studios during his years in the wilderness, Jobs is one of the few players who can move with ease between Hollywood and Silicon Valley. And so partnership with Apple appeals to men like Rupert Murdoch, who in 2011 launched *The Daily,* the first iPad-only newspaper, an Apple exclusive. But lest Apple's self-positioning seem merely cynical, it is worth remembering that their platform is a thing of enviable beauty, and the promise of real markets for writers and other creators is hardly trivial—for most it's a matter of life and death. Rather than push aside the old makers of content, Apple has built a bridge to the future for them, a move consistent with Apple's past. One original dream of the Macintosh still lives in the newer devices: to bring the blessings of the computer revolution to those not particularly interested in computers. Contrary to what geeks sometimes think, not everyone secretly dreams of writing their own code. While Google beckons us to think of everything differently, Apple promises a world that is the same only easier.

By March of 2010, Apple had surpassed Microsoft as the largest technology company in the world, with a valuation of over $240 billion. Steve Jobs, who resigned in August 2011 and passed away six weeks later, had finally built an information empire as mighty as any that had come before. But along the way he jettisoned Wozniak's vision. For all their success and glamour, the appliances betray Wozniak's pathbreaking inspiration to empower the individual user, the virtue of which even the casual user can appreciate in principle. The machines may have far more computational power than the PC of a decade ago, but that power is not really at one's disposal; it is harnessed for consumption, not creation. They put the individual exactly where Hollywood would: as another member of the audience. The difference this time is that the couch potatoes are ambulatory, and fixated on slightly smaller screens.

PROJECT ANDROID

Throughout the summer of 2007, rumors flew that some kind of Google phone was in the works. At the Googleplex, the firm's storied campus, a suspicious statue, a human-robot (or android), with red eyes showed up in a nondescript building across from the main campus. Finally, on November 5, 2007, Google effectively announced the Gphone—by letting it be known that there was no such thing.

In contrast with the unveiling of the iPhone, there was no stadium event, no screaming crowd, and most important, no product. Instead, there was just a blog post entitled "Where's My Gphone?"[16] An employee named Andy Rubin wrote the following: "Despite all of the very interesting speculation over the last few months, we're not announcing a Gphone. However, we think what we are announcing—the Open Handset Alliance and Android—is more significant and ambitious than a single phone."

Here it was: Google's first real foray into the world of the telephone, as distinct from the computer, the Internet, or the Web. The significance cannot be overstated. Until 2007, the Web and its allies had, in the main, been playing defense—attempting to preserve the status quo of net neutrality and limit the power of their rivals among other information enterprises. Coming out of this defensive crouch, Google took the fight to its adversaries, attempting to plant the flag of openness deep in the heart of telephone territory, Bell's holy land since the 1880s.

Project Android, at its launch, puzzled industry observers, for it had no obvious revenue model. Google was giving away Android for free, as it does most of its other products. Mind you, what Google is giving away is not a telephone or even a telephone service—users must still buy those—but rather an operating system for telephones, based on the Linux kernel, the Ur–free and open software beloved of tech geeks. By giving away a version adapted for telephony, Google was distributing a free set of tools for programmers of any affiliation to write applications.

Given what we now understand, it should be obvious that this move was, like so many other initiatives, a means to an end rather than an end in itself. Project Android is an effort to "convert" the mobile world into territory that is friendly to Google and its allies rather than to its enemies. It is, to return to our wild kingdom analogy, an effort to extend the world of ice and snow, where the polar bear cannot be defeated. For Google cannot win in a world of closed platforms. Android is its bid to keep some of the mobile world open, Web-friendly, and most of all, friendly to Google's business model of making sure customers spend enough time, every day, with Google products so as to protect its advertising revenue.

As soon as the Android was announced, Steve Jobs trashed it in the *New York Times*. "Android hurts them [Google] more than it helps them," said Jobs. "It's just going to divide them and people who want to be their partners." Or, quite possibly, provide Apple with its only real competition in the markets that matter most to it.

In 2008, when the project was still secret, I spoke with Android developer Rich Miner, who predicted with absolute confidence that his machines would struggle for the first year but then come to dominate the market. After all, open beats closed, as the Silicon Valley mantra goes. Thus, the PC had beaten out the mainframe in the 1980s and Microsoft had beaten Apple in the 1990s. So while Apple may have blazed the way with its iPhone, Android could soon be expected to carry away the mobile market.

Miner would be proved prescient. After a slow start, Google eventually signed up partners, and by early 2011, the Android was the top-selling smartphone in the United States and the world. As in the Macintosh circa 1994, Apple would remain a leader in technology and design but become a laggard in market share. Yes, that may be in part because Google gives Android software away for free, and uses the revenue from its search advertising business to subsidize its development efforts. Alternatively, it hints that Google had learned the paramount lesson of the 1990s—for, like Microsoft Windows, Android simply works on more devices, and therefore reaches more consumers.

The success of Android is significant enough to allow us to question whether the Cycle of information industries is different from the one that developed during the twentieth century. In the 1920s and 1930s, the progression toward integrated models seemed inevitable, simply the norm of industrial development. In the time of Adolph Zukor, Theodore Vail, and the rest, it had seemed quite natural, in a Darwinian way, that an integrated approach like Apple's was the key to fitness and dominance. But as Android thrives, two things become apparent: the Internet may have ushered in a new age of sustainable open systems, but the drift toward monopoly remains as irresistible as ever. And whether the success of Android proves that the Cycle is broken depends on one critical proposition: that its master, Google, really is a different kind of firm.

In the fall of 2010, I was on Google's campus speaking of cycles, of open and closed, centralization and decentralization. A senior employee raised his hand. "You have a good point," he said "When you're a new company, getting started, openness seems really great, because it offers a way in. But I have to admit, the bigger you get, the more appealing closed systems starts to look."

Both the Web and Internet are open systems with billions of users and thousands of firms operating on them. But as the history of the information industries shows, such ecosystems tend to be short-lived. Sometimes they are closed by existing powers who see new technologies as a threat. But often it is today's revolutionary who succumbs to the allure of being tomorrow's emperor. Is Google destined to arrive at its Napoleonic moment?

Writing in 2011, there are some signs to that effect. As Google's monopoly over search has ripened, the company has, in mostly subtle ways, begun a tell-tale effort to defend the engine that furnishes the revenues that make everything else easy. One is to continually improve the product; that is hardly something anyone can object to. Another tactic is to surround the search feature with so many complementary functions—Google Maps, Gmail, Google News, and the rest—that abandoning Google would also mean leaving a lot of other cool stuff behind. More controversial is the fact that, since the 2010s, many of Google's searches take you directly to Google-owned properties, which can be handy but also a way of diverting users from the competitors of these sites in the name of convenience. Whether all of this is a defense of its monopoly or simply serving consumer demands is hard to say.

Meanwhile, as the Android grows into a full-size robot, Google also faces the paradoxical reality that some of the most effective ways of competing with Apple involve becoming more like Apple. Like Apple, it has begun to block apps that interfere with the revenue models of itself or its telephone partners—like the apps that let you use your phone to connect your computer to the Internet. Since the launch of its open platform, Google has become enmeshed in the kind of tight partnerships it had always decried. In 2010 Google got so close to Verizon as to agree with the Bell company that net neutrality rules weren't really necessary for wireless, a heresy among those who profess openness as the true faith. Perhaps to shore up its openness bona fides, Google has often gone into overdrive with openness messaging like a political reformer accused of corruption. In 2011, amid rumors of a more-closed Android system, Google's Andy Rubin issued vehement denials, declaring "we will continue to work toward an open and healthy ecosystem because we truly believe this is best for the industry and best for consumers." Google has also continued to point to a sort of mission statement, to a document that many call its "openness manifesto," which can be summarized in a sentence: "Open systems win." Sometimes, it seems to be protesting too much.

In fairness, it must be allowed that Google has remained more committed to openness than any information empire before it. What now seems possible, if unprecedented, is a well-defended Internet monopolist running a mostly open system. If we reach that point, the future will depend on an equally unprecedented question: What matters more to a monopolist—openness or supremacy? It is a question never faced in the information industries, where "monopoly" has been synonymous with a closed system. Google may wind up squaring the circle in a way reminiscent of history's great anomalous monopolist, AT&T, volunteering itself for regulation rather than being maimed. It may seek out deals with governments in the United States and around the world that leave its monopoly intact and defended in exchange for doing what it does so well, running an open system in a spirit of public service. "Do No Evil" might become not a motto but a sworn duty. As Vail showed, such noblesse oblige can be very good indeed for the bottom line—for, over the long run, common carriage isn't a bad business.

Google is not the only Web-born revolutionary that seeks to make that idealistic invention its dominion. Social-networking sites, Facebook first and foremost, stealthily aim to conquer by offering themselves as Web alternatives. Many forms of content that once stood independent on the Web—personal pages, fan pages, e-vites, and so on—are now created instead on Facebook. That Facebook's pages are far easier to create and link to other Facebook features goes without saying. But the decisive difference is that unlike Web pages, Facebook pages are Facebook's property, and are deliberately not linked to the rest of the Web. This departure from the Web's founding principle of universality has led Tim Berners-Lee to sound an ominous alarm. A social networking site like Facebook, he warns, threatens to become "a closed silo of content, and one that does not give you full control over your information in it.... [T]he more this kind of architecture gains widespread use, the more the Web becomes fragmented, and the less we enjoy a single, universal information space." It is another instance of the seduction of convenience blinding us to what we are giving up, and what we are signing up for.

The banality of most people's Facebook pages should not blind us to the larger implications. True, in its short history Facebook has helped overthrow more governments than it has propped up. But should Facebook ever see a benefit in aligning itself with a government (as AT&T did when providing the Bush administration warrantless wiretaps), clearly it could serve as one of the better spying tools ever created. Once a firm or industry gains huge power over the majority of people, the possibility exists for government to make that firm an offer it can't refuse.

Facebook's ultimate ambitions may yet be a work in progress. Already, however, the struggle for primacy on the Web gives a strong indication that the network's special properties are not completely immune to the Cycle. Networks, it turns out, far from having an inherent character, are ultimately what we make them. As Berners-Lee wrote in 2010, "people seem to think the Web is some sort of piece of nature, and if it starts to wither, well, that's just one of those unfortunate things we can't help. Not so. We create the Web, by designing computer protocols and software; this process is completely under our control." Neither a character nor a fate can be presumed.

In this way, the future may all come down to what we want. But what we truly want is, unfortunately, a matter of ambiguity. Eric Schmidt, former Google CEO, insists that "the vote is clear that the end user prefers choice, freedom, and openness." But as every pollster knows, it's all a matter of how you put the question. Do you want total freedom? Sure. Would you settle for a little less in exchange for having all of Hollywood and New York's finest content at your command? All your friends in constant touch on Facebook? The whole world via the most reliable network on earth, effortlessly accessible on the most beautiful device you've ever seen, which is constantly growing in its capacities to anticipate and fulfill every human desire? Remind me: what am I giving up? The worst of the Internet—the spam, the faulty apps, the junky amateur content. With technology promising a paradise in exchange for the prerogative to do a bit of choosing for us, the red pill of openness may seem a bitter one indeed.

The openness movement, of which Google has been a de facto, if not always trusted, leader, remains based on a contrary notion of virtue, a different idea of Utopia. In the context of the information industries, it is one that can be traced back to the edenic world of 1920s radio. To restore us to such a blissful seat is what the apostles of openness long for, and it is nothing short of a social transformation. They idealize a world in which most goods and services are free or practically free, thereby liberating the individual to pursue self-expression and self-actualization as his primary purpose.[17] But to inhabit such a world, much is asked of us—much more, perhaps, than some want to give. It may be true, today, that the individual holds more power than at any time in the past century, and literally in the palm of his hand. Whether or not he can hold on to it is another matter.

NOTES

1. The quotes in this chapter from Steve Jobs and Eric Schmidt are drawn from the 2007 Macworld conference in San Francisco, or from a February 2010 interview with Eric Schmidt. Jobs's entire keynote address from the 2007 Macworld event may be viewed at www.apple.com/quicktime/qtv/mwsf07/ (last visited March 2010).

2. This title is official; see Google's "Corporate Information" website, www.google.com/corporate/execs.html (last visited March 2010).

3. Tim Bray's comment was made on a personal blog but cleared by Google and widely attributed to it. The blog post is at www.tbray.org/ongoing/When/201x/2010/03/15/Joining-Google.

4. This quote is drawn from the 1927 essay referenced throughout this book: Aldous Huxley, "The Outlook for American Culture," *Harper's Magazine,* August 1927.

5. One particularly interesting history of Wozniak and Jobs's initial meeting and development of what would eventually become Apple, as well as the reinvention of the company in recent years with the development of popular modern Apple technology, may be found in Michael Moritz, *Return to the Little Kingdom: Steve Jobs, the Creation of Apple, and How It Changed the World* (New York: Overlook, 2009). Other descriptions of the early history of Apple include Roy A. Allen, *A History of the Personal Computer: The People and the Technology* (London, Ontario: Allen Publishing, 2001), 36.

6. This quote, as well as much of the Wozniak centric information in this chapter, is drawn from Steve Wozniak's autobiography, *iWoz—Computer Geek to Cult Icon: How I Invented the Personal Computer, Co-Founded Apple, and Had Fun Doing It* (New York: W. W. Norton, 2006), 103.

7. Wozniak said this at his talk at Columbia University on September 28, 2006.

8. Matthew B. Crawford, *Shop Class as Soulcraft* (New York: Penguin, 2009); Robert Pirsig, *Zen and the Art of Motorcycle Maintenance: An Inquiry into Values* (New York: William Morrow, 1974). Pirsig's book, while generally taken as a meditation on spirituality and technology, actually spends more time on complex epistemological questions that are hard to summarize. Wozniak, *iWoz*, 291.

9. This quote is from Leander Kahney, "How Apple Got Everything Right by Doing Everything Wrong," *Wired*, March 18, 2008. In the article, Kahney also questions Apple and Google's supposedly close relationship: "By Google's definition, Apple is irredeemably evil, behaving more like an old-fashioned industrial titan than a different-thinking business of the future." The book he was promoting with this article: Leander Kahney, *Inside Steve's Brain* (New York: Penguin, 2008).

10. Herbert N. Casson, *The History of the Telephone* (Chicago: A. C. McClurg, 1910), 157.

11. The *New York Times* story is "Psychology of Telephone Girls," *New York Times*, April 4, 1912. The effect of the financial panic on the telephone girls is described in Casson, *History of the Telephone*, 155.

12. The idea of describing Google as a switch comes from my colleague Charles Sabel at Columbia.

13. This account is based on an interview with Tim Berners-Lee on April 22, 2011, and the account in Tim Berners-Lee, *Weaving the Web: The Original Design and Ultimate Destiny of the World Wide Web* (New York: HarperOne, 1999).

14. "At SBC, It's All About 'Scale and Scope,' " *BusinessWeek*, November 7, 2005.

15. According to Wozniak, in an interview with *Wired* magazine. See Rachel Metz, "iWoz Logs Leap from Geek to Icon," Wired.com, August 24, 2006, available at www.wired.com/gadgets/mac/news/2006/08/7164.

16. The blog post can be found at googleblog.blogspot.com/2007–11-wheres-my-gphone .html.

17. The best account of such a future is a novel by Cory Doctorow, *Down and Out in the Magic Kingdom* (New York: Tor, 2003); it is also the evident vision of the Burning Man festival. On the relationship between the tech world and Burning Man, see Fred Turner, "Burning Man at Google," 145.

QUESTIONS FOR MAKING CONNECTIONS
WITHIN THE READING

1. "In Hindu mythology," Wu writes, "deities and demons assume different incarnations to fight the same battles repeatedly." In what sense has the Internet's history involved an almost mythic opposition between the champions of openness and the proponents of centralization? Who have been the defenders of openness, and who have sought to advance monopolies over information? Wu makes the point that earlier technologies—telephones, for instance, and radio—moved from openness to monopoly. Why might the Internet meet a different fate?

2. We often think of technology as essentially value-neutral. Mobile phones or iPods can be used, after all, for benevolent or malicious purposes, depending on the context or the motives of the user. But when we consider technology from the standpoint of social life, values become important. What social values have accompanied the development of the Internet? Cooperation or competition? Equality or hierarchy? Democracy or top-down control? What broader conclusions can we reach about technology in general? Can it ever be value-neutral? Does technology always reflect the values of its creators, or does it sometimes escape the grasp of those who try to control it?

3. Drawing on Wu's account, describe the relations between technology and economics. In what ways do market forces facilitate technological innovation? In what ways do they actually constrain technology or prevent its free circulation? We often assume that innovation and the market work in harmony, but tensions sometimes challenge that view. How often in the case of the Internet has innovation been driven by the search for profit rather than by demand? In what ways have economic forces thwarted the intentions of altruistic pioneers like Tim Berners-Lee?

QUESTIONS FOR WRITING

1. Does the complexity and expense of technologies like the Internet increase or diminish the prospects for greater social equality? While innovators like Steve Wozniak imagined the Internet as democratic, other figures—like Steve Jobs and Bill Gates—were able to use the technology to increase centralization and erode the net's early openness. Is there something about the Internet that lends itself to centralized control regardless of the goals of the people involved? Do all technologies ultimately strengthen those already in power?

2. In the summer of 2013, Edward Snowden, a whistleblower employed by the National Security Agency, exposed the government's surveillance of the telephone and net communications of millions of Americans. The secretive Foreign Intelligence Surveillance Court (FISA), a branch of the federal

judiciary, had directed Verizon Business Network Services to turn over "on an ongoing basis" all "call detail records or 'telephony metadata' created by Verizon." In what ways does the possibility of secret government surveillance complicate the ongoing debate between openness and the centralization of the Internet?

QUESTIONS FOR MAKING CONNECTIONS
BETWEEN READINGS

1. Joseph Stiglitz is troubled by the increasing concentration of the nation's wealth in the hands of a financial elite that manipulates the economy. In what ways does the concentration of wealth that Stiglitz criticizes parallel the concentration of power over the Internet? Did Steve Jobs and Bill Gates each attempt to create a monopoly? What solutions does Stiglitz propose to cope with the problem of economic inequality? Might his proposals apply as well to the operations of the Internet? Should the government play a larger role in defending net neutrality?

2. Given the story Wu tells about the struggles over the ownership of the Internet, do you think that colleges and universities should follow Cathy Davidson's advice in "Project Classroom Makeover"? By placing education in the hands of the Internet's giants, will her "project" give greater scope to students' creative energies or will they find themselves locked in by a system that reduces them to passive spectators? Has Davidson overlooked the Net's dark side, or does Wu fail to understand its potential for creativity?

Eight Sample Assignment Sequences

SEQUENCE ONE

Andrew Solomon, Son
Azar Nafisi, *Selections from* Reading Lolita in Tehran
Jean Twenge, An Army of One: *Me*

1. We normally think of "family" as the most natural of all human relations. We begin our lives in families, and as we mature we move into a world that seldom seems as warmly supportive. Not only are the members of a family often bound together by ties of "blood," but they share a stock of common memories formed over many decades. Yet Andrew Solomon suggests that family may not be as natural as we think. Our horizontal relationships—defined by qualities like deafness, for example—may be no less "natural" than our relations to brothers, sisters, cousins, uncles, and aunts. How might horizontal identities complicate our thinking about what defines the relationships we call "natural"? Ultimately, can the case be made that all identities are equally natural—or equally invented? Is identity always something we create rather than something we inherit?

2. *Reading Lolita in Tehran* depicts a society most people in the West would describe as "authoritarian"—the Islamic Republic of Iran. Women are required to cover themselves, cannot travel far without a male chaperone, and are subject to harassment by the police for "immodest" behavior. It's easy for Westerners to condemn such restrictive treatment of women, but we might approach Azar Nafisi's testimony in another way—through the lens that Solomon provides. Can we describe the Republic as a society where vertical identity is too highly privileged at the expense of horizontal

relations? Do secular societies depend on strengthening horizontal ties? Is fundamentalism linked in some way to vertical identity?

3. Drawing on Solomon, Nafisi, and Jean Twenge, make an argument about the tensions between society and the self. In what ways does our society define who we are, sometimes by offering us choices, and sometimes by restricting the choices we can make? In what ways does our development as distinct individuals require us to resist society, and in what ways do we require society's support in order to become individuals? Are the self and society necessarily opposed, or does this opposition conceal their ultimate interdependence? At what point does society's power over us become oppressive, and at one point does personal identity tip over into narcissism?

SEQUENCE TWO

Karen Armstrong, *Homo religiosus*
Maggie Nelson, Great to Watch
Robert Thurman, Wisdom

1. "Like art," Karen Armstrong writes, "the truths of religion require the disciplined cultivation of different modes of consciousness." Normally, we conceive of religion as quite separate from art. Religion happens in synagogues or churches, involves rituals and imparts truths we often regard as eternal. Art is what happens in studios and museums. It involves skilled performances that push the envelope and help reshape how we see the world. In what ways does Armstrong ask us to rethink this conventional division between religion and the arts? How does her interest in "modes of consciousness" as opposed to beliefs or group identity put religion in a different light? What does she mean by "cultivation," and what forms of cultivation might religion and the arts make available? If religion in the Paleolithic was more like art than it is today, how might we account for the change?

2. As we have seen, Armstrong associates the arts with "different modes of consciousness." But what happens if art's modes of consciousness take us to places that are more like hell than heaven, as Maggie Nelson alleges in her critique of the avant-garde and its spin-offs in the mass media? Armstrong believes that religion can break free from its rigidity and narrow-mindedness by embracing the arts' openness to change and experimentation. But if religion can learn from the arts, what might contemporary *artists* learn from ancient religions? Have the arts lost touch with the possibility of living, in Nelson's words, "beyond the reach of hatred, greed, and anxieties about our status"? Consider the difference, for example, between John Cage's serene 4'33" and those forms of art and entertainment that inflict a "brutal sensory overload."

3.   Armstrong suggests that over time, religion has evolved in ways that reflect the changing needs of society. Different needs, she suggests, have required different forms of both "cultivation" and "consciousness." *Homo religiosus* ends with the "great sages" of the Axial Age more than two thousand years ago, but what clues might Nelson and Robert Thurman provide about the future direction of religion in our era? Why has ritual violence become so much a fixture of our popular culture, and what can we learn about our unmet needs from the recent interest in meditation and the experience of "selflessness"? Why might selflessness be useful now as a cultural ideal?

SEQUENCE THREE

Joseph Stiglitz, Rent Seeking and the Making of an Unequal Society
Ethan Watters, The Mega-Marketing of Depression in Japan
Michael Moss, The Extraordinary Science of Addictive Junk Food

1.   Does Joseph Stiglitz criticize rent seeking for purely economic reasons, or do his criticisms actually reflect ethical objections distinct from economic realities? In developing an answer, be sure to explain how, in Stiglitz's view, rent seeking worsens inequality. How does the growth of wealth at the top disadvantage people in the middle and at lower income levels? Why does "a rising tide" fail to "lift all boats"? That is, why might the growth of the economy fail to benefit everyone? Do the ill effects of rent-seeking suggest that economic issues are linked inextricably to ethical considerations—that is, to decisions about how we should live and how we should treat others? If ethics and economics are linked, should we see economics as a neutral science like physics or biology?

2.   What does Ethan Watters's objection to the marketing of antidepressants overseas have in common with Stiglitz's critique of rent seeking here at home? Initially, the two might seem completely unrelated. The marketing of drugs clearly fails to conform to the definition of "rent seeking," and the manufacturing of pharmaceuticals makes jobs for people in the United States. But Watters and Stiglitz both seem to believe that corporations have an obligation to the entire society. How might they describe those obligations, and how might they reply to those who say that the only obligation of a company is to make a profit for shareholders?

3.   Stiglitz, Watters, and Michael Moss all deal with institutions that have met with success rather than with failure. The financial sector Stiglitz writes about has recovered from the market collapse of 2008. Indeed, corporate earnings have swelled since then, as have bonuses for Wall Street financiers. Although still modest, antidepressant sales in Japan have climbed steadily.

And, of course, people eat more junk food than ever, while the spread of obesity continues unabated. Why might "success" be a poor metric for evaluating the effectiveness of our economy? What other metrics might be more appropriate?

SEQUENCE FOUR

Karen Ho, Biographies of Hegemony
Steven Johnson, The Myth of the Ant Queen
Martha Stout, When I Woke Up Tuesday Morning, It Was Friday

1. Use Karen Ho's research on the Ivy League to explore the question of how much we are responsible for our success and how much comes from happening to be in the right place at the right time. Does Wall Street seek out students from Harvard and Princeton because they have a special aptitude for finance, or do they develop that aptitude because Wall Street firms seek them out? Why might Wall Street overlook excellent students at other schools—the University of Michigan, for example, or Haverford College? In what ways does the cult of "smartness" help to justify special advantages enjoyed by students at the Ivies? In what way does the system actually create the success it claims to reward?

2. Steven Johnson's chapter might be understood as a celebration of change that rests on a virtually invincible optimism. No matter how chaotic change might appear, Johnson suggests that an invisible hand will always shape things for the best. In what ways might Ho's research complicate Johnson's optimistic account of change? Do the changes in the Ivy League, especially the domination of finance, improve or detract from the quality of education there? Are those changes likely to improve the lives of most Americans? Is it possible that the forces of change might be leading to a future where democracy and equality have become distant memories? Does the growing influence of Wall Street represent change from the bottom up? From the top down?

3. The focus of Martha Stout's chapter is the experience of dissociation. On the one hand, dissociation has the power to protect us from trauma and violence, but, on the other hand, it can also destroy our lives by increasing our isolation from the world and from other people. Is it possible for whole societies to fall prey to the malady of dissociation that Stout describes? "All human beings," she observes, "have the capacity to dissociate psychologically." If sanity really is a myth, as implied by the title of Stout's book—*The Myth of Sanity*—there could be thousands of Julias, Seths, and Lilas in America today. From the evidence provided by Ho, Johnson, and Stout, would you say that dissociation has become an important element in social life?

SEQUENCE FIVE

Leslie Bell, *Selections from* Hard to Get
Beth Loffreda, *Selections from* Losing Matt Shepard
Susan Faludi, The Naked Citadel

1. Leslie Bell explores what she describes as "the paradox of sexual freedom." Women are encouraged to pursue the same avenues of fulfillment that men have had access to for centuries, including sexual freedom. But when they actually attempt to exercise this freedom, women confront a new array of cultural contradictions. Those seeking independence and success may conclude that they will have to choose between careers and intimate relationships. Sexually adventurous women run the risk of manipulation by men who have no regard for their happiness. Although people normally look to the norms of their society as a guide, would you say that these norms are reliable, based on your reading of Bell?

2. Matt Shepard, whose murder is the subject of Beth Loffreda's report, might be said to have transgressed the norms of his community, the town of Laramie, Wyoming. Within that community, however, there were other communities that supported his behavior and fought to see justice done, such as the community of gays, lesbians, and bisexuals. One way to understand the conflict that followed in the wake of Shepard's death is to see it as a clash between the values of different communities. How are we to choose when we encounter contradictions of this kind, with each community claiming that its values are the right ones?

3. Like Loffreda's *Losing Matt Shepard*, Susan Faludi's "Naked Citadel" describes a conflict that erupts over gender and sexuality. Drawing on these two selections as well as Bell's *Hard to Get*, explain why gender and sexuality are so often cultural flashpoints. What is it about women's equality that some men find threatening? And why is sexuality so highly charged with moral, cultural, and political significance? Is it possible that culture always depends on excluding someone, or subordinating certain groups to the power of others? Or does the opposite hold true: are exclusion and inequality damaging even to those who hold power?

SEQUENCE SIX

Cathy Davidson, Project Classroom Makeover
Sherry Turkle, *Selections from* Alone Together
Tim Wu, Father and Son

1. Based on your reading of "Project Classroom Makeover," how would you describe Cathy Davidson's philosophy of education? That is, what does she

consider to be the proper aims of teaching and learning, and what methods does she appear to believe would best facilitate those ends? Would it be possible for Davidson to hold her current beliefs about reform if computers and the Internet did not exist? Does Davidson want the new technology to help in making a cultural change, or does she seem to think technology will make cultural change irrelevant? Does technology replace ideas? Can it do our thinking for us? Is it our tool, or do we become extensions of our technology?

2. Davidson embraces the new media as an alternative to what she sees as an educational system designed to stifle creativity and independent thinking. In what ways does Tim Wu's narrative challenge this optimism? If the Web is moving rapidly toward the same centralization that has overtaken other technologies, will bringing iPods into colleges have the liberating impact Davidson foresees? Or will it simply insert consumerism into education more deeply than ever? Will Davidson's reforms hasten the rise of Web-based monopolies, or will they help prevent such an event?

3. Use Sherry Turkle, Wu, and Davidson to development an argument about the impact of technology on our cultural lives. That is, how is technology transforming the ways we see ourselves and others, how we think and act, and what we value? Pay particular attention to the utopian rhetoric that has often accompanied the release of new commodities like iPads, Androids, Furbies, and so on. None of the writers in this sequence qualifies as a "luddite" or reflexive techno-pessimist, but Wu and Turkle attempt to inject an element of critical reflection into a discourse that typically equates change with social progress. Could technologies like the Web ultimately take away our freedom? Could they make us less creative? Are they making us less social?

SEQUENCE SEVEN

Charles Siebert, An Elephant Crackup?
Karen Armstrong, *Homo religiosus*
Malcolm Gladwell, The Power of Context

1. In "An Elephant Crackup?" Charles Siebert quotes Gay Bradshaw on the basic changes that humans need to make in order to ensure the survival of healthy elephant populations: "In addition to conservation, we need to educate people about how to live with wild animals like humans used to do, and to create conditions whereby people can live on the land and live with elephants without it being this life-and-death situation." Siebert takes this thinking one step farther by arguing that the elephants' survival depends on humans developing a deeper sense of identification with the natural world. In what ways does Siebert's own essay help to create that sense?

2.   Karen Armstrong's *Homo religiosus* describes a time, the Paleolithic Era, when humans lived more closely with animals, not only in physical proximity but in psychological proximity as well. But does the evidence that Armstrong provides suggest that our ancestors had achieved the kind of "identification" with nature that Siebert recommends? Animals appear on the walls of Lascaux caverns and hunters may have worshipped a "god known as the Animal Master," but do we still find 30,000 years ago a symbolic distance between *Homo sapiens* and other species? Does the evolution of religion, as Armstrong retraces it, widen this distance or narrow it? Even if the ancient religions failed to give animals a central place, do they provide some of the elements we need to create the new consciousness Siebert argues for?

3.   Malcolm Gladwell demonstrates that social change tends to happen in a nonlinear way. Sometimes small changes can trigger enormous shifts in the ways people think and act. Drawing on ideas like the Broken Windows Theory and the Power of Context, make an argument about how we might set the stage for a change in the way people think about the natural world. What tipping point might bring about the interspecies understanding Siebert wants us to see? What can we learn from Armstrong's account about how greater closeness to nature might require a different form of consciousness?

SEQUENCE EIGHT

Azar Nafisi, *Selections from* Reading Lolita in Tehran
Oliver Sacks, The Mind's Eye
Daniel Gilbert, Immune to Reality

1.   The members of Azar Nafisi's Thursday morning seminar are all subject to the policies of their oppressive government. Yet, we can observe subtle differences in the ways they have experienced oppression and in their responses to it. How might the seminar have allowed these and other differences to emerge? How does the seminar change the young women, and how is Nafisi herself affected? On the basis of Nafisi's account, make an argument about the links between literature, imagination, and the expression of differences. To what extent do the arts empower people to express themselves? Are literature and, more broadly, the arts inherently liberating, or does the answer depend on the way we use them?

2.   Oliver Sacks describes people who have lost their sense of sight but then reconstruct their perceptions of the world—and also transform their mental processing. Drawing on the evidence that Sacks provides as well as Nafisi's story of her reading group, make an argument about the relationship between human creativity and the real world. Is the real world as fixed and inflexible as people often suppose? Is there a single reality at all, or are there many realities? How are we limited in our ability to reshape the way we experience reality? Is every understanding of the world an act of creativity?

3. Daniel Gilbert is intrigued by our capacity to deceive ourselves through unconscious operations like "cooking the facts." He seems to take pleasure in pointing out how often we fail to understand ourselves well enough to find the happiness we seek, and why, even when we find happiness, we tend to lose it again. In what ways do Nafisi and Sacks complicate Gilbert's view of human self-deception? Are we as inept at finding happiness as Gilbert suggests? Are we as self-deceiving? Does our tendency to "cook the facts" also account for our creativity? Where does self-deception start and creativity stop?

Author and Title Index